Fodor's

W9-AXE-810

PORTUGAL

8th Edition

**Where to Stay and Eat
for All Budgets**

**Must-See Sights
and Local Secrets**

Ratings You Can Trust

Fodor's Travel Publications   New York, Toronto, London, Sydney, Auckland
www.fodors.com

FODOR'S PORTUGAL
Editor: Adam Taplin

Editorial Production: Tom Holton
Editorial Contributors: Mary McLean, Norman Renouf
Maps: David Lindroth, *cartographer*; Rebecca Baer and Bob Blake, *map editors*
Design: Fabrizio La Rocca, *creative director*; Guido Caroti, *art director*; Moon Sun Kim, *cover designer*; Melanie Marin, *senior picture editor*
Production/Manufacturing: Colleen Ziemba
Cover Photo (Seaweed Vessel, Aveiro): Picture Finders Ltd./eStock Photo

COPYRIGHT
Copyright © 2007 by Fodor's Travel, a division of Random House, Inc.

Fodor's is a registered trademark of Random House, Inc.

All rights reserved under International and Pan-American Copyright Conventions. Published in the United States by Fodor's Travel, a division of Random House, Inc., and simultaneously in Canada by Random House of Canada, Limited, Toronto. Distributed by Random House, Inc., New York.

No maps, illustrations, or other portions of this book may be reproduced in any form without written permission from the publisher.

Eighth Edition

ISBN 978–1–4000–1775–1

ISSN 0071–6510

SPECIAL SALES
This book is available at special discounts for bulk purchases for sales promotions or premiums. Special editions, including personalized covers, excerpts of existing books, and corporate imprints, can be created in large quantities for special needs. For more information, write to Special Markets/Premium Sales, 1745 Broadway, MD 6-2, New York, New York 10019, or e-mail specialmarkets@randomhouse.com.

AN IMPORTANT TIP & AN INVITATION
Although all prices, opening times, and other details in this book are based on information supplied to us at press time, changes occur all the time in the travel world, and Fodor's cannot accept responsibility for facts that become outdated or for inadvertent errors or omissions. So **always confirm information when it matters,** especially if you're making a detour to visit a specific place. Your experiences—positive and negative—matter to us. If we have missed or misstated something, **please write to us.** We follow up on all suggestions. Contact the Portugal editor at editors@fodors.com or c/o Fodor's at 1745 Broadway, New York, NY 10019.

PRINTED IN THE UNITED STATES OF AMERICA

10 9 8 7 6 5 4 3 2 1

Be a Fodor's Correspondent

Your opinion matters. It matters to us. It matters to your fellow Fodor's travelers, too. And we'd like to hear it. In fact, we *need* to hear it.

When you share your experiences and opinions, you become an active member of the Fodor's community. That means we'll not only use your feedback to make our books better, but we'll publish your names and comments whenever possible.

Here's how you can help improve Fodor's for all of us.

Tell us when we're right. We rely on local writers to give you an insider's perspective. But our writers and staff editors—who are the best in the business—depend on you. Your positive feedback is a vote to renew our recommendations for the next edition.

Tell us when we're wrong. We're proud that we update most of our guides every year. But we're not perfect. Things change. Hotels cut services. Museums change hours. Charming cafés lose charm. If our writer didn't quite capture the essence of a place, tell us how you'd do it differently. If any of our descriptions are inaccurate or inadequate, we'll incorporate your changes in the next edition and will correct factual errors at fodors.com *immediately.*

Tell us what to include. You probably have had fantastic travel experiences that aren't yet in Fodor's. Why not share them with a community of like-minded travelers? Maybe you chanced upon a beach or bistro or B&B that you don't want to keep to yourself. Tell us why we should include it. And share your discoveries and experiences with everyone directly at fodors.com. Your input may lead us to add a new listing or highlight a place we cover with a "Highly Recommended" star or with our highest rating, "Fodor's Choice."

Give us your opinion instantly at our feedback center at www.fodors.com/feedback. You may also e-mail editors@fodors.com with the subject line "Portugal Editor." Or send your nominations, comments, and complaints by mail to Portugal Editor, Fodor's, 1745 Broadway, New York, NY 10019.

You and travelers like you are the heart of the Fodor's community. Make our community richer by sharing your experiences. Be a Fodor's correspondent.

Boa Viagem!

Tim Jarrell, Publisher

CONTENTS

ABOUT THIS BOOK

Our Ratings

Sometimes you find terrific travel experiences and sometimes they just find you. But usually the burden is on you to select the right combination of experiences. That's where our ratings come in.

As travelers we've all discovered a place so wonderful that its worthiness is obvious. And sometimes that place is so unique that superlatives don't do it justice: you just have to be there to know. These sights, properties, and experiences get our highest rating, **Fodor's Choice,** indicated by orange stars throughout this book.

Black stars highlight sights and properties we deem **Highly Recommended,** places that our writers, editors, and readers praise again and again for consistency and excellence.

By default, there's another category: any place we include in this book is by definition worth your time, unless we say otherwise. And we will.

Disagree with any of our choices? Care to nominate a place or suggest that we rate one more highly? Visit our feedback center at www. fodors.com/feedback.

Budget Well

Hotel and restaurant price categories from ¢ to **$$$$** are defined in the opening pages of each chapter. For attractions, we always give standard adult admission fees; reductions are usually available for children, students, and senior citizens. Want to pay with plastic? **AE, D, DC, MC, V** following restaurant and hotel listings indicate whether American Express, Discover, Diners Club, MasterCard, and Visa are accepted.

Restaurants

Unless we state otherwise, restaurants are open for lunch and dinner daily. We mention dress only when there's a specific requirement and reservations only when they're essential or not accepted—it's always best to book ahead.

Hotels

Hotels have private bath, phone, TV, and air-conditioning and operate on the European Plan (aka EP, meaning without meals), unless we specify that they use the Continental Plan (CP, with a Continental breakfast), Breakfast Plan (BP, with a full breakfast), or Modified American Plan (MAP, with breakfast and dinner) or are all-inclusive (including all meals and most activities). We always list facilities but not whether you'll be charged an extra fee to use them, so when pricing accommodations, find out what's included.

Many Listings
- ★ Fodor's Choice
- ★ Highly recommended
- ⊠ Physical address
- ✛ Directions
- 🕮 Mailing address
- ☎ Telephone
- 🖷 Fax
- 🌐 On the Web
- ✉ E-mail
- 🎫 Admission fee
- ⊘ Open/closed times
- ▶ Start of walk/itinerary
- Ⓜ Metro stations
- ▭ Credit cards

Hotels & Restaurants
- 🏨 Hotel
- ↩ Number of rooms
- ⚲ Facilities
- ⫶◯⫶ Meal plans
- ✕ Restaurant
- ⚏ Reservations
- 🏛 Dress code
- ↘ Smoking
- ⚇ BYOB
- ✕🏨 Hotel with restaurant that warrants a visit

Outdoors
- 🏌 Golf
- 🛆 Camping

Other
- ☕ Family-friendly
- ☎ Contact information
- ⇨ See also
- ⊠ Branch address
- ☞ Take note

WHAT'S WHERE

LISBON 	Lisbon is a captivating place. It's one of Europe's smallest capitals and easy to navigate on foot. It's a city that dips and rises over seven hills with the dusty cobbled streets of Alfama resembling the set of a medieval blockbuster in dramatic contrast to Chiados upmarket cafés and boutiques. This collision of the centuries is in evidence throughout the capital: Out of 17th-century buildings skip designer-clad youths; the fish market at Cais do Sodré resonates with traditional sights and smells; and a short walk from the 18th-century aqueduct sits the modernistic Amoreiras shopping center. Lisbon has an enviable roll call of sights within strolling distance of each other. Alternatively, hop on the funicular, tram, or metro.
LISBON'S ENVIRONS 	"A glorious Eden" is how Lord Byron described Sintra, a magical place studded with magnificent palaces, gardens, and luxury *quintas* (manor houses). At Cascais and Estoril, upmarket facilities cater to the summer onslaught of beach-going tourists. That said, these tasteful resorts are also Portuguese working communities where you can join the locals in such time-honored pastimes as a stroll along the shore, a seafood meal, or a flutter at the casino. To the north, around Guincho's rocky promontory and the Praia das Maças coast, the Atlantic is often windswept and rough, which means that, while it may not be so conducive to kicking back on a sun bed, it is excellent for wind- and kite-surfing and sailboarding, as well as stunning coastal drives. For sweeping sandy beaches head south of the Rio Tejo (River Tagus) on the Setúbal Peninsula.
ESTREMADURA & RIBATEJO 	The regions of Estremadura and Ribatejo extend north and east of Lisbon, following a line drawn by the wide valley of the Rio Tejo. This is a region replete with architectural splendor and historical pomp, and is home of several World Heritage Sites, including the headquarters of the Knights Templar, the Convento de Cristo. There is plenty of greenery in this region, as well, with pine forests, hills, and valleys, while the coastline reveals some of the most charming seaside resorts, like Nazaré and Ericeira. Out of the capital, and across the Tejo, you're soon in Ribatejo, famous as a bull-breeding district, whose mainly flatlands fade into the vast plains of the southern Alentejo region.

ÉVORA & THE ALENTEJO 	Évora is a real gem; medieval walls encircle an elegant town with palatial buildings, stylish restaurants, and a magnificent Roman temple. Ironically, this architecturally rich town is in one of Portugal's poorest regions; once known as the granary of Portugal, the Alentejo is a thinly populated, largely agricultural region of grain fields and cork and olive trees. The Alentejo is as remote in its way as Trás-os-Montes in the north, although the Lisbon–Estremoz highway has made the whole region more accessible. There are some impressive Atlantic beaches (whipped year-round by a strong wind), and a striking eastern section, where the Rio Guadiana forms the frontier with Spain. Alentejo summers start early (March), and there's little shade from the sun.
THE ALGARVE 	Dividing the Alentejo from Portugal's southernmost coastal province is a continuous range of dramatic mountains—the Serra de Monchique and the Serra de Caldeirão. The Algarve is Portugal's most popular area for tourists, here for the unadulterated sunshine (some 3,000 hours a year), sweeping beaches, attractive coastal resorts and water sports. Venture inland and you'll find the unspoiled beauty of villages like Monchique. Faro, the regional capital, is an attractive town with an old quarter, superb beaches, and plenty of accommodation and restaurant choice. Head west for the coastal drama and rocky cliffs of Sagres—and some of the best surfing in the country. Coastal winter days are warm and bright, the wildflowers strung across the low hills start to bloom in February, and temperatures stay high until late October.
COIMBRA & THE BEIRAS 	The central Beiras region contains Portugal's most spectacular mountain range, the Serra da Estrela, which reaches a height of 6,530 feet and offers the country's best hiking. In the Beira Alta (Upper Beira)—between Viseu, Guarda, and Covilha—the winter frost is fierce, and the wind whistles through a string of hill towns that, while little known to foreigners, are at the heart of Portugal's history and home to some superb Renaissance art. The unspoiled coast itself, the pine-forested Costa da Prata (Silver Coast), is one of the finest sandy stretches in the country, and inland from the main resort of Figueira da Foz lies one of Portugal's most dynamic and fascinating cities. Coimbra has plenty going for it, including a magnificent 13th-century university, a lively student life, elegant shopping streets, and cobbled backstreets where you can find some of the best *fado* bars in the country.

WHAT'S
WHERE

PORTO & THE NORTH 	Portugal's northern region is a dramatic patchwork of soaring mountains, rolling hills, and dense forests. This upper Minho area is also home to *vinho verde,* Portugal's distinctive young green wine, while Porto—famous for an eponymously named beverage—is a captivating mix of the medieval and modern. Porto successfully combines a slick commercial hub with the charmingly dilapidated riverfront district—a well-deserved World Heritage Site. Across the water is Vila Nova de Gaia, the headquarters of a thriving port trade. Moving to the mountainous northeast you'll find the seldom-visited region with the Shangri-la name of Trás-os-Montes (Beyond the Mountains)—an unspoiled area of rugged beauty, with tumbling rivers, expansive forests, hilltop castles, and quiet villages. In the milder, more-fertile southern part lie the vineyards of the Douro Valley, whose grapes are used to make the above-mentioned port wine. Touching the Atlantic and stretching from the northern border south to Porto, the Minho contains the lush hinterland of the rivers Minho, Lima, and Douro. In this mass of predominantly green landscape is the Costa Verde (Green Coast), the beautiful pine-tree-lined northern coast. Winters are mild here, with plenty of rain, and the Minho is heavily cultivated. Summers are short and temperate.
MADEIRA 	Off the coast of Morocco, about 600 km (372 mi) due west of Casablanca, lies the subtropical Madeiran archipelago, an autonomous possession of Portugal. It consists of Madeira (the largest island of the group), nearby Porto Santo, and the uninhabited islets of Ilhas Desertas and Ilhas Selvagens. (The Azores, whose remote location and relative poverty keep them somewhat unvisited, are Portugal's other autonomous possession; they aren't covered in this book.) Best known to some wine aficionados for its velvety fortified wine, Madeira is dominated by a mountain range, volcanic in origin, which rises to spectacular summits; its highest peak, Pico Ruivo, reaches a heady altitude of 6,102 feet. On the lush northern coast, cliffs pierce the sea, and to the west is the arid Paúl da Serra plateau. South along the coast, the landscape becomes gentler, and much more populated. Funchal, the flower-bedecked capital, is near the southeastern corner of the island.

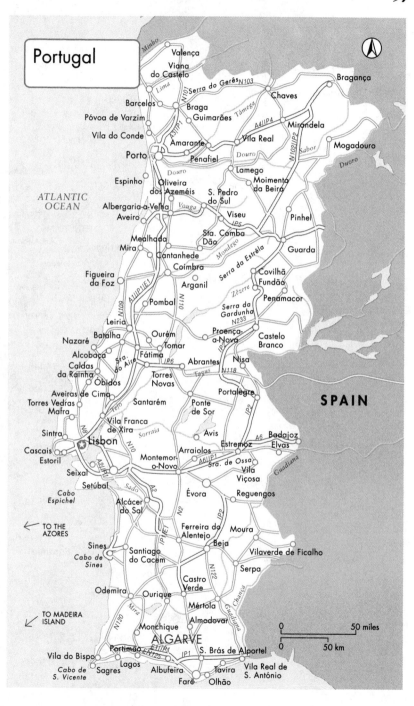

Europe

Gulf
of
Bothnia

FINLAND

Oslo

SWEDEN

Helsinki

Gulf of Finland

Tallinn

St. Petersburg

ESTONIA

Stockholm

Göteborg

Kattegat

Riga

LATVIA

Moscow

Copenhagen

LITHUANIA

Kaunas

Baltic Sea

RUSSIA

Vilnius

R U S S I A

Kaliningrad

Minsk

Berlin

POLAND

BELARUS

MANY

Warsaw

Kraków

Kiev

Prague

CZECH
REPUBLIC

UKRAINE

SLOVAKIA

ch

Vienna

Bratislava

Salzburg

Budapest

MOLDOVA

AUSTRIA

HUNGARY

Chișinău

EIN

SLOVENIA

Ljubljana

Zagreb

ROMANIA

ce

CROATIA

Novi Sad

BOSNIA AND
HERZEGOVINA

Belgrade

Bucharest

Sarajevo

SERBIA

Black Sea

YUGOSLAVIA

Rome

MONTENEGRO

KOSOVO

BULGARIA

Adriatic Sea

Podgorica

Priština

Sofia

ITALY

Skopje

Istanbul

MACEDONIA

Naples

Tirane

Ankara

ALBANIA

TURKEY

ian Sea

GREECE

*Aegean
Sea*

*Ionian
Sea*

Sicily

Athens

Mediterranean Sea

CYPRUS

MALTA

Crete

QUINTESSENTIAL PORTUGAL

Pastelarias

Only the staunchest dieter will not be tempted by Portugal's deliciously calorific cakes and pastries. The window displays are real cream-cake affairs, invariably wedged between trendy boutiques catering to fashionable beanpoles. Every region has its specialty sweet treat, generally known as *doces conventuais* (convent desserts), which usually originates from the respective local convent. And, yes, they really *are* a touch of heaven. In the Algarve, the Moorish influence is evident in the marzipan and almond biscuits, while farther north in Abrantes the egg pastries known as *bolo de anjo* (angel cake—those nuns again) have a melt-in-the-mouth fluffy topping. If you are seeking true sublimity, however, bite into a warm *pasties de nata*, straight from the oven. These gorgeous custard tarts are made with flaky light pastry, creamy egg custard, and sprinkled cinnamon.

Feiras

The Portuguese love to party and here (as in neighboring Spain) there are countless annual celebrations and fiestas. Don't miss out when you are traveling around and be sure to check at the local tourist office for upcoming events. For the Portuguese the country's fairs and festivals are far more than holidays from the year's work. They are occasions in which to be immersed with passion and commitment. At saints' days, harvest festivals, pilgrimages, and *feiras* (fairs), you can expect everything from ceremonial pomp and religious processions to wild street parties and quaint traditions. St. John's in Porto (June 23) is a good example of the latter, with everyone hitting each other over the head with plastic hammers or leeks while enjoying a night of drinking, revelry, and dance from dusk to dawn in the city streets.

If you want to get a sense of contemporary Portuguese culture, and indulge in some of its pleasure, start by familiarizing yourself with the rituals of daily life. These are a few highlights—things you can take part in with relative ease.

Bacalhau

Few people understand the bounty of the sea more than the Portuguese. One singularly appetizing delicacy called *bacalhau* (dried, salted cod) appears on the menu at virtually every restaurant, though it is definitely an acquired taste. Shop fronts are chockablock with the stuff: think fossilized white strips of leather and you will be on the right track. There are reputedly 365 ways of preparing this curious delicacy, ranging from roasted with onions and potatoes to fish pie. The Portuguese love affair with seafood encompasses just about everything that swims in the sea, including limpets (normally braised with garlic). In Lisbon there is an entire street—Rua dos Bacalhaus (Codfish Street)—dedicated to the lowly cod. Grilled sardines are prevalent as well, but don't expect the tinned variety you might be accustomed to. The Portuguese prefer to serve them whole, head and all.

Fado

The dramatic image of a black-shawled fado singer, head thrown back, eyes closed with emotion, has become an emblem of Portugal; the swelling, soulful song with the plaintive guitar accompaniment seems to embody Portugal's romantic essence. Fado's importance is such that when the great *fadista* Amália Rodrigues died in 1999, the government declared three days of national mourning and awarded her a state funeral. When the singing begins in a fado house, all talking ceases and a reverent silence descends on the tables. A world of immutable sadness appears, populated by many types of people: the lost, the poor and oppressed, the abandoned and rejected. You should not miss an opportunity to witness this unique musical style.

ON THE CALENDAR

	Religious celebrations, called *festas* (feasts or festivals), *feiras* (fairs), and *romarias* (pilgrimages or processions), are held throughout the year. Some of the leading annual events are listed below. Verify specific dates with the people at the Portuguese tourism office, who can also send you a complete list of events.
ONGOING February–March	**Carnaval** (Carnival), the final festival before Lent, is held throughout the country, with processions of masked participants, parades of decorated vehicles, and displays of flowers.
April	**Semana Santa** (Holy Week) festivities are held in Braga, Ovar, Póvoa de Varzim, and other cities and major towns, with the most important events taking place on Monday, Thursday, and Good Friday.
May	Legend has it that, in the early 16th century, a peasant who insisted on working on the Day of the Holy Cross saw a perfumed, luminous cross appear on the ground where he was digging. Ever since, Barcelos has held the colorful **Festas das Cruzes** (of the Crosses), with a large fair, concerts, an affecting procession, and a fireworks display on the Rio Cavado. During the **Romaria de Fátima,** thousands make the pilgrimage to the town from all over the world to commemorate the first apparition of the Virgin to the shepherd children on May 13, 1917.
June	Monção celebrates the **Festa do Corpo de Deus** (Corpus Christi), which includes a symbolic battle between good and evil. Amarante hosts the **Festa de São Gonçalo,** when St. Gonçalo is commemorated by the baking of phallus-shape cakes, which are then exchanged between unmarried men and women. Events also include a fair, folk dancing, and traditional singing. The **Festa de São João** is especially colorful in Porto, where the whole city erupts with bonfires and barbecues and every corner has its own *cascatas* (arrangements with religious motifs). Locals roam the streets, hitting passersby on the head with, among other things, leeks and plastic hammers.
June–September	For four weeks the **Noites de Queluz** (Queluz Nights) festival is staged in the gardens of the Palácio Nacional. Complete with costumed cast and orchestra, this event mimics the concerts, fireworks displays, and other activities held in the gardens to amuse Queen Maria I, who lived in the palace throughout her long reign (1777–1816) and whose eccentric behavior earned her the name "Mad" Queen Maria.

July	The **Festa do Colete Encarnado** (Red Waistcoat) in Vila Franca de Xira honors the *campinos* (cowboys) who guard the brave bulls in the pastures of the Ribatejo. Streets are cordoned off, and bulls are let loose as would-be bullfighters try their luck at dodging the beasts.
July–August	The **Festival da Música de Estoril** sees concerts by leading Portuguese and foreign artists in several towns along the Estoril Coast.
September	The **Romaria de São Gens** (St. Gens) brings ceramic vendors from all over the country to Freixo de Cima, west of Amarante. The **Festa das Vindimas** (Grape Harvest) in Palmela has a symbolic treading of the grapes and a blessing of the harvest, accompanied by a parade of harvesters, wine tastings, the election of the Queen of the Wine, and fireworks.
October	**Feira de Outubro** (October Fair) in Vila Franca de Xira, a short distance from Lisbon, has farming and agricultural activities, handicraft displays, bullfights, and a running of the bulls in the streets. The Algarve's **Feira de Outubro** gathers together crafts, goods, and produce from villages throughout the Serra de Monchique.
November	The **Festival Nacional de Gastronomia** (National Gastronomy Festival) in Santarém consists of traditional regional dishes, cooking contests, and lectures. The **Feira Nacional do Cavalo** (National Horse Fair) in Golegã coincides with a festival honoring St. Martin, combining parades of saddle and bullfighting horses with riding competitions, handicrafts exhibitions, and wine tastings.
December	**Festa de São Sylvester** (St. Sylvester), on New Year's Eve, transforms Funchal into a vast fairground, with bands of strolling dancers and singers, thousands of lights, and breathtaking fireworks.

IF YOU LIKE

Manueline Architecture

Named after King Manuel (1495–1521), this exuberant style mirrored the ostentation of explorers like Vasco da Gama and Pedro Álvares Cabral, who were grabbing at new lands overseas hand-over-fist. Unsurprisingly, the style incorporated maritime elements and discoveries brought from these voyages, and subsequently spread throughout the Portuguese Empire, to the islands of the Azores, Madeira, enclaves in North Africa, and even to Goa in India. Tragically, much of the original Manueline architecture in Portugal was lost in the 1755 Lisbon earthquake and subsequent tsunami. In Lisbon, King Manuel's magnificent Royal Palace was destroyed, along with the All-Saints Hospital and several churches. The city, however, still has some outstanding examples left.

- **Lisbon.** Chief among the many fabulous Manueline buildings in Lisbon is the Mosteiro dos Jerónimos, designed by Diogo Boitac and featuring filigree and elaborately carved stonework. Nearby, the multiturreted Torre de Belém is another Manueline extravaganza.

- **Tomar.** The Convento do Cristo here is the most extraordinary Manueline monument in Portugal; it's a riot of twisted and ornate carving with twisted knotted ropes of stone and strands of coral.

- **Batalha.** The flamboyantly designed Santa Maria da Vitória bristles with flying buttresses and balustrades. The interior is awesome as well with its vast star-vaulted chapel and the Royal Clausters with its tangle of carved Manueline symbols.

Hilltop Villages

The hilltop villages of Portugal are especially beguiling, as they are often made of stone sculpted out of the rock face. Most of them date to Roman times, when they were garrison towns, but they later came in handy during the 17th-century War of Restoration against the Castilians. If you can manage an overnight stay, dusk is the best time of all to visit these castles. Visitors have left and the narrow streets take on a misty otherworldly air.

- **Marvão.** A small population of 1,000 inhabit this dramatic hilltop village, located in the Alto Alentejo, which is surrounded by the original 17th-century city walls. A castle built in AD 715 still reigns supreme.

- **Monsaraz.** Another jewel in the Alentejo tiara, this tiny village is surrounded by fascinating Neolithic megaliths. Narrow lanes, lopsided cottages, and a handsome castle are here, together with stunning views of the surrounding olive groves which are planted in straight lines along the ancient Roman roads.

- **Óbidos.** Whitewashed houses bordering brilliantly colored bougainvillea make up this pretty medieval village, reputedly a wedding gift from Dom Dinis to his wife (beats a mere ring!). Óbidos has plenty of wining and dining choices and several places to stay.

Azulejos

Somehow, no matter how many catalogs you peruse and stores you tramp through, those tiles you end up decorating your bathroom or kitchen with at home just look so plain compared to Portugal's all-encompassing decorative *azulejos*. These brightly colored tiles are everywhere: houses, shops, monuments, and vast wall murals that brighten public spaces all over the country. The Moors first introduced azulejos here in the 8th century with classic geometric designs that are still in evidence today.

● **Lisbon.** The Museu Nacional do Azulejo traces the development of tile making from its Moorish roots. Don't miss the Cervejaria da Trindade, a vaulted beer hall on Rua Nova da Trinidade which has stunning azulejos with figurative designs typical of the late 19th century, or the metro stations with their contemplative azulejo designs, including Colégio Militar and Camp Pequeno.

● **Porto.** This is a fabulous city for azulejos, starting at the São Bento train station with its magnificent mural of battle scenes. Churches are literally smothered by tiles here, including the Igreja do Carmo and the Capela das Almas.

● **Sintra.** One of the best places to see the early-16th-century geometric tiles is Sintra's magnificent Palácio Nacional da Pena. Throughout the historic property you'll find beautiful palaces and mansions adorned with azulejos.

Family Pursuits

The Portuguese adore children and welcome them everywhere, including at bars and restaurants where families drink and dine together. If your young ones grow tired of such grown-up pursuits, Portugal also has a healthy dose of sights and activities geared towards children of all ages. This is a culture that revolves around family life throughout the day and well into the evening; bedtime is late here, with many children still up at midnight during the summer months.

● **Churches & Castles.** Children will love the fairy-tale quality of Portugal's magnificent churches and castles. Several stand out, including the Knights Templar Convento de Cristo, in Tomar, where kiddies can light a candle and wonder at its otherworldly Da Vinci Code feel. The castles at Sintra and Elvas are other winners.

● **Dinosaurs.** For a real Jurassic Park experience check out the fascinating Parque Natural das Serras de Aire e Candeeiros, near Fatima, where you can follow in the footsteps of the dinosaurs. There are special children's tours available, otherwise just follow the signs.

● **Algarve.** A major holiday destination, the Algarve offers plenty of choice, including water parks, zoos, boat trips, and horse riding. There are also miniature trains that chug around the various resorts and, of course, the cheapest activities of all: making sandcastles and splashing in the sea.

GREAT ITINERARY

HIGHLIGHTS OF PORTUGAL

You'll start in the Algarve, Portugal's southernmost region of gorgeous beaches, vibrant resorts, and secluded hill villages, and continue north via the country's major towns. Landscapes along the way include the picturesque coast and the arid plains of the south; vibrant Lisbon and its lush environs; and the rivers, valleys, forests, and mountains of the north.

Days 1 & 2: Faro

This town makes an ideal base for exploring the most attractive resorts and villages in the Algarve. Don't miss lovely riverside Tavira, bustling Lagos, and gorgeous mountain-based Monchique. If you are able, take the train that runs between Lagos and Vila Real; this coastal route is one of the most scenic in Portugal. ⇨ *Faro & Environs in Chapter 5.*

Days 3–5: Lisbon

Don your walking shoes and range across the seven hills of the Portuguese capital. If your knees can't cope, hop one of the vintage street trams that snake up and down the hills. You should plan on enjoying at least one meal in the Praça dos Restauradores; the views of the city are magnificent; you may want to consider a *fado* show, as well. ⇨ *Lisbon in Chapter 1.*

Day 6: Óbidos to Leiria

After all that trudging, take it easy with a meandering drive from Lisbon through the fertile Estremadura region. You'll pass Óbidos, the enchanting walled village once given as a royal wedding present. Move on to the stunning World Heritage Sites of Alcobaça and Batalha. At the journey's end drop by the magnificent medieval castle at the former royal residence of Leiria, one of Portugal's unsung gems. ⇨ *Estremadura in Chapter 3.*

Day 7: Coimbra

Coimbra, a delightful town abuzz with students, boasts heady architecture, a sophisticated shopping scene, and romantic squares and gardens. The place oozes history: Portugal's first king was born and buried here. It's a hilly city so be prepared, but the center is reasonably compact and you should be able to cover all the main sights easily in a day. Don't miss the quirky *elevador*—a combination of funicular, elevator, and walkway—or *fado,* the most characteristic of Portugal's folk music. ⇨ *Coimbra in Chapter 6.*

Days 8 & 9: Porto

Portugal's second city and gateway to the north, Porto has a beguiling air of faded grandeur with its peeling buildings and medieval tangle of river-frontage streets. Start by picking up a map at the tourist office and heading for the atmospheric Ribeira embankment, with their strung-with-washing buildings and superb tascas where you can tuck into fresh fish and admire the colorful lights of the impressive port lodges across the water. ⇨ *Porto in Chapter 7.*

Day 10: Braga

The country's religious nerve center, Braga is an ecclesiastical heavyweight with a massive archbishop's palace at the center. A tiara of impressive religious buildings and sanctuaries encircles the town, including the extravagant Bom Jesus baroque pilgrim church, located 5 km (3 mi) to the

Viana
do Castelo
MINHO
Lima River
Barcelos
Braga
Guimarães
DOURO
Porto
Estarreja
ATLANTIC
OCEAN
COASTAL
Mealhada
Coimbra
BEIRA
Batalha   Leiria
Alcobaça
ESTREMADURA   SPAIN
Óbidos
Lisbon
ESTORIL
COAST
Setúbal
Ferreira do
Alentejo
Castro
Verde
Monchique
ALGARVE
Lagos   Portimão   Tavira
Faro   Vila Real de
S. António

ings, superb restaurants, and sweeping beaches. Chug across the Rio Lima by ferry to the local strip of sand, stroll around the picturesque town center, and, if your timing permits, visit the bustling Friday market to pick up a few hand-embroidered linens as gifts for the folks back home. ⇨ *The Minho & the Costa Verde in Chapter 7.*

TIPS

❶ Trains and buses serve all the towns on this itinerary, but connections in the far south and far north can be time consuming, so allow plenty of time or, better still, rent a car.

❷ Bear in mind that August is the Algarve's hottest and busiest tourist month, so try to plan your trip around this, if possible.

❸ Drop into the Lisbon Welcome Centre and pick up a lifesaving map of the city. You may want to consider buying the Lisboa Card here, as well, as it will prove seriously euro-economizing on travel and admission to museums and monuments.

---

east. Braga is a city for strolling. If you have the time, it's an easy day trip from Braga to medieval Guimarães with its lovely town center and magnificent palace of the dukes of Bragança. ⇨ *The Minho & the Costa Verde in Chapter 7.*

Day 11: Viana Do Castelo

A low-key Portuguese resort and the country's folkloric capital, this elegant seaside town has grandiose 16th-century build-

GREAT ITINERARY

BYWAYS & BACKWATERS

This meandering tour of the northern rivers, valleys, and mountains steers clear of the hustle bustle of cities and tourist crowds, allowing you to absorb the local life and culture—Portugal's mellow pleasures.

Days 1 & 2: Monção

Now a peaceful spa town on a serene stretch on the Rio Minho, Monção is home to a castle that's the only reminder of more-tumultuous times. The local wine, the sprightly *vinho verde,* encourages long lunches and makes the perfect accompaniment to salmon and trout freshly caught from the Minho. The liveliest day to visit town is Thursday when the town swings into action with its weekly market. ⇨ *The Minho & the Costa Verde in Chapter 7.*

Day 3: Ponte de Lima

You can do this handsome town justice in a day. Its highlight is the ancient bridge with its 31 arches spanning the River of Oblivion, as it was known. Riverside promenades, mansions, elegant manor-house accommodations, museums, and churches are included in the attractions; pick up a map at the helpful tourist office. ⇨ *The Minho & the Costa Verde in Chapter 7.*

Day 4: Barcelos

If you like markets, you have come to the right place. Held every Thursday (just follow the shopping baskets), this is celebrated as one of Portugal's biggest and best. Despite the coachloads of visitors, the market is essentially organized by locals for locals and chockablock with ceramics, baskets, toys, fresh produce, agricultural supplies, clothes, shoes, and household equipment. We recommend Barcelos as a day trip, because the market is so well attended that overnight accommodations are scarce. ⇨ *The Minho & the Costa Verde in Chapter 7.*

Day 5: Amarante

If you're looking for love, touching the saintly effigy in the Convento de São Gonçalo is recommended by the locals. Judging by the smooth-as-glass white limestone, there have been plenty of hopefuls. The rest of the day, stroll across the pretty bridge, wander along the riverbanks, or rent a rowboat. ⇨ *The Coast & the Duoro in Chapter 7.*

Day 6: Chaves

Just a few miles from the Spanish border, pretty Chaves once bore the brunt of any attack. Its 14th-century castle is the most prominent feature, but the atmospheric medieval streets, tiled churches, local museums, and thermal springs provide more-passive pastimes. While there, rent a paddleboat from the river gardens for the best views of the ancient Roman Ponte Trajano bridge. ⇨ *Trás-os-Montes in Chapter 7.*

Day 7: Bragança

Within the walls of the Cidadela (citadel) is a superbly preserved medieval village. Wander the cobbles, and gaze at neighboring Spain from the castle walls, then descend to the modern town. Parking is refreshingly easy in this town, with plenty of places by the bus station and even up in the citadel itself. Just follow the signs. ⇨ *Trás-os-Montes in Chapter 7.*

Days 8 & 9: The Eastern Beiras

With fertile valleys, medieval villages, cas-

tles, and fortresses, this area is atmospheric and rugged with tucked-away villages and towns like Fundão, Castelo Rodrigo, and Almeida. Every castle wall tells a story, while every abandoned house or tower harbors a ghost or two. Note that a car is essential for this part of the route as the bus coverage is patchy and sporadic. ⇨ *The Eastern Beiras in Chapter 6.*

Day 10: Sortelha

It's not quite the land that time forgot, but Sortelha comes as close as anywhere in Portugal. Ancient walls, crumbling houses, cobbled streets, and simple back-to-basic accommodation all contribute to the stuck-in-a-time-warp atmosphere. Again, getting here by public transport is possible but problematic, as several of the bus lines only operate during school term time. ⇨ *The Eastern Beiras in Chapter 6.*

WHEN TO GO

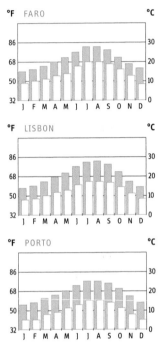

Peak season begins in spring and lasts through autumn. In midsummer it's never unbearably hot (except in parts of the Algarve and on the mainland plains); along the coast, cool breezes often spring up in the evening. In the Algarve, springtime begins in February with a marvelous range of wildflowers. Late September and early October herald Indian summer, which ensures warm sunshine through November. Winter is mild and frequently rainy, except in Madeira, where it feels like spring every day.

Climate

🔁 Forecasts **Weather Channel Connection** (☎ 900/932-8437 95¢ per min ⊕ www.weather.com).

Lisbon

WORD OF MOUTH

"It is clichéd to say that Lisbon is a city of hills, but what we were not prepared for was the wonderful dance of light and color revealed from each vista. . . . Reading about azulejos does not quite prepare you for the intricacy and ubiquity of this beautiful and functional art form. Nor were we really ready for the beautiful trees and flowers everywhere—our guesthouse had lemon and fig trees, a prickly pear cactus, and a myriad of gorgeous flowers."

—dwsnyder

Updated by
Norman
Renouf

LISBON BEARS THE MARK OF AN INCREDIBLE HERITAGE with laid-back pride. Spread over a string of seven hills north of the Rio Tejo (Tagus River) estuary, the city also presents an intriguing variety of faces to those who negotiate its switchback streets. In the oldest neighborhoods, stepped alleys are lined with pastel-color houses and crossed by laundry hung out to dry; here and there *miradouros* (vantage points) afford spectacular river or city views. In the grand 18th-century center, black-and-white mosaic cobblestone sidewalks border wide boulevards. *Elétricos* (trams) clank through the streets, and blue-and-white azulejos (painted and glazed ceramic tiles) adorn churches, restaurants, and fountains.

Of course, there are parts of Lisbon—particularly several suburbs beyond the city center—that lack charm. Even some of the handsome downtown areas have lost their classic Portuguese appearance as the city and its residents have become more cosmopolitan: shiny office blocks have replaced some 19th- and 20th-century art nouveau buildings and sit alongside others. And older, much-loved trams now share the streets with "fast trams" as well as with belching buses and automobiles.

Some of the modernization—particularly the infrastructure upgrades—has improved the city, though. To prepare for its role as host of the World Exposition in 1998, Lisbon spruced up its public buildings, overhauled its metro (subway) system, and completed an impressive bridge across the Rio Tejo. Today the expo site is an expansive riverfront development known as Parque das Nações, and the city is now a popular port of call for European cruise ships, whose passengers disembark onto a lively, revitalized waterfront.

But Lisbon's intrinsic, slightly disorganized, one-of-a-kind charm hasn't vanished in the contemporary mix. Lisboetas are at ease pulling up café chairs and perusing newspapers against any backdrop, whether it reflects the progress and commerce of today or the riches that once poured in from Asia, South America, and Africa. And quiet courtyards and sweeping viewpoints are never far away.

EXPLORING LISBON

Getting Around

The center city is small enough to cover on foot, but because of Lisbon's hills, it's easy to underestimate the distances or the time it takes to cover it. Places may appear close to one another on a map when they're actually on different levels, and the walk can be fearsomely steep. Public transportation is excellent, entertaining, and a bargain, to boot. Marvelous old trams, buses, the metro, and turn-of-the-20th-century funicular railways and elevators can transport you up the hills. If time is short or energy lags, taxis are a genuine bargain and can be summoned with a phone call. And, wherever you are, the Rio Tejo is never far away.

Navigating

The center of Lisbon stretches north from the spacious Praça do Comércio—one of Europe's largest riverside squares—to the Rossío, a smaller square lined with shops and cafés. The district in between is known as

A BIT OF HISTORY

It is Lisbon's geographical location, sitting alongside the wide and natural harbor of the Tejo river, that has made it strategically important as a trading seaport throughout the ages. The city was probably founded around 1200 BC by the Phoenicians, who traded from its port and called it *Alis-Ubo*. The Greeks came next, naming it Olisipo. But it wasn't until 205 BC that Lisbon prospered, when the Romans, calling it in their turn *Felicitas Julia*, linked it by road to the great Spanish cities of the Iberian Peninsula. The Visigoths followed in the 5th century and built the earliest fortifications on the site of the Castelo de São Jorge, but it was with the arrival of the Moors in AD 714 that Lisbon, then renamed *Ascbouna*, came into its own. The city flourished as a trading center during the 300 years of Moorish rule, and the Alfama—Lisbon's oldest district—retains its intricate Arab-influenced layout. In 1147 the Christian army, led by Dom Afonso Henriques and with the assistance of northern Crusaders, took the city after a ruthless siege. To give thanks for the end of Moorish rule, Dom Afonso planned a great cathedral, and the building was dedicated three years later. A little more than a century after that, in 1255, the rise of Lisbon was complete when the royal seat of power was transferred here from Coimbra by Afonso III, and Lisbon was declared capital of Portugal.

The next great period—that of *os descobrimentos* (the discoveries)—began with the 15th-century voyages led by the great Portuguese navigators to India, Africa, and Brazil. During this era, Vasco de Gama set sail for the Indies in 1497–99 and Brazil was discovered in 1500. The wealth realized by these expeditions was phenomenal: gold, jewels, ivory, porcelain, and spices helped finance grand buildings and impressive commercial activity. Late-Portuguese Gothic architecture—called Manueline (after the king Dom Manuel I)—assumed a rich, individualistic style, characterized by elaborate sculptural details, often with a maritime motif. Torre de Belém and the Mosteiro dos Jerónimos (Belém's tower and monastery) are supreme examples of this period.

With independence from Spain in 1640 and assumption of the throne by successive dukes of the house of Bragança, Lisbon became ever more prosperous, only to suffer calamity on November 1, 1755, when it was hit by the last of a series of earthquakes. Two-thirds of Lisbon was destroyed, and tremors were felt as far north as Scotland; 40,000 people in Lisbon died, and entire sections of the city were swept away by a tidal wave.

Under the direction of the prime minister, the Marquês de Pombal, Lisbon was rebuilt quickly and ruthlessly. The medieval quarters were leveled and replaced with broad boulevards; the commercial center, the Baixa, was laid out in a grid; and the great Praça do Comércio, the riverfront square, was planned. Essentially downtown Lisbon has an elegant 18th-century layout that remains as pleasing today as it was intended to be 250 years ago.

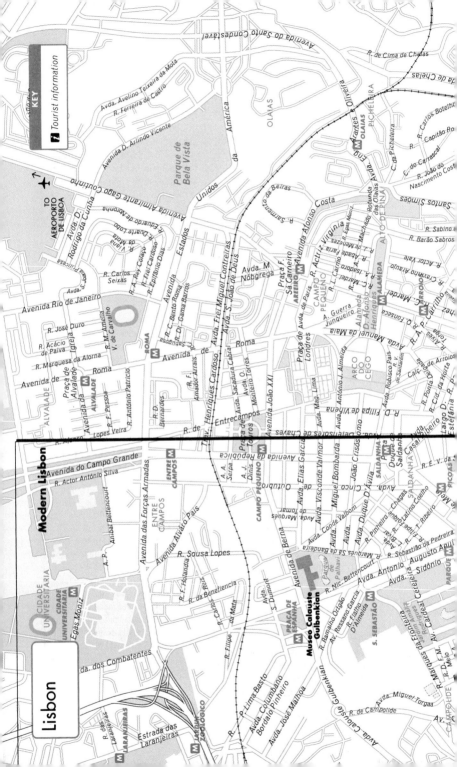

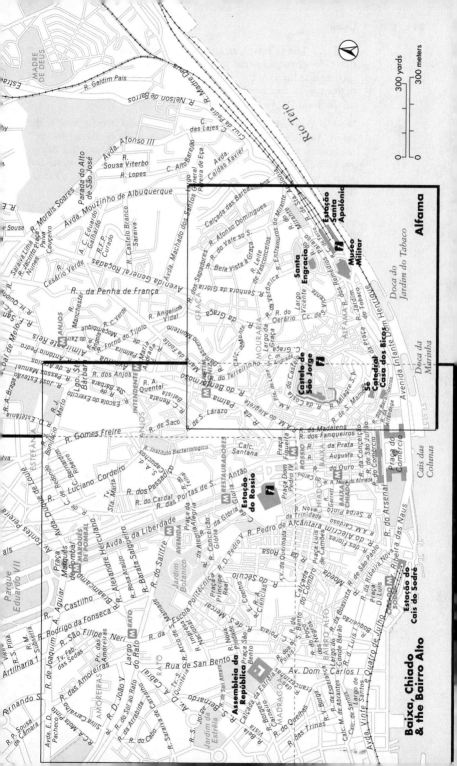

Baixa, Chiado
& the Bairro Alto

Alfama

Rio Tejo

300 yards
300 meters

MADRE
DE DEUS

R. Galdim Pais

R. Nelson de Barros

Cruz da Pedra

C. das Lajes

Avda. Afonso III

R. Sousa Viterbo

C. Alto Barejão

Avda. Pereira de Eça

R. Lopes

Avda. Caldas Xavier

Santos General

Avda. Mouzinho de Albuquerque

Parada do Alto de São José

R. Jacinto Praça

A. C. Eduard Galhardo

R.F.P. Curado

R. Castelo Branco Saraiva

Avda. Machado dos Santos

Calçada das Barbadinhas

R. Afonso Domingues

R. do Vale so S.

R. Bela Vista à Graça

R. dos Sanadores

R. Entremuros do Mirante

Estação Santa Apolónic

R. da Penha de França

R. Manchester

R. C. verde

R. Angelina Vidal

GRAÇA

R. da Graça

Largo Vicente

Santa Engrácia

Museu Militar

Doca do Jardim do Tabaco

ANJOS

Almirante Reis

R. Forno do Tijolo

Senhora da Glória

Largo do Oerário

Cc. de Vi

ALFAMA R. dos Remédios

R. Jardim do Tobaco

Doca da Marinha

R. Antonio Pedro

MOURARIA

Castelo de São Jorge

Casa dos Bicos

Avenida Infante Dom Henrique

INTENDENTE

R. da Palma

R. do Castelo

Sé Catedral

R. Mlaie S.A.

R. de S. Mamede

Cais das Colunas

R. Gomes Freire

R. de Saco

R. da Madalena

R. dos Fanqueiros

da Prata

Augusta

do Ouro

R. da Conceição

R. de São Julião

R. Nova do Almada

Praça do Comércio

Cais da

ESTEFÂNIA

Instituto Bacteriológico

Calç. Santana

Praça da Figueira

ROSSIO

BAIXA CHIADO

R. Luciano Cordeiro

Sta. Marta

R. dos Passadiço

R. do Cardal

R. das Portas de S.

Praça Dom Pedro IV

Estação do Rossio

Antão

Calç. Glória

R. Nova da Trinidade

R. do Alecrim

R. Serpa Pinto

Garrett

Praça Luís de Camões

BAIRRO ALTO

R. das Flores

MARQUÊS DE POMBAL

Praça Marquês de Pombal

Alexandre Herculano

R. Rosa Araújo

R. Barata Salgueiro

R. do Salitre

AVENIDA

Praça da Alegria

R. da Alegria

R. Conceição da Glória

R. D. Pedro V

R. Pedro de Alcântara

R. da Rosa

R. da Ribeira Nova de São Paulo

Estação do Cais do Sodré

CAIS DO SODRÉ

Ribeira das Naus

Parque Eduardo VII

Jardim Botânico

R. Escola Politécnica

Praça do Príncipe Real

R. do Século

R. do Moeda

MARATO

R. Rodrigo da Fonseca

R. São Filippe Neri

Tv. Fab. das Sedas

R. da Escola Politécnica

Praça São Mercal

R. Nova

Imprensa Nacional

R. D. Ciências

R. da Queimada

Calçada do Combro

R. do Poço dos Negros

BAIRRO ALTO

R. de S. Bento

R. dos Polais

Assembleia da República

Rua de San Bento

Praça São Bento

Calçada da Estrela

Av. Dom Carlos I

MADRAGOA

Jardim da Estrela

R. das Trinas

R. de Santos

Av. Vinte e Quatro de Julho

the Baixa (Lower Town), an attractive grid of parallel streets built after the 1755 earthquake and tidal wave. The Alfama, the old Moorish quarter that survived the earthquake, lies east of the Baixa. In this part of town are the Sé (the city's cathedral) and, on the hill above, the Castelo de São Jorge (St. George's Castle).

West of the Baixa, sprawled across another of Lisbon's hills, is the Bairro Alto (Upper Town), an area of intricate 17th-century streets, peeling houses, and churches. Five kilometers (3 mi) farther west is Belém, site of the famous Mosteiro dos Jerónimos, as well as a royal palace and several museums. A similar distance to the northeast, Lisbon's Parque das Nações pivots around the spectacular Oceanário de Lisboa.

The modern city begins at Praça dos Restauradores, adjacent to the Rossío. From here the main Avenida da Liberdade stretches northwest to the landmark Praça Marquês de Pombal, dominated by a column and a towering statue of the man himself. The praça is bordered by the green expanse of the Parque Eduardo VII, named in honor of King Edward VII of Great Britain, who visited Lisbon in 1902.

When to Go

It's best not to visit at the height of summer, when the city positively steams and lodgings are expensive and crowded. Winters are generally mild and usually accompanied by bright blue skies, but for optimum Lisbon weather, visit on either side of summer, in May or late September through October. The city's major festivals are in June; the so-called *santos populares* (popular saints) see days of riotous celebration dedicated to saints Anthony, John, and Peter.

The Alfama

The Moors, who imposed their rule on most of the southern Iberian Peninsula during the 8th century, left their mark on much of Lisbon but nowhere so evidently as in the Alfama district. Here narrow, twisting streets and soaring flights of steps wind up to an imposing castle on one of the city's highest hills. This is a grand place to get your bearings and take in supreme views. Because its foundation is dense bedrock, the district—a jumble of whitewashed houses with flower-laden balconies and red-tile roofs—has survived the wear and tear of the ages, including the great 1755 earthquake.

The timeless alleys and squares have a notoriously confusing layout, but the Alfama is relatively compact, and you'll keep circling back to the same buildings and streets. In the Moorish period this area thrived, and in the 15th century—as evidenced by the ancient synagogue on Beco das Barrelas—it was an important Jewish quarter. Although now a somewhat run-down neighborhood, it has a down-to-earth charm—particularly during the June festivals of the santos populares—and smart bars and restaurants are slowly moving in.

GETTING AROUND   The Alfama's streets and alleys are very steep, and its levels are connected by flights of stone steps, which means it's easier to tour the area from the top down. Take a taxi up to the castle or approach it by Tram 28 from Rua Conceição in the Baixa or Bus 37 from Praça da Figueira.

GREAT ITINERARIES

IF YOU HAVE 2 DAYS

To view all the major attractions in two days, you'll have to get up early. Start at the Rossío, the main downtown square, and stroll through the Baixa, pausing to window-shop or take a coffee. Wander into the Alfama quarter by way of the Sé, following the winding streets past lookout points and churches as far as the hilltop Castelo de São Jorge. The views here are magnificent, and you can grab lunch at one of the many nearby cafés and restaurants. A tram ride takes you back down to the Baixa, where, in the riverside Praça do Comércio, you pick up another tram for the rattling ride west to Belém and the magnificent Mosteiro dos Jerónimos, the acclaimed Torre de Belém, and the *Padrão dos Descobrimentos*. On the way back to the city center, stop off at the Museu de Arte Antiga.

Your second day can be less hectic. Head up to the Bairro Alto and the Chiado shopping area and spend the morning browsing in galleries and stores, visiting the Igreja de São Roque and popping into the Instituto do Vinho do Porto for a glass of port. Have lunch in one of the small taverns or restaurants, and then return to the Baixa via the Elevador da Glória. Take the metro uptown to the Fundação Calouste Gulbenkian, where you can spend a few hours viewing the collections in the Museu Calouste Gulbenkian and the adjacent Centro de Arte Moderna. Alternatively, take the metro to Parque das Nações to visit the Oceanário de Lisboa.

IF YOU HAVE 4 DAYS

Spend the first morning in the Baixa, where the shops and cafés are inviting. At the riverside Praça do Comércio, take a ferry across the river and back for fine city views. Have lunch in the suburb of Cacilhas, where the ferry docks, or return to Praça dos Restauradores, just north of the Rossío, where a side street just off the square—Rua das Portas de Santo Antão—is lined with well-known fish restaurants. Spend the afternoon in the Alfama, taking in the Sé, the Castelo de São Jorge, and the Museu-Escola de Artes Decorativas.

On your second day, catch a tram out to Belém. Spend half the day exploring the monastery and monuments; you'll also have time for at least one of the specialty museums—Museu da Marinha, or Museu Nacional de Coches. On your way to or from Belém, stop at the Museu de Arte Antiga.

Split your two remaining days between old and modern Lisbon. One full day should involve seeing the Chiado shopping area and exploring the Bairro Alto. Be sure to pop into the Convento do Carmo's archaeological museum and make a side trip to the Jardim da Estrêla, or you can spend more time at the Oceanário de Lisboa.

On the final day, walk the length of the boulevard-like Avenida da Liberdade to the city's main park, Parque Eduardo VII, where the greenhouses are a treat. From here, it's a simple metro ride to the Museu Calouste Gulbenkian and the Centro de Arte Moderna.

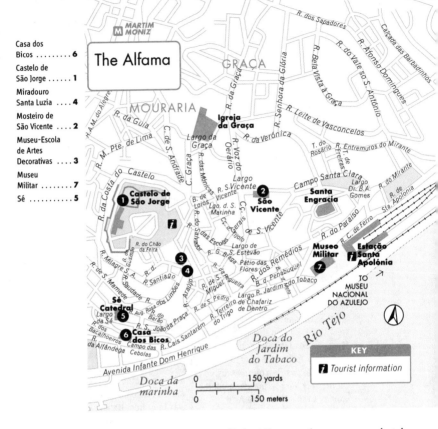

The Alfama

GRAÇA

MOURARIA

Igreja da Graça

Largo da Graça

Largo da Graça

Largo S.Vicente

Castelo de São Jorge ❶

São Vicente ❷

Santa Engracia

Campo Santa Clara

Largo de S. Estêvão

Largo de ❸
❹
Pátio das Flores

Museu Militar ❼

Estação Santa Apolónia

TO MUSEU NACIONAL DO AZULEJO

Sé Catedral ❺

Casa dos Bicos ❻

Rio Tejo

Doca do Jardim do Tabaco

Avenida Infante Dom Henrique

Doca da marinha

0 ___ 150 yards
0 ___ 150 meters

KEY

🛈 *Tourist information*

TIMING Allow two to three hours to walk the Alfama, perhaps more on a hot day, when you'll want to rest on the castle grounds or stop for drinks in a café. A visit to the Museu-Escola de Artes Decorativas will occupy at least an hour or two. Note that most museums are closed Monday, and that churches generally close for a couple of hours in the middle of the day.

What to See

❻ **Casa dos Bicos.** The House of Pointed Stones, an Italianate dwelling, was built in 1523 for Bras de Albuquerque, the son of Afonso, who became the viceroy of India and who conquered Goa and Malacca. It has a striking facade studded with pointed white stones in diamond shapes. The interior is similarly impressive. The top two floors were destroyed in the 1755 earthquake, and restoration did not begin until the early 1980s. ⊠ *Rua dos Bacalhoeiros, Alfama* ☎ *21/888–4827* 🎫 *Free* ⊙ *Weekdays 9:30–5:30.*

❶ **Castelo de São Jorge.** Although St. George's Castle was constructed by the

Fodor'sChoice   Moors, it's on the site that was the beginning of the city and had previ-
★   ously been fortified by Romans and Visigoths. At the main entrance is a statue of Dom Afonso Henriques, who in 1147 besieged the castle and ultimately drove the Moors from Lisbon. Within the walls are ramparts, towers, and remnants of a palace that was a residence of the kings of Por-

IF YOU LIKE

DINING

There's no doubt that Lisbon takes its food seriously; many businesses have *cut* their lunch break to an hour and a half.

Most places serve home-style Portuguese cuisine—grilled sardines and squid, simple steaks and cutlets drenched in olive oil and garlic, fresh seafood (always ask the price before ordering), spit-roasted chicken, lamb chops, and casseroles. Local specialties include *açorda* (a thick bread-and-shellfish stew sprinkled with cilantro), *ameijoas á bulhão pato* (clams in garlic sauce), and different varieties of *bacalhau* (dried salt cod) or *bife* (steak). *Caldeirada* is a simple fish stew that varies from restaurant to restaurant, and once a week any local place worth its salt dishes up a *cozido*—a boiled meat stew.

In addition, the capital serves the best of the country's regional foods, including *porco à alentejana* (pork and clams) from the Alentejo, lampreys from the Minho region of the north, and many seasonal items. If you want still more variety, try restaurants that specialize in colonial Portuguese food: Brazilian, Mozambican, and Goan (Indian).

Wine is good and reasonably priced, with the *vinho da casa* (house wine) usually more than drinkable. It's customary to finish your meal with a glass of port. If you stop by the renowned Instituto do Vinho do Porto during your visit, you can taste different varieties and pick your favorite. Locals set more store by a glass of Moscatel de Setúbal, a rich dessert wine from across the river that's available everywhere.

Almost all Lisbon restaurants permit smoking throughout. If you're averse to smoke, choose a large, high-ceilinged room such as those along the trendy riverfront, avoiding seats in any upper levels; dine alfresco; or plan to eat at top restaurants, which often have powerful filtration systems.

LODGING

In Lisbon you're spoiled for choice when it comes to finding a room—though accommodations aren't the bargains restaurants are.

You can still find reasonably priced rooms among the city's dozens of modest *pensões* (guesthouses), some of which cost less than €40 a night. Be warned, however, that the decor may leave something to be desired, the toilet may be down the hall, and you may have to share a shower. Quality varies greatly from one guesthouse to another, but the best are spotless and friendly, and many are downtown, around the Rossío and the Praça dos Restauradores, as well as in the Bairro Alto.

MUSEUMS

Lisbon has some splendid museums, and all of them are reasonably priced. Standouts include the Museu Calouste Gulbenkian and the Museu de Arte Antiga, which have the finest collections of art and artifacts in the country. The singular Museu Nacional do Azulejo concentrates on the art of the country's famous ceramic tiles.

tugal until the 16th century. From the Câmara Escura in the Torre de São Lourenço you can spy on visitors going about their business below. Named after Roman Lisbon, "Olisipónia" is a multimedia exhibit on the city's history of the city: images projected onto a large wall convey the drama of such episodes as the Great Earthquake of 1755. The rest of the well-kept castle grounds are home to swans, turkeys, ducks, ravens, and other birds, and the outer walls encompass the medieval church of Santa Cruz, a few simple houses, and some restaurants and souvenir shops. Panoramic views of Lisbon can be seen from the walls, giving a very clear perspective of the layout of the city, the broad harbor, and the towering Ponte 25 de Abril suspension bridge; be careful of the uneven footing. ⊠ *Entrances at Largo do Chão da Feira and Largo do Menino de Deus, Alfama* ☎ *21/880–620* ✉ *Castle €5* ⊙ *Mar.–Oct., daily 9–9; Nov.–Feb., daily 9–6.*

❹ Miradouro Santa Luzia. Hop off Tram 28 at this terrace-garden viewpoint that takes in the Alfama and the river. It catches the sun all day, and a nearby café serves welcome drinks. The adjacent Igreja de Santa Luzia (Church of Santa Luzia) is a sorry sight these days. Its exterior was once adorned with fine azulejos depicting the siege of the castle. They've been replaced by heartfelt graffiti—AQUI HAVIA HISTORIA-CULTURA. AGORA—0 ("Here there once existed history and culture. Now—nothing")—that makes its point. ⊠ *Largo da Santa Luzia, Alfama.*

❷ Mosteiro de São Vicente. The Italianate facade of the twin-towered St. Vincent's Monastery heralds an airy church with a barrel-vault ceiling, the work of accomplished Italian architect Filippo Terzi (1520–97). Finally completed in 1704, the church has a superbly tiled cloister depicting the fall of Lisbon to the Moors. The former refectory is the pantheon of the Bragança dynasty, who were the first rulers of an independent Portugal. Only Maria I and Pedro IV are not buried here, and among the solid tombs and weighty inscriptions lies Catherine of Bragança, who married Charles II of England in 1661. There's little to see—save a medieval cistern and a richly decorated entrance hall—but it's worth the admission fee to climb up to the towers and terrace for a look over the Alfama, city, and river. From here you can see the huge white dome of Santa Engraça—the church immediately behind and below São Vicente in Campo de Santa Clara—which doubles as the country's Panteão Nacional (National Pantheon), housing the tombs of Portugal's former presidents as well as cenotaphs dedicated to its most famous explorers and writers. ⊠ *Largo de São Vicente, Alfama* ☎ *21/882–4400* ✉ *Monastery €2, church free, pantheon €1.50* ⊙ *Monastery Tues.–Sun. 10–6; church Tues.–Fri. 9–6, Sat. 9–7, Sun. 9–12:30 and 3–5; pantheon Tues.–Fri. 10–6, Sat. 10–7, Sun. 10–5.*

❸ Museu-Escola de Artes Decorativas. The Museum-School of Decorative Arts, in the 17th-century Azurara Palace, has objects that date from the 15th through 19th century. Look for brightly colored Arraiolos—traditional, hand-embroidered Portuguese carpets based on imported Arabic designs—as well as silver work, ceramics, paintings, and jewelry. With so many rich items to preserve, the museum has become a major center for restoration. Crafts such as bookbinding, carving, and cabinetmaking are all undertaken here by highly trained staff; you can view the restoration work by appointment. ⊠ *Largo das Portas do Sol 2, Alfama* ☎ *21/881–4600* ⊠ *€5* ⊙ *Tues.–Sun. 10–5.*

At Largo das Portas do Sol there are a number of small café-bars with outside seats from which you can watch ships on the Rio Tejo. **Cerca Moura** (⊠ Largo das Portas do Sol 4, Alfama ☎ 21/887–4859)—named after the Moorish walls that surround the district—is one of the best.

❼ Museu Militar. The spirit of derring-do is palpable in the huge Corinthian-style barracks and arsenal complex of the Military Museum. As you clatter through endless, echoing rooms of weapons, uniforms, and armor you may be lucky enough to be followed—at a respectful distance—by a guide who, without speaking a word of English, can convey exactly how that bayonet was jabbed or that gruesome flail swung. In this beautifully ornate building there is also a collection of 18th- to 20th-century art. The museum is on the eastern edge of the Alfama, at the foot of the hill and opposite the Santa Apolónia station. It's easy to get here by Bus 9 or Bus 39. ⊠ *Largo de Santa Apolónia, Alfama* ☎ *21/ 884–2568* ⊠ *€2.50* ⊙ *Tues.–Sun. 10–5.*

MUSEU NACIONAL DO AZULEJO – To fully understand the craftsmanship that goes into making the ubiquitous azulejos, visit this magnificent museum at the 16th-century Madre de Deus convent and cloister. Some of the ceramics exhibited here date from the 1700s. Displays range from individual glazed tiles to elaborate pictorial panels. The 118-foot *Panorama of Lisbon* (1730) is a detailed study of the city and waterfront and is reputedly the country's longest azulejo piece. The richly furnished convent church contains some sights of its own: of note are the gilt baroque decoration and lively azulejo works depicting the life of St. Anthony. There are also a little café-bar and a gift shop that sells tile reproductions. ⊠ *Rua da Madre de Deus 4 (Bus 104 or 105 from Santa Apolónia station), Madre de Deus* ☎ *21/810–0340* ⊕ *www.mnazulejo-ipmuseus.pt* ⊠ *€3* ⊙ *Tues. 2–6, Wed.–Sun. 10–6.*

❺ Sé. Lisbon's austere Romanesque cathedral, Sé (which stands for *Sedes Episcopalis)*, was founded in 1150 to commemorate the defeat of the Moors three years earlier; to rub salt in the wound, the conquerors built the sanctuary on the spot where Moorish Lisbon's main mosque once stood. Note the fine rose window, and be sure to visit the 13th-century cloister and the treasure-filled sacristy, which, among other things, contains the relics of the martyr St. Vincent. According to legend, the relics were carried from the Algarve to Lisbon in a ship piloted by ravens. ⊠ *Largo da Sé, Alfama* ☎ *21/886–1081* ⊠ *Cathedral free, cloister and sacristy €2.50* ⊙ *Cathedral daily 10–7, cloister and sacristy daily 10–1 and 2–6.*

The Baixa

The earthquake of 1755, a massive tidal wave, and subsequent fires killed thousands of people and reduced proud 18th-century Lisbon to rubble. But within 10 years, frantic rebuilding under the direction of the king's minister, the Marquês de Pombal, had given the city a new look: a neoclassical grid design. You can still see this perfectly today in the impressive Baixa district—which these days includes shops, restaurants, small hotels, and other commercial enterprises—that stretches from the riverfront to the square known as the Rossío. Pombal intended the various streets to house workshops for certain trades and crafts, something that's still reflected in street names such as Rua dos Sapateiros (Cobblers' Street) and Rua da Prata (Silversmiths' Street). Near the neoclassical arch at the bottom of Rua Augusta, street stalls selling jewelry and ethnic items sometimes appear on weekends.

TIMING You could walk the Baixa in half an hour, but multiply that by four to allow time to explore the sights and poke into shops. Then add an hour or more for people-watching or lingering in a café, enjoying the Rossío's satisfying chaos.

What to See

★ ⑩ **Elevador de Santa Justa.** Built in 1902 by Raul Mésnier, who studied under Eiffel, the Santa Justa Elevator, inside a Gothic-style tower, is one of Lisbon's more extraordinary structures. After stepping outside the elevator compartment at the upper level, you can either take the walkway leading to the Largo do Carmo, or climb the staircase to the very top of the structure for views of the Baixa district and beyond. There's a windswept café up here, at an elevation of 147½ feet, though its prices, like its location, are sky high. ⊠ *Rua Aurea and Rua de Santa Justa, Baixa* ☎ *21/361–3054* 🎫 *€2.40 return* ☉ *Daily 9–9.*

❽ **Praça do Comércio.** When the Marquês de Pombal completed his plan for Lisbon, he offset the gridded streets you now see in the Baixa district with the enormous riverfront Praça do Comércio. Known also as the Terreiro do Paço, after the royal palace (the Paço) that once stood here, it's lined with yellow, arcaded, 18th-century buildings. Steps—once used by occupants of the royal barges that docked here—lead up from the water onto the square. The equestrian statue is of Dom José I, king at the time of the earthquake and subsequent rebuilding. In 1908, amid unrest that led to the declaration of a republic, King Carlos and his eldest son, Luís Filipe, were assassinated as they rode through the square in a carriage. Later, during the 1974 revolution, the Praça do Comércio and its surrounding government buildings were among the first places to be occupied by rebel troops. The square itself is a hub for public transportation (trams to Belém leave from here, and ferries cross the Tagus at this point), and it's also worth coming here on Sunday morning, when a market of old coins and banknotes takes place under the arches of the arcade. To the west of the square (your right if you're facing the waterfront) and along Rua do Arsenal is the smart **Lisbon Welcome Centre** (☎ 21/031–2700) with its information desk, modern art gallery, auditorium, tobacco shop, café, deli, and restaurant. It's open daily from 9 to 8.

⌐
NEED A
BREAK?

One of the original buildings on Praça do Comércio houses the **Café Martinho da Arcada** (⊠ Praça do Comércio 3, Baixa ☎ 21/887-9259), a literary haunt since 1782. The main rooms contain an expensive restaurant; adjacent to it is a more modest café-bar.

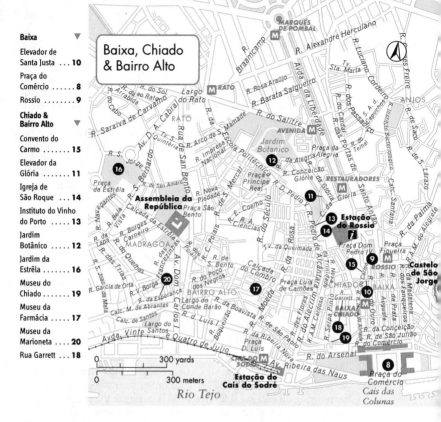

**Baixa, Chiado
& Bairro Alto**

⑨ Rossio. Lisbon's main square since the Middle Ages is popularly known as the Rossío, although its official name is Praça Dom Pedro IV (whom the central statue commemorates). Although rather overwhelmed by the traffic that circles it, the Rossío is a grand space, with ornate French fountains. Public executions were once carried out here; slightly less dramatic performances these days are on show in the mid-19th-century Teatro Nacional (National Theater). It's at the square's northern edge and was built on the site of the Palace of the Inquisition. You'll probably do what the locals do when they come to the Rossío, though: pick up a newspaper, sit at one of the cafés that line the square's east and west sides, and, perhaps, have one of the roaming shoe shiners give your boots a polish—just be sure to agree on a price first.

FodorsChoice ★

Sala Ogival. If you're curious about Portuguese wine—either as an expert or as a novice—be sure to stop by this new showroom for Vini Portugal, the organization responsible for promoting Portuguese wines domestically and internationally. Admission to the gorgeous marble showroom is free, and you'll have the opportunity to taste a flight of wines of your choosing. ⊠ *Praça do Comércio, Baixa* ☎ *21/342–0690* ☉ *Tues.–Sat. 10 AM–8 PM.*

Chiado & the Bairro Alto

West of the Baixa is the fashionable shopping district of Chiado. Although a calamitous 1988 fire destroyed much of the area, an ambitious rebuilding program has restored some of the fin de siècle facades. And a chic retail complex, hotel, and metro station on the site of the old Armazéns do Chiado—once Lisbon's largest department store—has given the district a modern focus. Along Rua Garrett and Rua do Carmo are some of Europe's best shoe stores as well as glittering jewelry shops, hip boutiques, and a host of cafés and delis. Chiado's narrow, often-cobbled streets lead to the Bairro Alto and often follow contours of the hills, which can make getting around confusing. Although the settlement of the Bairro Alto dates from the 17th century, most of the buildings are from the 18th and 19th centuries and are an appealing mixture of small churches, warehouses, antiques and art galleries, artisans' shops, and town houses with wrought-iron balconies.

Bairro Alto's streets are filled with the sounds of daily life: children scuffle amid the drying laundry, women carry huge bundles from shop to shop, and old men clog the doorways of barrooms. The neighborhood has always had a reputation as being rather rough-and-ready, and there's still a thriving red-light district and back alleys where it would be unwise to venture after dark. On the whole, however, it's safe to walk around; indeed, the Bairro Alto has more bars, restaurants, fado clubs, and discos than any other district.

TIMING   The Bairro Alto is remarkably compact, and it takes very little time to walk from one end to the other; an hour would cover it. But once you start diving off into the side streets and lingering in the shops, galleries, and bars, you'll find you can happily spend a morning or afternoon here. Neither the Igreja de São Roque nor the Convento do Carmo will occupy you for more than half an hour. Note that the Instituto do Vinho do Porto doesn't open until 2 PM. If you don't like crowds, avoid the Bairro Alto late at night, especially on weekends, when seemingly the whole of Lisbon comes here to eat, drink, and party.

What to See

⓮ Convento do Carmo. The partially ruined Carmelite Convent—once Lisbon's largest—was severely damaged in the 1755 earthquake. Today open-air summer orchestral concerts are held beneath its majestic archways. Its sacristy houses the **Museu Arqueológico do Carmo** (Archaeological Museum), a small but worthy collection of ceramic tiles, medieval tombs, ancient coins, and other city finds. Photographers take note: you're only allowed to take pictures of the exterior sections of the building. The convent is unlikely to delay you long, but the lovely square outside is a great place to pull up a café seat. ⊠ *Largo do Carmo, Chiado* ☎ *21/347–8629* ⊑ *€2.50* ☉ *Apr.–Sept., Mon.–Sat. 10–6; Oct.–Mar., Mon.–Sat. 10–5.*

⓫ Elevador da Glória. One of the finest approaches to the Bairro Alto is via this funicular railway on the western side of Avenida da Liberdade, near Praça dos Restauradores. It runs up the steep hill and takes only about a minute to reach the São Pedro de Alcântara Miradouro, a viewpoint that looks out over the castle and the Alfama. ✉ *Calçada da Glória, Bairro Alto* ☎ *21/363–2044* 💲 *€0.90 one-way* ⊙ *Daily 7 AM–midnight.*

⑭ Igreja de São Roque. Filippo Terzi, the architect who designed São Vicente on the outskirts of the Alfama, was also responsible for this Renaissance church. He was commissioned by Jesuits and completed the church in 1574. Curb your impatience with its plain facade and venture inside. Its eight side chapels have statuary and art dating from the early 17th century. The last chapel on the left before the altar is the extraordinary 18th-century Capela de São João Baptista (Chapel of St. John the Baptist): designed and built in Rome, with rare stones and mosaics that resemble oil paintings, the chapel was taken apart, shipped to Lisbon, and reassembled here in 1747. You may find a guide who will escort you around the church and switch on the appropriate lights so the beauty of the chapel is revealed. Adjoining the church, the **Museu de Arte Sacra** (Museum of Sacred Art) displays a surprisingly engaging collection of clerical vestments and liturgical objects: the capes and drapes are delicately embroidered in gold, and the jewel-encrusted crosses and goblets glitter in their cases. ✉ *Largo Trindade Coelho, Bairro Alto* ☎ *21/323–5381* 💲 *Church free; museum €1.50 Mon.–Sat., free Sun.* ⊙ *Church weekdays 8:30–5, weekends 9:30–5; museum daily 10–5* Ⓜ *Baixa-Chiado.*

★ ⑬ Instituto do Vinho do Porto. In the cozy, clublike lounge, you can taste some of the Port Wine Institute's more than 300 types and vintages of port—from extra-dry white varieties to red vintages. Service can be slow, but eventually someone will bring you a wine list, and you can order by the glass or bottle. ✉ *Rua de São Pedro de Alcântara 45, Bairro Alto* ☎ *21/347–5707* ⊕ *www.ivp.pt* 💲 *Free; prices of tastings vary, starting at €1* ⊙ *Mon.–Sat. 2 PM–midnight* Ⓜ *Restauradores (then take Elevador de Glória).*

⑫ Jardim Botânico. Lisbon's main botanical garden was first laid out in 1874. Hidden between backstreets about 2 km (1 mi) north of the Bairro Alto, it makes a restful stop, with 10 acres of paths, benches, and nearly 15,000 species of subtropical plants; there's also a 19th-century meteorological observatory. ✉ *Rua da Escola Politécnica 58; weekday entrance also at Rua do Alegria, near Av. da Liberdade, Principe Real* ☎ *21/396–1521* ⊕ *www.mnhn.ul.pt* 💲 *Gardens €1, observatory free* ⊙ *Gardens May–Oct., weekdays 9–8, weekends 10–8; Nov.–Apr., weekdays 9–6, weekends 10–6; guided tours (reservations required) year-round Sat. at 11. Museum weekdays 10–5.*

⑯ Jardim da Estrêla. Inside the attractively laid out Estrêla Garden, old men sit at tables playing card games. Watch them a while, stroll the shaded paths, and then pull up a chair in the café for a drink or a snack. Towering over the southwestern side is the 18th-century **Basilica da Estrêla**, which is open daily 7:45 AM–8 PM. This spacious baroque basilica has an unusually restrained interior and offers views of the city from its *zimborio* (dome). The gardens lie on the western edge of the Bairro Alto. You can walk here, although it's more pleasant to catch Tram 28, which runs from Rua do Loreto, near Praça Luís de Camões, just west of Largo do Carmo.

⑲ Museu do Chiado. The Chiado's prime art gallery—built on the site of a monastery—specializes in Portuguese art from 1850 to the present day, covering various movements: romanticism, naturalism, surrealism, modernism. The museum also hosts international films and temporary exhibitions of paintings and sculpture. The museum may close between exhibitions, so call ahead before visiting. ⊠ *Rua Serpa Pinto 4, Chiado* ☎ *21/343–2148* ⊕ *www.museudochiado-ipmuseus.pt* 🎟 *€3, free Sun. until 2* PM ☉ *Tues. 2–6, Wed.–Sun. 10–6.*

⑰ Museu da Farmácia. The Museum of Pharmacy, within an old palace, covers more than 5,000 years of pharmaceutical history, from prehistoric cures to the fantastic world of fictive potions à la Harry Potter. Ancient objects related to pharmaceutical science and art—from Mesopotamia, Egyptian, Roman, and Incan civilizations—are on display in well-lighted showcases, as are those from Europe. Whole pharmacies have been transported here intact from other parts of Portugal, even a traditional 19th-century Chinese drugstore from Portugal's former territory of Macau. Call ahead to arrange lunch in the very elegant restaurant with excellent food. A very convenient feature of the museum is that it has a private parking lot. ⊠ *Rua Marechal Saldanha 1, Chiado* ☎ *21/340–0682* ⊕ *www. anf.pt* 🎟 *€5* ☉ *Weekdays 10–6 and last Sun. of each month 2–6.*

☾ ⑳ Museu da Marioneta. The intricate workmanship that went into the creation of the puppets on display at this museum is remarkable, and it's not just kids' stuff, either: during the Salazar regime, puppet shows were used to mock the pretensions and corruption of the politicians. The collection encompasses both Portuguese and foreign puppets. Those from Santo Aleixo in the Alentejo region (just south of Lisbon) are particularly notable, measuring just over 6 inches high. ⊠ *Convento das Bernardas, Rua da Esperança 146, Madragoa* ☎ *21/394–2810* 🎟 *€2.50* ☉ *Tues.–Sun. 10–1 and 2–6.*

⑱ Rua Garrett. The Chiado's principal street is lined with old stores and turn-of-the-20th-century, wood-paneled coffee shops. The most famous of the cafés is **Café A Brasileira** (⊠ Rua Garrett 120, Chiado ☎ 21/346–9541), which has a life-size statue of Portugal's national poet, Fernando Pessoa, seated at an outside table.

The Modern City

The attractions of 19th- to 20th-century Lisbon are as diverse as they are far-flung. Near the large square Praça dos Restauradores, north of Rossío, the southern reaches of the modern city echo some of the Baixa. With its 10 parallel rows of trees, Avenida da Liberdade is an enchanting place in which to linger and an easy-to-find reference point if you get lost in the surrounding backstreets. North of the city's main park, Parque Eduardo VII, the modern city stretches into residential suburbs with only the occasional attraction. You can reach all of them by public transportation or, if time is short, by taxi.

TIMING   In expansive, modern Lisbon, choosing sights according to your mood and the weather isn't out of line. You really will have to make choices about what to visit if you have just one day—to see everything, allow two or three days. It could take three hours to do justice to the Gulbenkian alone—especially if you have lunch on the premises. The palace and its gardens justify another hour easily; add another for walking (or two if you eschew any travel by taxis or metro), and perhaps another hour for shopping and a coffee break on the Avenida da Liberdade.

What to See

㉕ Amoreiras. Before the Parque das Nações site was developed, Lisbon could count its postmodern architectural triumphs on one finger—namely the gigantic pink-and-blue Amoreiras, a striking commercial-and-residential complex west of Parque Eduardo VII. Designed by Tomás Taveira in 1985 and visible from just about everywhere in town, the gleaming complex still turns heads; inside, there's a huge shopping center, a 10-screen movie theater, a food court—even a chapel. On weekends it seems all of Lisbon turns out to roam the corridors. Just across the road, you will now find the tower block housing the massive Dom Pedro hotel, whose top floors have incredible views over the city. ⊠ *Av. Eng. Duarte Pacheco, Amoreiras* ☎ *21/381–0200* ⊕ *www.amoreiras.com* ☉ *Shops and restaurants daily 10* AM*–midnight* Ⓜ *Marquês de Pombal.*

㉖ Aqueduto das Aguas Livres. Lisbon was formerly provided with clean drinking water by means of the Aqueduct of Free Waters (1729–48), built by Manuel da Maia and stretching for more than 18 km (11 mi) from the water source on the outskirts of the city. It survived the 1755 earthquake, and today its most graceful section consists of 14 arches that soar 200 feet over the pretty neighborhood square of Largo das Amoreiras. The aqueduct itself is off-limits unless you book a group tour, but the square is also the site of the associated Mãe d'Agua, an internal reservoir capable of holding more than a million gallons of water. This extraordinary structure is used for art exhibitions and other cultural displays, giving you the chance to view the vast holding tank, the lavish internal waterfall, and the associated machinery. ⊠ *Largo das Amoreiras, Campolide* ☎ *21/854–0484 for tours of aqueduct.*

㉒ Avenida da Liberdade. In the Restauradores neighborhood, Liberty Avenue—downtown's spine—was laid out in 1879. What started as an elegant rival to the Champs Élysées has lost some of its allure: many of the late-19th-century mansions and art deco buildings that once graced it have been demolished; others have been turned into soulless office blocks. There are, however, still some high-class hotels on the lower and mid-level sections, mixed in with old-fashioned and inexpensive pensions. Vehicles roar down both sides. It's still worth a leisurely stroll up the 1½-km (1-mi) length of the avenue, from Praça dos Restauradores to the Parque Eduardo VII, at least once—if only to cool off with a drink in one of the *esplanadas* (garden cafés). There are two amid the plane trees in the middle of the avenue. Halfway up and on the avenue's western side, the few theaters that make up Lisbon's surviving downtown theater district congregate in Parque Mayer.

㉙ Centro de Arte Moderna. In the gardens outside the Fundação Calouste Gulbenkian, sculptures hide in every recess. You may want to spend a little time here before following signs to the Modern Art Center—the

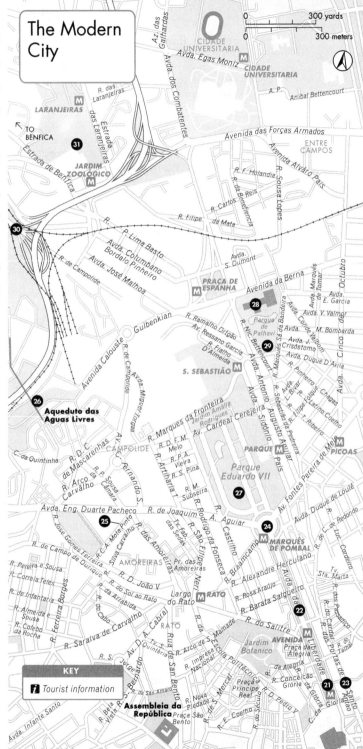

The Modern City

300 yards

300 meters

CIDADE
UNIVERSITARIA

Az. das Galhardas

Avda. Egas Moniz

CIDADE
UNIVERSITARIA

A. P.   Anibal Bettencourt

R. das
Laranjeiras

LARANJEIRAS

TO
BENFICA

Estrada das Laranjeiras

Avenida das Forças Armados

ENTRE
CAMPOS

Avenida Alvaro Pais

Avenida dos Combatentes

R. F. Hotandia

JARDIM
ZOOLÓGICO

Estrada de Benfica

Avenida Sousa Lopes

R. de Benefléncia

R. Carlos
da Mata

R. Filipe

R. da Benefléncia

R.   P. Lima Basto

Avda. Columbano
Bordalo Pinheiro

Avda. José Malhoa

R. de Campolide

Avda.
S. Dumont

PRAÇA DE
ESPANHA

Avenida da Berna

Avda. Marquês
de Tomar

Avda.
E. Garcia

Octubro

Avda. V. Valmor

Avda. Conde Valbon

R. Ramalho Ortigão

Gulbenkian

Av. Ressano Garcia

R. Flatho
D'Almeida

Parque
de
Palhavi

R. Nc Betencourt

R. Marquês Sá da Bandeira

M. Bombarda

Avda. J.
Crisóstomo

Avda. Cinco

Avda. Duque D'Avila

Avenida Calouste

R. de Campolide

Avda. Miguel Bomba

S. SEBASTIÃO

Avda. Antonio Augusto Aguiar

R. Pinheiro Chagas

R. L. Biva

R. Latino Coelho

R. Filipe Folque

R. T. Ribeiro

26 **Aqueduto das
Aguas Livres**

R. Marques da Fronteira

Jardim Amália
Rodrigues

Av. Cardeal Cerejeira

R. Sebastião da Pedreira

C. da Quintinha

R. D. C.
de Mascarenhas

CAMPOLIDE

R. D. F. M.
Melo

R. P. A.
Vieira

R. S. Pina

PARQUE

PICOAS

Avda. Sidónio Pais

Av. Fontes Pereira de Melo

R. Arco
Carvalho

R. P. Sousa
Camara

R. Fernando S.

R. Artiharia I

R. M.
Subserra

Parque
Eduardo VII

Avda. Duque de Loulé

Avda. Eng. Duarte Pacheco

R. de Joaquim

R. Rodrigo da Fonseca

R. A. Aguiar

27

24

R. C. de Redondo

Lic. Cordeiro

25

R. José Gomes Ferreira

R. C. A. Mota Pinto

Silva Carvalho

R. das Amoreiras

Tv. Fab.
das Sedas

R. São Filipe

MARQUÊS
DE POMBAL

R. Braamcamp

R. Alexandre Herculano

Tv.
Sta. Marta

R. de Campo de Ourique

AMOREIRAS

Pr. das
Amoreiras

Neri

R. Rosa Araújo

Avda. da

R. Pereira e Sousa

R. D. João V

R. Correia Teles

R. P. da Arrabida

Largo
do Rato

RATO

R. Barata Salgueiro

R. das Portas de

R. de Infantaria I

P. da Arrabida

R. do Sol ao Rato

R. Almeida e
Spusa

P. Cabo

Cabra

R. do Salitre

R. do Cardas

22

R. Cotelo
da Rocha

Ferreira Borges

R. Saraiva de Carvalho

RATO

R. de

R. Arço de S. Mamade

Jardim
Botanico

AVENIDA

Praça Liberdade

R. das Portas de

R. S.
Jorge

Av. D'Quintéria

Rua de San Bento

Escola Politécnica

Praça
da Alegria

R. Nova
Piedade

Praça
Principe
Real

R. Conceição
Glória

21 **23**

Santo Antão

Avda. Infante Santo

R. Bela
Vista

R. de San Amaro

**Assembleia da
República**

Praça São
Bento

R. Impresa
Nacional

R. de S. Marçal

R. E. Coelho

D. Pedro V

C. da Glória

KEY

ℹ *Tourist information*

20th-century art collection of the Calouste Gulbenkian Foundation, with its two floors of contemporary and modern works, the finest collection of its sort in Portugal. Naturally, Portuguese artists are best represented: look for pieces by Amadeo de Sousa Cardoso, whose painting style varied greatly in his short life; abstract works by Viera da Silva; and the childhood themes explored in the paintings of Paula Rego. There's also a special section set aside for drawings and prints. ⊠ *Rua Dr. N. Bettencourt, São Sebastião* ☎ *21/782–3000* ⊕ *www.gulbenkian.pt/arte/camjap.asp* ✉ *€3, combined ticket with the Calouste Gulbenkina Foundation €5; free Sun.* ◷ *Tues.–Sun. 10–5:45* Ⓜ *São Sebastião.*

㉛ Jardim Zoológico. With a menagerie of 2,000 animals from more than 370 species, the Zoological Garden is always a popular spot. Admission is pricey, but in addition to the usual habitats and enclosures there are a gorilla house, free range–style areas for larger animals, a children's zoo with miniature houses and small animals, a cable-car ride, and twice-daily animal shows (you have your pick of those that feature parrots, dolphins, or reptiles). You can pack a picnic lunch or eat at one of the on-site snack bars and restaurants. ⊠ *Estrada de Benfica 158, Sete Rios* ☎ *21/723–2910* ⊕ *www.zoolisboa.pt* ✉ *€12.50* ◷ *Late Apr.–Sept., daily 10–8; Oct.–mid-Apr., daily 10–6* Ⓜ *Jardim Zoológico or Sete Rios.*

㉘ Museu Calouste Gulbenkian. On its

Fodor'sChoice ★

own lush grounds, the museum of the celebrated Fundação Calouste Gulbenkian (Calouste Gulbenkian Foundation), a cultural trust, houses treasures collected by Armenian oil magnate Calouste Gulbenkian (1869–1955) and donated to the people of Portugal in return for tax concessions. The collection is split in two: one part is devoted to Egyptian, Greek, Roman, Islamic, and

> **DOWN DEEP**
>
> Free concerts are given some Sundays in the library atrium, and the foundation also has two concert halls, where music and ballet festivals are held in winter and spring. Modestly priced tickets are available at the box office.

Asian art and the other to European acquisitions. Both holdings are relatively small, but the quality of the pieces on display is magnificent, and you should aim to spend at least two hours here or even the better part of a day. English-language notes are available throughout the museum.

One of the highlights in the astounding Egyptian Room is a haunting gold mummy mask. Greek and Roman coins and statuary, Chinese porcelain, Japanese prints, and a set of rich 16th- and 17th-century Persian tapestries follow. The European art section has pieces from all the major schools from the 15th through the 20th century. A room of vivid 18th-century Venetian scenes by Francesco Guardi and paintings by Rembrandt, Peter Paul Rubens, Claude Monet, and Pierre-Auguste Renoir stimulate the senses, as do the Italian and Spanish ceramics, gleaming French furniture, textiles, and art nouveau jewelry.

If it's all too much to take in at one time, break up your visit with a stop in the basement's pleasant café-restaurant. There's an exhibition room here, too, with temporary displays. As you leave the museum, you can buy posters and postcards at the main desk. ⊠ *Av. de Berna 45, São Sebastião* ☎ *21/782–3000* ⊕ *www.museu.gulbenkian.pt* ▣ *€3, combined ticket with Modern Art Center €5; free Sun.* ☉ *Tues.–Sun. 10–5:45* Ⓜ *São Sebastião or Praça de Espanha.*

🕉 **Palácio dos Marqueses da Fronteira.** Built in the late 17th century, the Palace of the Marquises, often called the Palácio Fronteira, remains one of the capital's most beautiful houses, containing splendid reception rooms with 17th- and 18th-century tiles, contemporary furniture, and paintings. Note that visits may be limited to guided tours; phone ahead for information. The grounds harbor a terraced walk, a topiary garden, and statuary and fountains. Some of the city's finest azulejos adorn the fountains and terraces and depict hunting scenes, battles, and religious themes. ⊠ *Largo de São Domingo de Benfica 1, São Domingo de Benfica* ☎ *21/778–2023* ▣ *Palace €7.50; gardens weekdays €3, Sat. €2.50* ☉ *July–Sept., Mon.–Sat. for guided tours (must be booked in advance for groups only) at 10:30, 11, 11:30, and noon; Oct.–May, Mon.–Sat. 11 AM and noon* Ⓜ *Sete Rios.*

🕧 **Parque Eduardo VII.** Established at the beginning of the 20th century in the São Sebastião district, the city's main park was named to honor the British monarch's 1902 visit here during his brief reign. The sloping, formal gardens are used by surprisingly few of Lisbon's residents. There are, however, magnificent views from the avenue at the top of the park, where modernistic towers topped by concrete wheat sheaves stand like sentinels. The park also has Lisbon's best-kept horticultural secrets: the *estufa fria* (cold greenhouse) and *estufa quente* (hot greenhouse), which contain rare flowers, trees, and shrubs from tropical and subtropical climes. These are gorgeous grottoes in which to stroll, and concerts and exhibitions are held in the estufa fria from time to time. ☎ *21/388–2278 for information on greenhouses* ▣ *Greenhouses €1.20* ☉ *Park daily dawn–dusk. Greenhouses Apr.–Sept., daily 9–6; Oct.–Mar., daily 9–5* Ⓜ *Parque or Marquês de Pombal.*

🕤 **Praça Marquês de Pombal.** Dominating the center of Marquês de Pombal Square is a statue of the marquês himself, the man responsible for the design of the "new" Lisbon that emerged from the ruins of the 1755 earthquake. On the statue's base are representations of both the earthquake and the tidal wave that engulfed the city; a female figure with outstretched arms signifies the joy at the emergence of the refashioned

BULLFIGHTS

Campo Pequeno. Nothing grabs your attention quite so suddenly as the city's circular, redbrick, Moorish-style bullring, an over-the-top structure built in 1892 with small cupolas atop its four main towers. Recently totally renovated, the ring holds about 9,000 people who crowd in to watch weekly-Portuguese-style bull-fights, in which the bull is never killed in the ring, held every Thursday at 10 PM from June through September. At other times it's used as the venue that circuses and similar events. ⊠ *Praça de Touros do Campo Pequeno, Av. da República, Campo Pequeno* ☎ *21/793-2093* Ⓜ *Campo Pequeno.*

city. The square is effectively a large roundabout—known informally as the Rotunda—and a useful orientation point, since it stands at the northern end of Avenida da Liberdade (in the Baixa district) with Parque Eduardo VII (in the São Sebastião quarter) just behind. New buildings with classic facades are rising along the square's rim, and there are impressive entrances to the Marquês de Pombal metro station.

㉑ Praça dos Restauradores. Although this square, which is adjacent to Rossío train station, marks the beginning of modern Lisbon, it's technically part of the Baixa district. Here the broad, tree-lined Avenida da Liberdade starts its northwesterly ascent. *Restauradores* means "restoration," and the square commemorates the 1640 uprising against Spanish rule that restored Portuguese independence. An obelisk (raised in 1886) commemorates the event. Note the elegant 18th-century Palácio Foz, on the square's west side. Before World War I, it contained a casino; today it houses a tourist office. The only building to rival the palace is the restored Eden building, just to the south. The art deco masterpiece of Portuguese architect Cassiano Branco now contains the VIP Eden apartment-hotel and a Virgin Megastore.

㉓ Rua das Portas de Santo Antão. Everyone knows that if you want to eat seafood in the center of Lisbon, you come to the Baixa district's Rua das Portas de Santo Antão. Waiters lurk in the doorways of the many fish eateries that line this pedestrians-only street a block east of Praça dos Restauradores. Most establishments display fish on ice slabs and great tanks of lobsters; choose your meal and then sit at a table outside on the cobblestones to enjoy it. There are subtle contrasts here, too. Alongside the aforementioned restaurants there are tiny bars with an amazing selection of sandwiches, rolls, and other tasty bits and pieces. There's also **Gambrinus**, a restaurant considered one of the very best in Portugal, let alone Lisbon. Later, if you're daring, pop into one of the street's two surviving *ginginha* bars—cubbyholes where unshaven gents and local characters stand around throwing down shots of eye-wateringly strong cherry brandy.

Belém

Some of Lisbon's grandest monuments and museums are in the district of Belém (the Portuguese word for Bethlehem), at the city's southwestern edge. It was from here that the country's great explorers set out during the period of the discoveries. The wealth brought back from the New World helped pay for many of the neighborhood's structures, some of which are the best examples of the uniquely Portuguese late-Gothic architecture known as Manueline.

Although several buses and Tram 18 will get you here from Lisbon's center, the 30-minute ride on Tram 15 from the Baixa district's Praça do Comércio is very scenic. Tram 15 also passes close by or stops right at several of the important sights.

TIMING Set aside two or three hours for the Museu de Arte Antiga and another hour or two for the Mosteiro dos Jerónimos. This leaves an hour or two for one of the other museums and monuments—after that, you'll probably want to just flop into a chair at an Alcântara district bar or restaurant. Note that most of Belém's sights are closed Monday, and Sunday sees free or reduced admission at many attractions.

What to See

③④ Alcântara. The docks are alive with music in Alcântara, where late-night bars attract Lisbon's "in crowd." Here, in the lee of the huge Ponte 25 de Abril, the old wharves have been made over, and you can walk along the landscaped riverfront all the way to Belém (a 30-minute stroll). At Doca de Santo Amaro, under the bridge on its east side, a line of fashionable restaurants and clubs has emerged from the shells of former warehouses. These establishments are often more fashionable than culinary, though, and the constant rumble of cars passing over the bridge combined with occasional low-level airplanes preparing to land may disrupt your dining experience. Weigh the pros and cons carefully. Either way, the people-watching and potential for late-night mirth are extraordinary. On the terrace in front of the marina, the party goes on until late into the night. During the day, the easiest way to get here is by train from Cais do Sodré station or on Tram 15; at night, take a taxi.

④② Centro Cultural de Belém. Built of pink granite and marble, the modern Belém Cultural Center won few friends when it was constructed in 1991, although all of Lisbon appreciates its cultural offerings. The center, formerly the home of the Museu do Design, has a restaurant, a café, and a concert hall. Its roof gardens and terrace bar have fine views of the Mosteiro dos Jerónimos and the Rio Tejo. ⊠ *Praça do Império, Belém* ☎ *21/361–2400* ⊕ *www.ccb.pt* ☜ *Cultural center free* ☉ *Cultural center daily 8 AM–9:30 PM.*

③⑦ Jardim Botânico da Ajuda. Portugal's oldest botanical garden—laid out in 1768 by the Italian botanist Domenico Vandelli (1735–1816)—is an enjoyable place to spend an hour or so. You can stroll up here from the river at Belém, or take Tram 18 from downtown, which terminates near here. The many species of flora, labeled in Latin, are in several greenhouses covering 10 acres; if you call in advance, you may be able to arrange a guided tour. ⊠ *Calçada da Ajuda, Alto de Ajuda* ☎ *21/362–2503* ☜ *€2* ☉ *Thurs.–Tues. 10–5.*

③⑨ Mosteiro dos Jerónimos. Conceived and commissioned by Dom Manuel I, who petitioned the Holy See for permission to build it in 1496, Belém's famous Jerónimos Monastery was financed largely by treasures brought back from Africa, Asia, and South America. Construction began in 1502 under the supervision of Diogo de Boitaca (architect of the pioneering Igreja de Jesus at Setúbal) and his successor, João de Castilho, a Spaniard.

Fodor'sChoice
★

The monastery is a supreme example of the Manueline style of building (named after King Dom Manuel I), which represented a marked departure from the prevailing Gothic. Much of it is characterized by elaborate sculptural details, often with a maritime motif. João de Castilho was responsible for the southern portal, which forms the main entrance to the church: the figure on the central pillar is Henry the Navigator, and the canopy shows a hierarchy of statues contained within niches.

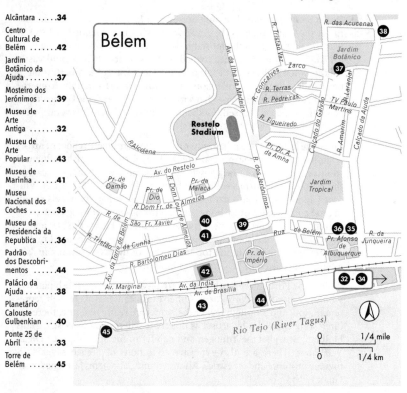

Inside, the remarkably spacious interior contrasts with the riot of decoration on the six nave columns, which disappear into a complex latticework ceiling. The Gothic- and Renaissance-style double cloister on the lower level was also designed to stunning effect by Castilho. The arches and pillars are heavily sculpted with marine motifs. It was meant to become, too, the pantheon of the new branch of the royal House of Aviz, of which Manuel I was the first monarch. Notice, also, the presence of elephants supporting tombs—these were derived from the colonies and considered a symbol of strength. The Hieronymite community lived in the monastery for over 400 years until the dissolution of religious orders in Portugal in 1833, when it was turned over to the state. ⊠ *Praça do Império, Belém* ☎ *21/362–0034* ⊕ *www. mosteirojeronimos.pt/* ⊠ *Cloister €4.50, free Sun.* ☉ *May–Sept., Tues.–Sun. 10–6:30; Oct.–Apr., Tues.–Sun. 10–5.*

NEED A BREAK?

For a real taste of Lisbon, stop at the **Antiga Confeitaria de Belém** (⊠ Rua de Belém 84–92, Belém ☎ 21/363-7423 ⊕ www.pasteisdebelem.pt), a bake shop–café that serves delicious, hot custard pastries sprinkled with cinnamon and powdered sugar. Although you can buy these treats throughout Lisbon, those made here, since 1837, are reputed to be the best.

③② Museu de Arte Antiga. The only museum in Lisbon to approach the status of the Gulbenkian is the Ancient Art Museum, founded in 1884. It was the first large public museum dedicated to the arts in Portugal. In a 17th-century palace, once owned by the Counts of Alvor, and vastly enlarged in 1940 when it took over the Convent of St. Albert, it has a beautifully displayed collection of Portuguese art—mainly from the 15th through 19th century—that superbly complements the Gulbenkian's general collection. Indeed, Gulbenkian himself donated several pieces to this museum, which opened in 1883.

Fodor'sChoice
★

Of all the holdings, the religious works of the Portuguese school of artists (characterized by fine portraiture with a distinct Flemish influence) stand out, especially the acknowledged masterpiece of Nuno Gonçalves, the *St. Vincent Altarpiece*. Painted between 1467 and 1470 for St. Vincent Chapel in Lisbon's cathedral, the altarpiece has six panels showing the patron saint of Lisbon receiving the homage of king, court, and citizens. Sixty figures can be identified, including Henry the Navigator; the archbishop of Lisbon; and sundry dukes, monks, fishermen, knights, and religious figures. In the top left corner of the two central panels is a figure purported to be Gonçalves himself.

Besides the Portuguese works, there are pieces by early Flemish painters who influenced the Portuguese. Other European artists are well represented, too, and although few of the works are really first rate, there are interesting examples by artists as diverse as Hieronymous Bosch, Hans Holbein, Brueghel the Younger, and painter to the Spanish court Diego Velázquez. There are also extensive collections of French silver, Portuguese furniture and tapestries, Asian ceramics, and items fashioned from Goan ivory.

Tram 15 from Praça do Comércio drops you at the foot of a steep flight of steps below the museum. Otherwise, Buses 27 and 49 from Praça Marquês de Pombal run straight to Rua das Janelas Verdes. Coming from Belém, Buses 27 and 49 run from Rua de Belém across from the monastery and stop near the museum on their way back to downtown Lisbon. ⊠ *Rua das Janelas Verdes, Lapa* ☎ *21/396–2825 or 21/396–4151* ⊕ *www.mnarteantiga-ipmuseus.pt* ⌸ *€3* ⊙ *Tues. 2–6, Wed.–Sun. 10–6.*

④① Museu de Marinha. In a complex of buildings adjoining the Mosteiro dos Jerónimos is the large, inviting Maritime Museum. Here you get a real grasp of the importance of the seafaring tradition in Portugal through maps and maritime codes, navigational equipment, full-size and model ships, uniforms, and weapons. ⊠ *Praça do Império, Belém* ☎ *21/362–0019* ⊕ *www.museu.marinha.pt* ⌸ *€3, free Sun. 10–1* ⊙ *Apr.–Sept., Tues.–Sun. 10–6; Oct.–Mar., Tues.–Sun. 10–5.*

★ ③⑤ Museu Nacional dos Coches. The National Coach Museum houses one of the world's largest collections of carriages in buildings that once accommodated a riding school. The oldest coach on display was made for Philip II of Spain in the late 16th century, and among the most stunning exhibits are three gold conveyances created in Rome for King John V in 1716. This dazzling collection of gloriously painted and/or gilded baroque vehicles is one of Lisbon's most popular sights. ⊠ *Praça Afonso* *de Albuquerque, Belém* ☎ *21/361–0850* ⊕ *www.museudoscoches-ipmuseus.pt* 💳 *€3, free Sun. 10–1* ⊘ *Tues.–Sun. 10–6.*

㊱ Museu da Presidencia da Republica (Museum of the President of the Republic). Seventeen presidents have governed Portugal since the Republic was established in 1910 (after the assassination of King Dom Carlos and his heir in 1908). That makes for more than 2,000 pieces on exhibit that include personal possessions, state gifts, and plenty of paperwork. Films depict the three phases of the Republic: the first republic, *Estado Novo* (the dictatorship), and democracy after the 1974 armed forces revolution. Another room presents a 14-minute virtual reality tour of the Belém Presidential Palace accompanied by a narrated history. Glass cases exhibit objects that belonged to the presidents, including the agenda of Americo Tomás, the puppet president during the dictatorship, and the sword of President Francisco da Costa Gomes, elected after the revolution. The mezzanine displays medals awarded by the presidents. ✉ *Praça Afonso de Albuquerque, Belém* ☎ *21/361–4600* ⊕ *www.museu.presidencia.pt* 💳 *Tues.–Fri. €2.50, Sat. €5* ⊘ *Tues.–Sun. 10–6.*

㊸ Padrão dos Descobrimentos. The white, monolithic Monument of the Discoveries was erected in 1960 to commemorate the 500th anniversary of the death of Prince Henry the Navigator. It was built on what was the departure point for many voyages of discovery, including those of Vasco da Gama for India and—during Spain's occupation of Portugal—of the Spanish Armada for England in 1588. Henry is at the prow of the monument, facing the water; lined up behind him are the Portuguese explorers of Brazil and Asia, as well as other national heroes, including Luís de Camões the poet, who can be recognized by the book in his hand. On the ground adjacent to the monument, an inlaid map shows the extent of the explorations undertaken by the 15th- and 16th-century Portuguese sailors. Walk inside and take the elevator to the top for river views. There are also 15- and 30-minute films about Lisbon's history. ✉ *Av. de Brasília, Belém* ☎ *21/303–1950* 💳 *€2.50; 15-min movie €2, 30-min movie €3* ⊘ *Tues.–Sun. 10–7.*

㊳ Palácio da Ajuda. According to legend, in the 16th century a shepherd found an image of the Virgin Mary in a cave close to here. In 1802 construction began on the Ajuda Palace, which was intended as a royal residence; its last regal occupant (Queen Maria) died here in 1911. Today the fussy building is home to a museum of 18th- and 19th-century paintings, furniture, and tapestries—hardly unique in Lisbon and, frankly, hardly an essential sight, although temporary exhibitions keep things interesting. It is also used for official ceremonies and functions by the Presidency of the Republic. It's a 20-minute walk north along Calçada da Ajuda from the Museu Nacional dos Coches, but Bus 14 and Tram 18 run this way, too. ✉ *Largo da Ajuda, Alto de Ajuda* ☎ *21/363–7095* 💳 *€4, free Sun. 10–2* ⊘ *Thurs.–Tues. 10–5.*

㊵ Planetário Calouste Gulbenkian. Behind the Museu de Marinha, the Calouste Gulbenkian Planetarium presents interesting astronomical shows and displays several times a week. A bulletin posted in the window announces the current program, or you can get updates from the

Prince Henry the Navigator

THE LINKAGE OF ENGLAND AND PORTUGAL and the beginning of Portugal's Age of Discovery can be traced back to the 14th century, when England's John of Gaunt gave his daughter, Philippa of Lancaster, in marriage to King João I. The couple's third son, Infante Dom Henrique, is known widely today as Prince Henry the Navigator (1394–1460). By the end of his lifetime, this multidimensional soldier-scientist had conceptualized, funded, and inspired discoveries beyond the borders of the world that Europe knew. No matter how they assess later misuses of exploration and conquest, scholars today generally agree that the prince paved the way for explorers such as Vasco da Gama and Ferdinand Magellan.

Unusual for a royal family in those (or any) times, João and Philippa raised six intelligent, apparently happy children. Alternately contemplative and restlessly athletic, Henry persuaded his father to let the four boys earn their knighthoods in an invasion of Morocco and the capture of its fortress at Ceuta. If the prince had not led his 70 soldier-filled ships to a victory worthy of Steven Spielberg replay, Portugal's Age of Discovery might have been very different.

At least three achievements secured Henry his place in the vanguard of explorers. In the Algarve, where he was governor, he founded a nearly legendary marine navigation school, which applied scientific principles to what was previously a haphazard endeavor. He also sent ships where none had gone before—especially around Cape Bojador, the "impassable wall" jutting out from West Africa at the end of the European-known Atlantic ocean. And he required that expeditions chart the seas as they sailed. Charts made of Cape Bojador later led Vasco da Gama to sail around it, then past the Cape of Good Hope and on to India.

Seen through the prism of history, Prince Henry seems a royal contradiction. He earned his knighthood defeating infidels and was eventually named Grand Master of the Order of Christ, the successor to the Knights Templar. But since he lived before the Inquisition began, he may have met some of the Latin-, Greek-, and Hebrew-speaking scholars who came to the royal court. Further, his ships engaged in Africa's lucrative slave trade, but he himself lived simply and, having given away his profits to fund further expeditions, died broke. The navigator-prince was not technically a navigator, and he rarely boarded a ship, but he pointed the way for generations of future explorers— such as yourself. In Lisbon, stop at breezy Belém on the Rio Tejo, where, at the prow of the ship-shaped *Padrão dos Descobrimentos* (Monument to the Discoveries), Prince Henry stands, leading other Portuguese explorers and even King Afonso V.

tourist office. ⊠ *Praça do Império, Belém* ☎ *21/362–0002* ⊕ *plane-tario.online.pt/entrada.asp* ✉ €3.

㉝ Ponte 25 de Abril. Completed in 1966 and originally dedicated to Dr. António de Oliveira Salazar, this bridge earned a name change after the 1974 revolution, which lurched into action on April 25 of that year. Lisbon's first suspension bridge across the Rio Tejo, linking the Alcântara and Almada districts, stands 230 feet above the water and stretches almost 2½ km (1½ mi). It's a spectacular sight from any direction, although most gasps are reserved for the view from the top downward. Crossing by car, bus, or train is a thrill every time—except, perhaps, during rush hours.

★ ㊹ **Torre de Belém.** The openwork balconies and domed turrets of the fanciful Belém Tower make it perhaps the country's purest Manueline structure. It was built between 1514 and 1520 on an island in the middle of the Rio Tejo, and dedicated to St. Vincent, the patron saint of Lisbon.

> ### DEALS
>
> If you plan to visit several of the park's attractions, consider buying (À15.50) a Cartão Parque das Nações. This card—sold at tourist offices, the Parque das Nações information desk, and at the area's various sights—gets you free admission to the aquarium and the tower; allows you to ride the excursion train and the cable car (one-way only) for free; and gives you discounts at the two pavilion attractions, the bowling center, and several restaurants. The card has to be activated at the selling point.

Today the chalk-white tower stands near what has become the north bank—evidence of the river's changing course. It was originally constructed to defend the port entrance, but it has also served as a customs control point, a telegraph station, a lighthouse, and even a prison from the late-16th through the 19th century. Cross the wood gangway and walk inside, not necessarily to see the rather plain interior but rather to clamber up the steep stone steps to the very top. From here you have a bird's-eye view of the river and central Lisbon. However, the best view of the torre itself is from the top of the nearby Padrão dos Descobrimentos. ⊠ *Av. de Brasília, Belém* ☎ *21/362–0034* 🎫 *€3* ⊗ *Tues.–Sun. 10–6:30.*

Parque das Nações

To prepare for the World Exposition in 1998, Lisbon's officials wisely kept in mind not only the immediate needs of the event, but also the future needs of the city. The result is Parque das Nações, a revitalized district on the banks of the Rio Tejo, 5 km (3 mi) northeast of Lisbon's center. Before it became the expo site, empty warehouses and refuse filled the district, which was once a landing area for seaplanes. Today it has apartment buildings, office complexes, hotels, restaurants, bars, and stores surrounded by landscaped parkland. It's also home to a marina; the Pavilhão Atlântico, a venue for major cultural and sporting events; the Bowling Internacional de Lisboa (BIL), Portugal's largest bowling alley; and the Feira Internacional Lisboa (FIL) convention center.

The centerpiece of the Parque das Nações is the popular Oceanário de Lisboa, an aquarium built for the expo. Near it are two museums: the Pavilhão do Conhecimento and the Pavilhão de Realidade Virtual. On Sundays in summer, open-air markets take place from 10 to 7 beside the river. Standing above it all is the Torre Vasco da Gama—from this tower, and from the Teleférico de Lisboa cable car that runs through the area, the views are fine.

TIMING You can spend anywhere from a couple of hours to all day (and all night) sightseeing, shopping, eating, and drinking here. Allot an hour or two for the Torre Vasco da Gama and about two hours for the Oceanário de Lisboa. On summer Sundays, set aside time to explore the markets at the north end of the park. Although some of the public transportation back to Lisbon's center stops running at midnight, taxis wait at the Estação de Oriente until all hours.

What to See

★ ☾ **Oceanário de Lisboa.** You cross a footbridge to reach this glass-and-stone complex, which rises from the river. With 25,000 fish, seabirds, and mammals, it's Europe's largest aquarium and the first ever to incorporate several ocean habitats (North Atlantic, Pacific, Antarctic, and Indian) in one place. You view the connected tanks and display areas from above and then from underwater; clever use of acrylic walls means that tropical fish and penguins look as if they inhabit the same space. Displays tell you more about the environments you're experiencing, and at the end you can sink onto a bench in one of the "contemplation" areas and just watch the fish swim by. ⊠ *Esplanada D. Carlos I (Doca dos Olivais), Parque das Nações* ☎ *21/891-7002 or 21/891-7006* ⊕ *www. oceanario.pt* ✑ *€10.50* ☾ *Apr.–Oct., daily 10–8 (last admission 7); Nov.–Mar., daily 10–7 (last admission 6).*

▌ **NEED A BREAK?** For pure nectar on a hot day, find one of the many stands or cafés displaying huge bowls of oranges. They have juice machines on which, for about €2, they'll squeeze what seems like a dozen of them for you.

Pavilhão do Conhecimento. The white, angular, structure designed by architect Carrilho de Graça for the expo seems the perfect place to house the Knowledge Pavilion, or Living Science Centre, as it's also known. All of the permanent and temporary exhibits here are related to math, science, and technology; most are also labeled in English (a manual is available for the few that aren't), and all are interactive. A cybercafé with free Internet access, a media library, a gift shop, and a bookstore round out the offerings. ⊠ *Parque das Nações* ☎ *21/891-9898* ⊕ *www. pavconhecimento.mct.pt/home* ✑ *€6* ☾ *Tues.–Fri. 10–6, weekends and holidays 11–7.*

Torre Vasco da Gama. At the park's easternmost edge and rising 480 feet above it, the graceful, white Vasco da Gama Tower is Portugal's tallest structure. Three glass elevators whisk you up 345 feet to the observation deck. In addition to taking in vistas across Lisbon and the Atlantic Ocean, you'll feel as if you're eye to eye with the 18-km (11-mi) Ponte Vasco da Gama (Vasco da Gama Bridge). You could lunch up here in the restaurant, but its menu is on the pricey side. ⊠ *Av. Pinto Ribeiro, Parque das Nações* ☎ *21/893-9550* ✑ *€2.49* ☾ *Daily 10–6.*

WHERE TO EAT

Meals generally include three courses, a drink, and coffee. Many restaurants have an *ementa turistica* (tourist menu), a set-price meal, most often served at lunchtime. Note that you'll be charged a couple of euros if you eat any of the *couvert* (or *coberto*) items—typically appetizers such as bread and butter, olives, and the like—that are brought to your table without being ordered.

Lisbon's restaurants usually serve lunch from noon or 12:30 until 3 and dinner from 7:30 until 11; many establishments are closed Sunday or Monday. Inexpensive restaurants typically don't accept reservations. In the traditional *cervejarias* (beer hall–restaurants), which frequently have huge dining rooms, you'll probably have to wait for a table, but usually not more than 10 minutes. In the Bairro Alto, many of the reasonably priced *tascas* (taverns) are on the small side: if you can't grab a table, you're probably better off moving on to the next place. Throughout Lisbon, dress for meals is usually casual, but exceptions are noted below.

WHAT IT COSTS In Euros					
	$$$$	**$$$**	**$$**	**$**	**¢**
AT DINNER	over €21	€16–€21	€11–€15	€7–€10	under €7

Restaurant prices are per person for a main course at dinner.

Alcântara & Belém

Continental

$$–$$$ ✕ **Kais.** Along the Avenida de Brasília that follows the river is a series of new restaurants. The most outstanding is the Kais, describing itself as "industrial chic." At the beginning of the 20th century, the space held a factory that produced electric generators. While waiting for the main meal, you'll be served a "chef's secret": a very small bowl of the daily soup. Some of the dishes on the menu include shrimp done in champagne sauce and steamed fish. Below the restaurant is a large rustic wine cellar with wooden tables and large wine casks. ⊠ *Cais da Viscondessa, Rua da Cintura, Santos* ☎ *21/393–2930* ⊕ *www.kais-k.com* ⊟ *AE, MC, V* ☾ *Closed Sun.*

Mediterranean

$$$ ✕ **Estufa Real.** Every Sunday starting at noon, a wonderful buffet with lots of salads (€33 per person, including a welcoming drink of orange juice or sparkling wine) is served inside the greenhouse of the Ajuda Botanical Gardens. As you sit surrounded by exotic trees and plants, you will be cordially welcomed with a glass of champagne on the house. On other days, the à la carte menu varies according to the season, and each month features a different herb. ⊠ *Jardim Botânico da Ajuda, Calçada do Galvão, Ajuda* ☎ *21/361–9400* ⊕ *www.estufareal.com* ⊟ *AE, DC, MC, V* ☾ *Closed Sat. No dinner.*

Portuguese

$$–$$$ ✕ **Alcântara Café.** Locals bring visitors here to impress them—it rarely fails. The café's mix of wood, leather, velvet, and steel elements combine to evoke a Lisbon of the 1920s. Portuguese dishes dominate the menu; try the prawns in lemon sauce. There's a large wine list, too, and a splendid bar if you want to sip an aperitif or stay on after dinner—drinks are served until 2 AM. The restaurant is near the Ponte 25 de Abril

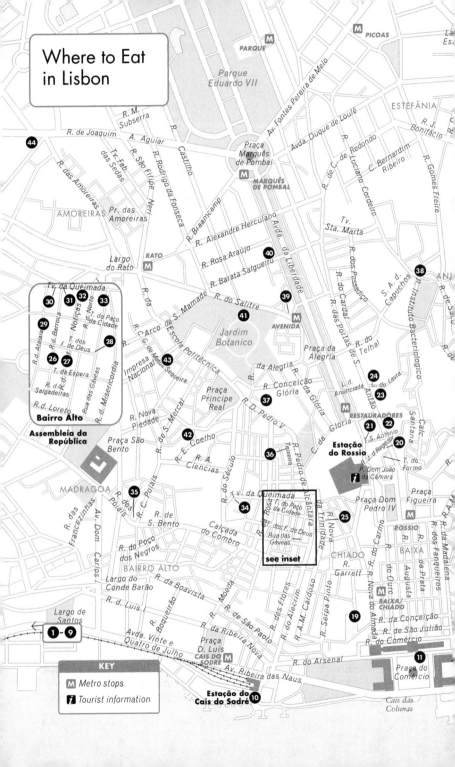

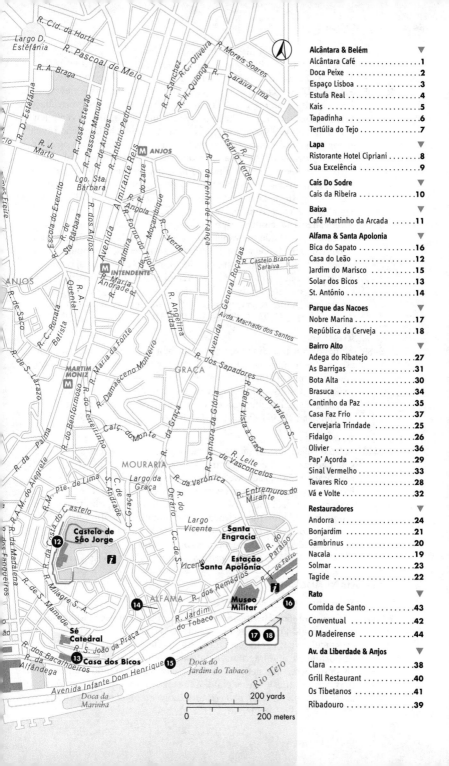

and close to the nightlife of the Doca de Santa Amaro; the kitchen is open until 1 AM. ☒ *Rua Maria Luísa Holstein 15, Alcântara* ☎ *21/363–7176* ⊕ *www.alcantaracafe.com* ▭ *AE, DC, MC, V* ⊘ *No lunch.*

$$–$$$ ✕ **Espaço Lisboa.** Don't worry if you can't get a table with a view of the Ponte 25 de Abril; there's plenty of space inside this former warehouse. Menu choices include chicken sausage invented—it's said—to help Jews who had supposedly converted to Christianity during the Inquisition avoid eating pork; *leitão assado* (suckling pig roasted in a wood-burning oven); and *encharcada do ovos* (a delicious concoction of eggs and sugar). After your meal, sink into a leather armchair in the candelabra-lighted bar. Find an excuse to check out the kiosk with old newspapers, the vintage grocery store, or the café museum. ☒ *Rua da Cozinha Econômica 16, Doca de Santo Amaro, Alcântara* ☎ *21/361–0212* ▭ *AE, MC, V.*

$–$$ ✕ **Tertúlia do Tejo.** Nothing is pretentious at this dockside restaurant. Large red umbrellas shade the esplanade tables. Plank floors set the tone in the downstairs dining room, and there's an agreeable madhouse of long tables and camaraderie upstairs. The *pratos do dia* (daily specials) are predictable, but if you try melon with smoked ham or *caldho verde* (green soup) as a starter, and then follow it with something grilled, you can't go wrong. Dinner reservations are advised. ☒ *Doca de Santo Amaro, Alcântara* ☎ *21/395–5552* ▭ *AE, DC, MC, V.*

Russian

$–$$ ✕ **Tapadinha.** Tapadinha has by far the best Russian food in Lisbon and especially the best beef tartare. Leave by taxi—because by the time you've sampled all their different-flavor vodkas you dare not drive. Constructivist posters and painted wooden dolls decorate the space, which is rather dark, but illuminated by candles. ☒ *Calçada da Tapada 41-A, Ajuda* ☎ *21/364–0482* ▭ *AE, DC, MC, V* ⊘ *Closed Sun.*

Seafood

$$–$$$$ ✕ **Doca Peixe.** The icy display of the day's catch at the entrance and the small aquarium clue you in to what's served here. In the center of the restaurant a staffer slices well-aged ham or weighs the fish that customers have chosen. You might start with a tomato-and-mozzarella salad or with oysters on the half shell. Sea bass or bream cooked in garlic, tomato, and onion and cod with turnip leaves are recommended main courses. *Bifinhas com molho de madeira* (small steaks in Madeira wine) is a meaty alternative. ☒ *Esplanada at Doca de Santo Amaro, Armazém 14, Alcântara* ☎ *21/397–3565* ⊕ *www.docepeixe.com* ▭ *AE, MC, V* ⊘ *Closed Mon.*

Alfama & Santa Apolónia

Eclectic

$$–$$$ ✕ **Casa do Leão.** The location—on the grounds of the Castelo de São Jorge—couldn't be better. In summer, terrace-garden seating grants spectacular views of the center of Lisbon. The food is a high-quality mix of Portuguese and international dishes. Squid comes on a skewer with shrimp, bacon, and peppers; the lamb chops are a standout entrée. You may want to finish with a plate of Portuguese cheeses. ☒ *Entrances to castle at Largo do Chão da Feira and Largo do Menino de Deus, Alfama* ☎ *21/887–5962* ▭ *AE, MC, DC, V.*

Japanese

$$–$$$$ ✕ **Bica do Sapato.** A favorite among Lisbon's "in crowd," the main attraction of this riverfront restaurant across from the Santa Apolónia train station is its stylish interior design. It includes original Knoll, Eero Saarien, and Mies van der Rohe chairs and rotating photographic panels. Diners choose between three separate dining experiences. Downstairs, a cafeteria serves exceptional food and has outdoor seating in summer. The restaurant serves nouvelle cuisine that leaves a serious dent in your credit card. Lastly, there's a sushi bar upstairs. ✉ *Av. Infante D. Henrique, Armazém B, Cais da Pedra, Santa Apolónia* ☎ *21/881–0320* ☐ *AE, DC, MC, V* ⊘ *Closed Sun. No lunch Mon.*

Mediterranean

$–$$ ✕ **St. António.** It's an interesting walk from the Casa dos Bicos, along Rua Terreiro do Trigo, and up some steps through the Travessa Terreiro do Trigo, one of Alfama's old side streets, to this restaurant. Black-and-white photos of famous artists, including a signed photo of pop singer Nelly Furtado, hang on the walls. The fried potato peels with mayonnaise as a dipping sauce are a surprising treat. They have a variety of appetizers such as carpaccio, mushrooms stuffed with Gorgonzola, or *joaquinzinhos fritos* (tiny fish fried in batter). Steak, fish, and duck dishes are accompanied by a baked potato with sour cream and steamed vegetables. During the Patron Saints of Lisbon festivities they set up tables outside under the grape arbor and grill sardines in the street. ✉ *Beco de São Miguel 7, Alfama* ☎ *21/888–1328* ☐ *AE, DC, MC, V* ⊘ *Closed Tues.*

Portuguese

$–$$ ✕ **Solar dos Bicos.** As the name implies, this charming restaurant with stone arches and beautiful azulejos offers typical Portuguese cuisine at very reasonable prices. ✉ *Rua dos Bacalhoeiros, 8-A, Alfama* ☎ *21/ 886–9447* ⊕ *www.solardosbicos.com* ☐ *MC, V.*

Seafood

$–$$ ✕ **Jardim do Marisco.** A white ceiling tops metal rafters high above the cool grays and warm woods of this restaurant overlooking the esplanade near Lisbon's major cruise-ship area. For a starter, consider traditional vegetable *sopa* (soup) or Portuguese oysters on ice, perhaps followed by a lavish portion of bean-based stew with meat or seafood or *espetadas de gambas piri piri* (spicy shrimp brochette). ✉ *Doca Jardim do Tabaco, Pavilion A/B, Av. Infante D. Henrique 21, Alfama* ☎ *21/882–4242* ⊕ *www.jardimdomarisco.pt* ☐ *AE, MC, V.*

Avenida da Liberdade

Eclectic

$$–$$$ ✕ **Grill Restaurant.** Because they're on the top floor of the Tivoli Lisboa hotel, the Grill and its O Terraço bar could let the vistas be the draw and not worry too much about the food. All praise, then, that the kitchen turns out high-quality prime rib and lamb cutlets. Here traditional salt cod is baked with potatoes and baby onions; for something different, try the mixed-fish curry. The restrained elegance makes this one of the few hotel restaurants worth the splurge; in summer there's no nicer place to sit than out on the terrace. ☒ *Av. da Liberdade 185, Liberdade* ☎ *21/ 353–2181* ⌣ *Reservations essential* ⊟ *AE, DC, MC, V.*

Seafood

$$ ✕ **Ribadouro.** One of Lisbon's oldest beer halls is also a seafood joint, with a counter full of fresh shellfish priced by weight—go easy, since this can be a costly way to eat. If you stick to the regular fish and meat dishes, you can't go wrong. When crowds spill out of the nearby theaters, you may have to wait for a table; try to arrive before 8 PM on weekends. ☒ *Av. da Liberdade 155, Liberdade* ☎ *21/354–9411* ⊟ *AE, DC, MC, V.*

Vegetarian

$ ✕ **Os Tibetanos.** It wouldn't be an exaggeration to say that most of Lisbon's vegetarians worship this restaurant run by a group of Tibetan Buddhism followers. A small shop at the entrance sells books on Buddhism, incense made by Nepalese monks, homeopathic medicine, and other natural products. You don't have to be a vegetarian to fall under the spell of the charming indoor garden and inventive menu. *Bife de seitan com cogumelos* (seitan steak with mushrooms), tofu *gratinado com queijo de cabra* (tofu au gratin with goat cheese), *tarte de papaia e requeijão* (papaya cheesecake), and a chocolate tart with chestnuts are all favorites. ☒ *Rua do Salitre 117, Liberdade* ☎ *21/314–2038* ⊕ *www. tibetanos.com* ⊟ *No credit cards* ⊘ *Closed weekends and holidays.*

Anjos

Portuguese

$$$–$$$$ ✕ **Clara.** Just a short taxi ride from the city center, this is an old Lisbon favorite. Found in an 18th-century mansion, and with a charming patio garden, this is a beautiful oasis in this busy city. Expect to find a delicious, and beautifully presented, selection of traditional Portuguese and international dishes—along with a fine selection of wine and cheeses—accompanied by the soothing tunes from the resident pianist. ☒ *Campo dos Mártires da Pátria 49, Anjos* ☎ *21/885–3053* ⊟ *AE, DC, MC, V* ⊘ *Closed Sun. No lunch Sat.*

Bairro Alto

Brazilian

$$$ ✕ **Brasuca.** The food is Brazilian, and the welcome is warm. With its open fire, its alcove, and its intimate dining rooms, this converted mansion makes you feel as if you're eating in someone's home. Dishes such as *picadinho á mineira* (minced beef with onions, peppers, and bananas) or *moqueca* (fish or shrimp in coconut milk) are always reliable. The beer is Brazilian, too, or you may prefer to sip a more potent *caipirinha* (cocktail made with *cachaça*, a rumlike Brazilian liquor, sugar, and lime). ☒ *Rua João Pereira da Rosa 7, Bairro Alto* ☎ *21/342–8542* ⊟ *AE, DC, MC, V* ⊘ *Closed Mon.*

Indian

$$–$$$ ✕ **Cantinho da Paz.** The trick is finding this place (take a taxi), but once you're through the unassuming entrance, you'll be glad you made the effort. It's a joyful mom-and-pop establishment that specializes in the cuisine of Goa—so spicy Indian curries abound. The shrimp curry is rich in coconut and cream. The English-speaking owner is happy to guide you through the menu. ⊠ *Rua da Paz 4, off Rua dos Poiais de São Bento, Bairro Alto* ☎ *21/396–9698* ⌂ *Reservations essential* ▤ *MC, V* ⊙ *Closed Sun.* ▤ *V.*

Mediterranean

$$$$ ✕ **Olivier.** Named after its owner, the son of famous Portuguese chef Michel, this restaurant has successfully won the hearts of Lisbon's gourmets. You go through a big white door into the cozy, sophisticated black-and-red interior where owner Olivier and his blue-shirted minions greet you. The restaurant prides itself on its 11 original appetizers—such as crab guacamole served on corn bread, tomato and feta cheese on the spit, foie gras with onion and port wine, mushrooms with pesto and cheese—and all are mouthwatering. ⊠ *Rua do Teixeira 35, Bairro Alto* ☎ *21/342–1024* ⊕ *www.restaurante-olivier.com* ▤ *AE, DC, MC, V* ⊙ *Closed Sun.*

Portuguese

★ **$$–$$$$** ✕ **Pap' Açorda.** What was once a bakery is now one of Lisbon's most happening restaurants. Art and media types scramble for the closely packed tables in the minimalist interior. The menu lists cutting-edge versions of Portuguese classics—grilled sea bass; breaded veal cutlets; and *açorda* itself, that bread-based stew, rich in seafood and flavored with cilantro. There's a good wine list (all Portuguese) and a long bar by the door where those unwise enough not to have made a reservation wait for a table. ⊠ *Rua da Atalaia 57, Bairro Alto* ☎ *21/346–4811* ⌂ *Reservations essential* ▤ *AE, DC, MC, V.*

★ **$$–$$$** ✕ **Sinal Vermelho.** At this update of a traditional *adega* (tavern), the split-level dining room is traditionally tiled, and the food is thoroughly Portuguese, but the prints on the wall are modern, the clientele firmly professional, and the wine list wide ranging. Consider starting with a plate of clams drenched in oil and garlic and follow it with a fresh seafood dish; the meat dishes are less inspiring, although if you feel daring, you might try the tripe or the kidneys. ⊠ *Rua das Gáveas 89, Bairro Alto* ☎ *21/343–1281* ⌂ *Reservations essential* ▤ *AE, MC, V* ⊙ *Closed Sun.*

$$ ✕ **Casa Faz Frio.** This convivial adega—complete with wood beams, stone floors, paneled booths, blue tiling, and bunches of garlic suspended from the ceiling—is of a type that's fast disappearing. The list of Portuguese dishes on the prix-fixe menu changes daily, and although there's not a large choice, you'll usually find steak, rice dishes, bacalhau, grilled pork, and quail. ⊠ *Rua de Dom Pedro V 96–98, Bairro Alto* ☎ *21/346–1860* ▤ *No credit cards.*

$–$$ ✕ **Adega do Ribatejo.** There are fado clubs aplenty in the Bairro Alto, but none so accessible as this tiled adega. The food is reasonably good; dishes such as steaks, bacalhau, veal, and fried fish are often on the changing menu. At the nightly singing sessions, professional musicians serenade you with earsplitting renditions of traditional songs. The manager works the tables and sings himself on occasion; even the cooks sometimes get in on the act. ⊠ *Rua Diário de Notícias 23, Bairro Alto* ☎ *21/346–8343* ▤ *MC, V* ⊙ *Closed Sun.*

$–$$ × **As Barrigas.** The clientele are a well-traveled lot, judging by the post-cards that line the walls of this cozy, wood-paneled adega, but the cooking stays firmly in Portugal. The specialty is a rich arroz *de polvo* (with octopus), and there are steaks, a fish of the day, and other tavern standards. And the restaurant's name? It means "the stomachs," which you'll appreciate once you've waded through their large portions. ⊠ *Travessa da Queimada 31, Bairro Alto* ☎ *21/347–1220* ▱ *V.*

$–$$ × **Bota Alta.** This wood-paneled tavern is one of the Bairro Alto's oldest and most favored eateries—lines form outside by 8 PM. There's little space between the tables, but this only enhances the buzz. Once you've secured a seat, choose from a menu strong on traditional Portuguese dishes—perhaps bacalhau cooked in cream, homemade sausages, steaks in wine sauce, or grilled fish. The house wine comes in ceramic jugs and is very good. ⊠ *Travessa da Queimada 37, Bairro Alto* ☎ *21/342–7959* ▱ *AE, DC, MC, V* ⊗ *Closed Sun. No lunch Sat.*

$–$$ × **Fidalgo.** The local intelligentsia have made this low-key, comfortable restaurant their refuge, though friendly owner Eugenio Fidalgo welcomes every sort of patron. He'll gladly help you with the Portuguese menu and the excellent wine list. Specialties include grouper with tomatoes and shrimp as well as several bacalhau dishes. If you've never had *medalhões de javali* (wild boar cutlets), try them here—they're incredibly succulent. ⊠ *Rua da Barroca 27, Bairro Alto* ☎ *21/342–2900* ⊕ *www.restaurantefidalgo.com* ▱ *AE, MC, V* ⊗ *Closed Sun.*

★ **¢–$$** × **Cervejaria Trindade.** The Trindade is a classic 19th-century cervejaria, with colorful tiles, vaulted ceilings, and frenetic service. You can pop in for a beer and a snack or eat a full meal. Hearty dishes such as açorda and steaks form the mainstay; if you opt for the grilled seafood, the tab will jump dramatically. The terrace is an enjoyable spot for dining in summer. ⊠ *Rua Nova da Trindade 20, Bairro Alto* ☎ *21/342–3506* ▱ *AE, DC, MC, V.*

¢–$$ × **Vá e Volte.** In what's little more than a bar with a couple of small dining rooms, the owner, his wife, the cook, and a small staff keep the meals coming with speed and good humor. Fried or grilled fish or meat dishes are served with enough salad, potatoes, and vegetables to keep the wolf from the door, and the *arroz doce* (rice pudding) is homemade. The house wine is fine, but even if you choose a regional specialty, the price won't break the bank. ⊠ *Rua Diário de Notícias 100, Bairro Alto* ☎ *21/342–7888* ▱ *AE, MC, V* ⊗ *Closed Mon.*

Baixa

Portuguese

$$ × **Café Martinho da Arcada.** This famous café-restaurant, founded in 1782 beneath the arcades of Praça do Comércio, was once frequented by the Portuguese poet Fernando Pessoa and other literary stars. These days the lunchtime crowd in its wood-paneled dining room is mainly businesspeople. The menu lists regional Portuguese cuisine; sometimes there's a colonial splash with the occasional Brazilian dish. Try a *cataplana* (clam stew) from the Algarve, especially if you won't be heading south on this trip. ⊠ *Praça do Comércio 3, Baixa* ☎ *21/886–6213* ▱ *MC, V* ⊗ *Closed Sun.*

Cais do Sodre

Portuguese

$–$$ ✕ **Cais da Ribeira.** An old fisherman's warehouse was converted into this small split-level restaurant. It specializes in fish grilled over charcoal, as well as a filling caldeirada (fish stew). Whatever you order, the views over the river will complement your meal nicely. ⊠ *Rua da Cintura, Armazém A, behind railway station, Cais do Sodré* ☎ *21/342–3611* ▤ *AE, DC, MC, V* ☺ *Closed Sun.*

Chiado

French

$$$–$$$$ ✕ **Tavares Rico.** Established as a café in 1784, and the oldest restaurant
Fodor'sChoice in the city, today Tavares Rico pleases its customers with a handsome
★ Edwardian dining room; outstanding service; superb, French-inspired fare; and an excellent wine list. Caviar pushes the price of a meal right up, but there's nothing wrong with lowering your sights—the sole cooked in champagne sauce is a classic, and there are game birds available in season, served roasted in a rich wine sauce. Cravings for Portuguese food can be assuaged by the bacalhau or the *sopa alentejana* (Alentejo-style soup that's a concoction of garlic, bread, and egg). ⊠ *Rua Misericórdia 35–37, Chiado* ☎ *21/342–1112* ⚞ *Reservations essential* ⌂ *Jacket and tie* ▤ *AE, DC, MC, V* ☺ *Closed Sun. No lunch Sat.*

Portuguese

$$$–$$$$ ✕ **Tagide.** In a fine old house that looks out over the Baixa and the Rio Tejo (reserve a table by the window), you can have one of Lisbon's great food experiences. The dining room lined with 17th-century tiles is a lovely backdrop for sampling regional Portuguese fare. Try the famous *presunto* (smoked ham) from Chaves, stuffed squid from the Algarve, or the classic *porco à alentejana* (Alentejo-style pork). ⊠ *Largo Academia das Belas Artes 18–20, at bottom of Rua Ivens, Chiado* ☎ *21/347–1880* ⚞ *Reservations essential* ▤ *AE, DC, MC, V* ☺ *Closed Sun. No lunch Sat.*

Lapa

Italian

$$–$$$$ ✕ **Ristorante Hotel Cipriani.** Why choose northern Italian cuisine in Portugal? Because Cipriani's food is exceptional. So is its service, whether you're a solo traveler scanning a book or part of a designer-clad quartet celebrating a milestone. Waiters whip off domed silver lids in time to the music of a 12-string Portuguese guitar that approaches concert quality. You could start with cannelloni stuffed with ricotta and zucchini, or a shrimp-and-spinach-stuffed puff pastry with oyster sauce. Sautéed monkfish on a bed of ratatouille or citrus-glazed duck might follow. Wine prices range from modest to monumental. ⊠ *Lapa Palace hotel, Rua Pau de Bandeira 4, Lapa* ☎ *21/394–9434* ⚞ *Reservations essential* ▤ *AE, MC, V.*

Portuguese

★ **$$–$$$** ✕ **Sua Excelência.** In this cozy little town-house restaurant, put yourself in the hands of the English-speaking owner, Mr. Queiroz, who will talk you through the outstanding Portuguese menu. Specialties include smoked swordfish (an Algarve favorite), baked bacalhau, and Angolan-style chicken. A meal here is an intimate experience—particularly refreshing after a hectic day of sightseeing. ⊠ *Rua do Conde 34, Lapa* ☎ *21/390–3614* ▤ *MC, V* ⊘ *Closed weekends and Sept.*

Parque das Nações

Eclectic

$–$$$ ✕ **República da Cerveja.** This large eating and drinking—or maybe drinking and eating—spot pulses with energy. It's not easy to categorize, with its German chef and Portuguese manager who arrived via Missouri, but it's appealing even if you're not tempted by the wide array of beers. Steak—perhaps flavored with oysters—is always on the blackboard of ever-changing specials. Pizzas and burgers dominate the late-night menu; food is served until 1 AM Sunday through Wednesday nights and until 4 AM Thursday through Saturday nights, when there's often live music or a show. ⊠ *Passeio das Tagides 2, Parque das Nações* ☎ *21/892–2590* ⊕ *www.republicadecerveja.com* ▤ *AE, MC, V.*

Portuguese

$–$$$$ ✕ **Nobre Marina.** This luxurious restaurant is highly praised for its sophisticated Portuguese cuisine. From the outside terrace that re-creates a large ship in glass and iron, you have magnificent views of the Tagus River, the marina, and the rest of the Parque das Nações. They serve a superb *sopa de santola* (crab soup) in a crab shell on a bed of coarse salt. ⊠ *Passeio dos Navegantes, Edifício Nau, Marina Expo, Parque das Nações* ☎ *21/893–1600* ▤ *AE, DC, MC, V.*

Rato

Brazilian

$$ ✕ **Comida de Santo.** Excellent Brazilian food served in a funky, brightly painted dining room and accompanied by lively Brazilian music keeps this place packed until closing time, at 1 AM. Come and enjoy classic dishes, such as *feijoada* (meat-and-bean stew) or *vatapá* (a spicy shrimp dish). Order a caipirinha while you're waiting. The restaurant is down a side street off Rua Escola Politécnica—easy to miss if you're not on the ball. You have to ring the bell for entrance. ⊠ *Calçada Engenheiro Miguel Pais 39, Rato* ☎ *21/396–3339* ⌑ *Reservations essential* ▤ *AE, DC, MC, V.*

Portuguese

$$$–$$$$ ✕ **Conventual.** Housed in an old convent, and decorated with religious artifacts, this is one of Lisbon's most classic restaurants and you will delight in the traditional Portuguese dishes served up here. Its clientele ranges from modern pop stars to politicians. ⊠ *Praça das Flores, Rato* ☎ *21/390–9196* ⌑ *Reservations essential* ▤ *AE, DC, MC, V.*

$$–$$$ ✕ **O Madeirense.** Although it's in the Amoreiras shopping complex, this restaurant makes you feel as if you're in Madeira: rural scenes adorn the walls; staffers wear traditional costumes; and the place is filled with wood, rattan, and plants. The service is good, and the cooking is assured. Try the tuna, the swordfish, or the *espetada* (a skewer of steak fillet, rubbed with salt and spices and hung above the table from a stand so you can serve yourself). ⊠ *Loja 3027, Av. Eng. Duarte Pacheco, Amoreiras* ☎ *21/381–3147* ⊕ *www.omadeirense.com* ⚲ *Reservations essential* ⊟ *AE, DC, MC, V* ⊗ *Closed Sun.*

Restauradores

Portuguese

$–$$$ ✕ **Andorra.** On the renowned Baixa street of fish restaurants, the Andorra is a perfect place for a simple lunch; from the terrace you can people-watch and smell the charcoal-grilled sardines. The friendly staff serves plates of well-cooked Portuguese favorites, and you can choose from a short wine list that caters to most tastes. ⊠ *Rua Portas de Santo Antão 82, Restauradores* ☎ *21/342–6047* ⊟ *MC, V.*

$–$$
Fodor'sChoice
★ ✕ **Bonjardim.** In an alley between Praça dos Restauradores and Rua Portas de Santo Antão, and known locally as "Rei dos Frangos" ("King of Chickens"), Bonjardim specializes in superbly cooked spit-roasted chicken, best eaten with fries and a salad. The restaurant is crowded at peak times (8 PM–10 PM), but you shouldn't have to wait long, and watching the frenzied waiters is entertaining. An overflow dining room on the opposite side of the alley serves the same menu and has the same good deals. ⊠ *Travessa de S. Antão 11, Restauradores* ☎ *21/342–4389* ⊟ *AE, DC, MC, V.*

¢ ✕ **Nacala.** There's no bar and there are just a couple of tables outside, but the basic food, including, octopus salad and bifanas, an enticing soup, is supplemented by a window full of mouthwatering sandwiches. It's a great place for an inexpensive lunch. ⊠ *Rua Portas de Santo Antão 63, Restauradores* ☎ *21/347–1483.*

Seafood

$$$–$$$$ ✕ **Gambrinus.** On a busy street that's full of fish restaurants, Gambrinus stands alone, with more than 70 years of experience in serving the finest fish and shellfish. In a series of somber, dark-paneled dining rooms, and even sitting at the bar, you're led through the intricacies of the day's seafood specials by waiters who know their stuff. Prawns, lobster, and crab are always available; seasonal choices such as sea bream, sole, and sea bass are offered grilled or garnished with clam sauce. There are meat dishes, too, but they're rather beside the point here. ⊠ *Rua Portas de S. Antão 23–25, Restauadores* ☎ *21/342–1466* ⊟ *AE, DC, MC, V.*

$$–$$$ ✕ **Solmar.** Items from the sea figure prominently on the menu and in the restaurant itself: there's a huge mosaic of an underwater scene. Some have complained that Solmar is resting on its laurels, but the cooking is more hit than miss. In winter the restaurant entices diners with wild boar or venison. There are also cheaper snacks available in the adjacent café, where locals pop in throughout the day for coffee and cakes. ⊠ *Rua Portas de S. Antão 106, Restauradores* ☎ *21/346–0010* ⊟ *AE, DC, MC, V.*

WHERE TO STAY

If you've arrived without accommodations, stop by the airport tourist information desk or the downtown tourist office. The staff at either location can provide you with a list of hotels and pensões. Though it's not a complete list, it will get you started in your search.

Even in the city's hotels, consider inspecting a room before taking it: street noise can be a problem, and, conversely, quieter rooms at the back don't always have great views (or, indeed, any views). Also, some hotels charge the same rate for each of their rooms, so by checking out a couple you might be able to get a better room for the same price. This is especially true of the older hotels and inns, where no two rooms are exactly alike. And, if rooms for nonsmokers are unavailable, stale smoke can permeate one room, yet be totally absent in its clone down the hall.

Lisbon hosts trade fairs and conventions and is busy year-round, so it's best to secure a room in advance of your trip. Peak periods are Easter–June and September–November; budget pensões are particularly busy in summer. Despite the high year-round occupancy, substantial discounts—sometimes 30%–40%—abound from November through February.

WHAT IT COSTS In Euros					
	$$$$	**$$$**	**$$**	**$**	**¢**
FOR 2 PEOPLE	over €275	€176–€275	€101–€175	€60–€100	under €60

Hotel prices are for a standard double room, including tax, in high season (off-season rates may be lower).

Amoreiras

$$$$ 🖼 **Hotel Dom Pedro Lisboa.** The slightly exotic lobby here hums with comings, goings, and clusters of conversation. Although it's in the Amoreiras business center, facing the shopping complex, the hotel has its own gallery of luxury boutiques as well. Rooms and suites have rich fabrics and polished wood furniture, including executive desks and other amenities for the prosperous business travelers who favor the hotel. Vacationers who love to shop also opt to stay here, owing to its location and its weekend rate reductions. The top floors offer amazing views over Lisbon, the river, and the 25 de Abril bridge. ⊠ *Av. Eng. Duarte Pacheco 24, Amoreiras, 1070-109* ☎ *21/389–6600* 🖷 *21/389–6601* ⊕ *www. dompedro-hotels.com* ⇆ *254 rooms, 9 suites* ⌂ *2 restaurants, room service, in-room safes, minibars, cable TV, 3 bars, laundry service, Internet, meeting rooms, no-smoking floors* ☰ *AE, DC, MC, V* ⏐◎⏐ *EP.*

$$ 🖼 **Fénix.** As the Praça Marquês de Pombal has emerged a better, brighter place, so has this hotel, which has recently been enlarged and renovated. Guest quarters are done in shades of pastel pink and have large closets, comfortable armchairs, and gleaming bathrooms. Rooms in front overlook the square; those in back face the park. The basement restaurant, O Bodegon, serves good Spanish and Portuguese food in rustic surroundings. ⊠ *Praça Marquês de Pombal 8, Amoreiras, 1269-133* ☎ *21/386–*

2121 ☏ *21/386–0131* ⊕ *www.hotelfenix.pt* ↪ *119 rooms, 4 suites* ↺ *Restaurant, room service, in-room safes, minibars, cable TV, in-room data ports, 2 bars, laundry service, meeting rooms* ▤ *AE, DC, MC, V* 🍽 *BP* Ⓜ *Rotunda.*

Avenida da Liberdade & Environs

★ **$$$–$$$$** 🏨 **Tivoli Lisboa.** There's enough marble in the public areas to make you fear for the future supply of the stone, but grandness gives way to comfort in the rooms, which are characterized by fresh decor, well-equipped bathrooms, and a moderate amount of space. In warmer months the outdoor pool and garden offer respite from the bustling city; the grill on the top floor presents wonderful river and city views. A filling morning buffet is served in a restaurant off the lobby. ✉ *Av. da Liberdade 185, Liberdade, 1269-050* ☏ *21/319–8900* ☏ *21/319–8950* ⊕ *www.tivolihotels.com* ↪ *299 rooms, 30 suites* ↺ *2 restaurants, coffee shop, room service, in-room safes, minibars, cable TV, 2 tennis courts, pool, 2 bars, shops, babysitting, laundry service* ▤ *AE, DC, MC, V* 🍽 *BP* Ⓜ *Avenida.*

$$$ 🏨 **Britânia.** The Britânia is in one of the few 1940s buildings near Avenida da Liberdade to have survived progress unscathed. The one-time town house was the work of architect Cassiano Branco, and it originally housed studio apartments, hence the larger than usual rooms. But it's the art deco touches throughout that really impress—from the original marble panels in the baths to the "porthole" windows in the facade, the columns and candelabra in the lobby, and the murals in the bar. Staff members are really friendly. ✉ *Rua Rodrigues Sampaio 17, Liberdade, 1150-278* ☏ *21/315–5016* ☏ *21/315–5021* ⊕ *www.heritage.pt* ↪ *32 rooms, 1 suite* ↺ *Dining room, in-room safes, cable TV, bar* ▤ *AE, DC, MC, V* 🍽 *EP* Ⓜ *Marquês de Pombal.*

$$$ 🏨 **Sofitel Lisboa.** Right in the middle of the Avenida da Liberdade, the handsome Sofitel has a high-tech edge to its design. Rooms are pleasingly contemporary—decorated in attractive colors and comfortably appointed. The intimate piano bar makes a good stop after a day's touring, and you can sit by a window in the Cais da Avenida restaurant for sidewalk views of the central artery. ✉ *Av. da Liberdade 123–125, Liberdade, 1269-038* ☏ *21/322–8300* ☏ *21/322–8310* ⊕ *www.sofitel.com* ↪ *167 rooms, 4 suites* ↺ *Restaurant, room service, bar, laundry service, business services* ▤ *AE, DC, MC, V* 🍽 *BP, MAP* Ⓜ *Avenida.*

$$ 🏨 **Dom Carlos Liberty.** On the corner of one of Lisbon's busiest avenues and in tune with the latest technologies, Dom Carlos Liberty offers four-star service at three-star prices. With boxed-in views of surrounding buildings, contemporary rooms are tastefully colored in different tones of beige, elegantly sober yet cozy and comforting with thick carpeting and padded bed panels. Although bathrooms carry nice white marble, they are a bit cramped, with little counter space. From noon on, the downstairs buffet breakfast area becomes a pleasant lounge with honorary bar and snacks, bookshelves, free newspapers, plasma TV, "tasteful" music playing in the background, and two computers with free Internet access making you feel at home. The rooftop has a bedroom with a terrace with two teak sun chairs, clay-potted bushes, and views of the river and castle to the east. ⊠ *Rua Alexandre Herculano 13, Liberdade, 1150-005* ☎ *21/317–3575* 🖷 *21/352–0272* ⊕ *www.domcarloshoteis. com* 🗩 *59 rooms* ⚲ *In-room safes, cable TV with movies, gym, Internet, parking (fee)* ▤ *AE, DC, MC, V* ⍥ *BP.*

★ **$$** ▣ **Lisboa Plaza.** This welcoming, family-owned hotel behind Avenida da Liberdade has been in business for almost half a century, and the experience shines through. The staff is friendly and helpful, and pastel colors, prints on the walls, attractive ornaments, dried-flower arrangements, and well-stocked marble baths lend character and a sense of comfort. The best rooms are at the back, looking up to the botanical gardens; those in front are closer to the main road and don't have the views, but double-glazed windows keep things quiet. Although it's not included in the room rate, the buffet breakfast is excellent. ⊠ *Travessa do Salitre 5, Liberdade, 1269-066* ☎ *21/321–8218* 🖷 *21/347–1630* ⊕ *www. heritage.pt* 🗩 *94 rooms, 12 suites* ⚲ *Restaurant, room service, cable TV, bar, laundry service, Internet, business services, meeting rooms, no-smoking rooms* ▤ *AE, DC, MC, V* ⍥ *EP* Ⓜ *Avenida.*

$$ ▣ **Sana Lisboa Park.** You're poised to enter the best shopping areas and sights from your base in this hotel near Praça Marques de Pombal and Avenida da Liberdade. As soon as you return from the bustling avenue into the spacious lobby, you enter a world of contemporary elegance, sober and discreet. At 5 PM the restaurant serves tea in traditional blue-and-white Vista Alegre porcelain, accompanied by finger sandwiches, hot scones, and cakes. Burn off calories downstairs in the "fitness and well-being center" with its invigorating aquatic colors where you can enjoy massages, Turkish baths, Jacuzzi, saunas, or a workout in the gym. ⊠ *Av. Fontes Pereira de Melo 8, Liberdade, 1069-310* ☎ *21/006–4300* 🖷 *21/006–4301* ⊕ *www.sanahotels.com* 🗩 *281 rooms, 6 suites* ⚲ *Restaurant, room service, in-room safes, minibars, cable TV, gym, hot tub, massage, spa, piano bar, shops, laundry service, Internet, parking (fee)* ▤ *AE, DC, MC, V* ⍥ *BP.*

$ ▣ **Flamingo.** If you're seeking reliable, good-value lodgings in the city center—and you don't need the creature comforts of a high-end hotel—then the Flamingo is worth a try. The staff is friendly, and the small, simply furnished rooms are pleasant enough for the price; despite double-glazed windows, though, those in front tend to be noisy. A stay here gets you discounts at the neighboring parking lot, a bonus in this busy area. ⊠ *Rua Castilho 41, Liberdade, 1250-068* ☎ *21/384–1200* 🖷 *21/ 384–1208* ⊕ *www.bestwestern.com/pt/hotelflamingo* 🗩 *39 rooms* ⚲ *Restaurant, in-room safes, minibars, cable TV, in-room data ports, bar, laundry service* ▤ *AE, DC, MC, V* ⍥ *BP* Ⓜ *Marquês de Pombal.*

$ ▣ **Ibis.** Of the various Ibis hotels around Lisbon, this one's location makes it the best positioned for sightseeing. There is nothing particularly spectacular about these hotels, but they are functional and offer basic facilities at a reasonable price. Although a little cramped, a lot of the rooms on the top floors have good views of the Tagus River and Lisbon's rooftops. The buffet breakfast is an extra €5 per person, and they have lots of parking space in their garage. ⊠ *Rua Barata Salgueiro 53, 1250-043* ☎ *21/330–0630* 🖷 *21/330–0631* ⊕ *www.ibishotel.com* 🗩 *70* *rooms ﾈ Snack bar, cable TV, bar, parking (fee)* ⊟*AE, DC, MC, V* ⑩*EP* Ⓜ *Avenida or Marquês de Pombal.*

Areeiro

¢ ▦ **Lar do Areeiro.** It's hard to beat the value of this recently renovated pension 1 km (½ mi) from the city center. It has both a taxi stand and a metro station at its doorstep that will link you to all the main sights. To some, the 1970s architectural layout in its bar and lounge might be outdated, but others might find it in sync with today's "retro" look. Reserve ahead for these cheerful rooms, which have showers rather than bathtubs. ⊠ *Praça Dr. Francisco Sá Carneiro 4, Areeiro, 1000-159* ☎ *21/849–3150* 📠 *21/840–6321* ⤢ *62 rooms* ﾈ *Some in-room safes, minibars, cable TV, bar, babysitting* ⊟*AE, DC, MC, V* ⑩*BP* Ⓜ*Areeiro.*

Bairro Alto

$ ▦ **Pensão Londres.** This modest bed-and-breakfast is a surprisingly agreeable choice in the "you-get-what-you-pay-for" category. Expect a modest but indisputably clean room—singles, doubles, or triples—with or without bath, starting on the third floor of a former residence in the Bairro Alto section. ⊠ *Rua Dom Pedro V 53, Bairro Alto, 1250-092* ☎ *21/346–2203* 📠 *21/346–5682* ⊕ *www.pensaolondres.com.pt* ⤢ *40 rooms, 13 with bath* ﾈ *Cable TV; no a/c* ⊟ *DC, MC, V* ⑩ *CP* Ⓜ *Avenida.*

¢ ▦ **Camões.** Typical of Bairro Alto guesthouses, the Camões has simple rooms on a couple of floors of an apartment building and is overseen by a bustling matron. For the price, don't expect great comfort; do expect clean, bright rooms with beds that don't sag. Rooms facing the street have little balconies—which make for noisy nights but give you a window onto Bairro Alto life. There's a small breakfast room, or you can step out into the neighborhood for coffee and pastries. ⊠ *Travessa do Poço da Cidade 38, Bairro Alto, 1200* ☎ *21/346–7510* 📠 *21/346–4048* ⤢ *19 rooms, 7 with bath* ⊟ *No credit cards* ⑩ *CP* Ⓜ *Baixa-Chiado.*

Baixa

$$$ ▦ **Avenida Palace.** Built in 1892, Lisbon's first luxury hotel is still a pretty penny. French architect Lucian Donnat breathed new life into the hotel when refitting it to its original romantic belle epoque style. Regal elegance combines with modern comfort here. Classically furnished rooms are completely soundproof, and bathrooms are lined in the finest Portuguese marble. Sumptuously furnished suites, fit for a king, are decorated in Louis XV, Louis XVI, D. Maria, D. José, and Empire styles. The Avenida Palace also has one of the finest locations in town. ⊠ *Rua 1° de Dezembro 123, Rossío, 1200-359* ☎ *21/321–8100* 📠 *21/342–2884* ⊕ *www.hotel-avenida-palace.pt* ⤢ *62 rooms, 20 suites* ﾈ *Room service, some in-room hot tubs, minibars, cable TV, bar, laundry service, free parking* ⊟ *AE, DC, MC, V* ⑩ *BP.*

$$ ▦ **Métropole.** From its balconied late-19th-century facade to its '20s-style bar and lounge, the Métropole has been known to put a grin on the face of many a guest. Its light- and antique-filled rooms are inviting. Those in front overlook the Rossío—with its flower sellers and cascading fountain—

the Alfama, and the Castelo de São Jorge; other quarters have views of the Baixa's constantly changing tableaux. What's more, you can also buy bottles of the famous Buçaco wines here. ⊠ *Rossío 30, Baixa, 1100-200* ☎ *21/321–9030* 🖷 *21/346–9166* ⊕ *www.almeidahotels.com* ⇨ *36 rooms ᴄ In-room safes, cable TV, bar* ⊟ *AE, DC, MC, V* ⦿ *EP* Ⓜ *Rossío.*

$$ 🏨 **Mundial.** Steps from the Rossío and Restauradores squares, this large property looks uncompromisingly modern, but inside there's lots of good, old-fashioned charm combined with modern facilities after a renovation in 2004. One wing overlooks the landscaping and fountains of Praça Martim Moniz. Rooms have elegant light-wood furniture, firm mattresses, and well-equipped bathrooms. Breakfast is served in the rooftop restaurant, Varanda de Lisboa, which has views of the Baixa on one side and the Alfama on the other—no wonder the hotel dubs itself "Lisbon's eighth hill." ⊠ *Rua Dom Duarte 4, Baixa, 1100-198* ☎ *21/884–2000* 🖷 *21/ 884–2110* ⊕ *www.hotel-mundial.pt* ⇨ *373 rooms ᴄ Restaurant, coffee shop, room service, minibars, cable TV with movies, bar, meeting rooms* ⊟ *AE, DC, MC, V* ⦿ *BP, MAP* Ⓜ *Rossío.*

$$ 🏨 **VIP Executive Suites Éden.** One of downtown's most exciting art deco buildings—the former Eden theater and movie house—has been converted into an "aparthotel." The understated lobby gives little hint at the comfort of the studios and one-bedroom apartments upstairs. Each unit overlooks a garden and the city and has modern furniture, a tiled bath, and a well-equipped kitchenette. But the biggest thrill is on the top floor, where a breakfast bar opens onto a terrace with castle views; the small pool here gets the sun all day. ⊠ *Praça dos Restauradores 24, Baixa, 1250-187* ☎ *21/321–6600* 🖷 *21/321–6666* ⊕ *www.viphotels. com* ⇨ *75 studios, 59 2-bedroom apartments ᴄ Kitchenettes, microwaves, refrigerators, cable TV, pool, bar, Internet, business services, meeting rooms* ⊟ *AE, MC, V* ⦿ *EP* Ⓜ *Restauradores.*

¢–$ 🏨 **Florescente.** Rooms at this inn are on five azulejo-lined floors and vary in size; all are bright and cheerful, with gleaming white-marble baths. Suites with a sleeping alcove are a good choice for budget-conscious families. Only breakfast is served, but you're one block from Praça dos Restauradores and on a street well known for its many seafood restaurants. ⊠ *Rua Portas de Santo Antão 99, Baixa, 1150-266* ☎ *21/342–6609* 🖷 *21/342–7733* ⊕ *www.residencialflorescente.com* ⇨ *64 rooms, 8 suites ᴄ Cable TV* ⊟ *AE, MC, V* ⦿ *BP* Ⓜ *Restauradores.*

¢ 🏨 **Insulana.** One of a series of long-standing, modest hotels in Baixa's shopping area, the Insulana has the edge over most and generally has space even when others are full—possibly because it's a little hidden away, up two flights of stairs through a clothes shop. Rooms are dark and dated, but they're clean and hospitable places to rest your head; ask for a room at the rear to minimize disturbance from street noise. ⊠ *Rua da Assunção 52, Baixa, 1100-044* ☎ *21/342–3131* 🖷 *21/342–8924* ⊕ *www. insulana.cjb.net* ⇨ *32 rooms ᴄ Cable TV, bar* ⊟ *AE, MC, V* ⦿ *CP* Ⓜ *Baixa-Chiado.*

Chiado

$$ 🏨 **Lisboa Regency Chiado.** Arriving at the entrance, you may assume the taxi—or Jaguar limo that's available on request—has dropped you at an office. Never assume. This boutique hotel is a showcase of style on the sixth to eighth floors of the Grandes Armazéns do Chiado shopping complex. From the public areas, you look through a three-story window at tile rooftops, the Sé, and the Castelo de São Jorge. Designer Pedro Espírito Santo has blended elements of 16th-century Portugal with those from former colonies, and guest rooms are a mix of antiques and 21st-century amenities. ⊠ *Rua Nova de Almada 114, Chiado, 1200-290* ☎ *21/ 325–6100 or 21/325–6200* 🖶 *21/325–6161* ⊕ *www.regency-hotels-resorts.com* 🛏 *38 rooms, 2 suites* ⚷ *Room service, in-room safes, cable TV, in-room data ports, bar, lounge, shops, laundry service* ☰ *AE, DC, MC, V* ⎮⚹⎮ *BP* Ⓜ *Baixa-Chiado.*

$ 🏨 **Borges.** The Borges is as old-fashioned as the glove shops and shoe-shine stands that dot the district surrounding it. The hotel is favored by European tour groups as well as those who love to shop. Rooms and bathrooms are fresh and tidy, and you'll have no trouble finding an English-speaking staff member. Although the rate includes a Continental breakfast, you're better off having coffee and a pastry at the famous Café A Brasileira, which is just steps away. ⊠ *Rua Garrett 108–110, Chiado, 1200-503* ☎ *21/346–1951* 🖶 *21/342–6617* ⊕ *www.hotelborges.com* 🛏 *96 rooms* ⚷ *Cable TV, bar* ☰ *MC, V* ⎮⚹⎮ *CP* Ⓜ *Baixa-Chiado.*

Graça

$$$$ 🏨 **Solar do Castelo.** This 18th-century mansion built within St. George's Castle walls is now a charming inn. It occupies what was once the kitchens of the Alcáçova Palace (Home of the Kings) and is still known as the Palacete das Cozinhas (little palace of the kitchens). The interior has contemporary classic decor and exudes a homey feel. Guest rooms offer bathrobes. Breakfast and drinks are served on the cobblestone interior patio amid potted plants, trees, and a gurgling fountain. If you're lucky, you might be graced by the presence of one of the peacocks living next door in the castle gardens. ⊠ *Rua das Cozinhas 2, Alfama, 1100-181* ☎ *21/880–6050* 🖶 *21/887–0907* ⊕ *www.heritage.pt* 🛏 *14 rooms* ⚷ *In-room safes, cable TV, in-room data ports, babysitting* ☰ *AE, DC, MC, V* ⎮⚹⎮ *EP.*

$$–$$$ 🏨 **Solar dos Mouros.** This melon-color Alfama house next to the castle is typical, but what's inside is not. Named for the view it has, each spacious, brightly colored room is individually decorated with genuine pieces of contemporary art as well as African art the owner/artist has collected. You can indulge your aural senses with the CD player. Light meals and salads are served in the bar. ⊠ *Rua do Milagre de Santo Antonio 6, Alfama, 1100-351* ☎ *21/885–4940* 🖶 *21/885–4945* ⊕ *www.solardosmouros.pt* 🛏 *11 rooms, 1 suite* ⚷ *Room service, in-room safes, minibars, cable TV, bar, laundry service* ☰ *AE, DC, MC, V* ⎮⚹⎮ *CP.*

$$ 🏨 **Albergaria Senhora do Monte.** The views from this small, unpretentious hotel in the oldest part of town are fine, especially at night, when the nearby Castelo de São Jorge is softly illuminated. To make the most of the location, opt for one of the junior suites, which have terraces. The top-floor bar–breakfast room has a panoramic picture window (making breakfast a real pleasure), and the neighborhood is quiet. It's a steep walk every time you return here, but Tram 28 runs nearby.

FodorśChoice
★

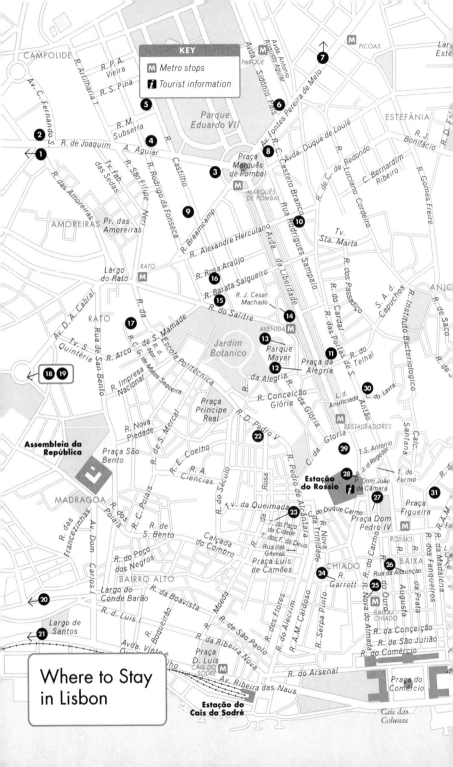

Where to Stay
in Lisbon

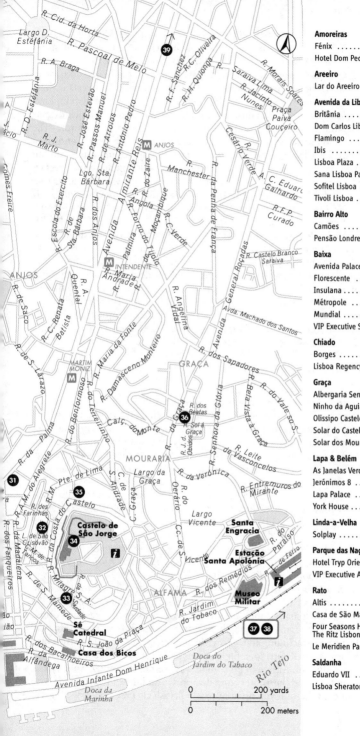

✉ *Calçada do Monte 39, Graça, 1170-250* ☎ *21/886–6002* 📠 *21/ 887–7783* ⊕ *www.maisturismo.pt/sramonte* ⟲ *24 rooms, 4 suites* ⚬ *Cable TV, bar, babysitting* ▤ *AE, DC, MC, V* ⦿ *BP.*

$$ 🏨 **Olissipo Castelo.** This small, elegant hotel is in the Bairro do Castelo between the Mouraria and Alfama quarters, where the streets in June are the scene of festivities celebrating the patron saints of Lisbon. Luxurious, pale textured fabrics, striped pastel wallpapering, thick carpeting, and elegant finishing give you a sense of pampered comfort. The bathrooms are done in white marble. Rooms on the second and third floors have lovely terraces with wooden tables and chairs where you can breakfast and sip an afternoon drink while contemplating the spectacular panoramic views over Lisbon's rooftops. Book well ahead. ✉ *Rua Costa do Castelo 112–126, Alfama, 1100-179* ☎ *21/882–0190* 📠 *21/ 882–0194* ⊕ *www.olissipohotels.com* ⟲ *22 rooms, 2 suites* ⚬ *Room service, minibars, bar, Internet, free parking* ▤ *AE, DC, MC, V* ⦿ *BP.*

¢ 🏨 **Ninho da Aguias.** This 200-year-old house "nesting" on the very top of the Alfama offers five-star views at budget prices. The rooms are simply furnished in white, including the antique iron beds. Be sure to ask for a room with a bath or you risk walking down the hall with towel in hand. An iron spiral staircase leads down to a garden shaded by passion-fruit trees and other exotic trees and flowers. There is no bar, but you can help yourself to the honor bar in the refrigerator and take your drink to the garden. ✉ *Costa do Castelo 74, Alfama, 1100-179* ☎ *21/ 885–4070* ⟲ *14 rooms, 6 with bath* ⚬ *No a/c, no room TVs* ▤ *No credit cards* ⊘ *Closed Christmas wk* ⦿ *EP.*

Lapa & Ajuda

$$$$ 🏨 **Lapa Palace.** A 19th-century town house in the leafy Lapa district contains Portugal's most elegant and welcoming hotels. Marble, antique furnishings, and fresh flowers are ubiquitous. So are such room amenities as a hot tub, high-speed Internet access, or a stereo with a CD collection. From your guest quarters you might see terraced lawns, a waterfall, the heated pool, or the city and river. Whatever the vista from your room, you can enjoy a 180-degree city view from the terrace of the Rio Tejo Bar, where comfortable chairs and sofas invite you to truly savor your drink or tea. ✉ *Rua Pau de Bandeira 4, Lapa, 1249-021* ☎ *21/ 394-9494* 📠 *21/395–0665* ⊕ *www.orient-expresshotels.com* ⟲ *109 rooms and suites* ⚬ *3 restaurants, room service, in-room safes, some in-room hot tubs, minibars, cable TV, in-room VCRs, pool, health club, bar, shops, babysitting, laundry service, Internet, business services, meeting rooms* ▤ *AE, DC, MC, V* ⦿ *BP.*

★ $$$ 🏨 **York House.** Although it was a convent in the 17th century, this inn is far from austere. Vine-covered staircases climb to the garden from the street, and a shady courtyard invites you to relax over a meal or a drink. Each guest room is unique, though all have good-quality reproduction furniture—including four-poster beds—and beautiful rugs, which also adorn the tiled corridors. Eight rooms have a classical décor, and 24 are more modern. Although it's a good way west of the center, York House is on tram and bus routes from downtown and near the Museu de Arte Antiga. It has a loyal, predominately British clientele; book well in advance. ⊠ *Rua das Janelas Verdes 32, Lapa, 1200-692* ☎ *21/396–2435* ☐ *21/397–2793* ⊕ *www.yorkhouselisboa.com* ⇆ *32 rooms* ♻ *Restaurant, bar* ☰ *AE, DC, MC, V* ⏀ *BP.*

$$–$$$ ▦ **Jerónimos 8.** Just around the corner from the famous monastery of the same name, this appealing hotel stands out for its location and style, in which a modern ambience harmoniously blends past and present. And, of course, since this is an Almeida hotel, patrons are entitled to purchase bottles of the very famous Buçaco wines. ⊠ *Rua dos Jerónimos 8, Belém, 1400-211* ☎ *21/799–1930* ☐ *21/793–0445* ⊕ *www. almeidahotels.com* ⇆ *65 rooms* ♻ *Bar, ethernet, safe, Wi-Fi, free parking* ☰ *AE, DC, MC, V* ⏀ *BP.*

★ $$ ▦ **As Janelas Verdes.** On the same street as the Museu de Arte Antiga, this late-18th-century mansion was once the home of Portuguese novelist Eça de Queirós. Fittings, furnishings, paintings, and tile work throughout are in keeping with the building's historic character. Its guest rooms are individually furnished and tasteful; some have access to the garden via an exterior staircase. On the ivy-covered patio, you can eat breakfast and imagine yourself in a different age. Reservations are vital for stays here. ⊠ *Rua das Janelas Verdes 47, Lapa, 1269-066* ☎ *21/396–8143* ☐ *21/396–8144* ⊕ *www.heritage.pt* ⇆ *29 rooms* ♻ *Dining room, in-room safes, cable TV, bar* ☰ *AE, DC, MC, V* ⏀ *EP* Ⓜ *Cais do Sodré.*

Linda-a-Velha

$$–$$$$ ▦ **Solplay.** This ultramodern hotel is 10 km (6 mi) from Lisbon, off the Cascais toll road in the town of Linda-a-Velha. To get to the golf courses in Belas and Cascais, to Lisbon, or to the airport you can take the hotel's free minibus or a chauffeur-driven car. One- and two-room apartments have fully equipped kitchenettes and spacious terraces with superb views. The roof not only holds a garden with palm trees, but a "top of the world" swimming pool spanned by an arched bridge. Public areas and rooms are decorated with works by well-known painter Victor Lages. Solplay is child friendly, with a special health club adapted for children, and DVDs for their entertainment. ⊠ *Rua Manuel da Silva Gaio 2, 2795-132* ☎ *21/006–6000* ☐ *21/006–6199* ⊕ *www. solplay.pt* ⇆ *119 apartments* ♻ *Restaurant, kitchenettes, cable TV, tennis court, indoor-outdoor pool, gym, hair salon, hot tub, sauna, steam room, piano bar, shop, babysitting, parking* ☰ *AE, DC, MC, V* ⏀ *BP, FAP, MAP.*

Parque das Nações

$$ ▦ **Hotel Tryp Oriente.** The riverfront, restaurants, and aquarium of Parque das Nações are just steps from the door of this hotel built for Expo'98 and refurbished in 2004, and the Vasco da Gama mall is just down the street. Rooms are comfortable and functional, if somewhat bland. Excellent train and metro transportation puts you downtown in about 15 minutes. The hotel fills up when there's a convention at FIL. ⊠ *Av. D. João II, Parque das Nações, 1990-083* ☎ *21/893–0000* ☐ *21/893–0099* ⊕ *www.solmelia.es* ⇆ *90 rooms, 26 suites* ♻ *Restaurant,* *in-room safes, cable TV, bar, laundry service, Internet, convention center, no-smoking rooms* ▤ *AE, MC, V* ¶⨀ *EP* Ⓜ *Oriente.*

$$ ▦ **VIP Executive Arts.** The high-ceilinged lobby bar suggests the film *2001: A Space Odyssey* with its futuristic black-and-white plastic chairs, which resemble carved-out cue balls. You are in contact with the riverside and all of the attractions of the World Exposition in 1998, including the Oceanarium. The red wall around the terrace window is the only element of color in the otherwise minimalist decor dominated by off-white. The futuristic theme is carried over into the bedrooms. ✉ *Av. Dom João II, lote 1-18, Parque das Nações, 1998-028* ☎ *21/002–0400* 🖷 *21/002–0401* ⊕ *www.viphotels.com* ⇨ *300 rooms* ⌂ *Restaurant, room service, in-room safes, minibars, cable TV, 2 bars, shops, babysitting, Internet, car rental, parking (fee)* ▤ *AE, DC, MC, V* ¶⨀ *BP, MAP.*

Rato

$$$$ ▦ **Altis.** This large, boxy, modern lodging has a broad range of facilities, including an art gallery and a heated indoor lap pool. Its virtue is reliability, which is why it hosts a lot of business travelers. The mezzanine bar-lounge above the lobby is a relaxing spot, and rooms are comfortable, if unexceptional; those on higher floors have fine views of Parque Eduardo VII, as does the top-floor restaurant. ✉ *Rua Castilho 11, Rato, 1269-072* ☎ *21/310–6000* 🖷 *21/354–8696* ⊕ *www.hotel-altis.pt* ⇨ *290 rooms, 13 suites* ⌂ *2 restaurants, room service, in-room safes, minibars, cable TV, indoor pool, gym, sauna, 3 bars, shops, laundry service, Internet, business services, meeting rooms* ▤ *AE, DC, MC, V* ¶⨀ *BP* Ⓜ *Rotunda.*

$$$$　**Four Seasons Hotel The Ritz Lisbon.** The luxury starts the minute you
Fodor'sChoice ▦ step into the marble reception area and the lounge-bar, whose terrace
★ overlooks the park. Public areas are filled with tapestries, fine paintings, and antique reproductions. Large, airy guest rooms have elegant furnishings and bathrooms as well as private terraces. Rooms in the back with park views are the best choice; on a clear day you can see Castelo de São Jorge and the Rio Tejo from the upper floors. A superb buffet breakfast—as well as lunch and dinner—is served at the Varanda restaurant, which also has a terrace. ✉ *Rua Rodrigo da Fonseca 88, Rato, 1099-039* ☎ *21/381–1471* 🖷 *21/383–1688* ⊕ *www.fourseasons.com* ⇨ *282 rooms and suites* ⌂ *Restaurant, snack bar, room service, in-room safes, minibars, cable TV, gym, bar, shops, babysitting, laundry service, Internet, meeting rooms, no-smoking floors* ▤ *AE, DC, MC, V* ¶⨀ *EP* Ⓜ *Marquês de Pombal.*

$$$$ ▦ **Le Meridien Park Atlantic.** Business travelers like the distinctive Park Atlantic for its location—right by Parque Eduardo VII—and facilities. There's plenty for vacationers to admire, too, including the split-level atrium with its cozy brasserie and separate conservatory-style bar. All the sleek rooms have smart bathrooms and soundproofing; more to the point, they all have fantastic views over the city and park. ✉ *Rua Castilho 149, Rato, 1099-034* ☎ *21/381–8705* 🖷 *21/389–0500* ⊕ *www.lemeridien.pt* ⇨ *313 rooms, 17 suites* ⌂ *Restaurant, cable TV, hair salon, sauna, bar, shops, babysitting, laundry service, Internet, business services, meeting rooms, no-smoking floors* ▤ *AE, DC, MC, V* ¶⨀ *EP* Ⓜ *Marquês de Pombal.*

$ ⌂ **Casa de São Mamede.** The Casa de São Mamede is a real survivor. One of the first private houses to be built in Lisbon after the 18th-century earthquake has been transformed into a relaxed guesthouse endowed with antique, country-style furniture; a tiled dining room; a grand staircase; and stained-glass windows. You're just a 10-minute walk from the Bairro Alto or a long, steep hike from the metro. ⊠ *Rua da Escola Politécnica 159, Rato, 1250-100* ☎ *21/396–3166* 🖷 *21/395–1896* 🛏 *28 rooms* ⌂ *Dining room; no room phones, no room TVs* ⊟ *No credit cards* ⏉ CP Ⓜ *Avenida.*

Saldanha

$$–$$$ ⌂ **Lisboa Sheraton & Towers.** Even those who eschew chain hotels appreciate this Sheraton overlooking modern Lisbon. Its many advantages include a huge reception area with a comfortable bar, a helpful staff, an agreeable restaurant, and modestly sized guest rooms with many amenities. Tower rooms have parquet floors, coffeemakers, a club lounge, and private check-in and checkout. Executive rooms have large desks and fax-modem outlets. The top-floor Panoramic Bar is the perfect place for an aperitif. Although the hotel is near Parque Eduardo VII and the Gulbenkian museum's gardens, most of your sightseeing days will start and end with a bus or taxi ride. ⊠ *Rua Latino Coelho 1, Saldanha, 1069-025* ☎ *21/357–5757* 🖷 *21/354–7164* ⊕ *www.sheraton.com* 🛏 *377 rooms, 7 suites* ⌂ *2 restaurants, room service, in-room safes, cable TV, some in-room data ports, pool, health club, massage, sauna, 2 bars, shops, laundry service, business services* ⊟ *AE, DC, MC, V* ⏉ BP Ⓜ *Picoas.*

$–$$ ⌂ **Eduardo VII.** Beyond the anonymous, 1930s exterior of this hotel, which is near the park of the same name, you'll find 10 floors of shipshape rooms that are short on space, but smart and comfortable. The hotel's singular attraction is the view of the Lisbon skyline from the top-floor restaurant and bar. ⊠ *Av. Fontes Pereira de Melo 5, Saldanha, 1060-114* ☎ *21/356–8800* 🖷 *21/356–8833* ⊕ *www.hoteleduardovii.pt* 🛏 *136 rooms, 4 suites* ⌂ *Restaurant, in-room safes, minibars, cable TV, some in-room data ports, billiards, bar, Internet, business services, meeting rooms* ⊟ *AE, DC, MC, V* ⏉ BP, MAP Ⓜ *Marquês de Pombal.*

NIGHTLIFE & THE ARTS

Lisbon has a thriving arts-and-nightlife scene, and there are listings of concerts, plays, and films in the monthly *Agenda Cultural* and the quarterly *Unforgettable Lisboa* booklets, both available from the tourist office. Also, the Friday editions of both the *Diário de Notícias* and *O Independente* newspapers have separate magazines with entertainment listings. Although written in Portuguese, listings are fairly easy to decipher.

It's best to buy tickets to musical and theatrical performances at the box offices, but you can also get them at several agencies, including the Fnac book, computer, and music store at the Colombo mall, the Valentim Carvalho music store in the Grandes Armazéns do Chiado shopping complex on Rua do Carmo, and the Ticket Line in the Colombo, Vasco da Gama, and Chiado malls. A special ticket office—called ABEP—on

Praça dos Restauradores, near the main post office, also sells tickets to sporting events.

Nightlife

Lisbon bars and discos open late (10 PM). On weekends the mobs are shoulder to shoulder in the street, as each passing hour heralds a move to the next trendy spot. Many places are dark and silent on Sunday; Monday, Tuesday, and (sometimes) Wednesday are also nights when bars are closed. For a less boisterous evening out, visit a café-bar or an *adega típica* (traditional wine cellar) that has fado shows. Still other venues host a variety of live events, from rock and roll to African music.

Bars

The Bairro Alto, long the center of Lisbon's nightlife, is the best place for barhopping. Most bars here are fairly small, and stay open until 3 AM or so. Larger, designer bars started opening a few years ago along and around Avenida 24 de Julho in the Santos neighborhood, where—because this isn't a residential area as the Bairro Alto is—bars can stay open until 5 or 6 AM. The latest hot neighborhood is farther along the riverbank, next to the bridge in Alcântara, where the Doca do Santo Amaro and the Doca de Alcântara have fashionable terrace-bars and restaurants, some converted from old warehouses.

Whichever district you choose, note that not all bars have signs outside; to find the latest places you may have to follow the crowds or try a half-open door. Don't expect to have a quiet drink: the company is generally young and excitable.

If you are looking for an older, more sophisticated crowd, visit **Blues Café** (✉ Rua de Cintura do Porto, Armazém H, Rocha Conde de Obidos ☎ 21/395–7085 ⊕ www.bluescafe.pt), which is inspired by colonial New Orleans. Live music is played every Thursday. For a quiet drink in an older part of town, seek out **Cerca Moura** (✉ Largo das Portas do Sol 4, Alfama ☎ 21/887–4859), which has outdoor seating and river views. The famous old art deco Condes cinema is now the **Hard Rock Cafe** (✉ Av. da Liberdade 2, Liberdade ☎ 21/324–5280). Lisbon can now send tourists off with a Hard Rock Cafe T-shirt, too.

Heading down toward Avenida 24 de Julho, the late-night crew stops off at **O'Gillin's** (✉ Rua das Remolares 8–10, Cais do Sodré ☎ 21/342–1899), an Irish bar across the road from the train station. It regularly hosts bands at night; Sunday afternoon a jazz group performs. If you can't make it to the famous "Peter's bar" on Faial Island in the Azores, you can visit Lisbon's **Peter Café Sport** (✉ Rua da Pimenta, Parque das Nações ☎ 21/895–0060) in front of the Garcia da Horta gardens. It's known for its gin and tonics and toasted ham-and-cheese sandwiches.

BAIRRO ALTO   **Apollo XIII** (✉ Travessa da Cara 8, Bairro Alto ☎ 21/342–4952) draws students into its tiny drinking den. The walls of **Artis** (✉ Rua Diário de Notícias 95, Bairro Alto ☎ 21/342–4795) are covered in movie posters, and various musical instruments are incorporated into the decor. Jazz recordings fill the air as friends enjoy drinks and Artis's popular toasted chicken sandwiches. **Clube da Esquina** (✉ Rua da Barroca 30, Bairro Alto ☎ 21/342–7149), on a street corner, is a trendy bar among the younger crowd. Those who can't squeeze inside hang out in the street with glass in hand. **Pavilhão Chinês** (✉ Rua Dom Pedro V 89, Bairro Alto ☎ 21/342–4729) is a comfortable 1900s-style bar with bric-a-brac—statues, tankards, ceramics, baubles, toys—from around the world.

The most refined place in Bairro Alto to start off your evening is the relaxed **Solar do Vinho do Porto** (✉ Rua de São Pedro de Alcântara 45, Bairro Alto ☎ 21/347–5707), a formidable old building where you can sink into an armchair and sample port. **A Tasca** (✉ Travessa de Queimada 13–15, Bairro Alto ☎ 21/342–4910) is a bright bar with tequila as its specialty drink.

ALCÂNTARA **Doca de Santo** (✉ Doca de Santo Amaro, Alcântara ☎ 21/396–3522 ⊕ www.docadesanto.pt) has a great palm-lined esplanade. Get ready for a lively night of salsa at **Havana** (✉ Doca de Santo Amaro, Armazém 5, Alcântara ☎ 21/397–9893). The right drink is a *mojito* cocktail (made with crushed mint and rum).

SANTOS **Steakhouse** (✉ Rua Cintura do Porto, Armazém 255, Santos ☎ 21/324–2910), a riverside bar-restaurant, is terrific in summer with a tropical garden. **Xafarix** (✉ Rua Dom Carlos I 69, Santos ☎ 21/396–9487) has been around for years. Its cramped basement hosting live concerts every night is a favorite among fans of Portuguese music.

Café-Bars & Pastelarias

Many of Lisbon's cafés are glorious: the old-timers often have rich interiors of burnished and carved wood, mirrors, and tiles. Many also have outdoor seating, so you can order a coffee, beer, or snack and watch the city pass by. Those that specialize in pastries and cakes are known as *pastelarias* (pastry shops), and their offerings are among the city's greatest contributions to the gastronomic arts: be sure to sample some. Most cafés remain open for at least the early part of the evenings on weekdays; a few have become late-night drinking haunts. Some cafés close early on Saturday and altogether on Sunday, however.

BAIXA **Café Martinho da Arcada** (✉ Praça do Comércio 3, Baixa) is a welcome stop for a *pastel de nata* (custard tart) before catching your tram to Belém. Tradition oozes from the tiled walls, and the waiters rush to and fro while bakers prepare scrumptious pastries. Note that it's closed Sunday. With its grand interior and suitably aloof waiters, the traditional **Café Nicola** (Praça Dom Pedro IV 24, west side of Rossío, Baixa) is one of the pricier spots for sitting down and taking in downtown. As its name suggests, **Leiteria A Camponeza** (✉ Rua dos Sapateiros 155–157, Baixa) is an old-fashioned *leiteria* (specializing in milk products and pastries) with blue-tiled walls that display bucolic scenes. You can enjoy its coffee, cakes, and sandwiches any day but Sunday, when the café is closed. The **Pastelaria Suiça** (✉ Rossío 96, Baixa) stretches all the way back to the adjacent Praça da Figueira. Outdoor tables are at a premium, but the relaxed ambience (even a single beer or coffee can hold your table for an hour) makes them worth the wait and slightly higher prices.

CHIADO In the heart of the shopping district, **Café A Brasileira** (⊠ Rua Garrett 120, Chiado) is the most famous of Lisbon's old haunts. A bronze statue of Portugal's poet-writer Fernando Pessoa sits just outside. For a feel of bygone days and enjoyment of the literary and art memorabilia on the walls, come before dark: at night every table is taken over by beer-drinking young people.

LAPA Dying for a cup of tea? **Cha da Lapa** (⊠ Rua Olival 8, Lapa), a cozy Victorian-style teahouse, serves hot scones, chocolate eclairs, and cheesecake as well as filtered leaves.

RATO All who wander into the small **Confeiteria Cister** (⊠ Rua da Escola Politécnica 107, Rato) feel they have discovered it. Choose an enticing cake or sandwich, then find a spot at one of the polished wood tables, where patrons, young and old, linger with a friend, a newspaper, or just a large cup of coffee.

SALDANHA There's not much that **Galeto** (⊠ Av. da República 14, Saldanha) doesn't serve, from cakes and sandwiches to full meals, from early to late every day. Pull up a stool at one of the long wooden counters. Founded in 1929, the **Versailles** (⊠ Av. de República 15, Saldanha) has retained its grand furnishings. Massive mahogany display cases groan with chocolates, port wines, and liqueurs. Homemade cakes and hot chocolate are specialties.

Dance Clubs

Most clubs are in the Bairro Alto and along the Avenida 24 de Julho, though more and more cool, upscale places are opening in the Santos and Alcântara districts. Most places charge a cover of about €10–€15 (perhaps more on weekends), which usually includes one drink. Some clubs have strict door policies; bouncers may scrutinize you and your clothes. Clubs are open from about 10 or 11 PM until 4 or 5 AM; few get going before midnight.

Fragil (⊠ Rua da Atalaia 126, Bairro Alto ☎ 21/346–9578) is a long-standing favorite that attracts a partly gay crowd. Fans of Buena Vista Social Club will feel at home at **La Gloria Cubana** (⊠ Rua Oliveira Miguéis 48, Alcântara ☎ 21/395–5977), where after midnight, the waiters start to play live Cuban music. Those who aren't playing music are on the dance floor teaching someone to salsa. **Indochina** (⊠ Rua da Cintura do Porto de Lisboa, Armazém H, Rocha Conde de Obidos ☎ No phone) lends an exotic touch to the night scene with its colonial Vietnam decor, but its music is modern top of the pops. **Kapital** (⊠ Av. 24 de Julho 68, Santos ☎ 21/395–5963) is typical of the high-fashion, high-price venues down on the avenida; its terrace is its nicest feature.

Keops (⊠ Rua da Rosa 157–159, Bairro Alto ☎ 21/342–8773) raises eyebrows with its funky Egyptian theme. It's rumored that John Malkovich is one of the owners of the hot club **Lux** (⊠ Av. Infante D. Henrique near Sta. Apolónia, Alfama ☎ 21/882–0890), which is in a remodeled riverside warehouse. **Plateau** (⊠ Rua Escadinhas da Praia 7, Santos ☎ 21/396–5116) attracts nostalgic Lisboetas longing to dance to classic rock. According to one of the DJs, the Rolling Stones visited here once.

Fado Clubs

Fado is a haunting music rooted in African slave songs. During colonial times it was exported to Portugal; later, Lisbon's Alfama was recognized as the birthplace of the style, and today most performances occur in the Bairro Alto. In the adegas típicas food and wine are served, and fado plays late into the night: the singing starts at 10 or 11, and the adegas often stay open until 3 AM. It's becoming increasingly difficult to find an authentic adega; ask around for a recommendation. Note that some establishments charge (according to the night and who is playing) a minimum food and drink consumption fee, usually around €10–€15.

One of the oldest fado clubs, **Adega do Machado** (⊠ Rua do Norte 91, Bairro Alto ☎ 21/322–4640), is busy every night but Monday, when it's closed. For fado at budget prices, consider a meal in the **Adega do Ribatejo** (⊠ Rua Diário de Notícias 23, Bairro Alto ☎ 21/346–8343), a popular local haunt, where there's live entertainment nightly. **Clube de Fado** (⊠ Rua S. João de Praça 92–94, Alfama ☎ 21/885–2704 ⊕ www.clube-de-fado.com) is popular with locals who come to hear the guitar playing of both established performers and rising stars.

Parreirinha d'Alfama (⊠ Beco do Espírito Santo 1, Alfama ☎ 21/886–8209) is a little club owned by fado legend Argentina Santos. She doesn't sing very often herself these days, but the club hires many other highly rated singers. **Senhor Vinho** (⊠ Rua do Meio à Lapa 18, Lapa ☎ 21/397–2681 ⊕ www.restsrvinho.com) is an institution and attracts some of Portugal's most accomplished fado singers. It's closed Sunday. **Timpanas** (⊠ Rua Gilberto Rola 24, Alcântara ☎ 21/390–6655), which is closed Wednesday, is one of the city's best fado clubs. This explains why it's popular with tour groups even though it's so far from the center of town.

Gay & Lesbian Clubs

Lisbon has a well-established gay and lesbian scene, concentrated primarily in and around the Bairro Alto. **As Primas** (⊠ Rua da Atalaia 154–156, Bairro Alto ☎ No phone) is referred to as a lesbian hangout, though everyone drops in to this tasca to hear the '80s music on the jukebox. **Finalmente** (⊠ Rua da Palmeira 38, Bairro Alto ☎ 21/372–6522) has one of the best sound systems in town and attracts a high-camp crowd. **Fragil** (⊠ Rua da Atalaia 126, Bairro Alto ☎ 21/346–9578), although not exclusively gay, does attract a good, mixed crowd. **Herois Louge Café** (⊠ Calça do Sacramento 14, Chiado ☎ 21/342–0077), a bar-cum-restaurant, might first be mistaken for an interior design shop with its retro-'60s white plastic chairs. Their original sandwiches are a good alternative to the ubiquitous *tosta mista*. The lesbian bar **Memorial** (⊠ Rua Gustavo de Matos Sequeira 42, Rato ☎ 21/396–8891) can get packed on the weekends. **Trumps** (⊠ Rua Imprensa Nacional 104b, Rato ☎ 21/397–1059) is the city's biggest gay disco.

Live Music

Plenty of places have live rock, pop, and jazz performances. Big-name American and British bands, as well as the superstar Brazilian singers so beloved in Portugal, often play in Lisbon's large concert halls and stadiums. African music is also immensely popular here, with touring groups from Cabo Verde and Angola playing regularly alongside home-grown talent.

The city's best jazz joint is the **Hot Clube de Portugal** (✉ Praça da Alegria 39, Rato ☎ 21/346–7369), which puts on a wide variety of gigs every night but Sunday and Monday, starting about 11. **Pê Sujo** (✉ Largo de São Martinho 6, Alfama ☎ 21/886–5929) specializes in live Brazilian music, which goes down smoothly with its potent caipirinhas. The **Ritz** (✉ Rua da Glória 55, Bairro Alto ☎ 21/342–5140) is Lisbon's biggest African club. It's on the edge of the Bairro Alto, in a rather seedy area, but is renowned as a friendly place where you can dance to live music.

The Arts

Classical music concerts are staged from about October through June by the Fundação Calouste Gulbenkian. Of particular interest is the Early Music and Baroque Festival, held in churches and museums around Lisbon every spring. You may also be in town during a performance of the Nova Filarmonica, a national orchestra that gives concerts around the country throughout the year. The Orquestra Metropolitana de Lisboa performs a regular program at various city venues.

Concert Halls & Theaters

The **Centro Cultural de Belém** (✉ Praça do Império, Belém ☎ 21/361–2400 ⊕ www.ccb.pt) puts on a full range of reasonably priced concerts and exhibitions, featuring national and international artists and musicians. The circular concert hall **Coliseu dos Recreios** (✉ Rua Portas de Santo Antão 96, Rossío ☎ 21/324–0580 ⊕ www.coliseulisboa.com) is a Lisbon cultural landmark. It hosts international performers and musicals as well as some of the best Portuguese stars.

There's a major concert and exhibition program mounted at **Culturgest** (✉ Caixa Geral de Depósitos, Rua Arco do Cego 1, Campo Pequeno ☎ 21/790–5155 ⊕ www.culturgest.pt), an auditorium and exhibition center sponsored by a Portuguese bank.

The main venue for rock concerts is the **Estádio de Alvalade** (✉ Rua Francisco Stromp, Alvalade ☎ 21/751–4000), a large stadium covered in a concoction of yellow, green, and white tiles. It was totally redesigned by postmodernist architect Tomás Taveira for the Euro 2004 soccer championship. The prime mover behind Lisbon's artistic and cultural scenes is the **Fundação Calouste Gulbenkian** (✉ Av. de Berna 45, São Sebastião ☎ 21/793–5131 ⊕ www.gulbenkian.pt), which not only presents exhibitions and concerts in its buildings but also sponsors events throughout the city.

The **Pavilhão Atlântico** (✉ Parque das Nações ☎ 21/891–9333 ⊕ www.pavilhaoatlantico.pt), the country's biggest indoor arena, hosts large-scale classical concerts, pop and rock bands, dance performances, and sporting events. Plays are performed in Portuguese at the **Teatro Nacional de Dona Maria II** (✉ Praça Dom Pedro IV, Baixa ☎ 21/325–0827 ⊕ www.teatro-dmaria.pt), Lisbon's principal theater. Performances are given August–June, and there's the occasional foreign-language production, too.

The **Teatro Nacional de São Carlos** (✉ Rua Serpa Pinto 9, Baixa ☎ 21/325–3000 ⊕ www.saocarlos.pt) hosts an opera season December–June.

Film

All films shown in Lisbon appear in their original language accompanied by Portuguese subtitles, and you can usually find the latest Hollywood releases playing around town. Ticket prices are around €3.50–€5 and are even cheaper on Monday; it's best to get to the movie theater early on any day to be assured a seat. There are dozens of movie houses throughout the city, including a couple on Avenida da Liberdade. Some theaters are in preserved art deco buildings and are attractions in their own right.

A modern cinema complex in the **Amoreiras** (✉ Av. Eng. Duarte Pacheco, Amoreiras ☎ 21/383–1275) shopping complex has 10 screens. There's a multiscreen cinema at the **Colombo** (✉ Av. Col. Militar, Benfica ☎ 21/711–3200) mall. Portugal's national film theater, the **Instituto da Cinemateca Portuguesa** (✉ Rua Barata Salgueiro 39, Marquês de Pombal ☎ 21/354–6279), has screenings Monday through Saturday at 6:30 and 9:30. This is the place to catch contemporary Portuguese films and art-house reruns. The **UCI Cinemas–El Corte Inglés** (✉ Av. António Augusto de Aguiar 31, São Sebastião ☎ 70723–2221) has the latest in modern screen technology.

Galleries

The Centro Cultural de Belém has an ever-changing program of art exhibitions, and Lisbon's major art museums and commercial buildings often put on temporary exhibitions alongside their permanent collections. In addition, the city's gallery count has passed 100 and is growing. If you're staying at the Meridien Park Atlantic, Altis, or Hotel Dom Pedro Lisboa, you needn't even step outside to peruse their galleries. Most galleries are closed Sunday and daily 1–3, and will insure and ship whatever you buy.

The **Galeria de Arte Cervejaria Trindade** (✉ Rua Nova da Trindade 20, Bairro Alto ☎ 21/342–3506), at the back of the famous beer-hall restaurant, is open only for exhibitions, though the splendid tiled walls of the cervejaria are a show in their own right. At the Centro Cultural de Belém, **Galeria Arte Periférica** (✉ Centro Cultural de Belém lj. 1, 5–6, Belém ☎ 21/361–7100 ⊕ www.arteperiferica.pt) is a good source of contemporary art, particularly by younger artists. **Galeria Barata** (✉ Av. de Roma 11A, Campo Grande ☎ 21/842–8352) is a modern art gallery that doubles as a bookshop—or vice versa.

If you're looking for contemporary Portuguese art that has yet to catch the eye of critics or collectors, try **Galeria Novo Século** (✉ Rua do Século 23A, Bairro Alto ☎ 21/342–7712). You might spot works of London-based Paula Rego at **Galeria 111** (✉ Campo Grande 113-A, Alvalade ☎ 21/797–7418 ⊕ www.galeria111.pt), arguably Portugal's best-known gallery. In Lisbon's historic cathedral area, **Loja da Calçada** (✉ Calçada de S. Vicente 96, Alfama ☎ 21/886–2780) is a small shop that concentrates on individual discoveries.

Movimento Arte Contemporânea (✉ Rua do Sol ao Rato 9, Rato ☎ 21/385–0789 ✉ Av. Álvares Cabral 58, Rato ☎ 21/386–7215) was founded in

1993 by Dr. Alvaro Lobato Faria, a Portuguese professor of mathematics. His goal was to aid in the cultural exchange between Portuguese artists and artists in Portuguese-speaking countries such as Brazil. Contemporary paintings, sculptures, ceramics, tapestries, jewelry, and coins are on display, 90% of which are by Portuguese contemporary artists and the other 10% of which are by contemporary Portuguese-speaking artists.

OUTDOOR ACTIVITIES

Boating
Clube Naval (⊠ Cais do Gás, Letra H, Cais do Sodré ☎ 21/346–9354), where you can arrange to sail and canoe, is directly on the river. The office is open weekdays 10–1 and 3–7.

Bowling
Bowling Internacional de Lisboa (⊠ Alameda dos Oceanos, near Oriente Station, Parque das Nações ☎ 21/892–2521) is worth the ride north. It's large, noisy, and popular, with 30 lanes in high demand on weekends.

Bullfighting
Bullfights are held on Thursday (and some Sundays) between Easter and October in the ornate Praça de Touros (bullring) at **Campo Pequeno.** Some people defend the Portuguese bullfight as entertainment because the bull isn't killed in the ring but rather is wrestled to the ground by a group of *forçados* (a team of eight men who fight the bull) dressed in traditional red-and-green costumes. Nonetheless, any bull injured during the contest is later killed. The first-class riding skills displayed by the *cavaleiro* (horseback fighter) during the event are undeniable. After the cavaleiro performs, the forçados goad the bull into charging them, and one man throws himself across the horns (which have been padded) while the other men pull the bull down by grabbing hold of whatever they can, including the beast's tail. Performances start at 10 PM and seats cost €20–€45. ⊠ *Praça de Touros do Campo Pequeno, Av. da República, Campo Pequeno* ☎ 21/793–2093 Ⓜ *Campo Pequeno.*

Golf
There are at least nine top-quality golf courses in Lisbon's environs, most of which are concentrated along the Estoril Coast. If you're planning to play golf and don't mind missing out on city-style dining, fado, or nightlife, consider staying at one of the hotels outside Lisbon with golf packages.

See Chapter 9, *Golf in Portugal: Where to Play* for a complete list of golf courses in the area.

The 18-hole, par 69 golf course at **Lisboa Sport Clube** (⊠ Casal da Carregueira, Belas ☎ 21/431–0077 ⊕ www.lisbonclub.com) is about 20 minutes by car from the city at Queluz. Greens fees are €45 weekdays and €60–weekends.

Soccer
Soccer is by far Portugal's most popular sport. Portugal hosted the Euro 2004 soccer championships, for which it built new stadiums and remod-

eled others in eight cities. Lisbon has three teams, which play at least weekly during the September–May season. Although you can buy tickets on the day of a game at the stadiums, it's best to get them in advance from the booth in the Praça dos Restauradores. Plan to arrive early, because there's usually a full program of entertainment first, including children's soccer, marching bands, and fireworks. (Note: always be wary of pickpockets in the crowd.)

The most famous of Lisbon's soccer teams is Benfica, which plays in the northwest part of the city at the **Estádio da Luz** (✉ Av. Gen. Norton Matos, Benfica ☎ 21/721–9555 ⊕ www.slbenfica.pt). It holds 65,000 spectators and is Portugal's largest, and also one of Europe's biggest, stadiums. A great rival of the famous Benfica soccer team, the Sporting Clube de Portugal (home club to soccer star Luis Figo) plays at the **Estádio José Alvalade** (✉ Rua Francisco Stromp, Alvalade ☎ 21/758–9021 ⊕ www.sporting.pt), near Campo Grande in the north of the city.

Swimming

The **Altis** (✉ Rua Barata Salgueiro 52, Rato ☎ 21/355–4110 or 21/314–2496) hotel opens its indoor lap pool to nonguests for about €15 an hour. The **Lisboa Sport Clube** (✉ Casal da Carregueira, Belas ☎ 21/431–0077 ⊕ www.lisbonclub.com) in Queluz has a swimming pool as well as a golf course. The central **Piscina do Ateneu** (✉ Rua Portas de Santo Antão 102, Baixa ☎ 21/342–2365) is open to the public at certain hours; call in advance.

The **Solplay** (✉ Rua Manuel da Silva Gaio 2, Linda-a-Velha ☎ 21/006–6000) hotel 10 km (6 mi) from Lisbon in the town of Linda-a-Velha has an excellent outdoor pool for nonguests for €20 per person for the whole day. They furnish towels, and use of the indoor pool, sauna, hot tub, steam bath, and gym is included in the €20. The outdoor pool, open 10 AM–6 PM, closes when the temperature drops low. The indoor pool is open 8 AM–10 PM all year.

Tennis

The two public tennis courts making up **Campos de Tennis do Campo Grande** (✉ Jardim do Campo Grande, Campo Grande) are amid gardens. The **Centro de Tennis de Monsanto** (✉ Parque Florestal de Monsanto, Estrada do Alvita, Monsanto ☎ 21/363–8073) is in Lisbon's large, lovely public park. The **Lisbon Racquet Center** (✉ Rua Alferes Malheiro, Alvalade) has nine courts.

SHOPPING

Small, independently owned stores are still quite common in Lisbon, and salespeople are courteous almost everywhere. Handmade goods, such as leather handbags, shoes, gloves, embroidery, ceramics, and basketwork, are sold throughout the city. Apart from top designer fashions and high-end antiques, prices are moderate. Most shops are open weekdays 9–1 and 3–7 and Saturday 9–1; malls and supermarkets often remain open until at least 10. Some are also open on Sunday. Credit cards—Visa in particular—are widely accepted.

Although fire destroyed much of Chiado, Lisbon's smartest shopping district, in 1988, a good portion of the area has been restored. The neighborhood has a large new shopping complex as well as many small stores with considerable cachet, particularly on and around Rua Garrett. The Baixa's grid of streets from the Rossío to the Rio Tejo have many small shops selling jewelry, shoes, clothing, and foodstuffs. The Bairro Alto is full of little crafts shops with stylish, contemporary ceramics, wooden sculpture, linen, and clothing. Excellent stores continue to open in the residential districts north of the city, at Praça de Londres and Avenida de Roma.

Department Store

Lisbon's largest department store, **El Corte Inglés** (⊠ Av. António Augusto de Aguiar 31 ☎ 21/371–1700 ⊕ www.elcortesingles.pt), a part of the major Spanish chain of the same name, was opened in November 2001 and sells fashion, leisure goods, household articles, and food. Its high-quality supermarket is a favorite among Lisboetas. Also, El Corte Inglés offers excellent service—hotel deliveries, interpreter services, 100% refunds on exchanged goods, and V.A.T. (Value-Added Tax) refunds for customers from non-EU countries.

Malls

Amoreiras (⊠ Av. Eng. Duarte Pacheco, Amoreiras ⊕ www.almoreiras.com), west of Praça Marquês de Pombal, contains a multitude of shops that sell clothes, shoes, food, crystal, ceramics, and jewelry. It also has a hairdresser, restaurants, and 10 movie screens; it's open daily 9 AM–11 PM.

Colombo (⊠ Av. Col. Militar, Benfica), one of the largest malls on the Iberian peninsula, has 19 department stores, more than 400 stores and restaurants, and a multiscreen cinema. The Col. Militar–Luz metro station has an exit right inside the complex, which is open daily 9 AM–11 PM.

As it rose from the ashes of a fire that destroyed much of the Chiado district in 1988, the **Grandes Armazéns do Chiado** (⊠ Main entrance on Rua do Carmo, Chiado ☎ 21/321–0600 ⊕ www.armazensdochiado. com) has been compared to a phoenix. Behind the restored facade of what was the city's main department store is a stylish complex of shops—designed by acclaimed Portuguese architect Álvaro Siza Vieira—just steps from the Avenida da Liberdade.

A short distance from some of the new hotels in the Liberdade area and in a triangle on the Avenida Fontes Pereira de Melo are three smaller shopping centers that cater to a more selective clientele. **Atrium Saldanha** (⊠ Praça Duque de Saldanha ☎ 21/319–2250) has a very good antiques shop, **Antiguidades no Atrium,** on the second floor. The **Monumental** (⊠ Av. Fontes Pereira de Melo ☎ 21/351–0500, 21/353–1856 cinemas) is famous for its movie theaters and its beer house, **Pasta Caffe,** which features different-flavored beers, pastas, and hamburgers. **Saldanha Residence** (⊠ Av. Fontes Pereira de Melo 42-E ☎ 21/351–0100) has a good selection of shops, including Hugo Boss and Mandarina Duck.

Portuguese suburbanites shop or catch a movie at the **Vasco da Gama** (⊠ Av. D. João II, Parque das Nações) complex, which is open 10 AM to 11 PM Sunday through Friday and 10 to midnight on Saturday. A shopping excursion here (take the metro to the Oriente stop) teams well with a visit to the Oceanário de Lisboa or a few games in the bowling center.

Markets

The best-known flea market is the **Feira da Ladra** (⊠ Campo de Santa Clara, Graça), held on Tuesday (8 AM–1 PM) and all day Saturday. For food, kitchenwares, and household items head to the covered **Mercado do Arroios** (⊠ Praça do Chile, Alto da Pina) at the Arroios metro station. It's open Monday–Saturday 7–2. Alfama locals shop at the **Mercado do Chão do Loureiro** (⊠ Calçada do Marq. do Tancos off Costa do Castelo, Alfama), open Monday–Saturday 8–2.

At the **Mercado da Ribeira** (⊠ Av. 24 de Julho, Cais do Sodré ☎ 21/031–2600 ⊕ www.espacoribeira.pt), opposite the Cais do Sodré station, the vendors are entertainment in themselves. The market is open Monday–Saturday 6–2. Every Sunday the marketplace is taken over by the **Feira de Coleccionismo** (Collectors' Market), open from 9 to 1. On the second Sunday of each month it is open until 6. The **Mercado 31 de Janeiro** (⊠ Rua E. V. da Silva, Saldanha) sells a little of everything, including produce, Monday–Saturday 8–2. It's near the Picoas metro stop and the Sheraton hotel. The **Praça de Espanha** (⊠ São Sebastião) market, near the metro stop of the same name, sells mostly clothes; it's open Monday–Saturday 9–5.

Specialty Stores

Antiques

Most of Lisbon's antiques shops are in the Rato and Bairro Alto districts along one long street, which changes its name four times as it runs southward from Largo do Rato: Rua Escola Politécnica, Rua Dom Pedro V, Rua da Misericórdia, and Rua do Alecrim. Look on the nearby Rua de São Bento for more stores. There's also a cluster of antiques shops on Rua Augusto Rosa, between the Baixa and Alfama districts.

Antiquália (⊠ Praça Luís de Camões 37, Chiado ☎ 21/342–3260) is packed with furniture, chandeliers, and porcelain. The owners of **Felner da Costa** (⊠ Rua do Alecrim 52–54, Chiado ☎ 21/342–6711) will guide you through their collection, which includes furniture, porcelain, and rarities. **J. Andrade Antiguidades** (⊠ Rua da Escola Politécnica 39, Bairro Alto ☎ 21/342–4964) is well known for its unusual objects, paintings, sculptures, and furniture. Near the cathedral, **M. Murteira Antiguidades** (⊠ Rua Augusto Rosa 19–21, Baixa ☎ 21/886–3851) carries antiques from the 17th and 18th centuries, including furniture, paintings, sculptures, and religious art. There's 20th-century artwork as well. One of the best-known antiques shops is **Solar** (⊠ Rua Dom Pedro V 68–70, Bairro Alto ☎ 21/346–552).

Ceramics

The **Atelier** (⊠ Rua dos Bacalhoeiros 12-A, Alfama ☎ 21/886–5563 ⊕ www.loja-descobrimentos.com), is located right next to the Casa dos

What to Wear Home from Lisbon

FASHION IN LISBON IS FLOURISHING, especially in the trendy Bairro Alto district, where Portuguese designers followed the nightlife with their boutiques. The brightly lighted modern shops make a stark contrast to the area's 16th-century layout and dark, narrow streets. Moda Lisboa (⊕ www.modalisboa.pt) is the most important fashion showcase in Portugal and the social event of the season, bringing together Portugal's most prominent designers—Ana Salazar, Fátima Lopes, Maria Gambina, José António Tenente, Luís Buchinho, and Manuel Alves, just to mention a few.

The Portuguese upswing began in the '70s when Ana Salazar shook up a national look that was stuck in the '50s. Intellectuals and artists embraced Salazar's asymmetrical shapes, ripped cloth, and cowl-effect drapings, and the international press hailed Salazar as a pioneer of "Made in Portugal" fashion. Her first shop on Rua do Carmo is still a landmark to fashion, and she has a second shop on Avenida Roma and another in Porto. Minimalist interior decor focuses attention on the clothes, which still use organza, mousseline, crepe, silk, and fishnet to create her trademark asymmetry.

Also hitting the scene in the '70s was Augustus. His unstructured shapes, strong colors, daring cleavages, and backless dresses are well known, and he mixes soft, flowing fabrics, embroidered tulle, natural silks, georgettes, chiffon, lace, and leather. He designed the dress first lady Mária José Rita wore to the royal wedding of Spain's Prince Philip in May 2004. He has a shop in the Amoreiras shopping mall and on Avenida Roma.

Ana Salazar's former apprentice José António Tenente now has his own line. His cocktail dresses have a classic look and an incredible attention to detail: hand embroidery with sequins, glass, and crystal. He also designs jeans, handbags, and eyeglasses.

Young designer Maria Gambina goes for a more carefree, sporty look. She uses prep school–like polos and sports clothes to create a schoolgirl look with a touch of devilish flirtation—bustiers and corsets or hook-and-eye fasteners with tied cords.

A show stealer at the Prêt-à-Porter in Paris, Fátima Lopes is one of Portugal's most internationally acclaimed designers. She has taken her fluid cuts, asymmetries, and unusual trimmings (such as her diamond-studded bikini) abroad and has opened shops in Paris. A Barbie doll has been made in her image with long black, shiny hair, accentuated bangs, and daring outfits.

Manuel Alves and José Manuel Gonçalves, a team praised for their skill in using luxurious materials to create very feminine, sophisticated looks, first opened a boutique at the D. Pedro Hotel in the Amoreiras district for their women's prêt-à-porter collections. They now have a store in the Bairro Alto.

Perhaps the best time to get familiar with these names in fashion are during winter sales in January and February, and summer sales in July and August. Savings can be as much as 50% (and sometimes up to 70%).

Bicos and specializes in hand-painted tiles. You can often see an artist at work here. What's more, they ship worldwide and you can even order online. The **Fábrica Sant'Ana** (⊠ Rua do Alecrim 95, Chiado ☎ 21/342–2537), founded in the 1700s, sells wonderful hand-painted ceramics and tiles based on antique patterns; the pieces sold here may be the finest in the city.

Portugal's most famous porcelain producer, **Vista Alegre** (⊠ Largo do Chiado 18, Chiado ☎ 21/346–1401), established its factory in 1824. A visit to the flagship store is a must even though you can buy perfect reproductions of their original table services and ornaments at dozens of shops. There are also eight other Vista Alegre–owned stores in the city, including at the Parque das Nações, the Colombo mall, and the airport. **Viuva Lamego** (⊠ Largo do Intendente 25, Graça ☎ 21/885–2408 ⊠ Calçada do Sacramento 29, Chiado ☎ 21/346–9692) sells the largest selection of tiles and pottery in Lisbon—and at competitive prices.

Clothing

Although Lisbon isn't on the cutting edge of clothing design, the city is becoming increasingly fashion-aware and according celebrity status to a rising tide of designers. ModaLisboa is an annual fashion event that promotes the creations of such Portuguese designers as Ana Salazar, Maria Gambina, and Miguel Viera. Their creations are sold alongside the more established labels in a variety of stores. Praça de Londres and Avenida de Roma—both in the modern city—form one long run of haute-couture stores and fashion outlets. Designer-clothing stores are also starting to slink into the Bairro Alto.

For women's designer clothes (at designer prices) visit **Ana Salazar** (⊠ Rua do Carmo 87, Chiado ☎ 21/347–2289). Organzas, crepe, silk jerseys, prewash, and fishnet are used to create her asymmetrical shapes in charcoal, khaki, red, and other colors. **Augustus** (⊠ Centro Comercial Roma, Loja 36, Av. de Roma, Alvalade ⊠ Av. Eng. Duarte Pacheco, Amoreiras ☎ 21/795–5224) is one of the city's most famous names in women's fashions. He's known for unstructured shapes, strong colors, daring cleavages, and backless dresses. **David and Monteiro** (⊠ Av. de Roma 9A, Alvalade ☎ 21/840–4296) has top-quality, midrange Portuguese and international fashions, such as Tommy Hilfiger and Lacoste. **Eldorado** (⊠ Rua do Norte 23–25, Bairro Alto ☎ 21/342–3935) sells a mix of new and secondhand clothing.

Fátima Lopes (⊠ Rua da Atalaia 36, Bairro Alto ☎ 21/324–0546), one of Portugal's most international fashion designers, has conquered the limelight with her outrageous, skimpy outfits, including a diamond-studded bikini. **José António Tenente** (⊠ Travessa do Carmo 8, Chiado ☎ 21/342–2560) has some great collections of women's clothing, especially cocktail dresses, featuring classical cuts with a strong graphic presence—hand-embroidered designs, sequins, and crystal applications. If there isn't a little girl in your life, the dresses in saucy prints at **Maison Louvre** (⊠ Rossío 106, Baixa ☎ 21/342–8619) will make you want to adopt one. **Manuel Alves & José Manuel Gonçalves** (⊠ Rua Serpa Pinto 15B, Bairro Alto ⊠ Rua das Flores, 105-1° Dt°, Amoreiras ☎ 21/346–0690) designs long, glamorous gowns with a strong sensual streak.

A new approach to children's fashion, **No Kidding** (✉ Rua do Norte 40–42, Bairro Alto ☎ 21/342–1801) offers a total makeover for kids under one roof: modern hairdos, trendy clothes, and the most sought-after brands of sneakers in the smallest sizes. **Outra Face da Lua** (✉ Rua do Norte 86, Bairro Alto ☎ 21/347–1570) is about as unconventional as Lisbon shopping gets. Is it named "Other Side of the Moon" because it doesn't open until late in the evening or because of its eclectic mix of retro clothes, music, gadgets, tea, and temporary tattoos?

Food & Wine

Several excellent delicatessens in the Baixa sell fine foods, including regional cheeses and wines, especially varieties of port—one of Portugal's major exports. Supermarkets also sell local wines, and so do—oddly enough—shops that purvey dried cod, which you'll see stacked outside on the sidewalk or hanging in the window. Rua do Arsenal has several such stores. Other popular gourmet items are the fresh chocolates, marzipan, dried and crystallized fruits, and pastries that are on sale in pastelarias.

Casa Pereira (✉ Rua Garrett 38, Chiado ☎ 21/342–6694) specializes in exotic coffees, teas, and chocolates. The **Pastelaria Suíça** (✉ Rossío 96, Baixa ☎ 21/321–4090) has a large selection of sweets.

Within the Centro Cultural de Belém, the **Coisas do Arco do Vinho** (✉ Rua Bartolomeu Dias, lojas n° 7–8, Belém ☎ 21/364–2031) has prizewinning wines and the owners, wine connoisseurs, can give you expert advice. The **Instituto do Vinho do Porto** (✉ Rua de São Pedro de Alcântara 45, Bairro Alto ☎ 21/347–5707) has more than 100 varieties to sample and bottles to buy. It also has a well-stocked duty-free store at the airport.

Manuel Tavares (✉ Rua da Betesga 1a, Baixa ☎ 21/342–4209), just off the Rossío, has cheese, chocolate, vintage ports, and wine. At **Napoleão** (✉ Rua dos Fanqueiros 70, Baixa ☎ 21/887–2042) the helpful staff speaks English and can recommend vintages.

Handicrafts

Almoravida (✉ Rua da Senhora da Glória 130, Graça ☎ 21/346–8967) is a showroom for traditional carpets. All things lace, especially the spidery *rendas de bilros* variety made in Portugal's north, is the specialty of **Arameiro** (✉ Praça dos Restauradores 62, Baixa ☎ 21/347–7875). Near the Castelo de São Jorge, you'll find **A Bilha** (✉ Rua do Milagre de Santo António 10, Alfama ☎ 21/888–2261), which sells embroidery, lace, copper, gold, and silver. For embroidered goods and baskets from the Azores, stop by **Casa Regional da Ilha Verde** (✉ Rua Paiva de Andrade 4, Baixa ☎ 21/342–5974). At **Francesinha** (✉ Rua da Barroca 96–98, Bairro Alto ☎ 21/347–4687), hand-painted ceramics sit alongside fabrics, wrought ironwork, and simple jewelry.

Nosso Design (✉ Rua Serpa Pinto 12 ☎ 21/325–8960) is dedicated to contemporary Portuguese design—glass objects, ceramics, furniture,

1

lamps, and jewelry. **Pais Em Lisboa** (⊠ Rua do Teixeira 25, Bairro Alto ☎ 21/342–0911) has wares from all over Portugal. **Pessoa de Carvalho** (⊠ Costa do Castelo 4, Alfama ☎ 21/886–2413) is an old Alfama house and sells candles, glassware, jewelry, and handicrafts. **Au Petit Peintre** (⊠ Rua de S. Nicolau 104, Baixa ☎ 21/342–3767), which has been around since 1909, has paper, art supplies, and small engravings and watercolors. **Tricana** (⊠ Av. Casal Ribeiro 15, Estefânia ☎ 21/315–5002) specializes in Oriental and French carpets and tapestries, including 19th-century Aubussons.

Jewelry

The Baixa is a good place to look for jewelry. What is now called Rua Aurea was once Rua do Ouro (Gold Street), named for the goldsmiths' shops installed on it under Pombal's 18th-century city plan. The trade has flourished here ever since.

For antique silver and jewelry visit **António da Silva** (⊠ Praça Luís de Camões 40, Chiado ☎ 21/342–2728). Renowned for its costume jewelry **Casa Batalha** (⊠ Armazéns do Chiado, Rua do Carmo 2, lj. 4.10a, Chiado ☎ 21/342–7313) has been around since 1635 (the original shop burned down in Lisbon's 1988 fire). If you are looking for original contemporary designer jewelry, visit **Galeria Teresa Seabra (Jóias de Autor)** (⊠ Rua da Rosa 160A, Bairro Alto ☎ 21/342–5383). **Sarmento** (⊠ Rua Aurea 251, Baixa ☎ 21/342–6774), one of the city's oldest goldsmiths, produces characteristic Portuguese gold- and silver-filigree work.

Leather Goods

Although there are shoe shops all over the city, they may have limited selections of large sizes, because the Portuguese tend to have small feet. The better shops, however, can make shoes to order. Gloves are sold or custom made in specialty shops on Rua do Carmo and Rua Aurea.

You'll find fine leather handbags and luggage at **Casa da Sibéria** (⊠ Rua Augusta 254, Baixa ☎ 21/342–5679). **Coelho** (⊠ Rua da Conceição 85, Baixa ☎ 21/342–5567) is excellent for leather belts and can also make leather-back fabric belts from your own material.

A reliable shoe store, with a good range of sizes and brands, is **Sapateria Bandarra** (⊠ Rua de Santa Justa 78, Baixa ☎ 21/342–1178). Visit **Ulisses** (⊠ Rua do Carmo 87, Chiado ☎ 21/342–0295) for leather gloves.

Music

For chart hits and music from just about everywhere in the world, head to the **Fnac** (⊠ Armazéns do Chiado, lj. 4.07, Rua do Carmo 2, Chiado ☎ 21/322–1800) inside the Armazéns do Chiado shopping center. It carries books and computer products, too. If you want to take home some soulful fado music, check out the CDs at **Valentim de Carvalho** (⊠ Rossío 59, Baixa ☎ 21/324–1570). They also offer an excellent selection of African music.

LISBON ESSENTIALS

Transportation

The best way to see central Lisbon is on foot. It's a small city by any standard, and most of the points of interest are within the well-defined older quarters. Just remember that the city is hilly and has cobblestone sidewalks that can make walking tiring (especially in the hot summer), even when you wear comfortable shoes. At some point you'll probably want to use the public-transportation system, if only to experience the old trams and funicular railways and elevators.

If you're staying in Lisbon for more than a few days, buy one of the various transport passes. The "7 Colinas" card for unlimited rides on a tram, bus, funicular, elevator, and metro costs €2.85 for one day's travel and five-day passes are €11.35. You pay an initial €0.50 to buy the card at metro stations, "7 Colinas" kiosks around the city (there is one on Praça Figueira and another at the Santa Justa Elevator), and at various newspaper and tobacco shops. It is rechargeable at any of these places.

All buses, trams, and elevators are operated by Carris, the city's public transportation company; the metro has a different ticketing system. You can buy passes or tickets for buses, trams, and elevators at the Cais do Sodré station, Restauradores metro station, and Carris kiosks throughout the city. If you decide not to use a pass, opt for advance tickets at €0.65 a ride. If you pay cash, the fare is €1.20 a ride.

Another option is the Lisboa Card, a special pass that allows free travel on all public transportation and free entry into 27 museums, monuments, and galleries—including all the major city attractions. You can buy cards that are valid for 24 hours (€13.50), 48 hours (€23), or 72 hours (€28). They're sold at the airport (in well-signed kiosks), at the Mosteiro dos Jerónimos, in the Lisbon Welcome Centre, at the tourist office in the Palácio Foz, and other places around the city.

A note of warning: avoid using public transportation, especially on the metro, during rush hours. Pickpockets ply their trade on crowded trains, buses, and trams. Keep an eye on your possessions, and carry wallets in inside pockets and bags and backpacks with the fastening facing your body. If your hotel lacks a convenient safe, consider stashing some documents and cash in a fashion-defying money belt.
🎬 Carris information line ☎ 21/361-3054 ⊕ www.carris.pt.

BY AIR
International and domestic flights land at Lisbon's small, modern Aeroporto de Lisboa, also known as Aeroporto de Portela, 7 km (4½ mi) north of the city. There's a tourist office here as well as a currency exchange bureau. TAP, the Portuguese national airline, flies to Lisbon from the New York area (Newark Liberty International Airport); it also links Lisbon with other European capitals. Continental has a daily service between Newark and Lisbon. Air France, British Airways, and Alitalia also fly to Lisbon.

Car-rental firms and the tourist-information office at the airport provide free maps of Lisbon and its environs. The trip to the city center takes 20–30 minutes, depending on traffic. There are no trains or subways between the airport and the city, but getting downtown by bus or taxi is simple and inexpensive.

A special bus, Aerobus 91, runs every 20 minutes, 7:45 AM–8:15 PM, from outside the airport into the city center. Tickets, which you buy from the driver, cost €3.10; TAP passengers can get a voucher entitling them to a ride for €2. The bus stops close to all the major hotels at several useful points, including Praça Marquês de Pombal, Avenida da Liberdade, the Rossío, Praça do Comércio, and the Cais do Sodré train station. As you board the bus, the driver will ask your hotel, note it on a sheet of paper, and call you when it's your stop.

City buses 44 and 45 cost only €1.20 one-way and depart every 15–30 minutes 5 AM–1:40 AM from the main road in front of the terminal building. They pass through Praça dos Restauradores en route to the Cais do Sodré train station (from here you can continue by rail to Estoril and Cascais).

Taxis in Lisbon are relatively cheap, and the airport is so close to the city center that many visitors make a beeline for a cab queue outside the terminal. To avoid any hassle over fares you can buy a prepaid voucher (which includes gratuity and luggage charges) from the tourist office booth in the arrivals hall. Expect to pay €13–€18 to most destinations in the city center and around €40 if you're headed for Estoril or Sintra.

🚩 Airport **Aeroporto de Portela** ☎ 21/841-3500 or 21/841-3700 ⊕ www.ana-aeroportos.pt.

🚩 Airline **TAP** ☎ 21/841-5000 or 707/205700.

BY BUS

City buses are operated by the public transportation company Carris and run 6:30 AM to midnight. Each stop is posted with full details of routes. For a spectacular journey across the Ponte 25 de Abril over the Rio Tejo take a bus from Praça de Espanha to Costa da Caparica or Setúbal. You can buy tickets for buses, elevators, and funiculars at Carris kiosks in the Praça de Figueira, at the foot of the Elevador de Santa Justa, in the Santa Apolónia and Cais do Sodré railway stations, and elsewhere around town. If you don't have a ticket, you can pay the operator on board, but it's twice the price and you must pay in cash (have small change on hand if possible). Either pay when boarding or simply insert your ticket in the ticket-punch machine behind the driver and wait for the pinging noise.

For a weekend beach trip, take the 75-PRAIA bus from Campo Grande to the beaches across the river at Caparica. There are stops along the way near hotels in Saldanha, Marques de Pombal, and Amoreiras. It runs on Saturday, Sunday, and holidays.

Lisbon's main bus terminal is the Gare do Oriente, adjacent to Parque das Nações, which also includes a railway and metro station. Most travel agents can sell you a bus ticket in advance; if you buy from the company ticket office at the main terminal, give yourself plenty of time to purchase before you depart. In summer it's wise to reserve a ticket at least a day in advance for destinations in the Algarve. There are four daily departures from Lisbon for the Algarve and Porto; towns closer to the capital have more frequent service. Most international buses and domestic express buses, including those to and from the Algarve, operate from within the Arco do Cego bus terminal, very near Praça Duque de Saldanha. The Saldanha and Picoas metro stations are within just a few minutes' walk.

Terminals at Praça de Espanha and Campo Pequeno—both of which have metro stops with the same name—serve Setúbal-Sesimbra and Portugal's northwest coast, respectively; the terminal at Campo das Cebolas, at the end of Rua dos Bacalhoeiros and east of Praça do Comércio, is for destinations in the Minho and the Algarve; buses to and from Mafra operate from Largo Martim Moniz, northeast of Praça da Figueira.

🚌 **Sete Rios bus terminal** ✉ Praça Humberto Delgado, Sete Rios ☎ 707/223344 service number, 21/354-5439, 21/354-5775. **Carris** ☎ 21/361-3054 ⊕ www.carris.pt.

BY CAR

Lisbon sees some of the most reckless driving in all of Portugal. Add to this the notoriously difficult parking situation in the city center and the cramped older quarters, and there's much to be said for not using a car in the capital. Nonetheless, new underground parking lots have been built, parking meters have been installed, and cars parked illegally can be clamped or towed away. Most parking meters are free on weekends, but in areas with nightlife such as the Chiado and Bairro Alto, parking is free on Sunday only (always check the parking signs for days and hours). Underground parking lots are expensive but safer. There is underground parking in Praça Camões, Chiado, Restauradores, Martin Moniz, Praça do Municipio in front of town hall, Avenida Alexandre Herculano, and Parque Eduardo VII. Most hotels in Lisbon have their own garages, but they usually charge guests to park in them. Most of the country's highways originate in Lisbon, including the fast roads west to Estoril (A5/IC15), south to Setúbal (A2/IP1, via the Ponte 25 de Abril), and north to Porto (A1/IP1). Crossing via the spectacular Ponte Vasco da Gama, north of the city center, is an alternative route to Setúbal and provides easier access for the main highways east to Spain.

CAR RENTAL It's often much cheaper to arrange car rental in conjunction with your airline ticket or by contacting a car company directly before you arrive. But if you've left it until your arrival in Portugal, all the major car-rental companies have offices at the airport and at Santa Apolónia station. In central Lisbon you'll find Avis, Budget, Europcar, and Hertz. Smaller local car-rental companies are also represented in Lisbon; try Autojardim or check with the tourist office for other options.

🚗 **Local Agency Autojardim** ✉ Rua Luciano Cordeiro 6A ☎ 21/354-9182, 21/846-2916 airport branch.

BY FUNICULAR & ELEVADOR

Small funicular-railway systems and an ingenious vertical elevator (both are called *elevador*) link some of the high and low parts of Lisbon. All are operated by Carris, the public transportation company, whose kiosks sell tickets (the fare is double the price if you pay upon boarding with cash rather than with a pre-bought ticket). Of the funicular railways, the most useful are the Elevador da Glória, which runs from Calçada da Glória, just behind Praça dos Restauradores, to Rua de São Pedro de Alcântara in the Bairro Alto, and the Elevador da Bica, which runs from Rua do Loreto down to Rua Boavista, northwest of Cais do Sodré. At this writing, the Elevador de Santa Justa functioned only as a tourist attraction—the walkway at the top leading to the Largo do Carmo in the Bairro Alto was closed for renovations. Departures on all three services are every few minutes from 7 AM to 11 PM.

🚏 **Carris** ☎ 21/361-3054 ⊕ www.carris.pt.

BY TAXI

Taxis are plentiful and relatively cheap. Drivers use meters but can take out-of-towners for a ride, literally, by not taking the most direct route. If you book a cab from a hotel or restaurant, have someone speak to the driver so there are no "misunderstandings" about your destination. The meter starts at €1.95 during the day and €2.30 at night and during weekends. You pay what is on the meter. Supplementary charges are added for luggage (€1.50) and if you phone for a cab (€0.75). The meter generally isn't used for journeys outside Lisbon, so you'll have to agree on a fare.

You may hail cruising vehicles, but it's sometimes difficult to get drivers' attention; there are taxi stands at most main squares. Remember that when the green light is on, it means the cab is already occupied. Tips—10% or so—for reliable drivers are appreciated.

🚕 Taxi Companies **Autocoope** ☎ 21/793-2756. **Rádio Táxis** ☎ 21/811-9000. **Télétaxi** ☎ 21/811-1100.

BY TRAIN

International trains from France and Spain and long-distance domestic trains from Porto and the north arrive at and depart from the Santa Apolónia station, on the riverfront to the east of Lisbon's center. One daily train runs to and from Paris; two daily trains run to and from Madrid; and there are frequent daily trains to and from Porto from 7 AM to midnight. Santa Apolónia station is connected to the metro network and links directly to Avenida da Liberdade. To reach the Rossío, change at Baixa-Chiado. Buses 9, 12, and 46 also run from outside Santa Apolónia to the center of town. Some long-distance and suburban trains stop at the Oriente station at the Parque das Nações, which is also connected to the metro system.

Local trains to Sintra and all destinations in Estremadura use the central Rossío station, an unmistakably neo-Manueline building that stands between Praça dos Restauradores and the Rossío itself. Trains to Sintra run daily every 15 minutes from 6 AM to 2:40 AM; three trains daily run to towns in Estremadura. For information, tickets, and platforms take the escalators through the station building to the top floor.

Trains along the coast to Estoril and Cascais arrive at and depart from the waterfront Cais do Sodré station, a 10-minute walk west of the Praça do Comércio. Departures both ways are regular—every 15–30 minutes,

5:30 AM–2:30 AM. Buses 45 and 58 run between Cais do Sodré and the central Lisbon squares; Cais do Sodré metro station provides easy access, or, if you prefer, there's a taxi stand outside the station.

The new line that heads to the Algarve and points south crosses over the Rio Tejo via the Ponte 25 de Abril; services added included a bar, restaurant, and business services. Both the InterCidade and the Alfa Pendular trains leave from the Oriente station, with a stop at Entrecampos, for Faro, Algarve's capital. The Intercidades leaves Oriente three times a day: 8:21 AM, 1:21 PM, and 7:21 PM, with a stop exactly 10 minutes later at Entrecampos. The fare is €14.50 for second class and €19 for first class. The Alfa Pendular offers a comfort class with telefax, mobile phone, and laptop jack at your seat. It leaves Oriente once a day: 5:21 PM, with a stop at Entrecampos at 5:31 PM. The fare is €19.50 second class and €26 for comfort class. Both trains take around three hours to reach Faro.

The Caminhos de Ferro Portugueses (CP) has general information lines that are really helpful only if you speak Portuguese. Your best bet is to check out the Web site.

🚊 **CP** ☎ 808/208208 ⊕ www.cp.pt. **Rail Europe** ☎ 800/942-4866, 800/274-8724, 0870/584-8848 U.K. credit-card bookings ⊕ www.raileurope.com.

🚊 **Stations Estação Barreiro** ☎ 21/207-3028. **Estação Rossío** ☎ 21/346-5022. **Estação Santa Apolónia** ☎ 21/888-4142.

BY TRAM

Lisbon's elétrico system, operated by the public transportation company Carris, is one of the most amusing and enjoyable ways to get around, especially if you can board one of the clunky old wooden ones (and remember to secure your bag and wallet against pickpockets). The sleek new supertrams are emblazoned with ads. For a taste of the old days, catch Tram 28 for an inexpensive tour of the city from the Alfama; Tram 15 will take you to Belém, passing by or near many of that district's sights; Tram 18 runs right to the Palácio de Ajuda, also in Belém. Stops are indicated by PARAGEM (stop) signs on the sidewalks, and every stop has a route indicator for each tram that passes that way. Buying tickets in advance at Carris kiosks will cost you half as much as paying the fare in cash when you board. The system operates 6:30 AM to midnight; insert your ticket in the ticket-punch machine by the driver.

🚊 **Carris** ☎ 21/361-3054 ⊕ www.carris.pt.

Contacts & Resources

BANKS & EXCHANGING SERVICES

Most major banks have offices in the Baixa, and there are currency-exchange facilities at the airport (open 24 hours) and at Santa Apolónia train station (open daily 8:30–8:30). Large hotels and some travel agencies also offer exchange facilities, but the rates are usually poor. Few savvy travelers use them anyway; ATMs are ubiquitous and have better rates.

EMERGENCIES

If you need medical attention, many doctors speak English. Ask the staff at your hotel or at the embassy to recommend a reliable one. For gen-

1

eral problems or in case of theft, the tourism police have an office open 24 hours. If you need to make a claim against your travel insurance, you must file a report there.

One clinic with English-speaking staff is Clínica Médica Internationale de Lisboa. Also, you can contact the British Hospital. Other hospitals include Hospital São José, Hospital de São Francisco Xavier, and Hospital Santa Maria.

🔝 **Ambulance** ☎ 21/942–1111. **Fire** ☎ 21/342–2222. **General emergencies** ☎ 112. **Police** ☎ 21/765–4242. **Tourism Police** ✉ Av. da Liberdade, in Palácio Foz, Restauradores ☎ 21/342–1623.

HOSPITALS   🔝 **British Hospital** ✉ Rua Saraiva de Carvalho 49, Campo de Ourique ☎ 21/394–3100 ✉ Rua Tomás da Fonseca, Edifício B, Torres de Lisboa ☎ 21/721–3400. **Clínica Médica Internationale de Lisboa** ✉ Av. António Augusto de Aguiar 40, São Sebastião ☎ 21/351–3310. **Hospital Santa Maria** ✉ Av. Prof. Egas Moniz, Alto da Pina ☎ 21/780–5111 ⊕ www.hsm.min-saude.pt. **Hospital de São Francisco Xavier** ✉ Est. Forte A. Duque, Belém ☎ 21/300–0300 ⊕ www.hsfxavier.min-saude.pt. **Hospital São José** ✉ Rua José A. Serrano, Saldanha ☎ 21/886–0710.

PHARMACIES   Hours of operation and listings of druggists that stay open late are posted on most pharmacy doors. Local newspapers also carry a current list of pharmacies that have extended hours.

🔝 **Farmácia Azevedo Filhos** ✉ Rossío 31, Baixa ☎ 21/342–7478. **Farmácia Barral** ✉ Rua Augusta 225, Baixa ☎ 21/342–5372. **Farmácia Durão** ✉ Rua Garrett 92, Chiado ☎ 21/347–6185.

MAIL

The *correio central* (main post office) on Praça do Comércio receives *poste restante* (general delivery) mail and is open Monday–Saturday 8:30–6. You'll need your passport to collect your mail. The post office on the eastern side of Praça dos Restauradores, at Number 58, is open Monday–Saturday 8 AM–10 PM and Sunday 9–6.

MEDIA

Many bookstores downtown carry at least a few English-language novels and guidebooks. Livraria Bertrand has a broader selection than most. The English-language selection at Livraria Buchholz far exceeds most vacation needs. CDs are downstairs, books upstairs, and classical music plays throughout. Livraria Britânica, across from the British Council, specializes in English-language books. For American and European newspapers, go to one of the several small newsstands at the bottom of Praça dos Restauradores or on the Rossío. The Fnac is a combination store of computer wares, music, and books. Its English-language section carries a good selection of best sellers.

🔝 **Fnac** ✉ Armazéns do Chiado, lj. 4.07, Rua do Carmo 2 ☎ 21/322–1800. **Livraria Barata** ✉ Rua da Roma 11A, Campo Pequeno ☎ 21/842–8350. **Livraria Bertrand** ✉ Rua Garrett 73, Chiado ☎ 21/346–8646. **Livraria Britânica** ✉ Rua Luís Fernandes 14, Bairro Alto ☎ 21/030–5587. **Livraria Buchholz** ✉ Rua Duque de Palmela 4, Amoreiras ☎ 21/317–0580.

TOUR OPTIONS

Beware of unauthorized guides who approach you outside popular monuments and attractions: they're usually more concerned with "guiding" you to a particular shop or restaurant.

BUS TOURS Many companies organize half-day tours of Lisbon and its environs and full-day trips to more distant places of interest. Reservations can be made through any travel agency or hotel; some tours will pick you up at your door. A half-day tour of Lisbon will cost about €27. A full-day trip north to Obidos, Nazaré, and Fátima will run about €75 (including lunch), as will a full day east on the "Roman Route" to Évora and Monsaraz.
🛈 Operators **Cityrama** ⊠ Av. Praia da Vitória 12-B, Saldanha ☎ 21/319-1085.

PRIVATE GUIDES For names of personal guides, contact Lisbon's main tourist office or the Syndicate of Guide Interpreters. It can provide an English-speaking guide for half-day (around €55) or full-day (around €95) tours; the price remains the same for up to 20 people. Office hours are weekdays 9–1 and 2–5:30.
🛈 **Syndicate of Guide Interpreters** ⊠ Rua do Telhal 4, Campo de Santana ☎ 21/346-7170.

WALKING TOURS City Hall organizes guided tours with various themes: Moorish Lisbon, Roman Lisbon, Lisbon from the Seven Hills, Silk Route, Bohemian Lisbon, and Luís de Camões's Lisbon. Tours leave City Hall at 10 AM each morning year-round. Call the City Hall's Cultural Department to reserve a spot on one of these free tours.
🛈 **City Hall** ⊠ Paços do Municipio, Baixa ☎ 21/322-7000.

VISITOR INFORMATION

The Lisbon branch of Portugal's tourist office—Investimentos, Comércio e Turismo de Portugal (ICEP)—is open daily 9–8. It's in the Palácio Foz, at the Baixa end of Avenida da Liberdade. There's also a branch at the airport that's open daily 6 AM to midnight. A much more rewarding place to get information is the Lisbon Welcome Centre, though you may have to wait patiently in a long line. The good news is that the information desk, which is open daily 9–8, is in a small complex with a café, a restaurant, a gallery, and a few shops. For general inquiries, you can try the Linha Verde Turista toll-free number.

For information on all the facilities and events at the Parque das Nações, stop at the information desk on Alameda dos Oceanos, in front of the Vasco da Gama center. The desk is open daily 9:30 to 8.
🛈 Tourist Information **ICEP** ⊠ Palácio Foz, Praça dos Restauradores, Baixa ☎ 21/346-3314, 21/845-0660 airport branch. **Lisbon Welcome Centre** ⊠ Praça do Comércio, Baixa ☎ 21/031-2810. **Parque das Nações Information** ⊠ Alameda dos Oceanos, Parque das Nações ☎ 21/891-9333 ⊕ www.parquedasnacoes.pt.

Lisbon's Environs

Updated by
Norman
Renouf

SUCH FAMOUS DESTINATIONS AS the Estoril Coast, Sintra, the palace at Queluz, the wonderful windswept beaches at Guincho—and even the city of Setúbal and its Manueline church—are all within an hour of Lisbon. Most are easily accessible by public transport, using the capital as your base. Within a 50-km (31-mi) stretch north and south of the Rio Tejo (Tagus River) you'll find a succession of attractive coastal resorts and important towns—each endowed with unique traditions and characteristics.

To the west and northwest of Lisbon is the most southerly part of the province of Estremadura. Estremadura was the first land Christians took back from the Moors in the 12th-century Reconquest, which had originated farther north in the region of the Rio Douro: *Estremadura* means "farthest from the Douro River," an indication of the early extent of the Christian advance against the Moors. Although the area encompasses glistening coastline, broad river estuaries, wooded valleys, and green mountains, its proximity to Lisbon means that its beaches, restaurants, and hotels are filled with people escaping from the city, and coastal roads are often congested.

Lisbon and its environs have served each other through history. Even the country's earliest rulers appreciated the importance of one to the other. It was the Moors who first built a castle northwest of the capital at Sintra as a defense against Christian forces, which, under Dom Afonso Henriques, moved steadily southward after the victory at Ourique in 1139. The castle at Sintra fell to the Christians in 1147, a few days after they defeated the Moors in Lisbon.

Once the Christian Reconquest had been consolidated in Estremadura, there was a less pressing need for defensive measures. The early Christian kings instead adopted the lush hills and valleys of Sintra as a summer retreat and designed estates that survive today. Similarly, Lisbon's 18th- and 19th-century nobility developed small resorts along the Estoril Coast; the amenities and ocean views are still greatly sought after (although the ocean itself isn't as clean as it could be). For swimming, modern Lisboetas look a little farther afield—south across the Rio Tejo to the beaches and resorts of the Costa da Caparica and the southern Setúbal Peninsula. Whichever direction you travel and whatever your interests, you'll be delighted with all that's within a day trip of Lisbon.

Exploring Lisbon's Environs

To the west of Lisbon, the Estoril Coast consists of a series of small beaches and rocky coves and is at its most delightful around the towns of Estoril and Cascais. Farther north, the Atlantic makes itself felt in the windswept beaches and capes beyond Guincho and up to the lighthouse at the Cabo da Roca—the westernmost point in Europe. Just a few miles inland, the Sintra hills are crisscrossed by minor roads and marked by old monastic buildings, estates, gardens, and market villages.

To the south, across the Rio Tejo, the contrast couldn't be more pronounced. The beaches of the Costa da Caparica combine to form a 20-

GREAT ITINERARIES

Numbers in the text correspond to numbers in the margin and on the Estoril Coast, Sintra & Queluz map and the Setúbal Peninsula map.

IF YOU HAVE 2 DAYS

Start in Lisbon and drive to **Estoril ❶**, where you can soak up the atmosphere in the gardens and on the seafront promenade. From here, it's only a short distance to ▦ **Cascais ❷**—the perfect place for an alfresco lunch. Afterward, explore the little cove beaches, and the **Boca do Inferno ❸**. The next day, it's less than an hour's ride north to **Sintra ❺**, where before lunch you'll have time to see its palace and climb to the **Castelo dos Mouros ❼**. After lunch, return to Lisbon, stopping in **Queluz ❷** to see the Palácio Nacional. For dinner, you might cross the Rio Tejo from Lisbon to **Cacilhas ❸** for seafood.

IF YOU HAVE 4 DAYS

From Lisbon, head for **Queluz ❷** and its Palácio Nacional. In the afternoon, make the short drive to ▦ **Sintra ❺**, where you can spend the rest of the day seeing the sights in and around the town. Consider having dinner in the adjacent village of **São Pedro de Sintra ❻**. Head out early the next day to the extraordinary **Palácio Nacional de Pena ❽**. To contrast this haughty palace with a more humble sight, travel west to the **Convento dos Capuchos ❿** before continuing to the headland of **Cabo da Roca ⓫**. Wind south to the wonderful beach at **Guincho ❹** to catch the late afternoon sun and have a bite to eat. Stick to the coastal road as it heads east toward ▦ **Cascais ❷**, where you can spend the night.

On the third day, drive back into Lisbon through **Estoril ❶**. Cross the Rio Tejo via the mighty Ponte 25 de Abril, and detour for lunch at either **Cacilhas ❸** or **Costa da Caparica ❿**. It's then only an hour's drive to the region's two attractive pousadas, one at ▦ **Palmela ⓯**, the other 10 km (6 mi) down the road in ▦ **Setúbal ⓰**. On the fourth morning drive through the **Serra da Arrábida ⓳**, stopping for lunch at an esplanade restaurant in **Sesimbra ⓴**. From here, you can return to Lisbon in around 90 minutes.

IF YOU HAVE 7 DAYS

Seven days exploring this region will allow the luxury of two nights in ▦ **Sintra ❺**, providing time to see all the surrounding sights with ease. On the third day, drive straight to **Cabo da Roca ⓫** and then south to **Guincho ❹**, if you fancy a half day at the beach, before following the coast around to ▦ **Cascais ❷**. Two nights spent here will allow you to really get to know the town and travel to and from **Estoril ❶**.

From Cascais, return to Lisbon and aim for lunch at either **Cacilhas ❸** or **Costa da Caparica ⓮**. Spend the night at the pousada in ▦ **Palmela ⓯** or the one in ▦ **Setúbal ⓰**. On the final day, plan to have lunch in **Vila Nogueira de Azeitão ⓲** and continue on a drive through the **Serra da Arrábida ⓳**. If you spend the night in the fishing port and resort town of ▦ **Sesimbra ⓴**, you'll have time to visit the windswept **Cabo Espichel ㉑** before driving back to Lisbon.

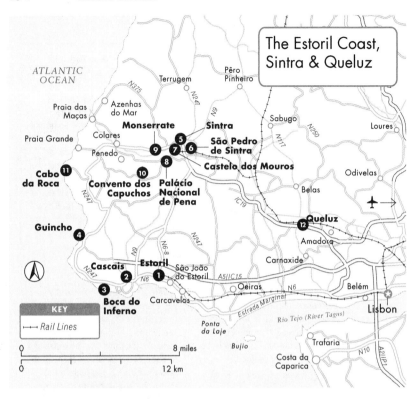

km (12-mi) sweep of sand, backed for the most part by the flat, wine-producing country of the Setúbal Peninsula. The landscape changes only in the south, where the peaks of the Serra da Arrábida rise above a rugged shore that shelters fishing villages and resorts. The only city of any size in the region, Setúbal, is just to the east of here, an obvious stop en route to Évora or the Algarve.

With a car you can cover the main sights north and south of the Rio Tejo in two days, although this gives you little time to linger. A week's touring wouldn't be too long to spend, particularly if you plan to soak up the sun at a resort or take an in-depth look at Sintra, whose beautiful surroundings alone can fill two or three days of exploring.

All the main towns and most of the sights are accessible by train or bus from Lisbon, so you can see the entire region on day trips from the capital. This is a particularly good way to explore the resorts on the Estoril Coast and the beaches of the Costa da Caparica, south across the Rio Tejo. The palace at Queluz also makes a good day trip: it's only 20 minutes northwest of Lisbon by train. Using the capital as your base, a realistic time frame for visiting the major sights is four days: one each for the Estoril Coast, Queluz and Sintra, Caparica, and Setúbal.

Restaurants & Cuisine

Restaurants on the coast stick to seafood and fish, whereas those farther inland may specialize more in grilled meats and codfish. Inexpensive restaurants don't generally take reservations, but it's advisable to reserve for the expensive ones. Dress for meals is usually casual, but people do dress up for dining at the Casino de Estoril or more expensive restaurants, namely those in luxury hotels.

City dwellers make a point of crossing the Rio Tejo to the suburb of Cacilhas for platefuls of *arroz de marisco* (rice with shellfish) or *linguado* (sole). One of Caparica's summer delights is the smell of grilled sardines wafting from restaurants and beachside stalls. Seafood is also the specialty along the Estoril Coast—even the inland villages here and on the Setúbal Peninsula are close enough to the sea to be assured a steady supply of fish.

In Sintra *queijadas* (sweet cheese tarts) are a specialty, and in the Azeitão region of the Setúbal Peninsula, locals swear by the *queijo fresco,* a delicious white cheese made either of goat's or sheep's milk. Lisbon's environs also produce good wines. From Colares comes a light, smooth red, a fine accompaniment to a hearty lunch; Palmela, the demarcated wine-growing district of Setúbal, produces distinctive amber-color wines of recognized quality; and the Fonseca winery produces a splendid dessert wine called Moscatel de Setúbal.

WHAT IT COSTS In Euros				
	$$$$	$$$	$$	$	¢
RESTAURANTS	over €21	€16–€21	€11–€15	€7–€10	under €7
HOTELS	over €275	€176–€275	€101–€175	€60–€100	under €60

Restaurant prices are per person for a main course at dinner. Hotel prices are for a standard double room, including tax, in high season (off-season rates may be lower).

About the Hotels

Outside Lisbon, you can stay in *pousadas,* inns that are members of the Turismo de Habitação organization. These are often in converted historic buildings, and they generally have superior facilities and restaurants. The three in this region are at Queluz, Setúbal, and Palmela. Since they typically have few rooms, availability is limited. Regardless of where you stay, in summer it's essential that you book in advance. Out of season, many places discount their prices substantially.

When to Go

If you're planning to visit in summer, particularly July and August, you *must* reserve a hotel room in advance. If you can, travel to the coastal areas in spring or early fall: the crowds are much thinner, and it could be warm enough for a brisk swim in April and October.

FESTIVALS   That said, most of the region's festivals are held in summer. In São Pedro de Sintra, the Festa de São Pedro (St. Peter's Day) celebration is on June 29; there are summer music and arts festivals in Sintra, Cascais, and Queluz; September in Palmela sees the Festa das Vindimas (Grape Harvest Festival); and the Feira de Santiago (St. James Fair) takes place in Setúbal at the end of July. Year-round markets include those in São Pedro de Sintra (second and fourth Sundays of every month) and Vila Nogueira de Azeitão (first Sunday of every month).

THE ESTORIL COAST

The Estoril Coast extends for 32 km (20 mi) west of Lisbon, taking in the major towns of Estoril and Cascais as well as smaller settlements that are part suburb, part beach town. It's a favored residential area, thanks to its proximity to (and milder winters than) the capital as well as its coastal charms. Some fancifully refer to the region as the Portuguese Riviera, and certainly the casino at Estoril and the luxurious seaside villas and hotels lend the area cachet.

In summer, count on crowds. And, not only are the towns and beaches crowded, but the ocean—sparkling from a distance—suffers from a long-standing pollution problem. The quality of the water varies greatly from beach to beach, and although ongoing work is slowly rectifying the situation, you should avoid swimming in an area unless the water has been declared safe. Look for a blue Council of Europe flag, which signals clean water and beach; consult local tourist offices if you're unsure.

Unless you intend to tour the wider region, it's better to travel by train from Lisbon rather than drive. This section has been arranged accordingly, with coverage of Estoril first, followed by Cascais, which marks the end of the train line; from here, it's a short walk to the Boca do Inferno and a brief bus ride to the magnificent beach at Guincho. If you drive, leave Lisbon via the Estrada Marginal (follow signs for Cascais and Estoril) and take the scenic coastal route (the N6), or the faster Auto-Estrada da Oeste (A5/IC15).

Estoril

❶ *26 km (16 mi) west of Lisbon; the train runs directly to Estoril, or get off at the previous station, São João do Estoril, and walk 2 km (1 mi) along the seafront promenade path, a fine route with excellent views.*

In the 19th century, Estoril was preferred by the European aristocracy, who wintered here in the comfort and seclusion of mansions and gardens. Although the town has elegant hotels, restaurants, and sports facilities, reminders of its genteel history are now few. It presents its best face right in the center, where today's jet set descends on the casino, at the top of the formal gardens of the Parque do Estoril.

Across the busy main road, on the beachfront Tamariz esplanade, are alfresco restaurants and an open-air seawater swimming pool. The best and longest local beach is at Monte Estoril, which adjoins Estoril's beach; here you'll find restrooms and beach chairs for rent, as well as plenty of shops and snack bars.

Estoril is also very much a sporting place, with major sailing events, windsurfing, tennis, horse shows, and motoring events at the old Formula 1 racetrack.

The **Museu Exilio,** inaugurated in 1942, above the post office, has a collection of memorabilia relating to Portugal's mid-20th-century history. It consists mostly of black-and-white photos with captions in Portuguese, focusing on Estoril's community of aristocratic exiles who fled here from northern Europe during World War II. There's also an exhibit devoted to the Nazi persecution of the Jews. ⊠ *Av. Aida* ☎ *21/ 482–5022* 🖼 *Free* ☉ *Weekdays 10–6.*

In addition to gambling salons, the **Estoril Casino**—one of the largest casinos in Europe—has a nightclub, bars, and restaurants. Tour groups often make an evening of it here, with dinner and a floor show, but it's a pricey night out. Most visitors, however, are content to feed one of the 1,200 slot machines in the main complex and then check out the other entertainment options: art exhibits, movies, nightly cabaret performances, and concerts and ballets (in summer). To enter the gaming rooms you must pay €4 (slots are free) and show your passport to prove that you're at least 21. Reservations are essential for the restaurant and floor show. For €37.50 you can see the show and have one drink on the house; €50 buys you entrance to the show and dinner. ⊠ *Parque do Estoril* ☎ *21/466–7700* ⊕ *www.casino-estoril.pt* ☉ *Daily 3 PM–3 AM; floor show nightly at 11.*

Where to Stay & Eat

$$–$$$$ ✕ **A Choupana.** Just east of town, this restaurant has views of Cascais Bay from its picture windows. It's a reliable establishment, where you can ask the English-speaking staff about the daily specials. Fresh seafood is the mainstay—try the *cataplana,* a tangy, typically Portuguese dish of clams and pork. Live music usually accompanies dinner, and in summer there's dancing nightly until 2. ⊠ *Estrada Marginal* ☎ *21/468–3099* ▭ *AE, DC, MC, V.*

$$–$$$$ ✕ **Cimas.** You're in for a good meal in these baronial surroundings of burnished wood, heavy drapes, and oak beams that have played host to royalty, high-ranking politicians, and other celebrities. The menu is an international hybrid: choose from game in season, fresh fish, chicken curry, even Indonesian *saté* (skewered, charcoal-broiled meats served with a peanut sauce). ⊠ *Av. Sabóia off Estrada Marginal* ☎ *21/468–0413* ▭ *AE, DC, MC, V* ☉ *Closed Sun. and 2nd and 3rd wks of Aug.*

$–$$$ ✕ **La Villa.** Whatever you do, book a table by a window at this seaside restaurant. Although the building is a Victorian landmark, it houses an elegant modern restaurant with the area's most interesting seafood dishes. Appetizers include fresh cod with cilantro marinated in gazpacho and soft-shell crab filled with broccoli purée. For an entrée you might try monkfish braised with pepper mustard over a baby onion and green pepper confit. Or go international with oysters, sushi, and sashimi. ⊠ *Praia do Tamariz* ☎ *21/468–0033* ▭ *AE, DC, MC, V* ☉ *Closed Mon.*

★ **$$$–$$$$** ✕🏨 **Palácio Estoril Hotel & Golf.** Exiled European courts waited out World War II in this luxurious 1930s hotel. Several of the well-appointed, Regency-style guest rooms have balconies, and public areas are adorned with monumental columns and chandeliers. A comfortable bar has views over the outdoor pool to the town's central park. There's no more-elegant spot in town to dine than the Four Seasons Grill

($$$–$$$$; reservations and a smart outfit are essential). Golfers who stay here can tee up at the Clube de Golfe do Estoril at reduced rates. ⊠ *Rua do Parque, Parque do Estoril, 2769-504* ☎ *21/468–0000* 🖷 *21/468–4867* ⊕ *www.palacioestorilhotel.com* 🛏 *129 rooms, 32 suites* 🛆 *2 restaurants, room service, in-room safes, minibars, cable TV, in-room data ports, golf privileges, 4 tennis courts, pool, gym, massage, sauna, horseback riding, squash, 3 bars, babysitting, Internet, business services, convention center, meeting rooms* 🖃 *AE, DC, MC, V* ⓘ *BP.*

$$–$$$ 🏨 **Inglaterra.** Displaying the splendor of an early-20th-century Portuguese colonial mansion, the hilltop Hotel Inglaterra—completely renovated in 2004—offers classy ambience. Although the interior decor is contemporary, the minimalist black wooden furniture, combined with exotic wooden cupboards and China-red embellishments, lends an Asian flavor. Most guest rooms have king-size beds, and the bathrooms covered in white azulejos match the rooms in their spaciousness. Some of the rooms have a private balcony overlooking either the Cascais Bay or the Sintra hills. If it weren't for the contemporary bathing suits by the pool, you could imagine you were in the Hollywood of the 1920s. ⊠ *Rua do Porto 1, 2765-271* ☎ *21/468–4461* 🖷 *21/468–2108* ⊕ *www.hotelinglaterra.com* 🛏 *55 rooms* 🛆 *Restaurant, in-room safes, minibars, cable TV, pool, 2 bars, babysitting, laundry service, Internet* 🖃 *AE, DC, MC, V* ⓘ *BP, FAP, MAP.*

� **$$** 🏨 **Estoril Eden Apartamentos Suites Hotel.** Looking for a good base with the kids? The comfortable studios and suites in this modern apartment hotel are reasonably sized and equipped with cable TV, fold-out beds, and a basic kitchenette. Ask for one of the front rooms, which have coastal views. Children might enjoy the free summer-entertainment program and the good sports facilities; parents can keep an eye on things from the poolside café. The ocean is just a few minutes' walk away via an underpass that starts behind the Monte Estoril train station. ⊠ *Av. Sabóia, 2769-502* ☎ *21/466–7600 or 800/604–4274* 🖷 *21/466–7601* ⊕ *www.hotelestorileden.pt* 🛏 *162 units* 🛆 *Restaurant, café, kitchenettes, cable TV, golf privileges, 2 pools (1 indoor), health club, massage, sauna, bar, nightclub, babysitting, children's programs (ages 6–12), convention center, meeting rooms* 🖃 *AE, DC, MC, V* ⓘ *EP.*

� **$$** 🏨 **Praia Mar.** Although it's in distant Carcavelos, a little to the east of Estoril, this charming hotel deserves serious consideration. The rooms, many overlooking the sea, are modern and contemporary but, contrastingly, the Rosa dos Ventos rooftop restaurant has a distinctly traditional ambience. The famous Buçaco wines are served here, and are also available to take home. ⊠ *Rua do Gurué, 2775-581* ☎ *21/458–5100* 🖷 *21/457–3130* ⊕ *www.almeidahotels.com* 🛏 *148 rooms, 6 suites* 🛆 *Restaurant, café, cable TV, pool, bar* 🖃 *AE, DC, MC, V* ⓘ *EP.*

$ 🏨 **Albergaria Valbom.** This bare-bones hotel is in the center of town near the main street with its pubs and shops. Rooms have outdated '70s-style furniture and different-colored bedspreads and curtains—striped or floral. ⊠ *Av. Valbom 14, 2750-508* ☎ *21/486–5801* 🖷 *21/486–5805* 🛏 *40 rooms* 🛆 *Bar* 🖃 *AE, DC, MC, V* ⓘ *BP.*

$ 🏨 **Hotel Lido.** On a quiet street overlooking the green hillside above Estoril, the Lido is a modest hotel whose amenities compensate for its lack of real style. The simple rooms all look the same—strong colors, clean lines, identical furniture—but they have balconies with fine views and there's a pool, a garden, and a lounge bar. Off-season discounts are substantial. The hotel is signposted for drivers from the casino; otherwise, it's a steep 15-minute walk from the center of Estoril. ⊠ *Rua do Alentejo 12, 2765-188* ☎ *21/468–4098* 🖷 *21/468–3665* 🌐 *www.hotellido. pt* ⌦ *56 rooms, 6 suites* ⚭ *Restaurant, cable TV, pool, billiards, bar, babysitting, meeting room* ⊟ *AE, DC, MC, V* ⦿ *BP.*

Nightlife

At night, the casino is a big draw, and most other barhopping takes place within the hotels. Most places are open 10 PM–3 AM. **Bauhaus** (⊠ Estrada Marginal ☎21/468–0965), next to the Estoril Eden hotel, attracts a lively clientele. The young and the restless head to **Forte Velho** (⊠ Estrada Marginal ☎ 21/468–1337), a medieval fort on the edge of town that has been converted into a dance club.

Outdoor Activities

GOLF *See* Chapter 9, *Golf in Portugal: Where to Play,* for a complete list of golf courses in the area.

> ### GOLF
>
> The superb golf courses near Lisbon attract players from far and wide. Most are the creations of renowned designers, and the climate means that you can play year-round. Many hotels offer golf privileges to guests; some places even have their own courses. Package deals abound.

Clube de Golfe do Estoril (⊠ Av. da República ☎21/468–0176) has an immaculate 18-hole par-69 championship course as well as a 9-hole course. The standard green fee for 18 holes is €57, but guests of the Hotel Palácio receive special rates and privileges. Note that on weekends only members can play here. On the Estoril–Sintra road, 7 km (4½ mi) north of Estoril, the **Estoril Sol** (⊠ N9, Linhó ☎ 21/924–0444) has a scenic 9-hole course on the fringes of the Serra de Sintra. The green fee is €21. **Penha Longa** (⊠ Estrada da Lagoa Azul, Linhó ☎ 21/924–9022), 9 km (5½ mi) north of Estoril, has superb views, an 18-hole course, a 9-hole course, putting greens, and golf clinics. The green fee for 18 holes is €90.

TENNIS Many of the larger hotels in Estoril have tennis courts, or you can contact the **Clube de Tenis do Estoril** (⊠ Av. Amaral ☎ 21/468–1675 or 21/466–2770), which has 18 courts and hosts international championships.

Shopping

Most general shopping is done in nearby Cascais. Each July and August sees the **Feira do Artesanato,** an open-air crafts fair near the casino. Stall vendors sell local art, crafts, and food every evening from 5 until midnight. The town of **Carcavelos,** 7 km (4½ mi) southeast of Estoril, has a busy Thursday market that sells food, clothes, and crafts; you can reach it by local train.

The **Galeria do Casino Estoril** holds three big art exhibitions during the year: in spring, talented young artists from Portuguese art schools are featured; naive art is the theme in summer; in October, Portuguese and international artists grab the spotlight. During the year there are also eight individual exhibitions. All the works—paintings, bronzes, ceramics, drawings, and sculptures, including marble pieces by Portugal's most famous sculptor, João Cutileiro—are for sale. Just off the main gallery is the Boutique de Arte, which sells smaller pieces by the same artists exhibited. ⊠ *Casino Estoril, Largo José Teodoro dos Santos* ☎ *21/466– 7700 (ask for art gallery)* ◷ *Daily 1:30 PM–1 AM.*

Cascais & Boca do Inferno

★ ❷ *3 km (2 mi) west of Estoril; the train runs directly here, or you can walk along the seafront promenade.*

Once a mere fishing village, the town of Cascais—with three small, sandy bays—is now a heavily developed resort packed with shops, restaurants, and hotels. Despite the masses of people, though, Cascais has retained some of its small-town character. This is most visible around the harbor, with its fishing boats and yachts, and in the old streets and squares off Largo 5 de Outubro, where you'll find lace shops, cafés, and restaurants. The beaches are very attractive, too, although bear in mind the pollution problems here: unless signs indicate otherwise, stay out of the sea.

The **Igreja de Nossa Senhora da Assunção** (Church of Our Lady of the Assumption), with its plain white facade, is the most graceful church in Cascais. Inside is an elegant golden altar, and there are fine paintings by 17th-century Portuguese artist Josefa de Óbidos—a rare instance of a female artist of that day gaining an international reputation. ⊠ *Largo da Assunção* ☎ *No phone* ⊠ *Free* ◷ *Daily 9–1 and 5–8.*

One of Cascais's 19th-century town houses serves as the **Museu dos Condes Castro Guimarães** (Counts of Castro Guimarães Museum) with displays of 18th- and 19th-century paintings, ceramics, and furniture as well as artifacts from nearby archaeological excavations. ⊠ *Av. Rei Humberto II de Itália* ☎ *21/ 482–5407* ⊠ *€1.50, free Sun.* ◷ *Tues.–Sun. 10–5.*

For an understanding of development in Cascais, visit the modern, single-story **Museu do Mar** (Sea Museum). Here, the town's former role as a fishing village is traced through model boats and fishing gear, period clothing, analysis of local fish, paintings, and old photographs. ⊠ *Rua J. Pereira de Melho* ☎ *21/486–1377* ⊠ *€1, free Sun.* ◷ *Tues.–Sun. 10–5.*

The most relaxing spot in Cascais, ☾ apart from the beach, is the municipal **Parque do Marechal Carmona,**

SHOPPING

Lisbon's environs have shopping opportunities galore, from clothes sold in smart Cascais and Estoril boutiques to the ceramics and woven and leather goods at roadside stalls and at weekly village markets. Quality and prices vary greatly, so shop around before buying. Prices are fixed almost everywhere, although with a firm command of Portuguese you may be able to negotiate a small discount at markets and roadside stalls.

which has a shallow lake, a café, a small zoo, and tables and chairs under the trees for picnickers. It's open daily 8:30 AM–7:45 PM in summer and until 5:45 PM in winter.

③ The most visited attraction in the area around Cascais is the forbiddingly named **Boca do Inferno** (Mouth of Hell), one of several natural grottoes in the rugged coastline, and just 2 km (1 mi) west of Cascais. It's best to visit at high tide or in stormy weather, when the waves are thrust high onto the surrounding cliffs. You can walk along the fenced paths to the viewing platforms above the grotto and peer down into the abyss. A path leads down to secluded spots on the rocks below, where fishermen cast their lines. Afterward, shop for lace, leather items, and other handicrafts at roadside stalls, and stop in one of the nearby cafés.

NEED A BREAK? On the coastal road west of Cascais, the café-terrace **Esplanada Santa Marta** (⌧ Estrada da Boca do Inferno ☎ 21/483–7779) overlooks the tiny Santa Marta Beach and a lighthouse. This is a perfect spot for a cool drink on the way to or from the Boca do Inferno, a 20-minute walk beyond.

Where to Stay & Eat

$–$$$ ✕ **Beira Mar.** One of several well-established and unpretentious restaurants behind the fish market, the Beira Mar has a comfortable, tiled interior. An impressive display of the day's catch shows you the best of the seafood, although, as ever, you can end up paying top dollar for dinner if you're not careful, since it's all sold by weight. Make sure you know the price first, or stick to the dishes with fixed prices—rice with clams or steaks cut from swordfish or tuna are always worth trying. ⌧ *Rua das Flores 6* ☎ *21/482–7380* ⊕ *www.beiramar-hoteleira.pt* ▤ *AE, DC, MC, V* ☾ *Closed Tues.*

$–$$$ ✕ **O Pescador.** Fresh seafood fills the menu at this folksy restaurant, a favorite since 1964, where a cluttered ceiling and maritime-related artifacts distract the eye. Sole is a specialty, and this is also a good place to try *bacalhau* (dried salt cod); it's often baked here, either with cream or with port wine and onions. ⌧ *Rua das Flores 10* ☎ *21/483–2054* ⊕ *www.restaurantepescador.com* ▤ *AE, DC, MC.*

$–$$ ✕ **Pizza Itália.** There are plenty of other pizza joints in Cascais, but Pizza Itália is probably the best of the bunch. In its indoor dining rooms or on its sunny terrace you can choose from a range of authentic pies and pastas. ⌧ *Rua do Poço Novo 1* ☎ *21/483–0151* ▤ *MC, V* ☾ *Closed Wed. No lunch.*

¢–$$ ✕ **Dom Manolo.** The surroundings aren't sophisticated in this Spanish-owned grill-restaurant, but for down-to-earth fare it's a good choice. The waiters charge back and forth delivering excellent spit-roasted chicken (*frango* in Portuguese) to a largely local clientele. Whatever your main dish, order potatoes or fries on the side; avoid the poor, overpriced salads and factory-made desserts. ⌧ *Av. Marginal 13* ☎ *21/483–1126* ▤ *No credit cards.*

$ ✕ **O Pereira.** Popular it may be, but this restaurant remains simple, with paper tablecloths and no decorations. The menu includes very cheap—and very good—dishes from every region in Portugal. The owner's cooking attracts many customers, so get there early: 12:30 for lunch and 7:30 for dinner. Don't expect much other than really good food. ⊠ *Rua Visconde da Luz 43* ☎ *21/483–1215* ▭ *No credit cards* ⊘ *Closed Thurs.*

★ $$$ ✕▥ **Hotel Albatroz.** On a rocky outcrop above the crashing waves, this gorgeous hotel was once the summer residence of the dukes of Loulé. Although expanded and modernized, its character has been retained, particularly in the fabric-lined corridors and the cozy terrace bar. The guest rooms combine elegance (old prints and floral drapes) with comfort (good beds and spacious bathrooms); it's worth paying extra for a sea view. The small pool and the terrace overlook the ocean. A fine buffet breakfast is served in the Albatroz restaurant ($$–$$$$; reservations and dressy-casual attire are essential), where fish dishes are the specialty. The hotels also rents three adjoining small villas. ⊠ *Rua Frederico Arouca 100, 2750-353* ☎ *21/484–7380* 🖷 *21/484–4827* ⊕ *www.albatrozhotels. com* ⇥ *37 rooms, 3 suites, 3 villas* ⚬ *Restaurant, room service, minibars, cable TV, golf privileges, saltwater pool, bar, shops, babysitting, Internet, meeting rooms* ▭ *AE, DC, MC, V.*

✪ $$$$ ▥ **Hotel Cascais Miragem.** Perfectly integrated into the landscape, the
Fodor's Choice newest and most luxurious of the hotels is built in steps up the side of the
★ hill above the sea. Each floor has different designer furniture and a different color scheme in which reds, oranges, and yellows predominate. View the sailboats on the sea from one of the many panoramic windows or from your balcony overlooking the bay. The infinity-edged pool has been spectacularly designed to give the illusion of extending into the sea. The hotel offers special services for children, including in-room toys and DVD cartoons, plus a children's pool. A minivan provides a shuttle into town and to golf courses. ⊠ *Av. Marginal 8554, 2754-236* ☎ *21/006–0600* 🖷 *21/006–0601* ⊕*www.cascaismiragem.com* ⇥*180 rooms, 20 suites* ⚬*3 restaurants, room service, cable TV with movies, 3 pools (1 indoor), health club, 3 bars, babysitting, parking (fee)* ▭ *AE, DC, MC, V* ❏ *BP.*

$$$ ▥ **Estalagem Villa Albatroz.** If Portugal's 18th-century writer Maria Amália de Carvalho could return today to her house on the harbor at Cascais Bay, she would surely check in and open up her laptop. Each light-filled room is individually furnished; some have balconies or fireplaces, and all have sea views. In the bathroom, the hair dryer, the phone, and the view of the greatly changed marina might surprise Dona Maria, but the huge tubs wouldn't. ⊠ *Rua Fernandes Tomas 1, 2750-342* ☎ *21/486–3410* 🖷 *21/484–4680* ⊕ *www.albatrozhotels.com* ⇥ *11 rooms* ⚬ *Restaurant, in-room safes, minibars, cable TV, in-room data ports, bar, meeting room* ▭ *AE, DC, MC, V.*

$$ ▥ **Hotel Baia.** This modern stone hotel fronted with white balconies overlooks fishing boats on the quayside and Cascais Bay. Your choice of rooms is straightforward: the 66 front rooms have balconies and sea views but are plain in the extreme; the rest face the town at the back but have been decorated with a bit more imagination. There's a private esplanade along the ground floor, with a lounge, restaurant, grill, café, and bar. ⊠ *Estrada Marginal, 2754-509* ☎ *21/483–1033* 🖷 *21/483–1095* ⊕ *www.hotelbaia.com* ⇥ *113 rooms* ⚬ *2 restaurants, café, cable TV, golf privileges, pool, bar, parking (fee), convention center* ▭ *AE, DC, MC, V* ❏ *BP, FAP, MAP.*

$ ▦ **Casa da Pérgola.** Set back from the road amid gardens, this intimate town house has been in the hands of the same family for more than 100 years. The painted-and-tiled facade sets a refined, solidly 19th-century tone that's continued inside by the heavy drapes, impressive stairway, period furniture, and art. In cooler weather you eat breakfast in the dining room surrounded by cabinets of old porcelain; on warmer days you can enjoy the day's first meal in the garden. Book well in advance to secure a room here. ☒ *Av. de Valbom 13, 2750-508* ☎ *21/484–0040* ⎙ *21/483–4791* ⊕ *www.pergolahouse.com* ⇌ *6 rooms* ⚖ *Dining room; no a/c in some rooms, no room TVs* ▭ *No credit cards* ⦿ *BP* ⊘ *Closed Dec.–Feb.*

Nightlife & the Arts

Cascais has plenty of bars on and around the central pedestrian street, Rua Frederico Arouca, and in Largo Luís de Camões. The marina is also a lively place to barhop, with a wide choice of places that stay open until around 2 AM.

Chequers (☒ Largo Luís de Camões 7 ☎ 21/483–0926) blasts rock music into the square nightly in summer.

You can hear fado, the mournful Portuguese folk music, at **Forte D. Rodrigo** (☒ Rua de Birre 961 ☎ 21/487–1373). On hot summer nights, customers of the English-style pub **John Bull** (☒ Largo Luís de Camões 8 ☎ 21/483–3319) spill out into the square.

Nuts Club (☒ Av. Rei Humberto II de Itália ☎ 21/484–4109), a popular disco close to the marina, has seven bars, two dance floors, and nice sea views from a terrace. Nothing much happens before midnight, but the action doesn't finish until 4 AM.

Outdoor Activities

FISHING **Turiboat** (☒ Marina de Cascais ☎ 91/782–2844 ⊕ www.turiboat.com) organizes deep-sea fishing outings.

GOLF *See* Chapter 9, *Golf in Portugal: Where to Play,* for a complete list of golf courses in the area.

Belas Clube de Campo (☒ Alamedo do Aqueducto, Belas Clube de Campo ☎ 21/962–6640 ⊕ www.belasgolf.com) is a prestigious 18-hole course designed by Rocky Roquemore. It makes good use of lakes and water courses, and it has a nice clubhouse. Green fees are €73–€84. **Quinta da Marinha** (☒ 4 km [2½ mi] west of Cascais ☎ 21/468–0100 for golf, 21/468–0180 for tennis, 21/486–9433 for horseback riding ⊕ www.quinta-da-marinha.pt) has an 18-hole course designed by Robert Trent Jones Jr. Green fees are €80–€88. There are also tennis courts, a pool, and an exceptional equestrian center where you can arrange horseback rides year-round.

WATER SPORTS You can rent surfing equipment from **Equinócio** (☒ Varandas de Cascais 3 ☎ 21/483–5354). Behind the train station, the dive shop **Exclusive Divers** (☒ Praia da Duquesa ☎ 21/486–8099 ⊕ www.exclusive-divers.net) offers scuba diving courses on the beach. Call a day in advance. A 2½-hour course costs €60. Their services also include specialized dive trips.

Call ahead and you can have lessons in kite surfing, windsurfing, and surfing from **Guincho Wind Factory** (✉ Villa Internacional, Aldeia de Juzo ☎ 21/484–1930 or 96/630–1378 ⊕ www.guinchowindfactory.com). You can either meet at the shop in Aldeia de Juzo, 1 km (½ mi) from Guincho beach, or arrange to meet right on the beach. Lessons are €25 for 1 hour, €80 for 5 hours (over the course of one or two days) or €160 for 10 hours (over a minimum of two days).

Shopping

Cascais is the best shopping area on the Estoril Coast, with pedestrian streets lined with stores and small market stalls. For smart fashions, gifts, and handmade jewelry, browse around Rua Frederico Arouca. Markets are held north of town at Rua Mercado (off Avenida 25 de Abril) on Wednesday and Saturday; you'll find fruit, vegetables, cheese, bread, and flowers. On the first and third Sunday of each month, a large market is held at the Praça de Touros (Bull Ring) on Avenida Pedro Álvares, west of the center. On the Marginal (coastal road) into Cascais from Lisbon, the **Cascais Villa** (✉ Av. Dom Pedro I ☎ 21/482–8250) shopping center has cinemas and shops carrying internationally known brands.

In **Ceramicarte** (✉ Largo da Assunção 3–4 ☎ 21/484–0170), Fátima and Luís Soares present their carefully executed, modern ceramic designs alongside more traditional jugs and plates. There's also a small selection of tapestries and artworks. The store is near the church.

In the Cascais shopping mall on the road between Cascais and Sintra, the bookstore/computer/record shop **Fnac** (✉ N9, Alcabideche ☎ 21/469–9000) sells English-language books as well as tickets to cultural events.

Manueis (✉ Frederico Arouca 91 ☎ 21/483–3452) sells tablecloths, bedspreads, and other fine linens. For typical Portuguese handmade jewelry such as filigree go to **Torres** (✉ Frederico Arouca 13 ☎ 21/483–0977), which has its own designers and trademark brand. For fine Portuguese porcelain visit **Vista Alegre Atlantis** (✉ Av. 25 de Abril 64 ☎ 21/483–8942).

Guincho

❹ *9 km (5½ mi) north of Boca do Inferno.*

There's a wide beach at Guincho, where Atlantic waves pound onto the sand even on the calmest of days, providing perfect conditions for windsurfing (the annual world championships are often held here in summer). The undertow here is notorious; even the best swimmers should take heed. Whether you surf or not, savor some fresh fish served at one of the restaurant terraces overlooking the beach. And if you don't want to drive—perhaps you would rather wash the meal down with wine and a glass of port?—it's a simple matter to come by bus, which leaves from outside Cascais's train station every two hours (7:45 AM–5:45 PM, journey time 25 minutes).

Where to Stay & Eat

$$$–$$$$ ✕ **João Padeiro.** "John the Baker," undoubtedly the most eclectic restaurant you are likely to find in this area, was named after the owner who opened a small restaurant in Cascais 40 years ago that catered to local fishermen. The place became so famous that it attracted Portuguese royalty. In 2001, John opened this establishment in what was once an indoor swimming pool—though he did keep the outdoor pool—in an isolated part of the Guincho beach. Now, under an elaborate wooden ceiling and surrounded by modern art and a wall of photographs showing guests of the old place, you can enjoy fabulous seafood dishes including the famous Cascais Dover Sole. ⊠ *Estrada do Guincho* ☎ *21/485-7141* ⊟ *AE, DC, MC, V* ⊘ *No dinner Sun. and during important football (soccer) matches.*

$–$$ ✕🖭 **Estalagem Muchaxo.** This inn is nestled in the rocks over Guincho beach. Although most of the rooms have ocean views, there are some at the back overlooking the nearby hills; the beach itself is just steps away. Much of the building is rustic, with stone floors, wood paneling, and maritime bric-a-brac. In the well-known restaurant ($$–$$$), fish specialties such as *caldeirada* (fish stew) are the order of the day. Meals are a little overpriced, and service isn't always top-notch, but what you're ultimately paying for is the unrivaled view through picture windows. ⊠ *Praia do Guincho, 2750-642* ☎ *21/487-0221* 🖷 *21/487-0444* ⊕ *www.muchaxo.com* ⇌ *60 rooms* ⚭ *Restaurant, minibars, cable TV, saltwater pool, squash, bar, Internet, meeting rooms; no a/c in some rooms* ⊟ *AE, DC, MC, V* ⦿ *BP, FAP, MAP.*

IN AND AROUND SINTRA & QUELUZ

The lush woods and valleys on the northern slopes of the Serra de Sintra (Sintra Mountains) have been inhabited since prehistoric times, although the Moors were the first to build a castle on the peaks. Later Sintra became the summer residence of Portuguese kings and aristocrats, and its late medieval palace is the greatest expression of royal wealth and power of the time. In the 18th and 19th centuries English travelers, poets, and writers—including an enthusiastic Lord Byron—were drawn by the region's beauty. The poet Robert Southey described Sintra as "the most blessed spot on the whole inhabitable globe." Its historic importance has been recognized by UNESCO, which designated it a World Heritage site in 1995.

Sintra is a good base for exploring the countryside. Driving is the easiest way to cover the area, but you could also take a guided tour (arranged through the tourist office) or see the sights by taxi. The nearest attractions are within walking distance or are accessible by bus or horse-drawn carriages. Trains will bring you to Sintra but not much farther.

Sintra

★ ❺ *30 km (18 mi) northwest of Lisbon, 13 km (8 mi) north of Estoril.*

The palaces, gardens, wooded paths, and viewpoints of Sintra are as enchanting as its horse-drawn carriages and old hotels. The region exudes its famous charm even at the height of the summer tourism season: tour buses are largely banned from the main square, and with a little effort you can escape any crowds by taking one of several walks in the countryside. To explore Sintra, you might start at the tourist office and—

armed with local walking information—begin your discoveries. For those who don't want to walk up the steep hills, you can take Bus 434, which leaves from the train station at 20- to 30-minute intervals beginning at 9:50 AM. Pay for your all-day ticket (€3.50) on the bus. It stops at all the palaces.

Sintratur offers old-fashioned **horse-and-carriage rides** (⊠ Rua João de Deus 82 ☎ 21/924–1238) in the Sintra area. A short tour of Sintra costs €30; longer trips run between €60 and €100 and go as far afield as Pena Palace and Monserrate.

Fodor'sChoice
★

Easily mistaken for a glaringly misplaced energy plant of some sort, the conical twin white chimneys of the **Palácio Nacional de Sintra** (Sintra Palace) are the town's most recognizable landmarks. Under those chimneys, meat turned on spits for the feasts of João I. There has probably been a palace here since Moorish times, although the current structure, also known as the Paço Real, dates from the late 14th century. It is the only surviving royal palace in Portugal from the Middle Ages. The property was the summer residence of the House of Avis, Portugal's royal line, and it displays a fetching combination of Moorish, Gothic, and Manueline architectural styles. Some of its rooms are exceptional, and bilingual descriptions in each of them let you enjoy the palace at your own pace. The kitchen, with its famous chimneys, is an intriguing stop, not least because of its sheer size (imagine the life of a scullery maid here). It's still used today when official banquets are held at the palace. The chapel has Mozarabic (Moorish-influenced) azulejos from the 15th and 16th centuries. The ceiling of the Sala das Armas is painted with the coats of arms of 72 noble families, and the grand Sala dos Cisnes has a remarkable ceiling of painted swans. One of the oldest rooms, the Sala das Pegas, figures in a well-known tale about Dom João I (1385–1433) and his dalliance with a lady-in-waiting. The king had the room painted with as many magpies as there were chattering court ladies, thus satirizing the gossips as loose-tongued birds. ⊠ *Largo Rainha D. Amélia* ☎ *21/910–6840* ⊠ *€4, free Sun. 10–2* ☉ *Thurs.–Tues. 10–5:30 (last admission 5).*

NEED A
BREAK?

Well placed in Sintra's central square—with fine views of the palace—Café Paris (⊠ Largo Rainha D. Amélia ☎ 21/923–2375) **makes a pleasant, if pricey, stop for a drink or even a meal. Outside seating can be difficult to score; the lucky ones can soak up the bustling street scenes.**

The tourist office's building also contains an art gallery, the **Galeria do Museu Municipal,** specializing in works associated with Sintra. ⊠ *Praça da República 23* ☎ *21/924–4772* ⊠ *Free* ☉ *Tues.–Fri. 9–noon and 2–6, weekends 2:30–7.*

2

The former fire station headquarters has been transformed into the **Museu do Brinquedo** (Toy Museum). Based on the collection of João Arbués Moreira, who began hoarding his toys when he was 14, the museum occupies more than four floors. Pick out your favorites from the thousands of toy planes, trains, and automobiles; dolls' furniture; rare lead soldiers; puppets; and a zillion-and-one other Christmas gifts and birthday presents—including some given to royal children. Of course, there's a playroom for kids with Legos—and computers. There's a café here, too. ⊠ *Rua Visconde de Monserrate* ☎ *21/924–2171* ⊕ *www. museu-do-brinquedo.pt* ⌨ *€4* ☉ *Tues.–Sun. 10–6.*

The steep, wooded slopes that rise from Sintra are home to many grand houses, including the intriguing **Quinta da Regaleira,** a five-minute walk along the main road past the tourist office. You have to call ahead to book a tour, and the entrance fee is high, but it's worth it. The estate was built in the early 20th century for a Brazilian mining magnate with a vivid imagination and a keen interest in freemasonry

---

FESTIVAL

The **Festival de Sintra** runs from June through September and features piano recitals, operas, and ballet in the town's palaces, churches, and parks. Performances in the gardens of the Palácio de Seteais are especially popular.

---

and the Knights Templars (who made their 11th-century headquarters on this very site). The main part of the tour takes in the gardens, where almost everything—statues, water features, grottoes, lookout towers—is linked to freemasonry or the Knights Templars. By the time you reach the spooky, 100-foot-deep Poço do Iniciáto (Initiation Well)—an inverted underground "tower"—you may be wondering what strange events might have gone on here (none did). From the well, you pass through inky tunnels, cross a small lake via stepping-stones, and emerge, gratefully, back into the light. Though the house—with its fantastic mix of styles, among them Gothic and Manueline—is flamboyant, it's something of an anticlimax after the garden tour. There's an uninspired exhibit on freemasonry, a café, and a restaurant. ⊠ *Rua Barbosa do Bocage 5* ☎ *21/910–6650* ⊕ *www.regaleira.pt* ⌨ *€5, guided tours (call ahead for tours in English) €10* ☉ *June–Sept. tours daily 10–5, every 30 mins; tours less frequent Oct.–May.*

If your stay is longer than a day or so, the **Museu Arqueológico de São Miguel de Odrinhas** (São Miguel de Odrinhas Archaeological Museum) is worth a visit. Its displays include locally found ancient and medieval objects. ⊠ *Av. Professor Dr. D. Fernando da Almeida* ☎ *21/961–3574* ⌨ *€2.50* ☉ *Wed.–Sun. 10–1 and 2–6.*

In a former palace, the **Sintra Museu de Arte Moderna–Colecção Berardo** (Contemporary Art Museum) has more than 1,500 works collected by Joe Berardo. It is the largest collection of its kind in Europe, with works by Andy Warhol, Pablo Picasso, Roy Lichtenstein, Salvador Dali, Julio Pomar, Francis Bacon, and many others. There is a permanent exhibition and other works are shown on a rotating basis. ⊠ *Av. Heliodoro*

Salgado ☎ *21/924–8170* ⊕ *www.berardomodern.com* ✉ € 3
◷ *Tues.–Sun. 10–6.*

Where to Stay & Eat

$$–$$$$ ✕ **Tacho Real.** Sintra locals come to this restaurant, at the top of a steep flight of steps, for a celebratory night out. They can count on confident, traditional dishes cooked with panache. Lamb, bacalhau *à brás* (with eggs, onions, and sliced potato), steaks, and game in season are all on the menu. ⊠ *Rua do Ferraria 4* ☎ *21/923–5277* ⊟ *AE, MC, V* ◷ *Closed Wed.*

$–$$$ ✕ **Curral dos Caprinos.** Formerly part of a sheep corral, this typical rustic restaurant is decorated with farming motifs. Clay pots, smoked hams, onions, and dried corn cobs hang from the ceiling, and the walls are lined in cork. The most spectacular of the excellent meat dishes is the *cabrito à moda de Oleiros,* a whole lamb for six roasted over laurel branches. Call to order it a day in advance. The *cogumelos à caprinos* (mushrooms with smoked ham, shrimp, and cream) is an unforgettable starter. ⊠ *Rua 28 de Setembro 13, Cabriz* ☎ *21/923–3113* ⊟ *AE, DC, MC, V.*

$–$$ ✕ **Neptuno.** Praia das Maçãs is a popular place to go for seafood restaurants on the beach. One of the favorites is Neptuno, a glassed-in restaurant practically on the sand. Hanging on the walls are photos of boats, big catches, and the sea—one photo shows the sea coming right up to the restaurant. Try the *peixe a bulhão pato* (fish with garlic, olive oil, and coriander) and *arroz de marisco* (seafood rice). ⊠ *Praia das Maçãs* ☎ *21/929–1222* ⊟ *AE, DC, MC, V* ◷ *Closed Thurs. No dinner Wed.*

$–$$ ✕ **Pátio Garrette.** Arches divide three rooms where long tables are covered in yellow tablecloths that match the chair cushions and curtains. Named after the restaurant, bacalhau *à garrette* (cooked with onions, garlic, peppers, and olive oil and garnished with coriander and boiled egg) is a good choice. Join the guests on the terrace who pose for pictures with views of the twin chimneys of the Paço Real, the church tower, and the distant beach. ⊠ *Rua Maria Eugénia Navarro* ☎ *21/924–3380* ⊟ *AE, DC, MC, V* ◷ *Closed Wed.*

¢–$ ✕ **Alcobaça.** The friendly owner bustles around to make sure guests are well served in this simple restaurant on a town-center side street. Try the excellent grilled fish, arroz de marisco, or tasty fresh clams *bulhão pato* (in garlic sauce). ⊠ *Rua das Padarias 7–11* ☎ *21/923–1651* ⊟ *MC, V.*

★ $$$$ ✕⌂ **Hotel Palácio de Seteais.** Built in the 18th century as a home for the Dutch consul to Portugal, this hotel is surrounded by pristine grounds 1 km (½ mi) or so from the center of Sintra. You enter under an arch that joins the building's two wings. In them, public rooms have period furnishings, delicate frescoes, and Arraiolos carpets, and guest rooms are individually styled, some with hand-painted wallpapers. The restaurant ($$–$$$; reservations essential; dressy attire requested) serves set, four-course, Continental meals. In summer, having coffee or tea on the terrace is a delight. ⊠ *Rua Barbosa do Bocage 8, 2725-517* ☎ *21/923–3200* ⊟ *21/923–4277* ⊕ *www.tivolpalaciosetais.com* ⇌ *30 rooms, 1 suite* ⌂ *Restaurant, cable TV, tennis court, pool, horseback riding, bar, Internet, meeting rooms* ⊟ *AE, DC, MC, V* ⵏⵁ *BP.*

2

$$$ ✕🏨 **Lawrence's Hotel.** When this 18th-century inn, the oldest on the penin-
Fodor's Choice sula, reopened as a luxury hotel late in the 20th century, the U.S. sec-
★ retary of state and the Netherlands' Queen Beatrix were among the first
guests. The intimate rooms are bathed in light from French windows,
and deluxe touches such as heated towel racks and crested linens abound.
The staff can arrange anything from jeep tours to babysitting. At
Lawrence's Restaurant ($$$–$$$$; reservations recommended) special-
ties—served on Portugal's Vista Alegre porcelain—might include fish soup
en croûte (served in hollowed-out bread) with coriander, roast duck, and
a dessert flambéed at your table. ⊠ *Rua Consigliéri Pedroso 38–40, 2710-
550* ☎ *21/910–5500* 🖷 *21/910–5505* ⊕ *www.lawrenceshotel.com*
↩ *11 rooms, 5 suites* ⚏ *Restaurant, in-room safes, cable TV, bar, li-
brary, Internet, meeting rooms* ▤ *AE, DC, MC, V* ⎆ *BP.*

$$ 🏨 **Quinta da Capela.** Built by the dukes of Cadaval, this long, low, 16th-
century manor house, largely rebuilt in Portuguese country style in
1773, has spacious rooms filled with period furniture. The grounds also
contain a garden, a chapel, and a tree-shaded pool. The views stretch
over to the Pena Palace. Because the manor house is 3 km (2 mi) west
of Sintra, off the road to Colares, a car is essential. ⊠ *Estrada de Monserrate, 2710* ☎ *21/929–0170* 🖷 *21/929–3425* ⊕ *www.quintadacapela.
com* ↩ *8 rooms, 2 suites* ⚏ *Dining room, pool, gym, sauna; no a/c,
no room TVs* ▤ *MC* ⎆ *BP* ⊘ *Closed Nov.–Feb.*

★ **$$** 🏨 **Quinta das Sequóias.** This 19th-century manor house on 40 wooded
acres underwent inspired renovations to transform it into a hotel. One
of the bathrooms was cleverly built around monolithic boulders, and a
tower was chosen as a place for a guest room as well as a flower-filled,
ground-floor sitting area. Antique touches proliferate: here an old para-
sol, there a period jewelry box. Buffet breakfasts (and light dinners on
request) are served in a large, galleried dining room. The gardens in-
clude a pool, a Jacuzzi, and a terrace. (Note there's a two-night mini-
mum stay in peak season.) ⊠ *2 km (1 mi) from Sintra, past the Palácio
de Seteais (Box 4), Monserrate 2710-801* ☎ *21/924–3821 or 21/923–
0342* 🖷 *21/910–6065* ⊕ *www.quintadassequoias.com* ↩ *5 rooms*
⚏ *Dining room, pool, hot tub, billiards, bar; no room TVs, no smok-
ing* ▤ *AE, DC, MC, V* ⎆ *BP.*

$$ 🏨 **Tivoli Sintra.** The Tivoli makes the most of its central location: in each
room, balconies afford valley and ocean views. Do whatever it takes to
score one of the superior rooms, where enormous balconies provide even
more tremendous vistas. Rooms are dark and have reproduction coun-
try-style antiques and tiled baths. ⊠ *Praça da República, 2710-616* ☎ *21/
923–7200* 🖷 *21/923–7245* ⊕ *www.tivolisintra.com* ↩ *73 rooms, 4 suites*
⚏ *Restaurant, in-room safes, minibars, cable TV, in-room data ports,
bar, Internet, convention center, meeting rooms* ▤ *AE, DC, MC, V* ⎆ *BP.*

★ **$–$$** 🏨 **Casa Miradouro.** Count yourself lucky if you've managed to book a
room at this candy-stripe 1890s house at the edge of Sintra. Its Swiss
owner, the charming Mr. Kneubühl, has a keen eye for style and comfort. Rooms have grand views, wrought-iron bedsteads, and polished
tile floors. Breakfast is served in the downstairs dining room, which opens
onto a terrace; although no other meals are served, you're only a (steep)
five-minute walk from Sintra's restaurants. ⊠ *Rua Sotto Mayor 55, 2710*

☎ 21/923–5900 🖷 21/924–1836 🌐 www.casa-miradouro.com ⇄ 6 rooms ♨ Cable TV, bar, lounge ▭ AE, DC, MC, V 🍽 BP ⊗ Closed mid-Jan.–Feb.

Outdoor Activities

Sintra's pretty surroundings positively beg to be seen at a leisurely pace on horseback. The **Centro Hípico da Costa do Estoril** (✉ Estrada da Charneca 186, Cascais ☎ 21/487–2064 🌐 www.centrohipicocosta estoril.com) offers rides in the Sintra hills and elsewhere. The **Grupo Ecológico de Cascais-GEC** (☎ 21/487–2646, 96/754–9492, or 91/965–1882) leads walks through the Sintra-Cascais Natural Park.

The equestrian center at the **Penha Longa Country Club** (✉ Estrada da Lagoa Azul, Linhó ☎ 21/924–9033) can arrange a variety of rides in the area.

From the town of Sintra itself, there are five walks through the hills and past the palaces. Information and maps are available at the **tourist office** (✉ Praça da República 23 ☎ 21/923–1157 or 21/924–1700), which is open 9–8 from June through September, and 9–5 from October through May.

Shopping

Sintra is a noted center for antiques, curios, and ceramics, although you'll need to choose carefully: prices are on the high side, and there's a fair amount of poor-quality goods. Keep an eye out for special in-store displays of hand-painted ceramics, many of them reproductions of 15th- to 18th-century designs, signed by the artists.

Almoraviva (✉ Rua Visconde de Monserrate 12–14 ☎ 21/924–0539) has handicrafts from all over Portugal, including embroidery from Madeira and the Azores, Vista Alegre porcelain, crystal from the north, Arraiolos rugs—you name it. Vintage port wines are on sale in **Camélia** (✉ Praça da República 2 ☎ 21/923–1704), whose owners can recommend vintages; you can buy local cheese here, too. **Casa Alegria** (✉ Escandinhas Felix Nunes 5 ☎ 21/923–4726) sells hand-painted tiles. They can also reproduce pictures or drawings you supply them. **Sr. Henrique Teixeira** (✉ Rua Onsiglieri Pedroso 2 ☎ 21/923–1043) sells antiques: 17th- and 18th-century tiles, sculptures, and bronze pieces. For hand-embroidered linen tablecloths, bedspreads, towels, and sheets, visit **Violeta** (✉ Rua das Padarias 19 ☎ 21/923–4095).

The small town of **Pêro Pinheiro** is known for its marble, and several shops here sell stacks of cachepots, plaques, and other garden objects. The town is on route N9, 9 km (5½ mi) northeast of Sintra.

Nightlife & the Arts

Festival de Sintra (✉ Praça Dr. Francisco Sá Carneiro ☎ 21/910–7110), the Sintra music and dance festival, takes place during June and July at the Centro Cultural Olga Cadaval as well as in the many palaces and gardens around Sintra and Queluz: Palácio Nacional de Sintra, Pena Palace, Quinta da Regaleira, Quinta da Piedade, Palácio de Seteais, and Queluz Palace. The Gulbenkian Symphony Orchestra and the Gulbenkian Ballet company as well as other international groups perform at the Olga Cadaval Cultural Center. The gardens of the Seteais Palace are well known for their open-air ballet and classical music performances. Tickets can be reserved and bought at the Olga de Cadaval Cultural Centre or at any Fnac store (there is one in the Cascais shopping mall) as well as the Lisbon Welcome Center. Programs are sometimes distributed at the arrivals area at the Lisbon airport.

São Pedro de Sintra

❻ *2 km (1 mi) southeast of Sintra.*

This little hillside village is most famous for its fair, the Feira de São Pedro, held every second and fourth Sunday of the month in the vast Praça Dom Fernando II (also called the Largo da Feira), where stalls are set up under the plane trees. Dating from the time of the Christian Reconquest, the fair is one of Portugal's best, with livestock and agricultural displays as well as local crafts, antiques, and food for sale. Even on nonfair days, it's worth coming to São Pedro to see the village church in its own enclosed little square. There are also several good restaurants in São Pedro, which makes it a good lunch stop.

The steep walk to São Pedro de Sintra along the main road from Sintra isn't much fun, although you can cut out much of the distance by climbing up through the gardens of the **Parque Liberdade** (☉ June–Sept., daily 9–8; Oct.–May, daily 9–6), which starts just east of Sintra. Otherwise, local buses leave from outside the Sintra train station (weekdays every 30–40 minutes, reduced service on weekends), and you can catch one as it passes the tourist office; or take a taxi.

Where to Eat

$-$$ ✕ **Adega do Saloio.** Families fill this popular rustic restaurant on weekends, drawn by the juicy steaks being cooked over the open fire as you walk in. The dining room is festooned with garlands of onions and garlic. House wine is served in brown clay jugs, and little plates of smoked ham, cheese, and black olives decorate the tables to whet the appetite. It's fun just watching the waiters bustling about with skewers of grilled meat and fish. The *espetada à madeira* (beef and laurel leaves on a skewer) that drips its juices as it's hung in front of you on the table is quite a spectacle. ⊠ *Rua Álvaro Reis 49* ☎ *21/923–1422* ⊟ *AE, DC, MC, V* ☉ *Closed Wed. and Thurs.*

$-$$ ✕ **Cantinho de São Pedro.** Imaginative Portuguese cuisine with a French twist is served at this busy, rustic restaurant in a small courtyard of artisans' workshops, just off the main square. Locals consider the food well worth the wait for a table. Try the trout with almonds and cream or look for the fresh shellfish on the list of *pratos do dia* (dishes of the day). ⊠ *Praça Dom Fernando II 18* ☎ *21/923–0267* ⊕ *www.cantinhosaopedro.com* ⊟ *AE, DC, MC, V.*

Shopping

The **Lojas do Picadeiro** (⊠ Praça Dom Fernando II) is a row of artisans' workshops that sell wooden toys, furniture, and art; a couple of taverns help restore flagging spirits.

Castelo dos Mouros

★ ❼ *3 km (2 mi) southwest of Sintra.*

Only the battlemented ruins of the 9th-century Moorish Castle still stand today, but the extent of these gives a fine impression of the solid fortress that finally fell from Moorish hands when it was conquered by Dom Afonso Henriques in 1147. It's visible from various points in Sintra itself—the steps of Sintra Palace is a favored vantage point—but for a closer look follow the steps that lead up to the ruins from the back of the town center, a walk that will take around 40 minutes going up and 25 minutes coming down. Buses run this way, too, or rent one of the horse-drawn carriages outside Sintra Palace for a more romantic trip. Panoramic views from the castle's serrated walls help explain why Moorish architects chose the site, and eagle-eyed visitors can also trace the remains of a mosque within the walls. ✉ *Estrada da Pena* ☎ *21/923–7300* ⊕ *www.parquedesintra.pt* ✉ *€4, guided tours €8* ⊗ *June–Sept., daily 9–8; Oct.–May, daily 9–7. Last admission 1 hr before closing.*

Palácio Nacional de Pena

❽ *4 km (2½ mi) south of Sintra.*

Fodor's Choice
★

The Disney-like, drawbridged Pena Palace is a glorious conglomeration of turrets and domes awash in pastels. In 1503 the Monastery of Nossa Senhora da Pena was constructed on this amazing site, but it fell into ruins after religious orders were expelled from Portugal in 1832. Seven years later the ruins were purchased by Maria II's consort, Ferdinand of Saxe-Coburg. Inspired by the Bavarian castles of his homeland, Ferdinand commissioned a German architect to build the castle of his fantasies. Work began in 1844 and was finished in 1885 when he was Fernando II. Pena Palace is a collection of styles

> **GETTING HERE IS HALF THE FUN**
>
> There are various ways to Palácio Nacional de Pena: you can take a local bus or a horse-drawn carriage, sign up for a tour, or make the long but very pleasant walk up from the center of Sintra (about 1½ hours). It is also possible to drive up, but there is very limited parking available once you get there. However you choose to arrive, note that the walk back down to Sintra is delightful: the route is through shaded woods with viewpoints under the cork trees.

that range from Arabian to Victorian. The surrounding park is filled with trees and flowers from every corner of the Portuguese empire. A tram takes you from the park gate up to the palace. The enormous statue on a nearby crag is thought to be Baron Eschwege (the building's German architect) cast as a medieval knight. A path beyond the Baron Eschwege statue leads to the **Cruz Alta**, a 16th-century stone cross that's 1,782 feet above sea level. It's an arduous climb, especially in the summer sun, but the views from this altitude are stupendous.

The final kings and queens of Portugal lived in the Pena Palace, the last of whom—Queen Amília—went into exile in England after the Republic was proclaimed on October 5, 1910. The pseudo-medieval structure, with its ramparts, towers, and great halls, has a rich, sometimes vulgar, and often bizarre collection of Victorian and Edwardian furniture, ornaments, and paintings. Given these extravagances, it is no wonder that the people of Portugal, not the richest of countries by any means at the time, decided to discard the monarchy. There are placards explaining each room. ⊠ *Estrada da Pena* ☎ *21/910–5340* 🎫 *Palace €4, combined ticket for park and palace €7, free Sun. 10–2. Tram €1.50* ⊙ *Mid-Sept.–mid-June, Tues.–Sun. 10–5 (last admission 4:30); mid-June–mid-Sept., Tues.–Sun. 10–7 (last admission 6:15).*

Monserrate

❾ *4 km (2½ mi) west of Sintra.*

The **palaces** here were laid out by Scottish gardeners in the mid-19th century at the behest of a wealthy Englishman, Sir Francis Cook. The grounds' centerpiece—the Moorish-style, three-domed **palace**—has been reopened to the public after 50 years of solitude. The original palace was built by the Portuguese viceroy of India. Sir Francis Cook restored it in the second half of the 19th century and it remained with his heirs for three generations. A history of the palace, *Castles, Caliphs and Christians* by Ida Kingsbury, is available at the palace reception area. Guided tours are at 10 AM and 3 PM. Be sure to book several days in advance. The gardens, with their streams, waterfalls, and Etruscan tombs, are worth a tour for their array of tree and plant species, though labels are few and far between. This is a popular picnic spot; it's easy to find your own glade somewhere along the winding paths. ⊠ *Estrada da Monserrate* ☎ *21/923–7300* 🎫 *€4, guided garden tours €3.50, palace tours (reserve in advance) €3.50* ⊙ *June–Sept., daily 9–8; Oct.–May, daily 9–7. Last admission 1 hr before closing.*

EN ROUTE
Past Monserrate the road leads west for 3 km (2 mi) to the small village of **Colares,** associated with the locally produced red wine. The town, its winding streets alive with colorful flowers and trees, is also known for its parish church, which is adorned with ceramic tiles, and its main square, bordered by 18th-century houses. For terrific views of the sea and surrounding mountains, take the winding road that climbs up to the village of **Penedo,** less than 2 km (1 mi) away from Colares.

Convento dos Capuchos

★ **❿** *13 km (8 mi) southwest of Sintra.*

The main entrance to this extraordinarily austere convent, with its simple tile roof and wooden beams lined with cork (to keep in what little warmth there might be), sets the tone for the severity of the ascetic living conditions. From 1560 until 1834, when it was abandoned, seven monks—never any more, never any less—inhabited the bare cells; prayed in the tiny chapel hewn out of the rock; and perhaps found some comfort in the washroom, kitchen, and refectory. Impure thoughts meant a spell in the Penitents' Cell, an excruciatingly small space. The 45-minute tour is obligatory, but, to their credit, the guides bring the history of the place to life with zest and humor. No vehicles are allowed close to the convent, so the peace is disturbed only by birdsong. ✉ *Convento dos Capuchos* ☎ *21/923–7300* ∰ *www.conventodoscapuchos.com* ⌦ *€4, guided tour €8* ☉ *June–Sept., daily 9–8 (last admission 7); Oct.–May, daily 9–6 (last admission 5).*

Cabo da Roca

★ **⑪** *15 km (9 mi) west of Sintra, 20 km (12 mi) northwest of Cascais.*

Between enchanting, culturally rich Sintra and the beach resort of Cascais you'll discover a totally different face of Lisbon's environs in this protected natural park. The windswept Cabo da Roca and its lighthouse mark continental Europe's westernmost point and are the main reason that most people make the journey. As with many such places, stalls purvey shell souvenirs and other gimmicks; an information desk and gift shop sells a certificate that verifies your visit. Even without the certificate, though, the memory of this desolate granite cape will linger. The cliffs tumble to a frothing sea below, and on the cape a simple cross bears an inscription by Portuguese national poet Luís de Camões. You can reach the cape from Cascais (30 minutes) or Sintra (40 minutes) by local bus, with regular departures from outside either town's train station.

**OFF THE
BEATEN
PATH**

The **ATLANTIC COAST –** North of Cabo da Roca, the protected national parkland extends through the successive Atlantic-facing resort villages of Praia Grande, Praia das Maçãs, and Azenhas do Mar. The first two have good beaches, and all have public swimming pools and small restaurants. A fun way to reach Praia das Maçãs is on the 19th-century Elétrico de Sintra, a tram that departs hourly from Ribeira de Sintra, 4 km (2½ mi) north of town, every day but Monday (the fare is €2.50). It passes through Banzão and offers engaging views as it approaches the beach. The park's many contrasts are readily apparent as you ride or drive through the microclimate of Serra de Sintra. ☎ *21/867–7681 for Elétrico de Sintra information.*

Queluz

⑫ *15 km (9 mi) east of Sintra, 15 km (9 mi) northwest of Lisbon.*

Halfway between Lisbon and Sintra (just off route N249/IC19) is the town of Queluz, dominated entirely by its magnificent palace. The drive from Lisbon takes about 20 minutes, making this a good half-day option or a fine stop on the way to or from Sintra. It's also easy to take the train: get off at the Queluz-Belas stop, turn left outside the station, and follow the signs for the 1-km (½-mi) walk to the palace.

Fodor'sChoice
★

The **Palácio Nacional de Queluz** (Queluz National Palace) was inspired, in part, by the palace at Versailles. Intended as a royal summer residence, the salmon-pink rococo edifice was ordered by Dom Pedro III in 1747, and work began under the supervision of architect Mateus Vicente de Oliveira. Within five years it was fit to receive its first royal inhabitants, but it took another 40 years and the artistic endeavors of Frenchman Jean-Baptiste Robillon for Queluz to acquire its famous romantic ap-

2

pearance. The building is fronted by a huge cobbled square and surrounded by Robillon's formal landscaping and waterways. The trees (brought from Amsterdam), statues (imported from London), ponds, canal, fountains, hedges—and the palace—all fit a carefully executed baroque plan that implies harmony and wholeness. After a 1934 fire, the palace was restored. It's used today for banquets, music festivals, and official meetings attended by world leaders, and as accommodations for visiting heads of state.

You can tour the apartments and elegant staterooms, including the frescoed Music Salon, the Hall of Ambassadors, and the mirrored Throne Room with its crystal chandeliers and gilt trim. Room furnishings and details—often of fine woods and precious metals from around the globe—are truly fit for a king. Walks in the formal gardens take you through orange groves and down avenues of oaks to azulejo-lined fountains and canals. ⊠ *Rte. IC19* ☎ *21/435–0039* 🎫 *€4, free Sun. 10–2* ⊙ *Wed.–Mon. 10–5 (last admission 4:30).*

Where to Stay & Eat

★ **$$** ✕🏨 **Pousada de Dona Maria I.** The Royal Guard quarters beneath the clock tower opposite the palace have undergone a stunning transformation: marble hallways lined with prints of old Portugal give way to crisp, high-ceilinged rooms furnished with exacting 18th-century reproductions. Only breakfast is served in the pousada itself, but the cooking hits the mark across the road in the old palace kitchens, now the Restaurante de Cozinha Velha ($$–$$$$; reservations essential), with its imposing open fireplace and a vast oak table. The Portuguese specialties on the ever-changing menu are occasionally tempered by a French touch. ⊠ *Rte. IC19, 2745-191* ☎ *21/435–6158* 🖷 *21/435–6189* ⊕ *www.pousadas.pt* ⊳ *24 rooms, 2 suites* ⚘ *Restaurant, cable TV, bar, meeting rooms* ▤ *AE, DC, MC, V* ⦿| *BP.*

THE SETÚBAL PENINSULA

The Setúbal Peninsula, south of the Rio Tejo, is popular for its Costa da Caparica beaches, which provide the cleanest ocean swimming closest to Lisbon. Other attractions include the major port of Setúbal, some Roman ruins, and the scenic mountain range—the Serra da Arrábida—that separates the port from the peninsula's southernmost beaches and fishing villages.

If you're intent on eating seafood at Cacilhas, spending the day at a beach, or simply touring the town of Setúbal, traveling by public transportation from Lisbon is easiest. If you want to see most of the sights covered in this section, however—and particularly if you want to tour the southern coastal and mountainous region—you should rent a car. Apart from the ferry ride to Cacilhas, connections between the Setúbal Peninsula and Lisbon are via the capital's two bridges. Returning on the impressive suspension bridge, the Ponte 25 de Abril, you're guaranteed terrific views of Lisbon. Avoid crossing during rush hour and on Friday and Sunday evenings, when the traffic can be horrendous. If you're heading directly for Setúbal, take the northern route across the Rio Tejo via the Ponte Vasco da Gama, from which the fast A12 highway cuts south and avoids the bottleneck over the Ponte 25 de Abril.

Cacilhas

⓭ *6 km (4 mi) south of Lisbon.*

Although a town in its own right, Cacilhas appears little more than a suburb of Lisbon, albeit one with the bonus of several reliable seafood restaurants along its main street, Rua do Ginjal. The town is immediately across the Rio Tejo from the capital; at night, and especially on weekends, it's a popular destination. Waiters armed with menus linger outside their doors, ready to pounce on passersby who can't decide where to eat; once inside, you're tempted with the best of the day's catch. The ferries run frequently from Terminal Fluvial, adjacent to Praça do Comércio, and from Cais do Sodré. One-way tickets cost €0.75, and the journey takes about 15 minutes.

The **Cristo Rei**—a huge, white statue of Christ, built in 1959—was modeled on the famous statue of Christ the Redeemer in Rio de Janeiro. The figure stands proudly above Cacilhas, its outstretched arms seemingly embracing the city of Lisbon across the water. Take the elevator to the platform beneath the statue's feet for panoramic city views. If your schedule is tight, though, opt for the vista from Lisbon's Torre Vasco da Gama. Buses from Cacilhas dockside can take you directly to the Cristo Rei statue every 20 to 30 minutes, daily 8 AM–9 PM. If you're driving, cross the Ponte 25 de Abril and follow the signs. ☎ *21/275–1000* ✉ *€4* ⊙ *Daily 9:30–6.*

Where to Eat

$–$$ ✕ **Atira-te ao Rio.** From Cais do Sodré in Lisbon, this Brazilian restaurant is just a boat ride across the Tagus River and a five-minute walk along the riverfront (the eatery's name means "jump into the river"). The many outdoor tables afford a splendid view of Lisbon and a romantic summer evening. On Saturday you can listen to live Brazilian music and fill up with the all-you-can-eat *feijoada* (black bean stew with different kinds of meats served with slightly toasted cassava flour, hot sliced cabbage, and slices of orange). Other dishes are grilled fish, and lasagna de bacalhau (codfish lasagna). The choice cocktail with kick is the *caipirinha* (cachaça—a spirit distilled from sugarcane—and crushed limes with crushed ice and sugar). ⊠ *Cais do Ginjal 69–70* ☎ *21/275–1380* ⊟ *DC, MC, V* ⊙ *Closed Mon.*

Costa da Caparica

★ ⓮ *14 km (8½ mi) southwest of Lisbon; 8 km (5 mi) west of Cacilhas; take the minor N377, a slower, more scenic route than the main IC20 route (off the A2/IP1).*

When Lisbon's inhabitants want to go to the beach, their preferred spot is the Costa da Caparica, a 20-km (12-mi) stretch of sand on the northwestern coast of the Setúbal Peninsula. The coastal strip centers on the

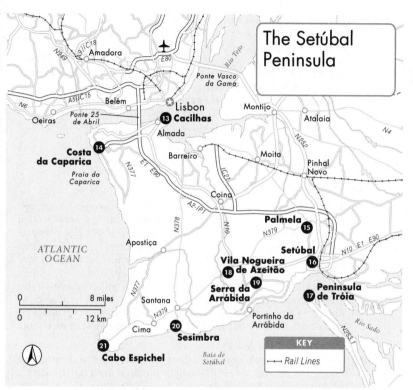

The Setúbal
Peninsula

2

lively resort of Caparica itself, at the northern end of the beach, less than an hour from the capital. Formerly a fishing village, it's now packed in summer with Portuguese tourists who come to enjoy the relatively un-polluted waters, eat grilled sardines, and stroll the seafront promenade. You may be able to avoid the crowds by heading south toward the less accessible dunes and coves at the end of the peninsula. From June through September, a small narrow-gauge train departs from Caparica and travels along an 8-km (5-mi) coastal route, making stops along the way; a one-way ticket to the end of the line costs €2.50. Each beach is different: the areas nearest Caparica are family oriented, whereas the more southerly resorts tend to attract a younger crowd (there are some nudist beaches as well).

Where to Eat

$$–$$$ ✕ **O Capote.** An outdoor terrace, red-tile roof, and rustic wooden ta-bles and chairs beckon passersby to this seafood restaurant. The fresh fish is sold by the kilo (2.2 pounds) and can be prepared either boiled or grilled. The meal *massa no caldo* is unique to the Caparica area: first you are served fish steamed with tomatoes, onions, and potatoes in a copper pot. When you are finished, the pot is taken back to the kitchen, where noodles, parsley, and mint are added to the leftover juice. The pot returns to your table holding a delicious soup. ⊠ *Rua dos Pescadores 40B* ☎ *21/290–1274* 🖃 *AE, DC, MC, V* ⊘ *Closed Oct. and Wed.*

$–$$ ✗ **Borda D' Água.** Either drive to Praia da Morena or catch the small train at Caparica and hop off in front of this Brazilian restaurant—a glassed-in wooden cabana built in the sand dunes. The owner's wife has done a wonderful job decorating with colorful pillows, hammocks, and weathered wooden tables. The menu features *picanha* (Brazilian grilled beef with an outer layer of fat) and feijoada, but they also have a selection of fresh fish to choose from. ⊠ *Praia da Morena* ☎ *21/296–2129* 🖃 *AE, DC, MC, V* ⊘ *Closed Jan.*

Palmela

⑮ *38 km (24 mi) southeast of Lisbon.*

The small town of Palmela lies in the center of a prosperous wine-growing area, and every September the community holds a good-natured Festa das Vindimas (Grape Harvest Festival) that draws inhabitants from their whitewashed houses and into the cobbled streets. The village is dominated by the remains of a 12th-century castle that was captured from the Moors and enlarged by successive kings. In the 15th century the monastery and church of Sant'Iago were built within the castle walls. The structures were damaged in the 1755 earthquake and lay abandoned for many years. After extensive restoration, a pousada was opened in the monastic buildings. From this height, on a clear day, you can see Lisbon.

Where to Stay & Eat

$$–$$$ ✗🏨 **Pousada de Palmela.** On a hill at the eastern end of the Arrábida range, this building was originally a medieval fortress and later a monastery. In 1979 it was converted into a luxury pousada, and the designers made inspired use of the flagstone corridors and old cloister (now a lounge). Most rooms have views of the valley and the sea; bathrooms are well equipped, and beds are comfortable. There's little trace of monastic asceticism in the monks' former refectory, now a dependable restaurant ($$–$$$$) that serves traditional Portuguese food and a good range of wines. ⊠ *Castelo de Palmela, 2950-997* ☎ *21/235–1226* 🖷 *21/233–0440* ⊕ *www.pousadas.pt* ⇗ *28 rooms* ⚏ *Restaurant, cable TV, bar, meeting rooms* 🖃 *AE, DC, MC, V* ⦿ *BP.*

Setúbal

⑯ *10 km (6 mi) south of Palmela, 50 km (31 mi) southeast of Lisbon.*

Many travelers use Setúbal as a spot to spend the night before driving on to the Algarve, since the Castelo de São Filipe has been converted into an exceptional pousada. Even if you decide to go on, you may want to dine here, or just pause to take in the views from the lofty castle. At the mouth of the Rio Sado, Setúbal is the country's third-largest port and one of its oldest cities. A significant industrial town in Roman times, it became one again during Portugal's Age of Discovery and took off during the 19th century. Its center remains an attractive blend of medieval and modern, and the handsome Igreja de Jesus in itself makes the city worth a stop.

2

Better still, spend half a day in the city, strolling cobbled pedestrian streets that open into pretty squares with cafés. The tourist office is built atop Roman ruins discovered during (and saved from) a construction project. Inside, you'll be standing above and peering down through the glass floor into a 5th-century fish-processing room. Near the port, an agreeable clutter of boats and warehouses is fronted by gardens, where you can stock up for a picnic at a huge indoor fish-and-produce market (open Tuesday–Sunday 7–2).

★ The 15th-century **Igreja de Jesus** (Church of Jesus), perhaps Portugal's earliest example of Manueline architecture, was built with local marble and later tiled with simple but affecting 17th-century azulejos. The architect was Diogo de Boitaca, whose work here predates his contribution to Lisbon's Mosteiro dos Jerónimos (Jerónimos Monastery). Six extraordinary twisted pillars support the vault; climb the narrow stairs to the balcony for a closer look. These details would soon become the very hallmark of Manueline style. Outside, you can still admire the original, although badly worn, main doorway and deplore the addition of a concrete expanse that makes the church square look like a roller-skating rink.

The church's original monastic buildings and Gothic cloister—on Rua Balneário Paula Borba—house the **Museu de Setúba**, a museum with a fascinating collection of 15th- and 16th-century Portuguese paintings, several by the so-called Master of Setúbal. Other attractions include azulejos, local archaeological finds, and a coin collection. ⊠ *Praça Miguel Bombarda* ☎ *265/537890* 🎟 *€1 suggested donation to church* ⊙ *Tues.–Sun. 9–noon and 2–5.*

Where to Stay & Eat

$–$$$ ✕ **Rio Azul.** This *marisqueira* (seafood restaurant) is hidden on a side street off Avenida Luisa Todi, on the way to the castle and west of the harbor. Although it's signposted from the main road, it's a little tricky to find. As you'd expect, the dishes to go for are the fresh fish grilled to perfection and the arroz de marisco. ⊠ *Rua Placido Stichini 1* ☎ *265/ 522828* ⊟ *AE, DC, MC, V* ⊙ *Closed Wed.*

★ $$–$$$ ✕🏠 **Pousada de São Filipe.** From the ramparts of this 16th-century castle-cum-pousada, the views of the town and the Rio Sado are fantastic. The approach to the main entrance takes you up a tunneled flight of stairs and past an 18th-century chapel decorated with azulejos depicting the life of São Filipe. The traditional guest rooms have carved headboards, tile floors, rugs, and white walls. The interior is also awash with azulejo tiling, especially in the bar. The restaurant ($$–$$$$) is strong on Portuguese cuisine, with such dishes as fish broth, stewed broad beans with cuttlefish, roast veal with Moscatel wine, and orange tart. ⊠ *Castelo de São Filipe, Estrada de São Filipe, 2900-300* ☎ *265/550070* 🖶 *265/ 532538* ⊕ *www.pousadas.pt* ✒ *16 rooms* ᘓ *Restaurant, cable TV, bar, meeting rooms* ⊟ *AE, DC, MC, V* ⎜◎⎜ *BP.*

$ 🏠 **Quinta do Patricio.** Open fireplaces and brightly colored rugs and paintings fill this homey manor house. From the large garden you'll get some nice views of the town. There are also two separate apartments for rent on the grounds, one with a kitchen, the other romantically converted from a former windmill. Breakfast is served, other meals are available on request, and reservations made well in advance are essential. Note that the wedding parties staged here most weekends can make things noisy. ⊠ *Estrada de São Filipe, 2900-300* 🖷🖷 *265/233817* ⊕ *www. hafesta.com* ↪ *3 rooms, 2 with bath; 2 apartments* ♿ *Pool, bar* ⊟ *No credit cards* ⏀ *BP.*

Peninsula de Tróia

⑰ *20 mins from Setúbal by boat.*

Across the estuary from Setúbal is the Peninsula de Tróia, a long spit of land blessed with fine beaches and clean water. The peninsula has been much developed, and the large Tróia Tourist Complex here includes the famous Tróia Golf Course. The area has managed to retain a little of its history, though: the peninsula is the site of the Roman town of Cetobriga, destroyed by a tidal wave in the 5th century. You can visit its scant ruins, opposite the marina. Car and passenger ferries to the peninsula run every 30 to 60 minutes (24 hours a day) from Setúbal's port.

Outdoor Activities

The **Tróia Golf Course,** an 18-hole championship course designed by Robert Trent Jones Sr., is considered by many to be Portugal's most difficult. It's on the coast, with small, narrow, well-protected greens and wide fairways. The main challenge is reaching the greens. The course is part of the **Complexo Turístico de Tróia** (⊠ Carvalhal, Grândola 🕾 265/494112), which has a driving range, putting greens, bunker and chipping areas, tennis courts, a restaurant, and a bar. Green fees are €72.50 weekends and €60.50 weekdays.

Vila Nogueira de Azeitão

⑱ *14 km (8½ mi) west of Setúbal.*

The region around the small town of Vila Nogueira de Azeitão, on the western side of the Serra da Arrábida, retains a disproportionately large number of fine manor houses and palaces. In earlier times, many of the country's noblemen maintained country estates here, deep in the heart of a wealthy wine-making region. Wines made here by the José Maria da Fonseca Company are some of the most popular in the country (and one of Portugal's major exports); the best known is the dessert wine called Moscatel de Setúbal.

For a close look at the wine business, seek out the headquarters of the **José Maria da Fonseca Company,** which stands on the main road

> ### TO MARKET
>
> Vila Nogueira de Azeitão's agricultural traditions are trumpeted on the first Sunday of every month, when a **country market** is held in the center of town. Apart from the locally produced wine, you can buy *queijo fresco* (sheep's milk)—a good choice for a picnic lunch—as well as excellent fresh bread from one of the market's bakery stalls.

2

through town. The intriguing tours (which must be booked in advanced) allow you to see all stages of production, and take around 20 to 40 minutes, depending on the size of the group. ⊠ *Rua José Augusto Coelho 11* ☎ *21/219–8940* ⊕ *www.jmf.pt* 🖼 *Free* ⊙ *Daily tours 10–noon and 2:15–4.*

Although it's not open to the public, the 16th-century Palácio de Tavora (Tavora Palace), on the central **Praça da República,** has an interesting history. In the 18th century, the Marquês de Pombal accused the Duke of Aveiro, who owned the palace, of collaborating in the assassination plot against the king, Dom José. Subsequently the duke was executed by the marquês, and the Tavora coat of arms was erased from the Sala das Armas in Sintra's National Palace.

The pride and joy of the **Quinta da Bacalhoa,** a late-16th-century L-shaped mansion, is its box-hedged garden and striking azulejo-lined paths. You can't tour the villa, which is a private house, but the garden is open to the public and contains a pavilion with three pyramidal towers—the so-called Casa do Fresco, which houses the country's oldest azulejo panel. Dating from 1565, it depicts the story of Susannah and the Elders. Scattered elsewhere are Moorish-influenced panels, fragrant groves of fruit trees, and enough restful spots to while away an afternoon. ⊠ *4 km (2½ mi) east of Vila Nogueira de Azeitão on N1* ☎ *21/218–0011* 🖼 *€1* ⊙ *Mon.–Sat. 1–5.*

Serra da Arrábida

🔞 *West of Setúbal, with access along the main N10 or minor N379; Portinho da Arrábida is 14 km (8½ mi) southwest of Setúbal.*

Occupying the entire southern coast of the Setúbal Peninsula is the Parque Natural da Arrábida, dominated by the Serra da Arrábida, a 5,000-foot-high mountain range whose wild crags fall steeply to the sea. There's profuse plant life at these heights, particularly in spring, when the rocks are carpeted with wildflowers. The park is distinguished by a rich geological heritage and numerous species of mammals, birds, butterflies, and other insects.

The main road through the park is the N10, which you can leave at Vila Nogueira de Azeitão to travel south toward the small fishing village of **Portinho da Arrábida,** at the foot of the mountain range. The village is a popular destination for Lisboetas, who appreciate the good local beaches. In summer, when the number of visitors makes parking nearly impossible, leave your car above the village and make the steep walk down to the water, where you'll find several modest seafood restaurants that overlook the port.

From Portinho da Arrábida, the lower, coastal road hugs the shore nearly all the way to Setúbal; the upper road leads to the ramshackle, white-walled **Convento de Arrábida,** an atmospheric 16th-century monastery built into the hills of the Serra da Arrábida. The views from here are glorious, but you'll have to contact the tourist office in Setúbal in advance to arrange a visit to the monastery.

Sesimbra

20 *40 km (25 mi) south of Lisbon, 30 km (18 mi) southwest of Setúbal.*

Sesimbra, a lively fishing village surrounded by mountains and isolated bays and coves, owes its popularity to its proximity to the capital. And, despite high-rise apartments that now mar the approaches to the town, its few surviving narrow, central streets reflect a traditional past. Moreover, the long beach is lovely, if a little crowded in summer, and perfectly fine for swimming. The waterfront is guarded by a 17th-century fortress and overlooked by outdoor restaurants serving fresh-fish meals. A short walk along the coast to the west takes you to the main port, littered with nets, anchors, and coils of rope and packed with fishing boats—which unload their catches at entertaining auctions. You can also take a 40-minute walk to the hilltop remains of a Moorish castle northwest of town.

Where to Stay & Eat

$–$$ ✕ **Café Filipe.** Set in a line of sidewalk restaurants overlooking the waterfront, the Filipe is always busy with diners digging into the terrific grilled fish—cooked outside on a charcoal grill—or arroz de marisco. There's no nicer spot for lunch, but you may have to wait in line for a table. It's worth it. ⊠ *Av. 25 de Abril* ☎ *No phone* ▤ *MC, V.*

$–$$$ ▦ **Sana Park Sesimbra.** This modern hotel is right across from the beach. Gold curtains and bedspreads in the white rooms contrast well with the deep blue of the sea outside the windows. You can breakfast at the little round table and chairs on your room's private terrace. On the sixth floor, yellow-and-white deck chairs around the wedge-shape heated pool are a nice place to take in the sun while viewing the sea. ⊠ *Av. 25 de Abril, 2970-634* ☎ *212/289000* ⊟ *212/289001* ⊕ *www.sanahotels. com* ⟿ *97 rooms, 3 suites* ⋄ *Restaurant, cable TV, indoor-outdoor pool, gym, hot tub, sauna, steam room, bar* ▤ *AE, DC, MC, V.*

¢–$ ▦ **Náutico Residencial.** A seven-minute walk from the beach in the center of town, this small inn is a good budget choice. The blue-and-white patterned curtains and bedcovers jazz up the otherwise very plain white walls and unornamented wooden furniture. For a little extra color, draw the curtains to reveal the palm trees in the garden below. Try to get one of the four rooms that have air-conditioning, although you can always just open a window and get a sea breeze. ⊠ *Av. dos Combatentes 19, 2970-628* ☎ *21/223–3233* ⊕ *www.residencialnautico.com* ⟿ *21 rooms* ⋄ *Cable TV, bar; no a/c in some rooms* ▤ *AE, DC, MC, V* ⫿◎⫿ *BP.*

Outdoor Activities

Sesimbra, a deep-sea fishing center, is renowned for the huge swordfish that are landed in the area. The **Clube Naval de Sesimbra** (⊠ Porto de Abrigo ☎ 21/223–3451) offers coastal fishing trips most Saturdays.

Cabo Espichel

21 *12 km (7 mi) west of Sesimbra.*

Espichel Cape, a salt-encrusted headland with a number of 18th-century pilgrim rest houses and a forsaken church, is the southwestern point of the Setúbal Peninsula. It's a rugged and lonely place, where the cliffs rise hundreds of feet out of the stormy Atlantic. To the north, unsullied beaches extend as far as Caparica, with only local roads and footpaths connecting them. There are six buses a day here from Sesimbra.

LISBON'S ENVIRONS ESSENTIALS

Transportation

BY BOAT & FERRY

LisboFerries cross the river to Cacilhas (7 AM–9 PM) from Fluvial terminal, adjacent to Praça do Comércio. One-way tickets cost €0.70, and the journey takes about 15 minutes. For information on car ferries from Cais do Sodré, check with the Lisbon tourist office. From Setúbal there's 24-hour ferry service for cars (€4.25) and foot passengers (€1) across to the Tróia Peninsula; the journey takes about 20 minutes. Departures are every 30–60 minutes.

🖪 **LisboFerries** ☎ 21/322-4000 ⊕ www.transtejo.pt.

BY BUS

Although the best way to reach Sintra and most of the towns on the Estoril Coast is by train from Lisbon, there are some useful bus connections between towns. Tickets are cheap (less than €3.50 for most journeys), and departures are generally every hour (less frequent on weekends); local tourist offices have timetables. Try to arrive 15 minutes before your bus departs.

At Cascais, the bus terminal outside the train station has regular summer service to Guincho (15 minutes) and Sintra (one hour). From the terminal outside the Sintra train station, there are half-hourly departures in summer to the resorts of Praia das Maçãs and Azenhas do Mar (30 minutes) in the west, and north to Mafra in Estremadura (one hour). There's also regular year-round service from Sintra to Cascais and Estoril (one hour). The most useful Sintra service, however, is the circular Stagecoach/Scotturb Bus 434 (daily, every 20–30 minutes, 10:20–5:45; €3.50 ticket valid all day), which connects Sintra station, the town center (the stop is outside the tourist office), Castelo dos Mouros, and the Pena Palace.

Buses to Caparica (45 minutes) depart from Praça de Espanha (Metro: Palhavã) in Lisbon, traveling over the Ponte 25 de Abril. Regular buses to Caparica also leave from the quayside bus terminal at Cacilhas, the suburb immediately across the Rio Tejo from Lisbon, which you can reach by ferry from the Fluvial terminal, adjacent to Praça do Comércio. Bus departures on both routes are as frequent as every 15 minutes in summer, and services run from 7 AM until well after midnight, but can be very crowded. There's also a special beach bus (No. 75) that runs to Caparica every 15–30 minutes from the beginning of June to the beginning of September; pick it up in Lisbon at Campo Grande, Saldanha, or Marquês de Pombal metro stations, or outside the Amoreiras shopping center.

Express buses to Setúbal (45 minutes) leave every hour from Lisbon's Praça de Espanha (Metro: Palhavã); a local service also calls at Vila Nogueira de Azeitão (45 minutes) before traveling on to Setúbal (one hour). At Setúbal bus station you can connect with local services north to Palmela (20 minutes) and southwest to Sesimbra (30 minutes). Six buses daily run a 30-minute trip from Sesimbra bus station to the southwestern Cabo Espichel.

🚌 **Cacilhas bus terminal** ⊠ Largo Alfredo Diniz 🕾 No phone. **Cascais bus terminal** 🕾 21/483-6357. **Palmela bus station** ⊠ Largo do Chafariz D. Maria I 🕾 21/235-0078. **Sesimbra bus station** ⊠ Av. da Liberdade 🕾 21/223-3071. **Setúbal bus station** ⊠ Av. 5 de Outubro 44 🕾 265/525051.

BY CAR

Fast highways connect Lisbon with Estoril (A5/IC15) and Setúbal (A2/IP1), and the quality of other roads in the region is generally good. Take care on hilly and coastal roads, though, and if possible, avoid driving out of Lisbon at the start of a weekend or public holiday or back in at the end. Both Rio Tejo bridges—especially the Ponte 25 de Abril but also the dramatic Ponte Vasco da Gama—can be very slow. Parking can be problematic, too, especially in summer along the Estoril Coast. When you do park, *never* leave anything visible in the car, and it's wise to clear out the trunk as well.

Lisbon is the initial point of arrival for almost all the destinations covered here; from the city, it's easy to take public transportation or drive to all the surrounding towns. Driving south from Peniche–Óbidos, you can take the N8/IC1, rather than the main highway, if you prefer to see Sintra before Lisbon. If you're traveling north from the Algarve, you reach the city of Setúbal and its peninsula before arriving in Lisbon.

CAR RENTAL There are better choices for car rentals in Lisbon, although the tourist offices in Cascais, Estoril, Sintra, and Setúbal can advise you of the local possibilities.

🚗 **Major Agencies** **Avis** ⊠ Tamariz Esplanade, Estoril 🕾 800/201002 ⊠ Av. Luisa Todi 96, Setúbal 🕾 265/538710. **Europcar** ⊠ Estrada Marginal, Centro Comércial Cisne, Bloco B, Lojas 4 and 5, Cascais 🕾 21/486-4438. **Hertz** ⊠ Av. Luisa Todi 277, Setúbal 🕾 265/527653.

BY TAXI

If you don't have your own car, it may pay—at least in time and convenience—to take a taxi to the towns around Lisbon. Cabs are relatively inexpensive, and you can usually agree on a fixed price that will include the round-trip to an attraction (the driver will wait for you to complete your tour). Tourist offices can give you an idea of what fares are reasonable for local trips, although Sintra should cost roughly €30, Queluz should be €20, and Estoril €35 one way.

🚕 **Central taxi lines** 🕾 21/466-0101 or 21/465-9500.

BY TRAIN

Electric commuter trains travel the entire Estoril Coast, with departures every 15–30 minutes from the waterfront Cais do Sodré station in Lisbon, west of the Praça do Comércio. The scenic trip to Estoril takes about

30 minutes, and four more stops along the seashore bring you to Cascais, at the end of the line. A one-way ticket to either costs €1.30; service operates daily 5:30 AM–2:30 AM. Trains from Lisbon's Rossío station, between Praça dos Restauradores and the Rossío, run every 15 minutes to Queluz (a 20-minute trip) and on to Sintra (40 minutes total). The service operates 6 AM–2:40 AM, and one-way tickets cost €1.10 to Queluz, €1.30 to Sintra.

Fertagus trains from Lisbon's Sete Rios and Entre Campos stations cross the Rio Tejo via the Ponte 25 de Abril. Passengers on the double-decker railcars benefit from fine views, air-conditioning, and background music during the seven-minute crossing. Taxis at stations across the river can take you on to Cacilhas, Setúbal, and other towns on the Setúbal Peninsula. Trains run between 5:30 AM and 2 AM. From June through September a narrow-gauge railway runs for 8 km (5 mi) along the Costa da Caparica from the town of Caparica, on the Setúbal Peninsula. It makes 20 stops at beaches along the way, and a one-way ticket to the end of the line costs €2.50.

🚈 **Fertagus** ☎ 21/294-9700. **Rail information line** ☎ 808/208208 ⊕ www.cp.pt.

Contacts & Resources

EMERGENCIES

In all the towns, a notice on the door of every *farmácia* (drugstore) indicates the name and address of the nearest all-night pharmacy.

🚈 **General emergencies** ☎ 112. **Police** ☎ 21/486-1127 in Cascais, 21/468-4207 in Estoril, 265/234823 in Setúbal, 21/923-0761 in Sintra. **Cascais hospital** ⊠ Av. Ultramar and Rua Padre J. M. Loureiro ☎ 21/482-7700. **Setúbal hospital** ⊠ Rua Camilo Castelo Branco ☎ 265/549000. **Sintra Health Center** ⊠ Rua Visconde de Monserrate 2 ☎ 21/910-6680.

MAIL

🚈 **Post Offices Cascais** ⊠ Rua Manuel J. Avelar ☎ 21/484-9380. **Setúbal** ⊠ Av. 22 de Dezembro ☎ 265/930140. **Sintra** ⊠ Praça da República 26 ☎ 21/910-6790.

TOUR OPTIONS

ORIENTATION TOURS

Most travel agents and large hotels in Lisbon or its environs can reserve you a place on a guided tour. Cityrama has half-day trips to Queluz, Sintra, and Estoril and a tour of the area's royal palaces (each €51); nine-hour tours of Sintra and Cascais (€76 including lunch); and even an evening visit to Estoril's famous casino (€71.50 including dinner). Gray Line Tours has day trips into Lisbon and the Arrábida Mountain range and to local crafts centers for around €71.

For guided tours of the Sintra area, ask at the tourist information center, which has current schedules and can sell tickets. Half-day tours typically encompass visits to all the principal sights and a wine tasting in Colares.

🚈 **Cityrama** ⊠ Av. Praia da Vitória 12-B, Saldanha, Lisbon ☎ 21/352-2594 ⊕ www.cityrama.pt. **Gray Line Tours** ⊠ Av. Praia da Vitória 12-B, Saldanha, Lisbon ☎ 21/352-2594 ⊕ www.cityrama.pt.

VISITOR INFORMATION

ICEP, the Portuguese national tourist office with its main Lisbon office in the Palácio Foz, has information on the city's environs. Local tourist offices are usually open June–September, daily 9–1 and 2–6, sometimes later in the tourist-resort areas. Hours are greatly reduced after peak season, and most offices are closed Sunday.

🚩 National Tourist Information **ICEP (Portugal national tourist office)** ⊠ Palácio Foz, Praça dos Restauradores, Baixa, Lisbon ☎ 21/346-3314 ⊕ www.portugalinsite.pt. 🚩 Regional Tourist Information **Cabo da Roca** ⊠ Azóia ☎ 21/928-0081. **Caparica** ⊠ Av. da República 18 ☎ 21/294-7000 ⊕ www.m-almada.pt. **Cascais** ⊠ Rua Visconde da Luz 14 ☎ 21/486-9277 ⊕ www.cm-cascais.pt. **Estoril** ⊠ Arcadas do Parque ☎ 21/467-8210. **Palmela** ⊠ Castelo de Palmela ☎ 21/235-0089. **Queluz** ⊠ Palácio Nacional de Queluz ☎ 21/434-2260. **Sesimbra** ⊠ Largo da Marinha 26, off Av. dos Naufragios ☎ 21/228-8540 ⊕ www.mun-sesimbra.pt. **Setúbal** ⊠ Travessa Frei Gaspar 10 ☎ 265/539120 ⊕ www.costa-azul.rts.pt. **Sintra** ⊠ Praça da República 23 ☎ 21/923-1157 or 21/924-1700 ⊕ www.cm-sintra.pt ⊠ Sintra train station ☎ 21/924-1623.

Estremadura & the Ribatejo

3

WORD OF MOUTH

"Use Óbidos as your base from which to see Al-cobaça and Batalha. You can get a taste of Óbidos in the evening and easily see both Batalha and Alcobaca in the same day without being overloaded."

—xxxx

Updated by
Mary McLean

WATER SHAPES THE CHARACTER OF THESE TWO PROVINCES. Estremadura stretches itself out along the coast, extending north from Lisbon to include the onetime royal residence of Leiria, 119 km (74 mi) from the capital. Closely tied to the sea, the narrow province is known for its fine beaches, coastal pine forests, and picturesque fishing villages. Some of these have evolved, for better or worse, into popular resorts. Fruits and vegetables grow in fertile coastal valleys, and livestock contentedly graze in rich pastures, but Estremadura hasn't always been so peaceful. During the Wars of Reconquest, which raged from the 8th through the 13th century, it was the scene of a series of bloody encounters between Christians and Moors. The province's name means "farthest from the Douro River," an indication of how far south of the Douro River the Christians had advanced against the Moors. In the aftermath of the wars, Portuguese sovereignty was secured with the defeat of the Spanish at Aljubarrota in 1385 and the turning back of Napoléon's forces in 1810 at Torres Vedras. The bloodshed left behind masterpieces of religious architecture—such as those at Alcobaça and Batalha—that commemorate Portuguese triumphs.

The Ribatejo region developed along both sides of the Rio Tejo (Tagus River), and it is this waterway, born in the mountains of Spain, that has shaped and sustained the province. In the north, inhabitants tend groves of olive and fig trees in a peaceful landscape that has changed little since Roman times.

Over the centuries Romans, Visigoths, Moors, and Christians built and rebuilt various castles and fortifications to protect the strategic Tejo. You'll see fine examples along the river at Belver, Abrantes, and Almourol. Tomar, spanning the banks of the Rio Nabão (a tributary of the Tejo), is dominated by the hilltop Convento de Cristo (Convent of Christ), built in the 12th century by the Knights Templar. In the brush-covered hills at the province's western edge lies Fátima, one of Christendom's most important pilgrimage sites. As it flows south approaching Lisbon, the Tejo expands, often overflowing its banks during the winter rains, and the landscape changes to one of rich meadows and pastures and broad, alluvial plains, where grains grow in abundance.

The Ribatejans are said to be more reserved than their fellow Portuguese—that is, until they step into the arena to test their mettle against a ton or so of charging bull. This is bullfighting country, the heartland of one of Portugal's richest and most colorful traditions. On the vast plains along the east bank of the Tejo, you'll encounter men on horseback carrying long wooden prods and often wearing the traditional waistcoats and stocking caps of their trade. These are *campinos,* the Portuguese "cowboys," who tend the herds of bulls and horses bred and trained for arenas throughout the country.

Exploring Estremadura & the Ribatejo

The sea is never far from sight in coast-hugging Estremadura, though seafaring days are but a memory in such places as Óbidos, where the harbor that once lapped against the village walls has long since silted

GREAT ITINERARIES

Three days will give you a sense of the region, five days will allow you to include a visit to the shrine at Fátima and the Convent of Christ, and a full week will give you enough time to cover the major attractions as well as explore the countryside. With additional days you can easily extend your itinerary to include Évora and the Alentejo or head north to Coimbra and the Beiras. It's best to explore these regions by car, unless you have a great deal of time and patience: trains don't serve many of the most interesting towns, and bus travel is slow.

Numbers in the text correspond to numbers in the margin and on the Estremadura & the Ribatejo map.

IF YOU HAVE 3 DAYS

Start with a visit to the imposing monastery and palace at **Mafra** ❶, then head for the coast, with a stop at the resort and fishing village of **Ericeira** ❷. Continue north along the shore to **Peniche** ❹, with its imposing fortress. Head inland to spend the night in the enchanting walled city of 🖼 **Óbidos** ❻. The next morning continue north, stopping at ceramics shops in **Caldas da Rainha** ❼. En route to 🖼 **Nazaré** ❽, tour the church and cloister at **Alcobaça** ❾. On your third day head inland to the soaring, multispired monastery church in **Batalha** ❿. Return to Lisbon along N1/IC2 with a stop in **Vila Franca de Xira** ⓬ (after

joining the A1 toll road at Aveiras da Cima) to visit the bullfighting museum. Alternatively, you could take N356 east from Batalha and then A1 down to Vila Franca from the Fátima junction, which will take slightly longer, but is handy if you want to visit Fátima en route.

IF YOU HAVE 5 DAYS

Follow the three-day itinerary to **Batalha** ❿, and then continue north to **Leiria** ⓫ and its hilltop castle. Take N113 east to the A1 and drive down to 🖼 **Fátima** ⓱, one of Christendom's most renowned destinations. The next morning, continue east on N113 to **Tomar** ⓲, an attractive town dominated by its hilltop convent. Later in the day, follow N110 south and then take N358-2, a scenic road that follows the Rio Zêzere, to its union with the Rio Tejo. Just west of their confluence, on an island in the Tejo, is the **Castelo de Almourol** ⓳, one of Portugal's finest. From here, follow N118 southwest along the Tejo, stopping in **Alpiarça** ⓯ to visit the Casa dos Patudos, a large country house containing the art collection of its former owner, and in **Almeirim** ⓰ to see the winery at the Quinta da Alorna. Spend the night in 🖼 **Santarém** ⓮, an important farming and livestock center with many fine sights. The next day return to Lisbon with a drive along the Tejo on N118 through the region of marshy plains known as the Lezíria.

up. Nazaré, however, still makes its living from the ocean—from fishing as well as from sunseekers. The same is true of the lively town of Ericeira, where sunbathers and surfers alike can indulge in their favorite pastimes. Coastal valleys once witnessed many a bloody fight between rival groups, including the Moors. These battles nonetheless left at least

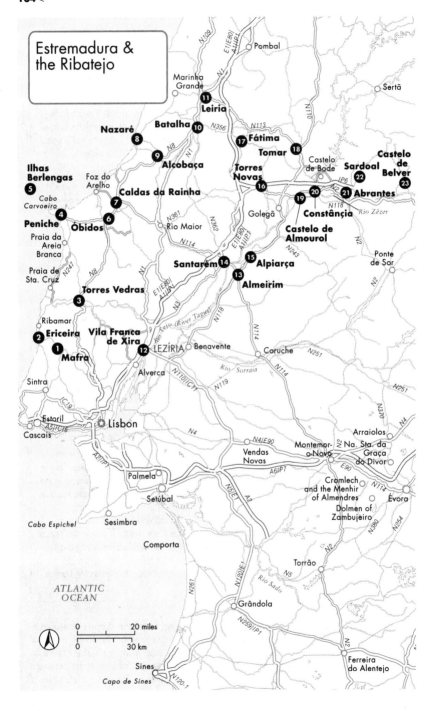

Estremadura & the Ribatejo

one positive legacy—extraordinary monasteries, such as the one at Batalha, built to celebrate Portuguese victories.

The Rio Tejo flows through the Ribatejo, where vast plains spread out from the riverbanks. Although fortifications line the river, the most famous monument is Fátima, where the Virgin Mary allegedly appeared to three young shepherds; millions of pilgrims still flock here every year to pay homage. In Tomar, the impressive Convento do Cristo, an amalgam of 12th- to 16th-century styles that was once the headquarters of the Knights Templar, is a reminder of the religious struggles that have defined the region.

Restaurants & Cuisine

Between mid-June and mid-September reservations are advised at upscale restaurants. Most moderate or inexpensive establishments, however, don't accept reservations. They also have informal dining rooms, where sharing a table with other diners is common. Dress is casual at all but the most luxurious places.

In Estremadura restaurants, the emphasis is on fish, including the ubiquitous *bacalhau* (dried salt cod fish) and *caldeirada* (a hearty fish stew). The seaside resorts of Ericeira, Nazaré, and Peniche are famous for lobster. In Santarém and other spots along the Rio Tejo, an *açorda* (bread soup) made with *savel*, a river fish also known as shad, is popular, as are *enguias* (eels) prepared in a variety of ways. Pork is a key component in Ribatejo dishes, and roast lamb and kid are widely enjoyed. Perhaps the result of a sweets-making tradition developed by nuns in the region's once-numerous convents, dessert menus abound with colorful-sounding—although often cloyingly sweet and eggy—dishes such as *queijinhos do céu* (little cheeses from heaven). The straw-color white wines from the Ribatejo district of Bucelas are among the country's finest.

About the Hotels

Estremadura has plenty of good-quality lodgings, especially along the coast. In summer, you'll need reservations. Most establishments offer substantial off-season discounts. *Estalagem* is the term for inn. The best accommodations in the Ribatejo are the government-run inns called *pousadas*. The pousadas are small, some with as few as six rooms, so reserving well in advance is essential. There are also a number of high-quality, government-approved private guesthouses. Look for signs reading TURISMO RURAL or TURISMO DE HABITAÇÃO.

WHAT IT COSTS In Euros				
$$$$	**$$$**	**$$**	**$**	**¢**
RESTAURANTS over €21	€16–€21	€11–€15	€7–€10	under €7
HOTELS over €275	€176–€275	€101–€175	€60–€100	under €60

Restaurant prices are per person for a main course at dinner. Hotel prices are for a standard double room, including tax, in high season (off-season rates may be lower).

When to Go

To avoid the busloads of visitors who inundate major monuments and attractions during July and August, visit the popular ones such as Óbidos and Mafra in the early morning. This also helps to beat the oppressive summer heat, particularly inland. The best time of year for touring is in early spring and from mid-September until late October. The climate during this period is pleasant, and attractions and restaurants aren't crowded. If throngs of people don't bother you, time your visit to Fátima to coincide with May 13, when between 500,000 and 1 million pilgrims overwhelm this otherwise sleepy country town. Less-spectacular pilgrimages take place year-round.

ESTREMADURA

The narrow province surrounding Lisbon and extending north along the coast for approximately 160 km (100 mi) is known as Estremadura, referring to the extreme southern border of the land the Portuguese reconquered from the Moors. This is primarily a rural region characterized by coastal fishing villages and small farming communities that produce mostly fruit and olives. A tour through the region includes visits to towns with some of Portugal's most outstanding architectural treasures, including Mafra, Alcobaça, Óbidos, Tomar, and Batalha.

Mafra

❶ *28 km (17 mi) northwest of Lisbon.*

The town of Mafra is one of the oldest in Portugal, with evidence of prehistoric settlements and remains of Roman and later Moorish occupation. Over the centuries the crown, church, and nobility have contested its ownership. In the 17th, 18th, and 19th centuries it was a favorite residence for nobility. The monastery dominates the town. Gold and riches brought from Brazil enabled its construction, which rivals the splendors of Versailles. The Mafra school of sculpture used marble from the surrounding countryside to produce much of the 18th-century sculpture seen here today. Mafra is also well known for its pottery: off-white with pale blue designs.

In 1711, after nearly three years of a childless union with his Hapsburg queen, Mariana, a despairing King João V vowed that should the queen bear him an heir, he would build a monastery dedicated to St. Anthony. In December of that same year, a girl—later to become queen of Spain—was born; João's eventual heir, José I, was born three years later. True ★ to his word, King João V built the enormous **Mosteiro Palácio Nacional de Mafra** (Monastery and Royal Palace), which looms above the small farming community of Mafra. The original project—entrusted to the Italian-trained German architect Friedrich Ludwig—was to be a modest facility that could house 13 friars. What emerged in 1750 after 18 years of construction was a rectangular complex containing a monastery large enough for hundreds of monks as well as an imposing basilica and a grandiose palace that has been compared to El Escorial outside Madrid, Spain. The numbers involved in the construction are mind-boggling: at times 50,000 workers toiled. There are 4,500 doors and windows, 300 cells, 880 halls and rooms, and 154 stairways. Perimeter walls that total some 19 km (12 mi) surround the park.

The one-hour guided tours are enlightening; those conducted by English-speaking docents take place at 11 AM and 2:30 PM. The highlight is the magnificent baroque library: the barrel-vaulted, two-tiered hall holds some 40,000 volumes of mostly 16th-, 17th-, and 18th-century works and a number of ancient maps. The basilica contains 11 chapels and was patterned after St. Peter's in the Vatican. The balcony of the connecting corridor overlooks the high altar and was a favorite meeting place for Dom João and Mariana, who had separate bedrooms. When you're in the gilded throne room, notice the life-size renditions of the seven virtues, as well as the impressive figure of Hercules, by Domingos Sequeira. On display in the games room is an early version of a pinball machine. Note the hard-planked beds in the monastery infirmary; the monks used no mattresses. You'll be fortunate if you arrive on a Sunday afternoon between 4 and 5, when the sonorous tones of the 92-bell carillon ring out. ☒ *Terreiro de D. João V* ☎ *261/817550* ☒ *€4, including tour* ☉ *Mon. and Wed.–Sun. 10–5:30 (last tour at 4:30).*

NEED A BREAK?

The **Pastelaria Fradinho** (☎ 261/815738), just across from the monastery, is a welcome respite from the rigors of sightseeing. Light, cheerful, and adorned with tiles, it specializes in little homemade, friar-shaped egg-and-almond pastries called, predictably, *fradinhos* (little friars).

The royal game reserve, the **Tapada Nacional de Mafra,** is about 2 km (1 mi) from the Mosteiro Palácio Nacional de Mafra, but 70% of the reserve burned in a fire in 2002. The huge wall-enclosed area was once the private hunting ground of João V and is stocked with deer and other local fauna. It is open to visitors on weekends and national holidays. You must call first to arrange a guided tour. If you want to visit on foot, you must arrive between 9:30 and 10 AM or 2 and 2:30 PM. The same hours apply if you want to rent a bike. ☎ *261/814240* ⊕ *www. tapadademafra.pt* ☒ *Grounds €4.50 on foot, €5.50 on walking tour; bicycle rental €20* ☉ *Weekends and holidays.*

Where to Stay & Eat

$ ✕ **Toca da Raposa.** A must-try of Portuguese cuisine, *cozido à portuguesa* (a boiled dinner with an assortment of meats, sausages, and vegetables), is served on Thursday and Sunday at this restaurant on a side street in front of the monastery. On other days, try their specialty, bacalhau *à toca* (fried codfish with bacon). ☒ *Rua 1° de Dezembro 6* ☎ *261/815122* ☐ *AE, DC, MC, V* ☉ *No dinner Sun. and Mon.*

$ ▥ **Hotel Castelão.** A convenient location in the center of Mafra and budgets rates are the draws. The large, modern hotel also has a traditional wine cellar and a restaurant that serves regional fare. ☒ *Av. 25 de Abril, 2640-456* ☎ *261/816050* ☐ *261/816059* ⇌ *19 rooms* ♿ *Restaurant, minibars, cable TV, bar, recreation room; no a/c in some rooms* ☐ *AE, DC, MC, V* ⏀ *BP, FAP.*

Ericeira

❷ *11 km (7 mi) northwest of Mafra.*

Ericeira, an old fishing town tucked into the rocky coast, is a popular seaside resort. Its core fans out from the sheer cliff, beneath which boats are hauled up onto a small, sheltered beach. The growth of summer tourism has caused a proliferation of bars, pubs, discos, pizzerias, and the like in the increasingly gentrified but still-attractive town center. But along the waterfront are a number of traditional seafood restaurants that are popular with both locals and visitors. Either end of the town has good sand for sunbathing, but the south end is preferred by surfers.

Where to Stay & Eat

$$–$$$$ ✕**Viveiros do Atlântico.** Live seafood crawling around in a vivarium shaped like a blue-and-white fisherman's boat at the entrance gives you an idea of what to find on the menu. Pick out the shellfish of your choice to be prepared especially for you, such as *sapateira recheiada* (stuffed crab) brought to the table in its shell. Try the *cataplanas* (mixed seafood served in a copper steamer). The restaurant has fantastic views—some stretch all the way to Peninha de Sintra—and there are only a few places from which you can't see the ocean. ✉ *Strada Nacional 247, Ribamar* ☎ *261/860300* ▤ *AE, DC, MC, V.*

$–$$$ ✕ **O Barco.** This quiet family-run restaurant resides on the harbor at the bottom of the town. Except for its big glass window with a view of the sea, the setting and decor are very simple, but people come for its excellent food. Their specialty is *tamboril na canoa com gambas* (monkfish with tomato and shrimp served in an earthenware pot). ✉ *Capitão João Lopes* ☎ *261/862759* ▤ *AE, DC, MC, V* ☉ *Closed Thurs.*

$–$$ ✕ **Mar à Vista.** This revived Portuguese fisherman's tavern has a genuine feel—fishing nets and baskets hang from walls, and the loud service adds to its character. Seafood is the only option, and most diners come for big *mariscadas* (seafood stews). The heaps of empty shells piled on plates are testimony to the feasts that took place. You have to go elsewhere for coffee afterward. ✉ *Rua Santo António 16* ☎ *261/862928* ▤ *No credit cards* ☉ *Closed Wed.*

$–$$$ ▥ **Hotel Vila Galé.** This luxurious hotel with its white facade and green tiled roof overlooks the Atlantic from the center of Ericeira. It has been aesthetically modernized, retaining traditional Portuguese features: claypotted geraniums hang outside room windows, the floors are of red tiles, and *azulejos* (glazed tiles) decorate the walls. Bedrooms have yellow-and-green fabrics and are equipped with every modern amenity; half have ocean views. There are three ocean-side swimming pools, including one salt water and one children's. In summer the bar opens its prow-shape terrace overlooking the sea. You feel like you are sailing away on a cruise ship. ✉ *Largo dos Navegantes, 2655-320* ☎ *261/869900* 🖷 *261/869950* ⊕ *www.vilagale.pt* 📞 *202 rooms* ⚐ *Restaurant, cable TV, in-room safes, minibars, 3 pools, gym, health club, hot tub, sauna, bar, public Internet* ▤ *AE, DC, MC, V* ⦿| *CP.*

$ ▥ **Hotel Pedro O Pescador.** If you prefer your hotels on the small side, then you'll like this intimate, pastel blue, family-run place near the beach. Cheerful rooms surround a central courtyard and have hardwood floors, floral print fabrics, and Alentejo furniture. Be sure to visit the lively bar. ✉ *Rua Dr. Eduardo Burnay 22, 2655-370* ☎ *261/869121* 🖷 *261/862321* ➪ *25 rooms* ⚙ *Bar, lounge, cable TV* ⊟ *AE, DC, MC, V* ⦿ *CP.*

Torres Vedras

➌ *20 km (12 mi) northeast of Ericeira.*

A bustling commercial center crowned with the ruins of a medieval castle, Torres Vedras is best known for its extensive fortifications—a system of trenches and fortresses erected by the Duke of Wellington in 1810 as part of a secret plan for the defense of Lisbon. It was here, at the Lines of Torres Vedras, that the surprised French army under Napoléon's Marshal Masséna was routed. You can see reconstructed remnants of the fortifications on a hill above town and throughout the area.

Where to Stay & Eat

$–$$ ✕ **Lampião.** Nationally renowned for its traditional Portuguese cuisine, this restaurant was awarded first prize in 2004 for best restaurant in the *Oeste* region (western part of Estremadura). Master chef Armando Santos and his family prepare meals in a cozy atmosphere. The decor is simple, but the food is excellent and customers get attentive service. *Cabrito assado* (roasted kid) is one of the specialties. The restaurant is 7 km (4½ mi) from the center of Torres Vedras in Turcifal, near the Serra do Socorro. ✉ *Largo Eng. João Carlos Alves 3, Turcifal* ☎ *261/951142* ⊟ *No credit cards* ⊘ *Closed Sun. No dinner Sat.*

$–$$ 🏨 **Hotel Golf Mar.** The idyllic location—on a rise overlooking a broad, sandy beach—and the golf course are the main reasons to stay here. The huge, concrete-block facade is hardly alluring and the interior lacks imagination, but there are lots of ways to work out or relax, including at a hydrotherapy center with Turkish bath and in a restaurant with panoramic sea views. The hotel is near the town of Lourinhã, 16 km (10 mi) northwest of Torres Vedras. ✉ *Praia do Porto Novo, 2560-100* 🖷 *261/980800* ⊕ *www.eav.pt* ➪ *252 rooms, 9 suites* ⚙ *Restaurant, 9-hole golf course, 2 tennis courts, 2 pools (1 indoor), hair salon, massage, sauna, spa, billiards, horseback riding, 3 bars, dance club, video game room, meeting rooms, in-room data ports, Wi-Fi* ⊟ *AE, DC, MC, V* ⦿ *BP, FAP, MAP.*

$ 🏨 **Hotel Império Jardim.** This bright, cheerfully appointed hotel is a good deal. It has several on-site eateries and shops, and it's right in the center of town as well. ✉ *Praça 25 de Abril 17, 2560-285* ☎ *261/314232* 🖷 *261/321901* ⊕ *www.imperio-online.com/hotel* ➪ *47 rooms* ⚙ *Restaurant, café, patisserie, minibars, public Wi-Fi, room service, cable TV, bar, shops, laundry service, meeting rooms, free parking* ⊟ *AE, MC, V* ⦿ *BP.*

Outdoor Activities

The therapeutic properties of the waters at the **Termas do Vimeiro** (✉ *Fonte dos Frades* ☎ *261/984484* ⊕ *www.termasvimeiro.com*) are good for respiratory, digestive, circulatory, and skin problems. Treatments last a minimum of eight days, and you have to make an initial appointment with a doctor. The thermal water treatment center is open from the end of June to the end of October.

The 9-hole **Clube do Golfe do Vimeiro** (⊠Praia do Porto Novo ☎261/980800 ⊕ www.eav.pt), designed by Frank Pennink, is on the beach and is part of the Hotel Golf Mar. Guests of the hotel golf for free; both guests and nonguests must reserve greens in advance. Fees range from €20 to €25.

Peniche

❹ *32 km (20 mi) northwest of Torres Vedras.*

In the lee of a rocky peninsula, Peniche is a major fishing-and-canning port that's also a popular summer resort known for its fine lace. The busy harbor is watched over by a sprawling 16th-century **Fortaleza Museu** (Fort Museum). At one time the fort's dungeons were full of French troops captured by the Duke of Wellington's forces. During Portugal's dictatorship, which ended in 1974, it was a prison for opponents of the regime. With the restoration of democracy, it became a museum covering all of its eras. You can tour the former cells and take in a small archaeological exhibit. For a good view of the fortress and the harbor, drive out to Cabo Carvoeiro; the narrow road winds around the peninsula, along the rugged shore, and past the lighthouse and bizarre rock formations. ▣ €1.30 ⊙ *Tues.–Sun. 10:30–12:30 and 2–6; closes at 5 in winter.*

The most interesting of the area's several churches is the 13th-century **Igreja de São Leonardo** (Church of St. Leonard) in the village of Atouguia da Baleia. ☎ *262/759142 town council office* ⊙ *Apr.–Oct., daily 9–12:30 and 2–5:30.*

Where to Stay & Eat

$$–$$$$ ✕ **Corteçais.** This modern restaurant is built into a cliff overlooking the sea, a favorable location to cast your line into the water and fish while you eat. *Festival de Mariscos,* a tray of seven different kinds of seafood, including lobster, oyster, and sea spiders, is served on a bed of natural seaweed and is a real feast. ⊠ *Porto de Areia-Sol* ☎ *262/787117* ▭ *DC, MC, V* ⊙ *Closed Wed., except in Aug.*

$–$$$$ ✕ **Nau dos Corvos.** On the Cabo Carvoeiro cliffs with a dramatic view of the sea and the lighthouse, this restaurant specializes in traditionally prepared seafood dishes. Be sure to try the *arroz de tamboril com gambas* (rice casserole with monkfish and prawns). ⊠ *Cabo Carvoeiro* ☎ *262/789004* ▭ *AE, DC, MC, V* ⊙ *Closed Wed. and Thurs.*

GREAT DRIVES

For the most scenic drive to Peniche, return to the coast and follow N247 north for 43 km (27 mi) to Cabo Carvoeiro. About 3 km (2 mi) north of Torres Vedras is the archaeological site Castro do Zambujal, the remains of an Iron Age settlement of people who worked the copper mines that once existed here. Farther on, the jagged coast is interrupted by fine beaches at Ribamar, Santa Cruz, and Areia Branca.

$ ⌘ **Hotel Atlântico Golfe.** Even if you're not a golfer, the views from your balcony (all rooms have them) over the links and the long beach will appeal. The hotel is on a sandy stretch famed for the health-giving properties of its waters, which are attributed to the local rock. The hydrotherapy center at the hotel uses tap water for its treatments, but there are thermal baths 2 km (1 mi) away. ⊠ *Praia da Consolação, 2525-150* 📞 *262/757700* ⊕ *www.atlanticogolfehotel.com* 📞 *90 rooms* ⌂ *Restaurant, in-room safes, in-room data ports, cable TV, 9-hole golf course, tennis court, indoor-outdoor pool, health club, hot tub, sauna, spa, bar, meeting rooms, some pets allowed* ⊟ *AE, DC, MC, V* ⍾⎮ *BP.*

$ ⌘ **Hotel Praia Norte.** This well-equipped, modern hotel is on a green lawn near the sea at the outskirts of Peniche. Guest rooms aren't very large, but they're light, pleasantly furnished, and well appointed. ⊠ *Av. Monsenhor Manuel Bastos, 2520-206* 📞 *262/780500* ⊕ *www.hotelpraianorte. com* 📞 *89 rooms, 3 suites* ⌂ *Restaurant, cable TV, in-room data ports, golf privileges, tennis court, 2 pools (1 indoor), hot tub, sauna, Turkish bath, volleyball, bar, playground, meeting rooms, some pets allowed* ⊟ *AE, DC, MC, V* ⍾⎮ *BP.*

$ ⌘ **Sol Peniche.** The nice thing about this modern hotel is that only a street and sand dunes separate it from the Cova da Alfarroba beach in the middle of Peniche Bay. Shaped like an L, the hotel has rooms with terraces overlooking the swimming pool or with views of the ocean. For additional comfort ask for a room with a king-size bed. ⊠ *Estrada do Baleal, 2520* 📞 *262/780400* ⊕ *www.solmelia.com* 📞 *102 rooms* ⌂ *Restaurant, 2 pools (1 indoor), bar, in-room safes, in-room data ports, laundry service* ⊟ *AE, DC, MC, V.*

Outdoor Activities

Peniche Sportagua is a large water-park complex with slides and separate adults' and children's swimming pools. The park also has a restaurant and snack bar. ⊠ *Av. Monsenhor Manuel Bastos* 📞 *262/789125* ⊕ *www.sportagua.com* 📧 *€10 for adults, €8 for children* ⊙ *Mid-July–mid-Sept., daily 10–7.*

Ilhas Berlengas

5 *10 km (6 mi) northeast of Cabo Carvoeiro.*

The harbor at Peniche is the jumping-off point for excursions to the Berlenga Islands. These six islets are part of a nature reserve and a favorite place for fishermen and divers. Berlenga, the largest of the group, is the site of the Forte de São João Baptista, a 17th-century fortress built to defend the area from pirates. The island has a campground, as well as a bar and restaurant, **Pavilhão Mar e Sol** (📞 262/750331), that has five rooms for rent (€78 for a double, open June–September). For information about accommodations in Peniche, contact the Peniche tourist office.

Viamar (📞 262/785646), €17 round-trip, operates regular summer boat services from Peniche to Berlenga. From May 15 to June 30 and again September 1 to September 15 there is one round-trip daily leaving at 10 AM and returning at 4:30 PM. In July and August there are round-trips daily at 9:30 AM and 11:30 AM, plus an evening boat that leaves at 5:30 and returns at 6:30. You can also stay overnight. The sea is often rough, so don't be alarmed by the rows of buckets under your seats!

Outdoor Activities

FISHING The most commonly caught fish are sea bass, bream, and red mullet. A fishing license isn't required. The charter-boat company **Nautipesca** (⊠ Rua das Ancoras 31, Peniche ☏ 262/789648, 936/ 222658, or 917/588358) offers deep-sea fishing excursions. Boats leave when conditions permit and when a minimum of 10 people are interested in heading out. Per-person rates are €30 on weekdays, €38 on weekends.

SCUBA DIVING The clear (and somewhat chilly) waters and bizarre rock formations off the Ilhas Berlengas are popular with scuba divers and snorkelers. The **Mergulhão** (⊠ Porto de Pesca de Peniche, Armazen 4 ☏ 966/008487 ⊕ www.mergulhao.net) dive center has two boats that take groups of six people out to explore underwater shipwrecks and caverns. One-tank trips cost €50–€60, depending on the destination. Be sure to book in advance.

> **WATER SPORTS**
>
> The clear waters and bizarre rock formations along Estremadura's coast make it a favorite with anglers, snorkelers, and scuba divers. A wet suit is recommended for diving and snorkeling, as the chilly waters don't invite you to linger long, even in summer. The area's most commonly caught fish are sea bass, bream, and red mullet. The placid waters of the Rio Zêzere (Zêzere River) provide excellent conditions for waterskiing.

Óbidos

★ ❻ *20 km (12 mi) east of Peniche.*

Once a strategic seaport, Óbidos is now high and dry—and 10 km (6 mi) inland—owing to the silting of its harbor. On the approach to town, you can see bastions and crenellated walls standing like sentinels over the now-peaceful valley of the Ria Arnoia. It's hard to imagine fishing boats and trading vessels docking in places that are today filled by cottages and cultivated fields.

As you enter town through the massive, arched gates, it seems as if you've been transported into medieval Portugal. The narrow Rua Direita, lined with boutiques and white, flower-bedecked houses, runs from the gates to the foot of the castle: you may want to shop for ceramics and clothing on this street. The rest of the town is crisscrossed by a labyrinth of stone footpaths, tiny squares, and decaying stairways. Each nook and cranny offers its own reward. Cars aren't permitted inside the walls except to unload luggage at hotels. Parking is provided outside town.

Óbidos has a long association with prominent Portuguese women. Young Queen Isabel was so enchanted with Óbidos—which she visited with her husband, Dom Dinis, shortly after their marriage in 1282—

that the king gave it to her as a gift, along with Abrantes and Porto de Mós; the town remained the property of the queens of Portugal until 1834. Queen Leonor (the wife of João II) came here in the 15th century to recuperate after the death of her young son; the town pillory bears her coat of arms. Famous primitive painter and daughter of an Óbidos artist, Josefa de Óbidos lived in the Capelaria mansion just outside town during the 17th century. She is buried in the São Pedro Church in Óbidos.

The walls of the fine medieval **castelo** (castle) enclose the entire town, and it's great fun to walk their circumference, viewing the town and countryside from their heights. Extensively restored after suffering severe damage in the 1755 earthquake, the multitower complex has both Arabic and Manueline elements. Since 1952 parts of the castle have been a pousada.

> **FUN FESTIVALS**
>
> Every July, the 10-day market **Mercado Medieval** (☎ 262/959231 tourism office) enlivens the town. Each day there is a parade of people in medieval costumes around the city walls. You can rent costumes and take part, too. To buy some of the typical products of the region—ceramics, cheeses, hams, and flowers—exchange your money for medieval coins and symbolic torreos. Battles and court scenes are dramatized daily and music animates the market all day up to midnight. As for a meal, consider a hunk of the wild boar being roasted over spits.

The 17th-century artist Josefa de Óbidos came as a small child and lived here until her death in 1684. You can see some of her work in the azulejo-lined **Igreja de Santa Maria** (St. Mary's Church), which was a Visigoth temple in the 8th century. The church is in a square off Rua Direita. ☎ *No phone* ☉ *Daily 9:30–12:30 and 2:30–7.*

Where to Stay & Eat

$$–$$$ ✕ **A Ilustre Casa de Ramiro.** Portuguese architect José Fernando Teixeira **Fodor's**Choice reworked this old building outside the castle walls into a rustic-chic restau-
★ rant with Moorish motifs. The main culinary feature is the open grill, where authentic regional dishes are prepared. Try the *arroz de pato* (rice with duck), a favorite dish among the Portuguese, who often serve it at their own dinner parties. ⊠ *Rua Porta do Vale* ☎ *262/959194* ▤ *AE, DC, MC, V* ☉ *Closed Thurs.*

$–$$ ✕ **Alcaide.** From the upstairs dining room and terrace of this rustic tavern you can enjoy a lovely view of rooftops with the countryside beyond. The Alcaide is often jammed with hungry sightseers, especially from May through October; this isn't a quiet hideaway. The food, however, is always carefully prepared, and the service is attentive. Try the bacalhau *à casa* (with chestnuts and roasted apples). ⊠ *Rua Direita* ☎ *262/959220* ▤ *AE, DC, MC, V* ☉ *Closed Wed. Nov.–June.*

★ **$$–$$$** ✕▣ **Pousada do Castelo.** Except for the electric lights and the relatively modern plumbing, the style of the Middle Ages prevails in this pousada, which occupies parts of the castle that Dom Dinis gave to his young bride, Isabel, in 1282. Room 2, in one of the massive stone towers, is especially evocative of ancient times; other rooms are individually furnished with 16th- and 17th-century reproductions. The restaurant's ($$–$$$$) food and service are worthy of royalty; there's a curtained alcove where you can dine in privacy and still enjoy a view of the castle walls and valley below. Try the cabrito assado (roast kid). ⊠ *Paço Real, 2510-999* ☎ *262/959105* ⊕ *www.pousadas.pt* ⤳ *6 rooms, 3 suites* ⸖ *Restaurant, bar, minibars, cable TV* ▤ *AE, DC, MC, V* ⧖ *BP.*

¢–$ ✕⊡ **Albergaria Josefa d'Óbidos.** This flower-bedecked inn is built into the hillside at the main gate. Rooms have comfortable 18th-century reproductions, including massive wooden pieces that greatly mask the fact that the place was built in 1983. Several reproductions of works by the 17th-century artist Josefa de Óbidos hang in the bar. The large rustic restaurant ($$) has an open brick grill and serves regional specialties: try the *arroz de tamboril* (casserole with monkfish and rice) or one of the bacalhau dishes. The peace in the dining room is sometimes disturbed by large tour groups. ⊠ *Rua D. João de Ornelas, 2510-074* ☎ *262/959228* ⤳ *34 rooms, 2 suites* ⸖ *Restaurant, bar, pub, cable TV* ▤ *AE, DC, MC, V* ⧖ *EP.*

$$$–$$$$ ⊡ **Praia d'el Rey Marriott Golf and Beach Resort.** The pride and joy of the western region is this five-star luxury resort hotel 16 km (10 mi) west of the walled city Óbidos. You have easy access to the Praia d'el Rey beach and special rates at the Praia d'el Rey Golf and Country Club's 18-hole seaside golf course and its tennis courts. Morning comforts in the rooms include coffeemakers and bathrobes. The luxurious indoor pool is surrounded by white columns reminiscent of a Roman bath. The Atlantic Grill and the Romy restaurant specialize in Mediterranean and nouvelle cuisine. Live jazz on Friday and Saturday night takes place in the Atlantic Bar. ⊠ *Av. D. Inês de Castro, Vale de Janelas, Amoreira, 2510-451* ☎ *262/905100* ☐ *262/905101* ⊕ *www.marriott.com/lisdr* ⤳ *179 rooms* ⸖ *2 restaurants, in-room safes, minibars, refrigerators, cable TV with movies, golf privileges, 2 tennis courts, 2 pools (1 indoor), health club, hot tub, beach, mountain bikes, bar, shop, in-room data ports, Wi-Fi* ▤ *AE, DC, MC, V* ⧖ *FAP, MAP.*

$–$$ ⊡ **Estalagem do Convento Hotel Óbidos.** This 19th-century convent-turned-inn is outside the town walls and a five-minute walk from the castle. The antique furnishings are rustic, but the conveniences are modern, though there is no air-conditioning. The restaurant serves dinner and the wine cellar is well stocked. ⊠ *Rua D. João de Ornelas, 2510-074* ☎ *262/959216* ⊕ *www.estalagemdoconvento.com* ⤳ *27 rooms, 4 suites* ⸖ *Restaurant, minibars, cable TV, bar; no a/c* ▤ *AE, MC, V* ⧖ *BP, MAP.*

$ ⊡ **Casa d'Óbidos.** Standing in the midst of extensive lawns, gardens, and orchards is this white manor house dating from the 19th century. There are views of the castle from its swimming pool and from all over the property. It is elegantly decorated with selected antiques and traditional Portuguese tiling by local craftsmen. There are six rooms in the main house, plus two spacious apartment-like accommodations in the 18th-century two-story cottage. ⊠ *Quinta de S. José, 2510-135* ☎ *262/950924* ⊕ *www.casadobidos.com* ⤳ *6 rooms, 1 cottage, 1 apartment* ⸖ *Tennis court, pool, billiards; no a/c, no rooms TVs* ▤ *No credit cards* ⧖ *BP.*

¢ 🏨 **Residencial Alcaidaria Mor.** To avoid the exorbitant prices of luxury hotels in the region, book one of the five rooms at this pension 6 km (4 mi) from Óbidos and 4 km (2½ mi) from the Marriott golf course. Three rooms are above the restaurant, and two lead off the downstairs terrace. You'll have views of the countryside and forest. Rooms do not have TVs, but the friendly service will provide one if you request it. ✉ *Praça Dr. Azeredo Perdigão 6–8, Amoreira 2510-408* ☎ *262/969948* ➥ *5 rooms* ⚒ *Restaurant, coffee shop, recreation room; no a/c* ☐ *No credit cards* ⏧ *BP.*

Outdoor Activities

There are three pleasant walks to take in Óbidos. It's just a 1-km (½-mi) trek from the city gate through farmlands, a grove of poplar trees, and along the Arnoia River to the Eburobritium Roman ruins (established 1 BC to AD 5), where you can see ancient baths and a forum. Another walk is through the free Lagoa de Óbidos Observatory, which has aquatic birds and birds of prey. There's also a park behind the walls of the town. Maps and brochures are available at the **tourist office** (☎ 262/959231) in the parking lot at the gate into the city wall.

The 18-hole, seaside golf course at the **Praia d'el Rey Golf and Country Club** (✉ Praia d'el Rey, Vale de Janelas ☎ 262/905005 ⊕ www.praia-del-rey.com) is among the best golf courses in Europe. It's open to everyone, and guests at the Praia d'el Rey Marriott Golf and Beach Resort get special prices. Weekdays cost €90 per person and weekends €110 per person (18 holes). Tuition for one hour costs €50. It's open daily from 8 AM until nightfall.

Caldas da Rainha

❼ *5 km (3 mi) north of Óbidos.*

Caldas da Rainha (Queen's Baths), the hub of a large farming area, is best known for its sulfur baths. In 1484 Queen Leonor, en route to Batalha, noticed people bathing in a malodorous pool. Having heard of the healing properties of the sulfurous water, the queen interrupted her journey for a soak and became convinced of the water's beneficial effects. She had a hospital built on the site and was reputedly so enthusiastic that she sold her jewels to help finance the project. There's a bronze statue of Leonor in front of the hospital, which continues to treat patients today for rheumatism and respiratory diseases.

The expansive wooded park surrounding the spa contains the **Museu Malhoa,** a museum with works mostly by local painter José Mal-

SHOPPING

The regions around Alcobaça and Leiria are well known for their high-quality crystal and hand-blown glass. Traditional hand-painted ceramics are sold at shops and roadside stands throughout Estremadura. Caldas da Rainha, a large ceramics-manufacturing center, produces characteristic cabbage-leaf and vegetable-shaped pieces. Traditional cable-stitch Portuguese fishermen's sweaters are for sale in towns all along the coast.

hoa (1854–1933). ⊠ *Parque D. Carlos I* ☎ *262/831984* 🎫 *€2* ⊘ *Tues.–Sun. 10–12:30 and 2–5.*

The **Museu de Cerâmica** (Ceramics Museum) is in the house of the noted 19th-century artisan Rafael Bordalo Pinheiro, who was also a well-known painter, cartoonist, and caricaturist. Some of his most famous ceramic figurines, done in gaudy colors, are the fat peasant "Zé Povinho," "Ama das Caldas" (the Caldas da Rainha wet nurse), the civil guard, and John Bull. Other amusing figures include a pig's head on a platter and leaping frogs. The collection contains ceramic works from all over the region, as well as works by Bordalo Pinheiro himself. There are a gift and book shop and a cafeteria here as well. ⊠ *Rua Dr. Ilídio Amado* ☎ *262/840280* ⊕ *www.ipmuseus.pt* 🎫 *€2, free Sun. morning* ⊘ *Tues.–Sun. 10–12:30 and 2–5.*

Where to Stay & Eat

$$–$$$$ ✗ **Sabores d'Itália.** This widely acclaimed restaurant is the place to go for genuine Italian food in Portugal. Everything—the pasta, bread, ice cream—is homemade by the owner Norberto Marcelino and his wife. Salmon carpaccio with truffles, lobster with moscatel sauce, green lasagna with monkfish and shrimp, tagliatelle with foie gras, and risotto with champagne and truffles are among the mouthwatering dishes on the menu. You can wash everything down with a bottle of Chianti or a good Portuguese wine from the extensive wine list. ⊠ *Rua Engenheiro Duarte Pacheco 17* ☎ *262/845600* ⊟ *AE, MC, V* ⊘ *Closed Mon.*

$$–$$$ ✗ **A Lareira.** Nestled in the pinewoods between Caldas da Rainha and the Foz do Orelho beach is this elegant modern restaurant that's a favorite with locals for special occasions. Try their prizewinning *folhado de caranguejo* (crab with flaky pastry), the salmon fillet with caviar sauce, or, for the more daring, the *ensopado de enguia* (stewed eel). Note that weekend meal prices are more expensive than the weekly set menu option. ⊠ *Rua da Lareira, Alto do Nobre* ☎ *262/823432* ⊟ *DC, MC, V* ⊘ *Closed Tues.*

$–$$ ✗ **São Rafael.** Many of the artisan Bordalo Pinheiro's ceramic pieces are displayed in glass showcases that line the wall of this restaurant adjoining the Bordalo Pinheiro Factory Museum. The windows are hung with the famous Alcobaça "Chita" cloth stamped in blue and burgundy floral motifs. While dining you can entertain yourself by looking at all the different ceramics figures. The menu includes traditional Portuguese cuisine and international dishes served on Bordalo Pinheiro plates and blue table mats. ⊠ *Rua Rafael Bordalo Pinheiro 53* ☎ *262/839383* ⊟ *MC, V.*

$–$$ ✗ **Supatra.** This renowned family-run Thai restaurant is good for those who want to savor the flavor of the East. The house recommends the pineapple rice with chicken and prawns. They also have a separate menu for vegetarians and a Sunday buffet lunch. ⊠ *Rua General Amilcar Mota* ☎ *262/842920* ⊟ *AE, DC, MC, V* ⊘ *Closed Mon.*

★ $–$$ 🏠 **Quinta da Foz.** Brazilian immigrants built this large manor house early in the 19th century. The property is surrounded by lawns at the edge of the Óbidos Lagoon, some 15 minutes' walk from the beach. Explore Caldas da Rainha, which is 9 km (5½ mi) away, or the other area towns from this quiet base. The bedrooms are large and comfortably furnished and there are two cottages on the grounds, which are available for stays of a minimum of three nights. ⊠ *Largo do Areial, Foz do Arelho 2500-457* ☎*262/979369* 🖷*262/979369* ⊕*www.manorhouses.com* ➴*6 rooms, 2 cottages* ᧒ *Billiards, pool; no a/c in some rooms* ⊟ *No credit cards* ⦿⊣ *BP.*

$ 🏨 **Cristal Caldas Hotel.** Business travelers choose this modern eight-story hotel because it's near the town center. In public areas, marble floors and wooden details are polished to perfection. Rooms are comfortable, though there aren't many details to indicate you're in Portugal. ⊠ *Rua António Sergio 31, 2500-130* ☎ *262/840260* 🖷 *262/842621* ⊕ *www. hoteiscristal.pt* ➴ *111 rooms, 2 suites* ᧒ *Restaurant, in-room safes, in-room data ports, minibars, cable TV, pool, sauna, bar, free parking* ⊟*AE, DC, MC, V* ⦿⊣ *EP.*

Outdoor Activities

Escola de Vela da Lagoa is the large wooden clubhouse with a sailing school on the north banks of the lagoon near Foz de Arelho. Rentals are by the hour: small sailboat €20, Windsurfer €14, canoe €8, and catamaran €20–€30. They also run a kite-surfing course costing €130 for six hours of private tuition. Its snack bar serves hamburgers, salads, fresh fruit juices, and milk shakes. ⊠ *Rua Dr. João Soares, Marginal da Lagoa, 2½ km (1½ mi) after the traffic circle at Foz* ☎ *262/978592* ⊕ *www.escoladeveladalagoa.com* ☾ *June–Oct., daily 10–dusk. Call ahead rest of yr.*

Kiro Karting, a well-run go-kart track, is a three-minute drive from the Lisbon–Leiria A8 N11 turnoff. It also has a children's track for ages above six (or for those who can reach the pedals). Prices vary depending on the car, but the average is €18 per person for 15 minutes. Call ahead, because sometimes the track is rented for private races. ⊠ *Quinta do Falcão, Bombarral* ☎ *262/609330* ⊕ *www.kiro-karting.com* ☾ *Mon. and Thurs.–Sun. 10–1 and 2:30–7, Wed. 2:30–7.*

The **Laguna de Óbidos** at Foz do Arelho is a lagoon that's popular with windsurfers. You can rent equipment from the Escola de Vela da Lagoa, near the beach: the cost for just the rig is €14 per hour; rental and lessons cost about €25 per hour. You can also rent sailing boats by the hour for €20. (⊠ Rua dos Reivais 40 ☎ 262/978592)

Shopping

Caldas da Rainha is famous for its cabbage-leaf and vegetable-shaped ceramic pieces produced in several of the town's factories and workshops, which you can visit if you reserve ahead of time. **Fábrica Rafael Bordalo Pinheiro** (⊠ Rua Rafael Bordalo Pinheiro 53 ☎ 262/839380), a factory named after the artist who made the Caldas da Rainha–style ceramics famous, is worth touring. **SECLA** (⊠ Rua São João de Deus ☎262/842151) is one of the area's leading ceramics workshops. Its shop is open Monday to Saturday from 9:30 to 7.

Nazaré

❽ *24 km (15 mi) northwest of Caldas da Rainha. For the most interesting route, head west from Caldas along the lagoon to the beach town of Foz do Arelho, then take the coast road 26 km (16 mi) north.*

Not so long ago you could mingle on the beach with black-stocking-capped fishermen and even help as the oxen hauled boats in from the crashing surf. But Nazaré is no longer a village and has long ceased to be quaint. The boats now motor comfortably into a safe, modern harbor, and the oxen have been put to pasture. The beachfront boulevard is lined with restaurants, bars, and souvenir shops, and in summer the broad, sandy beach is covered with a multicolor quilt of tents and awnings.

To find what's left of the Nazaré once hailed by many as "the most picturesque fishing village in Portugal," come in winter, and either climb the precipitous trail or take the funicular to the top of the 361-foot cliff called **Sítio**. Clustered at the cliff's edge overlooking the beach is a small community of fishermen who live in tiny cottages and seem unaffected by all that's happening below.

Where to Stay & Eat

$–$$$$ ✕ **A Celeste.** Owner Celeste personally greets guests at the entrance to her well-known seafood restaurant on the Atlantic seafront. She recommends *espadarte à celeste* (swordfish with cream-and-mushroom sauce) and squid or monkfish on the spit. This coast is famous for its caldeirada (a Portuguese version of bouillabaisse with nine kinds of seafood and fish). Try Celeste's. The most spectacular dish is the *cataplana de marisco* for two (a variety of steamed seafood that's served with a flourish). ⊠ *Av. República 54* ☎ *262/551695* ⊟ *AE, DC, MC, V.*

$ ✕⊞ **Adega Oceano.** Balconies overlook the beach at this white, pleasantly appointed hotel. The restaurant ($–$$$$), which has an outdoor seating area, serves typical Portuguese cuisine, including noteworthy caldeiradas. Hotel guests receive a 10% discount in the restaurant. ⊠ *Av. da República 51, 2450-101* ☎ *262/561161* ⊕ *www.adegaoceano. com* ⇖ *30 rooms* ⚭ *Restaurant, cable TV, beach, bar* ⊟ *AE, DC, MC, V* ❙❐❙ *BP.*

$ ✕⊞ **Albergaria Mar Bravo.** This modern guesthouse is right on the beach, just steps from both the sea and the center of town. All rooms have a water view from their balconies. The classy restaurant ($–$$$$) serves regional and international dishes; the seafood is always very fresh, with lobster plucked straight from the tank at the entrance. ⊠ *Praça Sousa Oliveira 71, 2450-159* ☎ *262/569160* 🖷 *262/569169* ⊕ *www.marbravo.com* ⇖ *16 rooms* ⚭ *Restaurant, in-room data ports, snack bar, cable TV, beach, bar, meeting rooms* ⊟ *AE, DC, MC, V* ❙❐❙ *CP.*

$$ ⊞ **Hotel Miramar.** The sea and town views from this inn are fantastic: it's about 1 km (½ mi) *above* Nazaré, in the village of Pederneira. The inn's smooth white facade is con-

---

BEACHES

Starting with Ericeira and extending north to São Pedro de Moel by Marinha Grande, there are a number of pleasant sandy beaches at convenient intervals along the coast. Some of the more popular stretches—with the customary range of facilities, hotels, and restaurants—are in Nazaré, Peniche, and Foz do Arelho. All beaches in Portugal are public.

trasted by its terra-cotta-tile roof, turquoise-blue swimming pool, and emerald-green lawns. The carpeted apartments have sitting areas and refrigerators. ⊠ *Rua Abel da Silva, Pederneira 2450-060* ☎ *262/550000* ⊕ *www.hotelmiramar.com* ↻ *41 rooms* ↻ *Restaurant, cable TV, pool, gym, hot tub, billiards, sauna, refrigerators, bar, free parking* ⊟ *AE, DC, MC, V* ⦿ *CP.*

$ 🔲 **Hotel Maré.** The Maré is right in the town center with access to the beach via the flower-filled gardens. If you can't get a room with a view, head for the fifth-floor terrace to take in the panoramic vistas. ⊠ *Rua Mouzinho de Albuquerque 8, 2450-901* ☎ *262/561226* ⊕ *www.hotel-mare.com* ↻ *36 rooms* ↻ *Restaurant, snack bar, cable TV, pool, bar, in-room data ports, meeting rooms* ⊟ *AE, DC, MC, V* ⦿ *BP.*

Shopping

The many shops and stands along the beachfront promenade have a good selection of traditional fishermen's sweaters as well as a wide array of caps and plaid shirts (the best are made of wool rather than acrylic blends). It pays to shop around: prices vary widely, and bargaining is the order of the day.

Alcobaça

9 *10 km (6 mi) southeast of Nazaré, 20 km (12 mi) northeast of Caldas da Rainha.*

Alcobaça is known for its crystal and is the site of a museum devoted to wine making. But the town is known best for its impressive church and monastery. Like the monastery at Mafra, the **Mosteiro de Alcobaça** was built as the result of a kingly vow, this time in gratitude for a battle won. In 1147, faced with stiff Muslim resistance during the battle for Santarém, Portugal's first king, Afonso Henriques, promised to build a monastery dedicated to St. Bernard and the Cistercian Order. The Portuguese were victorious, Santarém was captured from the Moors, and shortly thereafter a site was selected. Construction began in 1153 and was concluded in 1178. The church, the largest in Portugal, is awe inspiring. The unadorned, 350-foot-long structure of massive granite blocks and cross-ribbed vaulting is a masterpiece of understatement: there's good use of clean, flowing lines, with none of the clutter of the later rococo and Manueline architecture. At opposite ends of the transept, placed foot-to-foot some 30 paces apart, are the delicately carved tombs of King Pedro I and Inês de Castro.

The graceful twin-tiered cloister at Alcobaça was added in the 14th and 16th centuries. The Kings Hall, just to the left of the main entrance, is lined with a series of 18th-century azulejos illustrating the construction of the monastery. ⊠ *Praça 25 de Abril* ☎ *No phone* 🎟 *€6* ⊘ *Apr.–Sept., daily 9–7, cloisters 9–6:30; Oct.–Mar., daily 9–5, cloisters 9–4:30.*

While in Alcobaça, you may want to visit the interesting **Museu Nacional do Vinho** (National Wine Museum) to see wine-making implements and presses. The museum is in an old winery, on N8 heading north and just off the edge of town. ⊠ *Rua de Leiria* ☎ *262/582222* 🎟 *€1.50* ⊘ *Tues.–Sun. 9–12:30 and 2–5:30.*

Pedro and Inês

THE STORY OF PEDRO AND INÊS, one of the most bizarre love stories in Portuguese history, was immortalized by Luís de Camões in the epic poem *Os Lusíads*.

Pedro, son of King Afonso IV and heir to the throne, fell in love with the beautiful young Galician Inês de Castro, a lady-in-waiting to Pedro's Castilian wife, Constança. Fearful of the influence of Inês's family on his heir, the king banished her from the court. Upon the death of Constança, Pedro and Inês secretly married, and she lived in Coimbra, in a house later known as the Quinta das Lagrimas (the House of Tears); two sons were born of this union. King Afonso, ever wary of foreign influence on Pedro,

had Inês murdered. Subsequently, Pedro took the throne and had Inês's murderers pursued: two of the three were captured and executed, their hearts wrenched from their bodies. Pedro publicly proclaimed that he had been married to Inês and arranged an elaborate and macabre funeral for his wife. Before the procession, Inês's body, in royal garb, was enthroned beside him, and the courtiers were forced to kiss her lifeless hand. She was then placed in the tomb in Alcobaça that Pedro had designed, which lay, according to his wishes, opposite his own—so that on Judgement Day the lovers would ascend to heaven facing each other.

Where to Stay & Eat

$–$$ ✕ **Trindade.** The intimate dining room of this unpretentious restaurant is lined with old photos of local scenes that reveal some of Alcobaça's history. Try the specialty, *açorda de marisco* (with shellfish), and for dessert, the homemade pastry. ⊠ *Praça D. Afonso Henriques 22* ☎ *262/582397* ⊟ *AE, DC, MC, V* ⊘ *Closed Thurs. and Oct.–May.*

¢ ✕🏠 **Pensão Corações Unidos.** Facing the monastery, this simple pension has a good restaurant with home cooking featuring *frango na pucara* (chicken in a clay pot cooked with onions and port wine). Waiters speak English and French. Each room is different. Some have modern, sober wooden furniture, others, antiques with floral patterns carved in the wood. Bedcovers are made of the famous Alcobaça "Chita" cloth stamped in blue and pink, with patterns of flowers, rare birds, and Oriental designs copied from those brought by Vasco da Gama upon his return from India. ⊠ *Rua Frei António Brandão 39, 2460-047* ☎ *262/582142* 🖶 *262/582142* 🛏 *18 rooms* ⚭ *Restaurant, cable TV; no a/c* ⊟ *AE, DC, MC, V* ⧖ *CP.*

¢–$ 🏠 **Casa da Padeira.** This family-run guesthouse 5 km (3 mi) outside Alcobaça is named after a baker who fought the Spaniards with a wooden shovel—and pushed them into her oven—during the Battle of Aljubarrota in 1385. You're free to wander the well-tended gardens and mingle with the family. The large guest rooms are furnished with period reproductions. Homemade bread, fresh from the oven, is the highlight of breakfast; dinner is available on request. ⊠ *Hwy. N8, 19, Aljubarrota 2460-711* ☎ *262/505240* 🖶 *262/505241* ⊕ *www.casadapadeira.*

com ⟋ *8 rooms, 1 suite* △ *Miniature golf, pool, gym, billiards, bar; no a/c* ▤ *No credit cards* ⦿ *BP.*

¢ ⊞ **Hotel Santa Maria.** Gardens surround this hotel, and the monastery faces it. Some rooms have balconies; all rooms are simply furnished, comfortable, and, according to the manager, "good for the soul." There's no restaurant, but the wood-paneled bar is agreeable. ✉ *Rua Dr. Francisco Zagalo 20–22, 2460-041* ☎ *262/590160* 🖷 *262/590161* ⟋ *80 rooms* △ *Minibars, cable TV, bar, free parking* ▤ *AE, DC, MC, V* ⦿ *CP.*

Shopping

Casa Lisboa (✉ Praça 25 de Abril ☎ No phone), across from the monastery, has a good selection of fine lead crystal. The Atlantis outlet shop **Cristal Atlantis** (✉ Zona Industrial de Casal da Areia ☎ 262/540248 ◷ Mon.–Sat. 10–7, Sun. and holidays 2–7) sells both its first-rate crystal and its seconds. If you don't want to pay high prices for their normal wares, look through the second-choice pieces. Groups of more than five can visit the factory and the museum for €1.25 per person. Factory visits are conducted Tuesday–Saturday at 10:30, 11:15, noon, 2:30, 3:45, and 5 (English-speaking guides are available). **Fábrica Spal** (✉ Ponte da Torre, Valado dos Frades ☎ 262/597604), the Spal outlet shop for seconds, is a great place to buy porcelain. The defects are minimal, and they'll box and ship for you.

Batalha

★ ❿ *18 km (11 mi) northeast of Alcobaça.*

Batalha, which means "battle" in Portuguese, is the site of another of the country's religious structures that memorialize a battle victory. The monastery here is classified as a UNESCO World Heritage Site.

The church monastery **Santa Maria da Vitória** (St. Mary of Victory) was built to commemorate a decisive Portuguese victory over the Spanish on August 14, 1385, in the Battle of Aljubarrota. In this engagement the Portuguese king, João de Avis, who had been crowned only seven days earlier, took on and routed a superior Spanish force. In so doing he maintained independence for Portugal, which was to last until 1580, when the crown finally passed into Spanish hands. The heroic statue of the mounted figure in the forecourt is that of Nuno Álvares Pereira, who, along with João de Avis, led the Portuguese army at Aljubarrota.

The monastery, a masterly combination of Gothic and Manueline styles, was built between 1388 and 1533. Some 15 architects were involved in the project, but the principal architect was Afonso Domingues, whose portrait, carved in stone, graces the wall in the chapter house. In the great hall lie the remains of two unknown Portuguese soldiers who died in World War I: one in France, the other in Africa. Entombed in the center of the Founder's Chapel, beneath the star-shaped, vaulted ceiling, is João de Avis, lying hand in hand with his English queen, Philippa of Lancaster. The tombs along the south and west walls are those of the couple's children, including Henry the Navigator. Perhaps the finest parts of the entire project are the Unfinished Chapels, seven chapels radiating off an octagonal rotunda, started by Dom Duarte in 1435 and left roofless owing to lack of funds. Note the intricately filigreed detail of the main doorway. ✉ €3.50, free Sun. ☉ Daily 9–6.

On N8, 5 km (3 mi) south of Batalha's monastery, a small **Museu Militar** documents conflicts with Spain from the early Middle Ages through the early 15th century. ✉ Campo Militar de São Jorge ☎ 244/482087 ✉ €2 ☉ Tues.–Sun. 10–noon and 2–5.

Where to Stay & Eat

★ **$$** ✕🏠 **Pousada do Mestre Afonso Domingues.** Named for the principal architect of the famous Batalha monastery, this pousada is full of modern comforts in a two-story, white-stucco building. The good-size guest rooms have patterned wallpaper and are furnished in 17th- and 18th-century style; several look out on the monastery, as does the first-floor restaurant ($$$), with its polished *calçada* (pavement with small black stones on a white background) and wooden ceiling. The menu includes several types of bacalhau and a lamb pie, and there's an extensive wine list. ✉ Largo Mestre Afonso Domingues 6, 2440-102 ☎ 244/765260 🖷 244/765247 ⊕ www. pousadas.pt ⛵ 19 rooms, 2 suites ⚐ Restaurant, minibars, cable TV, in-room data ports, bar ☰ AE, DC, MC, V ⊚ BP.

$$ 🏠 **Quinta do Fidalgo.** This two-story manor house close to the monastery is homey: you can gather and chat with other guests in the spacious living room. Rooms are comfortably and traditionally furnished with antiques. The dominant style is that of Queen D. Maria I. Breakfast takes place under the trees in summer. ✉ Av. D. Nuno Álvares Pereira, 2440-102 ☎ 244/765114 🖷 244/767401 ⛵ 4 rooms ⚐ Cable TV, bar, recreation room; no a/c ☰ No credit cards ⊚ BP.

$ 🏠 **Casa do Outeiro.** This cheerful little pension in one of the quietest areas of Batalha offers a superb view of the historic monastery. Rooms are individually decorated with touches of vibrant colors and have terraces. Breakfast is served beside the pool. ✉ Largo Carvalho do Outeiro 4, 2440 ☎ 244/765806 🖷 244/765806 ⊕ www.casadoouteiro.com ⛵ 15 rooms ⚐ Minibars, cable TV, pool, recreation room, public Wi-Fi, meeting room ☰ MC, V ⊚ BP.

$ 🏠 **Motel São Jorge.** This attractive motel complex with recreational facilities is an ideal place to bring children and be in touch with the outdoors. The diamond-shaped swimming pool with a section for children is surrounded by green lawns, sun chairs, and umbrellas. It has a simple rustic restaurant, but the bungalows are equipped for you to do your own cooking. ✉ Estrada Nacional 1, Casal da Amieira, 2440-011 ☎ 244/769710 🖷 244/769711 ⊕ www.motelsjorge.com ⛵ 57 rooms, 10 bungalows ⚐ Restaurant, cable TV, tennis court, pool, bar, recreation room, laundry service, meeting room ☰ AE, DC, MC, V ⊚ BP.

OFF THE BEATEN PATH

PARQUE NATURAL DAS SERRAS DE AIRE E CANDEEIROS – This sparsely populated region straddles the border between Estremadura and the Ribatejo and is roughly midway between Lisbon and Coimbra. Within its 75,000 acres of scrublands and moors are small settlements, little changed in hundreds of years, where farmers barely eke out a living. In this rocky landscape, stones are the main building material for houses, windmills, and the miles of walls used to mark boundary lines. In the village of Minde, you can see women weaving the rough patchwork rugs for which this region is known. The park is well suited for leisurely hiking or cycling. If you're driving, the N362, which runs for approximately 45 km (28 mi) from Batalha in the north to Santarém in the south, is a good route.

Leiria

🕦 *11 km (7 mi) north of Batalha.*

Leiria is a pleasant, modern, industrial town at the confluence of the Rios Liz and Lena, overlooked by a wonderfully elegant medieval castle. The region is known for its handicrafts, particularly the fine handblown glassware from nearby Marinha Grande. Leiria's **castelo**, built in 1135 by Prince Afonso Henriques (later Portugal's first king), was an important link in the chain of defenses along the southern border of what was at the time the Kingdom of Portugal. When the Moors were driven from the region, the castle lost its significance and lay dormant until the early 14th century, when it was restored and modified and became the favorite residence of Dom Dinis and his queen, Isabel of Aragon. With these modifications the castle became more of a palace than a fortress and remains one of the loveliest structures of its kind in Portugal. Within the perimeter walls you'll encounter the ruins of a Gothic church, the castle keep, and—built into the section of the fortifications overlooking the town—the royal palace. There's also a museum. Lined by eight arches, the balcony of the palace affords lovely views. ☎ *244/ 813982* 🖾 *Castle and museum €2* ⊙ *Apr.–Sept., Tues.–Sun. 10–6; Oct.–Mar., Tues.–Sun. 9–5.*

Marinha Grande, just west of Leiria, is known for its fine-quality lead crystal, which has been produced in the region since the 17th century. The former Royal Glass Factory, founded in the 18th century, is now the site of a **Museu do Vidro**, with a collection of glass and crystal from several periods and factories. A shop is in the reception area. ☒ *Praça Gulhereme Stevens, Marinha Grande* ☎ *244/560209* 🖾 *€1.50* ⊙ *June–Sept., Tues.–Sun. 10–7; Oct.–May, Tues.–Fri. 10–6.*

Where to Stay & Eat

★ **$–$$$** ✕ **O Casarão.** Five kilometers (3 mi) south of Leiria, in Azoia at the Nazaré turnoff, O Casarão occupies a large country house surrounded by gardens. The service and presentation are flawless without being pretentious, and the extensive menu includes several ancient recipes from nearby monasteries. One of the best dishes is bacalhau *tiborna* (with olive oil, corn bread, and potatoes). Be sure to leave room for the *bolo pinão* (pine-nut cake). The comprehensive wine list displays the labels of 120 varieties. ☒ *Cruzamento de Azoia* ☎ *244/871080* ⊟ *AE, DC, MC, V* ⊙ *Closed Mon.*

$$ ✕ **Casinha Velha.** This restaurant makes its home within an old house with rustic Portuguese furniture, 1 km (½ mi) from downtown. The menu includes a noteworthy bacalhau *com natas* (with cream) as well as cabrito assado (which isn't served on Wednesday and Friday). ☒ *Rua Professores Portelas 23, Marrazes* ☎ *244/855355* ⊟ *AE, DC, MC, V* ⊙ *Closed Tues.*

$$ ✕ **Tromba Rija.** The place to go in the region is this restaurant 1 km (½
FodorsChoice   mi) from Leiria on N109 in Marrazes. Arched stone walls lend it a me-
★   dieval atmosphere. A long table displays more than 35 different regional
appetizers in clay pots. Main dishes include *pato bravo com molho de
cogumelos* (wild duck with mushroom sauce) and *lombo de porco rec-
heado com ameixas* (loin of pork stuffed with prunes). It is a very well-
known restaurant, so make reservations, be prepared to wait, and be
aware that the appetizers, wines, cheeses, and desserts can add up to a
hefty bill. ✉ *Rua Professores Portelas 22, Marrazes* ☎ *244/855072* ☰ *AE,
DC, MC, V* ☺ *Closed Sun., Mon., and July 15–31.*

¢–$$ ✕ **Cervejaria Camões.** You'll find this popular modern restaurant in the
middle of the beautiful Luís de Camões Park by the Rio Lis. Their spe-
cialties are *bife à Camões* (fried beefsteak garnished with sliced apples,
mushrooms, and cream) and bacalhau *à Camões* (baked with oil and
garlic and served with unpeeled mashed potatoes). Their most expensive dish, the *bife de Lombo com molho de queijo da serra* (filet mignon
with Serra da Estrela cheese sauce) is worth ordering. Upstairs, the bar
Sabor Latino has live jazz on Sunday night and dancing every night with
Latin music. An instructor is available. ✉ *Esplanada de Leiria* ☎ *244/
838628* ☰ *AE, DC, MC, V* ☺ *No dinner Mon.*

$ ✕🏨 **Best Western Hotel Dom José III.** Although this deluxe hotel is near the
center of town, the area surrounding it is quiet. The panoramic restau-
rant ($$–$$$$) serves excellent Portuguese and international fare with a
splendid view of the castle. ✉ *Av. Dom João III, 2400-164* ☎ *244/
817888* ⊕ *www.bestwestern.com* ➥ *54 rooms, 10 suites* ⚴ *Restaurant,
minibars, cable TV, laundry service, free parking* ☰*AE, DC, MC, V* ꙳*BP.*

$ 🏨 **Eurosol.** A pair of modern, mid-rise hotels, the Eurosol and Eurosol
Jardim, occupy a hilltop that's about a 15-minute walk from the town
center. The lobbies and bedrooms are spacious and smart, with contem-
porary lines and furnishings. The eighth-floor restaurant is ringed with
picture windows that give bird's-eye views of town. ✉ *Rua Dom José
Alves Correia da Silva, 2414-010* ☎ *244/849849* ⊕ *www.eurosol.pt*
➥ *128 rooms, 7 suites* ⚴ *Restaurant, minibars, cable TV, pool, health
club, massage, sauna, bar, shops, meeting rooms, public Wi-Fi, free
parking* ☰ *AE, DC, MC, V* ꙳ *EP.*

¢ 🏨 **Hotel S. Luís.** This rather dated hotel in a quiet neighborhood over-
looking the town is a five-minute walk from the park in the town cen-
ter. Furnishings are very plain. Except for a picture of the castle and an
abstract painting hanging on the reception-area wall, there are no other
adornments. Rooms are large and comfortable, and the ones on the fifth
and sixth floors have partial views of the nearby castle. ✉ *Rua Hen-
rique Summer, 2410-089* ☎ *244/848370* ➥ *48 rooms* ⚴ *Cable TV, bar,
lounge* ☰ *AE, DC, MC, V* ꙳ *BP.*

¢ 🏨 **Residencial Dom Dinis.** This air-conditioned budget lodging is only a
short walk from the town center. The drab exterior and disappointing
lobby do not reflect the pleasant modern rooms upstairs, which are fur-
nished in light brown wood with brightly colored fabrics. There are large
sunny balconies with lovely views of the castle and town. ✉ *Travessa
de Tomar 2, 2410-188* ☎ *244/815342* ➥ *24 rooms* ⚴ *Cable TV*
☰ *AE, DC, MC, V* ꙳ *BP.*

Shopping

The **Santos Barrosa Vidros** (⊠ Zona da Estão–Cumeira ☎ 244/570100), a factory museum, displays all types of glass products. Call ahead of time to arrange for a tour, as hours are erratic. Admission is free.

Craftsmen do exhibitions of glassblowing at the **Jasmim Glass Studio,** halfway along the main road between Leiria and Marinha Grande. Glass pieces are on sale at a wide variety of prices. Each piece is a unique work of art. The shop is open every day until 7. ⊠ *Estrada de Leiria 227, Marinha Grande* ☎ *244/575590* ⊕ *www.jasmimglass.com* ⊗ *Shop daily 10–7. Factory Mon.–Sat. 10–12:30 and 2:30–7; Sun. and holidays 10–12:30 and 2:30–5.*

THE RIBATEJO

To the east of Estremadura, straddling both banks of the Rio Tejo, the Ribatejo is a placid, flat, fertile region known for its vegetables and vineyards. It's also famous for its horses and bulls; you may well see campinos in red waistcoats and green stocking caps moving bulls along with long wooden poles. As a consequence of its strategic location, the Ribatejo is home to a number of imposing castles as well as such diverse sights as the bullfighting centers of Vila Franca de Xira and Santarém and the shrine at Fátima.

Vila Franca de Xira

⑫ *30 km (18 mi) north of Lisbon via the A1.*

Vila Franca de Xira is an excellent place to see Portuguese bullfights, known as the *tourada,* which are held from Easter through October. Although it's different from any version of this ancient spectacle in Mexico or Spain, Portuguese and Spanish bullfights have a common origin. Both forms were born in the Middle Ages in the struggle between Moors and Christians for the Iberian Peninsula, both were essentially arts of the nobility, and both were practiced by horsemen. Bullfighting remained essentially the same in Portugal and Spain until the middle of the 18th century. Its subsequent development into two separate styles, the matador on foot becoming protagonist in Spain and the horseman continuing to play the leading role in Portugal, was caused by the disapproval of Bourbon monarch Felipe V, who ascended

FUN FESTIVALS

Had Ernest Hemingway and his buddies taken a wrong train and wound up in Vila Franca de Xira some 60 years ago, perhaps Pamplona would have remained an unsung, grimy industrial town, and the world would have flocked instead to the Ribatejo each year for one of Portugal's greatest parties. The first week of July sees the **Festa do Colete Encarnado** (Festival of the Red Waistcoat), during which the downtown streets are cordoned off, and the bulls are let loose as folks try their luck at dodging the charging beasts. At night the streets are alive with fado music and flamenco dancing.

Bullfighting

BULLFIGHTING IN PORTUGAL remains true to its equestrian origins. As part of their training, medieval Portuguese and Spanish knights honed their equestrian skills and developed the dexterity of their horses in combat with the notoriously belligerent and agile Iberian fighting bulls. Long after these dangerous exercises lost their military utility, the noblemen continued to practice them. Displays of skill and courage, staged in castle courtyards and town squares, gradually evolved into today's spectacles.

In Spain, the evolution of bullfighting has produced the dramatic figure of the matador, a solitary figure who fights a deadly duel with his opponent from a proletarian position, on the ground. In Portugal, however, the aristocratic tradition of the horseman bullfighter has remained intact (though following a decree by the Marquês de Pombal in the 18th century, bulls aren't killed in Portuguese rings). The star of the Portuguese show is the elegant cavaleiro, costumed as an 18th-century nobleman, with plumed hat and embroidered coat. The aim of the bullfight—known as the tourada—is to show off the courtly skills of the horse and its rider. Even today, horseback bullfighters tend to come from the wealthy and aristocratic segments of society, whereas the greatest matadors have typically come from more humble origins.

During a bullfight the horse must make precisely timed movements to avoid being gored and to best position its rider for placing the darts. Using exceptional equestrian skills, the cavaleiro provokes the bull and, just inches away from the animal's padded horns, deftly places a colorfully festooned bandarilha (dart) in a designated part of the bull's back. With each pass of an ever-shorter bandarilha, the danger to horse and rider increases—in spite of the bull's blunted horns. At the proper moment, when the bull is sufficiently fatigued, the final dart is placed, and with a flourish the cavaleiro exits the arena.

The stage is now set for the pega, an audacious display of bravery with burlesque overtones. A group of eight men—called the forcados—dressed in bright-crimson vests and green stocking caps parades into the arena, and the leader, hands on hips, confronts the tired but still-enraged bull. When the bull charges, the leader meets him head on with a leap and literally seizes the bull by the horns. While he tries to hang on to the furious bull's head, suspended between its horns, the other men rush in and, with one of them hanging on to its tail, try to force the animal to a standstill. At times this can be an amusing sight, but there's an ever-present element of danger (forcados have been killed during the pega). At the end of the spectacle, a few cows are led in to lure the bull from the ring. If he has shown exceptional bravery, the bull will be spared for stud purposes; otherwise, he will be slaughtered for the meat. The best place to view bullfighting today is in Vila Franca de Xira.

to the Spanish throne in 1700. The king's French sensibilities were offended by the gore and violence of bullfighting, and he soon prohibited the practice. Spain's noblemen were forced to comply. Bullfighting, however, had become too popular to disappear. The horsemen noblemen's retinue of grooms and other helpers took the art over for themselves.

The bullring here, **Praça de Touros,** is one of Portugal's finest. It contains a small museum with a collection of bullfighting memorabilia. ⊠ *Palha Blanco* ☎ *219/273057 museum* 🖾 *Museum free* ☉ *Museum Tues.–Sun. 10–12:30 and 2–6.*

◔ Not all the area sights are related to bullfighting. The **Museu do Ar** (Air Museum), in nearby Alverca, has a captivating collection of old airplanes. ⊠ *Airport, 8 km (5 mi) south of Vila Franca de Xira* ☎ *219/581294* 🖾 *€1.50* ☉ *Oct.–June, Tues.–Sun. 10–5; July–Sept., Tues.–Sun. 10–6.*

Where to Stay & Eat

★ **$–$$$$** ✕ **O Redondel.** This restaurant inside the walls of the famous bullring sees a lot of action. It's considered Vila Franca's top eatery, with a menu full of regional dishes. There are high-vaulted brick ceilings, and in keeping with the theme, the dining room is adorned with bullfight posters and memorabilia. You don't have to have attended a fight to eat here. ⊠ *Estrada de Lisboa–Arcadas da Praça de Touros* ☎ *263/272973* ᨚ *Reservations essential* ⊟ *AE, DC, MC, V* ☉ *Closed Mon. and June.*

★ **$–$$** ✕ **O Forno.** This century-old wine warehouse has been converted into a restaurant with open grill and an old wood-fire oven. Try the bacalhau assado *com batata a muro* (roasted with potatoes "a muro"—fist smashed) and arroz de tamboril com gambas (monkfish rice with shrimp). Wine bottles are displayed on big wooden barrels. ⊠ *Rua Dr. Miguel Bombarda 143* ☎ *263/282106* ⊟ *AE, DC, MC, V* ☉ *Closed Tues.*

¢ ✕🏨 **Residencial Flora.** For simple but well-maintained budget accommodations, try this contemporary hotel in the center of town. Its small, homey restaurant ($$–$$$$) and wine cellar make a stay here all the more worthwhile: the food is excellent. If you're not a guest of the hotel, it's best to make reservations. (Note that the restaurant is closed Sunday and from mid-August to mid-September.) ⊠ *Rua Noel Perdigão 12, 2600-218* ☎ *263/271272* 🛏 *22 rooms* ᨚ *Restaurant, cable TV; no a/c* ⊟ *AE, DC, MC, V* ⦿ *BP.*

★ **$–$$** 🏨 **Lezíria Parque Hotel.** This modern, four-story, hotel-and-apartment complex off the main Lisbon–Porto road is a comfortable base from which to explore the bull- and horse-breeding region across the Rio Tejo. Rooms are small and plainly furnished, but the ground-floor coffeeshop is quite pleasant. The hotel arranges jeep tours of the surrounding wetlands, as well as river cruises on the Tejo. ⊠ *Hwy. N1, Povos 2600-246* ☎ *263/276670* ⊕ *www.leziriaparquehotel.pt* 🛏 *67 rooms, 4 suites* ᨚ *Restaurant, minibars, cable TV, bar, Wi-Fi* ⊟ *AE, DC, MC, V* ⦿ *EP.*

$ 🏨 **Quinta do Alto.** Once you drive through the massive iron gates of this hotel, you may have a hard time leaving. On 50 choice acres of orchards, gardens, and vineyards in the hills high above the Tejo, just 30 minutes from the Lisbon airport, the Quinta do Alto was once the summer residence of a prominent Portuguese family. Red brick adorns the vaulted ceilings, and the tile floors are enhanced with Arraiolos carpets. ⊠ *Estrada* *de Monte Gordo, 2600-065* ☎*263/ 276850* 📠 *11 rooms* ♿ *Tennis court, pool, gym, sauna, squash; no room TVs* 🖃 *AE, DC, MC, V.*

⌐ EN ROUTE
On the Rio Tejo's east bank, between Vila Franca de Xira and Santarém, is a region of marshy plains and rich pasturelands known as the Lezíria. The area contains many stud farms, where Portugal's best bulls and horses are bred. As you drive through the town of Benavente and the surrounding countryside, look for campinos in the fields working the bulls and horses.

Almeirim

 40 km (25 mi) northeast of Vila Franca de Xira, 4 km (2½ mi) east of Santarém.

The **Quinta da Alorna** is a 500-acre farm and winery that was established in 1723 by the Marquês de Alorna, a viceroy of India. The chardonnay comes highly recommended. 🖃 *EN118 at Km 73* ☎ *243/ 570700* 🖃 *Tastings €10 (includes tour of winery [in English] for minimum of 5 people). Advance reservations essential* ☉ *Weekdays 9–6.*

> **LOCAL LEGENDS**
>
> Almeirim is visited mostly because it has a number of restaurants that serve a local delicacy called *sopa da pedra* (stone soup). A local legend says there was once a priest who begged for his food. He took a *pedra* (stone) and approached a housewife, saying, "I have a stone, but if I had a carrot, I could make a soup." He approached another housewife and said, "I have a stone and a carrot. If I had some beans, I could make a soup." He approached various village women until he had all the ingredients he needed for his soup: carrots, beans, meat, sausages, and other vegetables. Today the sopa da pedra isn't complete without a stone.

Santarém

🕙 *7 km (4½ mi) northwest of Almeirim.*

Present-day Santarém, high above the Tejo, is an important farming and livestock center. It holds the largest agricultural fair in the country. Even with a tradition of bull breeding and bullfighting, Santarém curiously has what is considered the ugliest bullring on the Iberian Peninsula. Santarém also has bull farms, a working stud farm, and a winery that can be visited.

Some historians believe that Santarém's beginnings date from as early as 1200 BC and the age of Ulysses. Its strategic location led several kings to choose it as their residence, and the Cortes (parliament) frequently met here. Thanks to its royal connections, Santarém is more richly endowed with monuments than other towns of its size. The Portuguese refer to it as their "Gothic capital."

Walk up to the **Portas do Sol,** a lovely park within the ancient walls. From this vantage point you can look down on a sweeping bend in the river and beyond to the farmlands that stretch into the neighboring Alentejo.

The **Museu Arqueológico** (Archaeological Museum), in the Romanesque church of São João de Alporão, has interesting relics, including the finely sculpted tomb of Duarte de Menezes, which according to legend contains a single tooth, all that remained of the nobleman after his brutal murder by the Moors in Africa. The museum is directly across from the bell tower known as the Torre das Cabaças. ⊠ *Rua Figueiredo Leal* ☎ *243/304462* ✆ *€2* ☉ *Tues., Wed., and weekends 9:30–12:30 and 2–5:30; Thurs. and Fri. 10–12:30 and 2–5:30.*

The 14th-century Gothic **Igreja da Graça** (Graça Church) contains the gravestone of Pedro Álvares Cabral, the discoverer of Brazil. There's also a tomb of the explorer in Belmonte, the town of his birth, but no one is really sure just what (or who) is in which tomb. Note the delicate rose window whose setting was carved from a single slab of stone. ⊠ *Largo Pedro Álvares Cabral* ☎ *No phone* ☉ *Tues., Wed., and weekends 9:30–12:30 and 2–5:30; Thurs. and Fri. 10–12:30 and 2–5:30.*

Where to Stay & Eat

$–$$ ✕ **Adiafa.** Excellent grilled meats and good service are the norm at this large typically Ribatejo restaurant by the bullring. Non-meat eaters can try the *mangusto com bacalhau assado* (açorda with roasted codfish and fresh herbs). In winter, a fire in the fireplace may well welcome you. ⊠ *Campo Emilio Infante da Câmara* ☎ *243/324086* ▭ *AE, MC, V* ☉ *Closed Tues.*

¢–$ ✕ **Taberna da Quinzena.** Photos of patrons vie for your attention with bullfighting posters at this restaurant in a former house. It's run by the great-grandson of the original owner. Specialties include *toiro bravo* (wild bull), *entrecosto com arroz de feijoca* (spareribs with red bean rice) and mangusto com bacalhau assado. ⊠ *Rua Pedro de Santarém 93* ☎ *243/ 322804* ▭ *No credit cards.*

$ 🏠 **Corinthia Santarém Hotel.** Rooms at this contemporary hotel owned by an international chain overlook the plains or the town. Some rooms have balconies, complimentary morning newspapers, bathrobes, and trouser presses; all are equipped with such gadgets as hair dryers and alarm clocks. ⊠ *Av. Madre Andaluz, 2000-210* ☎ *243/309500* ⊕ *www. corinthiahotels.com* ⇗ *105 rooms, 6 suites* ⚭ *Restaurant, coffee shop, snack bar, room service, in-room safes, minibars, cable TV with movies, 3 pools (1 indoor), health club, sauna, bar, lounge, laundry service, in-room data ports, meeting rooms, Wi-Fi, airport shuttle, free parking* ▭ *AE, DC, MC, V* ⍥ *BP.*

¢ 🏠 **Beirante.** The Beirante is near Santarém's historic center, with easy access to the toll road. Accommodations here are plain but comfortable; room rates are truly budget. ⊠ *Rua Alexandre Herculano 3, 2000-149* ☎ *243/322547* ⇗ *32 rooms* ▭ *No credit cards* ⍥ *BP.*

Alpiarça

⑮ *10 km (6 mi) northeast of Santarém.*

Alpiarça is a pleasant little town where you'll have the chance to see how a wealthy country gentleman lived at the beginning of the 20th century. The **Casa dos Patudos,** now a museum, was the estate of José Relvas, a diplomat and gentleman farmer. This unusual three-story manor house with its zebra-stripe spire is surrounded by gardens and vineyards and filled with an impressive assemblage of ceramics, paintings, and furnishings—including Portugal's foremost collection of Arraiolos carpets. ⊠ *N118* ☎ *243/558321* 🎫 *€2.50* ⊙ *Oct.–Apr., Tues.–Sun. 10–noon and 2–5; May–Sept., Tues.–Sun. 10–noon and 2–6.*

EN ROUTE

About 20 km (12 mi) northeast of Alpiarça, on the way to Torres Novas, is the town of **Golegã**, one of Portugal's most notable horse-breeding centers. During the first two weeks of November, this is the site of the colorful Feira Nacional do Cavalo (National Horse Fair), the most important event of its kind in the country. It has riding displays, horse competitions, and stalls that sell handicrafts.

Torres Novas

🔟 *39 km (24 mi) northwest of Alpiarça.*

Torres Novas is best known for its crenellated, 14th-century hilltop **castelo,** which encloses a delightful garden. At the foot of the structure stands a caricature statue of Dom Sancho I—son and royal successor of Afonso Henriques—created by João Cutiliero, a prominent contemporary sculptor.

Where to Stay & Eat

$–$$ ✕ **Pic's.** This rustic restaurant has a view of the castle, which is just a minute's walk away. The decor includes antiques and Alentejo-style furniture, hand-painted with flowers by the owner's wife. Unique dishes include pork loin with chestnuts and honey, roasted in the oven on a clay tile, and *carnes à antiga no caldeirão* (meats cooked in a caldron brought to the table). The buffet holds a remarkable 52 entrées and salads, and another has 32 desserts. ⊠ *Quinta das Vieiras–São Pedro* ☎ *249/825580* ⊟ *AE, DC, MC, V* ⊙ *Closed Mon. No dinner Sun.*

¢–$ ✕▥ **Hotel dos Cavaleiros.** Facing the main square, this modern three-story hotel blends in well with the surrounding 18th-century buildings. Rooms are of a decent size and have plain, light-wood furnishings; ask for one on the third floor with a terrace. In spite of its sterile, coffeeshop appearance, the restaurant (¢) serves generous portions of well-prepared traditional dishes. Try the *espetada mista* (grilled pork, squid, and shrimp on a spit). ⊠ *Praça 5 de Outubro, 2350-418* ☎ *249/819370* ⊕ *www.hoteldoscavaleiros.com.pt* ➷ *57 rooms, 3 suites* ♻ *Restaurant, cable TV, bar, free parking* ⊟ *AE, DC, MC, V* 🍴 *EP.*

Fátima

⑰ *20 km (12 mi) northwest of Torres Vedras, 16 km (10 mi) southeast of Batalha, 20 km (12 mi) southeast of Leiria.*

On the western flanks of the Serra de Aire lies Fátima, an important Roman Catholic pilgrimage site that is, ironically, named after the daughter of Mohammed, the prophet of Islam. If you visit this sleepy little Portuguese town in between pilgrimages, it will be difficult to imagine the thousands of faithful who come from all corners of the world to make this religious affirmation, cramming the roads, squares, parks, and virtually every square foot of space. Many of the pilgrims go the last miles on their knees.

Catholic Stories

IT ALL BEGAN MAY 13, 1917, when three young shepherds—Lucia dos Santos and her cousins Francisco and Jacinta—reported seeing the Virgin Mary in a field at Cova de Iria, near the village. The Virgin promised to return on the 13th of each month for the next five months, and amid much controversy and skepticism, each time accompanied by increasingly larger crowds, the three children reported successive apparitions. This was during a period of anticlerical sentiment in Portugal, and after the sixth reputed apparition, in October, the children were arrested and interrogated. But they insisted the Virgin had spoken to them, revealing three secrets. Two of these, revealed by Lucia in 1941, were interpreted to

foretell the coming of World War II and the spread of communism and atheism. In a 1930 Pastoral Letter, the Bishop of Leiria declared the apparitions worthy of belief, thus approving the "Cult of Fátima."

In May 2000, Francisco and Jacinta were beatified in a ceremony held at Fátima by Pope John Paul II. The third secret, which was revealed after the beatification, foretold an attempt on the life of the pope. On the 13th of each month, and especially in May and October, the faithful flock here to witness the passing of the statue of the Virgin through the throngs, to participate in candlelight processions, and to take part in solemn masses.

At the head of the huge esplanade is the large neoclassical **basílica** (built in the late 1920s), flanked on either side by a semicircular peristyle. ✉ *Albergaria Nossa Senhora das Dores* ☎ *249/539600* ⊕ *www.santuario-fatima.pt* 🎫 *Free* ☼ *Easter–Oct., daily 7:30 AM–9 PM; Nov.–Easter, daily 7:30 AM–8 PM.*

The **Capela das Aparições** (Chapel of Apparitions) is a 20th-century structure built on the site where the appearances of the Virgin Mary are said to have taken place. A marble pillar and statue of the Virgin mark the exact spot. Gifts, mostly gold jewelry and wax reproductions of body parts, are burned as offerings in the hope of achieving a miraculous cure. ✉ *Albergaria Nossa Senhora das Dores* ☎ *249/539600* ⊕ *www.santuario-fatima.pt* 🎫 *Free* ☼ *Easter–Oct., daily 7:30 AM–midnight; Nov.–Easter, daily 7:30 AM–midnight.*

The **Museu das Aparições** (Museum of Apparitions; ✉ Rua Jacinto Marto ⊕ www.museuaparicoes.com 🎫 €2.50 ☼ Nov.–Mar., daily 9–6; Apr.–Oct., daily 9–7) has representations of scenes depicting the appearances of the Virgin Mary to the young shepherds in 1917. Dialogues between the children and the Virgin Mary are recorded in various languages.

The **Museu de Arte Sacra e Etnologia** (Museum of Sacred Art and Ethnology) hosts a vast collection of Portuguese religious art as well as a rare collection of ethnographic objects from the various peoples the Portuguese missionaries came in contact with around the world: in the Amazon, Angola, Guinea, Mozambique, and the Far East. ✉ *Rua Francisco Marto*

52 ☎ 249/539470 ⊕ www.
consolata.pt ⚏€3.50 ⊙Nov.–Mar.,
Tues.–Sun. 10–5; Apr.–Oct.,
Tues.–Sun. 10–7.

☪ The **Museu de Cera** (Wax Museum),
in the center of town, has 30
tableaux depicting the events that
took place in Fátima when the child
shepherds first saw the apparitions
in 1917. ⊠ Rua Jacinto Marto
☎ 249/539300 ⊕ www.mucefa.pt
⚏ €4.50 ⊙ Apr.–Oct., daily
9:30–6:30; Nov.–Mar., daily 10–5.

The **Casa dos Pastorinhos** is a cot-
tage in the nearby hamlet of Aljustrel, where the three shepherd children who saw the Virgin Mary were born. To reach it, turn off Avenida
Papa João XXIII and take the N356 to Aljustrel. The cottage is looked
after by a local family and has no set opening hours. To be safe, visit
before lunch or early in the afternoon.

☪ The hills to the south and west of Fátima are honeycombed with limestone **caves.** Within about a 25-km (15-mi) radius of town are four major
caverns—São Mamede, Mira de Aire, Alvados, and Santo António—
equipped with lights and elevators. On a guided tour (ask for an English-speaking guide) you can see the subterranean world of limestone
formations, underground rivers and lakes, and multicolor stalagmites
and stalactites. The Fátima tourist office can assist you with further details, including open hours, which vary by season. ☎ 244/704302 to
São Mamede, 244/440322 to Mira de Aire, 244/440787 to Alvados, 249/
841876 to Santo António ⚏ €4 to each cavern.

Where to Stay & Eat

$–$$$ ✕ **Retiro dos Caçadores.** A big brick fireplace, wood paneling, and stone
walls set the mood in this cozy hunter's lodge, where the food is sim-
ple, but portions are hearty and the quality is good. This is the best place
in town for fresh game, especially coelho com arroz (rabbit with rice)
and perdiz (partridge). ⊠ Lombo Egua ☎ 249/531323 ▤ MC, V
⊙ Closed Wed.

★ $$ ✕ **Tia Alice.** Considered the area's best restaurant, Tia (Aunt) Alice is
concealed in an inconspicuous old house with French windows, across
from the parish church near the sanctuary at Cova de Iria. A flight of
wooden stairs inside leads to an intimate dining area with a wood-beam
ceiling and stone walls. The cabrito assado is worth trying, as is the Tia
Alice especial (codfish with béchamel sauce and shrimp), which serves
two. ⊠ Rua do Adro ☎249/531737 ▤AE, DC, MC, V ⊙ Closed Mon.
and July. No dinner Sun.

$ ✕▥ **Estalagem Dom Gonçalo.** There is a pastoral view of gardens and
pinewoods from every window in this elegant modern inn a quarter mile
from the Fátima Sanctuary. In addition to comfortable rooms and a beautiful setting, it has the restaurant O Convite ($$–$$$), a favorite in this

part of the country. The chef, Pedro Vital, is well known for his bacalhau *no forno com gambas Dom Gonçalo* (baked in the oven with shrimp) and *tamboril com lagosta* (monkfish with lobster). More economical dishes include rabbit and duck with orange. ⊠ *Rua Jacinto Marto 100, 2495-450* ☎ *249/539330* 🖷 *249/539335* ⊕ *www.estalagemdomgoncalo.com* ⇥ *42 rooms* 🛆 *Restaurant, in-room safes, in-room data ports, cable TV, bar, playground* ⊟ *AE, DC, MC, V.*

$ 🖭 **Fátima Plaza.** This modern six-story pink-and-white hotel rises from among a grove of trees in the center of the town, a seven-minute walk from the basilica. The pink-and-white theme of the outside facade is carried over into the interior. As you enter a room, your attention is immediately drawn to the focal point, an elegant cherrywood bed set against a pink wall. ⊠ *Av. Beato Nuno, 2495-901* ☎ *249/530410* ⇥ *85 rooms* 🛆 *Restaurant, minibars, cable TV, public Wi-Fi, bar, free parking* ⊟ *AE, DC, MC, V* ⸗ *BP.*

$ 🖭 **Hotel de Fátima.** The closest hotel to the sanctuary is a modern four-story structure, generally considered Fátima's top lodging establishment. Light-wood furniture complements royal blue fabrics in the guest rooms, which have many amenities. ⊠ *Rua João Paulo II, Apartado 11, 2496-908* ☎ *249/533351* ⊕ *www.hotelfatima.com* ⇥ *126 rooms, 9 suites* 🛆 *Restaurant, minibars, cable TV, bar, shops, meeting rooms, free parking* ⊟ *AE, DC, MC, V* ⸗ *EP.*

$ 🖭 **Travel Hotel.** This pleasant hotel in the center of town is next to the basilica. It provides a good view of the candlelight processions and other ceremonies and has its own chapel as well. The walls are covered with frescos of Fátima. ⊠ *Av. Beato Nuno 283, 2496-908* ☎ *249/530350* ⇥ *46 rooms* 🛆 *Restaurant, bar* ⊟ *MC, V* ⸗ *EP* ⊙ *Closed Jan.*

¢   🖭 **Casa Beato Nuno.** This large pink-stucco inn just a few minutes' walk from the sanctuary is run by the Carmelites but is open to visitors of all faiths. The austere rooms are clean and comfortable. ⊠ *Av. Beato Nuno 51, 2496-908* ☎ *249/530230* 🖷 *249/530236* ⇥ *112 rooms* 🛆 *Restaurant, cable TV; no a/c* ⊟ *AE, MC, V* ⸗ *CP.*

Tomar

⑱ *24 km (15 mi) east of Fátima, 20 km (12 mi) northeast of Torres Novas.*

Tomar is an attractive town laid out on both sides of the Rio Nabão, with the new and old parts linked by a graceful, arched stone bridge. The river flows through a lovely park with weeping willows and an old wooden waterwheel.

In the Old Town, walk along the narrow, flower-lined streets, particularly Rua Dr. Joaquim Jacinto, which takes you to the heart of the Jewish Quarter and the modest **Museu-Sinagoga Luso-Hebraico Abraham Zacuto Sinagoga de Tomar.** Built in the mid-15th century, this is Portugal's oldest synagogue, though it's no longer used as such. Inside is a small museum with exhibits chronicling the Jewish presence in the country. The once-sizable community was considerably reduced in 1496 when Dom Manuel issued an edict ordering the Jews either to leave the country or convert to Christianity. Many, who became known as Marranos, converted but secretly practiced Judaism. ⊠ *Rua Dr. Joaquim Jacinto 73* ☎ *249/322427* 🖭 *Donations accepted* ⊙ *Daily 10–1 and 2–6.*

★ Atop a hill rising from the Old Town is the remarkable **Convento de Cristo** (Convent of Christ). You can drive to the top of the hill or hike for about 20 minutes along a path through the trees before reaching a formal garden lined with azulejo-covered benches. This was the Portuguese headquarters of the Knights Templar, from 1160 until the order was forced to disband in 1314. Identified by their white tunics emblazoned with a crimson cross, the Templars were at the forefront of the Christian armies in the Crusades and during the struggles against the Moors. King Dinis in 1334 resurrected the order in Portugal under the banner of the Knights of Christ and reestablished Tomar as its headquarters. In the early 15th century, under Prince Henry the Navigator (who for a time resided in the castle), the order flourished. The caravels of the Age of Discovery even sailed under the order's crimson cross.

The oldest parts of the complex date from the 12th century, including the towering castle keep and the fortresslike, 16-sided Charola, which, like many Templar churches, is patterned after the Church of the Holy Sepulchre in Jerusalem and has an octagonal oratory at its core. The paintings and wooden statues in its interior, however, were added in the 16th century. The complex's medieval nucleus acquired its Manueline church and cluster of magnificent cloisters during the next 500 years. To see what the Manueline style is all about, stroll through the church's nave with its many examples of the twisted ropes, seaweed, and nautical themes that typify the style, and be sure to look at the chapter house window, probably the most photographed one in Europe. Its lichen-encrusted sculpture evokes the spirit of the great Age of Discovery. ☎ *249/ 313481* 🖭 *€4.50* ⊙ *May–Sept., daily 9–6; Oct.–Apr., daily 9–5:30.*

In the gardens by the Rio Nabão there's an enormous working wooden **waterwheel.** It's typical of those once used in the region for irrigation and thought to be of either Arabic or Roman origin. ⊠ *Av. Marquês Tomar.*

Across the Rio Nabão is the 13th-century **Igreja de Santa Maria do Olival,** where the bones of several Templar knights are interred, including those of Gualdim Pais, founder of the order in Portugal. Popular belief—supported by some archaeological evidence—has it that the church was once connected with the Convent of Christ by a tunnel. ⊠ *Rua Prof. Andrade* ☎ *No phone* 🖭 *Free* ⊙ *Weekdays 10–5, weekends 11–5.*

In Pegões, some 5 km (3 mi) northwest of Tomar, is a 5-km-long (3-mi-long) **aqueduct,** built in the 16th century to bring water to Tomar. It joins the walls of the Convent of Christ.

Where to Stay & Eat

★ $$ ✕ **Chico Elias.** This restaurant owes its fame to owner and chef Maria do Céu's creativity. Guests are recommended to call a day ahead of time because the special dishes take time to prepare. What can be more creative than *feijoada de caracóis* (beans with snails) or *coelho na abóbora* (rabbit in a pumpkin)? Her other specialty is bacalhau *com broa* (with corn bread). ✉ *Rua Principal 70, Algarvias* ☎ *249/311067* ▭ *No credit cards* ☉ *Closed Tues.*

★ ¢–$$ ✕ **A Bela Vista.** The date on the calçada reads "1922," which was when the Sousa family opened this attractive little restaurant next to the old arched bridge. For summer dining there's a small, rustic terrace with views of the river and the Convent of Christ. Carrying on the family tradition, Eugenio Sousa presides over the kitchen, which turns out great quantities of hearty regional fare. Try the cabrito assado or the *dobrada com feijão* (tripe with beans), and wash it down with a robust local red wine. ✉ *Rua Fonte do Choupo 6* ☎ *249/312870* ▭ *No credit cards* ☉ *Closed Tues. No dinner Mon.*

★ $$ ✕▦ **Hotel dos Templários.** A large, modern hotel in a tranquil park along the Rio Nabão, the Templários has many units with views of the Convent of Christ. The big, airy dining room ($–$$) has picture windows facing the park and serves interesting regional dishes. With its spacious grounds, reasonable rates, and many amenities, the hotel makes a good base for exploring the whole area and can arrange boat tours. ✉ *Largo Candido dos Reis 1, 2304-909* ☎ *249/310100* ⊕ *www.hoteldostemplarios.pt* ⟿ *171 rooms, 5 suites* ⟐ *Restaurant, in-room safes, minibars, cable TV, tennis court, 3 pools (1 indoor), health club, hair salon, hot tub, sauna, billiards, bar, video game room, babysitting, playground, meeting rooms, free parking, public Wi-Fi, no-smoking rooms* ▭ *AE, DC, MC, V* ⦿ *BP.*

$ ▦ **Cavaleiros de Cristo.** The Cavaleiros de Cristo (Knights Templars) is a three-story modern pension in the historic center near the Nabão River. Displayed in the lobby are landscape painting, city scenes, and *tabuleiros*—platters piled high with 30 loaves of bread fixed on rods, interspersed with flowers and topped with a crown. Girls wear these unusual headpieces in a festival that honors the Holy Spirit, but the festival actually dates back to the time of mother goddess worship. Rooms, in which the color yellow predominates, are spacious and comfortable. ✉ *Rua Alexandre Herculano 7, 2300-554* ☎ *249/321203* ⟿ *16 rooms* ⟐ *Minibars, cable TV, bar, lounge* ▭ *AE, DC, MC, V* ⦿ *BP.*

$ ▦ **Estalagem de Santa Iria.** Named for the 7th-century martyred nun Iria, whose body floated downstream to Tomar, this inn sits in a park on a small island in the middle of the Nabão River. It's reachable by a small bridge. Rooms are modern, with balconies and pleasant views. ✉ *Parque do Muchão, 2300-586* ☎ *249/313326* ⟿ *13 rooms, 1 suite* ⟐ *Restaurant, cable TV* ▭ *AE, DC, MC, V.*

¢ ▦ **Residencial Sinagoga.** This small three-story pension in the old part of town is just a five-minute walk from the historic synagogue. The public area is a touch drab with wooden furniture, wood paneling, and brown leather sofas. The same look is carried into the rooms but is relieved by white walls and light-cream-color draperies. ✉ *Rua Gil Avô 31, 2300-586* ☎ *249/323083* ⊕ *www.residencialsinagoga.planetaclix.pt* ⟿ *22 rooms* ⟐ *Some minibars, cable TV, bar* ▭ *AE, DC, MC, V* ⦿ *BP.*

EN ROUTE From Tomar you can take N113 northwest to Ourem and visit its walled medieval castle, including its palace, church with crypt, and Gothic fountain built by king Afonso IV in the 15th century. To reach Castelo de Bode from Tomar, take EN 110 south. Set between hills and forests with inviting sandy beaches and placid waters, the lake (Estalagem Vale Manço) offers boating, fishing, and water sports.

Castelo de Almourol

16 km (10 mi) south of Tomar, 16 km (10 mi) east of Torres Novas. From Tomar take the N110 for 8 km (5 mi) south, turn off on the N358-1 toward Constância until you come to the river, turn right, and you will see the castle.

★ ⑲ For a close look at the **Castelo de Almourol**, a storybook edifice on a craggy island in the Rio Tejo, take the 1½-km-long (1-mi-long) dirt road leading down to the water from N3. The riverbank in this area is practically deserted, making it a wonderful picnic spot. (In summer you can take a boat to the island.) It could hardly be more romantic: an ancient castle with crenellated walls and a lofty tower sits on a greenery-covered rock in the middle of a gently flowing river. The stuff of poetry and legends, Almourol was the setting for Francisco de Morais's epic *Palmeirim da Inglaterra (Palmeirim of England)*.

Where to Stay & Eat

¢–$ ✕ **Restaurante Almourol.** A good lunch stop on the N3, this restaurant is in a lovely old house with gardens, orange trees, and a terrace overlooking the castle. It specializes in river fish dishes, especially savel (shad) and enguias (eels). ⊠ *Av. Cais de Tancos, Vila Nova da Barquinha* ☎ *249/720100* 🖃 *AE, DC, MC, V.*

$–$$$ ✕▦ **Residencial Sol Tejo.** Rooms here are decorated with green-stained pine furniture and flowered fabrics in pastel greens and pinks. Some have views of the Tagus River. In the restaurant, try the grilled or fried *fataça* fished out of the Tagus River. The hotel is 4 km (2½ mi) down the N3 from Castelo de Almourol and overlooks the town of Vila Nova da Barquinha. ⊠ *Soltejo Estrada N3, Vila Nova da Barquinha 2260-418* ☎ *249/720150* ↗ *13 rooms* ⟡ *Restaurant, coffee shop, cable TV* 🖃 *AE, DC, MC, V* ⦿ *BP.*

Constância

⑳ *4 km (2½ mi) east of Castelo de Almourol.*

Peaceful little Constância is at the confluence of the Zêzere and the Tejo. It's best known as the town where poet Luís de Camões was exiled in 1548, the unfortunate result of his romantic involvement with Catarina de Ataíde, the "Natercia" of his poems and a lady-in-waiting to Queen Catarina. There's a bronze statue of the bard in a reflective pose at the riverbank.

Where to Stay & Eat

★ $ ✕▦ **Quinta de Santa Barbara.** If you're looking for a place to immerse yourself in the Portuguese countryside, look no farther. The Quinta, a short drive from town, has several sprawling buildings—a few of which date from the 16th century—on some 45 acres of farmland and pine forests overlooking the Tejo. Each of the seven spacious rooms in the main house is individually decorated with 18th-century Portuguese reproductions and has a modern tiled bathroom. The small restaurant ($$), with a barrel-vault ceiling and stone walls, specializes in local dishes. ⊠ *2 km (1 mi) east of Constância on IP6; follow directions on sign at traffic circle, Refeitório Quinhentista, 2250-092* ☎ *249/739214* ⊕ *www. quinta-santabarbara.com* ⊲☞ *7 rooms* ⚬ *Restaurant, cable TV, tennis court, pool, horseback riding, bar* ⊟ *MC, V* ⊚⨍ *CP.*

Outdoor Activities

The English-speaking guides at **Glaciar-Desportos Bar** (⊠ Av. das Forças Armadas ☎ 962/503986 ⊕ www.glaciar-sportsbar.com) lead a wide variety of adventure activities on both the Tagus and the Zêzere rivers and in the surrounding forest, the Xarneca Alentejana. Half-day excursions include those by canoe, all-terrain bike (BTT), or horseback, or on foot. Food is not included unless you make arrangements beforehand. You can always grab a bite at their meeting point's Bar Esplanada do Zêzere on the riverbank. They also organize multiday camping trips for children. The per-person rates range from €8 for biking, to €20 for canoeing and €50 for horseback riding. They also offer special bike excursions from Marinha Grande to São Pedro de Moel and São Pedro de Moel to Nazaré.

Abrantes

㉑ *16 km (10 mi) east of Constância.*

Abrantes became one of the country's most populous and prosperous towns during the 16th century, when the Rio Tejo was navigable all the way to the sea. With the coming of the railroad and the development of better roads, the town's commercial importance waned. Walk up through the maze of narrow, flower-lined streets to the 16th-century **castelo.** Much of it is in disrepair, but with a bit of imagination you can conjure visions of what an impressive structure this must have been. The garden between the twin fortifications is a wonderful place to watch the sun set: the play of light on the river and the lengthening shadows along the olive groves provide a stirring setting for an evening picnic.

Where to Stay & Eat

$–$$ ✕ **Cristina.** You'll have a pretty garden view from this agreeable restaurant. The specialties include açorda de savel and *lombinhos com migas* (loin of pork served with bread crumbs). When in season, enguias *fritas* (fried eel) is also served. ⊠ *Estrada Nacional N3, Rio de Moinhos* ☎ *241/881177* ⊟ *AE, MC, V* ⊙ *Closed Mon. No dinner Sun.*

$–$$ ✕ **O Fumeiro.** This pleasant, spacious restaurant is handily situated in the old part of town over a café. The food is simple but good, consisting almost entirely of regional specialties. Try the cabrito assado if it's available. ⊠ *Rua do Pisco 9* ☎ *241/363893* ⊟ *No credit cards* ⊙ *Closed Sun.*

$ ✕▥ **Hotel de Turismo.** This Best Western hotel's hilltop location is so spectacular that it's a shame the architect couldn't have come up with something more innovative than an exterior of pink stucco. Inside is a different story: there's an inviting, clubby lounge with a fireplace and comfy leather chairs. Guest rooms are small but comfortable; some have terraces with wonderful vistas. The dining room (¢–$$) also has intoxicating views and is an excellent place to sample *palha de Abrantes* (straw of Abrantes), a dessert consisting of a thick egg and almond paste topped with yellow threadlike wisps made of eggs and sugar. ⊠ *Largo de Santo António, 2200-349* ☎ *241/361261* ⊕ *www.bestwestern.com* ⇆ *41 rooms ⚐ Restaurant, room service, minibars, cable TV, 2 tennis courts, pool, bar, laundry service, meeting rooms, free parking, no-smoking rooms* ▭ *AE, DC, MC, V* ❙❂❙ *BP.*

Sardoal

㉒ *12 km (7 mi) north of Abrantes on N244-3, 20 km (12 mi) northeast of Constância on N358-2.*

Sardoal, an island of white houses with yellow trim and red-tile roofs in a sea of wooded hills, is an enchanting place of narrow streets paved with pebbles from nearby streams. Flowers seem to be everywhere—hanging from windows and balconies and lining the winding lanes and alleys. In such a spot you might expect art to flourish, and the 17th-century parish church *does* contain a collection of fine 16th-century paintings by the "Master of Sardoal," an unknown painter whose works have been found in other parts of the country and whose influence on other artists has been noted.

Castelo de Belver

㉓ *30 km (18 mi) southeast of Sardoal. Follow N244-3 through the pine-covered hills to Chão de Codes; take N244 south toward Gavião.*

A fairytale castle planted on top of a cone-shape hill, the fortress of Belver was built in the last years of the 12th century by the Knights Hospitallers under the command of King Sancho I. The castle commands a superb view of the Tejo. In 1194 this region was threatened by the Moorish forces who controlled the lands south of the river, except for Évora. The expected attack never took place, and the present structure is little changed from its original design. The walls of the keep, which stands in the center of the courtyard, are some 12 feet thick, and on the ground floor is a great cistern of unknown depth. According to local lore, an orange dropped into the well will later appear bobbing down the river.

ESTREMADURA & THE RIBATEJO ESSENTIALS

Transportation

BY AIR

Estremadura and the Ribatejo are served by Lisbon's Aeroporto de Portela, 7 km (4½ mi) north of the city.

No trains run directly between the Airport and Estremadura and the Ribatejo, but you can catch one at Lisbon's Campo Grande or suburban Cacém stations. If you are landing in Lisbon and traveling directly to this area your best bet is to rent a car.

🚹 Airport **Aeroporto Portela** ☎ 21/841-3500 or 21/841-3700 ⊕ www.ana-aeroportos.pt.

BY BUS

There are few, if any, places in this region that aren't served by at least one bus daily. Express coaches run by several regional lines travel regularly between Lisbon and the larger towns such as Santarém, Leiria, and Abrantes. If you have the time and patience, bus travel is an inexpensive way to get around. It's best to do your booking through a travel agent. If you know some Portuguese, you can also get a schedule and fee information by calling the bus stations.

🚹 **Rede Nacional de Expressos** ☎ 707/223344 ⊕ www.rede-expressos.pt. **Fátima** ✉ Av. D. José Alves Correia Silva ☎ 249/531611. **Leiria** ✉ Av. Herois de Angola ☎ 244/811507. **Santarém** ✉ Av. Brasil 41 ☎ 243/333200. **Tomar** ✉ Varzea Grande ☎ 249/312299.

BY CAR

It's easy to reach Estremadura and the Ribatejo from Lisbon, since both provinces begin as extensions of the city's northern suburbs. There are two principal access roads from the capital: the A1 (also called E80 and IP1), which is the Lisbon–Porto toll road, provides the best inland access; the A8 (also called IC1) is the fastest route to the coast. From Porto there's easy access via the A1 tollway.

The roads are generally good, and traffic is light, except for weekend congestion along the coast. There are no confusing big cities in which to get lost, although parking can be a problem in some of the towns. Hotels don't usually charge for parking. Drive with extreme caution. Affable as they are on foot, the Portuguese are among Europe's most aggressive drivers.

CAR RENTAL There are major car-rental agencies in Leiria and Nazaré, as well as in Lisbon.

🚹 **International Agencies Avis** ☎ 262/562190 in Nazaré. **Hertz** ☎ 244/826781 in Leiria, 800/238238 toll-free.

BY TRAIN

Travel by train within central Portugal isn't for people in a hurry. Service to many of the more remote destinations is infrequent—and in some cases nonexistent. Even major attractions such as Nazaré and Mafra have no direct rail links. Nevertheless, trains will take you to most of the strategic bases for touring the towns in this chapter.

The Lisbon–Porto line (Santa Apolónia station) provides reasonably frequent service to Vila Franca de Xira, Santarém, Torres Novas, Tomar, and Fátima. Towns in the western part of the region, such as Torres Vedras, Caldas da Rainha, Óbidos, and Leiria, are served on another line from Lisbon's Rossío station.

🚹 **CP** ☎ 21/888-4025, 800/200904, or 808/208208 ⊕ www.cp.pt.

Contacts & Resources

EMERGENCIES

All sizable towns have at least one pharmacy open weekends, holidays, and after normal store hours. Local newspapers usually keep a schedule, and notices are posted on the door of every pharmacy.

🖪 **General emergencies** ☎ 112. **Caldas da Rainha Hospital Distrital** ✉ Rua Diário de Notícias ☎ 262/830300. **Leiria Hospital Distrital** ✉ Largo D. Mel. Aguiar ☎ 244/817000. **Tomar Hospital Distrital** ✉ Av. Dr. Candido Madureira ☎ 249/321100.

MAIL

🖪 **Fátima** ✉ Rua Conago Dr. M. Formigão ☎ 249/539080. **Leiria** ✉ Rua Sá de Miranda, Lote 1 ☎ 244/830980. **Tomar** ✉ Av. Marquês de Tomar ☎ 249/323094.

TOURS OPTIONS

ORIENTATION TOURS
Few regularly scheduled sightseeing tours originate within the region, but many of the major attractions are covered by a wide selection of one-day tours from Lisbon. For information contact Cityrama.

🖪 **Cityrama** ✉ Av. Praia da Vitória 12-B, Saldanha, Lisbon 1049-054 ☎ 21/319-1090 📠 21/356-0668 🌐 www.cityrama.pt.

BOAT TOURS
Boat trips along the Rio Zêzere depart at noon in summer from a dock at the Estalagem Lago Azul, upstream from the Castelo de Bode dam. The four-hour cruises cost €36.41, including a buffet lunch with wine, but they take place only when there are enough passengers; this is most likely to happen on weekends and national holidays. For reservations and information, contact Hotel dos Templários in Tomar.

🖪 **Estalagem Lago Azul** ✉ Hwy. N348, Ferreira do Zêzere, Castanheira ☎ 249/361445. **Hotel dos Templários** ✉ Largo Candido dos Reis 1, Tomar ☎ 249/310100 🌐 www.hoteldostemplarios.pt.

VISITOR INFORMATION

ESTREMADURA
🖪 Tourist Offices **Alcobaça** ✉ Praça 25 de Abril ☎ 262/582377. **Batalha** ✉ Praça Mouzinho de Albuquerque ☎ 244/765180. **Caldas da Rainha** ✉ Praça 25 de Abril ☎ 262/839700. **Ericeira** ✉ Rua Eduardo Burnay 46 ☎ 261/863122. **Leiria** ✉ Jardim Luís de Camões ☎ 244/848770. **Mafra** ✉ Terreiro D. João V ☎ 261/817170. **Nazaré** ✉ Av. República 17 ☎ 262/561194. **Óbidos** ✉ Outside town walls, at entrance to parking lot ☎ 262/959231. **Peniche** ✉ Rua Alex. Herculano ☎ 262/789571. **Torres Vedras** ✉ Rua 9 de Abril ☎ 261/314094.

THE RIBATEJO
🖪 Tourist Offices **Abrantes** ✉ Largo 1 de Maio ☎ 241/362555. **Constância** ✉ Câmara Municipal ☎ 249/730050. **Fátima** ✉ Av. José Correia A. da Silva ☎ 249/531139. **Santarém** ✉ Rua Capelo e Ivens 63 ☎ 243/304437. **Tomar** ✉ Rua Serpa Pinto 1 ☎ 249/329000. **Torres Novas** ✉ Largo dos Combatentes da Segunda Guerra Mundial 4-5 ☎ 249/813019. **Vila Franca de Xira** ✉ Rua Almirante Cándido dos Reis 147 ☎ 263/285605.

Évora &
the Alentejo

WORD OF MOUTH

"Marvão is a town up on a hill that looks out over the plain on all sides. It's a breathtaking view, it has an unbelievable castle, it's magical. At night, it's one of those places where you see the stars everywhere and breathe clean air deeply and just appreciate being alive and able to enjoy it all."

—Ireynold1

Updated by
Mary McLean

THE ALENTEJO, WHICH MEANS "THE LAND BEYOND THE RIO TEJO" (Tagus River) in Portuguese, is a vast, sparsely populated area of heath and rolling hills punctuated with stands of cork and olive trees. It's the country's largest region, stretching from the rugged west-coast beaches all the way east to Spain and from the Tejo in the north to the low mountains on the border of the Algarve, Portugal's southernmost region. Its central hub, Évora, is rich with traditional Portuguese architecture. Over the centuries the pastoral countryside has been the scene of innumerable battles: between Romans and Visigoths, Moors and Christians, Portuguese and Spaniards, Portuguese and French, and finally (in the 1830s) between rival Portuguese factions in a civil war. Few hilltops in the region are without at least a trace of a castle or fortress.

Portugal is the world's largest producer of cork, and much of it comes from the Alentejo. This industry is not for people in a hurry. It takes two decades before the trees can be harvested, and then their bark can be carefully stripped only once every nine years. The numbers painted on the trees indicate the year of the last harvest. Exhibits at several regional museums chronicle this delicate process and display associated tools and handicrafts.

The undulating fields of wheat and barley surrounding Beja and Évora, the rice paddies of Alcácer do Sal, and the vineyards of Borba and Reguengos de Monsaraz are representative of the region's role as Portugal's breadbasket. Traditions here are strong. Herdsmen tending sheep and goats wear the *pelico* (traditional sheepskin vest), and women in the fields wear broad-brim hats over kerchiefs and colorful patterned dresses over trousers. Dwellings are dazzling white; more elegant houses have wrought-iron balconies and grillwork. The windows and doors of modest cottages and hilltop country *montes* (farmhouses) are trimmed with blue or yellow, and colorful flowers abound. The best time to visit the Alentejo is spring, when temperatures are pleasant and the fields are carpeted with wildflowers. Summer can be brutal, with the mercury frequently topping 37°C (100°F). As the Portuguese say, "In the Alentejo there is no shade but what comes from the sky."

Exploring Évora & the Alentejo

The Alentejo contains a wide variety of attractions—from the rugged west-coast beaches to the Roman and medieval architecture of Évora. The area is divided roughly into two parts: the more mountainous region north of Évora, and the flatter Lower Alentejo, in the southern part of the region.

Restaurants & Cuisine

In the Alentejo, the country's granary, bread is a major part of most meals. It's the basis of a popular dish known as *açorda,* a thick, stick-to-the-ribs porridge to which various ingredients such as fish, meat, and eggs are added. Açorda *de marisco*—bread with eggs, seasonings, and assorted shellfish—is one of the more popular varieties. Another version, açorda *alentejana,* consists of a clear broth, olive oil, garlic, slices of bread, and poached eggs. *Cação,* baby shark, is a white-meat fish

GREAT ITINERARIES

You can make convenient loops starting and finishing in Lisbon, or you can extend your travels by continuing south to the Algarve from Beja or Santiago do Cacém. You should allow 10 days to get a feel for the region, exploring Évora and visiting some outlying attractions such as Monsaraz, Castelo de Vide, and Mértola. This will also allow time for a day or two of sunbathing on a west-coast beach. If you skip the beach, you can cover the most interesting attractions at a comfortable pace in seven days. Three days will give you time to explore Évora and its surroundings along with one or two additional highlights.

Numbers in the text correspond to numbers in the margin and on the Évora, the Upper Alentejo, and the Lower Alentejo maps.

IF YOU HAVE 3 DAYS
Be sure to include 🏠 **Évora** ❶–❶⑥, one of Portugal's most beautiful cities, in your first day of exploring. The following morning visit the rug-producing town of **Arraiolos** ❷⓪ and then continue on to **Estremoz** ❷④ and its imposing fortress, which doubles as a pousada. Head east past Borba and its marble quarries

to **Vila Viçosa** ❷③, site of the Paço Ducal. Then continue south to the whitewashed village of 🏠 **Terena** ❷②. In the morning visit the fortified hilltop town of **Monsaraz** ❷① before returning to Lisbon.

IF YOU HAVE 7 DAYS
After a day and night in 🏠 **Évora** ❶–❶⑥, head to the **Aqueduto da Agua da Prata** ❶⑦ and the prehistoric sites just outside town, which include the **Cromlech and the Menhir of Almendres** ❶⑧ and the **Dolmen of Zambujeiro** ❶⑨. On the way to your next overnight stop in 🏠 **Estremoz** ❷④, take a break in **Arraiolos** ❷⓪. From Estremoz head east to the fortified town of 🏠 **Elvas** ❷⑥, stopping en route at the Paço Ducal in **Vila Viçosa** ❷③. The following day continue to **Monsaraz** ❷①, with a stop along the way at **Terena** ❷②. From Monsaraz head south to 🏠 **Beja** ❸⑤, inspecting the Roman ruins at **São Cucufate** ❸③ en route. The next day head west to 🏠 **Santiago do Cacém** ❸⑨ for more Roman ruins and a few hours at the beach. On your seventh day return to Lisbon, stopping along the way to see the castle at **Alcácer do Sal** ❹⓪.

with a single bone down the back and is mostly served in a fish soup or as part of a porridge.

Pork from the Alentejo is the best in the country and often is combined with clams, onions, and tomatoes in the classic dish *carne de porco à alentejana*. One of Portugal's most renowned sheep's milk cheeses—tangy, but mellow when properly ripened—is made in the Serpa region. Alentejo wines—especially those from around Borba and Reguengos de Monsaraz—are regular prizewinners at national tasting contests.

Elvas, near the Spanish border, is known for its tasty sugar plums. *Ameixas D'Elvas* (Elvas plums) were exported with port wine to England and the Americas and became a popular Christmas sweet among

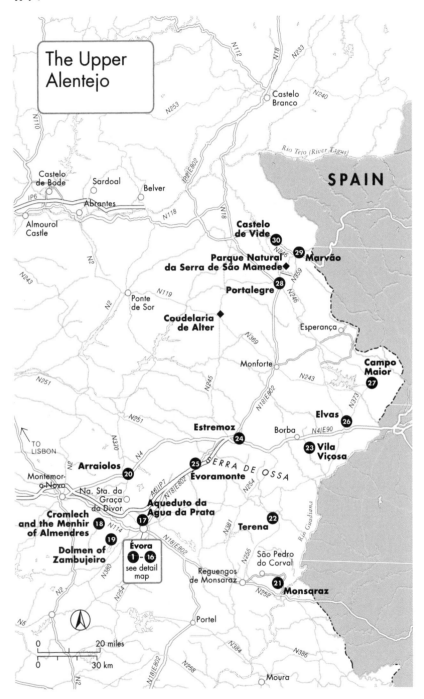

The Upper
Alentejo

the English. The plums are the green, very sweet Rainha Cláudia variety. The Alto Alentejo region offers the best climate for growing them and pesticides aren't used. As the supply is small and the demand is great, the plums are considered a gourmet treat. They can be eaten fresh, as prunes, dipped in a sugar syrup, candied, or as a jam.

Between mid-June and mid-September reservations are advised at upscale restaurants. Many moderate or inexpensive establishments, however, don't accept reservations and have informal dining rooms where you share a table with other diners. Dress at all but the most luxurious restaurants is casual.

About the Hotels

The best accommodations in this region are the *pousadas*. Indeed, some of the finest in the country are in the Alentejo, including one in the old Lóios convent in Évora and another in the castle at Estremoz. Many of the pousadas are small, some with as few as six rooms, so reserving well in advance is essential. There are also a number of high-quality, government-approved private guesthouses in the region. Look for signs that say TURISMO RURAL or TURISMO DE HABITAÇÃO. In summer, air-conditioning is absolutely necessary in Évora, where temperatures can soar to more than 44°C (110°F).

WHAT IT COSTS In Euros					
	$$$$	$$$	$$	$	¢
RESTAURANTS	over €21	€16–€21	€11–€15	€7–€10	under €7
HOTELS	over €275	€176–€275	€101–€175	€60–€100	under €60

Restaurant prices are per person for a main course at dinner. Hotel prices are for a standard double room, including tax, in high season (off-season rates may be lower).

When to Go

Spring comes early to this part of Portugal. Early April to mid-June is a wonderful time to tour, when the fields are full of colorful wildflowers. July and August are brutally hot, with temperatures in places such as Beja often reaching 37°C (100°F) or more. By mid-September things cool off sufficiently to make touring this region a delight.

ÉVORA & ENVIRONS

Dressed in traditional garb, shepherds and farmers with faces wizened by a lifetime in the baking sun stand around the fountain at Praça do Giraldo; a group of college girls dressed in jeans and T-shirts chat animatedly at a sidewalk café; a local businessman in coat and tie purposefully hurries by; and clusters of tourists, cameras in hand, capture the historic monuments on film—all this is part of a typical summer's day in Évora. The flourishing capital of the central Alentejo is also a university town with an astonishing variety of inspiring architecture. Atop a small hill in the heart of a vast cork-, olive-, and grain-producing region, Évora stands out from provincial farm towns the world over: the

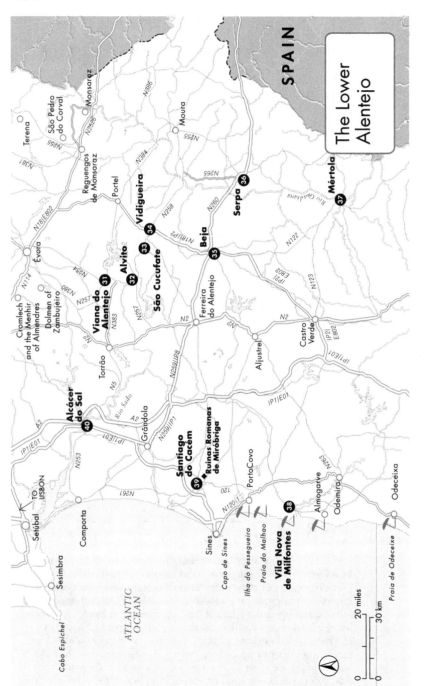

The Lower Alentejo

A BIT OF HISTORY

Although the region was inhabited some 4,000 years ago—as attested to by the dolmens and menhirs in the countryside—it was during the Roman epoch that the town called Liberalitas Julia in the province of Lusitania first achieved importance. A large part of present-day Évora is built on Roman foundations, of which the Temple of Diana, with its graceful Corinthian columns, is the most conspicuous reminder.

The Moors also made a great historical impact on the area. They arrived in 715 and remained more than 450 years. They were driven out in 1166, thanks in part to a clever ruse perpetrated by Geraldo Sem Pavor (Gerald the Fearless). Geraldo tricked Évora's Moorish ruler into leaving a strategic watchtower unguarded. With a small force, Geraldo took control of the tower. To regain control of it, most of the Moorish troops left their posts at the city's main entrance, allowing the bulk of Geraldo's forces to march in unopposed.

Toward the end of the 12th century Évora's fortunes increased as the town became the favored location for the courts of the Burgundy and Avis dynasties. It attracted many of the great minds and creative talents of Renaissance Portugal. Some of the more prominent residents at this time were Gil Vicente, the founder of Portuguese theater; the sculptor Nicolas Chanterene; and Gregorio Lopes, the painter known for his renderings of court life. Such a concentration of royal wealth and creativity superimposed upon the existing Moorish town was instrumental in the development of the delicate Manueline-Mudéjar (elaborate, Moslem-influenced) architectural style. You can see fine examples of this in the graceful lines of the Palácio de Dom Manuel and the turreted Ermida de São Bras.

entire inner city is a monument and was declared a UNESCO World Heritage site in 1986.

Évora is, above all, a town for walking. Wherever you glance as you stroll the maze of narrow streets and alleys of the Cidade Velha (Old Town), amid arches and whitewashed houses, you'll come face to face with reminders of the town's rich architectural and cultural heritage. West of Praça do Giraldo, between Rua Serpa Pinto and Rua dos Mercadores you have the old Jewish quarter of narrow streets lined with medieval houses. A tourist bus (€1 for all-day ticket) sponsored by the city follows a blue line marked on the street through the historic center. To get on just raise your hand anywhere along the blue line; you can get off whenever you wish. The area surrounding Évora is a rich agricultural region with scattered small villages and some of Portugal's earliest inhabited sites.

Note that, of the churches mentioned below, only the Sé and the Igreja de São Francisco have regular visiting hours. To view the interiors of the others you may have to sit in on a mass (times for services are usually posted on church doors) and look around afterward.

Évora

❶–⓰   *164 km (102 mi) southeast of Lisbon.*

Fodor's Choice
★

TIMING   Allow at least 2½ hours to tour Évora, or even 3, depending on how long you decide to spend relaxing with a drink in the gardens.

What to See

Ermida de São Bras (St. Blaise Chapel). A curious structure built in the late 15th century, this was the first important building in the Alentejo to join Gothic and Moorish elements and form the Gothic-Mudéjar style. The fortified church, a few hundred feet south of the city walls, is characterized by massive battlement-topped walls and a series of round towers crowned with steep spires. ⊠ *Rua da República* ☎ *No phone.*

⓫ Igreja de Espírito Santo (Church of the Holy Spirit). This 16th-century church is a squat structure fronted by five arches. It was originally part of the ancient Évora University. The interior contains some fine azulejos and paintings, including artist Gregorio Lopes's painting of the *Last Supper.* ⊠ *Largo do Colégio* ☎ *No phone.*

❼ Igreja dos Lóios (Lóios Church). This church is next to the former Convento dos Lóios, which is now the Pousada dos Lóios. The sanctuary, dedicated to St. John the Evangelist, was founded in the 15th century by the Venetian-based Lóios Order. Its interior walls are covered with 18th-century azulejo panels created by Oliveira Bernardes, the foremost master of this unique Portuguese art form. The blue-and-white tiles depict scenes from the life of the church's founder, Rodrigo de Melo, who, along with members of his family, is buried here. The bas-relief marble tombstones at the foot of the high altar are the only ones of their kind in Portugal. Note the two metal hatches on either side of the main aisle: one covers an ancient cistern, which belonged to the Moorish castle that predated the church (an underground spring still supplies the cistern with potable water), and beneath the other hatch lie the neatly stacked bones of hundreds of monks. This bizarre ossuary was uncovered in 1958 during restoration work. Enhanced by the 16th-century Renaissance gallery, the cloister is now an integral part of the Pousada dos Lóios. ⊠ *Largo do Conde de Vila Flor* ☎ *266/704714* ✉ *€3* ☉ *Tues.–Sun. 10–12:30 and 2–6.*

⓭ Igreja de Misericórdia (Mercy Church). The interior of this 16th-century church is lined with large azulejo panels depicting scenes from the life of Christ; the unsigned 18th-century tiles are thought to be the work of António de Oliveira de Bernardes. ⊠ *Rua da Misericórdia* ☎ *No phone.*

⓮ Igreja a Nossa Senhora da Graça (Our Lady of Grace Church). A splendid piece of classic Italian-style architecture, this church represents the first breath of the Renaissance in provincial Portuguese architecture. Note the massive figures on columns at either side of the portal. According to local legend, these four figures represent the first victims put to death in the Inquisition in Évora in 1543. ⊠ *Largo da Graça* ☎ *No phone.*

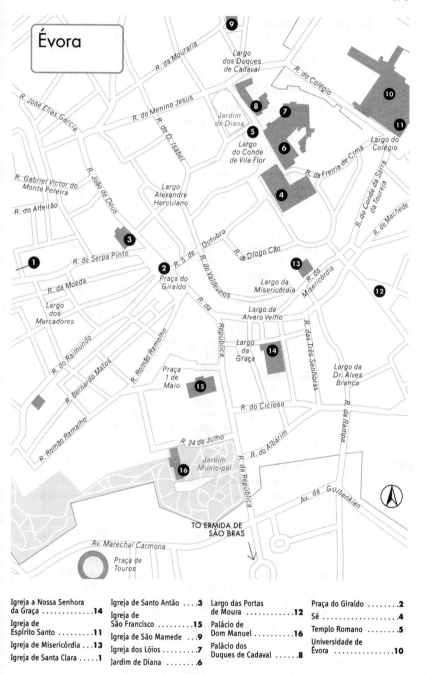

Évora

① Igreja de Santa Clara. This church temporarily houses a limited collection of pieces of sculpture paintings belonging to the Évora Museum, which is undergoing renovations. Highlights such as the primitive paintings by 16th-century Flemish priest Frei Carlos and Flemish paintings of the Bruges school and archaeological artifacts are on display. ⊠ *Rua Serpa Pinto* ☎ *266/702604* 🎫 *€1.50* ☉ *Wed.–Sun. 10–6, Tues. 2–6.*

③ Igreja de Santo Antão. Note the striking white Renaissance facade of this church, which stands near the fountain at the north end of Praça do Giraldo. A medieval hermitage of the Knights Templar was razed in 1553 to make way for this church, which has massive round pillars and soaring vaulted ceilings. The marble altar in bas-relief is a holdover from the primitive hermitage. ⊠ *Praça do Giraldo.*

⑮ Igreja de São Francisco. After the Sé, this is the grandest of Évora's churches. Its construction in the early 16th century, on the site of a former Gothic chapel, involved the greatest talents of the day, including Nicolas Chanterene, Oliver of Ghent, and the Arruda brothers, Francisco and Diogo. The magnificent architecture notwithstanding, the bizarre **Capela dos Ossos** (Chapel of Bones) is the main attraction. The translation of the chilling inscription over the entrance reads WE BONES WHO ARE HERE ARE WAITING FOR YOURS. The bones of some 5,000 skeletons dug up from cemeteries in the area line the ceilings and supporting columns. With a flair worthy of Charles Addams, a 16th-century Franciscan monk placed skulls jaw-to-cranium so they form arches across the ceiling; arm and leg bones are neatly stacked to shape the supporting columns. ⊠ *Praça 1 de Maio* ☎ *266/704521* 🎫 *€1* ☉ *Sun.–Fri. 9–1 and 2:30–5:30.*

⑨ Igreja de São Mamede (St. Mamede's Church). This small church contains a vaulted ceiling decorated with baroque frescoes. Note the fine azulejos that cover the nave's wall. The marble bust of Renaissance humanist Andre de Resende on the east wall was created by João Cutileiro, a well-known contemporary Portuguese sculptor. ⊠ *Rua da Mouraria* ☎ *No phone.*

NEED A BREAK? Off Rua 24 de Julho, a few steps from the Igreja de São Francisco, the **Jardim Municipal** (Municipal Gardens) is a pleasant place to rest after the rigors of sightseeing. The extensive and verdant gardens are landscaped with plants and trees from all over the world.

⑥ Jardim de Diana (Diana Garden). Opposite the Templo Romano, the restful, tree-lined park looks out over the aqueduct and the plains from the modest heights of what is sometimes grandiosely referred to as "Évora's Acropolis." You can take in nearly 2,000 years of Portuguese history from here. One sweeping glance encompasses the temple, the spires of the Gothic Sé, the Igreja dos Lóios, and the 20th-century pousada housed in the convent. A garden café at the corner of the park is a great spot to reflect on the architectural marvels before you. ⊠ *Largo do Conde de Vila Flor.*

⑫ Largo das Portas de Moura. One of Évora's most beautiful squares is characterized by paired stone towers that guard one of the principal entrances to the walled old city. The spires of the Sé rise above the towers, and in the center of the square is an unusual Renaissance fountain. The large white-marble sphere, supported by a single column, bears a commemorative inscription in Latin dated 1556. Overlooking the fountain is the Cordovil Mansion (closed to the public), on whose terrace are several particularly attractive arches decorated in the Manueline-Mudéjar style. ⊠ *Bounded by Ruas D. Augusto Eduardo Nunes, Enrique da Fonseca, Mendes Esteves, de Machede, and Miguel Bombarda, a 5-min walk southeast of the Sé.*

16 **Palácio de Dom Manuel.** Located at the entrance to the Jardim Municipal, only a part of this former royal palace remains. The existing wing was restored after a fire in 1916 and displays a row of paired, gracefully curved Manueline windows. On the building's south side there's a notable arcade of redbrick sawtooth arches. Currently used as an art gallery, the palace has witnessed a number of historic events since its construction in the late 15th century. It was here, for instance, in 1497, that Vasco da Gama received his commission to command the fleet that would discover the sea route to India.

8 **Palácio dos Duques de Cadaval** (Palace of the Dukes of Cadaval). The palace is readily identified by two massive stone towers that have pointed battlements. These towers, once part of a medieval castle that protected the town, were later incorporated into this former residence of kings João I and João IV. A small gallery contains historic documents, paintings, and the unusual Flemish-style bronze tomb of Rui de Sousa, a signatory of the Treaty of Tordesillas. In 1494 the treaty divided the world into two spheres of influence: Spanish and Portuguese. Today, much of the palace is used by the city, but the ground-floor gallery is open to the public. ⊠ *Largo do Conde de Vila Flor* ☎ *266/704714* ⊠ *€3* ⊗ *Daily 10–12:30 and 2–6.*

2 **Praça do Giraldo.** The arcade-lined square in the center of the old walled
Fodor'sChoice city is named after Évora's liberator, Gerald the Fearless. During Cae-
★ sar's time the square, marked by a large arch, was the Roman forum. In 1571 the arch was destroyed to make room for the fountain, a simple half sphere made of white Estremoz marble and designed by the Renaissance architect Afonso Álvares.

NEED A BREAK? The **Café Arcada,** opposite the fountain on Praça do Giraldo, is an Évora institution. The large hall, divided into snack bar and restaurant sections, is decorated with photos of the big bands that played here in the 1940s. Tables on the square are just the place from which to watch the city on parade.

Rua 5 de Outubro. The narrow cobblestone pedestrian thoroughfare is lined with souvenir shops and whitewashed houses with wrought-iron balconies. It's one of the town's most attractive streets and connects the Praça do Giraldo and the cathedral.

★ **4** **Sé.** Two, massive, asymmetrical towers and battlement-ringed walls give the Sé a fortresslike appearance. The transitional Gothic-style cathedral was constructed in 1186 from huge granite blocks. It has been enhanced over the centuries with an octagonal, turreted dome above the transept; a blue-tile spire atop the north tower; a number of fine Manueline windows; and several Gothic rose windows. At the entrance, Gothic arches are supported by marble columns bearing delicately sculpted statues of the apostles. With the exception of a fine baroque chapel, the granite interior is somber. The cloister, a 14th-century Gothic addition with Mudéjar vestiges, is one of the finest of its type in the country. Statues of the evangelists decorate the corners. Housed in the Sé's towers and chapter room is the **Museu de Arte Sacra da Sé** (Sacred Art Museum). Of particular interest is a 13th-century ivory *Virgin of Paradise,* whose body opens up to show exquisitely carved scenes of her life. Her head is a 16th-century wooden replacement, strangely out of proportion with her figure. ⊠ *Largo Marquês de Marialva* ☎ *266/759330* 🖾 *Museum and cloisters €4* ⊙ *Museum daily 9–noon and 2–4:30, cathedral daily 9–noon and 2–5.*

⑤ Templo Romano (Roman Temple). The well-preserved ruins of the Roman Temple dominate Largo do Conde de Vila Flor. The edifice, considered one of the finest of its kind on the Iberian Peninsula, was probably built in the 1st to 2nd century AD. Although it has long been referred to as the Temple of Diana, historians believe that the use of the Corinthian order of architecture in its columns and entablature indicates that it was dedicated to an emperor. The temple, largely destroyed during the invasions of the barbarian tribes in the early 5th century, was later used for various purposes, including that of municipal slaughterhouse in the 14th century. It was restored to its present state in 1871. ⊠ *Largo do Conde de Vila Flor.*

Fodor'sChoice ★

⑩ Universidade de Évora. From 1555 until its closure by the Marquis de Pombal in 1759, this university was a Jesuit college; in 1979, after a lapse of more than 200 years, Évora University resumed classes. Although the enrollment is small, the college's presence enlivens this ancient city. The large courtyard is flanked on all sides by graceful buildings with double-tier, white-limestone, arched galleries in Italian Renaissance style. From the main entrance you'll see the imposing baroque facade of the gallery, known as the Sala dos Actos (Hall of Acts), which is crowned with allegorical figures and coats of arms carved in white marble quarried in the region. Lining the gallery's interior are azulejo works depicting historical, mythological, and biblical themes. ⊠ *Rua do Colégio.*

SHOPPING

The brightly colored hand-painted plates, bowls, and figurines from the Upper Alentejo are popular throughout Portugal. The best selection of this distinctive type of folk art is in and around Estremoz, where the terra-cotta jugs and bowls are adorned with chips of marble from local quarries. Saturday morning the *rossio* (town square) is chock-full of vendors displaying their wares. Redondo and the village of São Pedro do Corval, near Reguengos de Monsaraz, are also good sources of this type of pottery, as is Évora. The village of Arraiolos, near Évora, is famous for its hand-embroidered wool rugs.

Where to Stay & Eat

★ **$$–$$$** ✕ **O Fialho.** Amor and Gabriel Fialho are the third generation of Fialhos to operate this popular, traditional restaurant. It may be rustic—with a beamed ceiling and painted plates hung on its walls—but the food is quite sophisticated. Start with the excellent *salada de polvo* (marinated octopus salad) and, as a main course, try the *perdiz de convento a cartuxa* (roast partridge with potatoes and carrots), which is made according to a recipe from a nearby monastery. There's a wide selection of Alentejo wines. ✉ *Travessa das Mascarenhas 16* ☎ *266/703079* ▤ *AE, DC, MC, V* ⊘ *Closed Mon.*

★ **$–$$$** ✕ **Cozinha de Santo Humberto.** One of Évora's oldest restaurants was once a wine cellar. Try the *sopa de peixe alentejana* (a mixed fish soup) or the *carne de porco com ameijoas* (small pieces of pork sautéed with clams). Game dishes such as grouse, wild boar, and partridge are particularly good in season (Santo Humberto, is, after all, the patron saint of hunters). The list of Alentejo wines is excellent. There's a cheaper café attached. ✉ *Rua da Moeda 39* ☎ *266/704251* ▤ *AE, DC, MC, V.*

$–$$ ✕ **Tasquinha do Oliveira.** Nobody has gone to any pains decorating this tiny restaurant, but the food is something else. Such game dishes as *arroz de lebre* (hare cooked with rice) and alentejan classics like *pézinhos de coentrada* (pigs' trotters with coriander) are superbly prepared. ✉ *Rua Cándido dos Reis 45-A* ☎ *266/744841* ▤ *AE, MC, V* ⊘ *Closed Sun. and Aug. 1–15.*

$ ✕ **Adega do Alentejano.** The food is hearty and simple in this pleasantly rustic Alentejo wine cellar. Try the special tomato soup, which is a meal in itself, with meat on the side, or the black pork steaks (black pork is flavorful and fattier than your average pork). Stick to the very reasonable local wine from the barrel, and you'll be agreeably surprised by the bill. ✉ *Rua Gabriel Vito do Monte Pereira 21-A* ☎ *266/744447* ▤ *No credit cards* ⊘ *Closed Sun.*

★ **$$$** ✕▥ **Pousada dos Lóios.** This luxurious pousada is in the 15th-century monastery opposite the Templo Romano. Except for the small size of the rooms, which were formerly the monks' cells, and the need for anyone over 5 feet 2 inches to duck when entering, there's no trace of monastic austerity here. Opulent period furnishings compensate for the cramped quarters, and elegant public rooms deserve a visit even if you don't plan to spend the night. Superbly prepared Alentejo specialties are served in the restaurant ($–$$$), a marvel of Manueline details. ✉ *Largo do Conde de Vila Flor, 7000-804* ☎ *266/730070* 🖷 *266/707248* ⊕ *www.pousadas.pt* ⤴ *31 rooms, 1 suite* ⚬ *Restaurant, cable TV, pool, bar, Wi-Fi* ▤ *AE, DC, MC, V* ▥ *BP.*

$ ✕▥ **Évora Hotel.** On the route to Montemor-o-Novo, just outside town, you'll find this pleasant, modern establishment. Guest rooms are generous in size and have small balconies. Public areas are light and spacious, as is the dining room ($–$$), which presents a delicious buffet of regional specialties on Sunday. ✉ *Quinta do Cruzeiro (N114), 7000-171* ☎ *266/748800* 🖷 *266/748806* ⤴ *166 rooms, 4 suites* ⚬ *Restaurant, cable TV, tennis court, 2 pools (1 indoor), ethernet, hot tub, sauna, bar* ▤ *AE, DC, MC, V* ▥ *BP.*

$$ ⊞ **Hotel da Cartuxa.** Building a two-story hotel—one that's simultaneously rustic *and* modern—inside a 14th-century walled city is no small feat. This establishment, just steps from Praça do Giraldo in the old part of town, proves that it can be done successfully, though. The comfortable public areas are furnished with antiques, and the large guest rooms have tiled baths. Ask for a room at the back for a view of the garden, pool, and Roman walls. ⊠ *Travessa da Palmeira 4/6, 7000-546* ☎ *266/ 739300* 🖶 *266/739305* ⊕ *www.hoteldacartuxa.com* ⬐ *79 rooms, 6 suites* ⚬ *Restaurant, cable TV, minibars, pool, bar, Wi-Fi, parking (fee)* ☰ *AE, DC, MC, V* ⓞ *FAP, MAP.*

$$ ⊞ **Hotel D. Fernando.** Most of the airy, well-equipped rooms in this modern hotel have balconies overlooking the lawn-surrounded swimming pool, which is very inviting after a day of summer sightseeing. Public areas are pleasant and spacious. The hotel is just outside Évora's old walls, a short stroll from the historic center. ⊠ *Av. Dr. Barahona 2, 7000-756* ☎ *266/737990* 🖶 *266/741716* ⬐ *101 rooms, 2 suites* ⚬ *Restaurant, cable TV, Wi-Fi, pool, bar* ☰ *AE, DC, MC, V* ⓞ *EP.*

$ ⊞ **Santa Clara.** What this unpretentious hotel lacks in facilities it makes up for in location—it's close to Praça do Giraldo and the center of Évora. Rooms are on the small side but are pleasantly furnished and adequately equipped. ⊠ *Travessa da Milheira 19, 7000-545* ☎ *266/704141* 🖶 *266/706544* ⬐ *43 rooms* ⚬ *Bar* ☰ *AE, DC, MC, V* ⓞ *CP.* ·

$ ⊞ **Solar de Monfalim.** In a historic building with a delightful arched gallery overlooking the street, this comfortable, family-run guesthouse provides quiet, old-fashion hospitality in the heart of the old city. The rooms, although small, are comfortably furnished, as is the TV lounge. ⊠ *Largo da Misericórdia 1, 7000-646* ☎ *266/750000* 🖶 *266/742367* ⊕ *www. monfalimtur.pt* ⬐ *26 rooms* ⚬ *Cable TV, bar, parking (fee)* ☰ *AE, MC, V* ⓞ *BP.*

¢ ⊞ **Hotel Ibis.** Just outside the city gate, this international hotel chain is a safe bet for those who want nothing more than comfortable, well-maintained rooms. ⊠ *Quinta da Tapada, Urbanização da Muralha, 7000-980* ☎ *266/760700* 🖶 *266/744632* ⊕ *www.ibishotel.com* ⬐ *87 rooms* ⚬ *Restaurant, snack bar, cable TV, bar, free parking, Wi-Fi, some pets allowed (fee)* ☰ *AE, DC, MC, V.*

¢ ⊞ **Pensão Residencial Giraldo.** Set in a three-story historic building near Praça do Giraldo, this pension offers plain rooms with white walls, wooden furniture, and blue-and-white bedspreads. Some of the floors have carpets and others tiles. Be sure to ask for a room with a bath or you will risk having to share one in the hall, although this may be okay if you are euro-economizing, as they cost around €10 less. ⊠ *Rua dos Mercadores 27, 7000-530* ☎ *266/705833* ⬐ *28 rooms, 18 with bath* ⚬ *Cable TV* ☰ *AE, DC, MC, V.*

Nightlife & the Arts

Casa do Vinho (⊠ Praça 1° de Maio 14 ☎ 266/709445) is an elegant wine bar with more than 200 different labels from the Alentejo. It also serves *petiscos* (tidbits) until 2 AM. The dance club **Praxis Clube** (⊠ Rua de Valdevinos 21 ☎ No phone) has two dance floors, one for house music and the other for chart favorites.

Every July the Casa Cadaval hosts the **Festival Évora Clássica** (✉ Jardim do Paço ☎ 266/744300), during which national and internationally renowned classical musicians perform, including the Gulbenkian Orchestra. Performances are held at the Garcia de Resende Theater and the Palácio das 5 Quinas. Tickets cost €10–€15.

Shopping

Rua 5 de Outubro is lined with shops selling regional handicrafts such as painted furniture, hand-painted ceramics, leather, cork, basketwork, ironwork, rugs, and quilted blankets.

O Pierrot (✉ Rua 5 de Outubro 65-A ☎ 266/703021) sells Alentejo regional handicrafts, from cork and leather to furniture and Alentejo wines. Young artists make and sell contemporary ceramics in their studio, **Cerâmica Contemporânea** (✉ Oficina da Terra, Rua do Raimundo 51-A ☎ 266/746049).

Outside the city gate, the workshop of Portugal's most internationally known sculptor, **João Cutileiro** (✉ Estrada de Viana 13 ☎ 266/703972 🖷 266/742849), can be visited upon appointment. He works in the finest Alentejo and imported marble. Some of his best pieces are female nudes, historical figures, and trees. To arrange a visit, you must first call between noon and 1, or 4 and 8 to make an appointment, or send an e-mail.

Outdoor Activities

Professor Murteira Reis of **Mendes e Murteira** (✉ Rua 31 de Janeiro, 15-A ☎ 266/739240 or 917/236025 ⊕ www.evora-mm.pt) organizes historical walking tours for groups of two to five people. These also can include visits to prehistoric sites in the region, nature walks, bird-watching, and ballooning. A half-day walking tour costs €80, not including monument fees. Tours by car are an additional €30.

FOUR-WHEEL DRIVING & BIKE TOURS

TurAventur (✉ Rua João de Deus 21 ☎ 266/743134 ⊕ www.turaventur.com) organize jeep tours to megaliths and other sights, as well as bike tours in the surrounding countryside.

GO-KARTS

Lucena Karting (✉ Quinta Lucena ☎ 266/896680 ⊕ www.kartevora.pt), a go-kart track on the outskirts of Évora (take N114 toward Montemor-o-Novo), provides an outlet for pent-up youthful energy. It costs €6.50 to take a five-minute spin; for €40 you can ride around for an hour. The track is open Tuesday through Sunday from 9 to 1 and 2 to 7, 10 AM to 11 PM in August.

HORSEBACK RIDING

The **Equeturi** (✉ Quinta do Bacêlo ☎ 266/742884) horseback-riding center is about 2 km (1 mi) from Évora on the road to Montemor-o-Novo. It gives lessons and conducts escorted rides in the countryside. Reservations are advised.

Évora Environs

A trip through the countryside surrounding Évora will take you to some of the earliest-inhabited sites in Portugal.

⓱ Aqueduto da Agua da Prata. The graceful arched Silver Water Aqueduct, which once carried water to Évora from the springs at Graça do Divor, is best seen along the road to Arraiolos (EN 144-4). You can also see a section of it within Évora, along the Rua do Cano in the city's northwest corner. Constructed in 1532 under the patronage of Dom João III, the aqueduct was designed by the famous architect Francisco de Arruda. Extensive parts of the system remain intact and can be seen from the road. ⊠ *Extends 18 km (11 mi) north of Évora.*

⓲ Cromlech and the Menhir of Almendres. The village of Guadalupe has a 17th-century chapel, but it's better known for its prehistoric relics. Near the agricultural cooperative's grain storage bins is the Menhir of Almendres, an 8-foot-tall Neolithic stone obelisk believed to have been used in fertility rites. Several hundred yards away is the cromlech, 95 granite monoliths arranged in an oval in the middle of a large field on a hill. The monoliths face the sunrise and are believed to have been the social, religious, and political center of the agro-pastoral, seminomadic population. The site is also believed to be linked to astral observations and predictions, fertility rites, and the worship of the mother goddess. ⊠ *15 km (9 mi) west of Évora, Guadalupe.*

⓳ Dolmen of Zambujeiro. The 20-foot-high Dolmen of Zambujeiro is the largest of its kind on the Iberian Peninsula. This prehistoric monument is typical of those found throughout Neolithic Europe: several great stone slabs stand upright, supporting a flat stone that serves as a roof. These structures were designed as burial chambers. ⊠ *12 km (7 mi) southwest of Évora. From N380 (the Évora–Alcáçovas road) take the turnoff to Valverde.*

Arraiolos

⓴ *22 km (14 mi) northwest of Évora.*

Arraiolos, dominated by the ruins of a once-mighty walled fortress, is a typical hilltop Alentejo village of whitewashed houses and narrow streets. What distinguishes it is its worldwide reputation as a carpet-producing center. In the 16th century, as Portuguese trade with the East grew, an interest developed in the intricate designs of the carpets from India and Persia, and these patterns served as models for the earliest hand-embroidered Arraiolos carpets. The colorful rugs aren't mass-produced in factories but are handmade by locals in their homes and cottages. An authentic Arraiolos rug, made of locally produced wool, has some 4,000 ties per square foot. To discourage imitations, in 1992 the town council designed a blue seal of authenticity to be affixed to each carpet. There's a permanent exhibition of Arraiolos carpets in the **Câmara Municipal** (Town Hall). Contact the tourist office, which is in the Town Hall, for more information. ⊠ *Praça Lima e Brito 27* ☎ *266/490240 for tourist office* 🖼 *Free* ⊙ *Weekdays 9–12:30 and 2–5:30, weekend hrs vary.*

Where to Stay & Eat

$–$$ ✗ **O Alpendre.** Next to the parish church in the center of town, this restaurant decorated in typical Alentejo style serves regional dishes such as *migas* (thick bread soup made with corn bread) with asparagus and *sopa de cação* (baby shark soup). Try the *carne de porco preto* (black pork). ⊠ *Bairro Serpa Pinto* ☎ *266/419024* ⊟ *AE, DC, MC, V* ⊗ *No dinner Mon.*

$$$ ✕⊞ **Pousada da Nossa Senhora da Assunção.** If you need to sleep on your decision about which carpet to buy, consider an overnight stay in this picturesque pousada. It's a little more than a kilometer (½ mi) outside of town in the Convento dos Lóios, an old convent that has been restored and tastefully padded with modern comforts. The restaurant ($–$$) decor is contemporary, but the menu favors traditional regional dishes. ⊠ *Val das Flores (take E370 to Pavia), Apartado 61, 7044-909* ☎*266/419340* 🖷*266/419280* ⊕*www.pousadas.pt* 🛏*30 rooms, 2 suites* ⟁ *Restaurant, minibars, cable TV, tennis court, pool, squash, bar, Wi-Fi, free parking* ⊟ *AE, DC, MC, V* ⦿⧵ *BP.*

¢ ⊞ **Solar Cor de Rosa.** This 19th-century pink manor house is in the center of town. Imitation Gothic arches, red clay–tile floors, and azulejo walls in the public areas give it a medieval character. Breakfast is served in a room with a view of Arraiolos. ⊠ *Rua Melo Mexia 29, 7040-067* 🖷🖷 *266/419050* 🛏 *4 rooms* ⟁ *Bar, lounge* ⊟ *No credit cards* ⦿⧵ *BP.*

Outdoor Activities

HORSEBACK
TOURS Horseback tours are available through the Arraiolos countryside on thoroughbred Lusitanian horses. Try **Coralie Baldrey** ⊠ *Moinho da Boavista, Arraiolos* ☎ *938/549489.*

Shopping

The main street of Arraiolos is lined with showrooms and workshops featuring the town's famous hand-embroidered wool rugs. One of the town's best rug selections can be found at **Calántica** (⊠ Rua Alexandre Herculano 20 ☎ 266/499356 or 914/537749). **Isilda Vieira** (⊠ Rua Bombeiros Voluntários 7 ☎ 266/429057) is a small rug shop in Arraiolos. The owner, Isilda, does rug restoration while she is in the shop.

THE UPPER ALENTEJO

The Upper Alentejo is the hillier, rockier half of the great Alentejo plain and has the region's highest mountain ranges—the Serra de São Mamede and the Serra de Ossa. Neither is very lofty, though, and the undulating fields, heaths, and cork plantations that make up most of the landscape leave the bigger impression. Quarries scar the landscape around Borba, Estremoz, and Vila Viçosa, but they produce Portugal's finest marble. (Portugal is second to Italy in marble exports.) Modern winemaking techniques have revolutionized production in the Upper Alentejo's vineyards, and some of Europe's finest wines are now produced in areas such as Borba, Reguengos de Monsaraz, and Portalegre.

Monsaraz

★ ㉑ *50 km (31 mi) southeast of Évora.*

The entire fortified hilltop town of Monsaraz is a living museum of narrow, stone-surfaced streets lined with ancient white houses. The town's 150 or so permanent residents (mostly older people) live mainly off tourism, and because they do so graciously and unobtrusively, Monsaraz has managed to retain its essential character.

Old women clad in black sit in the doorways of their cottages and chat with neighbors, their ever-present knitting in hand. At the southern end of the walls stand the well-preserved towers of a formidable 13th-century castle. The view from atop the pentagonal tower sweeps across the plain to the west and to the east over the Rio Guadiana (Guadiana River) to Spain. Within the castle perimeter is an unusual arena with makeshift slate benches at either end of an oval field. Bullfights are held here several times a year and always in the second week of September (during the festival of Senhora Jesus dos Passos, the village's patron saint).

The small **Museu Monsaraz,** next to the parish church, displays religious artifacts and the original town charter, signed by Dom Manuel in 1512. The former tribunal contains an interesting 15th-century fresco that depicts Christ presiding over figures of Truth and Deception. ⊠ *Praça Nuno Álvares Pereira* ☎ *No phone* ▧ *€1* ⊙ *Daily 10–1 and 2–6.*

The area around Monsaraz is dotted with megalithic monuments. The 18-foot-high **Menhir of Outeiro,** 3 km (2 mi) north of town, is one of the tallest ever discovered.

Where to Stay & Eat

★ **$–$$** ✕ **Casa do Forno.** The labor of love of two ambitious women (Gloria and Mariana), Casa do Forno is a popular restaurant. At the entrance is a huge, rounded oven with an iron door, hence the name (*forno* is Portuguese for "oven"). Picture windows line the dining room and afford a spectacular view over the rolling plains. The Alentejan menu appropriately features roasts; one special dish worth trying is the *borrego assado no forno* (roast lamb prepared according to an ancient recipe of the nearby monastery). ⊠ *Travessa da Sanabrosa* ☎ *266/557190* ▤ *AE, MC, V* ⊙ *Closed Tues.*

¢–$ ✕ **Lumumba.** This little restaurant in one of the old village houses has a devoted clientele that hails from both sides of the Portuguese–Spanish border. The dining room is small, but there is a terrace for outside dining with views over the valley to distant mountains. The menu is classic Alentejo, with good lamb and kid roasts and casseroles. Although their main specialty is *ensopado de borrego* (lamb stew), when available, the grilled fish dishes are also excellent; try the *chocos grelhados* (grilled squid) or the *peixe espada grelhada* (charcoal-grilled blade fish). ⊠ *Rua Direita* ☎ *266/557121* ▤ *AE, DC, MC, V* ⊙ *Closed Mon.*

$–$$ ▨ **Horta da Moura.** This hotel is set within a working farm. The main house, whose white-stucco facade has blue trim and an arched portico, is typical of Alentejo-style architecture. The cozy interior has vaulted brick ceilings with wooden beams and traditional furnishings. The outlying buildings include stables, a riding school, a crafts room, a winery, and a recreation center with a large fireplace. The helpful staff arranges walking, horseback riding, and cycling trips along the river, as well as four-wheel-drive and canoe excursions and fishing trips. ⊠ *Horta da Moura, Monsaraz, Apartado 64, Reguengos de Monsaraz 7200-999* ☎ *266/550100* ▤ *266/550108* ⊕ *www.hortadamoura.pt*

🛏 *6 rooms, 7 suites, 1 apartment* ⚅ *Minibars, cable TV, tennis court, pool, fishing, bicycles, horseback riding, recreation room* ▤ *AE, DC, MC, V* ◯ *BP.*

¢ ▦ **Casa Dom Nuno.** This small, rustic guesthouse—a true romantic hideaway—occupies an old, restored, white home on the main street of the walled town. The clean guest quarters have modern furnishings and fantastic valley views—the sunsets alone are worth the price of a room. ⊠ *Rua do Castelo 6, 7200-175* ☎ *266/557146* 🖷 *266/557400* 🛏 *8 rooms* ▤ *AE, DC, MC, V* ◯ *BP.*

Shopping

Reguengos de Monsaraz, 16 km (10 mi) west of Monsaraz, is a sleepy little Alentejo town often simply called Reguengos. It's the center of a large wine-producing region and is also known for its handwoven rugs. The 19th-century neo-Gothic church here was built by the same Lisbon architect who built Lisbon's bullfight arena. The tiny hamlet of **São Pedro do Corval,** 5 km (3 mi) northeast of Reguengos, is one of Portugal's major centers for inexpensive hand-painted pottery.

Herdade do Esporão, the famed wine estate that produces Esporão, one of Portugal's top labels, offers 40-minute tours of its wine-producing facilities and a free glass of wine at the end. You can sample wines at the bar Tuesday–Sunday from 10:30 to 5 (you pay according to the number of wines tasted). Pair wines with sophisticated Portuguese cuisine in their elegant restaurant ($–$$$; lunch only, reserve ahead). Famed chef Julia Vinagre prepares dishes with wine, olive oil, and vinegar from the estate, which, along with other products, are also on sale at the shop. Restaurant guests can take a free tour. ⊠ *Herdade do Esporão, from Reguengos follow signs to Esporão/Zona Industrial and then signs for Turismo Rural, Reguengos de Monsaraz* ☎ *266/509280* ⊕ *www.esporao.com* 🖾 *€2.50 with a tasting of 2 wines, €10 with a tasting of 4 wines* ◷ *Shop daily 9:30–6. Tours daily at noon, 3, and 4:30.*

Terena

㉒ *28 km (17 mi) north of Reguengos.*

Terena, with its castle on a hill, has a charter dating from 1262 and is a place where tourists are still a curiosity. Drive—or better yet, stroll—along the narrow Rua Direita past the white houses, some with Gothic doorways, others with baroque or Renaissance ones. The small, well-preserved castle was one of several built in this area to defend the border with Spain, which lies across the Rio Guadiana, 11 km (7 mi) east.

Where to Stay

★ $ ▦ **Casa de Terena.** A restored 18th-century house in out-of-the-way Terena has been turned into a charming inn. It has six comfortably furnished guest quarters, with a blend of Portuguese and African decor. ⊠ *Rua Direita 45, 7250-065* ☎ *268/459132* 🖷 *268/459155* ⊕ *www.casadeterena.com* 🛏 *5 rooms, 1 suite* ⚅ *Fans, bar; no a/c* ▤ *MC, V* ◯ *EP.*

Vila Viçosa

 18 km (11 mi) northeast of Terena.

A quiet town with a moated castle, Vila Viçosa is in the heart of the fertile Borba plain. It has been closely linked with Portuguese royalty since the 15th century, but this association hasn't always been a happy one: in 1483 King João II, seeking to strengthen his grip on the throne, moved to eliminate the second Duke of Bragança, his brother-in-law and most formidable rival, who controlled more than 50 cities, castles, and towns from Vila Viçosa. After much intrigue and counter intrigue, the unfortunate duke was beheaded in Évora's main square.

Court life in Vila Viçosa flourished in the late 16th and early 17th centuries, when the huge palace constructed by the fourth Duke of Bragança (Jaime) was the scene of great royal feasts, theater performances, and bullfights. This all came to an abrupt end in 1640, when King João IV, the eighth Duke of Bragança and the first Portuguese to occupy the throne after 60 years of Spanish domination, elected to move his court to Lisbon. Thereafter, Vila Viçosa slipped into relative oblivion. In more recent times Portugal's second-to-last king, Carlos I, and the young Prince Luís Filipe spent their last night in the palace. The following day, February 1, 1908, in response to a royal decree that mandated exile for "political" crimes, they were assassinated by members of a secret political society while riding in an open carriage.

The **Paço Ducal** (Ducal Palace) and the nearby *castelo* (castle) draw a great many visitors. Built of locally quarried marble, the palace's main wing extends for some 360 feet and overlooks the expansive Palace Square and the bronze equestrian statue of Dom João IV. At the north end of the square note the Porta do Nó (Knot Gate) with its massive stone shaped like ropes—an intriguing example of the Manueline style.

The palace's interior was extensively restored in the 1950s and contains all you'd expect to find: azulejos, Arraiolos rugs, frescoed ceilings, priceless collections of silver and gold objects, Chinese vases, Gobelin tapestries, and a long dining hall adorned with antlers and other hunting trophies. The enormous kitchen's spits are large enough to accommodate several oxen, and there's enough gleaming copper to keep a small army of servants busy polishing. Dom Carlos, the nation's penultimate king, spent his last night here before being assassinated in 1908; his rooms have been maintained as they were. Carlos was quite an accomplished painter—some say a better painter than he was a monarch—and many of his works (along with private photos of Portugal's last royal family) line the walls of the apartments. The palace itself as well as its armory, its treasury, and the castle and hunting museum can each be visited in separate guided tours.

The ground floor of the castle has displays of objects ranging from Paleolithic to 18th century and mainly Roman artifacts discovered during excavations. These include pieces from ancient Mediterranean civilizations—Egypt, Rome, Carthage, and pre-Columbian. Also on view are coaches from the 17th to the 20th century. Hunting, rather

Azulejos

IT'S DIFFICULT TO FIND AN OLD BUILDING OF ANY NOTE IN PORTUGAL that isn't adorned somewhere or other with the predominantly blue-toned ceramic tiles called *azulejos*. The centuries-old marriage of glazed ornamental tiles to Portuguese architecture is a match made in heaven.

After the Gothic period, large buildings made entirely of undressed brick or stone became a rarity in Portuguese architecture. Most structures had extensive areas of flat plaster on their facades and interior walls that cried out for decoration. The compulsion to fill these empty architectural spaces produced the art of the fresco in Italy; in Portugal, it produced the art of the azulejo.

The medium is well suited to the deeply rooted Portuguese taste for intricate, ornate decoration. And, aesthetics aside, glazed tiling is ideally suited to the country's more practical needs. Durable, waterproof, and easily cleaned, the tile provides cool interiors during Portugal's hot summers and exterior protection from the dampness of Atlantic winters.

The term *azulejo* comes not from the word *azul* (blue in Portuguese), but from the Arabic word for tiles, *az-zulayj*. But despite the long presence of the Moors in Portugal, the Moorish influence on early Portuguese azulejos was actually introduced from Spain in the 15th century.

The very earliest tiles on Portuguese buildings were imported from Andalusia. They're usually geometric in design and were most frequently used to form panels of repeated patterns. As Portugal's prosperity increased in the 16th century, the growing number of palaces, churches, and sumptuous mansions created a demand for more tile. Local production was small at first, and Holland and Italy were the main suppliers. The superb Dutch-made azulejos in the Paço Ducal in Vila Viçosa are famous examples from this period. The first Portuguese-made tiles had begun to appear in the last quarter of the 15th century, when a number of small factories were established, but three centuries were to pass before Portuguese tile making reached its peak.

The great figure in 18th-century Portuguese tile making is António de Oliveira Bernardes, who died in 1732. The school he established spawned the series of monumental panels depicting hunting scenes, landscapes, battles, and other historical motifs that grace many stately Portuguese homes and churches of the period. Some of the finest examples can be seen in the Alentejo—in buildings such as the university in Évora and the parish church in Alcácer do Sal—as well as at the Castelo de São Felipe in Setúbal. In Lisbon's Museu do Azulejo you can trace the development of tiles in Portugal from their beginnings to the present.

Portuguese tile making declined in quality in the 19th century, but a revival occurred in the 20th century, spearheaded by leading artists such as Almada Negreiros and Maria Keil. Today, some notable examples of tile use by contemporary artists can be seen in many of the capital's metro stations.

than war, is the dominant theme of the armory that holds more than 2,000 objects. The treasury displays crucifixes from Vila Viçosa and those belonging to Dona Catarina de Bragança as well as more than 200 pieces of jewelry, paintings, crystal, and ceramics. The porcelain collection is made up of blue-and-white china from the 15th to 18th century. ⊠ *Terreiro do Paço* ☎ *268/980659* ◻ *Palace €5; armory, treasury, castle, porcelain collection €5 each* ⊙ *Apr.–Sept., Tues.–Fri. 9:30–1 and 2:30–5:30, weekends 9:30–1 and 2:30–6; Oct.–Mar., Tues.–Sun. 9:30–1 and 2–5.*

After the tour of the Ducal Palace you can visit the nearby **Museu dos Coches** (Coach Museum), with its collection of horse-drawn conveyances and antique automobiles. Note that if you've seen or plan to see Lisbon's coach museum, you can skip this one; it's interesting but isn't in the same league as the one in the capital. ⊠ *Terreiro do Paço* ☎ *268/ 980659* ◻ *€1.50* ⊙ *Apr.–Sept., Tues.–Fri. 9:30–1 and 2:30–5:30, weekends 9:30–1 and 2:30–6; Oct.–Mar., Tues.–Sun. 9:30–1 and 2–5.*

Where to Stay & Eat

$$–$$$ ╳▥ **Pousada de D. João IV.** If you're hooked on Vila Viçosa's history, this inn next door to the palace has all the atmosphere you'll need. It's in a restored 16th-century convent that's furnished with period reproductions. Its restaurant ($$–$$$$) even serves dishes based on old convent recipes. Walking tours and hot-air ballooning can be arranged by the hotel. ⊠ *Terreiro do Paço, 7160* ☎ *268/980742* ⊟ *268/980747* ⊕ *www.pousadas.pt* ⌐ *31 rooms, 5 suites* ⌂ *Restaurant, cable TV, pool, bar, Wi-Fi* ⊟ *AE, DC, MC, V* ﴾◯﴿ *BP.*

$ ▥ **Casa dos Peixinhos.** Just a little over ½ km (¼ mi) from town, you can retreat to a 17th-century manor house surrounded by an orange grove. Rooms are spacious with period decor, and the building's construction keeps rooms cool without having air-conditioning. If you're there in winter, you can enjoy the salon with its fireplace. ⊠ *Estrada de Peixinhos, 7160-000* ☎ *268/980472* ⊟ *268/881348* ⊕ *www.casadospeixinhos.pa-net.pt* ⌐ *8 rooms* ⌂ *Cable TV, bar; no a/c* ⊟ *No credit cards* ﴾◯﴿ *BP.*

EN ROUTE On the main road between Vila Viçosa and Estremoz, you'll see dirt-and-rock piles strewn about the countryside. These tailings are the residue of centuries of extracting high-quality marble from the region's many quarries. The town of Borba, about 4 km (2½ mi) northwest of Vila Viçosa, has a pleasant conglomeration of modest whitewashed houses, noble mansions, and small churches—all beautifully decorated with marble. Borba is one of the Alentejo's major wine producers, and the town's vintners have won many national prizes. With an advance reservation, you can stop by a vineyard for a tasting.

Estremoz

㉔ *31 km (19 mi) northwest of Vila Viçosa.*

Estremoz, which lies on the ancient road that connected Lisbon with Mérida, Spain, has been a site of strategic importance since Roman times, and the castle, which overlooks the town, was a crucial one of the Alentejo's many fortresses. Estremoz is most closely associated with Isabel of Aragon, although she spent only a short time here. Married to Dom Dinis—a Portuguese king—in 1282, she arrived in 1336 and after a brief stay became ill and died. The luxurious Pousada da Rainha Santa Isabel, which occupies the castle, was named for her. It was also in Estremoz in 1367 that the queen's grandson Pedro, the lover and secret husband of Inês de Castro, died. The Portuguese people loved Queen Isabel and over the ages have handed down many tales and legends of her humility and charity. She

CASTLES

In much of the Alentejo, you can't drive far without seeing a castle or a fortress crowning one of the hills. Some, such as the castles at Estremoz and Alvito, have been restored and converted into luxurious *pousadas* (inns). Others, including those at Castelo de Vide and Viana do Alentejo, are open for you to clamber about their battlements.

4

was beatified in the 16th century, then canonized in 1625 by Pope Urban VIII. A statue in the castle square commemorates her. From atop the castle tower you'll have a magnificent view over the Alentejo plains.

The **Museu Municipal** is housed in a lovely 17th-century almshouse across from the castle. Its displays chronicle the development of the region and range from Roman artifacts to contemporary pottery, including a collection of the brightly colored figurines for which Estremoz is famous. ⊠ *Largo D. Dinis* ☎ *268/339200* 💷 *€1.10* ☉ *Tues.–Sun. 9–12:30 and 2–5:30.*

The lower town, a maze of narrow streets and white houses, radiates from the **Rossio,** a huge, central square. Stands lining it sell the town's famous colorful pottery. In addition to the multicolored, hand-painted plates, pitchers, and dolls, note the earthenware jugs decorated with bits of local white marble.

NEED A BREAK?
There are several refreshment stands and snack bars along the Rossio, but for more substantial fare try the **Café Alentejano.** From this popular 60-year-old café and its first-floor restaurant, you can watch the goings-on in the square. Inexpensive accommodation can be found upstairs.

Where to Stay & Eat

$$–$$$ ✕ **São Rosas.** The castle in the historic center of town also keeps this gastronomic landmark. Margarida Cabaço, owner and chef, offers traditional Alentejo savories. When in season, wild asparagus, wild mushrooms, and truffles appear on the menu. Specialties include *tarte de perdiz* (partridge pie) and *sela de borrego* (baked lamb). For fish try the trout with *chouriço* (smoked sausage) and *poejos* (native herb) or the sopa de cação. ⊠ *Largo D. Dinis 11* ☎ *268/333345* ▤ *AE, DC, MC, V* ☉ *Closed Mon.*

★ **$–$$** ✕ **Adega do Isaias.** Hidden away on a narrow side street a few minutes' walk from the square, this is the best place in town for hearty, no-nonsense roasts and grilled meats. The front part of the former wine cellar is a rough-looking bar; walk through to the dining area—a sloping, concrete-floor cave that's lined with huge terra-cotta wine jugs. The furnishings are basic—benches at planked tables—and you can expect the service to be casual, at best. But the food will be great, and the place will probably be packed. ⊠ *Rua do Almeida 21* ☎ *268/322318* ▭ *No credit cards* ⊘ *Closed Sun.*

★ **$$$** ✕▥ **Pousada da Rainha Santa Isabel.** One of Portugal's most luxurious pousadas is in Estremoz's hilltop castle. The sumptuous lobby and other public rooms display literally tons of gleaming Estremoz marble as well as 15th-century tapestries, Arraiolos rugs, and original paintings. The generous-size bedrooms are furnished with 17th- and 18th-century reproductions; some rooms have elaborate four-poster beds. Just to sit in the baronial dining hall ($$–$$$$) is a treat, and the food and service are fit for a queen. The accent is on traditional Alentejo dishes and old-fashioned recipes. The *perdiz caçador* (partridge in red wine) is very good in autumn. ⊠ *Largo D. Dinis 1, 7100* ☎ *268/332075* ▤ *268/332079* ⊕ *www.pousadas.pt* ↩ *23 rooms* ⌂ *Restaurant, cable TV, pool, Wi-Fi, bar* ▭ *AE, DC, MC, V* ⧖ *BP.*

$$ ▥ **Estalagem Páteo dos Solares.** This modern hotel occupies a large old house that has been restored using traditional materials and lots of marble. It is near the old walls in the center of town. ⊠ *Rua Brito Capelo, 7100-562* ☎ *268/338400* ▤ *268/338419* ⊕ *www.maisturismo.pt/ psolares* ↩ *42 rooms, 1 suite* ⌂ *Restaurant, cable TV, Wi-Fi, for each pool, bar, some pets allowed* ▭ *AE, DC, MC, V* ⧖ *BP.*

¢ ▥ **Hospedaria D. Dinis.** Rooms are spacious and comfortable at this small, modern hotel in the town center. Its bathrooms are lined with the famous marble of the region. It has no restaurant, but a good selection of them are footsteps away. ⊠ *Rua 31 de Janeiro 46, 7100-114* ☎ *268/332717* ▤ *268/322610* ↩ *7 rooms* ⌂ *Minibars, cable TV* ▭ *AE, DC, MC, V.*

Évoramonte

㉕ *17 km (10 mi) southwest of Estremoz, 42 km (26 mi) northeast of Évora.*

Évoramonte is a medieval town that sits along the western flank of the Serra de Ossa at an altitude of 1,550 feet. Drive up to the castle for a view that extends as far as the Serra da Estrela. The castle here, built in Italian Renaissance style, is distinguished by a massive round tower at each of its four corners. Also note the heavy Manueline ropes that run, like ribbons on a Christmas package, around the exterior; they're joined at the entrance with two tidy concrete knots.

The famous Alentejo soup, made with stale bread, garlic, olive oil, coriander, and water, is said to have originated in Évoramonte. The convention held here in 1834 to end the civil war between the Liberals and the Miguelists took so long that by the end only stale bread was left to eat—and thus was born the popular *sopa alentejana.*

Elvas

㉖ *40 km (25 mi) east of Estremoz, 15 km (9 mi) west of Spain.*

Elvas, extensively fortified because of its proximity to the Spanish town of Badajoz, was from its founding an important bastion in warding off attacks from the east. Portugal's most formidable 17th-century fortifications are characterized by a series of walls, moats, and reinforced towers. The size of the complex can best be appreciated by driving around the periphery of the town.

The 8-km (5-mi) **Aqueduto Amoreira** (Amoreira Aqueduct) took more than a century to build and is still in use today. It was started in 1498 under the direction of one of the era's great architects, Francisco de Arruda—who also designed the Aqueduto da Agua da Prata north of Évora. The first drops of water didn't flow into the town fountain until 1622. Some parts of the impressive structure have five stories of arches; the total number of arches is 843.

The 16th-century **Igreja da Nossa Senhora da Assunção** (Church of Our Lady of the Assumption) at the head of the town square, the Praça da República, has an impressive triple-nave interior lined with 17th-century blue-and-yellow azulejos. The church was designed by Francisco de Arruda, architect of the Elvas aqueduct, but underwent subsequent modifications. It was a cathedral until the diocese was moved to Évora in the 18th century. ⊠ *Praça da República* ☎ *No phone.*

From the Church of Our Lady of the Assumption walk up the hill past a pillory and two stone towers (spanned by a graceful Moorish loggia) to the **castelo.** At the battlements you'll have a sweeping view of the town and its fortifications. ⊠ *Praça da República* ☎ *No phone* 🎫 *€1.30* 🕙 *Oct.–May, daily 10–1 and 2–5; June–Sept., daily 2:30–6:30.*

Where to Stay & Eat

$–$$$ ✕ **A Bolota Castanha.** People drive miles to dine at this well-known restaurant 16 km (10 mi) from Elvas in the town of Terrugem. Run by famous restaurateur Júlia Vinagre, it serves traditional Alentejan food in an elegant setting. The house takes pride in its *cozido de grão* (boiled dinner with pork, smoked sausages, cabbage, and chickpeas), but their menu also lists international dishes such as spinach with shrimp au gratin and delicious sorbets for dessert. ⊠ *Quinta Janelas Verdes, Rua Madre Teresa, Terrugem* ☎ *268/657401* 🖃 *AE, DC, MC, V* 🕙 *Closed Mon. No dinner Sun.*

★ $$ ✕▥ **Pousada de Santa Luzia.** Portugal's first pousada is in a two-story, Moorish-style building 12 km (7 mi) from one of the major border crossings between Spain and Portugal. The cheerful, decent-size guest rooms have bright floral fabrics, hand-painted Alentejo furniture, and modern tiled bathrooms that are small but adequate. The large restaurant ($$–$$$$) has arched windows overlooking a garden and is a favorite with Elvas residents. One of the most popular dishes is *bacalhau dourado* (cod sautéed with eggs, potatoes, and onions). ⊠ *Av. de Badajoz, 7350-097* ☎ *268/637470* 🖶 *268/622127* 🌐 *www.pousadas.pt* 🛏 *25 rooms* 🍴 *Restaurant, cable TV, 2 tennis courts, pool, bar* 🖃 *AE, DC, MC, V* ❑ *BP.*

Campo Maior

㉗ *19 km (12 mi) northeast of Elvas.*

Surrounded by rows of gentle hills covered with the Alentejo's ubiquitous cork and olive trees, Campo Maior is a quiet, sparsely populated corner of the country where little has changed over the years. You may notice the smell of roasting coffee lingering in the air: it isn't coming from a nearby café but from the several coffee-roasting plants in the area.

Try to make it to this town during the first week of September, when nearly 100 streets and squares are covered with a rainbow-color mantle of paper flowers and decorations. The decorations for each neighborhood are a closely held secret for months, as the women nimbly assemble the paper flowers and the men construct the wooden framing. When the festival (*Festa das Flores*) opens, all is revealed in a blaze of color. Check with the local or regional tourist office for exact dates.

At the top of the hill is a castle that was reconstructed after lightning hit a gunpowder storage area in 1732. The disastrous explosion claimed the lives of more than 1,400. The Capela dos Ossos (Chapel of Bones) next to the parish church is lined with the bones of the victims. As you walk around the fortifications, you'll notice some tiny whitewashed dwellings with laundry fluttering about like flags in the breeze. The little buildings are the old army barracks, the only part of the military complex still occupied. Before leaving Campo Maior, stroll through the lower part of town, where the narrow streets are lined with many fine examples of wrought-iron grillwork and balconies, giving the town a Spanish appearance.

Portalegre

28 *47 km (29 mi) northwest of Campo Maior.*

Portalegre is the gateway to the Alentejo's most mountainous region as well as to the Parque Natural da Serra de São Mamede. The town is at the foot of the Serra de São Mamede, where the parched plains of the south give way to a greener, more inviting landscape. Although Portalegre lacks the charm of the whitewashed hamlets in the south of the province, it has long been noted worldwide for the quality of its handmade tapestries, which fetch high prices.

From the park in the center of the lower town, walk uphill past a maze of shops and old houses to the twin-towered **Sé** (Cathedral), a 16th-century church and the town's most prominent landmark. The 18th-century facade is highlighted with marble columns and wrought-iron balconies. Inside are early-17th-century azulejos depicting the Virgin Mary. ⊠ *Praça do Município* ☎ *245/330321* ⊘ *Mon.–Sat. 8:30–noon and 3–6, Sun. 9–noon.*

The **Museu Municipal,** in a former seminary next to the cathedral, contains a wealth of religious art, including a gilded, 16th-century Spanish pietà. ⊠ *Rua José Maria da Rosa* ☎ *245/300120* ⊠ *€2* ⊘ *Wed.–Mon. 9:30–12:30 and 2–6.*

From the cathedral square, head east about 400 yards to the ruins of a once-formidable **castelo,** whose tower walls afford a splendid view of the cathedral and its surroundings.

Roughly midway between the cathedral and the castle, the **Casa-Museu José Regio** (José Regio House and Museum), just off Avenida Poeta José

Regio, was named for a local poet who died in 1969. He bequeathed his varied collection of religious and folk art to the museum, which is in his former home. ⊠ *Largo de Boa Vista* ☎ *245/203625* 🎫 *€2* ⊙ *Tues.–Sun. 9:30–12:30 and 2–6.*

The **Museu de Tapeçaria Guy Fino** (Guy Fino Tapestry Museum) displays 46 tapestries designed by Portugal's most famous artists of the last half century. ⊠ *Rua do Figueiro* ☎ *245/307980* 🎫 *€2* ⊙ *Mon., Tues., and Thurs.–Sun. 9:30–1 and 2:30–6.*

You can enter the **Parque Natural da Serra de São Mamede** roughly 5 km (3 mi) northeast of Portalegre. The nature park extends north to the fortified town of Marvão and the spa town of Castelo de Vide, and south to the little hamlet of Esperança on the Spanish border. The sparsely inhabited 80,000-acre park region is made up of small family plots, and sheepherding is the major occupation. The area is rich in wildlife, including many rare species of birds, as well as wild boars, deer, and wildcats. This isn't a spectacularly scenic park but rather a quiet place for hiking, riding, or simply communing with nature. For information about activities, contact the park office. ⊠ *Praceta Herois da India 8* ☎ *245/203631.*

OFF THE BEATEN PATH

COUDELARIA DE ALTER – If you're interested in horses, you must visit the Coudelaria de Alter (Alter Stud Farm), 22 km (14 mi) southwest of Portalegre. It was founded by Dom João V in 1748 to furnish royalty with high-quality mounts. Dedicated to preserving and developing the extraordinarily beautiful Alter Real (Royal Alter) strain of the Lusitania breed, the farm has had a long, turbulent history. After years of foreign invasion and pillage, little remains of its original structures. Fortunately, the equine bloodline, one of Europe's noblest, has been preserved, and you can watch these superb horses being trained and exercised on the farm (phone ahead to make sure a visit is practical on the day you want to go). There are also three small but interesting museums here: one documents the history of the farm, one has a collection of horse-drawn carriages, and one has displays on the art of falconry. You can also watch falcons going through their daily training sessions. The town of Alter do Chão itself, with the battlements of a 14th-century castle overlooking a square, is also worth a stroll. ⊠ *The farm is on a dusty track 3 km (2 mi) northwest of Alter do Chão* ☎ *245/610080* 🎫 *Free* ⊙ *Farm daily 9:30–noon and 2–4:30.*

Where to Stay & Eat

$$ ✕ **O Rolo.** Near the center of town. Francisco Rolo's restaurant is famous for its charcoal-grilled meats and fish. Rolo prides himself on his 40 different appetizers—wild hare with beans, migas with asparagus, and others served in hot clay pots. You have to be careful to save some space for the main dish, such as the *posta de novilho alentejano* (thick veal steak) or *rolinhos de pork com ameixas de Elvas* (rolled pork with Elvas prunes), and one of his 15 different convent desserts and regional cheeses. ⊠ *Av. Pio XII* ☎ *245/205646* 🞸 *AE, DC, MC, V.*

$–$$ ✕ **O Abrigo.** On a quiet street around the corner from the cathedral you'll find this small, husband-and-wife-run restaurant. You enter the cork-lined dining area through a snack bar. One of the best dishes on the menu is the *migas alentejanas* (a tasty fried-pork-and-bread-crumbs concoction), served on a terra-cotta platter. ⊠ *Rua de Elvas 74* ☎ *245/331658* ⊟ *MC, V* ⊘ *Closed Tues.*

¢–$ ✕⌸ **Dom João III.** This modern multistory hotel is across from the city park. Although the lobby and hallways are somewhat institutional, the rooms are pleasant; many have balconies overlooking the park. The large top-floor restaurant, a favorite with local businessmen, is ringed with picture windows overlooking the town. The menu has international dishes as well as regional specialties. ⊠ *Av. da Liberdade, 7300-065* ☎ *245/ 330192* 🖶 *245/330444* ✑ *58 rooms, 2 suites* ⚭ *Restaurant, cable TV, pool, bar* ⊟ *AE, DC, MC, V* ⋈ *BP.*

▌ **EN ROUTE** For the most scenic approach to Marvão and the Serra de São Mamede from Portalegre, take N359 18 km (11 mi) to Marvão. The narrow but well-surfaced serpentine N359 rises to an elevation of 2,800 feet, past stands of birch and chestnut trees and small vegetable gardens bordered by ancient stone walls. At Portagem take note of the well-preserved Roman bridge.

Marvão

★ ㉙ *25 km (15 mi) northeast of Portalegre.*

The views of the mountains as you approach the medieval fortress town of Marvão are spectacular, and the town's castle, atop a sheer rock cliff, commands a 360-degree panorama. The village, with some 300 mostly older inhabitants, is laid out in several long rows of tidy, white-stone dwellings terraced into the hill. Although you can drive through the constricted streets, Marvão is best appreciated on foot.

You can climb the tower of the **castelo** and trace the course of the massive Vauban-style stone walls (characterized by concentric lines of trenches and walls, a hallmark of the 17th-century French military engineer Vauban), adorned at intervals with bartizans, to enjoy breathtaking vistas from different angles. Given its strategic position, it's no surprise that Marvão has been a fortified settlement since Roman times or earlier. The present castle was built under Dom Dinis in the late 13th century and modified some four centuries later, during the reign of Dom João IV.

At the foot of the path leading to the castle is the **Museu Municipal,** in the 13th-century Church of Saint Mary. The small gallery contains a diverse collection of religious artifacts, azulejos, costumes, ancient maps, and weapons. ⊠ *Largo de Santa Maria* ☎ *245/909132* ✑ *€1* ⊘ *Daily 9–12:30 and 2–5:30.*

Scattered among the chestnut groves at **Santo António das Areias,** 5 km (3 mi) northeast of Marvão, are some two dozen prehistoric dolmens.

Where to Stay & Eat

★ $$ ✕⌸ **Pousada de Santa Maria.** In 1976 several old houses within the city walls were joined to create the Pousada de Santa Maria. The rooms are decorated with traditional Alentejo furnishings, and the restaurant ($–$$) serves some of the best regional dishes in the village. ⊠ *Rua 24 de Janeiro 7, 7330* ☎ *245/993201* 🖷 *245/993440* ⊕ *www.pousadas.pt* ⌁ *29 rooms* ⚲ *Restaurant, cable TV, bar* ▤ *AE, DC, MC, V* ⦿ *BP.*

$ ✕⊡ **Albergaria El Rei Dom Manuel.** A house inside the castle walls was completely renovated to create this inn. Five of its rooms have fantastic cliff-side views. The restaurant ($$) serves regional fare. ⊠ *Largo da Olivença, 7330* ☎ *245/909150* 🖷 *245/909159* ⊕ *www.turismarvao. pt* ⌁ *15 rooms* ⚲ *Restaurant, cable TV, bar* ▤ *AE, DC, MC, V* ⦿ *BP.*

¢ ⊡ **Casa D. Dinis.** This Marvão house from the 18th century has stone arches and thick walls. Original murals depicting scenes from the Alentejo adorn the rooms. Drinks and breakfast are served on a panoramic terrace overlooking the valley, the ideal place to relax after a day of sightseeing. In winter, you can relax to the crackling sound of burning wood in the fireplace in the cozy lounge. Its snack bar, Castelo Bar, is across the street and serves small dishes and salads. ⊠ *Rua Dr. António Matos Magalhães 7, 7330-121* ☎ *245/993957* 🖷 *245/993959* ⊕ *www.casaddinis.pa-net.pt* ⌁ *8 rooms* ⚲ *Bar, lounge* ▤ *AE, DC, MC, V* ⦿ *BP.*

Outdoor Activities

Five kilometers (3 mi) northwest of Marvão on N246-1 is the **Ammaia Clube de Golfe de Marvão** (⊠ Quinta do Prado ☎ 245/993755 ⊕ www. marvaogolfe.com), an 18-hole golf course with stunning views of the São Mamede mountain range. Green fees range from €35 a day on weekdays to €45 a day on weekends.

EN ROUTE An intriguing backcountry lane connects Marvão with Castelo de Vide. About halfway down the hill from Marvão, turn to the right toward Escusa (watch for the sign) and continue through the chestnut- and acacia-covered hills to Castelo de Vide.

Castelo de Vide

③⓪ *8 km (5 mi) west of Marvão.*

A quiet, hilltop town, Castelo de Vide is a picturesque place with pots of geraniums and dazzling flower beds throughout town. There are steep cobbled streets that provide beautiful views of the whitewashed town against a backdrop of olive groves and hills. As you walk along, notice the many houses with Gothic doorways in various designs. (The tourist brochures proclaim that Castelo de Vide has the largest number of Gothic doorways of any town in Portugal.)

The large, baroque Praça Dom Pedro V is bordered by the Igreja de Santa Maria (St. Mary's Church) and the town hall. An alleyway to the right of the church leads to the town symbol, a canopied, 16th-century marble fountain. A cobblestone alley leads from the fountain up to a Juderia (Jewish Quarter).

A bare little room in a modest one-story cottage is all that remains of a medieval *sinagoga* (synagogue) that was once the center of a thriving Jewish community. In the Middle Ages, as the town prospered, many

Jews and Marranos (Jews forced to convert to Christianity) settled here. ⊠ *Rua da Judairia* 🕾 *No phone* 🎫 *Free* ☉ *June–Sept., daily 10–8; Oct.–May, daily 10–5:30.*

From the Judairia it's a short climb to the ruins of the **castelo.** Go up into the tower and inside the well-preserved keep to the large Gothic hall, which has a picture window looking down on the town square and the church. 🎫 *Free* ☉ *June–Sept., daily 10–8; Oct.–May, daily 10–5:30.*

On the last Friday of every month an open-air market, the **Mercado Franco** is held in Sitio do Canapé, next to the Municipal Market. You can find bargains in everything from T-shirts, shoes, and jewelry, to electronic equipment.

Where to Stay & Eat

$–$$$ ✕ **Sr. Marinos.** This comfortable, wood-paneled restaurant on the main square has an unusually eclectic menu for this part of the country. A number of French and Italian plates appear alongside some outstanding regional fare. The multilingual host will help out with translations. The wine list is as long as your arm. ⊠ *Praça Dom Pedro 6* 🕾 *245/901408* ▭ *AE, DC, MC, V* ☉ *Closed Sun. No lunch Mon.*

$ ✕▥ **Hotel Garcia d'Orta.** Named after a notable 16th-century Jewish doctor and naturalist who lived in Castelo de Vide (his bust by modern sculptor João Cutileiro is in the garden), this tastefully appointed hotel is one of the area's best values. Its restaurant, A Castanha ($$), is renowned for great Alentejan cooking and polished service. A stay here gets you a discount at the 18-hole Ammaia Golf Course, just a few miles away. ⊠ *Estrada de São Vicente, 7320* 🕾 *245/901100* 🖷 *245/901200* ⊕ *www.hgo.8m.pt* ⇱ *52 rooms, 1 suite* ♿ *Restaurant, cable TV, golf privileges, pool, bar* ▭ *AE, MC, V* ⎢◯⎢ *EP, FAP, MAP.*

$ ✕▥ **Sol e Serra.** The large rooms in this three-story Mediterranean-style hotel—just a 10-minute walk from the castle—have balconies looking over the park. The spacious bar, which overlooks the pool, is one of the town's most popular gathering places, and the restaurant ($$–$$$$), with its wooden beams, is one of the few places in Portugal that has a kosher menu. It also has live music and folk-dancing performances every Friday and Saturday June–September. ⊠ *Estrada de São Vicente, 7320* 🕾 *245/900000* 🖷 *245/900001* ⊕ *www.grupofbarata.com* ⇱ *82 rooms* ♿ *Restaurant, cable TV, pool, bar, Wi-Fi* ▭ *AE, DC, MC, V* ⎢◯⎢ *EP, FAP, MAP.*

THE LOWER ALENTEJO

Extending south of Évora and from the rugged west-coast beaches east to the border with Spain, the Lower Alentejo is a vast, mostly flat region of wheat fields, cork oaks, and olive trees. It rains very little here, and the summer months are particularly hot. Shepherds wearing broad-brim hats and sheepskin vests still tend their sheep in the fields. Gypsies still set up camp with makeshift tents, horse carts, and open fires. These scenes from a rapidly disappearing way of life contrast sharply with the modernization taking place in the region.

Viana do Alentejo

③ *37 km (23 mi) southeast of Évora.*

The attractive castle at Viana do Alentejo—with its rough stone walls, brick battlements, and round turrets—was constructed in 1313 to the very specific orders of Portuguese king Dom Dinis. He decreed that the pentagonal walls should be tall enough that a horseman with a lance measuring 9 *côvados* (an ancient unit of measure equal to 66 centimeters [26 inches]) couldn't injure anyone on the battlements. The fortified parish church within the walls of the castle—designed by the famous Diogo de Arruda—has a pleasing combination of battlements, spires, and ornate Manueline elements. Below the castle a delightful Renaissance fountain enhances the town square. Viana do Alentejo is also noted for a primitive-style pottery, sold in several small shops in town.

Where to Eat

¢–$ ✕ **S. Luis.** In the vaulted rooms of what was a medieval hospital adjoining the castle, this little family-run restaurant serves some of the area's best food. It's packed on weekends (and the staff gets somewhat overstretched). The menu is short, simple, and composed entirely of local dishes. Try the *carne de porco assado com puré de patatas* (roast pork with mashed potatoes). ✉ *Rua António Isidoro de Sousa 36* ☎ *266/953116* 🖃 *No credit cards.*

Alvito

㉜ *12 km (7 mi) south of Viana do Alentejo.*

Alvito is a typical, sleepy Alentejo town on a low hill above the Rio Odivelas. Noted for its fortresslike 13th-century parish church, the town also has a 15th-century castle converted into a pousada and a number of modest houses with graceful Manueline doorways and windows. The castle was built in 1482 by the Baron of Alvito, the first individual permitted to have his own castle. King Manuel I was born and died here.

Where to Stay & Eat

$ ✕ **O Camões.** Northwest of Alvito (7 km [4½ mi]), the main attraction of this large, popular restaurant is its wood-burning oven in which delicious legs of lamb, pork, and other meats are cooked to perfection. They're first marinated in coriander, oregano, and aromatic herbs that grow in the region. Owner Sr. Camões is also well known for his açorda dishes, the most popular being *açorda de cação* (baby shark porridge). ✉ *Rua 5 de Outubro, Vila Nova da Baronia* ☎ *284/475209* 🖃 *No credit cards.*

★ $$–$$$ ✕🖼 **Pousada do Castelo de Alvito.** This pousada is within the walls of the fortress at the edge of the village. The essential architectural elements of a castle, including crenellated battlements and massive round towers, have been retained, and there's a large garden, and a courtyard. Vaulted Gothic ceilings, red clay–tile floors, oil paintings with gold-leaf picture frames, and red-and-gold patterned upholstery add to the medieval atmosphere. Rooms fit for a king have beautiful arched Manueline windows and stone window benches. The cozy restaurant ($–$$$)

serves a variety of Alentejo specialties, including an excellent *bacalhau caldeirada* (codfish stew). ✉ *Largo do Castelo, 7920* ☎ *284/480700* 🖷 *284/485383* ⊕ *www.pousadas.pt* 🛏 *20 rooms* 🍴 *Restaurant, cable TV, pool, public Wi-Fi, bar* ⊟ *AE, DC, MC, V* 🍴 *BP.*

São Cucufate

㉝ *11 km (7 mi) southwest of Alvito.*

It's believed that these 2,000-year-old ruins of a two-story Roman villa were part of an extensive Roman settlement. Coins and other artifacts that have turned up indicate a 1st-century Roman presence. The villa's ground floor was probably used as a barn, with the living quarters above it. Remnants of the original heating and drainage systems are visible. The building was later adapted and used in the 13th century as a monastery. The frescoes in the little chapel that still stands on the site were painted in the late 15th and early 16th centuries. There's an information center and a café. ✉ *Estrada de Vila Alva (IC 258 from Vila Alva to Vidigueira), Vila de Frades* ☎ *284/441113* 🖾 *€2* ☉ *May–Sept. 15, Tues.–Sun. 9:30–12:30 and 3–6:30; Sept. 16–Apr., Tues.–Sun. 9–12:30 and 2–5.*

Vidigueira

㉞ *5 km (3 mi) southeast of São Cucufate.*

Vidigueira, a quiet farm town in the middle of the Alentejo plain, is best known as the onetime home of Vasco da Gama, the Portuguese explorer whose voyage in 1497 opened the sea route to India. A statue of him stands in the main square. At the edge of town, in a setting of gardens and ponds, is a Carmelite chapel where the explorer's body lay from the time it was returned from India in 1539 until it was moved in 1898 to Lisbon's Mosteiro de Jerónimos (Jerónimos Monastery).

Beja

㉟ *23 km (14 mi) southeast of Vidigueira.*

Midway between Spain and the sea is Beja, the Lower Alentejo's principal agricultural center that spreads itself across a small knoll. Much of the oldest part of town retains a significantly Arabic flavor—students of Portuguese even claim that the local dialect has Arabic characteristics—the legacy of more than 400 years of Moorish occupation.

Beja, founded by Julius Caesar and known as Pax Julia, was an important town in the Roman province of Lusitania during the 1st century. The name Pax Julia was chosen because it was here, after a long struggle, that peace was finally established between the Lusitanian chiefs and Julius Caesar. You can see Roman artifacts and other tokens of Beja's long history at the regional museum in the Convento da Conceição and at the excavations in nearby Pizões.

Many of the town's most interesting monuments were destroyed in the 19th century during the population's fury against the church's domination. In spite of that, Beja has an important valuable heritage, and it can all be explored on foot.

Facing a broad plaza in the center of the oldest part of town, the **Convento de Nossa Senhora da Conceição** (Our Lady of the Conception Convent) was founded in 1459 by the parents of King Manuel I. Favored by the royal family, this Franciscan convent became one of the richest of the period. It now houses the **Museu Regional Rainha Dona Leonor** (Queen Leonor Regional Museum), whose exhibits are of more interest to scholars of local history than to casual visitors. The church and cloisters display some fine azulejos from the 16th and 17th centuries, including panels depicting scenes from the life of St. John the Baptist, and a section of multicolored Moorish tiles. At the far end of the second-floor gallery is the famous Mariana Window. ⊠ *Largo da Conceição* ☎ *No phone* 💷 €*2 (includes admission to Museu Visigótico)* ۞ *Tues.–Sun. 9:30–12:30 and 2–5:15.*

> **LOCAL LEGEND**
>
> As the story goes, young Beja nun Mariana Alcoforado (1640–1723) fell in love with a French count named Chamilly, who was in the Alentejo fighting the Spaniards. When he went back to France, the nun waited longingly and in vain at the window for him to return. The affair was made public when five passionate love letters attributed to Mariana to the count were published in France in 1669 (the popular collection was known as the *Portuguese Letters*). The scandal brought a measure of lasting international literary fame to this provincial Alentejo town. It's likely that another Frenchman penned the letters after hearing of the love story.

The **Igreja de Santa Maria** (St. Mary's Church), across the square from the Convento de Nossa Senhora da Conceição, was once a mosque, and can be easily recognized by its massive round pillars, Mudéjar arches, and its bell tower similar in design to that of the famed Giralda Tower in Seville. ⊠ *Largo de Santa Maria* ☎ *284/328438.*

NEED A BREAK? **Café Pastelaria Santa Maria** (⊠ Largo de Santa Maria), opposite the Igreja de Santa Maria, has outside tables looking out on the convent square and is a pleasant spot for cake and coffee or a light lunch.

Castelo de Beja is an extensive system of fortifications, whose crenellated walls and towers chronicle the history of the town from its Roman occupation through its 19th-century battles with the French. ⊠ *Largo de Santo Amaro* 💷 *Free* ۞ *June–Sept., Tues.–Sun. 10–1 and 2–6; Oct.–May, Tues.–Sun. 9–noon and 1–4.*

The **Museu Visigótico** (Visigoth Museum), next to the Castelo de Beja in a 6th-century church, houses an impressive collection of tombstones, weapons, and pottery that documents the Visigoth presence in the region. ⊠ *Largo de Santo Amaro* ☎ *284/321465* 💷 €*2 (includes admission to Convento da Conceição)* ۞ *Tues.–Sun. 10–12:30 and 2–5:30.*

Where to Stay & Eat

¢–$$ ✕ **Teotónius.** Dine on traditional Alentejan fare in this agreeable restaurant with vaulted ceilings. You can also take a seat alfresco beneath fruit trees in the inner courtyard. The carne de porco à alentejana (pork with clams) is recommended. Other specialties include snails and fondue. ⊠ *Rua do Touro 8* ☎ *284/328010* ▤ *AE, DC, MC, V* ⊘ *Closed Mon.*

$ ✕ **A Esquina.** Good, plain local cooking—served with care in pleasant surroundings—is the attraction here. There are few better places to try *lebre com feijão* (hare with beans) in season. The wine list is short, but there's usually a good selection of Serpa cheeses. ⊠ *Rua Infante D. Henrique 26* ☎ *284/389238* ▤ *AE, V* ⊘ *Closed Sun.*

$$ ✕▥ **Pousada do Convento de São Francisco.** Surrounded by spacious gardens is an old convent that has been tastefully converted into a comfortable pousada. The former chapel has been preserved and incorporated into the complex. Alentejo dishes fill the menu in the restaurant ($$–$$$$); the *bacalhau com natas* (salt cod cooked with a cream sauce) is delicious. ⊠ *Largo Dom Nuno Álvares Pereira, 7801-901* ☎ *284/313580* 🖷 *284/ 329143* ⊕ *www.pousadas.pt* ⇗ *34 rooms, 1 suite* � *Restaurant, cable TV, 2 tennis courts, pool, bar, Wi-Fi* ▤ *AE, DC, MC, V* ▯◉ *BP, MAP.*

¢ ▥ **Cristina.** This comfortable *pensão* (pension) occupies a modern five-story building on one of the main shopping streets. Guest rooms are light and airy, albeit a bit sterile. Still, doubles are spacious and clean and cost just under €50 including breakfast. ⊠ *Rua de Mértola 71, 7800* ☎ *284/323035* 🖷 *284/329874* ⇗ *28 rooms, 3 suites* ಟ *Cable TV, bar* ▤ *AE, DC, MC, V* ▯◉ *BP.*

¢–$ ▥ **Monte Horta do Cano.** A kilometer and a half (1 mi) from Beja on the road to Ferreira do Alentejo, this rustic inn—once a farming estate— has six handsome rooms. On tap for the energetic are tennis, swimming, and clay-pigeon shooting. For those otherwise inclined there's an old wine cellar converted into a bar where you can linger over fine Alentejo wines and snacks of regional bread, cheeses, and cured sausage. ⊠ *Santiago Maior, Apartado 1018, 7800-249* ☎ *284/326156* ⇗ *6 rooms, 1 suite* ಟ *Tennis court, pool, mountain bikes, bar, some pets allowed* ▤ *No credit cards* ▯◉ *EP.*

Serpa

③⑥ *27 km (17 mi) southeast of Beja.*

In this sleepy agricultural town, men pass the time by gathering together in the compact Praça da República under the shadow of an ancient stone clock tower. Unemployment is high, and there's little else for many to do. In cubbyholes along narrow, cobbled streets, carpenters, shoemakers, basket weavers, and other craftsmen work in much the same manner as their forefathers.

SERPA MOMENT

If you're lucky, you may hear a group of Alentejo men, dressed in typical garb of sheepskin vest and trousers, singing medieval songs (*cante alentejano*), similar to Gregorian chants. These singers are famous all around Portugal.

One of Portugal's most renowned sheep's milk cheeses is still made in small factories around the town. You can buy the famous Serpa cheese in the historic town center at **Rouparia** (⊠ Rua de Nossa Senhora ☎ 284/549612), a small cheese factory owned by José Bule.

An aqueduct forms an integral part of the walls of the 13th-century **castelo,** from which there's a stunning view of town. The huge ruined sections of wall tottering precariously above the entrance are the result of explosions ordered by the Duke of Ossuna during the 18th-century War of the Spanish Succession. Within the castle walls there's a small **Museu Arqueológico** (Archaeological Museum; ☎ 284/540100 ⌚ Free ☾ Tues.–Sun. 9–12:30 and 2–5:30) with artifacts dating from the Paleolithic to the Islamic period.

Museu Etnográfico (Ethnographic Museum) in the old market building exhibits old traditional crafts such as cheese, basket, and chair making, as well as ironwork and pottery. ⊠ *Largo do Corro* ⌚ *Free* ☾ *Tues.–Sun. 9–12:30 and 2–5:30.*

The **Museu do Relógio** (Clock Museum) displays a collection of 1,100 clocks in the domed rooms of the former Convento do Mosteirinho (Mosteirinho Convent). ⊠ *Rua do Assento* ☎ *284/543194* ⊕ *www. museudorelogio.pa-net.pt* ⌚ *€2* ☾ *Tues.–Fri. 2–6, weekends 10–6.*

Where to Stay & Eat

$ ✕ **Molhó Bico.** Huge wine barrels sit at the entrance to this restaurant in a restored wine cellar near Praça da República. In winter, the specialty is grilled pork; in summer try the gazpacho to start, followed by the fried fish. The Serpa cheese and the Alentejo wines are good at any time of year. Keep an ear out for some cante alentejano at this restaurant. ⊠ *Rua Quente 1* ☎ *284/549264* ▤ *AE, DC, MC, V* ☾ *Closed Wed.*

¢–$ ✕ **Cervejaria Lebrinha.** At the entrance of town near the Abade Correia da Serra (public gardens), this spacious *cervejaria* (beer house) is said to have been pouring the best beer in Portugal since 1957. They don't brew the Sagres beer, but it's said the secret is in the pour. Old pictures adorning the walls take you back in time to the way Serpa used to be. Wild asparagus with eggs is a good choice for a starter, and then try the grilled carne de porco preto (black pork) which is always a tasty choice. As in most cervejarias, the service is fast and good. ⊠ *Rua Calvário 68* ☎ *284/549311* ▤ *No credit cards* ☾ *Closed Tues. and Sept. 1–15.*

★ $$ ▥ **Pousada de São Gens.** On a hill above Serpa's fortifications, this modern, white-domed, Moorish-style pousada is relaxed and informal. The Arabic influence continues as you walk through the green-tile entrance to the lobby, with its many arches and vaulted ceilings. Each of the rooms has a small terrace; bright, cheery fabrics nicely offset the white walls and ceilings. ⊠ *Alto de São Gens, 2 km (1 mi) south of Serpa (off N260 to Spain), 7830-099* ☎ *284/540420* ▤ *284/544337* ⊕ *www. pousadas.pt* ⇨ *16 rooms, 2 suites* △ *Restaurant, cable TV, pool, bar, Wi-Fi* ▤ *AE, DC, MC, V* ❤ *BP.*

¢–$ ▥ **Casa de Serpa.** Its labyrinth of passageways, whitewashed walls, vaulted ceilings, and interior open courtyard reflect the Arabic influence in this 200-year-old manor house near the Igreja do Salvador. Each charming room has a character of its own, where the Alentejo and Arabic are fused in an elegant combination. The breakfasts are special with fresh orange juice, honey from the region, and *queijadinhas* (cheese biscuits). The manor is in the center of town and within walking distance of restaurants. Owner Miguel Bentes will arrange bicycle tours of the town for you. ⊠ *Largo do Salvador 28, 7830-330* ☎ *284/549238* ⊕ *www. casadeserpa.com* ⊠ *6 rooms* ⌂ *Bar* ▭ *No credit cards* ¶⨂ *BP.*

Mértola

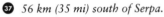 *56 km (35 mi) south of Serpa.*

The ancient walled-in town of Mértola is on a hill overlooking the Rio Guadiana and its Roman quay. Its occupiers have included the Phoenicians, Carthaginians, Romans, and Arabs. Under the Romans, it was an important copper-mining center, and it was the capital of the Moorish kingdom in Portugal until 1238, when the Christians—under the command of Santiago "Mata Mouros" (Moor Killer)—seized it.

Mértola has seen several archaeological excavations in recent years. The artifacts from these digs are all part of the Museu Arqueológico (Archaeology Museum), which has branches—each with displays from different periods—in several locations around town. At any one of them you can buy a combined ticket for €5 that covers the entrance to all the town's museums.

Built in 1292, the **Castelo de Mértola** contains carved stone from the Roman, Moorish, and Christian periods. The courtyard has a very deep cistern in the center. ☎ *No phone* ⊠ *€3 (ticket gains entrance to castle, several museums, and the Igreja Matrix)* ◷ *Oct.–June, Tues.–Sun. 10–12:30 and 2–5:30; July–Sept., Tues.–Sun. 10–1 and 3–7.*

Rising from the slopes above the river are the 12 white towers of the 12th-century **Igreja Matrix** (Parish Church). It was once a mosque and retains many of its original Islamic features, including a mihrab (a prayer niche that indicates the direction of Mecca). ⊠ *Rua da Igreja* ☎ *286/611101* ⊠ *Free* ◷ *Wed.–Sun. 10–12:30 and 2–5:30.*

Amid displays of jewels and metal items, the **Núcleo Islâmico** (Islamic Branch of the Museu Arqueológico) has an important collection of ceramics that date from the 9th to the 13th century. ⊠ *Rua da Igreja* ☎ *No phone* ⊠ *€2* ◷ *Oct.–June, Tues.–Sun. 10–12:30 and 2–5:30; July–Sept., Tues.–Sun. 10–1 and 3–7.*

You'll find statues, vases, and other Roman-period artifacts in the **Núcleo Romano**, the Roman Branch of the Museu Arqueológico. It's in the basement of the Câmara Municipal (City Hall). ⊠ *Praça Luís Vaz de Camões* ☎ *No phone* ⊠ *€2* ◷ *Weekdays 9–12:30 and 2–5:30.*

At the **Núcleo Visigótico–Basílica Paleocristã** (Visigoth Branch–Paleo-Christian Basilica) division of the Museu Arqueológico you can see Paleo-Christian writings on tombstones. ⊠ *Praça Rossio do Carmo* ☎ *No phone* ⊠ *€2* ◷ *Oct.–June, Tues.–Sun. 10–12:30 and 2–5:30; July–Sept., Tues.–Sun. 10–1 and 3–7.*

Where to Stay

¢ ⊞ **Residencial Beira Rio.** Some guest rooms in this former mill have balconies overlooking the Rio Guadiana; others face town. There are also two sitting rooms and a dining room. A buffet-style breakfast is served on the terrace. ⊠ *Rua Dr. Afonso Costa 108, 7750-352* ☎ *286/611190* 🖷 *286/611192* ⊕ *www.beirario.co.pt* ⤳ *15 rooms* ♿ *Dining room, cable TV, free parking* ☰ *AE, DC, MC, V* ⍟ *EP.*

Vila Nova de Milfontes

③⑧ *162 km (101 mi) northwest of Mértola.*

This small resort town is at the broad mouth of the Rio Mira, which is lined on both sides by sandy beaches. Overlooking the sea is an ivy-covered, late-16th-century fortress that protected Milfontes from the Algerian pirates who regularly terrorized the Portuguese coast. It was built on ancient Moorish foundations, for it was believed that the spirits there would ward off the pirates. The fortress has been restored and converted into a small guesthouse.

Where to Stay & Eat

$–$$$$ ✕ **Restaurante O Pescador.** Locals fondly refer to this bustling, air-conditioned *marisqueira* (seafood restaurant) as *"o Moura"* (Moura's place, a reference to the owner's name). Moura and his wife started off as fish sellers in the nearby market, so you know the seafood quality will be good. Though meals are quite affordable here, as at any seafood house, large lobsters can claim a price as high as €60. ⊠ *Largo da Praça 18* ☎ *283/996338* ☰ *No credit cards* ⊘ *Closed Thurs. Oct.–Apr.*

$ ✕⊞ **Hotel Social.** You're likely to have a water view at this hotel near the castle, be it the Rio Mira, the Atlantic, or the swimming pool (the latter is the cheapest). The restaurant ($) has panoramic views of the sea, which is spectacular on a clear day. Good, down-to-earth Portuguese dishes include *açorda de marisco* (seafood porridge), *sopa de peixe* (fish soup), and a variety of grilled fish that the Portuguese prepare so well. For those who prefer meat, try the *borrego à casa* (lamb stew). ⊠ *Av. Marginal, 7645-272* ☎ *283/996517* 🖷 *283/996324* ⤳ *28 rooms* ♿ *Restaurant, cable TV, pool, free parking* ☰ *No credit cards* ⍟ *BP* ⊘ *Restaurant closed Tues. Nov.–Jan.*

$$ ⊞ **Castelo de Milfontes.** In the town's castle, this inn is run along the lines of an old-fashioned guesthouse: the door closes at midnight, and dinner (included in the room rate) is served at a set time with the guests seated around a common table. Guest rooms are atmospheric and comfortable; ask for one with a sea view. ⊠ *Vila Nova de Milfontes 7645* ☎ *283/998231* 🖷 *283/997122* ⤳ *7 rooms* ♿ *Dining room, bar; no a/c* ☰ *No credit cards* ⍟ *MAP.*

$$ ⊞ **Duna Parque.** This two-story apartment-hotel complex is a 10-minute walk from town and a 5-minute walk from the beach. Guest quarters are in apartments and semidetached villas, all of which have living-room areas, kitchens, and open fireplaces. Some have balconies or roof terraces. The bar-restaurant, with its rustic beams and stonework, serves regional cooking. There's a three-night minimum stay in July

and August, and you can write home on the broadband Internet terminal. ⊠ *Eira da Pedra, 7645-291* ☎ *283/996451* 🖷 *283/996459* ⊕ *www.dunaparque.com* ⇆ *45 units* ⟁ *Restaurant, kitchens, cable TV, miniature golf, tennis court, indoor-outdoor pool, exercise equipment, hot tub, sauna, bar, playground, laundry facilities, ethernet; no a/c* ⊟ *V* ⟉⟊ *FAP, MAP.*

Beaches

The calm waters of the Franquia River beach, extending from the castle all the way to the Farol beach, are good for water sports and families with children. There are several scenic beaches between Porto Covo and Vila Nova de Milfontes. Rock formations stud Ilha do Pessegueiro beach, which is across from a tiny rocky island with a ruined fort, accessible by boat. The Aivados beach attracts fishermen, nudists, and surfers. The long Malhão beach is very popular and backed with dunes and fragrant scrubland. There are good access points and plenty of parking.

Santiago do Cacém

㊴ *40 km (25 mi) northeast of Vila Nova de Milfontes.*

Santiago do Cacém, about 16 km (10 mi) inland from the Atlantic at the junction of N120 and N261, is a quiet regional market town. The castle, built by the Knights of the Order of Santiago (St. James) on the site of Moorish ruins, dominates the community and affords sweeping views to the sea, marred only by the oil refineries at Sines. Inside the parish church, you can see a sculpture of St. James battling the Moors. The oldest part of town, just below the castle, is a maze of narrow streets with several well-preserved 17th- and 18th-century manor houses.

The **Museu Municipal,** in a former prison at the center of town, has several exhibits on Alentejo life, including one that shows the stages of and implements used in cork production. ⊠ *Praça do Município* ☎ *269/ 827375* 🖾 *Free* ☉ *Tues.–Fri. 10–noon and 2–5, weekends 2–5.*

Just outside town, off N121 to Ferreira do Alentejo, you can explore the excavations of the city of **Miróbriga.** The Celts originally settled this site in the 4th century BC; in the 1st century AD, it became a Roman town. The ruins, although not nearly as extensive or well preserved as those at Conímbriga near Coimbra, contain the interesting sanctuaries of Venus and Esculapius (god of medicine). ⊠ *Cumeadas* 🖾 *€2* ☉ *Tues.–Sat. 9–12:30 and 2–5:30, Sun. 9–noon and 2–5:30.*

Where to Stay & Eat

★ **$-$$** ✕ **Cerro da Inês.** The regional food is excellent, and so are the vistas. The restaurant is atop a water tower with views of the historic town and the countryside. ⊠ *Torre de Agua, Cerro da Inês* ☎ *269/823883* ⊟ *No credit cards* ☉ *Closed Mon.*

★ **$$** ✕🖾 **Quinta da Ortiga.** This lovely old estate, just 5 km (3 mi) from Santiago do Cacém, is amid 10 acres of trees and farmland. With wood-panel ceilings and Arraiolos carpets, it evokes life in a rural villa—rustic but with touches of luxury. The intimate restaurant ($$–$$$), which serves cuisine of the region, is more like a family dining room than a commercial establishment. ✉ *Off IP8 to Sines, Apartado 67, 7540* ☎ *269/ 822074* 🖷 *269/822073* 🛏 *13 rooms* ⚱ *Restaurant, cable TV, pool, bar* ▤ *AE, DC, MC, V* ⏻*BP.*

Outdoor Activities

The sparse population and minimal automobile traffic make this region a delight for equestrian outings. Whether for a few hours or a few days, you'll get an authentic perspective of the Alentejo on horseback. Overnight tours include lodging at bed-and-breakfasts and meals both on the trail and at local restaurants. Trails provide a variety of backdrops—including castles, villages, and prehistoric sites. Sines beach is good for horseback riding. For instruction and for riding on the beach at Sines, contact **Centro Equestre de Santo André** (✉ Monte V. Cima, Santo André ☎ 269/761235).

BEACHES

Some of Europe's finest and least crowded beaches are on the rugged stretch of Portugal's west coast that extends from the southern extreme of the Alentejo at Odeceixe north to where Sines rests on the tip of the Tróia Peninsula. Some beaches—such as Praia do Carvalhal and Praia Grande at Almograve—don't have any facilities and are uncrowded even in July and August. The beaches at Vila Nova de Milfontes and at Porto Covo have restaurants and the usual beach facilities. Exercise great care when swimming on the west coast: the surf is often high, and strong undertows and riptides are common.

Discover beautiful Alentejo scenery—coastlines, windmills, cork trees, and rolling hills that in spring are blanketed in flowers—on a donkey (safe even for grandmothers). On the road to Cercal, 14 km (8½ mi) from Santiago do Cacém, a sign on a dirt road points left to **Os Moinhos do Paneiro** (✉ Vale Seco ☎ 269/906222 ⊕ burros.planetaclix.pt). A half-day donkey ride for two is €35; a full day is €60 plus €10 an hour for a guide.

To experience the adventure of an African safari in the middle of the Alentejo, head to **Badoca Park,** home to tigers, giraffes, zebras, chimpanzees, yaks, buffalo, antelope, and other animals that roam free. For the best photo ops, join the one-hour safari tour that takes you around the park on a minitrain. There's a wooded picnic area for packed lunches, or you can eat at the restaurant, which is spectacularly decorated as an African lodge. ✉ *Herdade da Badoca, Alentejo-Santo André, Exit the A2 at the Grandola/Sines exit onto the IC33; the park entrance is at Km 34 (6 km [4 mi] southwest of Santiago do Cacém)* ☎ *269/708850* ⊕ *www.badoca.com* 🎟 *€13.50 entrance and safari tour* ☉ *Daily 9–8.*

Alcácer do Sal

⓵ *52 km (32 mi) northeast of Santiago do Cacém.*

Salt production here has nearly disappeared, but it was because of this mineral that Alcácer do Sal became one of Portugal's first inhabited sites. Parts of the castle foundations are around 5,000 years old. The

Greeks were here, and, later, the Romans, who established the town of Salatia Urbs Imperatoria—a key intersection in their system of Lusitanian roads. During the Moorish occupation, under the name of Alcácer de Salatia, this became one of the most important Muslim strongholds in all of Iberia. In the 16th century Alcácer prospered as a major producer of salt, and a brisk trade was conducted with the northern European countries, which used it to preserve herring. The hilltop castle is the town's most prominent attraction. Red-tile-roof buildings descend from the castle to the riverbank in long horizontal rows.

The marshlands and the estuary of the Rio Sado that extend to the west of Alcácer form the **Reserva Natural do Sado.** The riverbanks are lined with salt pans and rice paddies, and the nature reserve gives shelter to wildlife such as dolphins, otters, white storks, and egrets. From the beach town of Comporta, Route N261 runs south along the coast through a mostly deserted stretch of dunes and pine trees with some undeveloped sandy beaches.

Where to Stay & Eat

$–$$ ✕ **Hortelã da Ribeira.** Beneath the castle, this restaurant is named for the wild mint *(hortelã)* that grows on riverbanks. Owner Helena Fideles uses this herb and other Alentejo herbs in many delicious fish dishes—*arroz de tamboril* (rice with monkfish), *chocos* (squid), and *ameijoas* (clams). An interesting feature in the restaurant is its walls adorned with animal-motif tiles hand-painted by the local villagers. ⊠ *Estrada Santa Luzia, lj. 2* ☎ *265/612235* ▭ *AE, DC, MC, V* ☻ *Closed Mon.*

$–$$ ✕ **Porto Santana.** You can take your lunch outside with a view of the Rio Sado. Dinner is served indoors as at night the outdoor area becomes a bar. The specialty here is sopa de cação. ⊠ *Rua Senhora Santana* ☎ *265/ 622344* ▭ *AE, DC, MC, V* ☻ *Closed Tues.*

$$$ ⊞ **Pousada de Dom Afonso II.** In the ancient castle that overlooks the Rio Sado, this very attractive pousada looks out over the rooftops of the town and the green plains across the river. Guest rooms are comfortable and tastefully appointed with elegant wooden furniture, blue sofa chairs, and Oriental rugs to match. Public areas are medieval inspired with stone and brick walls, stone floors, wooden furniture, and illumination imitating medieval torches. There is plenty of sunning space around the rectangular pool at the edge of the castle wall and turret. ⊠ *Castelo de Alcácer, 7580* ☎ *265/613070* 🖷 *265/613074* ⊕ *www.pousadas.pt* ⇩ *33 rooms, 2 suites* ⚭ *Restaurant, cable TV, pool, wading pool, bar, Wi-Fi* ▭ *AE, DC, MC, V* ❙❘❙ *BP, FAP, MAP.*

¢ ⊞ **Albergaria da Barrosinha.** This typical whitewashed, one-story Alentejo country house is set in the midst of a huge farm estate surrounded by cork and pine trees. Red-and-white striped curtains and bedcovers elegantly match the red clay–tile floors. To contrast with the red, bathrooms are decorated in blue-and-white Alcobaça tiles. The inn organizes horseback riding, hiking, and biking tours for you. Game lovers can feast in the restaurant. ⊠ *Estrada Nacional 5, Barrosinha, 7580-251* ☎ *265/612032* 🖷 *265/612833* ⇩ *17 rooms, 2 suites* ⚭ *Restaurant, cable TV, pool, bicycles, horseback riding* ▭ *AE, DC, MC, V* ❙❘❙ *MAP.*

ÉVORA & THE ALENTEJO ESSENTIALS

Transportation

BY AIR

You can fly into Lisbon's Portela Airport or the airport in Faro and then take ground transportation into the region. Évora is roughly 160 km (100 mi) from Lisbon and about 245 km (152 mi) from Faro.

🛈 Airports **Faro Airport** ☎ 289/800617 or 289/800801. **Portela Airport** ☎ 21/841-3500 or 21/841-3700.

BY BUS

There are few places in this region that aren't served by at least one bus daily. Express coaches run by several regional lines travel regularly between Lisbon and the larger towns such as Évora, Beja, and Estremoz. Because several companies leave for the Alentejo from different terminals in Lisbon, it's best to have a travel agent do your booking.

🛈 **Belos Transportes S.A.** ⊠ Terminal Rodoviário, Évora ☎ 266/769410 ⊠ Rossio do Marquês de Pombal 88, Estremoz ☎ 268/322282. **Eva Transportes** ⊠ Rua Tavares 2, Beja ☎ 284/313620 ⊕ www.eva-bus.com. **Rede Nacional de Expressos** ⊠ Av. Duque D'Avila, Arco do Cego, Lisbon ☎ 21/358-1460.

BY CAR

Driving will give you access to many out-of-the-way beaches and villages. Although you'll encounter construction on many of the region's main routes, the roads are generally good, and traffic is light. There are no confusing big cities in which to get lost, although parking can be a problem in some of the towns such as Évora.

The toll highway A6, which branches off A2 running south from Lisbon, takes you as far as the Spanish border at Caia, where it links up with the highway from Madrid. This road provides easy access to Évora and the Upper Alentejo. The A2 runs south to the Algarve, as does the nontoll IP1/E01. Farther inland and south of Évora, the IP2/E802 is the best access for Beja and southeastern Alentejo. The N521 runs 105 km (65 mi) from Caceres, Spain, to the Portuguese border near Portalegre. To the south, the N433 runs from Seville, Spain, to Beja, 225 km (140 mi) away.

BY TAXI

Cabs within Évora's city limits and outside the city limits charge €0.45 per kilometer. Note that if you travel to another town from Évora, such as Beja, you'll have to pay for the taxi's return trip. To get a cab, head for one of the many taxi stands around town, such as the one in Praça do Giraldo (you can't hail them on the street) or call Radio Taxis Évora.

🛈 **Radio Taxis Évora** ☎ 266/734734.

BY TRAIN

Travel by train in the vast Alentejo is not for people in a great hurry. Service to the more remote destinations is infrequent—and in some cases nonexistent. A couple of towns, including Évora and Beja, are connected with Lisbon by several trains daily. The Intercidades train leaves from Lisbon's Oriente Station in the Parque da Nações to the Alentejo. You can also catch the Intercidades train at Lisbon's Entrecampos Station.

🚆 **Beja CP Train Station** ✉ Largo da Estação ☎ 284/326135. **Évora CP Train Station** ✉ Largo da Estação ☎ 266/742336.

Contacts & Resources

EMERGENCIES

Beja and Évora have hospitals with emergency rooms, and their approaches are marked HOSPITAL; the emergency room is marked URGÊN-CIAS. All sizable towns have at least one drugstore that's open weekends, holidays, and after normal store hours. Local newspapers usually keep a schedule, and notices are posted on all pharmacy doors.

🚆 **Évora Police** ☎ 266/702022. **General emergencies** ☎ 112. **Hospital Distrital** ✉ Rua Dr. António F. C. Lima, Beja ☎ 284/310200. **Hospital Distrital Espírito Santo** ✉ Largo Sr. da Pobreza, Évora ☎ 266/740100.

MAIL

🚆 **Post Offices Beja** ✉ Largo dos Correios ☎ 284/326135. **Évora** ✉ Rua de Olivença ☎ 266/745480.

TOUR OPTIONS

ORIENTATION TOURS
Few regularly scheduled sightseeing tours originate within the region, but many of the major attractions are covered by a wide selection of one-day tours from Lisbon. For information in Lisbon, contact Cityrama.

🚆 **Cityrama** ✉ Av. Praia da Vitória 12-B, Saldanha, Lisbon ☎ 21/319-1085 ⊕ www.cityrama.pt.

WALKING TOURS
Walking tours of Évora are available through Mendes and Murteira, and the company can also organize bus tours of the district's archaeological sites.

🚆 **Mendes and Murteira** ✉ Rua 31 de Janeiro 15-A, Évora ☎ 266/739240 or 917/236025.

VISITOR INFORMATION

ÉVORA & ENVIRONS
🚆 Tourist Offices **Arraiolos** ✉ Câmara Municipal ☎ 266/490240. **Évora** ✉ Praça do Giraldo 73 ☎ 266/702671. **Região de Turismo de Évora** ✉ Rua de Aviz 90, Évora ☎ 266/742534.

UPPER ALENTEJO
🚆 Tourist Offices **Campo Maior** ✉ Rua Major Talaja ☎ 268/688936 ⊕ www.cm-campomaior.pt. **Castelo de Vide** ✉ Rua Bartolomeu Álvares da Santa 81 ☎ 245/901361. **Estremoz** ✉ Largo da República ☎ 268/333541. **Évoramonte** ✉ Rua de Santa Maria ☎ 268/959227. **Marvão** ✉ Largo de Santa Maria ☎ 245/933886. **Monsaraz** ✉ Praça Dom Nuno Álavares ☎ 266/557136. **Portalegre** ✉ Palácio Póvoas-Rossio ☎ 245/331359. **Região de Turismo de São Mamede** ✉ Estrada de Santana 25, Portalegre ☎ 245/300770. **Vila Viçosa** ✉ Câmara Municipal ☎ 268/881101.

LOWER ALENTEJO
🚆 Tourist Offices **Alcácer do Sal** ✉ Rua da República 66 ☎ 265/622565. **Alvito** ✉ Largo das Alcacarias ☎ 284/485440. **Beja** ✉ Rua Capitão João Francisco de Sousa 25 ☎ 284/311913. **Mértola** ✉ Rua Alonso Gômes ☎ 286/612573. **Região de Turismo da Planície Dourada** ✉ Praça da República 12, Beja ☎ 284/310150. **Santiago do Cacém** ✉ Praça do Mercado Municipal ☎ 269/826696. **Serpa** ✉ Largo D. Jorge de Melo 2 ☎ 284/544727. **Viana do Alentejo** ✉ Praça da República ☎ 266/939938. **Vila Nova de Milfontes** ✉ Rua António Mantas ☎ 283/996599.

The Algarve

WORD OF MOUTH

"The most beautiful spot I have been to in Portugal was Sagres, which is in the Algarve, on the western tip. Almost completely surrounded by the sea, it's not hard to imagine the dreams of Henry the Navigator. Sagres is only 270 kms from Lisbon, and shouldn't take more than 4 hours if done leisurely."

—lol930

Updated by
Norman
Renouf

APPEALING, YES—PERHAPS TOO APPEALING for its own good. The Algarve is deservedly popular with millions of annual vacationers who throng here for sun, sandy beaches, superb golf, and all the other enticements of the seaside resorts. Along with the region's popularity has come progress, and during the past two decades, the Algarve has been heavily developed, with parts of the once pristine, 240-km (149-mi) coastline now overbuilt. In some areas the shore is almost wall-to-wall with villa complexes, hotels, dance clubs, and bars.

Until the construction of the airport at Faro in the '60s, the Algarve was rarely visited by tourists, and for centuries before that it remained isolated from the rest of Europe. Phoenicians, Romans, and Visigoths established fishing and trading communities here, but it wasn't until the arrival of the Moors in the 8th century that the region became an important strategic settlement. It was the Moors who gave the province its name—El Gharb (the Land to the West)—and who established their capital at the inland town of Silves (then called Chelb). In those days it had direct access to the sea and at its peak was a grand city with a population of more than 30,000.

Silves fell to the Christians in 1189, but the Moors weren't completely out of the region until the middle of the 13th century, leaving many tangible reminders of their 500-year rule: Arabic place-names; the white, cubelike houses in the coastal fishing villages; the popular fruits and sweets of the region; and the physical features of many of the people. In the 15th century Prince Henry the Navigator established a town and a pioneering navigation school near Sagres, where principles were developed that would enable 16th-century Portuguese mariners to explore much of the world. After this flurry of activity, though, the Algarve once again settled into obscurity.

The Algarve measures a mere 40 km (25 mi) north to south, bordered on the north by the Serra de Monchique (Monchique Mountains) and the Serra de Caldeirão (Caldeirão Mountains) and on the east by the Rio Guadiana (Guadiana River). Its location in the south, protected by hills, makes the Algarve much warmer than any other place in the country in winter; and in summer, the coast is cooled by sea breezes. The vegetation is far more luxuriant; the land, originally irrigated by the Moors, supports a profusion of fruits, nuts, and vegetables; and the fishing industry has always flourished.

Even where development is at its heaviest, construction takes the form of landscaped villas and apartment complexes, which are generally made of local materials and blend well with the scenery. And there are still small, undeveloped fishing villages and secluded beaches, particularly in the west. The west is also home to extraordinary rock formations and idyllic grottoes. In the east a series of isolated sandbar islands and sweeping beaches balances the crowded excesses of the middle. To see the Algarve at its best, though, you may have to abandon the shore for a drive inland. Here, rural Portugal still survives in hill villages, market towns, and agricultural landscapes, which, although only a few miles from the coast, seem a world away in attitude.

GREAT ITINERARIES

Give yourself at least three days to take in the more important sights. In five days you can see the sights, have a little time at the beach, linger over a delicious seafood lunch (or two) at a beachfront restaurant, and still have time to get away from the built-up coastal strip to some of the more remote inland villages. A seven-day stay will allow you to, perhaps, get in a game of golf or spend a few days simply relaxing on some of the many excellent beaches. After all, it was the discovery of these sandy stretches by sun-starved northern Europeans that transformed this sleepy province into one of the continent's most popular vacation spots.

IF YOU HAVE 3 DAYS

Begin with a day exploring the provincial capital, ⊞ **Faro** ❶– ❾, and its surroundings. The following morning, head west to the lighthouse at **Cabo São Vicente** ❸❺ and the fortress and exhibition center at **Sagres** ❸❹, where you can have lunch overlooking the cliffs. It's a two-hour drive and traffic can be heavy in summer. In the afternoon, return to Faro, stopping along the way in **Lagos** ❷❽– ❸❷ or

Portimão ❷❻. On Day 3, drive east to **Vila Real de Santo António** ❶❺, at the border with Spain. En route you can explore **Olhão** ❶❶, with its Moorish-style architecture, and **Tavira** ❶❸, one of the Algarve's most attractive towns.

IF YOU HAVE 5 DAYS

After a day in and around ⊞ **Faro** ❶– ❾, drive west to visit **Portimão** ❷❻ and the nearby beach resort of **Praia da Rocha** ❷❺. Continue west to overnight in ⊞ **Lagos** ❷❽– ❸❷, a city whose origins go back to Carthaginian times. After seeing the sights in Lagos, head to **Cabo São Vicente** ❸❺ for views from the lighthouse and then to ⊞ **Sagres** ❸❹. The next morning, follow N268 along the west coast to Aljezur, where you take N267 through a remote part of the Algarve to the hill town of **Monchique** ❷❼. Enjoy lunch at one of the terrace restaurants that afford views across the countryside to the sea. After lunch, head down the mountain on N266 to the coastal road N125 and swing east to **Olhão** ❶❶ and ⊞ **Tavira** ❶❸. On your last day, visit the border town of **Vila Real de Santo António** ❶❺.

5

Exploring the Algarve

The Algarve's main roads—the N125 and the IP1/E1—and its train line connect towns and villages along the entire coast, though rail travelers should beware that the train service is very slow and stations are often some way from the center of the town, resort, or village they purport to serve. If you rent a car, you can see all of the region in a week, albeit at a fairly brisk pace. Even if you plan to stay at one resort for several days, make an effort to see both the eastern and western ends of the province and an inland town or two; each has a distinct character.

For touring purposes, the province can conveniently be divided into four sections, starting with Faro—the Algarve's capital—and the nearby beaches and inland towns. The second section encompasses the region east to the border town of Vila Real de Santo António, from which you can cross into Spain. The most built-up part of the coast, and the section with the most to offer vacationers, runs from Faro west to Portimão. The fourth section covers Lagos, the principal town of the western Algarve, and extends to Sagres and Cabo São Vicente.

Restaurants & Cuisine

Unless otherwise noted, casual dress is acceptable throughout the Algarve. Reservations are not needed off-season, but in summer, you'll need them at most of the better restaurants.

Algarvian cooking makes good use of local seafood. The most unusual of regional appetizers, *espadarte fumada* (smoked swordfish), is sliced thin, served with a salad, and best when accompanied by a dry white wine. Restaurants generally serve their own version of *sopa de peixe* (fish soup) as well as a variety of succulent shellfish: *percebes* (barnacles), *santola* (crab), and *gambas* (shrimp). Main courses often depend on what has been landed that day, but there's generally a choice of *robalo* (sea bass), *pargo* (bream), *atum* (tuna), and espadarte.

At simple beach cafés and harbor stalls the unmistakable smell of *sardinhas assadas* (charcoal-grilled sardines) permeates the air—they make a tempting lunch served with fresh bread and smooth red wine. Perhaps the most famous Algarvian dish is *cataplana*—a stew of clams, pork, onions, tomatoes, and wine, which takes its name from the lidded utensil used to steam the dish. You have to wait for cataplana to be specially prepared, but once you've tasted it, you won't mind waiting again and again.

In inland rural areas, game highlights most menus, with many meat dishes served *o forno* (oven roasted). Specialties include *cabrito* (kid), *leitão* (suckling pig), and *codorniz* (quail), as well as *ensopado de borrego* (lamb stew).

The Algarve is known for its almonds, oranges, and figs, but these rarely appear in restaurants, where the choice of dessert is often limited to flan, ice cream, and perhaps a fresh fruit salad. Typical Algarvian sweets include rich egg, sugar, and almond custards that reflect the Moorish influence, including *doces de amendoa* (marzipan cakes in the shapes of animals and flowers), *bolos de Dom Rodrigo* (almond sweets with egg-and-sugar filling), *bolo Algarvio* (cake made of sugar,

ALGARVE MARKET DAYS

All the main towns and villages have regular food markets, usually open daily from 8 until around 2. Among the best are those in Olhão, Tavira, Lagos, and Silves. Larger weekly and monthly markets, where a wider variety of produce and goods is sold, are held in:

- Albufeira: first and third Tuesday of the month
- Loulé: first and fourth Sunday of the month
- Lagos: first Saturday of the month
- Portimão: first Monday of the month
- Sagres: first Friday of the month
- Silves: second Monday of the month

IF YOU LIKE

BEACHES

The Algarve's generally clean and impressive beaches are some of the finest in Europe. There are hundreds from which to choose on the long stretch of coast. Most (especially those in the main resorts) have snack bars and showers, and many have water-sports equipment for rent. Although you can wade out for a swim from most shores, heed local warnings about currents and steeply sloping seabeds.

The best cove beaches are at Lagos. Interesting stretches with enormous rock formations include those at Albufeira and Praia da Rocha. If you require more breathing space, particularly if you're traveling with young children, try the strands near Olhão and Tavira; these and the beaches near Sagres are less populated than those at major resorts.

There are anchorage and harbor facilities at Faro, Lagos, Olhão, Portimão, Praia da Rocha, Sagres, and Vila Real de Santo António. Snorkeling and scuba diving are especially good in the western Algarve, where certified, experienced divers can explore caves and rock formations. Wind- and board surfing are popular at a number of spots as well. In fact, several of the more remote west-coast beaches attract surfers from all parts of Europe.

BULLFIGHTS

Unlike the Spanish, the Portuguese don't kill their bulls at the end of the fight, although the severely injured ones are slaughtered immediately afterward, out of sight of the public. You can attend fights in the towns of Albufeira and Lagos; aficionados of the sport recommend attending the events held in August, which are fought by the country's top cavaleiros. Bullfights are held every Saturday at 5:30 PM April–June, September, and October; in July and August they're held at 10 PM, when the day's heat has dissipated.

GOLF

Golf is a year-round game here, and you'll find some of Europe's best courses, designed by the likes of Henry and William Cotton and Frank Pennink. All courses have a clubhouse with a bar and restaurant, practice grounds, and equipment rentals. Many Algarve hotels promote the area's golf facilities, and although green fees are never included in room rates, they're often discounted, and guests at certain hotels are given preference when it comes to booking tee times. See Chapter 9, Golf in Portugal: Where to Play, for a list of golf courses in the area.

NIGHTLIFE

In the major resorts you'll find plenty of bars and dance clubs. If you prefer a quieter evening, the Algarve's open-air cafés are perfect for a drink and people-watching, and sometimes a musician will stroll by. Many hotels also put on performances of fado and other traditional music. To gamble, head for one of the Algarve's three casinos—at Praia de Rocha, Vilamoura, and Monte Gordo—and remember to bring your passport as well as your wallet.

almonds, eggs, and cinnamon), and *morgado de figos do Algarve* (fig-and-almond paste). You will find these on sale in *pastelarias* (cake shops) and in some cafés.

About the Hotels

There are busy beachside hotels and secluded retreats in posh country estates. Apartment and villa complexes with luxurious amenities are often built on the most beautiful parts of the coast. They may be 5 km (3 mi) from the nearest town, but most have bars, restaurants, shops, and other facilities. Budget lodgings are also available.

In most towns and resorts, you'll be approached by people offering very reasonably priced *quartos* (rooms) in private houses, which are almost always clean and cheerful, if small and with shared bathrooms. Don't expect to pay less than around €25 for a reasonable double room per night. Also don't agree to take a room without seeing it first; it may be farther from the town center than you were led to believe.

In summer, reservations at most places are essential, and rates often rise by as much as 50% above off-peak prices. Since the weather from September through May is still good, you might want to consider an off-peak trip to take advantage of the lower prices.

WHAT IT COSTS In Euros					
	$$$$	**$$$**	**$$**	**$**	**¢**
RESTAURANTS	over €21	€16–€21	€11–€15	€7–€10	under €7
HOTELS	over €275	€176–€275	€101–€175	€60–€100	under €60

Restaurant prices are per person for a main course at dinner. Hotel prices are for a standard double room, including tax, in high season (off-season rates may be lower).

When to Go

Winter is mild: if you seek solitude and don't mind limiting your swimming to heated hotel pools, it's the perfect time to visit. There are plenty of bargains to be had as well. Algarvian springs, with their rolling carpets of wildflowers, are delightful. Late in the season, you can just about take a dip in the ocean, and there's plenty of space to lay out your beach blanket. Summer (July and August) is high season, when lodging is at a premium, prices are at their highest, and crowds are at their thickest. But summer also brings warmer seas, piercing blue skies, and warm, golden sands at the foot of glowing ocher-red cliffs.

FARO & ENVIRONS

Many people fly in to Faro and pass straight through on their way to beaches east and west, which is unfortunate. The city's harbor and Cidade Velha (Old Town) are both worthy of a night's stay or more, and its many facilities make it a fine base for touring the region. The towns that ring Faro contain their own sights worth seeing, from beaches and markets to churches and ruins.

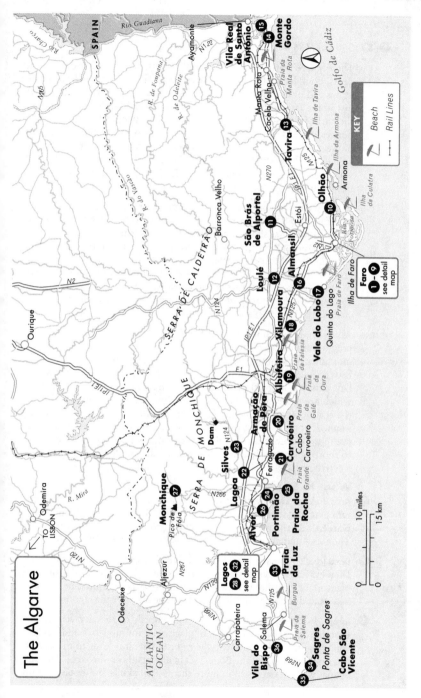

The Algarve

KEY
Beach
Rail Lines

Faro

❶–❾ *300 km (186 mi) southeast of Lisbon.*

The Algarve's prosperous provincial capital has around 100,000 residents. Founded by the Moors, the city was taken by Afonso III in 1249, at the end of the Arab domination. Much of its early architecture was lost in the late 16th century, when it was sacked by the English under the earl of Essex. It was further damaged by two 18th-century earthquakes, the latter of which, in 1755, also destroyed Lisbon. Remnants of the medieval walls and some historic buildings, however, can still be seen in the delightful Cidade Velha (Old Town). Here, quiet streets and squares, where balconies and tile work adorn even the most unappealing facade, are perfect for a stroll.

East of the harbor, in the pedestrian shopping streets around Rua de Santo António, you'll find much of what makes Faro tick as a tourist town: bars, restaurants, shops, and sidewalk hawkers touting souvenirs and snacks. During the 19th century a prosperous community of Jews from Gibraltar and Morocco settled in Rua de Santo António, boosting the growth of local trade. Around 1830, this community took the initiative of building two synagogues and a cemetery, which later, with the almost complete disappearance of the Jewish population, fell into ruins. The cemetery is still visible.

TIMING Allow about two hours to tour Faro's historic quarter in leisure, stopping when a pastry display case calls your name. The distances between monuments and museums here are short and the streets are easily navigated. Avoid touring in the heat of the day in summer, as the streets have little shade and the town is virtually treeless except for orange trees, which are not exactly shade givers. Allow a good 20 minutes to tour the ethnographic museum and 40 minutes for the archaeological museum. If you are a church fan, the Sé will not disappoint. Don't miss the Igreja do Carmo's Chapel of the Bones, which takes half an hour to thoroughly digest, although the Igreja de São Pedro is far more attractive inside.

What to See

❸ Arco da Vila. The entrance to the Cidade Velha is through this 18th-century gate that stands in front of the Jardim Manuel Bivar (Manuel Bivar Garden). At the top is a niche sheltering a white-marble statue of St. Thomas Aquinas, plus storks that nest here permanently.

❶ Doca (dock). The small dock—flanked by Faro's main square, the Praça Dom Francisco Gomes, and the Jardim Manuel Bivar—is filled with small pleasure craft rather than working fishing boats. A good time to come here is at dusk when the sun sets dramatically over the lagoon.

❾ Igreja do Carmo (Carmo Church). Just north of the city center, this baroque church looks very out of place amid the modern buildings surrounding it. Inside, a door to the right of the altar leads to the Capela dos Ossos (Chapel of the Bones) set in an outside garden area. The tiny chapel walls are covered in more than 1,000 skulls and bones dug up

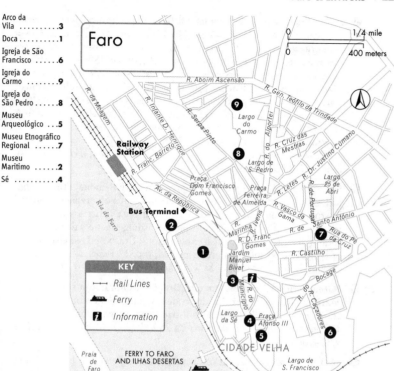

from the adjacent monks' cemetery—an eerie sight, to say the least, but a fairly common custom in Portugal. ⊠ *Largo do Carmo* ☎ *289/824490* ◨ *€0.75* ⊙ *Weekdays 10–1 and 3–5, Sat. 10–1.*

⑥ Igreja de São Francisco (Church of St. Francis). The plain facade of the Igreja de São Francisco gives no hint of the richness of its baroque interior. Inside are glorious 18th-century blue-and-white azulejos and a chapel adorned with gilt work. There aren't any set visiting hours. Ask at the tourist office or push the bell by the church's door; late afternoon is usually the best time to try. ⊠ *Largo de São Francisco* ☎ *No phone.*

NEED A BREAK?

The **Café Aliança** (⊠ Rua Francisco Gomes 7–11 ☎ 289/801621) is a timeworn coffeehouse, between Rua Francisco Gomes and Rua Marinha. Service is somewhere between slow and dead slow (wave vigorously to catch a waiter's attention), but it's worth it to see a glimpse of the Faro of an earlier time.

⑧ Igreja do São Pedro (St. Peter's Church). This 16th-century church is perhaps the prettiest of Faro's churches, and it has an unusual altar set to the left of the main altar. It's entirely carved in gilded chestnut wood and a delicate frieze depicts the Last Supper. ⊠ *Largo de S. Pedro* ☎ *No phone* ⊙ *Daily 9–1 and 3–7.*

⑤ Museu Arqueológico e Lapidar Infante D. Henrique (Prince Henry Archaeological and Lapidary Museum). The 16th-century Convento de Nossa Senhora da Assunção (Convent of Our Lady of the Assumption) houses this museum—the first to be opened in the Algarve, in 1894—which makes good use of the two-story cloister. The best displays are the Roman artifacts from local settlements predating Moorish Faro as well as Roman statues from the excavations at Estoi. Perhaps the most stunning artifact is the one unearthed near the train station: a well-preserved 3rd-century Roman mosaic of Neptune surrounded by the four winds. ⊠ *Praça Afonso III 14* ☎ *289/897400* ☑ *€2* ⊙ *July–Oct., Tues.–Fri. 10 AM–8 PM, weekends 1:30 PM–8 PM; Nov.–June, Tues.–Fri. 9 AM–6 PM, weekends 11:30 AM–5:30 PM.*

⑦ Museu Etnográfico Regional do Algarve (Algarve Regional Ethnographical Museum). Providing a bit of culture in an area otherwise dominated by stores and eateries this museum, housed in the District Assembly building, sheds light on local agricultural and fishing practices through models and diagrams, and English explanations. Crafts and reconstructions of typical house interiors are displayed, too. ⊠ *Praça da Liberdade 2* ☎ *289/827610* ☑ *€1.50* ⊙ *Weekdays 9–12:30 and 2–5:30.*

☾ ② Museu Marítimo Almirante Ramalho Ortigão (Admiral Ramalho Ortigão-Maritime Museum). At this dockside museum, models of local fishing craft are displayed alongside full-size boats of war and exploration. ⊠ *Capitania do Porto de Faro* ☎ *289/894990* ☑ *€1* ⊙ *Weekdays 9:30–noon and 2:30–5.*

④ Sé (Cathedral). The squat, mostly Renaissance-style Sé, built in 1251 over a former mosque and originally belonging to the Order of Santiago, faces the Largo da Sé a grand square bordered by orange trees and whitewashed palace buildings. The cathedral retains a Gothic tower but is mostly of interest for its interior full of 17th- and 18th-century azulejos. On one side of the nave is a red chinoiserie organ, dating from 1751. Best of all, however, is the view from the top of the church tower, looking out over Cidade Velha rooftops and across the lagoon. ⊠ *Largo da Sé* ☎ *No phone* ☑ *€2* ⊙ *Mon.–Sat. 10–5:30; tower 10–2.*

Beaches

The closest beach to town is the long, sandy **Praia de Faro,** on the Ilha de Faro (Faro Island), a sandbar 5 km (3 mi) southwest of town. It's near the airport and is a 25-minute ride from town on Bus 16, which runs every hour 8 AM–10 PM. You can catch it at the boat basin or opposite the bus terminal. Crowds pack in during peak season and on weekends. There's no surfing here, nor are water-sports rentals available.

Where to Stay & Eat

¢–$$ ✕ **Adega Nova.** A seating arrangement of long wooden tables lined by benches keeps things lively at this down-to-earth *adega* (wine cellar), where the Portuguese dishes are expertly prepared. You'll find more good cheer, as well as drinks, in the tile-covered bar. It's a good thing, too, as this place is close to the train station in an otherwise dreary area. ⊠ *Rua Francisco Barreto 24* ☎ *289/813433* ▭ *No credit cards.*

¢–$$ ✕ **Dois Irmãos.** In business since 1925, this large, central restaurant (one of several good places on this street) specializes in cataplana, as evidenced by the utensils that hang from its wood-beam ceiling. Almost any of the other seafood dishes are worth trying, too. Just save room for the flan. Choose your wine from one of the hundreds of bottles that line the upper walls. ✉ *Largo do Terreiro do Bispo 14–15* ☎ *289/823337* 🗐 *AE, DC, MC, V.*

¢–$ ✕ **Mesa dos Mouros.** The Moors' Table occupies an ancient stone house right by the Sé. You can either eat indoors or dine alfresco on a raised wooden terrace looking across the cobbled square, which is fringed with orange trees. Despite the antiquity of its surroundings, this is a very stylish restaurant that serves good fish dishes and Spanish tapas. ✉ *Largo da Sé* ☎ *289/878873* 🗐 *MC, V.*

$$$ ✕🖭 **Monte do Casal.** This 18th-century villa hotel is slightly out of Faro, near Estoi. The British owner and chef Bill Hawkins trained in the kitchens of Claridges and the Savoy, which makes dining here a highlight well accompanied by a formidable wine list. Rooms have old brass-cornered furniture, and nearly all have private patios overlooking the pool and gardens. From Faro take the N2 north toward São Bras and exit for Estoi. Follow signs for Moncarapachio for 2½ km (1½ mi), where the hotel is signposted on the left. Children under 16 are not allowed (except in July). ✉ *Cerro do Lobo, 8000-661* ☎ *289/991503* ⊕ *www.montedocasal.pt* 🛏 *12 rooms* ⌂ *Restaurant, in-room safes, cable TV, pool, bar; no kids under 16* 🗐 *MC, V* ⦿ *BP, MAP.*

★ $$ 🖭 **Hotel Eva.** From this well-appointed hotel on the main square, you have views of the boat basin and the Cidade Velha. There's a bar with occasional evening entertainment, as well as a rooftop pool and top-floor restaurant. Rooms are modern and comfortably furnished; ask for one overlooking the harbor area. There's also a courtesy bus to the town beach on nearby Ilha de Faro. ✉ *Av. da República 1, 8000-0078* ☎ *289/001000* 🛏 *148 rooms* ⌂ *Restaurant, coffee shop, snack bar, in-room safes, minibars, cable TV, pool, hair salon, bar, laundry service, meeting rooms* 🗐 *AE, DC, MC, V* ⦿ *BP, FAP, MAP.*

$ 🖭 **Residencial Algarve.** The original building was constructed in the 1880s for a wealthy maritime family. It was renovated to mirror the original style and is now one of Faro's nicest budget hotels. Even the bathrooms recall those in much more upscale establishments. Rooms are bright and have pine furnishings, stone floors, and simple pastel-color throw rugs. The hotel is just a few steps from the center of town. ✉ *Rua Infante Dom Henrique 52, 8000-0078* ☎ *289/895700* ⊕ *www.residencialalgarve.com* 🛏 *14 rooms* ⌂ *Cable TV* 🗐 *MC, V* ⦿ *BP.*

¢ 🖭 **Residencial Madalena.** The hotel is convenient to both the bus and train terminals, and once you arrive, the chirpy staff will help you navigate around town. Most rooms have spotless, modern en-suite bathrooms and are snug and warm in winter, a good commodity in Faro, where winter months can be bitter. Basic breakfast includes excellent coffee. ✉ *Rua Conselheiro Bivar 109, 8000-255* ☎ *289/805806* 🛏 *20 rooms* ⌂ *Cable TV* 🗐 *MC, V* ⦿ *CP.*

Nightlife

Café goers throng Faro's central pedestrian streets at night. Rua do Prior, in particular, is known for its wide selection of late-closing bars. Friday night is the best time for barhopping. Possibly the only bar playing industrial and gothic music in Algarve, **Gothic Bar** (✉ Rua da Madalena 38, off Rua do Prior ☎ 289/807887) attracts a crowd with body piercings. Don't be put off by the silly name: **Kingburger** (✉ Rua do Prior 40 ☎ 289/828085) rocks until well into the morning. If you're after a full-fledged dance club, visit trendy **24 Julho** (✉ Rua do Prior 38 ☎ 289/282468), which is patronized almost exclusively by the locals on weekends, when it stays open until 7 AM.

> ## FESTIVAL
>
> The Algarve's **Festival Internacional da Música Clássica**—a series of classical music performances by leading Portuguese and foreign artists—is held in Faro, Tavira, Albufeira, Portimão, and Lagos during the months of May to July.

Olhão

10 *8 km (5 mi) east of Faro.*

During the Napoleonic Wars, the inhabitants of this 18th-century port town on the Ria Formosa (a *ria* is a briny river) defied the French blockade on trade with Britain and profited from smuggling. With the proceeds, they built North African–style, cube-shaped whitewashed houses. In 1808, local fishermen reputedly sailed to Brazil to inform the exiled Dom João VI that the French had departed from Portugal. Because of their loyalty and courage (they sailed without navigational aids), the fishermen's hometown was granted a town charter. Although modern construction has destroyed much of its charm, Olhão's port is still colorful, and its intricate Cidade Velha is appealing. To get a bird's-eye view climb the parish church's bell tower.

The **Roman ruins** at Milreu, about 10 km (6 mi) northwest of Olhão, were first excavated in 1877. The settlement was once known as Roman Ossonoba, and the remains—including a temple (later converted into a Christian basilica) and mosaic fragments adorning some of the 3rd-century baths—date from the 2nd through the 6th century. A few of the more portable pieces are on display in Faro's archaeological museum. 🎟 €2 🕐 *Apr.–Sept., Tues.–Sun. 9:30–12:30 and 2–6; Oct.–Mar., Tues.–Sun. 9:30–12:30 and 2–5.*

Beaches

Adding to the allure of this area's beaches is the designation of this entire section of coastline, including islands and river inlets, as a nature reserve, thanks to the great number of migratory birds that flock here on their way south for winter. To reach beaches on the nearby islands, take a ferry from the jetty at the east end of the municipal gardens. A small kiosk there posts timetables and sells tickets. If it's closed, buy the tickets on board. From June to September, ferries run hourly each day; from October through May there are three or four trips daily. Schedules are available at the tourist office. The fare is about €1.

The **Ilha da Armona,** about 15 minutes east of Olhão, has some fine, isolated stretches of sand as well as vacation villas and café-bars. The sandy **Ilha da Culatra,** 15 minutes by ferry from Olhão, has several ramshackle fishing communities; at the southern village of Farol, you'll find agreeable beaches.

Shopping

★ One of the Algarve's best food markets, the **Mercado dos Pescadores** (☉ Mon.–Sat. 7–2), is held in the riverfront buildings in the town gardens. Feast your eyes on the shellfish for which Olhão is renowned; mussels, in particular, are a local specialty.

São Brás de Alportel

⓫ *18 km (11 mi) northwest of Olhão.*

Inland, São Brás is a regional center for processing cork. It's an unremarkable place, but there are two reasons why it makes a refreshing break from the developed coastline: its museum of traditional dress and its *pousada* (inn).

Just a short walk from the center of town is the **Casa do Cultura António Bentes, Museu do Traje Algarvio** (Antonio Bentes Cultural Center, Algarve Costume Museum), a charmingly old-fashioned collection of local costumes—featuring black lacework, bright colors, and the rooster emblem of Portugal—and various other regional rural bygones. ⊠ *Rua Dr. José Dias Sancho 61* ☎ *289/840100* 🖃 *€2* ☉ *Weekdays 10–1 and 2–5, weekends 2–5.*

Where to Stay & Eat

$$ ✕🖃 **Pousada de São Brás.** The Algarve's only inland pousada is atop a hill where the air is pure and the views are splendid. It was built in the 1940s, and though it has been lavishly refurbished for the 21st century, most of the original look has been kept intact. In public areas bright yellow rattan furniture has splashy green upholstery, and latticework dividers provide a sense of privacy. Guest rooms and their tile baths are well appointed. In the restaurant ($$–$$$$) look for such Portuguese fare as clams with coriander or roast kid with rosemary; the quality of the food is variable. ⊠ *Estrada de Lisboa, 8150* ☎ *289/842305* ⊕ *www.pousadas.pt* 🛏 *31 rooms, 2 suites* ⚶ *Restaurant, cable TV, tennis court, pool, bar* 🖃 *AE, DC, MC, V* ⊺⊙⊺ *BP, MAP.*

Loulé

⓬ *13 km (8 mi) west of São Brás de Alportel.*

This little town is known for its crafts and its vibrant Saturday-morning fair, held in and around the landmark central market, which is enclosed and topped by a red onion dome. The narrow cobbled streets—particularly Rua da Barbacã—around the castle and the church are lined with whitewashed houses and workshops (closed Saturday afternoons and Sunday) where a few artisans still make lace, leather, and copper items. Note the many houses with very finely sculpted (or filigreed) plasterwork on their white chimneys—a typical old Algarve sight. The rest of Loulé is overwhelmed by the main boulevard and modern buildings, but there's a pleasant municipal park at the top of town.

Once a Moorish stronghold, Loulé has preserved the ruins of the medieval **Castelo de Loulé** (Loulé Castle), which was enlarged in 1268 after the site had been occupied and fortified since Neolithic times. These days, it houses the historical museum and archives as well as the tourist office. ✉ *Largo Dom Pedro I* ☎ *289/400642* ✎ *Free* ☉ *Weekdays 9–5:30, Sat. 10–2.*

The restored 13th-century **Igreja Matriz** (Parish Church) has handsome tiles, wood carvings, and an unusual wrought-iron pulpit. ✉ *Largo Pr. C. da Silva* ☎ *No phone* ☉ *Mon.–Sat. 9–noon and 2–5:30.*

Where to Stay

$ 🏨 **Loulé Jardim Hotel.** Portuguese business travelers are drawn to this hotel, which is well off the main road on a small square in the old part of town, yet only a short drive (8 km [5 mi]) from the coast. Rooms are modest and clean; prices leave you with extra money to buy some of those items crafted in town. ✉ *Praça Manuel D'Arriaga, 8100-665* ☎ *289/413094* ⊕ *www.loulejardimhotel.com* ↪ *52 rooms* ♿ *In-room safes, cable TV, pool, 2 bars, lounge, laundry service, meeting room; no a/c* ⊟ *AE, MC, V* ⊙*❙ BP.*

THE EASTERN ALGARVE

The eastern portion of the province, known as the Sotavento, is a region of flat, sandy beaches that are more difficult to access than those in the western Algarve because of their locations on spits, sandbars, and islands. Mudflats between Faro and the Spanish border are protected areas for breeding birds. Although there has been some development along the coast, this is primarily a quiet, low-key area, though its principal town, Tavira, is an important fishing port.

Tavira

🔟 *30 km (18 mi) east of Loulé, 28 km (17 mi) east of Faro.*

Fodor$Choice At the mouth of the quiet Rio Gilão, Tavira is immediately endearing, ★ with its castle ruins, riverfront gardens, and old streets. Many of the town's white, 18th-century houses retain their original doorways and coats-of-arms; others have peculiar four-sided roofs that rise pyramid-like, and still others are completely covered in tiles. The town also has more than 30 churches, most dating from the 17th and 18th centuries. One of two river crossings—the low bridge adjacent to the arcaded Praça da República—is of Roman origin, although it was rebuilt in the 17th century and again in recent times after sustaining damage from floodwaters.

From the battlemented walls of the ruined central 13th-century **castelo** you can look down over Tavira's many church spires and across the river delta to the sea. ✉ *Stepped street off Rua da Liberdade* ✎ *Free* ☉ *Daily 9–5.*

One of the town's two major churches, **Santa Maria do Castelo** (St. Mary of the Castle) was built on the site of a Moorish mosque in the 13th century. Although it was almost entirely destroyed by the 1755 earthquake, the church retains its original Gothic doorway. ⊠ *Alto de Santa Maria (next to castelo)* ☎ *No phone* ▧ *€1* ⊙ *Daily 9:30–12:30 and 2–5:30.*

The **Igreja da Misericórdia** (Mercy Church) is a Renaissance structure with a portal that dates from 1541. On Good Friday, a 10 PM candlelight procession begins here. From May through July, the church occasionally hosts musical performances during the Algarve International Classical Music Festival. ⊠ *West of Praça da República* ☎ *No phone* ⊙ *Daily 9–12:30 and 2–6.*

> ### CATCH OF THE DAY
>
> Because Tavira is a tuna-fishing port, you'll find plenty of local color and fresh fish; tuna steaks, often grilled and served with onions, are on restaurant menus all over town at remarkably low prices. In the harbor area, you can sample no-frills dining at its best, alongside the fishermen, at any of the café-restaurants across from the tangle of boats and nets.

The **Torre de Tavira** is an old water tower that was converted into a camera obscura of the Leonardo da Vinci fashion in 1931. An oversize photographic camera here takes images of the panoramic views it commands of the town. The visit makes a fascinating exploration into the world of photography and a cool, shady afternoon retreat from the sweltering afternoon sunshine. ⊠ *Calçado da Galeria 12* ☎ *No phone* ▧ *€3* ⊙ *Daily 10–5.*

Beaches

★ Directly offshore and extending west for some 10 km (6 mi) is the **Ilha de Tavira,** a long sandbar with several good beaches. Ferries run to the island every half hour in July and August and every hour May through June and September through mid-October. The fare is about €1 round-trip. In summer a bus (marked QUATRO ÁGUAS) runs between the center of town and the jetty 2 km (1 mi) east.

About 12 km (7 mi) east of Tavira is Manta Rota, a small community with a few bars, restaurants, hotels, and the **Praia de Manta Rota.** At this exceptional beach, sandbars merge with the shore. A particularly nice strand is the offshore sandbar at the village of Cacela Velha. From Manta Rota to Faro the underwater drop-offs are often steep and you can quickly find yourself in deep water.

Where to Stay & Eat

$–$$$ ✕ **Restaurante Imperial.** This restaurant behind the riverside gardens is well known for its fish: clams, tuna, a tasty mixed fried-fish plate—you name it. In summer, there's seating on the sidewalk. Waiters are good at their job but a little aloof: after 40 years of service, the Imperial doesn't have to try hard to attract customers. Desserts are a tad disappointing. ⊠ *Rua José Pires Padinha 22–24* ☎ *281/322306* ⊕ *www.restaurante-imperial.com* ▭ *MC, V* ⊙ *Closed Wed. Oct.–May.*

¢–$$ ✕ **Beira Rio.** Named for its riverbank location, the Beira Rio offers the best water views in town. Locals tend to eat in the azulejo-lined dining room; visitors are often drawn to the peaceful terrace, where watching the moon rise over the Roman bridge is alone worth the price of dinner. Well-prepared Portuguese specialties such as pork with port-wine sauce share the menu with steaks, pizzas, and pasta. ⊠ *Rua Borda de Agua de Assêca 46–48* ☎ *281/323165* ⊟ *AE, DC, MC, V* ⊗ *No lunch.*

¢–$$ ✕ **Venezia.** On the edge of the main square opposite the town hall are a number of good cafés where you can sit out and watch the world go by. The Venezia offers light Portuguese appetizers and very good homemade soups and ice cream. Service is prompt, quite a rare quality in this part of the world. ⊠ *Praça da República 11* ☎ *281/323781* ⊟ *No credit cards.*

¢–$ ✕ **Ponto de Encontro.** Cross the Roman bridge to this typical Portuguese restaurant with tiled walls and tables immaculately draped with linens. You can also relax at outside tables to view the passing scene on the small square, which in summer is abloom with flowers and closed to traffic. Algarve-style swordfish grilled with garlic, tuna fried with onion, and other fresh fish dishes are specialties. ⊠ *Praça Dr. António Padinha 39* ☎ *281/323730* ⊟ *AE, DC, MC, V.*

$ ✕▦ **Marés Residencial e Restaurante.** Only a stone's throw from the waterfront (and the summer ferry to the Ilha de Tavira), this tiny hotel is above an excellent Portuguese restaurant ($$–$$$$). Some of the rooms have balconies that offer river or town views; all provide basic comforts and have bathrooms decorated with rustic tile work. A rooftop terrace looks out over Tavira's distinctive pyramid-shaped roofs. The boat out to Tavira island leaves from directly in front of this hotel. ⊠ *Rua José Pires Padinha 134/140, 8800* ☎ *281/325815* ⊕ *www.residencialmares.com* ⇆ *24 rooms* ⚐ *Restaurant, cable TV* ⊟ *AE, DC, MC, V* ¶⚐¶ *BP.*

$–$$ ▦ **Hotel Vila Galé Albacora.** This is an absolutely charming hotel in a lovely location at the confluence of two rivers, just in front of the beaches. In fact, in the summer months boats depart from here to take you to the beach. It's traditional in architectural style, modern in decor, and not far from Tavira—it has a minibus service to and from town. ⊠ *Quatro Águas, 8800-901* ☎ *281/380800* ⊕ *www.vilagale.pt* ⇆ *157 rooms, 5 suites* ⚐ *2 restaurants, room service, in-room safes, minibars, cable TV, 2 pools (1 indoor)* ⊟ *AE, DC, MC, V* ¶⚐¶ *BP, FAP, MAP.*

Monte Gordo

⓮ *22 km (14 mi) east of Tavira.*

Pinewoods and orchards break up the flat landscape around this large resort area, just 4 km (2½ mi) from the Spanish border. Relentlessly modern, Monte Gordo has plenty of hotels, restaurants, and nightspots but falls well short on charm and character.

Beach

The flat, 12-km-long (7-mi-long) **Praia de Monte Gordo** is a very popular beach. The seawater here has the highest average temperature in the country, but it, too, can go from warm to ice cold within a day.

Where to Stay & Eat

¢–$$ ✕ **Mota.** Large, lively, and unpretentious, this well-established restaurant is on the sands of the Praia de Monte Gordo. Seating is on a large covered terrace facing the ocean. During the day you can drop in for a snack or salad if you don't want a full meal; in the evening you're served regional dishes while live music plays in the background. ☒ *Praia de Monte Gordo* ☎ *281/512340* ⊟ *No credit cards.*

$$ 🏨 **Alcázar.** Outside, white balconies contrast with a redbrick facade; inside, sinuous arches and low, molded ceilings recall a cave's interior—or that of an Arab tent. Rooms have their own terraces and window boxes. The staff is accommodating, and the location—two blocks from the beach—is convenient. ☒ *Rua de Ceuta 9, 8900-435* ☎ *281/510140* ✍*hotelalcazar@mail.telepac.pt* ⤶*130 rooms* ⊘ *Restaurant, coffee shop, in-room safes, some in-room hot tubs, some minibars, cable TV, some ethernet, tennis court, 2 pools, bar, piano bar, dance club, recreation room, shops, playground, laundry service* ⊟ *AE, DC, MC, V* ⭗*BP, MAP.*

$ 🏨 **Casablanca Hotel.** Not being on the main drag is a major advantage at this cozy, cavelike hotel with Moorish tile work in the guest rooms and restaurant. The 1970s style and layout is best captured in the outdated split-level lounge bar, dance floor, and extravagant buffet restaurant with a domed, mirrored ceiling. Guest rooms have extras such as a coffeemaker, hair dryer, and ironing board. The solarium and the heated indoor pool help ward off any out-of-season chill. ☒ *Praceta Casablanca, 8900-426* ☎ *281/511444* ⤶ *42 rooms* ⊘ *Restaurant, in-room safes, cable TV, ethernet, 2 pools (1 indoor), bar, dry cleaning* ⊟ *AE, DC, MC, V* ⭗*BP, MAP.*

Nightlife

In addition to a wealth of nightclubs and discos, Monte Gordo has a **casino** (☒ Av. Infante ☎ 281/530800 ⊕ www.solverde.com) with black-jack and roulette, among other games, as well as a slot-machine room. From July through September, you can have dinner and see a cabaret show for €75; from October through June the cost is €50. You must be 18 or older to enter (bring your passport), and dressy-casual attire is best.

Vila Real de Santo António

⑮ *4 km (2½ mi) east of Monte Gordo, 47 km (29 mi) east of Faro.*

This community on the Rio Guadiana is the last stop before Spain. The original town was destroyed by a tidal wave in the 17th century and wasn't rebuilt until the late 18th century, when the Marquês de Pombal constructed a new, gridded town. Consequently, Vila Real, which took only five months to complete, is a showpiece of 18th-century planning. Like most border towns, it's a lively place, with plenty of bars and restaurants and some traffic-free central streets that encourage evening strolls. If you're interested in a short excursion across the border, visit Ayamonte, the town's Spanish counterpart, and a far livelier place to visit. Just across the Guadiana River, Ayamonte can be reached during the day and early evening on the charmingly old-fashioned ferryboat.

The company **Riosul Viagens e Turismo** (⊠ Rua Tristão Vaz Teixeira 15 C, Monte Gordo ☎ 281/510200 ⊕ www.riosultravel.com) arranges day-long river cruises that include lunch, a stop for a swim, and a final stop in the timeless village of Foz de Odeleite before returning by boat to Vila Real. It also offers jeep safaris. The company has shuttle service from all eastern and central Algarve hotels to the Vila Real de Santo António dock. The cost is €38 to €49, depending on pickup location.

THE CENTRAL ALGARVE

The central Algarve, between Faro and Portimão to the east, has the heaviest concentration of resorts, but there are also exclusive, secluded hotels and villas. In between built-up areas are quiet bays and amazing rock formations of arches, sea-stacks, caves, and blowholes. Shell-encrusted ocher-and-red cliffs contrast beautifully with the brilliant blues and greens of the sea. With a car it's easy to travel the few miles inland that make all the difference: minor roads lead into the hills and to towns that have resisted the changes wrought upon the coast.

Almansil

16 *10 km (6 mi) northwest of Faro.*

Almansil, which straggles along the N125, is near two of the region's biggest draws: the seaside resort areas of Quinta do Lago, roughly 5 km (3 mi) to the south, and Vale do Lobo, about 5 km (3 mi) to the southwest. Wealthy Europeans love these complexes for their superb hotels and sports facilities. Golf is the thing here, but tennis and horseback riding are also popular. Almansil's biggest draw is the **Igreja de São Lourenço** (Church of St. Lawrence), built in 1730. Notable are the church's blue-and-white, floor-to-ceiling azulejo panels and its intricate gilt work. ⊠ *São Lourenço* ☎ *No phone* 🎟 *€3* ⊙ *Tues.–Sat. 10–1 and 2:30–6.*

A pair of 200-year-old cottages downhill from the Igreja de São Lourenço have been transformed into the **Centro Cultural de São Lourenço.** The center has exhibits of contemporary Portuguese works, and it holds occasional classical music concerts. Don't miss the delightful sculpture garden to the rear. ⊠ *São Lourenço* ☎ *289/395475* 🎟 *Free* ⊙ *Tues.–Sat. 10–7.*

Where to Stay & Eat

$$–$$$ ✕ **Sr. Franco.** The finger-lickin' chicken that's grilled over charcoal pits in this large, spotless restaurant has won awards for owner Joaquim Guerréiro (he concocts a special seasoning of local herbs). For an even better dining experience order a side salad (with tomatoes, onions, and ample fresh oregano) and top everything off with a bottle of Portuguese *vinho verde,* a fruity, faintly sparkling wine. The food is well worth the 5-km (3-mi) trip southwest from Almansil. ⊠ *Estrada de Quarteira, Escanxinas* ☎ *289/393756* ▭ *AE, DC, MC, V.*

$$$$ ✕🏨 **Hotel Quinta do Lago.** Since this once-exclusive hotel was taken over by the Ria Park hotel chain, standards in service have dropped and it has become overpriced. But the many celebrities who own villas within the complex are still a draw, and a stay here does win you substantial discounts at area golf courses. Numerous other sporting activities, from horseback riding to clay-pigeon shooting, can be arranged at a price. Set amid hundreds of acres of parkland, the hotel's extensive manicured lawns and sterile "nature trails" have displaced the natural habitat for local birds and rare species in the Ria Formosa nature reserve. The beach and sandbar are accessed via a wooden bridge—don't miss the beach massage service provided. ⊠ *Quinta do Lago, 8135-024* ☎ *289/350350* ⊕ *www.quintadolagohotel.com* ⇥ *121 rooms, 20 suites* ♿ *2 restaurants, room service, in-room safes, minibars, cable TV, in-room VCRs, ethernet, golf privileges, 2 tennis courts, 2 pools (1 indoor), gym, health club, massage, sauna, beach, bicycles, billiards, Ping-Pong, 3 bars, shops, laundry service, Internet, business services, convention center, meeting rooms, no-smoking floor* ▤ *AE, DC, MC, V* ☺ *BP, MAP.*

Outdoor Activities

GOLF   *See* Chapter 9, *Golf in Portugal: Where to Play,* for reviews of golf courses in the area.

The Portuguese Open Championship has been held seven times at the **Campo de Golfe da Quinta do Lago** (☎ 289/390700 ⊕ www. quintadolagogolf.com), which has two 18-hole courses on the superb Quinta do Lago estate. Green fees cost €150 for non-Quinta residents, and €75 for Quinta residents.

WATER PARK   Just east of Vilamoura, and north of Quarteira, you'll find **Aquashow** (⊠ E.N. 396, Quarteira ☎ 289/389396 ⊕ www.aquashowpark.com ☎ €18 ☉ May–Sept.), a large water park that also includes daily shows of birds of prey and parrots, as well as the Oasis Tropical Park with more than 60 exotic species.

Vale do Lobo

⑰ *5 km (3 mi) southwest of Almansil.*

Vale do Lobo is a gated luxury villa complex that attracts the superrich and famous from the world over (but yes, it's still open to all). Le Meridien Dona Filipa Hotel has two prestigious 18-hole golf courses, and other greens include extensive and well-tended gardens lined with palms and exotic shrubbery. A private security firm keeps a close eye on things while you make use of the helipad, health spa, indoor riding school, fitness centers, the David Lloyd Tennis Club, a yachting club, polo pitches, and a host of restaurants, bars, and cafés. The area is a second home to wealthy Europeans. The local beach is one of the cleanest in the Algarve and remains relatively quiet during peak months. You can access the beach from below the Dona Filipa Hotel, where most of the restaurants are clustered.

Where to Stay & Eat

★ $$$$ ✕▦ **Le Meridien Dona Filipa Hotel.** Rooms at this striking hotel are pleasant and have balconies, most of which overlook the sea. The service is superb, and the landscaped grounds are extensive. Although the hotel has its own tennis courts, it's also very close to the locally renowned

Vale do Lobo Tennis Center. A stay here gets you reduced green fees and preferential tee times at the prestigious San Lorenzo Golf Club, which is owned by the hotel. Dining choices ($$$–$$$$) include the Dom Duarte restaurant, which has a Portuguese menu; the Primavera, which serves Italian cuisine; and the Grill, which offers local and international fare. ✉ *Vale do Lobo* ✆ *Almansil 8135-901* ☎ *289/357200* 🌐 *www.starwoodhotels.com* *147 rooms* *3 restaurants, room service, in-room safes, minibars, cable TV, 18-hole golf course, miniature golf, 3 tennis courts, pool, 2 bars, shops, children's programs (ages 6–12), playground, laundry service, Internet, business services, meeting rooms, no-smoking floors* ▭ *AE, DC, MC, V* 🍽 *BP.*

DOWN DEEP

Walk along the beach heading left (facing the sea) and you will come across a string of three beach bars, all of which are well known for their fresh seafood barbecues.

Outdoor Activities

GOLF *See* Chapter 9, *Golf in Portugal: Where to Play,* for reviews of golf courses in the area.

The Hotel Le Meridien Dona Filipa's **Campo de Golfe San Lorenzo** (✉ Vale do Lobo ☎ 289/396522) has 18 of Europe's finest holes. If you're not a guest of the hotel, the green fee is €150; hotel guests pay €65. The **Vale do Lobo Golf Club** (✉ Take N396 off N125 to Quarteira; continue to Vale do Lobo and follow signs ☎ 289/393939) has two 18-hole courses: the Royal (green fees €155), and the Ocean (green fees €145).

HORSEBACK RIDING At **Horses Paradise** (✉ Rua Cistoval Tires Norte ☎ 289/394189) riding rates per hour range from €19 to €40.

TENNIS The **Vale do Lobo Tennis Academy** (✉ Vale do Lobo ☎ 289/357850 🌐 www.algarvetenis.com) has 14 all-weather courts, a bar, a pro shop, a pool, a gym, a steam room, and a restaurant. Court fees start at €26.

Vilamoura

18 *10 km (6 mi) west of Almansil.*

What was once a prosperous Roman settlement is today a prosperous resort community with the Algarve's biggest marina—an enormous, self-contained, 1,000-berth complex with apartments, hotels, bars, cafés, restaurants, shops, and sports facilities. The town of Vilamoura and the area surrounding it also have several luxury hotels and golf courses as well as a major tennis center and casino.

Just off a corner of the marina, the excavations of Roman ruins at the site known as Cêrro da Vila, where Vilamoura was first established, have revealed an elaborate plumbing system as well as several mosaics. The small, well-laid-out **Museu de Cêrro da Vila** gives access to the site and exhibits pieces found here. ✉ *Av. Cerro do Vila* ☎ *289/312153* 🎟 *€2* ⏲ *Nov.–mid-Apr., daily 9:30–12:30 and 2–6; mid-Apr.–Oct., daily 9:30–1 and 2:30–7.*

Where to Stay & Eat

$$–$$$$ ✕⊞ **Tivoli Marinotel.** The luxurious and huge Tivoli Marinotel overlooks Vilamoura's marina and has direct access to a beach. Its rooms are well equipped and its facilities are wide ranging (including a Children's Club). From the marina, you can head out on sailboat or motorboat excursions or deep-sea fishing trips, or go scuba diving. Many people think this hotel has the best places to eat ($$$–$$$$) in town: the Grill Sirius, overlooking the boats, specializes in fish and has live music; the Aries restaurant faces the hotel gardens and serves top-quality international dishes. ✉ *Vilamoura Marina, 8126-901* ☎ *289/303303* ⊕ *www.tivolihotels.com* ↘ *393 rooms* ♿ *2 restaurants, room service, in-room safes, minibars, cable TV, in-room VCRs, ethernet, Wi-Fi, golf privileges, 2 tennis courts, 3 pools (1 indoor), health club, boating, marina, 2 bars, dance club, recreation room, shops, laundry service, Internet, business services, convention center, meeting rooms* 🖃 *AE, DC, MC, V* ⧖❘ *BP, FAP, MAP.*

$$$ ⊞ **Hotel Dom Pedro Golf.** Part of a highly successful vacation complex, the Dom Pedro is close to the casino, not far from a splendid beach, and five minutes from the marina. Rooms are attractively furnished, and there's a garden in which to relax. The hotel also has a comprehensive range of facilities and a free shuttle service to local golf clubs. ✉ *Rua Atlântico, 8125-478* ☎ *289/300700* ⊕ *www.dompedro.com* ↘ *266 rooms* ♿ *Restaurant, room service, in-room safes, minibars, cable TV, golf privileges, 3 tennis courts, 2 pools, hot tub, bar, shops, babysitting, Internet, convention center, meeting rooms* 🖃 *AE, DC, MC, V* ⧖❘ *BP, FAP, MAP.*

☾ **$–$$** ⊞ **Hotel Apartamento do Golfe.** You can opt for a very affordable, self-catered holiday in these roomy studio and one-bedroom apartments neatly set around a central swimming pool. Maid service is optional. Golf players will be in their element, as the hotel is flanked on all sides by high-quality courses. A buffet barbecue (¢–$$) is laid out each night in summer with unlimited food and plenty of sangria flowing. The suave hotel manager entertains guests with impromptu karaoke performances (ask him to try out his Frank Sinatra impression). The hotel is also within 10 minutes' drive of a casino, riding center, local tennis club, fishing club, shooting range, cinema complex, bowling, and the Vilamoura Marina. ✉ *Quarteira, 8125-507* ☎ *289/303140* ⊕ *www.vilamouragolfe.com. pt* ↘ *35 apartments* ♿ *Restaurant, room service, in-room safes, kitchenettes, minibars, cable TV, pool* 🖃 *AE, DC, MC, V* ⧖❘ *BP, FAP, MAP.*

Nightlife

A big part of Vilamoura's nightlife scene is its **Casino Vilamoura** (✉ Set back from marina, behind Marinotel hotel ☎ 289/310000 ⊕ www. solverde.pt), open nightly 4 PM–3 AM. You'll find two restaurants, a dance club, and the usual selection of games on 20 tables, and more than 500 slot machines. For €12.50 you can see the nightly show and have a free drink. Dress is smart-casual, and you must be 18 to enter.

Outdoor Activities

GOLF See Chapter 9, *Golf in Portugal: Where to Play,* for a complete list of golf courses in the area.

Vilamoura Golf Club (⊕ www.vilamouragolf.com) has four superb 18-hole championship courses: the **Old Course** (☎ 289/310341), the **Laguna** (☎ 289/310180), the **Pinhal** (☎ 289/310390), and the **Millennium course** (☎ 289/310188). Green fees range from €75 to €120, depending on the course and the season.

HORSEBACK RIDING Horses are available for lessons and for trail rides at the **Centro Hípico da Estalagem de Cegonha** (✉ Estalagem de Cegonha ☎ 289/302577). Rates start at €18.

SAILING To rent a sailboat, just walk around Vilamoura Marina and inquire at any of the various kiosks that deal with water sports. **Polvo Watersports** (✉ Vilamoura Marina ☎ 289/388149 ⊕ www.marina-sports.com) offers a wide range of water activities including Jet Ski and sailboat rentals, dolphin-watching trips, and parachute rides behind a speedboat. **Portugal Sail & Power** (✉ Vilamoura Marina ☎ 289/366993 ⊕ www.euro-sail.co.uk) specializes in sailing courses and multi-day trips.

If you'd like to relax and let someone else do the work, book a "Route of the Grottoes" cruise on the **Llana Cruises** (✉ Vilamoura Marina ☎ 289/302318 ⊕ www.algarve-seafaros.com), which has 5½- and 3-hour cruises for €30 and €13, respectively. The company also offers big-game fishing at €50 for those fishing and €30 for those spectating, and reef fishing at €30 and €20, respectively.

Albufeira

★ ⑲ *12 km (7 mi) west of Vilamoura.*

Taken by the Arabs in AD 716 and named Al-Buhera—Castle of the Sea—brash Albufeira has mushroomed from a fishing village into the Algarve's largest and busiest resort. The town beach attracts thousands of visitors daily, and the noisy center is full of cafés, bars, restaurants, discos, and souvenir shops. Albufeira ages a bit during the shoulder seasons when it draws older (often retired) visitors, mainly from northern Europe.

One of the last Algarve towns to hold out against the Christian army in the 13th century, Albufeira still has a distinctly Moorish flavor, most apparent in the steep, narrow streets and whitewashed houses snuggled on the hill that marks the center of the Cidade Velha. (A few words of caution: streets leading into the older parts of town may be difficult for some people to climb.)

Zoo Marine, 6 km (4 mi) northwest of Albufeira, is a popular and very pleasant marine park with low-key rides, swimming pools, performing parrots, and dolphin and sea lion shows. Those with the nerve, and willingness to part with €135, can take part in a dolphin interaction experience. The latest innovation is the new 4-D cinema that features an ecological friendly story that can be very touching in parts. Hotel pickups are available. ✉ *N125, Km 65, Guia* ☎ *289/560300* ⊕ *www.zoomarine.com* 🎟 *€12.50* ⊙ *Nov.–Mar., daily 10–5; Apr.–June and mid-Sept.–Oct., daily 10–6; July–mid-Sept., daily 10–7:30.*

Beaches

On most summer days, the **town beach,** which is reached by tunnel from Rua 5 de Outubro, is so crowded that it may be hard to enjoy its interesting rock formations, caves, and grottoes, not to mention sand and sea. If you want more space, you'll have to move farther afield. **Praia da Oura,** just 2 km (1 mi) east of Albufeira, is pretty but extremely crowded throughout most of the year. The beautiful **Praia da Galé,** 4 km (2½ mi) west of Albufeira, has the classic Algarve rock formations; just don't expect it to be deserted. There's free parking at all the beaches.

Where to Stay & Eat

$–$$$ ✕ **La Cigale.** This beachfront restaurant, 9 km (5½ mi) east of Albufeira, is renowned among locals for its excellent French and Portuguese cooking. The terrace is the most sought-after place to dine; reserve a table on it well in advance. The only drawback here is the parking situation—you must park up in the town and walk down the steep street to the harbor. ✉ *Praia de Olhas d'Agua* ☎ *289/501637* 🌐 *www.restaurantelacigale.com* 💳 *DC, MC, V* ⏲ *Closed Dec.–Feb.*

★ $$ ✕ **A Ruina.** For charcoal-grilled seafood, especially sardines or tuna steaks, this big, rustic restaurant is the place to go. Start with a shellfish salad and choose your main course from the display. You can sit on the beach or in one of two simple but attractively furnished dining rooms. There's a roof terrace and a top-floor bar, too. ✉ *Cais Herculano, Praia dos Pescadores* ☎ *289/512094* 🌐 *www.restaurante-ruina.com* 💳 *MC, V.*

★ $–$$ ✕ **Cabaz da Praia.** You'll have views of the beach from the cliff-side terrace of this long-established restaurant. Its name means "beach basket," and it has been converted from an old fisherman's cottage. There's fine French-Portuguese cooking here—fish soup, grilled fish served imaginatively, and chicken with seafood. Try the soufflé, perhaps the restaurant's most popular dish. ✉ *Praça Miguel Bombarda 7* ☎ *289/512137* 💳 *MC, V* ⏲ *Closed Thurs. No lunch Sat.*

$$$$ **Fodor'sChoice ★** ✕🏨 **Grande Real Santa Eulália.** Grande in name and grand in style and location, the Santa Eulália is in a privileged, locked-gate, beachfront position yet just a stone's throw from shops, bars, and more. It has large, modern, rooms—insist on one that faces the sea—and a whole host of facilities, not least of which is the impressive Real Spa Thalasso. The restaurant of choice here is Le Club where, surrounded by a soothing modern ambience reflecting the natural light and overlooking the bay, you can enjoy the finest of creative Italian and international cuisine. ✉ *Praia da Santa Euláliá, 8200-916* ☎ *289/598000* 🌐 *www.hoteisreal.com* *344 rooms and suites* *5 restaurants, in-room safes, minibars, cable TV, golf privileges, 2 tennis courts, 4 pools, massage, sauna, spa, steam room, 6 bars, laundry service, concierge, Internet room, free parking* 💳 *AE, DC, MC, V* *BP, MAP.*

$$$$ **Fodor'sChoice ★** ✕🏨 **Vila Joya.** This German-run exclusive jewel is set in lush, exotic gardens with no luxury spared. The highlight is definitely the cuisine ($$$–$$$$) of the finest and highest-rated restaurant in Portugal (two Michelin stars). Austrian chef Dieter Koschina buys lobster, crayfish, and turbot from the local fishermen but brings truffles, goose liver, and caviar from the best markets in Europe. Guest rooms and arabesque suites have a stylish, almost boudoir quality about them but are anything but tacky. Suites overlook the heated pool and semiprivate beach where a bar serves margaritas, caipirinhas, and a host of other exotic cocktails. ⊠ *Praia da Galé, 8201-902* ☎ *289/591795* ⊕ *www.vilajoya.com* ↩ *12 rooms, 5 suites* ⟁ *Restaurant, in-room safes, minibars, cable TV, golf privileges, 2 tennis courts, pool, massage, sauna, steam room, 2 bars, laundry service, Internet* ⊟ *AE, DC, MC, V* ¶⊙¶ *BP, MAP.*

$$ ⊞ **Hotel Vila Galé Cerro Alagoa.** One of Albufeira's most comfortable lodgings is just a 10-minute walk from the main square. Smart, well-equipped rooms have private balconies; be sure to ask for one with a sea view, or you may end up facing the busy main road. A courtesy bus runs you to nearby beaches. Book well in advance for summer stays here, as package-tour operators tend to book whole blocks of rooms. ⊠ *Via Rápida, 8200-916* ☎ *289/583100* ⊕ *www.vilagale.pt* ↩ *279 rooms, 31 suites* ⟁ *Restaurant, in-room safes, minibars, cable TV, golf privileges, 2 pools (1 indoor), gym, health club, hot tub, pub, recreation room, shop, meeting rooms* ⊟ *AE, DC, MC, V* ¶⊙¶ *BP, MAP.*

Nightlife

The owner, the music, and the clientele are all mellow at the cliff-side ★ **Bizarro's** (⊠ Rua Latino Coelho ☎ 289/512824). It's the perfect bar from which to watch the sun go down. **Club 7½** (⊠ Rua São Gonçalo de Lagos 5 ☎ No phone) stays open for drinking and dancing until 7 AM. Its dress code is on the strict side. The long-established club **Kiss** (⊠ Off Av. Dr. Francisco Sá Carneiro, Montechoro ☎ 289/515639) is crowded and glitzy and often has DJs. It's not for the prudish: scantily clad female go-gos dance on various stages.

Shopping

Every night in the height of summer, stalls with fairy lights wind their way through the center, selling handicrafts and tourist trinkets. It's fun to browse, and you may pick up the occasional interesting piece. A market is held on the first and third Tuesday of the month at the fairgrounds. You can buy anything from lightbulbs to cheap shoes and clothes, but it isn't a produce market. For high-quality Portuguese ceramics, crystal, and porcelain go to **La Lojas** (⊠ Rua Candido dos Reis 20 ☎ 289/513168).

Bookworms (⊠ Rua Manuel Teixeira Gomes Lofa, Edificio Telhas Verdes ☎ 289/543576 or 91/698–4030), the best little shop of its kind, offers a wide selection of new English-language books, secondhand books, leather and personalized bookmarks, and commercial and handmade cards. Soccer equipment and team shirts are big business in Europe, and **Destination Football** (⊠ Av. Sa Carneiro 13 ☎ 289/542593 ⊕ www. destinationfootballonline.com), with two stores close to each other, has the widest array of shirts for teams from across Europe, and the biggest selection of high-end soccer shoes, trainers, and more.

Armação de Pêra

⓴ *14 km (8½ mi) west of Albufeira.*

At this bustling resort, it's best to reserve your room near the sea, rather than behind the main road where apartment-hotels are crammed together.

Year-round, local boats can take you on two-hour cruises to caves and grottoes west along the shore, past the Praia Nossa Senhora da Rocha (Beach of Our Lady of the Rocks)—a beach named after the Romanesque chapel above it. To arrange tours, head to Praia Armação de Pêra—a wide sandy beach with a promenade—or Praia Nossa Senhora da Rocha and speak with the fishermen directly.

Aside from ferrying vacationers to and from adjacent cove beaches, the fishermen no longer work from the shores of **Carvoeiro**, 6 km (4 mi) west of Armação de Pêra. Still, it has just about maintained the character of a fishermen's settlement. The town has a harbor with shell-shape beaches, and a short walk or boat journey away—at Algar Seco—are interesting rock formations.

Where to Stay & Eat

★ **$$–$$$** ✕ **Indian Bollywood.** A cult following of faithful customers returns each year to this culinary and architectural landmark set opposite the fishermen's beach Praia Nossa Senhora da Rocha (you can't miss the turbaned turrets). Though hot and spicy tandoori dishes are the draw, mild options are plentiful, as are vegetarian dishes. A take-out service is available. ⊠ *Rua da Praia, Edifício Vista Mar 1, Praia do Carvoeiro* ☎ *282/313755* ▤ *AE, MC, V.*

$$$$ ▨ **Vila Vita Parc.** The pampering begins as soon as the wrought-iron gates open to welcome you. Gentle colors, dark-wood details, fireplaces, and Mediterranean-Moorish touches make this resort an exclusive oasis. From its cliff-top setting, landscaped gardens wind down to two sequestered beaches. All rooms, beautifully furnished and in different styles, are spacious and have either a sea or garden view or both. The Vila Vita Vital is a luxurious spa offering all kinds of relaxing treatments. ⊠ *Armação de Pêra 8365-911* ☎ *282/310100* ⊕ *www.vilavitaparc.com* ⊷ *91 rooms, 74 suites ☾ 6 restaurants, room service, in-room safes, minibars, cable TV, driving range, 9-hole golf course, golf privileges, miniature golf, putting green, 5 tennis courts, 3 pools (1 indoor), health club, hot tub, Japanese baths, massage, sauna, spa, steam room, Turkish bath, beach, windsurfing, boating, waterskiing, fishing, boccie, squash, volleyball, 8 bars, dance club, shops, babysitting, children's programs (ages 8–15), playground, laundry service, concierge, Internet, business services, convention center, meeting rooms, car rental, helipad, travel services* ▤ *AE, DC, MC, V* ⦿| *BP, FAP, MAP.*

$$$ ▨ **Hotel Garbe.** The bar, lounge, and restaurant—all with terraces that provide unhindered sea views—maximize the superb location of this squat, white complex. It's atop a low cliff at the western end of the beach and is built on several levels, with steps to the sands below. Public rooms are bright and appealing; guest rooms have modern furnishings. Service is friendly and charming here. ⊠ *Av. Marginal, 8365-909* ☎ *282/ 315187* ⊕ *www.hotelgarbe.com* ⊷ *189 rooms and suites ☾ 2 restaurants, room service, cable TV, pool, hair salon, 2 bars, recreation room, shop* ▤ *AE, MC, V* ⦿| *BP, FAP, MAP.*

$$–$$$ ▨ **Pestana Viking Resort.** About 1 km (½ mi) west of town, the Viking stands directly above the beach, and has recently been taken over by this prestigious group and totally refurbished. Its manicured grounds include swimming pools (one for children) and bars that are between the main building and the cliff top. ⊠ *Praia Nossa Senhora da Rocha, 8400-450* ☎ *282/314876* ⊕ *www.pestana.com* ⇨ *182 rooms* ⬧ *3 restaurants, room service, in-room safes, minibars, cable TV, tennis court, 2 pools, health club, hair salon, hot tub, massage, sauna, beach, boating, squash, 4 bars, dance club, recreation room, shops, children's programs (ages 6–12), playground, laundry service, convention center, meeting rooms, car rental* ⊟ *AE, DC, MC, V* ⦿ *BP, MAP.*

Outdoor Activities

Aqualand. Just north of town, and close to Alcantarilha, you'll find this fun water park that has just celebrated its 20th anniversary. Considered the largest such park on the Algarve, Aqualand is home to the Banzai Boggan and the highest ride in Portugal, the Kamikaze. ⊠ *E.N. 125 Alcantarilha* ☎ *282/320230* ⊕ *www.aqualand.pt* ⊡ *€16.50* ⊙ *Late May–mid-Sept.*

Carvoeiro

㉑ *5 km (3 mi) west of Armação de Pêra.*

This busy resort town maintains much of its fishing village charm, which is what drew increasing numbers of foreigners to settle here in the first place. An abundance of high-quality restaurants and lodgings makes this the ideal base for access to both east and west coasts. Small beaches lie at the foot of steep, rocky cliffs. Waves have sculpted the distinctive yellow rock into intricate archways and stacks encrusted with fossilized shells.

Where to Stay & Eat

★ ⓒ ✕ **Primavera Jardim.** Go up along the Estrada do Farol and at the top
$$–$$$ of the hill on your right is one of the Algarve's most enduring restaurants. It's well known to local expats for its friendly service and warm atmosphere. Meals range from German-influenced steak with potatoes followed by apple strudel to Italian delicacies such as mozzarella salad and seafood gnocchi. You can sit outside underneath the beer garden's palms, where a less expensive menu is served. The owners, the German Schram family, cook, serve, and mingle with remarkable charm and professionalism. ⊠ *Rua das Flores 2, Praia do Carvoeiro* ☎ *282/358342* ⊟ *AE, MC, V.*

$–$$$ ✕ **La Grande Muralha.** Tasty chopstick adventures await you on the main Estrada do Farol close to the town center. This outstanding Chinese restaurant has garnered a good reputation for its noodle, duck, and shrimp rice dishes. If you are looking for a break from the charcoaled chicken and fish routine, this is the place to break the monotony. ⊠ *Estrada do Farol, Praia do Carvoeiro* ☎ *282/357380* ⊟ *AE, MC, V.*

$–$$ ✕ **O Indiano.** There are three Indian restaurants in Carvoeiro, and this one has the best location right by Carvoeiro's beach. The sumptuous menu of kebabs, tandoori, light and spicy curries, and vegetarian dishes is also available to go. ⊠ *Edifício 2M, Estrada do Farol, Praia do Carvoeiro* ☎ *282/356999* ⊟ *AE, MC, V.*

☺ **$–$$** ✕🖃 **Tivoli Almansor.** This hotel took 30 years to complete but was worth the wait. The stunning cliff scenery can be had from every room, and although it is slightly worn at the edges, the excellent service and cuisine make up for any shortfall. Kids love this hotel, and so do budding divers, who can use the on-site Dutch/German-run diving school, perhaps the best in the Algarve. A steep, stone stairwell leads down to a private beach that has amazing cave formations even by Algarve standards. The deep blue bay shines a translucent magenta in bright sunshine, and clear waters mean snorkeling is a must. ✉ *Vale do Covo, 8401-911* ☎*282/310100* ⊕*www.tivolihotels.com* ⇌*289 rooms, 4 suites* ⚴ *2 restaurants, room service, in-room safes, minibars, cable TV, driving range, 9-hole golf course, golf privileges, miniature golf, putting green, 2 tennis courts, pool, health club, massage, sauna, spa, steam room, Turkish bath, beach, dive shop, windsurfing, boating, 2 bars, babysitting, children's programs (ages 8–18), playground, laundry service, concierge, Internet, business services, convention center, meeting rooms, car rental* ▭ *AE, DC, MC, V* ❮◉❯ *BP, FAP, MAP.*

Outdoor Activities

The **Carvoeiro Clube de Ténis Club** (✉ Vale Currais ☎ 282/357847 ⊕ www.carvoeiroclubedetenis.com) has 12 courts as well as a fitness center, a swimming pool, and a restaurant.

The **Tivoli Almansor Diving Centre** (✉ Vale do Covo 8401-911 ☎ 282/351194 ⊕ www.tivoli-diving.com) is an excellent diving school offering many different PADI courses suited to the individual. It offers dives twice daily from a modern speedboat that takes you up to 3 nautical miles from the coastline. You can dive between 32 and 115 feet of depth. From the boat you will see a reef, underwater caves, wrecks, corals, and an amazing variety of sea life. Rates for one day are €29.50; six days €145–€205 or 10 days €239–€325. The staff all speak English.

Lagoa

㉒ *10 km (6 mi) northwest of Armação de Pêra; 15 km (9 mi) northwest of Carvoeiro.*

This market town is primarily known for its wine, *vinho Lagoa*; the red is particularly good. The principal winery, **Cooperativa de Lagoa** (✉ N125 ☎ 282/342181), is on the main road just after the Carvoeiro junction, on the left. Call if you're interested in joining a prearranged group tour. At any time during normal working hours you can pop in to the office (at the side of the building) to sample the wine and buy a bottle or two.

Outdoor Activities

☺ The biggest of the Algarve's several water parks is **Slide & Splash,** east of Lagoa. The rides, such as the huge Black Hole and Blue Hole, are also the most exciting of their kind in the region. The park is open daily at 10 AM from Easter through October; closing times vary greatly, so call ahead to confirm. ✉ *Vale de Deus, just off the N125 (signposted), Estombar* ☎ *282/341685* ⊕ *www.slidesplash.com* 🎫 *€16.50* ☉ *Easter–Oct., daily beginning at 10.*

5

Shopping

Along N125 in nearby Porches, you can stop at roadside shops that sell both mass-produced and handmade pottery. **Olaria Pequena** (✉ N125, between Porches and Alcantarilha, Estombar ☎ 282/381213), which means "the small pottery," is owned and run by a friendly young Scot, Ian Fitzpatrick, who has worked in the Algarve for years. He sells his handmade pieces at very reasonable prices. The shop is open Monday through Saturday from 10 to 1 and 3 to 6.

Silves

② *7 km (4½ mi) northeast of Lagoa.*

Fodor's Choice
★

Once the Moorish capital of the Algarve, today Silves is one of the region's most intriguing inland towns. Rich and prosperous in medieval times, it remained in Arab hands until 1249, although not without attempts by Christian forces to take it. In 1189, after a siege led by Sancho I, the city was sacked by Crusaders, who subsequently put thousands of Moors to the sword. Silves finally lost its importance after its almost complete destruction by the 1755 earthquake. Today it's an enjoyable excursion from the coast; trains, buses, and a river service using traditional Portuguese gondola-like boats make the 20-km (12-mi) trip north from Portimão.

In the 12th century the Moors built a sandstone **fortaleza** (fortress) with an irregular polygonal plan that survived untouched until the Christian sieges. Its impressive parapets were restored in 1835 and still dominate the upper part of town. You can walk around the fort's remaining walls or clamber about its crenellated battlements, taking in the views of Silves and the hills. (Keep an eye open: some places have no guardrails.) Its gardens are watched over by a statue of King Dom Sancho I, and its capacious water cistern is now a gallery space devoted to temporary exhibitions, some of which have nothing to do with the fort. ☎ 282/445624 ⛭ €1.25 ⊘ June–Sept., daily 9–8 (last admission 7:30); Oct.–May, daily 9–6 (last admission 5:30).

The 12th- to 13th-century **Santa Maria da Sé** (Cathedral of St. Mary), built on the site of a Moorish mosque, saw service as the principal cathedral of the Algarve until the 16th century. The 1755 earthquake and indifferent restoration have left it rather plain inside, but its tower—complete with gargoyles—is still a fine sight. ✉ *Rua da Sé* ☎ *No phone* ⛭ *Free; donations accepted* ⊘ *Mon.–Sat. 9–6:30, Sun. 8:30–1.*

Although the labels are in Portuguese, the items on display at Silves's **Museu Arqueológia** (Archaeology Museum) still give interesting insights into the area's history. A primary attraction is an Arab water cistern, preserved in situ, with

---

TO MARKET

Silves's **mercado** (produce market), liveliest in the morning, is at the foot of town, close to the medieval bridge. If you arrive at lunchtime, have a delicious meal of spicy grilled chicken or fish from the outdoor barbecue at one of the simple restaurants here. The market is closed Sunday.

a 30-foot-deep well. The museum is a few minutes' walk below the cathedral, off Rua da Sé. ⊠ *Rua das Portas de Loulé* ☎ *282/442325* 🖃 *€1.50* 🕘 *Daily May.–Sept., Tues.–Sun. 10–7; Oct.–Apr., Tues.–Sun. 9–6.*

Where to Eat

¢–$$$ ✕ **Rui Marisqueira.** The fish and shellfish are remarkably good value, which is the main reason why the crowds from the coast come up into the hills to dine here. Grilled sea bream and bass are usually available, and there's locally caught game—wild boar, rabbit, and partridge—in season. ⊠ *Rua Comendador Vilarinho 27* ☎ *282/442682* 🖃 *AE, MC, V* 🕘 *Closed Tues.*

¢–$ ✕ **Churrasqueira Valdemar.** At this grill room on the riverfront behind the market, whole chickens are barbecued outside over charcoal. Eat under the stone arches and enjoy your *piri-piri* (spicy) chicken with salad, fries, and local wine. ⊠ *Facing river, behind market* ☎ *No phone* 🖃 *No credit cards.*

Portimão

㉔ *15 km (9 mi) southwest of Silves.*

Portimão is the Algarve's most important fishing port. Even before the Romans arrived, there was a settlement here, at the mouth of the Rio Arade (Arade River). Devastated in the 1755 earthquake, the town was revived by the fish-canning industry in the 19th century. Although colorful boats now unload their catch at a modern terminal across the river, contemporary Portimão, sprawling with concrete high-rise buildings, remains a cheerful, busy place.

Rather than staying in Portimão, most visitors choose one of the excellent local beach resorts and visit Portimão as a day trip, especially to shop. If you prefer to stay in town, the local tourist office can help you find accommodations at one of the hotels or *pensões* (pensions), which are of reasonable quality. The marina, **Marinha do Portimão,** has a wealth of boutiques, upscale restaurants, and bars. Lunch outdoors at the Doca da Sardinha ("sardine dock") between the marina and the old bridge is a must. You sit at one of many inexpensive establishments, eating the excellent charcoal-grilled sardines (a local specialty), chewy fresh bread, and simple salads and drinking local wine. Around you, the air is thick with barbecue smoke and the tang of the sea.

Beach

Across the bridge from and 5 km (3 mi) east of Portimão is the former fishing hamlet of Ferragudo. Despite its fine beach, **Praia Grande,** Ferragudo shows no sign of going down the mass-market tourist route. Right on the beach is the restored 16th-century Castelo de São João (St. John's Castle), built to defend Portimão and now privately owned. There are plenty of restaurants and bars near the beach as well as places to rent sailboards.

Where to Stay & Eat

$$–$$$$ ✕ **Dockside.** Set amidst the rows of bars and eateries around Portimão's marina, Dockside is an upscale marquee restaurant specializing in gen-

erous quantities of live shellfish and *francesinhas* (toasted rye sandwiches filled with ham, fried steak, and pork sausage, covered with melted cheese and coated with a spicy seafood sauce), and a variety of cataplanas. Good local and imported draft beer is served at the table. Reservations are recommended. ⊠ *Marinha do Portimão* ☎ *282/417268* ⊟ *AE, DC, MC, V.*

¢–$$ × **Flor da Sardinha.** This is one of several open-air eateries next to the bridge, by the fishing harbor, whose staff grills fresh sardines on quayside stoves and serves them to crowds seated at plastic tables. A plateful of these delicious fish, with boiled potatoes (never fries!) and a bottle of the local wine, is one of Portugal's best treats. ⊠ *Cais da Lota* ☎ *282/424862* ⊟ *No credit cards.*

¢–$ × **Kibom.** On a narrow pedestrian street in a typical Algarvian house, Kibom has represented the town in gourmet food competitions. The traditional Portuguese food here is highly recommended. Dishes include *arroz de marisco* (shellfish with rice), *feijoada de choco* (octopus with beans), and cataplana de *lagosta* (a spiny lobster). ⊠ *Rua Damião L. Faria e Castro, off Rua Judice Biker* ☎ *282/414623* ⊟ *AE, DC, MC, V* ⊙ *Closed Sun.*

$$–$$$ ⊞ **Tivoli Arade.** This hotel has a simple but stylish 1970s retro interior
Fodor'sChoice cleverly laid out around two large swimming pools complete with
★ wooden deck bars and palm gardens. The spacious rooms have kitchens, all you need to prepare a meal, and private terraces. Blocks of rooms are colored ocher, burnt sienna, and beige to match the changing shades of the *falesia*, or Algarve cliffs. If you are traveling by boat, this is the perfect place to base yourself at a moderate price. The beach is a 10-minute walk to the other side of the marina below the old town. ⊠ *Marina da Portimão, 8500* ☎ *282/460200* ⊕ *www.tivolihotels.com* ⇔ *196 suites* ⚋ *Restaurants, room service, in-room safes, kitchenettes, refrigerators, cable TV, golf privileges, 2 saltwater pools, gym, dive shop, 2 bars, piano bar, recreation room, playground, Internet, meeting rooms* ⊟ *AE, DC, MC, V* ⊚ *BP, MAP.*

Shopping

Portimão's main shopping street is Rua do Comércio. Shops on Rua de Santa Isabel specialize in crafts, leather goods, ceramics, crystal, and fashions. The enormous **Modelo Shopping Center** (⊠ N124 at Av. Miguel Bombarda, toward Praia da Rocha), open daily 10–10, has a plethora of shops and restaurants under one roof.

SHOPPING

Probably the best town in which to shop is Portimão, where you can spend at least half a day browsing. In summer, the main resorts have a lot of roadside stalls (a good area is outside the lighthouse at Cabo São Vicente), at which you can buy jewelry, handicrafts, art, and clothes. Look for reasonably priced hand-knit sweaters in stores throughout the Algarve. The best places to look for handmade copper items and other metal crafts are Portimão, Lagos, and Loulé. Small woven sisal baskets make good souvenirs and are available nearly everywhere.

Gabys (⌧ Rua Direita 5 ☎ 282/411988) sells good-quality leather items. For ceramics, porcelain, crystal, and handmade copper items, visit **O Aquario** (⌧ Rua Vasco da Gama 42 ☎ 282/426673 ⌧ Rua Vasco da Gama 41 ☎ No phone). There are high-class shoes and leather goods at **St. James** (⌧ Rua de Santa Isabel 26 ☎ 282/424620).

Outdoor Activities

Santa Bernarda. Take a sailing trip on the twin-masted pirate ship *Santa Bernarda* that departs from the harbor and offers either a Caves Expedition or a Sailing & Caves of Carvoeiro expedition for €25, or a full-day Robinson Tour for €50. (⌧ Rua Júdice Fialho 11 ☎ 967/023840 ⊕ www.santa-bernarda.com)

Praia da Rocha

㉕ *3 km (2 mi) southeast of Portimão.*

Praia da Rocha was one of the first resorts in the Algarve to undergo a transformation for the mass market, and it's now dominated by high-rise apartments and hotels. Its excellent beach is made all the more interesting by a series of huge colored rocks worn into strange shapes by the wind and sea. Buses run throughout the day between the town and Portimão.

The 16th-century **Fortaleza de Santa Catarina** (⌧ Av. Tomás Cabreira) was a defensive castle and provides wonderful views out to sea and across the Rio Arade to Ferragudo. Directly below the fortress, on the river side, is one of the Algarve's growing number of marinas. On the other side a long concrete jetty extends into the Atlantic.

Where to Stay & Eat

$$$ 🏨 **Hotel Algarve-Casino.** The sea vistas from this classy hotel are spectacular, so be sure to book a room with a view. The Moorish-style public rooms are bright, the spacious guest rooms have tile floors and balconies, and the casino has a restaurant as well as shows. ⌧ *Av. Tomás Cabreira, 8500-802* ☎ *282/402000* ⊕ *www.solverde.pt* ⇥ *192 rooms, 16 suites ⎔ 3 restaurants, room service, minibars, cable TV, 2 tennis courts, 2 pools, hair salon, casino, shops, convention center, meeting rooms, car rental* ▤ *AE, DC, MC, V* ⏍ *BP, MAP.*

★ **$$** 🏨 **Bela Vista.** The 19th-century home of a wealthy family, this three-story, blockish mansion is larger than its 16 guest rooms suggest. It lords over the beach below like a castle. Decorating the interior are original 17th- and 18th-century azulejos, leaded stained-glass panels, a wonderful staircase, and a large fireplace. In summer, a popular but low-key cocktail evening is held in the palm tree garden. Early reservations are essential for high-season stays. ⌧ *Av. Tomás Cabreira, 8500-802* ☎ *282/450480* ⊕ *www.hotelbelavista.net* ⇥ *14 rooms, 2 suites ⎔ Room service, minibars, cable TV, bar, laundry service; no a/c* ▤ *AE, DC, MC, V* ⏍ *CP.*

Alvor

㉖ *5 km (3 mi) west of Portimão.*

Characterized by a maze of streets, lanes, and alleys that intersect one another, the handsome old port of Alvor is one of the Algarve's best examples of an Arab village. In summer, many vacationers are attracted to Alvor's excellent beaches.

Beaches

If the small, covelike **Praia dos Três Irmãos** is too crowded, there's always space to spare on one of the beaches to either side.

Where to Stay & Eat

★ $$$ ✕⊞ **Le Meridien Penina Golf & Resort.** The Meridien has everything you would expect from one of the world's leading hotel chains, including well-groomed grounds. Significantly reduced green fees are offered at the adjacent 18-hole golf course designed by Henry Cotton. A bus shuttles you to and from the hotel beach, which has a restaurant (reservations essential) and water-sports facilities. A supervised children's village has its own pool and restaurant. There's a choice of six restaurants ($$$–$$$$), including the Grill Room, which serves excellent Portuguese dishes, and the Sagres Restaurant, with its lively theme evenings. ✉ *Montes de Alvor, Penina 8501-952* ☎ *282/420200* ⊕ *www.starwoodhotels.com* ⤶ *196 rooms* ♿ *5 restaurants, room service, in-room safes, minibars, cable TV, driving range, 3 golf courses, 6 tennis courts, pool, gym, sauna, beach, windsurfing, boating, horseback riding, 2 bars, shops, children's programs (ages 8–16), playground, laundry service, concierge, Internet, business services, convention center, meeting rooms, car rental, helipad, travel services, no-smoking rooms* ⊟ *AE, DC, MC, V* ⵏⵟ *BP, FAP, MAP.*

$$$ ✕⊞ **Pestana Alvor Praia.** Rooms at this split-level hotel have views of
Fodor'sChoice the sea or the Serra de Monchique. Decor is extra funky, with lime, red
★ currant, and white Italian-designed sofas and easy chairs. You won't be at a loss for home entertainment with a CD and DVD player. The hotel has opened a spa with treatments, heated indoor pool, massage, and beauty salons. Although it's an easy walk to the pleasant sands below, there's an elevator that can take you down to the beach. The dining room has picture windows overlooking the coast, and there's a deck with a snack bar. All of the restaurants ($$–$$$) are first class: O Almofariz serves Algarvian specialties, Sale e Pepe offers Tuscan cuisine, and Harira has Moroccan fare. ✉ *Praia dos Três Irmãos, 8500-904* ☎ *282/400900* ⊕ *www.pestana.com* ⤶ *195 rooms and suites* ♿ *3 restaurants, snack bar, room service, in-room safes, minibars, cable TV, driving range, golf privileges, miniature golf, 7 tennis courts, 2 saltwater pools (1 indoor), hair salon, massage, sauna, Turkish bath, beach, 3 bars, shops, children's programs (ages 7–15), playground, laundry service, Internet, convention center, meeting rooms* ⊟ *AE, DC, MC, V* ⵏⵟ *BP, MAP.*

Monchique

② *25 km (15 mi) northeast of Alvor, 20 km (12 mi) north of Portimão.*

The winding road up to Monchique from Portimão or Silves brings the surprise of lush greenery and an oasis of brightly colored villas surrounded by waterways and fruit groves. This is **Caldas de Monchique** (Monchique

Thermal Complex; ☎ 282/910910 ⊕ www.monchiquetermas.com), which is renowned for its healing spa waters that bubble out of the ground to create a paradise microclimate where "anything grows." The small chapel of Caldas is where many go for a blessing or to pray in thanks for the health of those who drink its waters. The **Thermas de Monchique** is just below the chapel and is intrinsic to the area. Visitors come not only for the water's healing properties but for pampering spa treatments. Modern spa facilities complement those for health treatments concerned with digestive, bone, kidney, and respiratory problems. Follow the road north and within 10 minutes you will be in Monchique. This tiny market town is known for its rich handicrafts, including leather, basketwork, woodwork, and embroidery. A short drive west on N266-3 brings you to the highest point in the Serra de Monchique. At 2,959 feet, the **Pico de Fóia** affords panoramic views—weather permitting—over the western Algarve. There's also a café here.

Where to Stay & Eat

★ ¢–$ ✕ **Teresinha.** Just west of Monchique, modest Teresinha has good country cooking, a simple interior, and an outdoor terrace that overlooks a valley as well as the coast. The ham and the grilled chicken are particularly tasty. ⊠ *Estrada da Fóia* ☎ *282/912392* ▤ *MC, V.*

$ ✕▥ **Inn Albergeria Bica-Boa.** Inspired by the many springs welling up from this thickly wooded mountainside above Monchique, this small hotel may be on the roadside, but there's very little traffic, and guest rooms face the back. It's a great place to get away from it all, especially if you like walking. The Bica-Boa restaurant (¢–$$$$) is popular with locals and expats from along the coast. Try the sole, stuffed squid, or lobster (which you should order in advance). The English owner, Susie, can organize walks for you and has added a range of dishes for vegetarians to the restaurant menu. ⊠ *Estrada da Lisboa 266, 8550* ☎ *282/912271* ⊲ *4 rooms* ⅏ *Restaurant, pool, bar, lounge* ▤ *AE, DC, MC, V* ⅋ *BP.*

¢–$ ✕▥ **Estalagem Abrigo da Montanha.** This pleasant, rustic inn—in the heart of the Serra de Monchique—has magnolia trees, a camellia-filled garden, and panoramic views. A leisurely lunch in the restaurant ($$–$$$$), where dependable regional dishes are prepared, makes for an enjoyable afternoon. If you want to stay longer to take in the scenery, be sure to reserve in advance for one of the welcoming rooms (all with views). ⊠ *Corto Pereiro, Estrada da Fóia, 8550* ☎ *282/912131* ⊕ *www. abrigodamontanha.com* ⊲ *15 rooms* ⅏ *Restaurant, cable TV, pool, bar* ▤ *AE, DC, MC, V* ⅋ *BP.*

LAGOS & THE WESTERN ALGARVE

From the bustling town of Lagos, the rest of the western Algarve is easily accessible. This is the most unspoiled part of the region, with some genuinely isolated beaches and bays along an often wind-buffeted route that reaches to the southwest and the magnificent Cabo São Vicente.

Lagos

★ ㉘–㉜ *13 km (8 mi) west of Portimão, 70 km (43 mi) northwest of Faro.*

An attractive, busy fishing port with some cove beaches nearby, Lagos draws an international crowd. And yet, the inhabitants seem to follow a way of life that goes beyond catering to visitors.

The town has a venerable history. Its deepwater harbor and wide bay have made it a natural choice for various groups of settlers, starting with the Carthaginians, who founded the town around 400 BC. Under the Moors, Lagos was a center for trade between Portugal and Africa. Even after the town fell to the Christians in 1241, trade continued and was greatly expanded under Prince Henry the Navigator, who used Lagos as his base. It later became capital of the Algarve, a role it lost after the great earthquake of 1755 reduced much of it to rubble. Nonetheless, some interesting buildings remain, as does the circuit of defensive walls, built between the 14th and 16th centuries over older, Moorish bastions. Some of the best-preserved sections can be seen from near the expansive Praça da República, at the southwest end of Avenida dos Descobrimentos. The main pedestrian streets leading off the central Praça Gil Eanes are lined with stores (including several good antiques shops), restaurants, cafés, and bars—all of which do a roaring business in summer. As with many cities and towns along the Algarve, trying to find a parking place here stretches one's patience to the extreme.

TIMING Although the main historic sights of the old town are all in close proximity, allow at least two hours for a tour. Be prepared to join lines for museums and, if it is summertime, to negotiate bustling crowds of backpackers, sightseers, and shoppers who throng the many bars, cafés, restaurants, and clothing and crafts shops. The Casa da Alfândega will probably occupy you for half an hour alone. Allow plenty of time to explore the Igreja de Santo António: it is striking in appearance from the outside and is full of surprises once you get inside. The churches between Praça da República and Rua do Castelo dos Governadores have unusual architectural styles that make them well worth a visit, but photography is discouraged within them.

What to See

㉘ **Casa da Alfândega.** Prince Henry the Navigator brought the first African slaves to Portugal for his personal use in 1441. He later established a slave market in West Africa to cope with increasingly large and barbaric slave auctions; by 1455 around 800 slaves were transported to Portugal each year. The first African slave market in Europe was held under the arches of the old Casa da Alfândega. The building now contains an art gallery with changing exhibits and is sometimes used for concerts and theater productions. It's open only during exhibitions and shows; ask at the tourist office for details. ⊠ *Praça da República* 🕾 *No phone* 🕮 *Free.*

㉙ **Castelo dos Governadores** (Governor's Palace). It was from the Manueline window of this palace that the young king Dom Sebastião is said to have addressed his troops before setting off on his crusade of 1578.

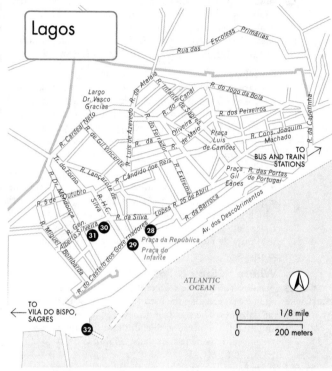

Lagos

The palace is long gone, though the section of wall with the famous window remains and can be seen in the northwest corner of the Praça da República. The crusade was one of Portugal's greatest-ever disasters, with the king and some 8,000 men killed in Morocco at Alcácer-Quibir. (Dom Sebastião is further remembered by a much maligned, modernistic statue that stands in Praça Gil Eanes.)

㉜ Forte Ponta da Bandeira. This 17th-century fort defended the entrance to the harbor in bygone days. From inside the fort you can look out at sweeping ocean views. For an interesting perspective on the rock formations and grottoes of the area's shoreline, take one of the short boat trips offered by the fishermen near the Ponta da Bandeira. Check for departure times on the quayside boards. ✉ *Av. dos Descobrimentos* ☎ *282/761410* 💶 *€2.20* ◷ *Tues.–Sun. 9:30–12:30 and 2–5.*

★ **㉛ Igreja de Santo António.** This early-18th-century baroque building is Lagos's most extraordinary structure. Its interior is a riot of gilt extravagance made possible by the import of gold from Brazil. Dozens of cherubs and angels clamber over the walls, among fancifully carved woodwork and azulejos. ✉ *Entrance via Museu Regional on Rua General Alberto Silveira* ☎ *282/762301* 💶 *€2.20; includes entry to Museu Regional* ◷ *Tues.–Sun. 9:30–12:30 and 2–5:30.*

③ **Museu Regional** (Regional Museum). This museum houses an amusing jumble of exhibits, including mosaics, archaeological and ethnological items, and a town charter from 1504—all arranged haphazardly. ⊠ *Rua General Alberto Silveira* ☎ *282/762301* 🎫*€2.20; includes entry to Igreja de Santo António* ⊙ *Tues.–Sun. 9:30–12:30 and 2–5:30.*

Beaches

The largest beach near town and one of the best centers for water sports is the 4-km (2½-mi) stretch of **Meia Praia,** to the northeast. You can walk to it in less than five minutes simply by crossing the footbridge. If you want to go farther along, however, you can take a bus from the riverfront Avenida dos Descobrimentos, and in summer there's a ferry service a few hundred yards from Forte Ponta da Bandeira.

You can reach the prettiest beach south of town—**Praia de Dona Ana**—by car or on an enjoyable 30-minute walk along a cliff top. If you hoof it, pass the fort, turn left at the fire station, and follow the footpaths, which go to the most southerly point. A short way beyond Praia de Dona Ana is the attractive **Praia do Camilo.** Just beyond this beach is the Ponta da Piedade, a much-photographed group of rock arches and grottoes.

Where to Stay & Eat

¢–$$$$ ✕ **Italia.** You may be reluctant to try Italian cuisine in Portugal, but it's **Fodor'sChoice** one way to broaden the use of fresh local seafood: on pizzas and in fill- ★ ing calzones. The shellfish dishes are particularly well done—spaghetti and ravioli are mixed with clams and shrimp; mussels and even lobster are put into divine pasta salads. ⊠ *Rua Garrett 26–28* ☎ *282/760030* 🖃 *AE, DC, MC, V.*

$$–$$$ ✕ **No Patio.** This cheerful restaurant with an inner patio is run by a Danish couple, Bjarne and Gitte. The outstanding fare is best described as international with a Scandinavian accent. Specialties include herring, duck-liver mousse, and tenderloin of pork with a Madeira and mushroom sauce. ⊠ *Rua Lançarote de Freitas 46* ☎ *282/763777* 🖃 *AE, MC, V* ⊙ *Closed Sun. and Mon.*

$–$$ ✕ **Café do Mar.** In a great location just outside town and overlooking the dramatic Praia da Batata and the Lagos bay, the Café do Mar serves good, modest fare. Eat inside, or at the outside tables, and you'll find a variety of fresh fish available, along with pasta and salads. What's more, there's a small public parking area just yards away—a rarity in this busy town. ⊠ *Av. Descobrimentos* ☎ *282/788006* 🖃 *MC, V.*

★ **¢–$$** ✕ **Dom Sebastião.** Portuguese cooking, especially charcoal-grilled fish specials, and unobtrusive service are the draws here. You can dine inside at elegant candlelighted tables on a cobblestone floor or outside on a sidewalk terrace. You may wish to start your meal with smoked swordfish, followed by grilled tuna or the cataplana—all extremely good. ⊠*Rua 25 de Abril 20* ☎ *282/762795* 🖃 *AE, DC, MC, V.*

¢–$$ ✕ **Mirante.** Just south of the town center and above the Praia de Dona Ana, Mirante shouts its fishermen's credentials loudly: a cork ceiling, ropes, and nets decorate the narrow interior. It makes an excellent lunch stop or a place for an early dinner, particularly in summer. Try the tuna steak stewed with onions and, for dessert, the homemade cream tart.

The staff is friendly and efficient. ⊠ *Praia de Dona Ana* ☎ *282/762713* ⊟ *MC, V.*

¢–$$ ✕ **Piri-Piri.** On one of the main streets this small, low-key restaurant—done in understated pastels—has an inexpensive but extensive menu. The long list of Portuguese dishes includes a variety of market-fresh fish, but the specialty is the zesty piri-piri chicken that gives the restaurant its name. ⊠ *Rua Afonso d'Almeida 10* ☎ *282/763803* ⊟ *MC, V.*

¢–$ ✕ **O Galeão.** Tucked away on a backstreet is this bustling, informal, local restaurant—it's so popular that you'll wait in line unless you've made a reservation. The food is first-rate, particularly the steaks—for once, fish, although well cooked, isn't the main event. A reasonably priced wine list encourages you to sample regional choices. ⊠ *Rua da Laranjeira 1* ☎ *282/763909* ⊟ *AE, DC, MC, V* ⊗ *Closed Sun.*

★ $$–$$$ ▥ **Tivoli Lagos.** At the eastern edge of the old town and an easy walk from the town center, this state-of-the-art hotel has an unusual design: it's strung across several levels with gardens, lounges, and patios. Guest rooms are large and elegantly appointed, with attractive tiling behind the bed headboards and in the bathrooms, and even on some lamps and tabletops. A bus shuttles you to Meia Praia, where the hotel has very good beach and water-sports facilities. The hotel's terrace grill restaurant remains one of the best choices for seafood and service in Lagos. There is also a very good Italian restaurant that bakes pizza in a wood-burning oven. ⊠ *Rua António Crisógno dos Santos, 8600-678* ☎ *282/790079* ⊕ *www.tivolihotels.com* ⇆ *312 rooms, 12 suites* ♿ *3 restaurants, room service, in-room safes, some minibars, cable TV, golf privileges, 3 tennis courts, 2 pools (1 indoor), gym, health club, 2 bars, piano bar, recreation room, shops, meeting rooms* ⊟ *AE, DC, MC, V* ⓞ *BP, MAP.*

★ $ ▥ **Casa da Moura.** It's a little hard to find at first and you must phone before you arrive, because the door is locked. Once inside, it's like being in your own apartment with no lobby personnel. The Moroccan interior is superb, as is the private pool area surrounded by cacti. Rooms are named after Moroccan towns (such as Agadir and Taza) and vary from doubles to large suites. All are stylishly decorated in the same somber Arab theme throughout. A highlight is the buffet breakfast served on the rooftop terrace with charming panache. Fresh fruits, honey, and pancakes abound, or if you prefer, an omelet will instantly be prepared to your liking. ⊠ *Rua Cardeal Neto 10, 8600-537* ☎ *282/770730* ⊕ *www.casadamoura.com* ⇆ *3 rooms* ♿ *Cable TV, pool, hot tub, Internet* ⊟ *No credit cards* ⓞ *EP.*

¢ ▥ **Pensão Mar Azul.** It's not hard to befriend fellow travelers in the comfortable community lounge of this simple, central pension. Rooms—some with a terrace—are clean and cheerful, though not all have full private baths (some have just a shower with shared toilet outside the room). Avoid guest quarters that face the pedestrian thoroughfare, which can be noisy in high season. ⊠ *Rua 25 de Abril 13, 8600-763* ☎ *282/770230* ⇆ *18 rooms, 11 with bath* ♿ *Cable TV, lounge; no a/c* ⊟ *MC, V* ⓞ *EP.*

★ ¢ ▥ **Surf Experience.** This very spacious and central house is open to all who have an interest in surfing, regardless of age. The owners of the house run a surf camp and offer special packages for surfers including accommodation, breakfast, and lunch plus facilities such as board repair and off-road transport as well as airport pickup. The daily rates work out to be very reasonable, considering that the large classic town house is modern, comfortable, and comes with maid service and spectacular views of the Lagos beaches from two large terraces. ⊠ *Rua dos Ferreiros 21, 8600* 📠 *282/761943* ⊕ *www.surfexperience.com* ⇌ *8 rooms, 4 with bath* ⌂ *Kitchen, cable TV, lounge, recreation room, laundry facilities, Internet; no a/c* ▭ *No credit cards* ⓧ| *BP, FAP, MAP.*

Nightlife

There are a number of bars at the end of Rua 25 de Abril, most playing music that's brutally loud. Perhaps the most refined of these is **Bon Vivant** (⊠ Rua 25 de Abril ☎ 282/768329), with a rooftop terrace way above the din. An excellent bar is **Mullens** (⊠ Rua Cândido dos Reis 86 ☎ 282/761281), whose enthusiastic staff helps keep things swinging until 2 AM; full meals are served, too. For dancing or cuddling on couches by a fireplace, try **Phoenix** (⊠ Rua 5 de Outubro 11 ☎ 282/760503), which plays disco and pop until 5 AM. The classy **Stevie Ray's Blues Jazz Bar** (⊠ Rua Senhora da Graça ☎ 282/760683) serves imported beers and French champagne.

Outdoor Activities

See Chapter 9, *Golf in Portugal: Where to Play,* for a complete list of golf courses in the area.

The 18 holes of the **Campo de Golfe de Palmares** (⊠ Monte Palmares, Meia Praia ☎ 282/790500 ⊕ www.palmaresgolf.com) overlook Lagos Bay. Green fees range from €56.50 to €85.50.

If you want to see dolphins, and do so with a company that supports their protection, then head for **Algarve Dolphins** (⊠ Marina de Lagos ☎ 282/764670 ⊕ www.algarve-dolphins.com), which for €35 will take you on a 90-minute ocean trip. They guarantee that you'll see dolphins because, if you don't, you go on another trip for free!

Praia da Luz

③③ *6 km (4 mi) west of Lagos.*

There was once an active fishing fleet here, and a favorite pastime was to watch the boats being hauled onto the broad, sandy beach that lends the community its name. The boats are gone, but this is still an agreeable destination—despite the development that has hit it. At the western edge of town a little church faces an 18th-century fortress that once guarded against pirates and is now a restaurant. Many of the accommodations available in Luz are in private villas and apartments; the tourist office in Lagos may be able to advise about them.

For a break from the coast and its buzz, you can head inland to the small, quiet town of **Vila do Bispo** at the western terminus of the N125 highway. The interior of its parish church, in the Praça do Igreja at the center of town, is covered with 18th-century azulejos. To see it, come on a Sunday morning; the church is open only for services at 11:30.

Beaches

Four kilometers (2½ mi) west of Praia da Luz is **Burgau,** a fishing village with narrow, steep streets leading to it. Although the town has partly succumbed to the wave of tourism that has swept over the Algarve, its fine beach remains unchanged. The relaxed, low-key village of **Salema,** 5 km (3 mi) west of Burgau, is blessed with a 1,970-foot-long beach at the foot of green hills.

Where to Stay & Eat

★ **$–$$$** ✕ **Cabanas Velhas.** Take the rough road west from Burgau, and then an even rougher one down to the Praia Almadena. You'll be rewarded with this delightful surprise on a deserted cove. In fairly recent times there might have been a rustic *chiringuito* (food stall) here, but these days, and thanks to new laws, restaurants have to be permanent establishments. Many, like this one, have transformed themselves into places that would be at home in any city. ⊠ *Praia Almadena* ☎ *282/697834* ▤ *MC, V* ☻ *No lunch in winter.*

¢–$ ✕ **Café Correia.** Favorites at this rustic family-run restaurant in the inland town of Vila do Bispo are the stuffed squid and the rabbit cooked with beer and an onion sauce. The wine list, presented in a well-worn ledger, contains 180 varieties. ⊠ *Rua José Cardoso 34, Vila do Bispo* ☎ *282/442455* ▤ *No credit cards* ☻ *Closed Sat.*

★ **$$** ▥ **Bela Vista.** This family-owned hilltop hotel's horseshoe configuration gives all the spacious guest quarters a great sea view. Rooms and suites have terraces as well as many modern conveniences. The restaurant is excellent, and the nearby beach is fine. ⊠ *Praia da Luz, 8600* ☎ *282/788655* ⊕ *www.belavistadaluz.com* ⟿ *39 rooms, 6 suites* ⚭ *Restaurant, in-room safes, cable TV, tennis court, 2 pools, fitness classes, gym, health club, bar, playground* ▤ *AE, DC, MC, V* ¶⊙¶ *BP.*

★ **$$** ▥ **Romantik Natur.** Set within verdant gardens complete with sculptures, this holiday village west of Praia da Luz offers an ambience of calm and peacefulness that will soothe the soul. ⊠ *Sítio Cama da Vaca, 8600* ☎ *282/697323* ⊕ *www.romantur.com* ⟿ *20 rooms, 40 apartments* ⚭ *Restaurant, cable TV, tennis court, 3 pools, bar, playground* ▤ *MC, V* ¶⊙¶ *BP.*

Outdoor Activities

See Chapter 9, *Golf in Portugal: Where to Play,* for a complete list of golf courses in the area.

Ten kilometers (6 mi) west of Praia da Luz you'll find the 18-hole course at **Campo de Golfe Parque da Floresta** (⊠ Budens ☎ 282/690054 ⊕ www. parquedafloresta.com). Green fees are €70–€85.

Lessons with certified scuba instructors, wreck dives, and night dives are available at **Blue Ocean Divers** (⊠ Center Motel Ancora, Estrada de Porto de Mós ☎▤ 282/782718 ⊕ www.blue-ocean-divers.de). Praia da Luz's broad bay provides an excellent venue for windsurfing. Instruction and equipment rental are available directly on the beach.

Sagres

⬤ 34   *30 km (18 mi) southwest of Praia da Luz, 3 km (2 mi) southeast of Cabo*
Fodor'sChoice   *São Vicente.*
★

In the 19th century, this village, amid harsh, barren moorland, was re-built over earthquake ruins. Today there's little of note apart from a fort and a series of fine, sweeping beaches.

Views from the **Fortaleza de Sagres** (Sagres Fortress), an enormous run of defensive walls high above the crashing waves, are spectacular. Its massive walls and battlements make it popular with kids. The importance of this area dates to as early as the 4th century BC, when Mediterranean seafarers found it to be the last sheltered port before the wild winds of the Atlantic. In the late 8th century, according to local religious tradition, the mortal remains of the 4th-century martyr of Zaragoza, St. Vincent, washed up here. This led to a Vincentine cult that attracted pilgrims here until the destruction of the sanctuary in the mid-12th century. The fortress was rebuilt in the 17th century, and although some historians have claimed that it was the site for Prince Henry's house and famous navigation school, it's more likely that Henry built his school at Cabo São Vicente. But this doesn't detract from the powerful atmosphere. Certainly the **Venta da Rosa** (Wind Compass, or compass rose) dates from Prince Henry's period. Uncovered only in the 20th century, this large circular construction made of stone and packed earth is in the courtyard just inside the fortress. The simple Graça Chapel is of the same age.

A stark, modern building within the fort houses an **exhibition center** (☎ 282/620140 🖂 €3 ⊙ May–Sept., daily 10–8:30; Oct.–Apr., daily 10–6:30), with revolving exhibits documenting the region's history, flora, fauna, and nautical themes. The tunnel-like entrance to the fortress is about a 15-minute walk from the village; three buses a day run this way on weekdays.

Where to Stay & Eat

$$–$$$$ ✕ **Vila Velha.** Traditional Portuguese cuisine is given a twist of healthy, organic flavor here, and dishes include a range of international vegetarian options. From the terrace grill you can watch the sunset over Cabo São Vicente (Cape St. Vincent). Because of the popularity of this restaurant with local expats, it's recommended that you book in advance. 🖂 *On headland between fishing harbor and Praia da Mareta* ☎ *282/624788* 🞓 *MC, V* ⊙ *Closed Mon.*

¢–$$ ✕ **Restaurante Waza.** As popular with surfers as it is with local businessmen, this surprisingly international restaurant specializes in big portions of fresh fish and potatoes, rich burgers, and exotic chocolate desserts. The calorie count is high here, so throw out ideas of ordering something light. Waza also has a snack bar that operates during the day and late at night for drinks and cocktails. 🖂 *On headland at Praia da Beliche* ☎ *282/624125* 🞓 *AE, DC, MC* ⊙ *Closed Tues. and Wed.*

¢–$ ✕ **O Retiro do Pescador.** This outdoor grill is incredibly good value and serves a range of meats as well as the most flavorful fresh fish in Sagres. The homemade brandy is worth a try, as are the typical regional desserts prepared by the owner's wife and family. ⊠ *Vale das Silvas* ☎ *282/624438* 🖃 *No credit cards.*

★ **$–$$** ✕🖳 **Pousada do Infante.** In a two-story country house across the bay from the Fortaleza de Sagres, this pousada has a glorious view of the sea and the craggy cliffs. Guest rooms are homey, and public areas are comfortable—particularly the terrace bar, which is a perfect place to watch sunsets. Throughout the pousada are Moorish embellishments such as minarets and arches alongside the pool. The service and the Portuguese food in the well-respected restaurant ($$$$) are accomplished; expect seafood specials such as fried squid or clams with pork and, for dessert, perhaps almond cake. ⊠ *On headland between fishing harbor and Praia da Mareta, 8650-385* ☎ *282/620240* ⊕ *www.pousadas.pt* 🛏 *51 rooms* ⌂ *Restaurant, cable TV, tennis court, pool, bar, meeting rooms* 🖃 *AE, DC, MC, V* ⫟⦿⫟ *BP.*

Nightlife

Sagres is a well-known haunt of young travelers, and there are several music bars near the village square. The loud, lively **Last Chance Saloon** (⊠ Road to Praia da Mareta ☎ No phone) is on the pub-crawl route for most young merrymakers passing through Sagres. **A Rosa dos Ventos** (⊠ Praça da República ☎ 282/624480) is the town's most popular bar, attracting a motley crowd of European travelers. It also serves local snacks, burgers, and salads.

Outdoor Activities

The best fishing in Sagres is in winter when seas are rough; *sargo* (big bream bass) and *dourada* (mahimahi) are the main catches. Smaller bream, mullet, mackerel, and bass can be caught during the more settled summer months. **Baleeira** is a small fishing port of Sagres, which houses up to 100 fishing boats, some more than 65 feet in length. You can hire a local fisherman and his boat for a three-hour fishing trip from Salema to Sagres and back with possible swimming stops at lonely beaches along the way.

Cabo São Vicente

㉟ *6 km (4 mi) northwest of Sagres, 95 km (59 mi) west of Faro, 30 km (18 mi) southwest of Lagos.*

At the southwest tip of Europe, where the land juts starkly into the rough Atlantic waters, is Cabo São Vicente, called *O Fim do Mundo* (The End of the World) by early Portuguese mariners. Legends attach themselves easily to this desolate place, which the Romans once considered sacred (they believed it was where the spirits of the light lived because with sunset the light disappeared). It takes its modern name from the martyr St. Vincent, whose relics were brought here in the 8th century; it's said that they were transported to Lisbon 400 years later in a boat guided by ravens.

It's believed that Prince Henry built his house and the school of navigation here in the 15th century to train his captains—including Vasco da Gama and Ferdinand Magellan—before they set out on their voyages of discovery. The ancient buildings were long ago destroyed by pirates and earthquakes. This is not the crowded, overdeveloped Algarve of the south coast. From here you can see the spectacular cliff tops at Murração looking onto seemingly endless deserted beaches. Vast flocks of migratory birds round Cape St. Vincent and the Sagres headlands each year with the navigational precision that would have truly astounded Columbus. He learned how to navigate at the school of navigation after the armed convoy he was traveling with was attacked by pirates off Cape St. Vincent in 1476. Sixteen years later he set sail from here to discover the Americas.

Fodor'sChoice ★ The keeper of the isolated **Faro de São Vicente** (St. Vincent Lighthouse) opens it to visitors at his discretion. The beacon is said to have the strongest reflectors in Europe—they cast a beam 96 km (60 mi) out to sea. The views from the lighthouse are remarkable. Turquoise water whips across the base of the rust-color cliffs below, the fortress at Sagres is visible to the east, and in the distance lies the immense Atlantic.

Vila do Bispo

36 *10 km (6 mi) north of Cabo São Vicente.*

Though not particularly attractive itself, Vila do Bispo lies at the crossroads between west and south coastal roads and makes a good base for local beaches. What draws people to this area is the Parque Natural Sudoeste Alentejano e Costa Vincentina—a less traveled region of designated park area that contains some of the Algarve's wildest beaches and has become a mecca for surfers from all over the world. Portugal's best surfing beach is Amado, which at almost 13 km (8 mi) in length has enough room for the dozens of surfing camps and schools that have sprung up around it. Aljezur, a far prettier town, lies about 20 km (12 mi) northeast, but still lacks good hotels and restaurants, which can be found in the Vila do Bispo environs.

Where to Stay & Eat

★ **$$-$$$$** ✕ **O Sitio do Rio.** The family that runs this place believes in healthful cooking and high-quality, homemade produce, and using as few additives as possible. Daily fresh fish comes in all shapes and sizes, vegetarian dishes are on offer, and you can also choose from goat, pork, or lamb cutlets cooked in white wine or seasoned with rosemary. ⊠ *Praia do Bordeira, Carrapateira* ☎ *282/973119* ▭ *MC, V.*

★ **¢-$$$** ✕ **A Eira do Mel.** This restaurant excels at mixing local recipes and produce with sophisticated international cuisine. The flavors and artful presentation attract a youthful and vibrant crowd of faithful regulars. ⊠ *Estrada do Castelejo, Mercado Municipal* ☎ *282/639016* ▭ *MC, V* ☉ *Closed Sat.*

$-$$ ✕ **Chill In.** The name of this restaurant is actually a play on words, as its specialty is chili con carne and any Mexican-style dish that involves chili beans, tortillas, and chili peppers. The result works, but perhaps too well, as the place has become so popular it seems as if they are short of staff. Portions could be bigger and served faster. The sheer number of diners, traffic at the bar, and bright Latin American decor adds to the animated atmosphere. The restaurant is 2 km (1 mi) outside Aldeia

Velha towards Lagos. ⊠ *Estrada Lagos-Lisboa (E.N. 120), Aldeia Velha* ☎ *91/9193850* ▤ *MC, V* ✆ *Closed Mon. and Tues.*

★ ¢ ✕ **O Sitio do Forno.** This very simple restaurant is run by a fishing family who catch the menu early in the morning and cook it without any frills. Charcoal-grilled tiger prawns, shrimp, *percebes* (goose-neck barnacles), mussels, haddock, and sole are served with lemon, or coriander. Bread, local sausage *(chouriço)*, and potatoes in olive oil and olives complement the fish. There's cheap local red wine to wash it all down. The waiter, apart from being the fisherman's son, also happens to be the local mayor—the youngest in Portugal. Local fishermen mingle with curious travelers, making for a good and unusual atmosphere. ⊠ *Praia do Amado, Carrapateira* ☎ *96/3558404* ▤ *No credit cards* ✆ *Closed Mon.*

$ 🏨 **Monte Velho.** This converted farmhouse offers hip, luxurious accom-
Fodor'sChoice modation with stunning panoramic views toward the beaches of Amado
★ and Murração. The charming owners, Henrique and Vera, are perfect hosts, and the hotel offers all kinds of activities such as a 4-km (2½-mi) donkey ride to the beach, quad motorbikes, surfing classes, and massage. Breakfasts are long, drawn-out affairs (served from 9 to 11 AM) with a sumptuous spread of local delicacies to sample while chatting to the typically trendsetting guests. The seven individually decorated suites come with their very own hammocks for the semiprivate patios. ⊠ *Herdade do Monte Velho, Carrapateira 8670-230* ☎ *282/973207* ⊕ *www.wonderfulland.com/montevelho* ⬎ *7 suites* ⅋ *Massage, boating, bicycles, horseback riding* ▤ *MC, V* ⎟◎⎟ *BP, FAP, MAP.*

THE ALGARVE ESSENTIALS

Transportation

BY AIR

TAP Air Portugal has regular daily service from Lisbon and Porto. Flying time from Lisbon to Faro is 45 minutes; from Porto, 90 minutes. All international and domestic airlines use Faro Airport, which is 6 km (4 mi) west of town. It's easy to find your way into Faro: after around 4 km (2½ mi), signs along the road from the airport direct you right into town.

From mid-May to the end of October there's free Aerobus service from Faro Airport to the town center. Except for Tuesday when it doesn't run at all, the free service runs every 45 minutes from 8 to 8 daily; just show your airplane ticket when boarding. A taxi from the terminal building to the center of Faro costs around €10 (there's a small extra charge for baggage). Ask the staff at the airport tourist office for a list of prices for rides to other destinations in the region. Always make sure that you agree on a price with the taxi driver before setting off. Buses 14 and 16 shuttle between Faro town and the airport hourly, 8 AM–9 PM (until 11 PM July–mid-September); buy tickets on board (€1).

🇫 **Faro Airport** ☎ 289/800617, 289/800801 for flight information ⊕ www.ana-aeroportos.pt. **TAP Air Portugal** ☎ 289/818538.

BY BUS

Various companies run daily express buses between Lisbon and Lagos, Portimão, Faro, Tavira, and Vila Real de Santo António. Allow for 3½–4½ hours' travel time for all these destinations. Generally this is more comfortable than traveling by train, and some of the luxury coaches have a restroom, TV, and food service. Any travel agency in Lisbon can reserve a seat for you; in summer, book at least 24 hours in advance.

The main form of public transportation in the Algarve is the bus, and every town and village has its own terminal. You may have to walk from the main road to the more isolated beach areas, however. Tickets are relatively inexpensive, although a bus ride always costs more than the comparable train journey. Most ticket offices have someone who speaks at least a little English. The booklet *Guia Horário*, which costs €3 and is available at main terminals, lists every bus service, with timetables and information in English. Some local services are infrequent or don't run on Sunday.

🚊 Terminals **Albufeira** ✉ Parque Ribeira ☎ 289/589755. **Faro** ✉ Av. da República ☎ 289/899760. **Lagos** ✉ Rossío de São João ☎ 282/762944. **Portimão** ✉ Av. Guanaré ☎ 282/418120. **Vila Real de Santo António** ✉ Av. da República ☎ 281/511807.

BY CAR

To reach the Algarve from Lisbon—an easy 300-km (186-mi) drive south—cross the Ponte 25 de Abril and take the toll road to Setúbal. Beyond here, the main IP1 highway runs via Alcácer do Sal, Grândola, and Ourique, eventually joining N125, the main east–west thoroughfare near Guia, north of Albufeira. To reach Portimão, Lagos, and the western Algarve, turn right; go straight to reach Albufeira; and turn left for Faro and the eastern Algarve. The drive from Lisbon to Faro, Lagos, or Albufeira takes about three hours, longer in summer, on weekends, and on holidays.

In the east, a suspension bridge crosses the Rio Guadiana between Ayamonte in Spain and Vila Real de Santo António in Portugal. The east–west N125 extends 165 km (102 mi) from the Spanish border all the way west to Sagres. It runs parallel to the coast but slightly inland, with clearly marked turnoffs to the beach towns. Be very careful on this route, as it's one of Europe's most dangerous. In summer expect traffic jams in several places along it. In addition, portions of highway are under construction everywhere, and roadwork and diversions add to the traffic near the busy resorts. The high-speed IP1 and IC4 extend from the Spanish border to Bensafrim, just northwest of Lagos; eventually it will run to Sagres.

Beware that Portugal has some of the worst accident statistics in Europe. Always drive defensively. In inland areas, minor country roads aren't always well maintained; when driving at night in rural areas, look out for mopeds without lights. Signage throughout the region can be very confusing, but don't despair. Local officials have started replacing older tangles of signs with streamlined versions.

🚗 Local Agency **Auto Jardim** ✉ Av. da Liberdade, Albufeira ☎ 289/589688 ✉ Faro Airport ☎ 289/800881.

BY TAXI

If you intend to take a cab from Faro Airport, look for the board in the arrivals hall that lists regulated rates to major tourist destinations. In

Faro, you can call for taxis or hail them on the street, and around €4–€5 will get you across town (traffic permitting). Beware, however: a significant number of drivers will have meters that are mysteriously "not working"; always agree on a fare before you set off.

BY TRAIN

There are regular daily departures to the Algarve from Lisbon's Barreiro station on the south banks of the Tagus. Purchase your ticket for a boat ride at Terminal Fluvial in front of the Praça do Comércio, which takes you across the river to the train station for all trains traveling in a southerly direction. The route runs through Setúbal to the rail junction of Tunes (three hours from Barreiro) and continues on to Albufeira (another 10 minutes), Faro (another 40 minutes), and all stations east to Vila Real de Santo António (another two hours). For the western route to Silves (another 20 minutes) and Lagos (another hour), you must change trains at Tunes.

The railroad connects Lagos in the west with Vila Real de Santo António in the east—running close to N125. Several trains a day run the entire often-scenic route, which takes three to four hours; tickets are very reasonably priced, and the trip is pleasant. Some of the faster trains don't stop at every station, and some of the stations are several miles from the towns they serve, although there's usually a connecting bus. The main train stations generally have someone who speaks some English, but it's easier to get information at tourist offices. At the Faro and Lagos offices, timetables are posted.

🚉 **Major Stations Faro** ✉ Largo da Estação ☎ 808/208208. **Lagos** ✉ Largo da Estação ☎ 282/762987.

Contacts & Resources

EMERGENCIES

Each region has a health center for primary medical (outpatient) treatment; local tourist offices can supply addresses and phone numbers. There are hospitals in Faro, Lagos, and Portimão. Each town has at least one pharmacy that stays open all night; consult the notice posted on every pharmacy's door for current schedules.

🚑 **General Emergencies** ☎ 112. **Police** ✉ Rua Serpa Pinto, Faro ☎ 289/803887 ✉ Rua General Alberto Silveira, Lagos ☎ 282/762930.

🚑 **Hospitals Faro** ✉ Rua Leão Penedo ☎ 289/803411. **Lagos** ✉ Rua do Castelo dos Governadores ☎ 282/763034. **Portimão** ✉ Av. São João de Dios ☎ 282/415115.

MAIL

In Faro, there's a post office in Largo do Carmo. In Lagos, there's a branch in Praça Gil Eanes. Both are open Monday through Saturday from 8:30 to 6:30.

TOUR OPTIONS

Many companies and individual fishermen along the coast rent out boats for excursions. These range from one-hour tours of local grottoes and rock formations to full-day trips that often involve a stop at a beach for a barbecue lunch. Main centers for coastal excursions are Albufeira, Vilamoura, Portimão, Tavira, Lagos, Sagres, Vila Real, and Armação de Pêra. Consult the tourist offices in these towns for details or simply wander down to the local harbor, where the prices and times of the next cruise will be posted.

Jeep "safaris" are a unique way to see fascinating inland villages. Lunch is usually included in the price. Algarve operators include Megatur and Zebra Safari. Riosul Viagens arranges cruises up the Rio Guadiana, which runs between Portugal and Spain. It also has half-day overland tours by jeep and full-day cruise-jeep tours that take you off the beaten path up to the village of Foz de Odeleite. Turinfo can organize boat trips, jeep tours, and other activities around the Sagres Peninsula.

🚩 **Megatur** ✉ Rua Conselheiro Bivar 80, Faro ☎ 289/807485 ⊕ www.megatur.pt. **Riosul Viagens e Turismo Lda** ✉ Rua Tristão Vaz Teixeira 15C, Monte Gordo ☎ 281/510201 ⊕ www.riosul-tours.com. **Turinfo** ✉ Praça da República, Sagres ☎ 282/620003. **Zebra Safari** ✉ Arcadas de S. João, Albufeira ☎ 289/583300 ⊕ www.zebrasafari.com.

VISITOR INFORMATION

FARO & ENVIRONS 🚩 Tourist Offices **Faro** ✉ Airport ☎ 289/818582 ✉ Rua da Misericórdia 8–12 ☎ 289/803604. **Loulé** ✉ Edifício do Castelo ☎ 289/463900. **Olhão** ✉ Largo Sebastião Martins Mestre 6A ☎ 289/713936.

EASTERN & CENTRAL ALGARVE 🚩 Tourist Offices **Albufeira** ✉ Rua 5 de Outubro ☎ 289/585279. **Armação de Pêra** ☎ 282/312145. **Monchique** ✉ Largo dos Choroes ☎ 282/911189. **Monte Gordo** ✉ Av. Marginal ☎ 281/544495. **Portimão** ✉ Av. Zeca Afonso ☎ 282/531800. **Praia da Rocha** ✉ Av. Tomás Cabreira ☎ 282/419132. **Silves** ✉ Rua 25 de Abril ☎ 282/442255. **Tavira** ✉ Rua da Galeria 9 ☎ 281/322511.

LAGOS & THE WESTERN ALGARVE 🚩 Tourist Offices **Lagos** ✉ Sitio de São João ☎ 282/763031. **Sagres** ✉ Rua Comandante Matoso ☎ 282/624873.

Coimbra &
the Beiras

WORD OF MOUTH

"Coimbra is a terrific lively city and one of the best places to hear authentic fado, especially in one of the tiny atmospheric *tascas* where the students hang out. Another high point—literally—has to be the spectacular Serra da Estrela; the region's highest mountain range and *the* place to head for if you're into hiking or cycling in the great outdoors."

—Mary McLean

Updated by
Mary McLean

IT'S NOT FAR FROM ONE POINT IN THE BEIRAS TO ANY OTHER. In fact, you can drive from the Atlantic shore to the lonely fortified towns along the Spanish border—only 160 km (100 mi)—in the time it takes many residents of Los Angeles or London to commute to work. But within this small area there's tremendous diversity among the beaches, lagoons, and mountains.

To the east, Portugal's highest mountains, the Serra da Estrela, rise to nearly 6,600 feet and provide a playground of alpine meadows, wooded hills, and clear streams. High in this range's granite reaches, a tiny trickle of an icy stream begins a tortuous journey to the sea. This is the Rio Mondego, praised in song and poetry as the most Portuguese of all rivers. The longest river entirely within the country and the lifeblood of the Beiras, it provides vital irrigation to fruit orchards and farms as it flows through the region's heart. Coimbra, the country's first capital and home to one of Europe's earliest universities, rises above its banks. Closer to the sea, under the imposing walls of Montemor Castle, the river widens to nurture rice fields before merging with the Atlantic at the popular beach resort of Figueira da Foz.

Exploring Coimbra & the Beiras

The Beiras region encompasses the provinces of the Beira Litoral (Coastal Beira), the Beira Baixa (Lower Beira), and the Beira Alta (Upper Beira), which together make up roughly one-quarter of continental Portugal's landmass. On the verge of being discovered, the Beiras contain some of the last remaining areas in Europe unscathed by mass tourism.

Portugal's first capital, the ancient university town of Coimbra (pronounced *queembra*), provides a good introduction to this part of the country. The region's western portion contains the seaside resort of Figueira da Foz and the canals and lagoons in and around the delightful old port of Aveiro. Farther inland it includes Viseu, with its wonderful parks and historic old quarter. The mountain resort of Caramulo and the belle epoque towns of Luso and Curia are some of the country's most popular spas. The region's eastern area includes Portugal's highest mountains—the Serra da Estrela—the renowned Dão wine region, and a chain of ancient fortified towns along the Spanish border.

Restaurants & Cuisine

With the exception of some luxury hotel dining rooms, restaurants are casual in dress and atmosphere, although a bit less casual than in the southern parts of the country. The emphasis is generally more on the food than on the trappings. Except for pizza and the occasional Chinese restaurant, foreign food is virtually nonexistent.

At almost any of the ubiquitous beach bar–restaurants, you can't go wrong by ordering the *peixe do dia* (fish of the day). In most cases it will have been caught only hours before and will be prepared outside on a charcoal grill. You'll usually be served the whole fish along with boiled potatoes and a simple salad. Wash it down with a chilled white Dão wine, and you have a tasty, healthful, relatively inexpensive meal. In Figueira

A BIT OF HISTORY

This region has played an important role in Portugal's development. The Romans built roads, established settlements, and in 27 BC incorporated into their vast empire the remote province known as Lusitania, which encompassed most of what is now central Portugal, including the Beiras. They left many traces of their presence, including the well-known and well-preserved ruins at Conímbriga, near Coimbra. The Moors swept through the territory in the early 8th century and played a leading role for several hundred years. Many of the region's elaborate castles and extensive fortifications show a strong Moorish influence. The towns along the Spanish frontier have been the scene of many fierce battles—from those during the Wars of Christian Reconquest to those during the fledgling Portuguese nation's struggle against invaders from neighboring Castile.

The Beiras also played a part in Portugal's golden Age of Discovery. In 1500 Pedro Álvares Cabral, a nobleman from the town of Belmonte on the eastern flank of the Serra da Estrela, led the first expedition to what is now Brazil. Much of the wealth garnered during this period, when tiny Portugal controlled so much of the world's trade, financed the great architectural and artistic achievements of the Portuguese Renaissance. Throughout the region there are fine examples of the Manueline style, the uniquely Portuguese art form that reflects the nation's nautical heritage. The cathedrals at Guarda and Viseu, the Igreja e Mosteiro de Santa Cruz (Church and Monastery of Santa Cruz) in Coimbra, and the Convento de Jesus (Convent of Jesus) in Aveiro are especially noteworthy.

During the 19th-century Peninsular War, between Napoléon's armies and Wellington's British and Portuguese forces, a decisive battle was fought in the tranquil forest of Buçaco. Later in the same century, this area witnessed a much more peaceful invasion, as people from all corners of Europe came to take the waters at such well-known spas as Luso, Curia, and Caramulo. Around the turn of the 20th century, when the now tourist-packed Algarve was merely a remote backwater, Figueira da Foz was coming into its own as an international beach resort.

6

da Foz and in the Aveiro region, *enguias* (eels), *lampreia* (lamprey), and *caldeirada* (a fish stew that's a distant cousin of the French bouillabaisse) are popular.

The inland Bairrada region, between Coimbra and Aveiro, and in particular the town of Mealhada are well known for *leitão assado* (roast suckling pig). In Coimbra the dish to try is *chanfana*; this is traditionally made with tender young kid braised in red wine and roasted in an earthenware casserole. In the mountains, fresh *truta* (trout) panfried with bacon and onions is often served, as is *javali* (wild boar). *Bacalhau* (salt cod) in one form or another appears on just about every menu in the region. Bacalhau *à brás* (fried in olive oil with eggs, onions, and pota-toes) is one of many popular versions of this common dish.

The Beiras contain two of Portugal's most notable wine districts: Bair-rada and Dão. The reds from these districts generally benefit from a fairly long stay in the bottle; 1983 and 1985 are particularly good years, and if you see a 1983 Porta dos Cavaleiros Reserva *tinto* (red) on a wine list, grab it. The full-bodied Dão goes wonderfully with chanfana or leitão assado. The flowery whites from around here should be drunk much younger.

This region is also justly famous for its contribution to the country's dessert menus, although many of these pastry delights, such as Coim-bra's *arrufada* (a small cinnamon-flavor pastry), are rarely found far from home. The tangy sheep's cheese of the Serra da Estrela is popular throughout the country.

About the Hotels

There are plenty of high-quality accommodations in the western reaches of the Beiras, but the options thin the farther inland you move; make reservations in advance if you plan to travel during the busy summer months. That said, the Beiras has a great variety of lodging choices, ranging from venerable old luxury hotels to gleam-ing, modern hostelries. Though small, the region has several *pou-sadas* (inns that are members of the Turismo de Habitação organization), which make the perfect bases for exploring the entire region. In addi-tion, there are Solares de Portugal lodgings, which are family owned and run and can range from mansions to cottages. Most establishments offer substantial off-season discounts. (High season varies by hotel but generally runs July 1–September 15.)

WHAT IT COSTS In Euros					
	$$$$	**$$$**	**$$**	**$**	**¢**
RESTAURANTS	over €21	€16–€21	€11–€15	€7–€10	under €7
HOTELS	over €275	€176–€275	€101–€175	€60–€100	under €60

Restaurant prices are per person for a main course at dinner. Hotel prices are for a standard double room, including tax, in high season (off-season rates may be lower).

When to Go

Although the Beiras's coastal beaches are popular in summer, the crowds are nothing like those in the Algarve. The water along this shore isn't as warm as it is farther south, and as a consequence the season is con-siderably shorter. Plan your beach time here between early June and mid-September.

With the exception of the eastern regions, the interior isn't subject to the blazing heat of the Alentejo or the Algarve's interior and so is well suited for summertime touring. Aside from occasional showers, the weather is comfortable between early April and mid-November. Win-ters, especially in the eastern mountain towns, are harsh.

GREAT ITINERARIES

If you have just three days, you can visit Coimbra and the coast, unless you head straight inland to the mountains. Don't let the distances fool you into being overambitious: the mountain roads may not be long, but they take a lot of time to drive. A week is enough time to experience Coimbra, visit a spa and the coast, and explore the Serra da Estrela.

IF YOU HAVE 3 DAYS

Spend your first morning in 🖼 **Coimbra ❶ –⓴**, with a stroll through the Cidade Velha (Old Town) and the university. In the afternoon visit the Roman ruins at **Conímbriga ㉑**. The next day, follow the Rio Mondego to the beach resorts of **Figueira da Foz ㉓** and Buarcos, head up the coast, and move inland to visit the china factory in **Vista Alegre ㉔** and the nearby Museu do Mar. Use the rest of the day and evening to explore **Aveiro ㉖**, the famous Ria de Aveiro, and the delightful little coastal villages along the sand spit, such as Costa Nova, south of Aveiro.

IF YOU HAVE 7 DAYS

Start in 🖼 **Coimbra ❶ –⓴** and **Conímbriga ㉑**, as above. The next day, stop to visit the castle at **Montemor-o-Velho ㉒** on your way to another night in 🖼 **Figueira da Foz ㉓**, from which you can visit the other beach resort, Buarcos, and drive out to Cape Mondego to enjoy the view and the sunset. Continue along the dune-lined coast on the third day, and after stops in Costa Nova, **Vista Alegre ㉔** and a visit to the nearby Museu do Mar, unpack your toiletries in 🖼 **Aveiro ㉖**. The following morning, take a boat trip

through the narrow waterways and marshlands that make up the Ria de Aveiro, and after lunch continue on to 🖼 **Viseu ㉘** by way of **Ovar ㉗** and the castle at Santa Maria da Feira.

On your fifth day, continue east from Viseu and make a loop that includes visits to the fortified towns of **Celorico da Beira ㊸**, **Trancoso ㊹**, **Castelo Rodrigo ㊺**, and **Almeida ㊻**—a pleasant drive through the sparsely settled countryside over little-traveled roads. Spend the night in the mountain bastion of 🖼 **Guarda ㊼** or at one of the charming country hotels within the Serra de Estrela. The next morning, either visit the cathedral and museum in Guarda, or devote the whole day to exploring the magnificent high reaches of the Parque Natural da Serra da Estrela, with its fabulous views, great walks, exciting wildlife and birds, and beautiful flowers. Leave the park at Seia. Continue by way of **Penacova ㉞** to the forest of 🖼 **Buçaco ㉝**, just north of Coimbra. Be sure to visit the opulent Palace Hotel and, if it's within your budget, spend the night; there are more modest accommodations in the nearby spa town of 🖼 **Luso ㉜**. On your last day, explore the options of the local spas before returning to Coimbra.

6

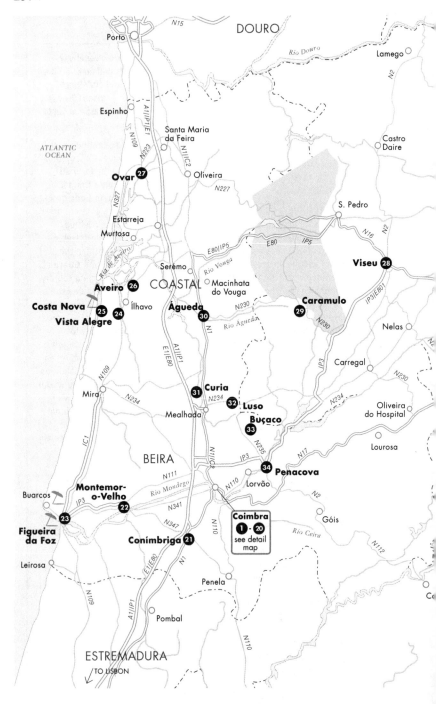

The Beiras

N226

Leomil

Rio Douro

Vila Nova
de Foz Côa

Rio Águeda

UPPER   BEIRA

N221

**Castelo
Rodrigo** 45

Aguir
da Beira

44 **Trancoso**

Pinhel

N102/IP2

46 **Almeida**

N324

N340

N226

Freixedas

N221

**Celorico
da Beira**

E80/IP5

43

E80/IP5

Castelo
Mendo

N17

Mangualde

N324

Linhares

47 **Guarda**

Aldeia
da Ponte

N231

42 **Gouveia**

N18-1 N18

N233-3

N339

PARQUE NATURAL DA SERRA DA ESTRELA

N233-3

Seia

Valhelhas

Manteigas

Centum Cellas

38 **Sabugal**

Torre

40

39

Penhas
da Saude

41 **Covilhã**

Belmonte

Sortelha

Serra de Malcata

N339

Rio Zêzere

N18

E802/

N346

37 **SPAIN**

Fundão

36

N345

Penamacor

N238

Alpedrinha

E802/N18

Monsanto

Cambas

LOWER   BEIRA

N112

N233

E802/N18

N240

20 miles

0

0

30 km

E802/
IP6

35 **Castelo Branco**

COIMBRA

❶–⓴ *197 km (123 mi) northeast of Lisbon.*

Fodor'sChoice
★

Coimbra is best known for its university. Although it was first estab-lished in Lisbon by King Dinis I in 1290 and subsequently transferred back and forth between Coimbra and Lisbon, it was finally installed on its present site in 1537. Since then the university has played an impor-tant role in the life of both the city and the nation. During the 1960s, it was a center of the unrest preceding the 1974 revolution. Many cur-rent political leaders were educated here, and Dr. António Salazar, the country's dictator from 1932 until 1968, once taught economics in its lecture halls. Today, the students add much life to the city. They proudly wear the traditional black capes and adorn their briefcases with colored ribbons denoting which faculty they attend (red for law and yellow for medicine, for example). After final exams in May, they burn their rib-bons with great exuberance in a ceremony called Queima das Fitas (Burning of the Ribbons).

TIMING   Allow at least two hours for the walk around the old town; double that if you are intending to visit the attractions along the way. If you want to continue across the bridge, you'll probably need a couple more hours. The hill is very steep. For this reason, the tour starts at the top of it and works itself down.

Exploring

❼ Arco de Almedina. Located on the Baixa district's Rua Ferreira Borges—one of the city's principal shopping streets—the Arco de Almedina is a tall, graceful opening in a massive stone wall that leads to a courtyard. The 12th-century arch is one of the last vestiges of the medieval city walls, and above it are a Renaissance carving of the Virgin and Child and an early Portuguese coat of arms. The adjacent tower houses the city's his-torical archives. Its *sino de correr* (warning bell) was used from the Mid-dle Ages until 1870 to signal the populace to return to the safety of the city walls. The tower also holds an art gallery. ⊠ *Rua Ferreira Borges.*

▌NEED A BREAK?   Why not succumb to the temptation of the pastry-filled windows of the cafés along the Rua Ferreira Borges? The **Café Nicola** (⊠ Rua Ferreira Borges 35, Baixa) is a good choice for sampling *arrufada*, Coimbra's most notable contribution to the world's great pastries. This curved confection is said to represent the Rio Mondego's tortuous course.

⓯ Convento de Santa Clara-a-Nova (New Santa Clara Convent). This con-vent on a hill was built in the 17th century to house the Poor Clair nuns who were forced by floods from their old convent. The remains of Queen Isabel were also moved here. The barrackslike exterior protects a sumptuous baroque church and noble cloisters that shouldn't be missed. Queen Isabel's silver shrine is behind the main altar in the church, installed there by Coimbra townspeople in 1696. The queen's original tomb—she ordered it for herself in 1330—stands in the lower

A BIT MORE HISTORY (COIMBRA)

Since its emergence as the Roman settlement of Aeminium, this city on the banks of the Rio Mondego has played an influential and often crucial role in the country's development. In Roman times, it was an important way station, the midway point on the road connecting Lisbon with Braga to the north, and a rival of the city of Conímbriga, across the river to the south. But by the beginning of the 5th century the Roman administration was falling apart, and Aeminium fell under the dominance of Alans, Swabians, and Visigoths in turn. By the middle of the 7th century, under Visigoth rule, its importance was such that it had become the regional capital and center of the bishopric of Conímbriga. Upstart Aeminium had finally gained ascendancy over its rival Conímbriga.

The Moorish occupation of Coimbra is believed to have occurred around the year AD 714, and it heralded an era of economic development: for the next 300 years or so, Coimbra was a frontier post of Muslim culture. North of the city there are no traces of Moorish architecture, but Coimbra has retained tangible fragments of its Muslim past—remains of old walls as well as a small gate, the Arco de Almedina, once an entrance to a medina—and the surrounding country is full of place-names of Moorish origin.

After a number of bloody attempts, the reconquest of Coimbra by Christian forces was finally achieved in 1064 by Ferdinand, King of León, and Coimbra went on to become the capital of a vast territory extending north to the Rio Douro and encompassing much of what are now the Beiras. The city was the birthplace and burial place of Portugal's first king, Dom Afonso Henriques, and was the capital from which he launched the attacks against the Moors that were to end in the conquest of Lisbon and the birth of a nation. Coimbra was the capital of Portugal until the late 13th century, when the court was transferred to Lisbon.

The figure who has remained closest to the heart of the city was the Spanish-born wife of King Dinis, Isabel of Aragon. During her life, while her husband and son were away fighting wars, sometimes against each other, Isabel occupied herself with social works, battling prostitution and fostering education and welfare schemes for Coimbra's young women. She helped found a convent, and had her own tomb placed in it. She bequeathed her jewels to the poor girls of Coimbra to provide them with wedding dowries. When she died on a peacemaking mission to Estremoz in 1336, her body was brought back to Coimbra, and almost immediately the late queen became the object of a local cult. Isabel was beatified in the 16th century, then canonized in 1625 by Pope Urban VIII after it was determined that her body had remained undecayed in its tomb.

6

Coimbra

choir at the other end of the church. Carved out of a single block of stone, the splendid Gothic sarcophagus is decorated with sculpted polychrome figures of Franciscan friars and nuns. An effigy of the queen dressed in her Poor Clair habit lies on top. During the Peninsular War, the French general Massena used the convent as a hospital for 300 troops wounded during the battle of Buçaco. The carefully hidden convent treasures escaped the desecration inflicted on so many Portuguese monuments during this period. Part of the convent is now used as the **Military Museum,** which has a small collection of arms and artifacts, many dating from the Napoleonic Wars. ✉ *Rua Santa Isabel* ☎ *239/441674* 🖃 *Church free, cloister €1, museum €1.50* ⊙ *Daily 10–noon and 2–5.*

16 **Convento de Santa Clara-a-Velha** (Old Santa Clara Convent). Centuries-old flood deposits are still being excavated from this ruined Gothic church by restorers, so the church can be viewed only from the outside. Founded as a Poor Clair convent in the early 14th century by Queen Isabel, widow of King Dinis and patron saint of Coimbra, the building was beset by periodic flooding and was finally abandoned in 1677. Both Queen Isabel and the tragic Inês de Castro were originally interred here. ✉ *Rua de Baixo* 🖃 *€3 Tues.–Sun., guided tours at 10, 11, 2, 3, 5, and 6.*

⑨ Igreja e Mosteiro de Santa Cruz (Church and Monastery of Santa Cruz). The stark, 12th-century stone facade of this church is enhanced by a Renaissance entrance, added as part of renovations in 1507. This is Portugal's national pantheon, and inside, the high altar—whose delicate carvings were done by Nicolas Chanterene in 1521—is flanked by the intricately detailed tombs of Portugal's first two kings, Dom Afonso Henriques and his son Dom Sancho I. In the sacristy are several notable examples of 16th-century Portuguese painting. The lower portions of the interior walls are lined with azulejos (painted and glazed ceramic tiles) depicting various religious motifs. From the sacristy, a door opens to the Casa do Capitulo (Silent Cloister); this double-tier Manueline cloister contains scenes from the Passion of Christ, attributed to Chanterene. ✉ *Praça 8 de Maio* ☎ *239/822941* ✆ *Church free; sacristy, chapter room, and cloister €2.50; cloister only €1* ⊙ *Mon.–Sat. 9–noon and 2–5:45, Sun. 4–6.*

NEED A BREAK?

The **Café Santa Cruz** (✉ Praça 8 de Maio ☎ 239/833617) is one of the most unusual watering holes north of Lisbon. Until its conversion to more pedestrian uses in 1927, this was an auxiliary chapel for the monastery. Now its high-vaulted Manueline ceiling, stained-glass windows, and wood paneling make it a great place in which to indulge a favorite Portuguese pastime: sitting in a café with a strong, murky *bica* (Portugal's answer to espresso) and a brandy, reading the day's newspaper. It's closed Sunday.

① Jardim Botânico (Botanical Garden). Find relief from Coimbra's oppressive summer heat in this wonderful shady garden near the university. Designed by British architect William Elsden and by two natural history teachers, Domingos Vandelli and Dalla Bella, this was created during the reform of the university in 1772 by the Marquis of Pombal. It's still a place of serious scientific study, and the 50 acres is home to more than 1,200 species of plants. ✉ *Alameda Dr. Júlio Henriques* ☎ *239/822897* ✆ *Weekdays free, weekends and holidays €2* ⊙ *Sept. 16–Feb., daily 9–5; Mar.–June, daily 9–7; July–Sept. 15, daily 9–8. Guided tours by request, daily 9–noon and 2–5.*

⑧ Jardim de Manga (Manga Garden). A small park with an odd assortment of domed, rose-color turrets grouped around a fountain, this garden was designed by Jean de Rouen in the 16th century and once belonged to the cloisters of the Mosteiro de Santa Cruz. The fountain symbolizes the fountain of life, and the eight pools radiating from it represent the rivers of paradise. ✉ *Rua Olímpio Fernandes.*

⑭ Largo da Portagem. This triangular plaza with cafés and shops is at the foot of the Ponte Santa Clara, on the beautiful riverbank of Coimbra's Baixa (Lower Town) district. The statue of Joaquim António de Aguiar, with pen in hand, represents the signing in 1833 of a decree banning religious orders throughout Portugal (the result of an anticlerical liberalism that had infused political thought throughout Europe at this time).

Museu Machado de Castro (Machado de Castro Museum). Closed for restoration until 2010, the museum contains a fine collection of sculpture, including works by Jean de Rouen and Master Pero, and an intriguing little statue of a mounted medieval knight. The Bishop's Chapel, adorned with 18th-century azulejos and silks, is a highlight of the upstairs galleries, which contain a diverse selection of Portuguese paintings and furniture. The building, itself a work of art, was constructed in the 12th century to house the prelates of Coimbra; it was extensively modified 400 years later and was converted to a museum in 1912. Don't miss the basement's well-preserved vaulted passageways—built by the Romans as storerooms for the forum that was once here—and be sure to take in the view from the terrace of the Renaissance loggia. As you exit the museum, note the large 18th-century azulejo panel depicting Jerónimo translating the Bible. ⊠ *Largo Dr. José Rodrigues* ☎ *239/823727* ☞ *€3, free Sun. 9:30–12:30* ⊙ *Closed for restoration until 2010. When open, times are Tues.–Sun. 9:30–12:30 and 2–5:30.*

⑪ Palácio da Justiça (Hall of Justice). The stately 16th-century building that houses the Hall of Justice was once the College of St. Thomas. To the left of the main entrance is a large azulejo panel depicting the goddess of justice watched over by a Knight Templar. The three panels in front read WORK, JUSTICE, and ORDER. Gracing the interior is a two-tier cloister, decorated with azulejo panels depicting historical themes associated with Coimbra. ⊠ *Rua da Sofia* ☞ *Free* ⊙ *Weekdays 9–12:30 and 2–5:30.*

⑤ Palácio de Sobre Ribas (Palace above the Riverbanks). The palace occupies a tower in the ancient walls in the lower part of the Cidade Velha. The building's exterior is graced by several Manueline doorways and windows. ⊠ *Rua Sobre Ribas.*

⑫ Pátio da Inquisição (Patio of the Inquisition). Headquarters of the Portuguese Inquisition from 1548, this fine building, now an art gallery and exhibition space, is made up of a series of houses, homes of the Inquisitors, and dungeons and torture chambers used to house the accused (mostly Jews who had actually, or only in appearance, converted to Christianity). All of these face onto a deceptively peaceful cloister and garden courtyard. ⊠ *Rua Pedro da Rocha* ☎ *239/826178* ☞ *Free* ⊙ *Tues.–Sun. 10–7, Fri. 10–10.*

☾ ⑰ Portugal dos Pequenitos (Portugal of the Little Ones). At Coimbra's small, open-air theme park, children poke around the models of Portugal's most important buildings, built to the scale of a five-year-old child. Then they can compare them with what they've seen firsthand. It's within walking distance of the Ponte Santa Clara. ⊠ *Rossío de Santa Clara* ☎ *239/441225* ☞ *€6* ⊙ *Sept. 16–Feb. 20, daily 10–5; Feb. 21–May, daily 10–7; June–Sept. 15, daily 9–8.*

⑬ Praça do Comércio. One of the Baixa district's busiest and most attractive plazas, this was the site of the circus in Roman times. Today it's ringed with fashionable shops in 17th- and 18th-century town houses, and street vendors sell everything from combs to carpets on its corners. The Rua Eduardo Coelho, which fans out from the square, is lined with shoe stores and was once known as the Street of the Shoemakers.

Closed to the public, the Igreja de Sant'Iago, on the square's northeast corner, is a small, late-13th-century stone church with finely carved Romanesque columns. On the opposite corner, the Igreja de São Bartolomeu dates from 957. Destroyed several times, it was rebuilt in its present form in 1756.

⓲ Quinta das Lágrimas (House of Tears). Popular history has it that Dom Pedro and Inês de Castro lived with their children on this estate. It was here on a black January night in 1355 that Inês was killed by agents of Dom Pedro's father, Afonso IV. The 18th-century manor house on the grounds—which has nothing to do with the Inês tragedy—has been turned into a hotel. You can visit the gardens and the celebrated Fonte dos Amores (Fountain of Love), whose waters are said to be Dona Inês's tears. ⊠ *Estrada das Lages* ☎ *239/802380* ⚟ *€0.75* ⊗ *Daily 9–5.*

⓾ Rua da Sofia. This broad, busy street is one of the city's main thoroughfares. Developed in the 16th century, the road is famous for its many fine religious monuments, including the Carmo, Graça, São Pedro, and Santa Justa churches. The entire street has been classified as a national monument.

❻ Rua Quebra Costas. This is the main pedestrian link between the Baixa district and the Sé Velha. The street name translates to "back-breaker"; try carrying a heavy load of groceries up this steep incline, and you'll understand why it's an apt name.

❸ Sé Nova (New Cathedral). The 17th-century Jesuit cathedral was patterned after the baroque church of Il Gesù in Rome, as were many such churches of the day. It took a century to build and shows two distinct styles as fashion changed from classical cleanliness to the florid baroque. The woodwork, from the gilded altarpiece to the blackwood choir stalls, moved across from the Sé Velha (Old Cathedral), are particularly worth a look. There are two organs, both dating to the 18th century. The church became the local cathedral in 1772, 13 years after the abolition of the Jesuit Order by the Marquis of Pombal. ⊠ *Largo da Sé Nova* ⚟ *Free* ⊗ *Tues.–Sat. 9:30–12:30 and 2–6:30.*

NEED A BREAK?

The cathedral square is ringed with cafés and restaurants. **Café Sé Velha** (⊠ **Rua da Joaquim António Aguiar 136** ☎ **239/834547**), decorated with azulejos depicting local scenes, is one of the most inviting.

❹ Sé Velha (Old Cathedral). Made of massive granite blocks and crowned by a ring of battlements, this 12th-century cathedral looks more like a fortress than a house of worship. (Engaged in an ongoing struggle with the Moors, the Portuguese, who were building and reconstructing castles for defense purposes throughout the country, often incorporated fortifications in their churches.) The harsh exterior is softened somewhat by graceful 16th-century Renaissance doorways. The somber interior has a gilded wooden altarpiece, a late-15th-century example of the Flamboyant Gothic style, created by the Flemish masters Olivier of Ghent and Jean d'Ypres. The walls of the Chapel of the Holy Sacrament are lined with the touching, lifelike sculptures of Jean de Rouen, whose life-size Christ figure is flanked by finely detailed representations of the

Fodor's Choice
★

6

apostles and evangelists. The cloisters (closed 1 PM–2 PM), built in the 13th century, are distinguished by a well-executed series of transitional Gothic arches. ⊠ *Largo da Sé Velha* ☎ *239/825273* ✉ *Cathedral free, cloisters €3* ⊙ *Mon.–Thurs. and Sat. 10–6, Fri. 10–1.*

★ ❷ **Universidade Velha** (Old University). Coimbra University is one of the oldest academic institutions in Europe, founded in Lisbon in 1290 and transferred to the Royal Palace of Coimbra in 1537. It is still one of the country's most important universities, and it dominates the city both physically (taking up most of the hill in the center of the old town) and in numbers, with some 20,000 students. Built in 1634 as a triumphal arch, the **Porta Férrea** (⊠ Praça Porta Férrea) marks the entrance to the principal university courtyard and is adorned with the figures of the kings Dinis and João III. The courtyard itself holds a statue of Dom João III; it was during his reign that the university moved permanently to Coimbra. Walk to the far end of the courtyard for a view of the Mondego and across it to the Convento de Santa Clara-a-Nova. The double stairway rising from the courtyard leads to the graceful colonnade framing the Via Latina (Latin Way), the scene of colorful student processions at graduation time. Amid much pomp and ceremony, doctoral degrees are presented in the Ceremonial Hall's **Sala dos Capelos,** which is capped with a fine paneled ceiling and lined with a series of portraits of the kings of Portugal.

The 18th-century **clock-and-bell tower,** rising above the courtyard, is one of Coimbra's most famous landmarks. The bell, which summons students to class and in centuries past signaled a dusk-to-dawn curfew, is derisively called the *cabra* (she-goat; an insulting term common in other parts of Europe, particularly the Mediterranean, and used here to express the students' dismay at being confined to quarters). In the courtyard's southwestern corner is a building with four huge columns framing massive wooden doors: behind them is one of the world's most beautiful libraries, the baroque **Biblioteca Joanina.** Constructed in the early 18th century, it has three dazzling book-lined halls and a large painting of the monarch responsible for its construction—Dom João V. The library is open Monday through Saturday from 10 to noon and from 2 to 5; admission is €3. Next to the Biblioteca Joanina is the **Capela de São Miguel** (⊠ Largo da Porta Férrea ☎ 239/859900 ✉ Each monument €2.50, €4 for all 3 ⊙ Oct.–Apr. 4, daily 9:30–noon and 2–5; Apr. 5–Sept., daily 9–7:30), with a fine 16th-century Manueline portal opening onto the courtyard. Begun in 1517, the chapel's glories are nevertheless from the 18th century. Its baroque organ, mannerist main altar, and rococo side altars are stunning.

Although there are modern dormitories and apartments, many of the students, some because of tradition and some for economic reasons, prefer the old *repúblicas* (student cooperatives) scattered around the university quarter. Those who live in these ramshackle houses—with the bare minimum of creature comforts—share costs and chores, allowing themselves the one indulgence of a cook. The dwellings were hotbeds of anti-Salazar activity during the years of the dictatorship, and they historically attract people who lean to the left of the political spectrum.

Fado

THE WORD *FADO* means "fate" in Portuguese, and like the blues, fado songs are full of the fatalism of the poor and the deprived, laments of abandoned or rejected lovers, and tales of people oppressed by circumstances they cannot change. The genre, probably an outgrowth of a popular sentimental ballad form called the *modinha*, seems to have emerged some time in the first half of the 19th century in the poor quarters of Lisbon. At first, fado was essentially a music of the streets, a bohemian art form born and practiced in the alleys and taverns of Lisbon's Mouraria and Alfama quarters. By the end of the century, though, fado had made its way into the drawing rooms of the upper classes. Portugal's last king, Dom Carlos I, was a fan of the form, and a skilled guitar player to boot.

Strictly an amateur activity in its early years, fado began to turn professional in the 1930s with the advent of radio, recording, and the cinema. The political censorship exercised at the time by Portugal's long-lasting Salazar dictatorship also influenced fado's development. Wary of the social comments *fadistas* might be tempted to make in their lyrics, the authorities leaned on them heavily. Fado became increasingly confined to fado houses, where the singers needed professional licenses and had their repertoires checked by the official censor.

Nowadays, although the tradition of fado sung in taverns and bars by amateurs (called *fado vadio* in Portuguese) is still strong, the place to hear fado—the Lisbon form of it, at least—is in a professional fado house. Called *casas de fado*, the houses are usually restaurants, too, and some of them mix the pure fado with folk dancing shows. Casas de fado are frequented by Portuguese, so don't be wary of one being a tourist trap.

There are two basic styles of fado: Coimbra and Lisbon. In both forms the singer is typically accompanied by three, or sometimes more, guitarists, at least one of whom plays the Portuguese guitar, a pear-shaped 12-string descendant of the English guitar introduced into Portugal by the British port wine community in Porto in the 19th century. It is the Portuguese guitar that gives the musical accompaniment of fado its characteristically plaintive tone, as the musician plays variations on the melody. The other instruments are usually classical Spanish guitars, which the Portuguese call *violas*.

Although the greatest names of Lisbon fado have been women, and the lyrics often deal with racy, down-to-earth themes, Coimbra fado is always sung by men, and the style is more lyrical than that of the capital. The themes tend to be more erudite, too—usually serenades to lovers or plaints about the trials of love. Coimbra fado is also a largely amateur expression, typically sung by university students.

6

The repúblicas aren't open to the public, but if you can get an invitation to step inside one, don't pass up the opportunity for a glimpse of student life. The **República Bota-Abaixo** (✉ Rua São Salvador 6), near the Museu Machado de Castro, is a typical example of this Portuguese-style cooperative.

Where to Stay & Eat

$$$$ ✕ **Quinta da Romeira.** In a quiet residential area about a 10-minute drive
Fodor'sChoice toward Penacova, this friendly, family-run restaurant is worth the trip.
★ The decor is a bit baroque, with walls and curtains in vibrant reds and
pinks, but the regional food and the wine list are excellent, and you will
have a chance to mix with Coimbra high society. ⊠ *Quinta da Romeira,
lt. 56* ☎ *239/781301* ▤ *AE, MC, V* ☺ *No dinner Sun., no lunch Mon.*

★ **$$** ✕ **Dom Pedro.** The entrance to this restaurant—just a few steps along
the riverfront from the tourist office and next to a car dealer—is hardly
impressive, but inside it's a different story. A tasteful blend of arches,
tile, and wood makes this just the right place in which to enjoy the ex-
cellent chanfana and *açorda de mariscos* (a sort of bread porridge mixed
with eggs and mounds of fresh shellfish). There's an extensive list of Por-
tuguese wines, and the service is efficient without being stuffy. ⊠ *Av.
Emídio Navarro 58* ☎ *239/829108* ▤ *AE, MC, V.*

$-$$ ✕ **O Trovador.** Seasoned travelers know that the rule of thumb is to stay
away from restaurants near major sights. But O Trovador—just a step
away from the old cathedral—has good service and regional food as well
as a manor house decor. There is nightly fado in summer and on Friday
and Saturday the rest of the year. Reservations are essential for the music.
⊠ *Largo da Sé Velha 15–17* ☎ *239/825475* ▤ *MC, V* ☺ *Closed Sun.*

¢ ✕ **Democrática.** Wine barrels add a touch of rustic Portugal to the otherwise functional interior of this popular old establishment. The students
and locals who frequent it come for the food and the conviviality, however. The fare is simple and inexpensive. A tasty *caldo verde* (potato soup
with shredded cabbage and sausage) and fresh grilled fish make a typical meal. ⊠ *Travessa da Rua Nova 7* ☎ *239/823784* ▤ *MC, V*
☺ *Closed Sun.*

¢-$ ✕ **À Capella.** This cheap and cheerful student-run bar is in an atmos-
Fodor'sChoice pheric old chapel (Capela de Nossa Senhora da Vitória) in the Jewish
★ Quarter. If you want to eat dinner here, call in advance to reserve a table
and place a meal order. Otherwise there are drinks and bar food to ac-
company the live fado music every night at 11. ⊠ *Largo da Vitória–Rua
Corpo de Deus (E4)* ☎ *239/833985* ⌂ *Reservations essential* ▤ *MC,
V* ☺ *No lunch.*

¢-$ ✕ **Zé Manel.** This back-alley hole-in-the-wall has simple wooden tables
and chairs, an open kitchen with a jumble of pots and pans, and walls
plastered with an intriguing assortment of scribbled poems and cartoons.
The food is great and cheap, so don't pass up the chance for a meal here—
if you can get in (it's a favorite with students). For such a small place,
it has an amazing choice of dishes, including a wonderful *sopa da pedra*
(a rich vegetable soup served with hot stones in the pot to keep it warm).
⊠ *Beco do Forno 12* ☎ *239/823790* ⌂ *Reservations not accepted*
▤ *No credit cards* ☺ *Closed Sun. No dinner Sat.*

$$ ✕▥ **Astória.** The domed, triangular Astória faces the Rio Mondego
and has been a Coimbra landmark since its construction in 1927. If you
like your hotels with old-world charm and almost-state-of-the-art com-
forts, then you'll like this veteran. Choose between a river view and the
floodlighted rooftops of the old town. The wood-paneled L'Amphitryon
Restaurant ($$$) is one of the city's finest for Portuguese fare and

Buçaco wines. ⊠ *Av. Emídio Navarro 21, 3000-150* ☎ *239/853020* ⊕ *www.almeidahotels.com* ⊅ *75 rooms* ⚲ *Restaurant, room service, cable TV, Wi-Fi, bar, concierge, meeting rooms* ⊟ *AE, DC, MC, V* ❘O❘ *BP, CP, FAP, MAP.*

\$\$ ✕⊞ **Quinta das Lágrimas.** A former palace, this small Relais & Chateau
Fodor'sChoice hotel is on the grounds of the estate where Inês de Castro was suppos-
★ edly killed at the order of her husband's father. The public rooms are laden with antiques, and guest rooms are furnished simply but with patrician style. The hotel has opened a modern extension (ask for rooms in the old section if possible) and a luxurious, ultramodern spa. At the Arcadas da Capela restaurant (\$\$\$\$), the menu sometimes offers recipes dating from the 18th century and often uses homegrown herbs, fruits, and vegetables. It has an excellent list of Portuguese and foreign wines. ⊠ *Rua António Augusto Gonçalves, 3040-901* ☎ *239/802380* ⊕ *www. quintasdaslagrimas.com* ⊅ *35 rooms, 4 suites* ⚲ *Restaurant, cable TV, driving range, 9-hole golf course, tennis court, pool, spa, bar, ethernet, public Wi-Fi* ⊟ *AE, DC, MC, V* ❘O❘ *BP, CP, FAP, MAP.*

\$\$ ✕⊞ **Tivoli.** Favored by businesspeople, the Tivoli is sleek, outfitted with all the latest gadgets, and near the main railway station in Coimbra's modern business district, a bus ride from the center. The only thing lacking is a sense of place: once in your comfortable room, you could be anywhere, but it does have an indoor pool to make up for it. The Porta Férrea restaurant (\$\$\$\$) has excellent international and regional dishes and subdued surroundings. ⊠ *Rua João Machado 4–5, 3000-226* ☎ *239/826934* ⊕ *www.tivoli.pt* ⊅ *90 rooms, 10 suites* ⚲ *Restaurant, room service, in-room safes, minibars, cable TV, indoor pool, health club, bar, laundry service, business services, meeting rooms, car rental, Wi-Fi, ethernet* ⊟ *AE, DC, MC, V* ❘O❘ *BP, CP, FAP, MAP.*

\$–\$\$ ⊞ **Dona Inês.** This modern glass-and-marble hotel is on the banks of the Mondego, just a few minutes' walk from the business district. Although simply furnished in a rather bland, 1970s style, the rooms are light and airy. ⊠ *Rua Abel Dias Urbano 12, 3000-001* ☎ *239/855800* ⊕ *www. hotel-dona-ines.pt* ⊅ *72 rooms, 12 suites* ⚲ *Restaurant, cable TV, tennis court, bar, meeting rooms, Wi-Fi* ⊟ *AE, DC, MC, V* ❘O❘ *BP, FAP, MAP.*

\$ ⊞ **Tryp Coimbra.** As its glass facade suggests, this hotel, formerly the Meliá Confort, is contemporary, uncluttered, and equipped to meet all your needs. Rooms are done in beiges, browns, and oranges and have light-wood furniture. The hotel is in a quiet residential zone, a 20-minute walk from the city center. You can also hop on the bus that stops outside the hotel's door every half hour or so. ⊠ *Av. Armando Gonçalves 20, 3000-059* ☎ *239/480800* ⊕ *www.solmelia.com* ⊅ *126 rooms, 14 suites* ⚲ *Restaurant, room service, minibars, cable TV, sauna, bar, shops, meeting room, Wi-Fi* ⊟ *AE, DC, MC, V* ❘O❘ *BP.*

¢ ⊞ **Casa Pombal.** A Dutch woman runs this charming, laid-back pension in a town house on the hill in the heart of the old town. The rooms are simple and basic, but the rooftop views are stunning, and it is a friendly place where travelers chat freely in the small courtyard. The buffet breakfast is more generous than most. Book ahead. ⊠ *Rua das Flores 18, 3000-442* ☎ *239/835175* ⊅ *10 rooms, 3 with bath* ⊟ *AE, MC, V* ❘O❘ *BP.*

¢ ▥ **Ibis.** If you've been in one of this chain's properties, you've been in them all, but for the money, the service is hard to beat. This pleasant, comfortable hotel also has a prime riverfront location in the center of Coimbra, not too far from its more distinguished rivals. ✉ *Av. Emídio Navarro 70, 3000-150* ☎ *239/852130* ⊕ *www.accorhotels.com* 🛏 *110 rooms* ⚘ *Restaurant, cable TV, bar, parking (fee), no-smoking rooms* ▭ *AE, DC, MC, V* ⏍ *BP.*

Outdoor Activities

O Choupal, a pleasant wooded area along the river at the city's west end, was originally a poplar grove planted as a buffer against floods. The park has a place in Coimbra's history as a setting for student serenades and poetic meditation. It's now used more by joggers than romantics. East of the old city on Praça da República, **Parque de Santa Cruz** (Santa Cruz Park) is a pleasant mixture of luxuriant vegetation, ornate fountains, and meandering walking paths.

BOATING **Basófias** (✉ Parque Dr. Manuel Braga ☎ 096/604–0695 ⊕ www. basofias.com) offers leisurely 45-minute boat trips on the river, Tuesday–Sunday throughout the year. In winter, there are departures at 3, 4, and 5. In summer, they leave at 11, 3, 4, 5, and 6. Boats depart from the pier in Parque Dr. Manuel Braga, just upriver from the Santa Clara Bridge. The cost is €5 per person.

June through September, the student-run **O Pioneiro do Mondego** (☎ 239/ 478385) conducts kayak trips on the Rio Mondego. You're picked up at 10 AM in Coimbra and taken by minibus to Penacova, a peaceful little river town 25 km (15 mi) to the north. The descent takes about three hours, but plan on a day for the whole outing. Call the English-speaking staff for information and reservations. Trips cost €18 per person, including kayak rental.

HIKING/ **Trans Serrano** (☎ 235/778938 ⊕ www.transserrano.com) is an outdoor
KAYAKING and adventure company based near Lousã Mountain, about 20 km (12 mi) southeast of Coimbra. They will provide transport and English-speaking guides for nature hikes, cultural rambles, and kayaking in the surrounding countryside.

HORSEBACK You can arrange to horseback ride for an hour or two or take longer
RIDING equestrian excursions at the **Centro Hípico de Coimbra** (✉ Mata do Choupal ☎ 239/837695). It's on the right bank of the Rio Mondego, 2 km (1 mi) or so downstream from the Santa Clara Bridge.

TENNIS At the **Clube Tenis de Coimbra** (✉ Av. Urbano Duarte, Quinta da Estrela ☎ 239/403469 ⊕ www.atcoimbra.com), nonmembers pay a €6-per-hour court fee that covers two to four players. Rackets are available for free, but you'll have to bring your own balls or buy them from the club.

Shopping

In addition to the ubiquitous lace and cockerels, numerous stores in the city sell delicate blue-and-white Coimbra ceramics, most of them reproductions of 17th- and 18th-century patterns. This style is very distinct from the jolly earthenware associated with Portugal and can be difficult to find in other regions.

The Baixa district by the river is crowded with shops, selling everything from souvenirs to underwear and tablecloths. Major shopping streets are Rua Ferreira Borges, Praça do Comércio, Rua Eduardo Coelho, Rua Fernão de Magalhães, and Rua Visconde da Luz. The Mercado Municipal (Municipal Market) in Rua Olímpio Nicolau Rui Fernandes has a good collection of fruits and vegetables, but is not particularly charming or photogenic.

THE WESTERN BEIRAS

The western Beiras encompass shore and mountain, fishing villages and country towns, wine country and serene forest. Sights to see range from castles to cathedrals, monasteries to museums. You can also just lie in the sun by the Atlantic or sample the restorative powers of the air and mineral water in one of the inland towns.

On the gentle-faced coast, long, sandy beaches and sunbaked dunes stretch from Figueira da Foz, on the Mondego River estuary, north toward the great lagoon at Aveiro, where colorful kelp boats bob beyond fine, white-sand beaches. A bit farther inland are the vineyards of the Dão region, the Serra do Caramulo range, the lush forests of Buçaco, and the sedate spa resorts of Curia and Luso.

Conímbriga

★ **㉑** *16 km (10 mi) southwest of Coimbra.*

Conímbriga, one of the Iberian Peninsula's most important archaeological sites, began as a small settlement in Celtic or possibly pre-Celtic times. In 27 BC, during his second Iberian visit, the emperor Augustus established a Roman province that came to be called Lusitania. It was in this period that, as the Portuguese historian Jorge Alarcão wrote, "Conímbriga was transformed by the Romans from a village where people just existed into a city worth visiting." It still is.

One enters the bucolic setting via a brick reception pavilion. Pools and gardens surround the museum in which the site's Iron Age origins, heyday as a prosperous Roman town, and decline after the 5th-century barbarian conquests are chronicled. The museum also contains artifacts unearthed at the site; it's best to tour it after seeing the excavations.

At the site's entrance is a portion of the original Roman road that connected Olissipo (as Lisbon was then known) and the northern town of Braga. If you look closely, you can make out ridges worn into the stone by cart wheels. The uncovered area represents just a small portion of the Roman city, but within it are some wonderful mosaic floors. The 3rd-century House of the Fountains has a large, macabre mosaic depicting Perseus offering the head of Medusa to a monster from the deep, an example of the amazing Roman craftsmanship of the period.

Across the way is the Casa do Cantaber (House of Cantaber), named for a nobleman whose family was captured by invading barbarians in 465. A tour of the house reveals the comfortable lifestyle of Roman nobility at the time. Private baths included a *tepidarium* (hot pool) and *frigidarium* (cold pool). Remnants of the central heating system that was beneath the floor are also visible. Fresh water was carried 3 km (2 mi) by aqueduct from Alcabideque; parts of the original aqueduct can still be seen. A bus that leaves from Rua João de Ruão 18—in the center of Coimbra and close to the river—drops you off right by the entrance to the ruins. The one-way fare is €1.50. ⊠ *Condeixa-a-Velha* ☎239/941177 ⊕ *www.conimbriga.pt* 🎟 *Ruins and museum €3* ☉ *Ruins daily 10–6. Museum Mar.–Oct., Tues.–Sun. 10–6; June–Sept., Tues.–Sun. 9–8.*

Where to Stay & Eat

★ $$–$$$$ ✕ **O Cabritino.** This friendly local village restaurant is strongly recommended by locals, including many people who head out from Coimbra to eat here. It has excellent traditional Portuguese food, including its signature kid, after which the restaurant is named. ⊠ *Rua Francisco Lemos 9, Condeixa-a-Nova* ☎ *239/944111* ▤ *AE, DC, MC, V.*

★ $$ ✕▦ **Pousada de Santa Cristina.** This modern pousada in the delightful town of Condeixa-a-Nova makes an ideal base for visiting the Roman ruins at Conímbriga, 1 km (½ mi) to the south, and Coimbra, 15 km (9 mi) to the northeast. The attractive inn contains spacious, comfortably furnished rooms, and one of the area's best traditional restaurants ($$–$$$). ⊠ *Rua Francisco Lemos, Condeixa-a-Velha 3150-142* ☎*239/ 944025* ⊕ *www.pousadas.pt* ⤂ *45 rooms* ⚐ *Restaurant, cable TV, tennis court, pool, bar, Wi-Fi* ▤ *AE, DC, MC, V* ⓞ *BP.*

Montemor-o-Velho

㉒ *20 km (12 mi) west of Coimbra, 16 km (10 mi) northwest of Conímbriga.*

On a hill overlooking the fertile Mondego basin between Coimbra and Figueira da Foz, Montemor-o-Velho figures prominently in the region's history and legends. One popular story tells how the castle's besieged defenders cut the throats of their own families to spare them a cruel death at the hands of the Moorish invaders; many died before the attackers were repulsed. The following day the escaping Moors were pursued and thoroughly defeated. Legend has it that all those slaughtered at Montemor were resurrected but forever carried a red mark on their necks as a reminder of the battle.

The most scenic route from Coimbra to the castle, N341, runs along the Rio Mondego's south bank. The route through the village to the castle is extraordinarily complicated; park in the main square and walk up the rest of the way. The castle walls and tower are largely intact, though thanks to damage done during the Napoleonic invasions in 1811, little remains inside the impressive ramparts to suggest this was a noble family's home that once garrisoned 5,000 troops. Archaeological evidence indicates the hill has been fortified for more than 2,000 years. Although the castle played an important role in the long-standing conflict between the Christians and Moors, changing hands many times, the structure seen today is primarily of 14th-century origin. There are threads of the story of Inês de Castro here, for in January 1355 Dom Afonso IV, meeting in the castle with his advisers, made the decision to murder her. The two churches on the hill are also part of the castle complex; the Igreja de Santa Maria de Alcaçova dates from the 11th century and contains some well-preserved Manueline additions. ☎ *239/680380* 🎟 *Free* ⊗ *July–Sept., daily 10–9; Oct.–June, daily 10–5:30.*

Where to Eat

$$–$$$$ ✕ **O Ramalhão.** This charming restaurant in a restored 16th-century village house is decorated in a comfortable rustic style. The food is typical of the region, with plenty of fish and game, and there is an excellent wine list stuffed with local specialties. ⊠ *Rua Tenente Valadim 24* ☎ *239/689435* ▭ *AE, DC, MC, V* ⊗ *Closed Mon. No dinner Sun.*

Figueira da Foz

㉓ *14 km (8½ mi) west of Montemor-o-Velho.*

There are various theories as to the origin of the name Figueira da Foz. The consensus around the busy fishing harbor at this seaside resort favors the literal translation: "the fig tree at the mouth of the river." The belief is that when this was just a small settlement, oceangoing fishermen and traders from up the river would arrange to meet at the big fig tree to conduct their business. Although today there are no fig trees to be seen, the name has stuck.

Shortly before the turn of the last century, with the improvement of road and rail access, Figueira, with its long, sandy beach and mild climate, developed into a popular resort. Today, although the beach is little changed, a broad four-lane divided boulevard runs along its length. The town side is lined with the usual mélange of apartments, hotels, and restaurants, but the beachfront has been spared from development.

One of Figueira da Foz's more curious sights is the 18th-century **Casa do Paço** (Palace House), the interior of which is decorated with about 7,000 Delft tiles. These Dutch tiles were salvaged from a shipwreck at the mouth of the harbor in the late 1600s. ⊠ *Largo Prof. Vitor Guerra 4, around corner from main post office* ☎ *233/401320* 🎟 *Free* ⊗ *Weekdays 9:30–12:30 and 2–5.*

The triangular 17th-century **Fortaleza da Santa Catarina** (Santa Catarina Fortress), adjacent to the beachfront tennis courts, was occupied by the French during the early days of the Peninsular War.

Just 2 km (1 mi) north of Figueira, the town of **Buarcos** has retained some of the character of a Portuguese fishing village in spite of a heavy influx of tourists. Here colorfully painted boats are still pulled up onto the sandy beach, fishermen sit around mending nets, and many of the houses are coated in brightly colored tiles.

NEED A BREAK?

There are roughly a dozen brightly painted wooden-shack restaurants on the beach. These are wonderful places for fresh grilled fish or just a cold drink. With a large sign proclaiming its name, A Plataforma (⊠ Buarcos) is one of the best.

Palácio Sotto Mayor, an elegantly furnished, French-style manor house, was constructed as part of the wave of development in the late 19th and early 20th century that made Figueira da Foz a world-class resort. Long in the hands of one of Portugal's leading families, the building now belongs to the owners of the casino, and local gossip has it that it was "donated" as payment for gambling debts. Its collection includes paintings and fine furnishings. ⊠ *Rua Joaquim Sotto Mayor* ☎ *233/422121* ⊡ *€1* ☉ *Sept.–June, weekends 2–6; July and Aug., daily 2–6.*

> **GREAT VIEWS**
>
> **Farol de Cabo Mondego.** Drive out to the cape where the Cape Mondego Lighthouse stands for a wonderfully uncluttered view of the coastline. The road traces a loop and returns to Buarcos.

Centro de Artes e Espectáculos (CAE), an impressive arts center designed by Luís Marçal Grilo, sits among the open green spaces of the Parque das Abadias. Inside, the space is flexible enough to host a variety of performance events and also includes exhibition space used for arts, crafts, and photography, plus a cinema. ⊠ *Rua Abade Pedro* ☎ *233/407200* ⊕ *www.figueiradigital.com/cae* ⊡ *Exhibits free* ☉ *Gallery Tues.–Fri. 10–6, weekends and holidays 2–6.*

Where to Stay & Eat

$$–$$$$ ✕ **Teimoso.** Although the menu choices are varied, seafood—sold by weight—is what put this seaside restaurant on the map. Locals and visitors alike gather in the dining room, which has large picture windows, to order the shellfish that comes fresh from huge saltwater tanks. ⊠ *Estrada do Cabo Mondego, Buarcos* ☎ *233/402720* ⊟ *AE, MC, V* ☉ *Closed Wed.*

$–$$$ ✕ **Quinta de Santa Catarina.** The fish dishes at this popular restaurant—in a garden on the outskirts of the town—are outstanding. The menu varies depending on the catch of the day, but ask if one of the *tambril* (monkfish) dishes is available. The house also does a really good *rojões á minhota* (Minho-style sautéed pork). ⊠ *Rua Joaquim Sotto Mayor 92* ☎ *233/423468* ⊟ *AE, MC, V* ☉ *Closed Mon.*

★ $–$$ ✕ **O Peleiro.** In the quiet village of Paião, 10 km (6 mi) from Figueira, this restaurant—all wood and tiles—was once a tannery, and that's what the name means. Heavy on regional specialties, the menu includes *sopa da pedra* (vegetable soup)—a must. Grilled pork or veal on a spit are also excellent, and there's a good wine selection. ⊠ *Largo Alvideiro 5, Paião* ☎ *233/940120* ⊟ *AE, MC, V* ☉ *Closed Sun. and 1st 2 wks of May and Sept.*

$–$$ ✕▦ **Mercure.** Tour groups favor this five-story, 1950s-vintage hotel, perhaps because it overlooks a broad, sandy beach. Public and guest rooms are spacious and airy with sea views costing slightly more than city views. Seafront rooms have small balconies, and the large pool has a view of the beach. The restaurant ($–$$$) serves international dishes as well as regional specialties. ⊠ *Av. 25 de Abril 22, 3080-086* ☎ *233/403900* ⊕ *www.accorhotel.com* ⇨ *102 rooms* ♢ *Restaurant, minibars, cable TV, pool, piano bar, babysitting, meeting room, Wi-Fi* ⊟ *AE, DC, MC, V* ⊺❙ *EP.*

☾ **$–$$** ⊡ **Casa da Azenha Velha.** An attractively converted flour mill on a farm a few kilometers out of town, this is a perfect place for families, with a lovely pool, games room, and host of animals from peacocks to ostriches and horses. With breakfast and the sitting room in the main house, the charmingly decorated bedrooms are all in converted outbuildings. There is a separate restaurant, Azenha ($$), on the farm. ⊠ *Caceira de Cima, 3080* ☎ *233/425041* ⟿ *5 rooms, 1 apartment* ⚲ *Horseback riding, tennis court, recreation room; no room TVs* ▭ *No credit cards* ⦿I *BP.*

$ ⊡ **Aparthotel Atlântico.** In this high-rise tower at the beach, the accommodations—one-room apartments with basically equipped kitchenettes, sleeping either two or four people—are small but adequate, with functional and rather gloomy furnishings. Some apartments have wonderful sea views and balconies. There is a swimming pool in a nearby hotel which guests may use. ⊠ *Av. 25 de Abril 20, 3080-086* ☎ *233/408900* ⟿ *70 apartments* ⚲ *Kitchenettes, cable TV, pool, bar* ▭ *AE, DC, MC, V* ⦿I *BP.*

★ **$** ⊡ **Ibis.** On a quiet street just a five-minute walk from the beach, this small three-star hotel is in an attractive remodeled stone building built in 1914. It has all the modern appointments Ibis fans expect, and offers well-maintained, comfortable rooms. ⊠ *Rua da Liberdade 20, 3080-168* ☎ *233/422051* ⊕ *www.ibishotel.com* ⟿ *50 rooms* ⚲ *Cable TV, bar, lounge, Wi-Fi* ▭ *AE, DC, MC, V* ⦿I *BP.*

¢ ⊡ **Pensão Esplanada.** This turn-of-the-last-century corner house is across from the beach. The floors creak, and the rooms have seen better days, but are clean and the price is right. Ask for a room with a sea view. ⊠ *Rua Engenheiro Silva 86, 3080-150* ☎ *233/422115* ⟿ *19 rooms* ▭ *No credit cards* ⦿I *EP.*

Nightlife

The 1886 gaming room of the **Casino da Figueira** has frescoed ceilings, chandeliers, and a variety of table games, including blackjack and American and Continental roulette. Banks of slot machines lie in wait in a separate room. Within the same building there's also a belle epoque show room—site of a nightly revue at 11—as well as two cinemas, a piano bar which also has regular fado, and a restaurant. The shows are free, but drinks are expensive. Although dress is casual, jeans and T-shirts aren't permitted. The minimum age to enter is 18; bring your passport. ⊠ *Av. Bernado Lopes* ☎ *233/408400* ⊕ *www.casinofigueira. pt* ▭ *Gaming room free* ⊙ *Table games daily 5 PM–3 AM, slot machines daily 3 PM–3 AM.*

Outdoor Activities

Activity centers on the water here. The fishing for sea bream, bass, and mullet is good at Cape Mondego and at Costa de Lavos and Gala beaches, just south of town. Carp and barbel are caught in the Quiaios Lakes, northeast of Buarcos.

You can rent sailboards and other water-sports gear from most resorts on the shore of either Figueira or Buarcos. The Quiaios Lakes are also popular for windsurfing. Board surfers often find 10- to 12-foot waves at Quiaios Beach (just north of Cape Mondego).

BICYCLING   In summer, you can rent bikes and mopeds by the day and week at the **AFGA Travel Agency** (✉ Rua Miguel Bombarda 79 ☎ 233/402222).

BOATING   Throughout the year, you can do boat and kayaking trips on the Mondego River with **Capitão Dureza** (✉ Rua Dr. Francisco Nico, 4–3¼ Esq. ☎ 233/427772 ⊕ www.capitaodureza.com).

TENNIS   There are good hard courts at the **Figueira da Foz Tennis Club** (✉ Av. 25 de Abril 1 ☎ 233/422287 ⊕ www.tennisclubdafigueira.com). Fees— per hour, per court—are €4.50 for individuals and €5 for doubles with an extra €0.60 per hour for lighting in the evening. Lessons with a pro are available, and you can rent rackets.

EN ROUTE   The most scenic route north from Buarcos is a winding road that climbs through a wooded area to the little village of Boa Viagem (Good Journey). From here you can trace the course of the Rio Mondego as it flows into the sea and then head north, following a narrow road that runs along the sand dunes to Aveiro, or turn inland to Vagos and pick up N109 to Vista Alegre.

Vista Alegre

㉔ *50 km (31 mi) northeast of Buarcos.*

Portugal's finest china is produced here by a business that was started in 1824 as a sort of commune. Housing was furnished for workers from all parts of the country, training was provided by French master craftsmen, and the clay came from the nearby town of Ovar. Today the settlement's large, tree-filled square is bordered by the factory, a china museum and gift shop, and a small 17th-century chapel with the delicately carved tomb of the chapel's founder.

Through its collection of hundreds of magnificent pieces, the **Museu Histórico da Vista Alegre** (Vista Alegre Historical Museum) traces the development of fine porcelain at the factory from the 1850s to the present day. ✉ *Off N109* ☎ *234/320600* ▦ *Free* ☉ *Tues.–Fri. 9–6, weekends 9–12:30 and 2–5.*

Two kilometers (1 mi) northeast of Vista Alegre is the small town of Ílhavo, with its brightly tiled art nouveau houses and its **Museu do Mar** (Museum of the Sea). Housed in a drab concrete building next to a fish-processing plant, the museum has an interesting collection documenting the region's close relationship with the sea and its mainstay of cod fishing. It also has some good early pieces of Vista Alegre china. ✉ *Rua Vasco da Gama, Ílhavo* ☎ *234/329608* ⊕ *www. museumaritimo.cm-ilhavo.pt* ▦ *€2* ☉ *June–Sept., Tues.–Fri. 9:30–12:30 and 2:30–5:30, weekends 2–5; Nov.–Jan., Tues.–Fri. 10–noon and 2–5, weekends 2–5.*

Costa Nova

㉕ *About 5 km (3 mi) west of Ílhavo.*

Take the bridge just south of Aveiro across to Praia de Barra and you arrive at the ribbon of small resorts strung along the south sand spit of the Ria de Aveiro. Of them all, the most delightful is Costa Nova, which has decked itself out from top to toe in jazzy candy stripes. There are no actual sights, but the town is a pleasant place to walk along the lagoon, have lunch in one of a host of small seafood restaurants, and cross over to the Atlantic side of the dunes for fabulous beaches and rolling waves.

Aveiro

㉖ *5 km (3 mi) northeast of Vista Alegre.*

Aveiro's traditions are closely tied to the sea and to the Ria de Aveiro, the vast, shallow lagoon that fans out to the north and west of town. Salt is extracted from the sea here, and kelp is harvested for use as fertilizer. Swan-necked *moliceiros* (kelp boats) still glide along canals that run through Aveiro's center. In much of the older part of town, sidewalks and squares are paved with *calçada* (traditional Portuguese hand-laid pavement) in intricate nautical patterns. The town's most attractive buildings date from the latter half of the 17th century. In the last couple of years, a massive restoration project has transformed the old fishermen's quarter, just off the main canal, into a delightful little area of small bars and restaurants. A central market square hosts live entertainment in summer months.

★ The **Ria de Aveiro**, a 45-km (28-mi) hydralike delta of the Rio Vouga, was formed in 1575, when a violent storm caused shifting sand to block the river's flow into the ocean. Over the next two centuries, as more and more sand piled up, the town's prosperity and population tumbled, recovering only when a canal breached the dunes in 1808. Today the lagoon is a unique combination of fresh and salt water, narrow waterways, and tiny islands. Salt marshes and pine forests border the area, and the ocean side is lined with sandy beaches. In this tranquil setting, colorful moliceiros, low-slung, wide-bottom boats with steeply curved and brightly painted prows and sterns, glide gracefully along, their owners harvesting seaweed.

> **TIP**
>
> The best place for viewing Aveiro's boats is along the Canal Central and Canal de São Roque, which is crossed by several attractive bridges. On the banks, to the west of these canals, are checkerboard fields of gleaming white salt pans. The industry dates back to the 10th century when salt was used for preserving fish. The bacalhau is still a staple of the Portuguese menu.

The **Troncalhada Ecomuseum** is a salt pan where traditional methods of making salt are on display. ✉ *Canal das Pirâmides* ☎ *234/406300* ⊕ *www.cm-aveiro.pt* 🎫 *Free* ☽ *Daily dawn–dusk.*

This isn't just a fishermen's town. A royal presence is what gave impetus to Aveiro's economic and cultural development. In 1472 Princess Joana, daughter of King Afonso V, retired against her father's wishes to the **Convento de Jesus** (Convent of Jesus)—established by papal bull in 1461—where she spent the last 18 years of her life. After four centuries, the Convento de Jesus was closed in 1874 upon the death of its last nun. It now contains the **Museu de Aveiro,** which encompasses an 18th-century church whose interior is a masterpiece of baroque art. The elaborately gilded wood carvings and ornate ceiling by António Gomes and José Correia from Porto are among Portugal's finest. Blue-and-white azulejo panels have scenes depicting the life of Princess Joana, who was beatified in 1693 and whose tomb is in the lower choir. Her multicolor inlaid-marble sarcophagus is supported at each corner by delicately carved angels. Note also the 16th-century Renaissance cloisters, the splendid refectory lined with camellia-motif tiles, and the chapel of São João Evangelista (St. John the Evangelist). Items on display, many brought from other convents, include sculpture, coaches and carriages, artifacts, and paintings—including a particularly fine 15th-century portrait of Joana by Nuno Gonçalves. ⊠ *Av. de Santa Joana Princesa* 🕿 *234/423297* 🎫 *€2* ☉ *Tues.–Sun. 10–5:30.*

> **NEED A BREAK?** Facing the canal, just down Rua João Mendonça from the tourism office, are several little **coffeehouses** that specialize in regional *doces* (sweets) such as *ovos moles* (egg-yolk sweets) and biscuits and wafers of various sorts.

On the **Praça da República,** look for the graceful, three-story Câmara Municipal (Town Hall), which has a pointed bell tower. The plaza's 18th-century **Igreja da Misericórdia** (Mercy Church; ⊠ Praça da República 🕿 234/426732 🎫 Free ☉ Mon.–Sat. 9–12:30 and 2–5) has an imposing baroque portal; the walls of the otherwise sober interior are resplendent with blue-and-white azulejos. There's a small museum here with vestments and other religious articles.

At Aveiro's northeast edge, on Rua João de Moura, the **Estação de Caminhos de Ferro** (Railway Station) displays some lovely azulejo panels depicting regional traditions and customs. For restless youngsters, the large **Parque Municipal** (City Park), south of Aveiro's center on Avenida Artur Ravara, has a well-equipped playground.

Where to Stay & Eat

★ **$–$$** ✕ **A Barca.** Devoted diners pack this small, family-run restaurant to feast on its fish dishes. Although the style is homey, the cooking has won national gastronomical prizes. Try the *fritada de peixe* (fish fry) and the *amêijoas á bulhão pato* (clams in a garlic and coriander sauce). ⊠ *Rua José Rabumba 5* 🕿 *234/426024* 🖃 *MC, V* ☉ *Lunch and dinner Mon.–Fri. (1–3 and 7–10 PM). Closed Sat. and Sun.*

¢–$$ ✕ **O Mercantel.** This restaurant is the brainchild of Senhor Costa (a.k.a. Costa da Lota), who spent 13 years working at the nearby *lota* (fish market). His skill with fish is locally renowned, and people have applauded his change of career. Specialties include fresh fish, fish stew, and *arroz* *de marisco* (shellfish with rice). ⊠ *Rua António dos Santos Le 16* ☎ *234/428057* ▭ *AE, DC, MC, V* ☾ *Closed Mon.*

¢–$$ ✕ **Porterhouse.** Although the kitchen is good with fish and shellfish, its top dishes are *bife porterhouse* (a juicy, grilled, porterhouse steak) and *espeitada de carne* (skewered meat grill). A fireplace lends warmth and cheer when Atlantic mists are blowing in. ⊠ *Rua João Afonso 13/15* ☎ *234/428156* ▭ *V.*

$$ ✕⌂ **Pousada da Ria.** This two-story
FodorśChoice inn is about a 30-minute drive
★ north of Aveiro, near Torreira and midway down the narrow, pine-covered peninsula that separates the Ria da Aveiro from the sea. It's filled with and surrounded by plants and flowers, and the wood-and-tile entry has a loft seating area. Through picture windows in

BOAT TOURS
Although you can drive through the Ria on back roads, the best way to see the area is by boat. From mid-June to mid-September, ☾ **boat trips** around the lagoon depart throughout the day from the main canal, just in front of the tourism office. The fare is Å7 for one hour and Å20 for a two-hour ride, lunch included. During the low season, boats are available with advance booking. It may also be possible to have a one-hour tour in a moliceiro; tickets can be purchased at the tourist office, or ask at the quay. ⊠ *Canal Central* ☎ *234/838397* 🖙 *Å7 or Å20* ☾ *Mid-June–mid-Sept., daily.*

10 of the cheerfully furnished rooms you can watch the colorfully painted moliceiros glide along the water. The spacious restaurant ($$–$$$) has equally lovely views, a summer terrace, and a highly recommended *ensopada de cabrito* (kid stew). ⊠ *Murtosa 3870-301* ☎ *234/860180* ⊕ *www.pousadas.pt* 🖙 *19 rooms* ⚿ *Restaurant, tennis court, pool, bar* ▭ *AE, DC, MC, V* ⏉ *BP.*

$–$$ ✕⌂ **Hotel Imperial.** The efficient, modern Imperial is in the heart of Aveiro. A Best Western hotel, the rooms are modern and comfortable; some on the upper floors have small balconies and nice views. The restaurant ($$–$$$$) is luxurious without being ostentatious and is popular with the business community. Specialties include *enguias fritas* (fried eels) and *bacalhau com natas* (dried salt cod with cream). The breakfast buffet is the best in town. ⊠ *Rua Dr. Nascimento Leitão, 3810-108* ☎ *234/ 380150* ⊕ *www.hotelimperial.pt* 🖙 *100 rooms, 8 suites* ⚿ *Restaurant, minibars, cable TV, 2 bars, laundry service, meeting rooms, ethernet* ▭ *AE, DC, MC* ⏉ *BP.*

★ $ ⌂ **Arcada.** At the foot of the bridge over the central canal, the location of this arched, four-story building couldn't be more convenient. It's a comfortable, family-owned classic with old-fashioned, no-frills comfort. Furnishings in the well-kept rooms vary from traditional Portuguese to blond-wood 1950s pieces. The lounge and bar recall a gentlemen's club, albeit one that's slightly past its prime. ⊠ *Rua Viana do Castelo*

4, 3800-275 ☎ 234/421885 ↘ 43 rooms, 6 suites ⚐ Cable TV, bar, lounge ⊟ AE, DC, MC, V ◉ BP.

$ ⊡ **Hotel As Américas.** Built around a 1920s art nouveau house that now holds the bar, breakfast room, and games room, this is essentially an unremarkable modern hotel with well-equipped rooms in an attached modern building. ⊠ Rua Engenheiro Von Hafe 20–22, 3800-176 ☎ 234/384640 ⊕ www.hotelasamericas.com ↘ 68 rooms, 2 suites ⚐ In-room safes, minibars, cable TV, ethernet, billiards, bar, lounge, meeting room ⊟ AE, MC, V ◉ BP.

¢ ⊡ **Residencial do Alboi.** This small, modern hotel is on a quiet backstreet a few blocks from the main canal. Rooms are comfortable, the bar is attractive, and the breakfasts are excellent. ⊠ Rua da Arrochela 6, 3810-052 ☎ 234/380390 ⊕ www.residencial-alboi.com ↘ 22 rooms ⚐ Cable TV, bar ⊟ AE, MC, V ◉ EP.

¢–$ ⊡ **Hotel Mercure.** Another link in the massive French chain, this Mecure stands out in its converted 1930s art deco mansion with a red-tiled roof and balconies. A fat palm tree sits in front, and you enter through an old wooden door. It's near the railway station, is pleasant and well run, and has a good restaurant. The rooms are spacious and pristine. ⊠ Rua Luis Gomes de Carvalho 23, 3800-211 ☎ 234/404401 ⊕ www.mercure.com ↘ 49 rooms ⚐ Restaurant, room service, in-room safes, minibars, cable TV, bar, no-smoking rooms, some pets allowed, Wi-Fi, parking (fee) ⊟ AE, MC, V ◉ BP.

Outdoor Activities

There's no swimming off the lagoon in town, as it's built up with ports, harbors, seafood farms, and salt pans. Within a 20-minute drive you can reach excellent beaches that stretch for miles along the massive sand spit to the north and south of town.

BICYCLING Near the tourist office on Rua João Mendonça and at other spots around town you'll find racks with bikes that you can use to tour Aveiro and its surroundings. To free a bike, insert a €1 coin as you would a shopping cart. When you return the bike, you get your money back. In case you were wondering, there are tracker devices on the bikes to ensure their return.

HORSEBACK RIDING **Escola Equestre de Aveiro** (⊠ Quinta do Chão d'Agra, Vilarinho ☎ 234/912108 ⊕ www.escolaequestreaveiro.com), about 6 km (4 mi) north of Aveiro on N109, gives classes for all levels and offers rides (reservations are necessary) into the wetlands around Aveiro. Prices range from €10 an hour for a group trek to €20 an hour for a single rider.

Shopping

The **Armazéms de Aveiro** (⊠ Rua Conselheiro Luís de Magalhães 1 ☎ 234/422107) sells leading Portuguese brands of high-quality ceramics and china, including Vista Alegre and Quinta Nova. The staff will ship purchases as well. The mall **Forum Aveiro** (⊠ Rua Batalhão Caçadores 10 ☎ No phone), beside the main canal in the center of town, has dozens of little shops and restaurants.

CLOSE UP

Beaches

THERE'S A VIRTUALLY CONTINUOUS STRETCH of good sandy beach along the entire coastal strip known as the Beira Litoral—from Praia de Leirosa in the south to Praia de Espinho in the north. One word of caution: if your only exposure to Portuguese beaches has been the Algarve's southern coast, be careful here. West-coast beaches tend to have heavy surf and strong undertows and riptides. If you see a red or yellow flag, do *not* go swimming. The water temperature on the west coast is usually a few degrees cooler than it is on the south coast.

You have your choice of beaches. There are fully equipped resorts, such as Figueira da Foz and Buarcos, or if you prefer sand dunes and solitude, you can lay your mat down at any one of the beaches farther north. Just point your car down one of the unmarked roads between Praia de Mira and Costa Nova and head west. The beaches at Figueira da Foz, Tocha, Mira, and Furadouro (Ovar) are well suited to children; they all have lifeguards and have met the European Union standards for safety and hygiene.

6

Ovar

㉗ *24 km (15 mi) north of Aveiro; head north on N109 from Aveiro to Estarreja, then turn west and follow N109-5 through quiet farmlands, and after crossing the bridge over the Ria, continue north on N327 to Ovar.*

At Ria de Aveiro's northern end, Ovar is a good jumping-off point for the string of beaches and sand dunes to the north. This small town, with its many tiled houses, is a veritable showcase of azulejos. The **Câmara Municipal** (Town Hall), built in the 1960s, is adorned with some unusually beautiful multicolor tile panels. The exterior of the late-17th-century **Igreja Matriz** (Parish Church) is completely covered with blue-and-white azulejos. ⊠ *Av. do Bom Reitor and Rua Gomes Freire* ☎ *No phone* ⊙ *Mon.–Sat. 9–12:30 and 2:30–5:30.*

The small **Museu de Ovar**, in an old house in the town center, has displays of traditional tiles, regional handicrafts, and costumes and tableaux re-creating scenes from provincial life in the past. There's also a small collection of mementos of popular 19th-century novelist Júlio Dinis, a native of Ovar and its most famous son. ⊠ *Rua Heliodoro Salgado 11* ☎ *256/572822* ⊠ *€1.50* ⊙ *Mon.–Wed. 9:30–12:30 and 2:30–5:30, Sat. 9:30–12:30.*

The fairy-tale-like **Castelo de Santa Maria da Feira** (Castle of Santa Maria da Feira) is 8 km (5 mi) northeast of Ovar. Its four square towers are crowned with a series of conical turrets in a display of Gothic architecture more common in Germany or Austria than in Portugal. Although the original walls date from the 11th century, the present structure is the result of modifications made 400 years later. From atop the towers you can make out the sprawling outlines of the Ria de Aveiro.

✉ *Largo do Castelo* ☎ *No phone* 🎫 *€1.50* ⊘ *Tues.–Sun. 9–12:30 and 2–6.*

Viseu

28 *82 km (51 mi) southeast of Ovar, 71 km (44 mi) southeast of Aveiro; you can take the scenic but twisting and bone-jarring N227 across the Serra da Gralheira or the smoother, faster, but much less interesting IP1 and IP5.*

A thriving provincial capital in one of Portugal's prime wine-growing districts, the Dão region, Viseu has remained a country town in spite of its obvious prosperity. Its newer part is comfortably laid out, with parks and wide boulevards that radiate from a central traffic circle.

The tree-lined **Praça da República,** also known as the Rossío, is framed at one end by a massive azulejo mural depicting scenes of country life. The heroic figure in bronze, standing sword in hand, is Prince Henry the Navigator, the first duke of Viseu. The stately building across from the tile mural is the **Câmara Municipal.** Walk inside to admire the colorful Aveiro tiles and fine woodwork, and be sure to see the courtyard. Just to the south of the square, a graceful stairway leads to the 18th-century, baroque Igreja dos Terceiros de São Francisco (Church of the Brotherhood of St. Francis), behind which is a large, wooded park with paths and ponds.

★ One of Portugal's most impressive squares, the **Largo da Sé,** is bounded by three imposing edifices—the cathedral, the palace housing the Museu de Grão Vasco, and the palacelike Igreja da Misericórdia.

The Sé (🎫 Cathedral free, museum €1.50 ⊘ Cathedral daily 9:30–12:30 and 2–5:30; museum Tues. 2–6, Wed.–Sun. 10–6), a massive stone structure with twin square bell towers, lends the plaza a solemn air. Construction on this cathedral was started in the 13th century and continued off and on until the 18th century. Inside, massive Gothic pillars support a network of twisted, knotted forms that reach across the high, vaulted roof; a dazzling, gilded, baroque high altar contrasts with the otherwise somber stone. The lines of the 18th-century upper level are harsh when compared with the graceful Italianate arches of the 16th-century lower level. The walls here are adorned with a series of excellent azulejo panels that depict various religious motifs. To the right of the mannerist main portal is a double-tier cloister, which is connected to the cathedral by a well-preserved Gothic-style doorway. The cathedral's Sacred Art Museum has reliquaries from the 12th and 13th centuries.

If the Sé looks more like a fortress, the white, rococo **Igreja da Misericórdia** (Church of Mercy; 🎫 €1.50 ⊘ Tues. 2–6, Wed.–Sun. 10–6), across from it looks like a residential palace. The fussy ornamentation around the windows and unusual entranceway are more impressive than the interior.

★ Housed in a palatial former seminary beside the cathedral, the lovely **Museu Grão Vasco** (Grão Vasco Museum) originally created to display the works of 16th-century local boy Grão Vasco, who became Portugal's most famous painter. In addition to a wonderful collection of altarpieces by him and his students, the museum has a wide-ranging collection of other art and objects, from Flemish masterpieces to Portuguese faience, and Oriental furniture. ⊠ *Paço dos Trê Escalões, Largo da Sé* ☎ *232/422049* ⊕ *www.ipmuseus.pt* ✉ *€3, free Sun. until 2* ⊙ *Tues. 2–6, Wed.–Sun. 10–6.*

★ The square **Praça de Dom Duarte** is one of those rare places where just the right combination of rough stone pavement, splendid old houses, wrought-iron balconies, and views of an ancient cathedral (it's just below the Largo da Sé) come together to produce a magical effect. Try to be here at night, when the romance is further enhanced by the soft glow of the streetlights. There's one restaurant and one café to dip into.

> ### MORE THAN MEETS THE EYE
>
> The history of Viseu actually goes back a lot farther than the medieval center suggests, with a thriving Iron Age settlement here before the Romans arrived. There are a number of prehistoric dolmens scattered across the surrounding countryside. A statue of a warrior stands on a rock at the edge of town, on the road to Aveiro. It's a monument to **Viriáto**, the leader of the Lusitanian resistance to the Roman invasion in the 2nd century BC. Some historians believe this was the site of his encampment.

Where to Stay & Eat

★ $–$$$ ✕ **O Cortiço.** Viseu's most celebrated restaurant is known for the sometimes comical names of its dishes as well as for its intelligent use of old local recipes. Try the *coelho bêbedo* (drunk rabbit), which is rabbit stewed in red wine, or the bacalhau *podre* (rotten), which is actually a savory dish of salt cod braised in a tomato-and-wine sauce. ⊠ *Rua Augusto Hilário 47* ☎ *232/423853* ⊟ *AE, DC, MC, V.*

$$ ⊞ **Montebelo.** The facade of this unusual high-rise is made up of cylinder-like walls of glass separated by bone-white supports. The massive complex spreads itself out horizontally as well. As modern as the structure is, the interior has classic furnishings and nature is not forgotten, with plenty of landscaped lawn. Public areas and guest rooms have brass details, rich wood furniture, and luxurious fabrics and carpets in deep reds, golds, and greens. ⊠ *Urbanização Quinta do Bosque, 3510-020* ☎ *232/420000* ⊕ *www.hotelmontebelo.pt* ➳ *84 rooms, 16 suites* △ *Restaurant, in-room safes, minibars, cable TV, golf privileges, tennis court, pool, health club, hot tub, sauna, piano bar, Wi-Fi, parking (fee)* ⊟ *AE, DC, MC, V* ⦿ *BP.*

$ ⊞ **Avenida.** Owned by a keen collector of African and Chinese antiques, which are liberally scattered across the public and guest rooms, this charming small town house has the eclectic feel of a bazaar. Deep turquoises and terra-cottas are redolent of a Moroccan market. The bedrooms are small but interestingly decorated, some with antique beds and Portuguese antiques. The breakfast buffet is more generous than most. ⊠ *Av. Alberto Sampaio 1, 3510-030* ☎ *232/423432* ⊕ *www.turism. net/avenida* ➳ *30 rooms* △ *Cable TV* ⊟ *AE, DC, MC, V* ⦿ *BP.*

Fodor'sChoice ★

6

★ $ 🏨 **Grão Vasco.** For many years the Grão Vasco was Viseu's leading hotel. Although it has been overtaken by newer properties, it is still a good choice and a great value. Its location in a wooded park just steps from the main square gives you the convenience of the city and the quiet of the countryside. Many of the rooms have balconies that look out on an oval pool. The restaurant serves a wide variety of principally Portuguese dishes; if it's in season, try the wild boar. ⊠ *Rua Gaspar Barreiros, 3510-032* ☎ *232/423511* ↪ *170 rooms, 3 suites* ⚭ *Restaurant, in-room safes, minibars, cable TV, pool, bar, babysitting, meeting rooms* ▭ *AE, DC, MC, V* ❙⊙❙ *EP.*

¢ 🏨 **Bela Vista.** This comfortable *residencial* (accommodation in what was once a private home) is on a quiet street about 1½ km (1 mi) from the center of town. The price is affordable, breakfast is included, and the trade-off is small, unexciting rooms. ⊠ *Rua Alexandre Herculano 510, 3510-035* ☎ *232/422026* ↪ *44 rooms* ⚭ *Parking* ▭ *No credit cards* ❙⊙❙ *BP.*

Shopping
Narrow Rua Direita, in the old part of town, is lined with shops displaying locally made wood carvings, pottery, and wrought iron. The surrounding rural areas, particularly north toward Castro Daire, are well known for their strong tradition of linen, basketry, and heavy woolen goods. The lengthily named **Fundação da Câ Municipal de Viseu para a Protecção do Artesanato** (⊠ Casa da Ribeira ☎ 232/429761) is the city-center sales outlet for many of these crafts.

Where to Stay
★ $ 🏨 **Casa de Darei.** This delightful agro-tourism property is on a working vineyard along the banks of the River Dão and next to a shallow lake. Despite the rural setting, spacious rooms have a modern boutique hotel style with cool, crisp, strong earth colors. Apartments can accommodate three to eight people. Indulge in the Casa's own delicious wines (tastings and tours available), homegrown fruits and vegetables, and activities that include anything from canoeing, fishing, and riding to helping with the harvest. ⊠ *Mangualde-Penalva exit off IP5, 2½ km (1½ mi) toward Penalva, Mangualde 3530-107* ☎ *252/613200* ⊕ *www.casadedarei.pt* ↪ *9 rooms, 4 apartments* ⚭ *Kitchens, fishing, horseback riding* ▭ *AE, DC, MC, V* ❙⊙❙ *BP.*

Caramulo
㉙ *24 km (15 mi) southwest of Viseu.*

In the early part of the last century, when tuberculosis was rife, people

---

WINE ROAD

Driving to Caramulo from Viseu takes you through the heart of the Dão region. Here you'll see many vineyards, some carefully terraced. The wines pressed from these grapes are some of Portugal's finest. The **Gabinete da Rota do Vinho Dão** (Office of Dão Wine Routes; ☎ 232/410060) can provide lists of vineyards and recommend routes to charming wine-growing villages such as Caramulo and Mangualde. **Mangualde,** about 15 km (9 mi) southeast of Viseu on the N234, has a number of fine historic buildings, including the magnificent 18th-century **Palácio dos Condes de Anadia.**

came here for the beneficial effects of the fresh mountain air. Although tuberculosis is no longer the problem it once was, Caramulo hasn't lost its appeal. People still come to enjoy the heather-clad wooded slopes and to walk through the parks and gardens. Mineral water bottled at the nearby spring is popular throughout the country.

The unusual museum in the **Museu do Caramulo–Fundação Abel de Lacerda** (Caramulo Museum–Abel de Lacerda Foundation) was established and supported by a local doctor. Its varied collections, all from donations, include jewels, ceramics, and a fine assortment of paintings that represent such diverse artists as Salvador Dali, Pablo Picasso, and Grão Vasco. Next door to the Fundação Abel de Lacerda is the **Museu do Automóvel,** whose collection of perfectly restored antique cars includes such rare items as a 1902 Darracq. Also on exhibit are vintage bicycles and motorcycles. ⊠ *Av. Abel de Lacerda* ☎ *232/861270 (both museums)* ⊕ *www.museu-caramulo.net* ⊠ *€6 (valid for both museums)* ⊙ *June–Sept., daily 10–1 and 2–6; Oct.–May, weekdays 10–1 and 2–5.*

CARAMULINHO – From the trailhead on N230-3 near the Hotel Caramulo, it's about a 30-minute climb to Caramulinho, at an elevation of 3,500 feet. Here at the tip of the Serra do Caramulo, you can look out across a vast panorama, taking in the coastal plain to the west and the Serra da Estrela to the southeast.

OFF THE BEATEN PATH

Where to Stay & Eat

★ **$$** ✕▦ **Hotel do Caramulo.** This four-star hotel and spa at nearly 3,000 feet above sea level is not the world's most glamorous building, but it is designed so that 43 of the 87 rooms have panoramic views from their balconies. The rooms are a bit impersonal, but have all the usual comforts, and there is a good restaurant ($$–$$$) and bar. The real draws, however, are the excellent spa and health center and the great outdoors, with a range of energetic activities from hill-walking to rock-climbing within the Serra do Caramulo on offer. ⊠ *Av. Dr. Abel Lacerda, 3475-031* ☎ *232/860100* ⊕ *www.hoteldocaramulo.pt* ⟰ *83 rooms, 4 suites* ⟁ *Restaurant, in-room safes, minibars, cable TV, in-room VCRs, 2 pools (1 indoor), fitness classes, gym, hot tub, sauna, spa, steam room, squash, bar, dance club, Wi-Fi* ⊟ *AE, DC, MC, V.*

★ **$** ✕▦ **Estalagem do Caramulo.** The exterior of this inn is reminiscent of an alpine chalet, which seems appropriate given this small pousada's location in the Serra do Caramulo. In the reception area, Arraiolos carpets hang on knotty-pine walls. The lounge, restaurant, and bar are divided by a see-through partition, and there's an inviting open fireplace. Rooms are small but adequate, and each has a marble bathroom and a small balcony. Views throughout the property are exceptional. The restaurant's ($–$$) fare is country style, with chanfana *de borrego* (roast lamb, instead of the more usual kid, with red wine) as one of the favorites. ⊠ *1 km (½ mi) from Caramulo on N230* ⊕ *Guardão 3475-031* ☎ *232/861291* ⟰ *12 rooms* ⟁ *Restaurant, pool, badminton, bar, lounge* ⊟ *AE, DC, MC, V* ❍ *BP.*

Águeda

③ *25 km (15 mi) west of Caramulo, 18 km (11 mi) southeast of Aveiro.*

This center for the production of paper products has an attractive parish church and several well-preserved manor houses. Águeda itself isn't particularly appealing, although it is worth visiting the richly decorated little **Igreja da Santa Eulalia,** which is dedicated to the local patron saint. There are a number of prehistoric and Roman sites in the surrounding area. What really makes a visit to this area worthwhile is the peaceful rolling fields and woodlands of the surrounding countryside.The **Museu Ferroviário** (Railway Museum) is 10 km (6 mi) north of Águeda on IC2 in the village of Macinhata do Vouga. Part of the village railway station, the museum's exhibits include four steam locomotives dating from 1886. ⊠ *Estação de Caminhos de Ferro* ☎ *222/002723* ⊠ *€1.50* ⊘ *Mon.–Sat. 9–1 and 2–5.*

Where to Stay & Eat

★ $ ✕▦ **Estalagem da Pateira.** The name *pateira* comes from *pato,* the Portuguese word for "duck." This modern inn is on Portugal's largest lake, which was the private duck reserve of King Manuel I in the 16th century. If you fancy the idea of being serenaded to sleep by croaking frogs after watching a lake sunset, this place—7 km (4½ mi) west of Águeda off Route 333—is for you. The restaurant ($–$$) serves some excellent fare, including a very good bacalhau. ⊠ *Rua da Pateira 84, Fermentelos 3750-439* ☎ *234/721219* ⊕ *www.pateira.com* ⇶ *58 rooms, 1 suite* ⟐ *Restaurant, café, 3 pools (1 indoor), gym, sauna, boating, bar, dance club* ⊟ *AE, DC, MC, V* |◎| *FAP, MAP.*

Curia

③ *16 km (10 mi) south of Águeda, 20 km (12 mi) north of Coimbra.*

This small but popular spa is in the heart of the Bairrada region, an area noted for its fine wines and roast suckling pig. The waters, with their high calcium and magnesium-sulfate content, are said to help in the treatment of kidney disorders. For the last 100 years, the spring has been contained within an elaborate treatment center that has provided rejuvenating pampering and medical treatment side by side. Curia is a quiet retreat of shaded parks—with a small lake and grand belle epoque hotels—just a half hour's drive from the clamor of the summer beach scene. Coimbra, Aveiro, Figueira da Foz, the Serra do Caramulo, and Viseu are all within an hour's drive.

Where to Stay & Eat

★ $–$$ ✕ **Pedro dos Leitões.** Of the several restaurants specializing in suckling pig, "Suckling Pig Pete" is the most popular. Having a meal here is a near must in this area. The size of the parking lot is a dead giveaway that this is no intimate bistro, and Pedro's spitted pigs pop out of the huge ovens at an amazing rate, especially in summer. In spite of the volume, quality is maintained. The restaurant lies about 3 km (2 mi) from Curia. ⊠ *Rua Alvaro Pedro 1 (N1), Mealhada* ☎ *231/209950* ⊟ *AE, MC, V* ⊘ *Closed Mon. and 2 wks in late June–early July.*

★ **$–$$** ✕🏨 **Grande Hotel da Curia.** One of the fanciest hotels in the vicinity of Curia's thermal springs was built in the 1890s. Everything seems polished to perfection, from the marble floors to the mahogany furniture and paneling; fine carpets and fabrics abound. The restaurant ($$–$$$), with its wood-plank floors and soft draperies, typifies the subdued elegance throughout. The menu is primarily international, with a few regional specialties. Medical staff in the state-of-the-art health center can help you with diet and exercise programs. ⊠ *Curia* ⏍ *Tamengos 3780-541* ☎ *231/515720* ⊕ *www.grandehoteldacuria.com* ⤳ *80 rooms, 6 suites* ♺ *Restaurant, in-room safes, cable TV, 2 pools (1 indoor), health club, hot tub, massage, sauna, Turkish bath, bar, library, meeting rooms, Wi-Fi* ⊟ *AE, DC, MC, V* ⍉ *BP.*

$ 🏨 **Quinta de São Lourenço.** This delightful 18th-century manor—surrounded by vineyards and pine groves—is in the tiny village of São Lourenço do Bairro. The house has six comfortable-size bedrooms with wooden floors, period furniture, and modern bathrooms. There's also a small apartment. Meals can be arranged upon request. ⊠ *3 km (2 mi) from Curia on N1 to Mugofores, São Lourenço do Bairro 3780-179* ☎ *231/528168* ⤳ *6 rooms, 1 apartment* ♺ *Billiards, bar, library, recreation room* ⊟ *No credit cards* ⍉ *BP.*

Luso

③② *8 km (5 mi) southeast of Curia, 18 km (11 mi) northeast of Coimbra.*

This charming town, built around the European custom of "taking the waters," is on the main Lisbon–Paris train line, in a little valley at the foot of the Buçaco Forest. Like Curia, it has an attractive park with a lake, elegant hotels, and medicinal waters. Slightly radioactive and with a low-sodium and high-silica content, the water—which emerges from the Fonte de São João, a fountain in the center of town—is said to be effective in the treatment of kidney and rheumatic disorders.

Where to Stay & Eat

¢–**$** ✕ **O Cesteiro.** At the western edge of town just past the Luso bottling plant, this popular local restaurant serves simple fare that includes several types of salt cod, roast kid, and fresh fish. ⊠ *Rua Dr. Lúcio Abranches* ☎ *231/939360* ⊟ *MC, V.*

$$ ✕🏨 **Grande Hotel de Luso.** This hulking, yellow-stucco complex, constructed in 1945, is a tad bombastic, but the interior is luxurious and serene. Rooms are large and airy, with modern, tiled bathrooms; some bedrooms have terraces that overlook the Olympic-size pool. The hotel is adjacent to the park and renowned Luso Spa, with its many therapeutic programs. The restaurant ($–$$) serves a good selection of international and regional foods in a pleasant environment with a view of the pool. The management also has bikes to rent. ⊠ *Rua Dr. Cid de Oliveira, 3050-230* ☎ *231/937937* ⊕ *www.hoteluso.com* ⤳ *143 rooms* ♺ *Restaurant, miniature golf, 2 pools (1 indoor), sauna, bar, bicycles, billiards, Wi-Fi, dance club* ⊟ *AE, DC, MC, V* ⍉ *BP.*

★ **$** 🏨 **Vila Duparchy.** As you pass through the old gate and go up the long, curved, tree-lined driveway, you'll soon realize this is no ordinary hotel. The two-story stucco house was built in the late 19th century but has been receiving guests only since 1988. Upstairs are just six rooms; each has a fireplace, a modern bath, and period furnishings. On the ground floor are three comfortable sitting rooms, which you share with the owners (who speak English) and other guests. The spacious grounds are full of trees and flowers. Evening meals can be arranged in advance. ⊠ *Rua José Duarte Figueiredo 148, just outside Luso on E234 to Mealhada, 3050-235* ☎ *231/930790* ◻ *6 rooms* ⌂ *Pool, recreation room* ▤ *AE, MC, V* ⦿ *BP.*

Buçaco

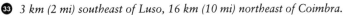 **33** *3 km (2 mi) southeast of Luso, 16 km (10 mi) northeast of Coimbra.*

In the early 17th century, the head of the Order of Barefoot Carmelites, searching for a suitable location for a monastery, came upon an area of dense virgin forest. Having rejected an offer to settle in Sintra because there were too many distractions, he chose instead the tranquil forest of Buçaco. A site was selected halfway up the slope of the greenest hill, and by 1630 the simple stone structure was occupied. To preserve their world of isolation and silence, the monks built a wall enclosing the forest. Their only link with the outside world was through one door facing toward Coimbra, which one of them watched over. The Coimbra Gate, still in use today, is the most decorative of the eight gates constructed since that time.

So concerned were the Carmelites for the well-being of their forest that they obtained a papal bull in 1643 calling for the excommunication of anyone caught cutting down even a single tree. They planted a number of exotic varieties, and the forest flourished. Attracted by the calm and tranquility of the forest, individual monks left the monastery to be alone with God and nature. They built simple hermitages, where they would stay, without human companionship, for several months at a time. You can still see vestiges of these hermitages as you walk through the forest.

In 1810 this serenity was shattered by a fierce battle in which the Napoleonic armies under Massena were repulsed by Wellington's British and Portuguese troops. An obelisk marks the site of the Battle of Buçaco, a turning point in the French invasion of the Iberian Peninsula. In 1834, owing to the rise in anticlerical sentiment and the country's need for money to rebuild the economy after the war of succession between the two sons of King John VI, the government issued a decree ordering the confiscation of all monasteries and convents. The monastery was virtually abandoned.

In the early years of the 20th century, much of the original structure was torn down to construct—under the supervision of Italian architect Luigi Manini—an opulent, multiturreted, pseudo-Manueline extravaganza that was to be a royal hunting lodge. With the exception of one brief vacation and a dubious romantic fling, this "simple hunting lodge" was never used by the royal family. It became a prosperous hotel—now the Palace Hotel do Buçaco—and in the years between the two world wars it was one of Europe's most fashionable vacation addresses. Tales told in local villages have it that during World War II, when neutral Portugal was a hotbed of espionage, Nazi agents ensconced in the tower rooms beamed radio signals to submarines off the coast. Today many come to Buçaco just to view this unusual structure, to stroll the shaded paths that wind through the forest, and to climb the hill past the Stations of the Cross to the Alta Cruz (High Cross), their efforts rewarded by a view that extends all the way to the sea.

The small **Museu Militar de Buçaco** (Buçaco Military Museum) houses uniforms, weapons, and various memorabilia from the Battle of Buçaco. ⊠ *On the left of N234, just outside forest grounds* ☎ *231/939310* 🎫 *€1* ⊙ *June–Sept., Tues.–Sun. 10–5:30; Oct.–May, Tues.–Sun. 10–4.*

Where to Stay & Eat

★ **$–$$$** ✕🏨 **Palace Hotel Buçaco.** A former royal hunting lodge in a 250-acre forest, the Palace is an architectural hodgepodge that includes everything from Gothic to neo-Manueline to early Walt Disney. There's an elevator, but who can resist walking up the grand, red-carpeted stairway, its walls lined with azulejo panels, and past the suit of armor? It's worth the steep price for the restaurant's prix-fixe meals just to sit at a finely laid table and take in the carved-wood ceiling, inlaid hardwood floors, and Manueline windows. An elegantly prepared *leitão* (suckling pig) perfectly complements the Buçaco wines stored in the hotel's immense cellars. These wines are available in the restaurants at all Almeida hotels, and also to all guests. ⊠ *Buçaco* 🏨 *Luso 3050-261* ☎ *231/937970* ⊕ *www.almeidahotels.com* ➲ *53 rooms, 6 suites* ⊘ *Restaurant, room service, pool, bar, shop, travel services, free parking, ethernet* ⊟ *AE, DC, MC, V* 🍴 *FAP, MAP.*

Penacova

③④ *12 km (7 mi) southeast of Buçaco, 12 km (7 mi) northeast of Coimbra; from Buçaco, the most scenic route is N235, through wooded countryside along the foot of the Serra do Buçaco; from Coimbra, take N110 along the Rio Mondego.*

A little town on a hill at the junction of three low mountain ranges, Penacova affords panoramic views wherever you look and wonderful hikes. The parish church in the town square was built in 1620.

Just outside Penacova, in a small wooded valley, is the village of Lorvão and the **Mosteiro de Lorvão.** This monastery is worth visiting not just to see what's still standing, but also to feel the vibes of a departed epoch. Its origins are obscure, but there's archaeological evidence of monastic life here dating as far back as the 6th century. In the 13th century Lorvão became a convent for Cistercian nuns and was the custodian of a famed library of 12th-century illuminated manuscripts. The convent was closed down by government order in the 19th century. By that time, the impoverished nuns were partly supporting themselves by making the forerunners of the exquisitely carved willow toothpicks that you can buy in Penacova and in handicrafts shops around the country. (The nuns originally used them to decorate the little cakes they made for sale.) Still standing is a baroque church that dates primarily from the 18th century and has beautifully carved choir stalls and an ornate wrought-iron choir grille. The adjacent museum contains archaeological pieces recovered from the site as well as several illuminated manuscripts. ⊠ *Turnoff on N110, 2 km (1 mi) south of Penacova, Lorvão* ☎ *239/474430* ☒ *Free* ⊘ *June–Sept., daily 9–12:30 and 2–6:30; Oct.–May, daily 9–12:30 and 2–5.*

Where to Stay & Eat

$$–$$$ ✕ **O Panorâmico.** It's easy to see how this small, family-run restaurant got its name: there's a wonderful panoramic view of the Rio Mondego as it snakes its way along to Coimbra. Be sure to try the house specialty, *lampreia à mode de Penacova* (lamprey cooked with rice). ⊠ *Largo Alberto Leitão* ☎ *239/477333* ☰ *DC, MC, V.*

$ 🏨 **Palacete do Mondego.** The pink-and-yellow paint job and art nouveau–style architecture may seem out of place given the bucolic, hilltop setting. But this hotel has a lot going for it and makes a good base for exploring the countryside. It's on a site where a castle is believed to have stood when the Moors and the Christians were facing off in these territories during the 11th and 12th centuries. The all-round views command both the Mondego and Alva rivers, giving some credence to the castle theory. Guest rooms are well equipped, attractively furnished, and comfortable. ⊠ *Av. Dr. Vissaya de Barreto 3, 3000-191* ☎ *239/470700* ⊕ *www.palacete-penacova.net* ⇆ *36 rooms, 2 suites* ⚑ *Restaurant, cable TV, pool, bar* ☰ *AE, DC, MC, V* ☉*I BP.*

Outdoor Activities

HIKING Several paths lead over the hills to the monastery in Lorvão or through the vineyards and fields down to the Rio Mondego. **Trans Serrano** (☎ 235/778938 ⊕ www.transserrano.com) will provide transport and English-speaking guides for nature hikes and kayaking in the surrounding countryside.

KAYAKING Between June and September, there are kayak trips down the Rio Mondego from Penacova to Coimbra. For more information contact the student-run **O Pioneiro do Mondego** (☎239/478385) or the local tourist office.

THE EASTERN BEIRAS

Life is difficult in the mountains and along the frontier with Spain. Winters are cold and harsh, and summers are broiling hot. The rugged mountains of the Serra da Estrela and the sparse vegetation of the stone-strewn high plateau present a sharp contrast to the sandy beaches, lush valleys, and densely forested peaks along the coast. As you drive east, the red-tile roofs and brightly trimmed white-stucco houses are replaced by stone-and-slate structures, reflecting the more somber environment.

Because crops don't flourish here, many inhabitants have supplemented their meager farming incomes by smuggling contraband across the Spanish border. Between 1950 and 1970, many of the villages lost their ablest workers to the factories of northern Europe; a half million Portuguese went to France alone. As a consequence, many towns are populated primarily by senior citizens.

Still, it's worth visiting this region to stand atop a centuries-old castle wall and look out on the landscape's rugged beauty. And in this part of the country, where visitors are still something of a curiosity, you'll find perhaps the warmest welcome. With many mellow old buildings uninhabited, this beautiful area is one of Europe's last great undiscovered gems for those wishing to buy a second home away from the madding crowd.

Castelo Branco

㉟ *150 km (93 mi) southeast of Coimbra.*

The provincial capital of Beira Baixa is a modern town of wide boulevards, parks, and gardens. Lying just off the main north–south IP2 highway, it's easily accessible from all parts of the country.

There's an older section of town, where you'll find the **Praça Luís de Camões,** the town's best-preserved medieval square. The building with the arched stone stairway is the 16th-century **Câmara Municipal** (Town Hall). At the top of the town's hill are the ruins of the 12th-century **Castelo Templario** (Templar's Castle). Not much remains of the series of walls and towers that once surrounded the entire community. Adjoining the Castelo Templario is the flower-covered **Miradouro de São Gens** (St. Gens Terrace), which provides a fine view of the town and surrounding countryside.

A small regional museum, the **Museu Francisco Tavares Proença Junior,** is housed in the old Paço Episcopal (Episcopal Palace). In addition to the usual Roman artifacts and odd pieces of furniture, the collection contains some fine examples of the traditional *bordado* (embroidery) for which Castelo Branco is well known. Adjacent to the museum is a workshop where embroidered bedspreads in traditional patterns are made and sold. ⊠ *Largo da Misericórdia* ☎ 272/344277 ⊕ *www.ipmuseus. pt* ☞ €2 ☉ *Tues.–Sun. 10–12:30 and 2–5:30.*

★ Take a stroll through the **Jardim do Antigo Paço Episcopal** (Garden of the Old Episcopal Palace). These 18th-century gardens are planted with rows of hedges cut in all sorts of bizarre shapes and contain an unusual assemblage of sculpture. Bordering one of the park's five small lakes are a path and stairway lined on both sides with granite statues of the apostles, the evangelists, and the kings of Portugal. The long-standing Portuguese disdain for the Spanish is graphically demonstrated here; the kings who ruled when Portugal was under Spanish domination are carved to a noticeably smaller scale than the "true" Portuguese rulers. Unfortunately, many statues were damaged by Napoléon's troops when the city was ransacked in 1807. ⊠ *Rua Bartolomeu da Costa* ☎ *No phone* ☞ €1.50 ☉ *May–Sept., daily 9–9; Oct.–Apr., daily 9–5.*

Where to Stay & Eat

★ **$$** ✕ **Praça Velha.** In a stone building on a lovely square (the plaque outside reads 1685), this is by far the best restaurant in town. Of the two dining rooms, the older section with the beamed ceiling and stone floors is best. One intriguing specialty is *bife na pedra* (steak served still cooking on a hot stone slab). ⊠ *Largo Luís de Camões 17* ☎ *272/328640* 🍴 *AE, DC, MC, V* ⊙ *Closed Mon.*

$-$$ 🏨 **Rainha Dona Amélia.** The Dona Amélia is a graceful, modern, five-story hotel in the center of the town, run as part of the Best Western chain. The no-frills rooms are pleasant, functional, and airy. Because of its proximity to the Serra da Estrela, this hotel is busiest during the ski season between November and May. ⊠ *Rua de Santiago 15, 6000-179* ☎ *272/348800* ⊕ *www.bestwestern.com/pt/hotelrainhadamelia* ⇱ *64 rooms* ⌂ *Restaurant, coffee shop, minibars, cable TV, hair salon, bar, shop, babysitting, free parking, no-smoking rooms* 🍴 *AE, MC, V* 🍴 *FAP, MAP.*

$ 🏨 **Tryp Colina do Castelo.** This modern business-style hotel atop a hill overlooking the town lacks individuality but has friendly, attentive staff. All the conveniences you could wish for are here, plus the luxury of exceptionally good views. ⊠ *Rua da Piscina, 6000-453* ☎ *272/349280* ⊕ *www.solmelia.com* ⇱ *97 rooms, 6 suites* ⌂ *Restaurant, snack bar, room service, in-room safes, minibars, cable TV, 3 tennis courts, indoor pool, gym, health club, hot tub, massage, sauna, Turkish bath, squash, bar, meeting rooms, Wi-Fi* 🍴 *AE, DC, MC, V* 🍴 *BP.*

Shopping

Tradition in Castelo Branco dictates that a new bride make an embroidered bedspread for her wedding night. This custom is still followed, and these delicately patterned, hand-embroidered linen-and-silk spreads are among the finest examples of Portuguese craftsmanship. There's a display-and-sales room next to the **Museu Francisco Tavares Proença Junior** (⊠ Rua Bartolomeu da Costa); expect to empty your purse.

EN ROUTE As you travel north on IP2, you cross a landscape of broad plains dotted with olive trees and with the peaks of the Serra da Estrela as a distant backdrop. Thirty kilometers (18 mi) north of Castelo Branco you'll come to the village of Alpedrinha, known for its fine fountains and well-preserved remnants of the Roman road that connected this fertile agricultural region with the Spanish town of Mérida.

Fundão

🕉 *36 km (22 mi) north of Castelo Branco, 16 km (10 mi) south of Covilhã.*

The pears and cherries grown in this region are the best in Portugal, and Fundão is the principal market town for the area's many orchards. It's also a convenient gateway to the fortified towns along the Spanish border. The 18th-century **Igreja Matriz** (Parish Church) is noted for its azulejos and decorative ceiling. ⊠ *Largo da Igreja* ☎ *No phone* ⊙ *Daily 9–7.*

Where to Stay & Eat

$ ✕🏨 **Estalagem da Neve.** Rooms in this tiny Victorian-style inn are small but comfortably furnished. The restaurant ($-$$), with its beamed ceiling and tiled walls, is an inviting place in which to enjoy a fine Portuguese meal. Try the trout or roast kid. ⊠ *Calçada de São Sebastião, 6230-347* ☎ *275/752215* ⇱ *6 rooms* ⌂ *Restaurant, pool, bar, some pets allowed, free parking* 🍴 *AE, DC, MC, V* 🍴 *EP.*

$ ✕🏨 **Hotel Samasa.** This comfortable if unexciting modern hotel in the town center is redecorating many of its rooms with colors that may leave you feeling as if you are living in a pot of mustard. The Hermínia Restaurant ($–$$) has rustic touches such as fieldstone on the walls, yet still feels a bit stiff. However, it offers some of the finest food in town, and if you close your eyes, the facilities are fine. ✉ *Rua Vasco da Gama, 6230-375* ☎ *275/751299* 🌐 *www.hotelsamasafundao.com* *50 rooms* *Restaurant, room service, billiards, bar, recreation room* ▭ *AE, DC, MC, V* 🍽 *EP.*

Penamacor

37 *28 km (17 mi) east of Fundão, 28 km (17 mi) southeast of Covilhã.*

Like many of the towns in this region, Penamacor is a mix of old and new. Dominated by the ruins of an ancient castle, it was a key link in the chain of strategically placed fortified communities. On its outskirts are newer stucco houses, many built by Portuguese emigrants with money earned working in France and Germany.

6

The **Castelo de Penamacor** (Penamacor Castle) once guarded the northern approaches to the Rio Tejo. In the wake of the 11th- and 12th-century campaigns to reconquer this region from the Moors, Penamacor lay in ruins. In 1180 Dom Sancho I ordered the reconstruction of the fortifications. Although you can still find traces from that period, much of what you now see, including the solitary watchtower, dates from the early 16th century. If the castle is closed, ask for the key at the tourist office.

The 16th-century **Igreja da Misericórdia** (Church of Mercy) is distinguished by a fine Manueline entrance. A rare octagonal **pillory** in front of the old town hall is worth a look.

The small but interesting **Museu Municipal** (Town Museum) is in a building that was a political prison until the 1974 revolution. One of the original cells has been kept intact, and among the other exhibits is the only complete Roman crematorium on the Iberian Peninsula. ✉ *Largo ex Quartel* ☎ *No phone* *Free* *Daily 9–12:30 and 2–5:30.*

Where to Stay

★ $ 🏨 **Estalagem Vila Rica.** This 19th-century converted farmhouse is surrounded by trees and gardens and is adjacent to a popular hunting area. The large guest rooms are simple but comfortable, and there is a rather stark restaurant serving local cuisine. ✉ *N233, 6090-535* ☎ *277/394311* *11 rooms* *Bar* ▭ *No credit cards* 🍽 *BP.*

Sabugal

38 *20 km (12 mi) northeast of Penamacor, 36 km (22 mi) northeast of Covilhã; from Penamacor, follow N233 north across the high plateau.*

The main attraction here is the 13th-century **Castelo de Sabugal** (Sabugal Castle), which sits majestically atop a grassy knoll and is noted for its unusual pentagonal tower. Some historians maintain that the five sides represent the five shields of the Portuguese national coat of arms. Climb the stone stairs in the courtyard and walk around the battlements. The castle overlooks the Rio Côa, an important tributary of the Douro. ⊠ *Câmara Municipal, Praça da Republica* ☎ *271/751040* ⊕ *www.cm-sabugal.pt* ⊠ *Free* ☉ *Mon.–Sat. 10–5.*

OFF THE BEATEN PATH

PARQUE NATURAL DA SERRA DA MALCATA – The 50,000-acre park along the Spanish border between Penamacor and Sabugal was created to protect the natural habitat of the Iberian lynx, which was threatened with extinction. Although this isn't a place of rugged beauty and spectacular vistas, it's nevertheless an attractive, quiet region of heavily wooded, low mountains with few traces of human habitation. In addition to the lynxes, the park shelters wildcats, wild boars, wolves, and foxes. The northern boundary begins about 10 km (6 mi) southeast of Sabugal.

Sortelha

39

Fodor's Choice
★

10 km (6 mi) southwest of Sabugal, 26 km (16 mi) east of Covilhã.

If you have time to visit only one fortified town, this should be it. From the moment you walk through its massive ancient stone walls, you feel as if you're experiencing a time warp. Except for a few TV antennas, there's little to evoke the 21st century. The streets aren't littered with souvenir stands, nor is there a fast-food outlet in sight. Stone houses are built into the rocky terrain and arranged within the walls roughly in the shape of an amphitheater.

Above the village are the ruins of a small but imposing **castelo** (castle). The present configuration dates back mainly to a late-12th-century reconstruction, done on Moorish foundations; further alterations were made in the 16th century. Note the Manueline coat of arms at the entrance. Wear sturdy shoes so that you can walk along the walls (you can circle the entire village this way). Children of all ages can let their fantasies run wild while taking in views of Spain to the east and the Serra da Estrela to the west. The three holes in the balcony projecting over the main entrance were used to pour boiling pitch on intruders. Just to the right of the north gate are two linear indentations in the stone wall. One is exactly a meter (roughly a yard) long, and the shorter of the two is a *côvado* (66 centimeters [26 inches]). In the Middle Ages, traveling cloth merchants used these markings to ensure an honest measure.

Where to Stay & Eat

★ **$–$$$** ✕ **Restaurante Dom Sancho.** This pleasant little restaurant in a restored stone house in the main square began life as a bar that was the pet project of a local engineer. Since then it has become one of the area's more presentable restaurants. It specializes in game dishes such as roast wild boar and venison. ⊠ *Largo do Corro* ☎ *271/388267* ⊟ *No credit cards* ☉ *Closed Tues.*

There aren't any hotels or pousadas in this medieval town, but several ancient stone houses offer comfortable, although not luxurious, accommodations at very low rates.

The largest and most upmarket is the **Casa da Cerca** (⊠ Largo do Santo António ☎ 271/388113), which has six air-conditioned rooms, a bar, and a restaurant, and does accept Visa. **Casas do Campanário** (⊠ Rua da Mesquita, 6320-536 ☎ 271/388198), next to the church, just inside the village walls, consists of two apartments; one can accommodate two people, the other eight people. It has a bar and restaurant but does not accept credit cards. **Casa da Villa** (⊠ Rua Direita, 6320-536 ☎ 271/ 388113) has two double rooms and a kitchenette (no credit cards).

Belmonte

40 *14 km (8½ mi) northwest of Sortelha, 20 km (12 mi) southwest of Guarda.*

Three things catch your eye on the approach to Belmonte. The first two, the ancient castle and the church, represent the historic past; the third structure, an ugly water tower, symbolizes the new industry of the town, now a major clothing-manufacturing center. Belmonte's importance can be traced back to Roman times, when it was a key outpost on the road between Mérida, the Lusitanian capital, and Guarda. You can still see elements of this road.

Ask a Portuguese, or better yet a Brazilian, what Belmonte is best known for, and the answer will undoubtedly be Pedro Álvares Cabral. In 1500 this native son "discovered" Brazil and in doing so helped make Portugal one of the richest and most powerful nations of that era. The **monument to Cabral,** in the town center, is an important stop for Brazilians visiting Portugal.

Of the mighty complex of fortifications and dwellings that once made up the **Castelo de Belmonte** (Belmonte Castle) only the tower and battlements remain. As you enter, note the scale-model replica of the caravel that carried Cabral to Brazil. On one of the side walls is a coat of arms with two goats, the emblem of the Cabral family (in Portuguese, *cabra* means "goat"). Don't miss the graceful but oddly incongruous Manueline window incorporated into the heavy fortifications. The castle ruins are on a rocky hill to the north overlooking town. 🎟 *Free* ☉ *Daily 10–12:30 and 2–5.*

Adjacent to the Castelo de Belmonte, a cluster of old houses makes up the **Juderia** (Jewish Quarter; ☎ 275/087766). Belmonte had (and, in fact, still has) one of Portugal's largest Jewish communities. Many present-day residents are descendants of the Marranos, the Jews who were forced to convert to Christianity during the Inquisition. For centuries, many kept their faith in secret, pretending to be Christians while practicing their true religion behind closed doors. Such was their fear of repression, that Belmonte's secret Jews didn't emerge fully into the open until the end of the 1970s. The community remained without a synagogue until 1995. It is possible to do group tours that cover the history of the community and the **synagogue** by phoning ahead.

The 12th-century stone **Igreja de São Tiago** (Church of St. James) contains fragments of original frescoes and a fine pietà carved from a single block of granite. The tomb of Pedro Cabral is also in this church.

6

Actually there are two Pedro Cabral tombs in Portugal, the result of a bizarre dispute with Santarém, where Cabral died. Both towns claim ownership of the explorer's mortal remains, and no one seems to know just who or what is in either tomb. If the church is closed, see if someone at the tourist office can help you gain entrance. ⊠ *Adjacent to Castelo de Belmonte* ☎ *275/911488* ☎ *Free* ⊙ *Weekdays 9:30–12:30 and 2–5:30, weekends by arrangement.*

The town's eco-museum, **Eco-Museu do Zêzere,** describes the surrounding geology and countryside. ⊠ *Rua Pedro Álvares Cabral* ☎ *275/ 910012 town hall* ☎ *Free* ⊙ *Daily 10–12:30 and 2–5:30.*

OFF THE BEATEN PATH

CENTUM CELLAS – A short way outside Belmonte, on a dirt track signposted off N18, is a strange archaeological sight that has kept people guessing for years: a massive, solitary, three-story framework of granite blocks. The building is thought to be of Roman origin, but experts are unable to explain its original function convincingly or provide many clues about its original appearance. Some archaeologists believe it was part of a much larger complex. Excavations of the surrounding area are planned.

Where to Stay & Eat

$$$ ✕▥ **Convento de Belmonte.** Just over a kilometer (½ mi) from Belmonte on the slopes of the Serra da Esperança, this attractive pousada is in a restored Franciscan monastery founded in 1563 by a descendant of Pedro Álvares Cabral, the first European to reach Brazil. The blend of ancient and modern has been accomplished with finesse. Rooms are well equipped, handsome, and have balconies with views of the surrounding hills. As ever in pousadas, the food ($$) is excellent, with a seasonal menu and regional variations such as stuffed partridge with spinach. ⊠ *Serra da Esperança* ✑ *Apartado 35, Belmonte 6250* ☎ *275/910300* ⊕ *www.pousadas.pt* ✑ *23 rooms, 1 suite* ⊘ *Restaurant, pool, fishing, bar, ethernet* ⊟ *AE, DC, MC, V* ⦿ *BP.*

¢ ✕▥ **Belsol.** Owner João Pinheiro is an enterprising hotelier who has opted for quality and good service over ostentation. In the guest rooms, rosy wood furniture and floors make a nice counterpoint to the white walls and striped, contemporary fabrics and area rugs in white, taupe, and lavender; several rooms have balconies with views of the Rio Zêzere. Stone terraces lead to swimming pools and landscaped areas. Local businesspeople favor the restaurant (¢–$$) for its excellent Portuguese food. Try the trout fresh from local waters. Note that you will need wheels if you stay here, the hotel is located around 8 km (5 mi) from town on the main N18 road. ⊠ *Quinta do Rio off IP2/N18* ✑ *Belmonte 6250* ☎ *275/912206* ⊕ *www.hotelbelsol.com* ✑ *53 rooms, 1 suite* ⊘ *Restaurant, cable TV, 3 pools, bar, billiards, playground, public Internet* ⊟ *AE, DC, MC, V* ⦿ *BP.*

Covilhã

41 *16 km (10 mi) southwest of Belmonte, 48 km (30 mi) north of Castelo Branco.*

Although its origins go back to Roman times, there's little in present-day Covilhã of historic significance. Nevertheless, it is an attractive town that is the main business center of and southern gateway to the Serra da Estrela. It's within easy access of the main ski area.

The town is closely linked to sheep raising and is Portugal's most important wool-producing center. The **Museu de Lanifícios** (Museum of Wool Manufacturing) stands within the university grounds, in a restored dye-works founded by the Marquis of Pombal in 1764. You'll learn about local wool production, its technology, and the lives of the wool workers. ⊠ *Rua Marquês D'Ávila e Bolama* ☎ *275/319700* 🎟 *€2* ⊘ *Tues.–Sun. 9:30–noon and 2:30–6.*

GREAT DRIVES

If you prefer to take in the scenery by car, the roads through the Serra da Estrela, although hair-raising at times, are well maintained. The drive between Covilhã and Seia on N339, the country's highest road, affords a breathtaking view of the Zêzere Valley. Along the way you'll pass a small fountain marking the source of the Rio Mondego. It's in this region that Portugal's noblest cheese, the tangy *queijo da Serra*, is made from the milk of ewes pastured on the rugged mountain slopes.

Where to Stay & Eat

$–$$$ ✕ **Ovelhita Restaurante.** This tastefully restored restaurant is in a town house just down the road from the tourist office. The food is excellent, with a modern twist on the local Portuguese specialties. The only thing you can hold against the fashionable place is its popularity with local businessmen, who tend to smoke like chimneys. ⊠ *Largo da Infantaria XXI 19* ☎ *912/509659* ▤ *MC, V* ⊘ *Closed Sun.*

$ ✕▥ **Hotel Turismo.** This hotel may be simple, modern, and functional but it's far from spartan, with exercise facilities and a dance club. Guest rooms are pleasant and well equipped. Among the local specialties served in the panoramic rooftop Piornos restaurant ($–$$) is fresh trout from nearby mountain streams. ⊠ *Acesso a Variante, Quinta da Olivosa* 🖉 *Covilhã 6200-909* ☎ *275/330400* ⊕ *www.imb-hotels.com* 🔀 *104 rooms* ⚭ *Restaurant, health club, massage, minibars, sauna, squash, 2 pools, Wi-Fi, bar, dance club, meeting rooms* ▤ *AE, DC, MC, V* ⊺◯⊺ *BP.*

$ ▥ **Tryp Dona María.** This modern three-star hotel makes up for somewhat boring, boxlike architecture with comfort amenities and great views. The rooms are a reasonable size, with simple, clean lines, wooden fittings, and white walls, but they do feel rather institutional. ⊠ *Alameda Pêro da Covilhã, about 1 km (½ mi) southeast of the town center, 6200-346* ☎ *275/310000* ⊕ *www.solmelia.com* 🔀 *81 rooms, 6 suites* ⚭ *Restaurant, pool, minibars, Wi-Fi, bar, laundry service* ▤ *AE, DC, MC, V* ⊺◯⊺ *BP.*

Parque Natural da Serra da Estrela

★ Until the end of the 19th century, this mountainous region was little known except by shepherds and hunters. The first scientific expedition to the Serra da Estrela was in 1881, and since then it has become one of the country's most popular recreation areas. In summer the high, craggy peaks, alpine meadows, and rushing streams become the domain of hikers, climbers, and trout fishermen. The lower and middle elevations are heavily wooded with deciduous oak, sweet chestnut, and pine. Above the tree line, at about 4,900 feet, is a rocky, subalpine world of scrub vegetation, lakes, and boggy meadows that are transformed in late spring into a vivid, multicolored carpet of wildflowers. The Serra da Estrela Natural Park is home to many species of animals, the largest of which include wild boar, badger, and, in the more remote areas, the occasional wolf.

Where to Stay & Eat

★ $ ✕ **Cabana do Pastor.** A cozy mountain restaurant with a fireplace and panoramas, this is a good place to try some Serra cheese. If you're lucky, the restaurant may have some at its optimum stage of maturity. The fine, locally cured *presunto* (cured ham) is also good here, and the place is famed for its *cabrito no forno*, a succulent dish of roast kid. The restaurant is 12 km (7 mi) southwest of Gouveia. ⊠ *Behind souvenir shop on N339, Seia* ☎ *238/313010* ▭ *V.*

★ $$–$$$ ✕▥ **Pousada de Convento do Desagravo.** Located in a delightful village with just 400 inhabitants, this gracious pousada began life as a convent in the late 18th century. Today its cool white rooms and shady arched corridors are simply but elegantly furnished to maintain a sense of peace and well-being, and the restaurant ($$–$$$) serves local specialties such as duck, game, and trout. ⊠ *Vila Pouca da Beira 3400-758* ☎ *238/670080* ⊕ *www.pousadas.pt* ⇩ *24 rooms* ♻ *Restaurant, tennis court, pool, bar* ▭ *AE, DC, MC, V* ▯◯▮ *BP.*

★ $$ ✕▥ **Pousada de São Lourenço.** At an elevation of 4,231 feet, this granite mountain lodge is in the heart of the Serra da Estrela, 13 km (8 mi) from the spa town of Manteigas. The cozy lounge has plush seating by a fireplace, and rooms are both elegant and rustic with dark-wood furniture and fabrics in deep colors. Ask for Room 207; it has a loft for sleeping and one of the best views. If you're just driving through, stop for lunch at the restaurant ($–$$) and try the unusual but delicious bacalhau *à lagareiro* (with corn bread, olive oil, and potatoes). ⊠ *On E232 to Gouveia* ⌖ *Manteigas 6260-200* ☎ *275/980050* ⊕ *www.pousadas. pt* ⇩ *21 rooms, 1 suite* ♻ *Restaurant, bar* ▭ *AE, DC, MC, V* ▯◯▮ *BP.*

$ ▥ **Estalagem Varanda dos Carqueijais.** At an altitude of 4,000 feet, about 15 km (9 mi) from Covilhã, this hotel curves around a tennis court and swimming pool. The rooms have all the usual conveniences of a four-star hotel without much aesthetic distinction, but who's complaining with the spectacular mountain views from the balconies? The hotel is convenient for summer hikes and using the Torre ski lifts in winter. ⊠ *Varanda dos Carqueijais, EN339, Serra da Estrela* ⌖ *Covilhã 6200* ☎ *275/319120* ⊕ *www.turistrela.pt* ⇩ *49 rooms, 1 suite* ♻ *Restaurant, tennis court, pool, bar, Wi-Fi* ▭ *AE, DC, MC, V* ▯◯▮ *BP.*

$ ▥ **Hotel Serra da Estrela.** Built in the early part of the 20th century as a tuberculosis sanatorium, this hotel 12 km (7 mi) from Covilhã has been completely renovated. Rooms are large, and those in the front have good valley views. At an elevation of 3,936 feet, the hotel provides an excellent base for a few days in the mountains and, in winter, is the focus of the local ski resort. ⊠ *Penhas da Saude (on road to Torre)* ⌖ *Covilhã 6203-073* ☎ *275/310300* ⊕ *www.turistrela.pt* ⇩ *38 rooms, 2 apartments, 22 villas* ♻ *Restaurant, snack bar, 2 tennis courts, pool, bar, Wi-Fi* ▭ *AE, DC, MC, V* ▯◯▮ *BP.*

Outdoor Activities

CAMPING There are several official campsites within the park (ask at the tourist office for details) with basic toilet and shower facilities. There are also a number of good commercial campsites in the area. The Web directory **Virtual Portugal** (⊕ www.portugalvirtual.pt/accommod/mountains) has a list of campsites, such as in Guarda and Belmonte, with details of their facilities and phone numbers.

HIKING This is a hiker's paradise, and there are plenty of well-marked trails. A comprehensive trail guide is available at tourist offices in the region, and although it's in Portuguese, the maps, elevation charts, and pictures are useful. There are also plenty of other adventure sports on offer, from hang gliding to climbing.

SKIING With the coming of winter and the first snows, the area becomes a winter playground, offering many Portuguese their only exposure to winter sports. The highest point in continental Portugal is **Torre** (☎ 275/314727), with an elevation of 6,539 feet, within the south part of Parque Natural da Serra da Estrela. Although it has five ski lifts and the facilities have been upgraded, it can't compete with other European ski resorts. Still you'll find a restaurant and sports-equipment shops, and you can rent gear. The weekday rates for lift passes run from €12 for a half day to €24 for a full day; rates are slightly higher on weekends and at night. Equipment hire ranges from €17 for snowboards to €27 for skis. For information, contact the Ski Station. In Manteigas, on the far side of the mountains, you can ski and snowboard year-round thanks to the synthetic run at the **Ski Parque** (☎ 275/982870) complex. It takes about three hours to drive between Torre and Ski Parque, both of which have accommodations. The direct route between them is the highest road in Portugal and a thrilling ride above the snow line and in the clouds.

FISHING There's excellent trout fishing in the Rio Vouga (Vouga River) and in the rivers and lakes of the Serra da Estrela—particularly in the Rio Zêzere, which cuts through one of Europe's deepest glacial valleys—and in the Comprida and Loriga lakes. The Beira Litoral is full of beaches and rocky outcroppings where you can try your luck with a variety of fish, including bass, bream, and sole. Check with the local tourist offices for information about obtaining permits. No permit is required for ocean fishing.

Gouveia

㊷ *28 km (17 mi) northwest of Covilhã.*

Nestled into the western side of the Mondego Valley, this quiet town of parks and gardens is a popular base from which to explore the Serra da Estrela. The exterior of the baroque **Igreja Matriz** (Parish Church) is covered with blue-and-white tiles, and well-executed azulejos depicting the Stations of the Cross line the inside walls of the small, dimly lighted chapel across the street. ⊠ *Praça de São Pedro* ☎ *No phone* ☉ *Daily 9–6.*

The **Museu Abel Manta,** in an 18th-century manor house, displays a good collection of the paintings by this artist, one of the country's most distinguished. He was born in Gouveia in 1888 and died in Lisbon in 1982. ⊠ *Rua Direita* ☎ 238/490219 🎟 *Free* ⊙ *Tues.–Sun. 9:30–12:30 and 2–6.*

OFF THE BEATEN PATH

CANIL MONTES HERMÍNIOS – Gouveia is the principal center for the Serra da Estrela sheepdogs, which are famous for their loyalty and courage. In earlier days, when marauding wolf packs were an ever-present menace, the dogs wore metal collars with long spikes to protect their throats. To learn more about the dogs, you can visit the Montes Hermínios Kennels, one of the major breeding kennels in the Vale do Rossim. ⊠ N232 *between Gouveia and Manteigas, Solar do Cão da Serra, Estrada da Serra* ☎ 238/492426 ⊙ *Visits by appointment.*

> **GREAT VIEWS**
>
> The fortified hamlet of Linhares—atop a rocky outcrop at an elevation of 2,625 feet and 16 km (10 mi) northeast of Gouveia—is a good place to take in Serra da Estrela views. The village's stone houses, church, and shops are encircled by walls, much of which remain intact, as do two square, crenellated towers from the time of King Dinis. There's a 16th-century pillory in front of the church.

Where to Stay & Eat

★ $ ✕ **O Júlio.** Thanks to the talents of its chef, owner, and namesake, Júlio, those who love good food travel to this unassuming restaurant from miles around. Try the *truta frita do Mondego* (fried trout from the Rio Mondego) or the *javali no forno* (roast wild boar). ⊠ *Travessa do Loureiro 11* ☎ 238/498016 ▭ MC, V ⊙ *Closed Tues.*

$ 🏨 **Hotel Gouveia.** This small, modern hotel on one of the main approaches to the Serra da Estrela has comfortable rooms furnished in traditional style. Several have small balconies. The ground-floor O Foural restaurant is popular with local businesspeople; service is attentive, and although the menu (and the prices) changes daily, a good bet is the roast kid. If you like tennis, there are two courts you can use for free in the nearby city park. ⊠ *Av. 1 de Maio, 6290* ☎ 238/491010 🛏 *45 rooms, 3 suites* ⚭ *Restaurant, bar, cable TV* ▭ AE, DC, MC, V ⊙l BP.

Celorico da Beira

❸ *23 km (14 mi) northeast of Gouveia, 16 km (10 mi) northwest of Guarda.*

Celorico da Beira is a major producer of Serra cheese, which is made from the best-quality ewe's milk, using traditional methods. Production takes place between December and March. One of Europe's largest cheese markets is held on the Praça Municipal every Friday from December to May, with a cheese fair in February. If you miss the market, you can always visit the tiny **Solar de Queijo Serra** (Serra Cheese Museum; ⊠ Largo 5 de Outubro ☎ 271/742105).

Celorico has the requisite **castelo** watching over it from a hilltop. A large portion of the walls and an impressive tower are intact. Before visiting the castle, be sure to stop by the town hall on Rua Sacadura Cabral for the key. ⊠ *Follow Rua Fernão Pacheco from main road up through remnants of the old town* 🎫 *Free* ⊙ *Mon.–Sat. 10–12:30 and 2–5.*

¢ ✕⊡ **Mira Serra.** Owner Fernando Batista was the manager of a luxury hotel in the Algarve before striking out on his own with this modern, four-story establishment. The rooms are comfortable and furnished in traditional style; some have small balconies. The restaurant ($$) prepares a delicious bacalhau à brás. ⊠ *Just off IP5, Bairro de Santa Eufemia* 🏠 *Celorico da Beira 6360* ☎ *271/742604* ✉ *miraserra@oninet. pt* 🛏 *40 rooms* ⚐ *Restaurant, room service, minibars, cable TV, tennis court, bar* ▤ *AE, DC, MC, V* ⦿ *EP.*

Trancoso

44 *18 km (11 mi) northeast of Celorico da Beira, 26 km (16 mi) northwest of Guarda.*

This town reached its pinnacle in 1282, when King Dinis chose it as the site for his marriage to Isabel of Aragon. Portions of its well-preserved castle walls and towers date from the 9th century. Above one of the gates, the **Porta do Carvalho,** you can make out the figure of a knight. This was a local lad who, during one of the many battles with the Spanish, left the safety of the castle walls to capture the Spanish flag. He was caught, but before being spirited away, he defiantly hurled the flag over the wall.

EN ROUTE The most scenic route to take from Trancoso is the tortuous N226 to Friexedas followed by the N221 to Pinhel, 38 km (24 mi) to the east. Atop a hill in the Marofa range, Pinhel was a key bastion during the wars of restoration. Its most striking 17th-century remnants are two solitary towers. On one of them, below the balcony facing the town, you can make out the graceful form of a Manueline window. Taking N221 north to Castelo Rodrigo, you'll cross the Serra da Marofa and a desolate, rocky moonscape. Now much improved, this stretch was once known as the Accursed Road, because of its many bends.

Castelo Rodrigo

45 *60 km (37 mi) northeast of Trancoso.*

This old fortified town is now mostly deserted, many of its former residents having emigrated to France and Germany. The ruins of the **fortaleza** (fortress) afford a panoramic view of the surrounding countryside. In neighboring Figueira de Castelo Rodrigo, the 18th-century **Igreja Matriz** contains several gilded wooden altars. It's open daily 9–6.

Almeida

⟲ **46** *18 km (11 mi) southeast of Castelo Rodrigo.*

Enclosed within a star-shaped perimeter of massive stone walls, moats, and earthen bulwarks lies the quiet little town of Almeida. Less than 10 km (6 mi) from the Spanish border, it has been the scene of much fighting over the centuries. This is a place for walking, clambering along the walls and bulwarks, and giving your imagination free rein—perhaps to conjure up ghosts of battles past. The drive from Castelo Rodrigo to Almeida is winding, mountainous, and dramatic.

Where to Stay & Eat

★ $$ ×⊞ **Pousada Nossa Senhora das Neves.** Portuguese architect Cristiano Moreira eloquently integrated a modern hotel into historic fortress walls. Public areas and guest rooms are spacious and light, and large terraces look out across the high tablelands into Spain. You can sip your afternoon glass of chilled white port and imagine Wellington's troops facing Napoléon's armies on this very spot. The restaurant ($–$$), divided into two plank-floor dining rooms, serves regional dishes, including *sopa de peixe do Rio Côa* (a rich tomato-based soup made with fish from the nearby Côa River). The wine list has more than 60 selections. ⊠ *Rua das Muralhas, 6350* ☎ *271/574283* ⊕ *www.pousadas.pt* ⤶ *21 rooms* ⚒ *Restaurant, minibars, fishing, bar, free parking* ⊟ *AE, DC, MC, V* ⏀⏀ *BP.*

¢ ×⊞ **A Muralha.** This modern residencial, just outside the fortifications, is the creation of former English teacher Manuel Dias, who manages the hotel, and his wife, Eliza, who runs the restaurant (¢–$). Cork-paneled hallways lead to homey, simply furnished rooms with cork floors. The restaurant's specialties include cabrito no forno and an excellent bacalhau. ⊠ *Bairro de São Pedro, 6350-211* ☎ *271/574357* ⤶ *24 rooms* ⚒ *Restaurant, bar* ⊟ *AE, MC, V* ⏀⏀ *BP.*

Guarda

47 *38 km (24 mi) southwest of Almeida, 36 km (22 mi) northeast of Covilhã, 60 km (37 mi) east of Viseu.*

At an elevation of about 3,300 feet, Guarda is Portugal's highest city and is aptly referred to by the four Fs: *forte, feia, fria, e farta* (strong, ugly, cold, and wealthy). A somber conglomeration of austere granite buildings in a harsh, uncompromising environment, Guarda is no charming mountain hamlet, but it is interesting historically and a good base from which to explore the mountains and the fortified villages along the Spanish border. Winters are cold and gloomy, often cutting into the short springtime.

From pre-Roman times, Guarda has been a strategic bastion on the northeastern flank of the Serra da Estrela, protecting the approaches from Castile. The town is thought to have been a military base for Julius Caesar. After the fall of the Roman Empire, the Visigoths and later the Moors gained control. Guarda was liberated in the late 12th century by Christian forces and, along with a number of towns in the region, enlarged and fortified by Dom Sancho I. The dukes of Braganca were closely related to the kings of Portugal, and with rank came the privilege and aforementioned wealth. For the rather dour and purposeful local mountain residents, Guarda is still a main trading and business center.

The **Torre de Menagem** (Castle Keep), on a small knoll above the cathedral, and a few segments of wall are all that remain of Guarda's once extensive fortifications. From atop the ruins is an impressive view across the rock-strewn countryside toward the Castilian plains.

Construction on the fortresslike **Sé** (Cathedral) started in 1390 but wasn't completed until 1540. As a consequence, the imposing Gothic building also shows Renaissance and Manueline influences. Although built on a smaller and less majestic scale, the cathedral shows similarities to the great monastery at Batalha. Inside, a magnificent four-tier relief contains more than 100 carved figures. The work is attributed to the 16th-century sculptor Jean de Rouen. ⊠ *Praça Luís de Camões* ☎ *No phone* ⊙ *Tues.–Sun. 9–12:30 and 2–5:30.*

The Sé occupies the north side of the **Praça Luís de Camões,** which is also the site of some fine 16th- and 18th-century houses and arcades. The statue standing in the center of the square is of Dom Sancho I.

The **Museu da Guarda** (Guarda Museum), in a stately early-17th-century palace adjacent to the 18th-century Igreja da Misericórdia (Church of Mercy), is worth a visit. It documents the region's history with a collection of prehistoric and Roman objects, old paintings, documents, arms, and ecclesiastical art. ⊠ *Rua Frei Pedro Roçadas 30* ☎ *271/213460* ⊠€2 ⊙ *Tues.–Sun. 10–12:30 and 2–5:30.*

Where to Stay & Eat

¢–$ ✕ **Belo Horizonte.** Guarda isn't noted for its good restaurants, but this modest establishment in the old quarter is one of the few exceptions. It serves hearty regional fare and a different dish of bacalhau daily. ⊠ *Largo de São Vicente 1* ☎ *271/211454* ⊟ *AE, MC, V* ⊙ *Closed Sat.*

★ $ ✕▥ **Hotel Vanguarda.** Right in the heart of Guarda, this ultramodern three-star hotel may be a cuckoo in the nest when it comes to the prevailing local architecture and the rooms may be a little small, but it is clean, comfortable, well run, and well equipped. Many rooms have balconies and excellent views. The sophisticated bar and dining room ($–$$) would not look out of place in New York or London and serves an interesting mix of modern European and traditional Portuguese dishes. ⊠ *Av. Monsenhor Mendes Do Carmo, 6300-586* ☎ *271/208390* ⊕ *www.hotelvanguarda.com* ⟿ *76 rooms, 6 suites* ⟆ *Restaurant, in-room safes, minibars, bar, Wi-Fi* ⊟ *AE, MC, V* ⦿❘ *BP.*

★ $ ▥ **Quinta da Ponte.** In the little village of Faia, 12 km (7 mi) from Guarda, in the foothills of the Serra da Estrela, this charming 17th-century manor house has been beautifully restored. There are light and airy rooms both in the old house and modern extensions, and breakfast is served in the old stable block. ⊠ *Faia, 6300-095* ☎ *271/926126* ⊕ *www. quintadaponte.com* ⟿ *2 rooms, 5 apartments* ⟆ *Restaurant, pool, bar* ⊟ *AE, DC, MC, V* ⦿❘ *EP.*

$ ▥ **Solar de Alarcão.** To absorb Guarda's history, book a room in this 17th-century granite house just around the corner from the Sé. Accommodations are comfortable and furnished with antiques; the only concessions to modernity are TVs and well-fitted bathrooms. There's also a small family chapel. ⊠ *Rua Dom Miguel de Alarcão 25, 6300-684*

🕿 *271/214392* 🖋 *3 rooms* 🅿 *Free parking* 🚫 *No credit cards* 🍴 *EP.*

¢ 🖵 **Filipe.** This residencial has plain but comfortable rooms and little else. In an under-equipped town such as Guarda it's a good choice if you don't plan to stay long and are looking for something inexpensive. ✉ *Rua Vasco da Gama 9, 6300-772* 🕿 *271/223658* 🖋 *40 rooms* 🅿 *Parking (fee)* 🚫 *AE, DC, MC, V* 🍴 *EP.*

COIMBRA & THE BEIRAS ESSENTIALS

Transportation

BY AIR

Coimbra is 197 km (123 mi) north of Lisbon and 116 km (72 mi) south of Porto. Both cities are connected to Coimbra via the A1 (E80) highway. Intercontinental flights usually arrive in Lisbon, but Porto has an increasing number of European connections, including through several budget airlines.

BY BUS

Buses of various vintages can take you to almost any destination within the region, and unlike train stations, which are often some distance from the town center, bus depots are central. Although this is a great way to travel and get close to the local people, it requires a great deal of time and patience.

Regional and local bus schedules are posted at terminals, and you can also get information at local tourist offices. Rede Expressos provides comfortable bus service between Lisbon, Porto, and Coimbra, and to other parts of the Beiras. International as well as regional services are available at the Rodoviário da Beira Litoral bus station in Coimbra and at the Rodoviário da Beira Interior stations in Castelo Branco and Covilhã.

Coimbra's yellow municipal buses make regular stops around the city from 6 AM to midnight. The tourist office has maps of the bus routes. 🚩 **Rede Expressos** ✉ Av. Fernão de Magalhães 2D, Coimbra 🕿 239/855270 🌐 www.rede-expressos.pt. **Rodoviário da Beira Interior** ✉ Rodrigo Rebelo 3, Castelo Branco 🕿 272/340120 ✉ Central de Camionagem, Covilhã 🕿 275/334914. **Rodoviário da Beira Litoral** ✉ Av. Fernão de Magalhães, Coimbra 🕿 239/855270. **Serviços Municipais de Transportes de Coimbra** (SMTUC) 🕿 239/941441.

BY CAR

The Beiras, with their many remote villages, are suited to exploration by car. Distances between major points are short; there are no intimidating cities to negotiate; and except for the coastal strip in July and August, traffic is light. Roads in general are good and destinations well marked; however, parking is a problem in the larger towns.

Although you can zip from Lisbon to Coimbra on the A1 toll highway in less than two hours or drive from Porto to Coimbra in under an hour, resist the temptation. The heart and soul of the Beiras are along the many miles of more minor roads—those squiggly little lines lacing Portugal's map.

Allow plenty of time for journeys the moment you are off the main highways. Many of the mountain roads are switchbacks that need to be treated with extreme caution. In addition, you are almost certain to get lost with appalling signposting (usually hidden around the corner or behind a tree) and nightmarish one-way mazes in every town, from the smallest hamlet to the largest city. If you get to your destination without going around the whole town three times, consider yourself lucky. Even the locals admit to getting lost on a regular basis.

Drive defensively at all times. Portugal has Europe's highest traffic fatality rate, and the worst road in the country for accidents is the IP5 heading inland from Aveiro to the Serra de Estrela.

BY TRAIN

Although the major destinations in the Beiras are linked by rail, service to most towns, with the exception of Coimbra, is infrequent. Using Coimbra as a hub, there are three main rail lines in the region. Line 110, the Beira Alta line, goes northeast to Luso, Viseu, Celorico da Beira, and Guarda. Line 100 extends south through the Ribatejo to intersect with Line 130, the Beira Baixa line, which runs from Lisbon northeast through Castelo Branco and Fundão to Covilhã, the gateway to the Serra da Estrela. Going north from Coimbra, Line 100 serves Curia, Aveiro, and Ovar and continues north to Porto and Braga.

Coimbra, Luso, Guarda, Ovar, and Aveiro are on the main Lisbon–Porto and Lisbon–Paris lines. Two trains arrive from and depart for Paris daily, and in summer a daily car-train operates between Paris and Lisbon. There are also regular trains linking the principal cities in the Beiras with Madrid, Lisbon, and Porto. There are three stations in Coimbra: Coimbra A (Estação Nova), along the Mondego River, a five-minute walk from the center of town (for domestic routes); Coimbra Parque just south of Ponte de Santa Clara (also for domestic routes); and Coimbra B (Estação Velha), 5 km (3 mi) west. International trains and trains from Lisbon and Porto arrive at Coimbra B, where there's a free shuttle to Coimbra A. There are also bus links between stations. Schedules for all trains are posted at all three stations.

🚄 Train information ☎ 808/208208 ⊕ www.cp.pt.

Contacts & Resources

EMERGENCIES

In all sizable towns, pharmacies operate on a rotating system for staying open after normal closing hours, including weekends and holidays. Consult a local newspaper or the notice posted on the door of every pharmacy. If you require medical assistance, hospitals in Castel Branco, Coimbra, Figueira da Foz, and Guarda have *urgências* (emergency rooms).
🚑 General ☎ 112.

Hospital Amato Lusitano ⊠ Av. Pedro A. Cabral, Castelo Branco ☎ 272/322133. **Hospital Distrital da Figueira da Foz** ⊠ Gala, Figueira da Foz ☎ 233/402000. **Hospital Sousa Martins** ⊠ Av. Reinha Dona Amalia, Guarda ☎ 271/222133. **Hospital da Universidade de Coimbra** ⊠ Praça Prof. Mota Pinto, Celas, Coimbra ☎ 239/400400.

MAIL

Coimbra's central post office, the CTT Estação Central, is adjacent to the train station and is the center for *poste restante* (general delivery). Most other towns have just one central post office, where poste restante is received.

🏤 Post Office **CTT Estação Central** ⊠ Av. Fernão de Magalhães 223, Coimbra.

TOUR OPTIONS

There are very few regularly scheduled guided tours originating in the Beiras. The Departamento Cultural (Cultural Department) in Coimbra's town hall organizes excellent one-day bus excursions to areas around Coimbra, but they take place once a month only. If you can catch one of these, the experience is worthwhile, as the tours usually include a rewarding introduction to regional home cooking. The Coimbra town hall tourist offices can supply details. There are also a couple of companies offering guided walking tours and activities in the mountains. Other than that, the only regular tours of the Beiras originate either in Lisbon or in Porto. For further information contact a travel agency.

🏤 **Coimbra tourist office** ☎ 239/488120.

VISITOR INFORMATION

COIMBRA 🏤 Tourist Office **Região de Turismo do Centro** ⊠ Av. Afonso Henriques 132, Coimbra ☎ 239/488120 ⊕ www.turismo-centro.pt.

THE WESTERN BEIRAS 🏤 Tourist Offices **Águeda** ⊠ Largo Dr. João Elísio Sucena ☎ 234/601412. **Aveiro** ⊠ Rua João Mendonça 8, Aveiro ☎ 234/423680. **Buarcos** ⊠ Largo Tomas de Aquino ☎ 233/433019. **Caramulo** ⊠ Av. Dr. Jerónimo de Lacerda ☎ 232/861437. **Curia** ⊠ Largo Dr. Luís Navega ☎ 231/512248 or 231/504442 ⊕ www.turismo-curia.pt. **Ílhavo** ⊠ Praça do Município ☎ 234/325911. **Luso** ⊠ Rua Emidio Navarro 136 ☎ 231/939133. **Ovar** ⊠ Edifício da Câmara Municipal, Rua Elias Garcia ☎ 256/572215. **Penacova** ⊠ Câmara Municipal, Largo Alberto Leitão 5 ☎ 239/470300. **Região de Turismo do Centro** ⊠ Praceta Dr. Marcos Viana, Av. 25 de Abril, Figueira da Foz ☎ 233/402820 ⊕ www.figueiraturismo.com. **Região de Turismo de Dão-Lafões** ⊠ Av. Calouste Gulbenkian, Viseu ☎ 232/420950. **Região de Turismo da Rota da Luz** ⊠ Rua João Mendonça 8, Aveiro ☎ 234/423680.

THE EASTERN BEIRAS 🏤 Tourist Offices **Belmonte** ⊠ Largo do Brasil, Castelo do Belmonte ☎ 275/911488. **Castelo Branco** ⊠ Câmara Municipal, Alameda da Liberdade ☎ 272/330339. **Fundão** ⊠ Av. da Liberdade ☎ 275/752770. **Gouveia** ⊠ Av. 25 de Abril ☎ 238/490243. **Guarda** ⊠ Praça Luís de Camões ☎ 271/205530. **Penamacor** ⊠ Av. 25 de Abril ☎ 277/394316. **Região de Turismo da Serra da Estrela** ⊠ Av. Frei Heitor Pinto, Covilhã ☎ 275/319560.

Porto &
the North

WORD OF MOUTH

"I can honestly say that the trip along the Douro river from Porto Campanha station to Regua is one of the most beautiful and scenic journeys I have ever made, period. The railway follows the river's every bend and most of the time runs right along the bank side. Just, well, mindblowing. The trip from Porto was cheap—making it an appealing day trip for anyone staying in the north of the country."

–Matt from England

ed by
Mary McLean

LINING THE RIVER THAT MADE IT A TRADING CENTER ever since pre-Roman times, vibrant and cosmopolitan Porto centers itself some 5 km (3 mi) inland from the Atlantic Ocean. The Moors never had the same strong foothold here that they did farther south, and the city remained largely unaffected by the great earthquake of 1755; as a result, Porto's architecture shows off a baroque finery lacking in Lisbon. Its grandiose granite buildings were financed by the trade that made the city wealthy: wine from the upper valley of the Rio Douro (Douro River, or River of Gold) was transported to Porto, from where it was then exported. You can follow that trail today by boat or on the beautiful Douro rail line.

The remote north can be beautiful, as it is in the valley of the Rio Douro and the deep, rural heartland of the Minho, a coastal province north of Porto. The Minho is surrounded by water. It takes its name from the river forming Portugal's northern border with Spain, meets the Atlantic in the west, and is cut by the long, peaceful and parallel rivers Lima and Cávado. The Minho coast, a sweeping stretch of beaches and fishing villages, has a lush, green landscape. Some locations have been appropriated by resorts, but there are still plenty of places where you can find solitary dunes or splash in the brisk Atlantic away from crowds. Inland you can lose yourself in villages with country markets and fairs that have hardly changed for hundreds of years.

To the northeast there's adventure at hand, in the winding mountain roads and remote towns and villages of the Trás-os-Montes (Beyond the Mountains) region. After centuries of isolation, the area is being accessed by ever more and ever better roads, but there's still great excitement in getting off the beaten track and taking rattling bus rides into the far northeastern corners. The imposing castle towers and fortress walls of this frontier region are a great attraction, but—unusual in such a small country—it's often the journey itself that's the greatest prize: traveling past voluminous man-made lakes, through forested valleys rich in wildlife, across bare crags and moorlands, and finally down to coarse, stone villages where TV aerials sit oddly in almost medieval surroundings.

The rugged uplands of the northern Trás-os-Montes are called the Terra Fria (Cold Land), where you may spot some unusual forms: Iron Age sculptures of boars with phallic attributes. It's believed these were worshipped as fertility symbols.

Exploring Porto & the North

The north of Portugal can be divided into four basic regions—Porto and its immediate environs, the Douro Valley, the evergreen Minho, and the somewhat remote and untamed Trás-os-Montes area to the east, a region still slightly short on amenities yet long on spectacular scenery and superb country cooking.

Restaurants & Cuisine

On the whole, restaurants in Porto and the north offer extremely good value, although the smaller ones often don't accept credit cards.

Dress throughout the region is informal, and reservations are usually unnecessary.

The cooking in Porto is rich and heavy. It's typified by the city's favorite dish, *tripas á moda do Porto* (Porto tripe), a concoction of beans, chicken, sausage, vegetables, and spices. Elsewhere in Portugal residents of Porto are known as *tripeiros* (tripe eaters)—a nickname earned when the city was under siege during the Napoleonic Wars and tripe was the only meat available. However, tripe doesn't dominate the menu in Porto, and dishes tend to resemble those served in the Minho region. *Caldo verde* (literally "green soup") is ubiquitous; it's made of potato and shredded kale in a broth and is usually served with a slice or two of *chouriço* sausage. Fresh fish is found all the way up the coast, and every town has a local recipe for *bacalhau* (dried salt cod); in the Minho it's often cooked with potatoes, onions, and eggs. *Lampreias* (lampreys)—eel-like fish—are found in Minho rivers from February through April and are a specialty of Viana do Castelo and Monção. Pork is the meat most often seen on menus, appearing in inventive stews and sausages. For adventurous palates a typically *Minhoto* dish is *papas de sarrabulho,* a hearty stew of shredded pork in a flour-thickened, cumin-scented, pig's-blood soup. Roast *cabrito* (kid) is very popular, too.

> ## FERTILE FIELDS
>
> Little of the green countryside is wasted. Vines are trained on poles and in trees high above cultivated fields, forming a natural canopy, for this is *vinho verde* country. This refreshing young "green wine"— light on alcohol but with fine digestive properties—is crisp. There are two types of vinho verde: red and white. The Portuguese drink the red more often and export more of the white. Whatever the color, vinho verde is a true taste of the north.

In the mountains wonderful *truta* (trout) is available at any town or village close to a river. Trás-os-Montes menus are enlivened by hearty meat stews, which usually include parts of the pig you may wish had been left out (an ear or a trotter, for example). Sausages are a better bet, particularly *alheira* (a legacy of the Sephardic Jews, who devised this mock sausage of chicken and spices to fool religious authorities) or chouriço, the spicy, smoked variety. The other smoked specialty of the region is *presunto de Chaves,* a delicious smoked ham from the town of Chaves. Most dishes will be served with *batatas* (potatoes) or *arroz* (rice), both fine examples of staples being raised to an art form. Potatoes here, whether roasted, boiled, or fried, have an irresistibly nutty and sweet flavor. Rice is lightly sautéed with chopped garlic in olive oil before adding water, resulting in a side dish that could easily be devoured as a main course.

The wine available throughout the north is of very high quality. The Minho region's vinho verde is a light, young, slightly sparkling red or white wine. The taste is refreshing, both fruity and acid. Both reds and whites are served chilled (most people prefer the white), and vinho verde goes exceptionally well with fish and shellfish. Vinho verde made from the *Alvarinho* grape in the region of Monção is prized throughout the country.

GREAT ITINERARIES

Porto is 3½ hours north of Lisbon by highway or express train, so even a short trip to Portugal can include a night or two here. From Porto, it's only another 2 hours through the Minho coastline up to the Spanish border, or another 3–4 hours east to the less visited Trás-os-Montes and the eastern border with Spain.

It takes only a day or two to experience the more urban pleasures of Porto and its wine lodges and the nearby coastal resorts. Several more days would permit a visit to the history-rich towns of Braga or Guimarães or a trip through the lovely Douro Valley. A full week would allow you to cover all of this and the peaceful inland towns and villages along the rivers Lima and Minho, or you could set off for the remote northeastern Trás-os-Montes and its fascinating towns of Bragança and Chaves.

IF YOU HAVE 3 DAYS
Devote the first morning to 🏛 **Porto** ❶– ⓭, followed by an afternoon tour of the port-wine lodges in Vila Nova de Gaia, across the Rio Douro. Before turning in, spend time enjoying the riverside cafés and restaurants. In the morning, drive north through the sandy coastal towns of **Vila do Conde** ⓮, **Póvoa de Varzim** ⓯, and **Ofir and Esposende** ⓰. After the bracing air, shopping to the sound of the waves, and a seafood lunch, head inland to the ancient city of 🏛 **Braga** ㉒, with its profusion of churches. Overnight here or in the delightfully medieval 🏛 **Guimarães** ㉑, which you should explore on Day 3. Worth

a side trip from either town is the fascinating Citânia de Briteiros, the hilltop site of an ancient Iron Age settlement.

Alternatively, you could spend your second two days savoring the pastoral Douro Valley. Follow the winding N108 east from Porto along the river's north bank. Don't miss the view at Entre-os-Rios, where the Douro and Tâmega rivers converge. Head back up toward 🏛 **Amarante** ⓲, one of the north's most picturesque towns, its halves joined by a narrow 18th-century bridge. It's worth overnighting here. On Day 3, wind your way southeast along the N101, passing through Mesão Frio, to the Douro, where you can follow the river east to **Pêso da Régua** ⓳, heart of the port-wine country, and tour a wine cellar or two. Across the river and a bit farther south is **Lamego** ⓴, with its impressive 18th-century pilgrimage shrine of Nossa Senhora dos Remédios. From either of these towns, it's not far to **Vila Real** ㉛, gateway to the remote and beautiful region of Trás-os-Montes. You could spend the night here and head east the next day, or return to Porto.

IF YOU HAVE 5 DAYS
Spend a day and night in 🏛 **Porto** ❶– ⓭, then head inland and north. Take two days to explore 🏛 **Braga** ㉒, including the Citânia de Briteiros, and 🏛 **Guimarães** ㉑. On Day 4 go west to **Barcelos** ㉓, folk-art center of the country; try to arrive on a Thursday, when the large weekly market is filled with purveyors of everything from live pigs to hand-painted pottery. Continue north to graceful 🏛 **Viana**

do Castelo ㉔, along the Rio Lima. Wander its narrow stone streets and stay the night in the art deco pousada on a hill overlooking town or drive up along the Costa Verde to **Caminha** ㉕ or one of the other partially walled castle towns along the Spanish border: 🔲 **Vila Nova de Cerveira** ㉖, **Valença do Minho** ㉗, and **Monção** ㉘.

On Day 5, head to quaint Arcos de Valdevez and rent a rowboat for a couple of hours on the river, then continue on to two nearby towns with beautiful bridges, **Ponte da Barca** ㉙, with its 15th-century arched passageway, and **Ponte de Lima** ㉚, graced with a long, low Roman footbridge. If you're in Ponte de Lima on the second Monday of the month, you can visit the country's oldest market. From here, return to Porto or Lisbon.

IF YOU HAVE 7 DAYS
Porto ❶– ⓯ is the ideal first day and night for your explorations. On Day 2, head inland for 🔲 **Amarante** ⓲, where you can have dinner in the romantic old part of town and spend the night. The next day, continue to 🔲 **Vila Real** ㉛, the capital and first sizable town in the Trás-os-Montes region. On Day 4, head northeast—passing through Murça, with its giant, granite *porca* (pig) of legend—to the attractive town of **Mirandela** ㉜. Visit the 17th-century Paço dos Távoras and then continue on the IP4 into the Serra de Nogueira toward the country's northeastern corner. Eventually you'll see the great castle at 🔲 **Bragança** ㉝ rising in the distance; plan on spending two nights here. On Day 5, visit the sights of the city, which dates from about 600 BC. The next day, head west along the N103, one

of the country's most spectacular drives. You'll pass through **Vinhais** ㉞ on the way to **Chaves** ㉟, originally a Roman military base and popular today for its thermal springs. From Chaves, you could head back toward Vila Real and on to a final night in Porto.

Another alternative would be to stay on the N103 and continue west until you reach the lake and hydroelectric dam system along the Rio Cávado. The winding road allows for marvelous views and has several access points into the **Parque Nacional da Peneda-Gerês,** where you could quite understandably choose to stay overnight (the São Bento Pousada overlooks the Caniçada dam) for a bit of hiking in the woods, or you could continue down the road to 🔲 **Braga** ㉒, spend the night, and then return to Porto.

7

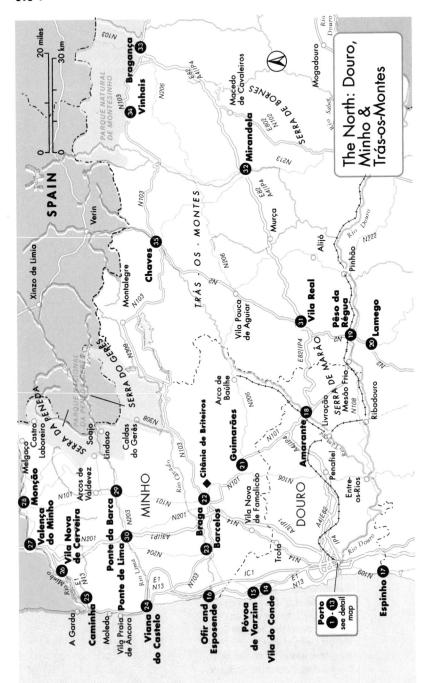

The North: Douro, Minho & Trás-os-Montes

20 miles
30 km

SPAIN

PARQUE NATURAL DE MONTESINHO

33 Bragança
34 Vinhais
N103
N103

Macedo de Cavaleiros
E82/IP4
32 Mirandela
N213

Mogadouro
Rio Sabor
E802 N102

SERRA DE BORNES

Murça
N206
Alijó
N222
Rio Douro

Verin
35 Chaves
Montalegre
N103

TRÁS - OS - MONTES
N2

Vila Pouca de Aguiar

Pinhão
31 Vila Real
19 Pêso da Régua
20 Lamego
N2

Xinzo de Limia
Rio Limia

SERRA DO GERÊS
N308
N908

SERRA DA PENEDA
PARQUE NACIONAL DA PENEDA

Castro Laboreiro
Lindoso
Soajo
Caldas do Gerês

Arco de Baúlhe
N206

SERRA DE MARÃO
E82/IP4
Mesão Frio
Livração
18 Amarante
N108
Ribadouro

Melgaço
28 Monção
27 Valença do Minho
26 Vila Nova de Cerveira
N101
N203
N201

Arcos de Valdevez
29 Ponte da Barca
30 Ponte de Lima
Rio Cávado

MINHO
N103
N201
N101

Citânia de Briteiros
Guimarães
21
N101

Penafiel
A4/E82
Entre-os-Rios
IP4
N106
N15

DOURO
Rio Douro

22 Braga
23 Barcelos
A3/IP1
N204
N14

Vila Nova de Famalicão

Trofa
N14

A Garda
Moledo
Vila Praia de Âncora
25 Caminha
24 Viana do Castelo
Rio Minho
E1 N13
Rio Lima
E1 N13
N103

16 Ofir and Esposende
15 Póvoa de Varzim
14 Vila do Conde
IC1

17 Espinho
N109

1 - 13 Porto
see detail map
E1 N13

Port enjoys the most renown of the local wines (ask for *vinho do Porto*), but the Douro region, where port comes from, also produces some of Portugal's finest table wines. Other good regions for wine include the area around Chaves, particularly at Valpaços, which produces some excellent, full-bodied, and almost creamy reds.

About the Hotels

In Porto hotel rates rival those in Lisbon, and you should reserve rooms well in advance to avoid disappointment. Lodgings in the Minho and Trás-os-Montes regions are very reasonably priced compared with their counterparts elsewhere in the country. The Turismo no Espaço Rural (Rural Tourism) network allows you to spend time at a variety of historic manor houses, country farms, and little village cottages scattered throughout the north. Many of these converted 17th- and 18th-century buildings are found in the lovely rural areas around Ponte de Lima, in the Minho region. *Pousadas* (inns) offer a variety of settings in the north, from a 12th-century monastery in Guimarães to more rustic, hunting-lodge digs in such places as the Marão mountain ridges near Amarante or a hilltop in Bragança.

WHAT IT COSTS In Euros					
	$$$$	**$$$**	**$$**	**$**	**¢**
RESTAURANTS	over €21	€16–€21	€11–€15	€7–€10	under €7
HOTELS	over €275	€176–€275	€101–€175	€60–€100	under €60

Restaurant prices are per person for a main course at dinner. Hotel prices are for a standard double room, including tax, in high season (off-season rates may be lower).

Timing

It's best to visit the north in summer, when Porto and the Minho region are generally warm, but be prepared for drizzling rain at any time. Coastal temperatures are a few degrees cooler than in the south. Inland, and especially in the northeastern mountains, it can be very hot in summer and cold in winter.

PORTO

Industrious Porto—Portugal's second-largest city, with a population of roughly 250,877 and a location 321 km (199 mi) north of Lisbon—considers itself the north's capital and, more contentiously, the country's economic center. Locals support this claim by quoting a typically down-to-earth maxim: "Coimbra sings, Braga prays, Lisbon shows off, and Porto works." Certainly wherever you look, there's evidence of a robust city. Massive developments on the outskirts give way to a fashionable commercial area in the heart of town; shops and restaurants bustle with big-spending locals; and the city's buildings, churches, and monuments—both old and new—impress with their solid construction. A new metro has also helped propel Porto into the 21st century. There's poverty here, of course, primarily down by the river in the ragged older areas, parts of which are positively medieval. But in the shopping centers, the stately stock exchange building, and the affluent port-wine industry, Porto oozes confidence.

This emphasis on worth rather than beauty has created a solid city rather than a graceful one. The public buildings tend to be sober. Gray and ocher tones often dominate facades. But the city abounds in fine structures and interesting perspectives. It's quite impressive at first sight if you approach from the south, and its glorious location on a steep hillside above the Rio Douro affords exhilarating views.

WHAT'S IN A NAME?

The importance of the river trade to the city is reflected in its current name, whose use began in early medieval times. *Porto* means simply "port," and over the centuries the city has traded widely in fish, salt, and wine. English and Spanish speakers' name for Porto—Oporto—is a result of a misunderstanding. When the Portuguese said "o Porto" (the port), traders assumed the "o" was part of the city's name.

The river has influenced the city's development since pre-Roman times, when the town of Cale on the left bank prospered sufficiently to support a trading port, called Portus, on the site of today's city. Under the Romans this twin town of Portus-Cale became a thriving commercial center, and it continued to be successful despite the later ravages of Moorish occupation and Christian reconquest. Given the outward-looking nature of its inhabitants, it's fitting that Henry the Navigator—the great explorer king—was born here at the end of the 14th century.

As the result of the Methuen agreement with England in 1703, which gave commercial preference to Portuguese wines in detriment to French ones, the Douro Valley vineyards found a new market and shipped ever-increasing quantities of wine out of Porto. It was around this time that the practice of mixing Douro Valley wine with brandy began. This was meant to preserve the wine better for the journey to England, and to improve its taste over time. This practical measure became responsible for today's port wine flavor. Port wine trade is still big business, based just across the river in the suburb of Vila Nova de Gaia (site of the Roman town of Cale), and in many *quintas* (wine estates) in the Douro Valley.

Exploring Porto

You can walk around most of central Porto. To reach the few outlying attractions, you can take buses, taxis, funiculars, or the metro. This comprises four metropolitan lines which all converge at the Trinidade stop. An additional line running from the airport to the center is scheduled to open in late 2007. For an update and metro map check the tourist office or Web site www.metrodoporto.pt. If you are on foot be prepared for the hills, which can prove tiring in the summer heat. The city is very congested, so leave your car at your hotel. Central parking is difficult to find, and much of the downtown area (in particular, the riverside and the winding streets of the Old Town below the cathedral) isn't accessible to cars.

What to See

❷ Avenida dos Aliados. This imposing boulevard is lined with bright flower beds and grand buildings and is essentially the heart of the central business district. In addition to corporate businesses and banks, you'll find clothing and shoe stores, plus restaurants and coffeehouses. At one end of it is the broad Câmara Municipal (Town Hall). A tall bell tower sprouts from the roof of this palacelike, early-20th-century building, inside of which an impressive Portuguese wall tapestry is displayed. Praça da Liberdade—the hub from which Porto radiates—is at the other end of the avenue. Two statues adorn the square: a cast of Dom Pedro IV sitting on a horse and a modern statue of the great 19th-century Portuguese poet and novelist Almeida Garrett.

NEED A BREAK? Many of Porto's old-style coffeehouses—which once rivaled Lisbon's in opulence and literary legend—have disappeared. Two notable ones have survived and are perfect places to sit and imbibe both a *cimbalino* (espresso) and the city. The ornate **Majestic Café** (⊠ Rua de Santa Catarina 112 ☎ 22/200-3887 ⊕ www. cafemajestic.com ☼ 9 AM-midnight) has piano music and temporary art exhibitions. It's on a busy pedestrian shopping street, a short walk from Avenida dos Aliados. Just around the corner from the Majestic Café is the attractively restored **Confeitaria do Bolhão** (⊠ Rua Formosa 339 ☎ 22/339-5220).

❻ Cais da Ribeira (Ribeira Pier). A string of fish restaurants and *tascas* (taverns) are built into the street-level arcade of timeworn buildings along this pier. In the Praça da Ribeira, people sit and chat around an odd, modern, cubelike sculpture; farther on, steps lead to a walkway above the river that's backed by tall houses. The pier also provides the easiest access to the lower level of the middle bridge across the Douro. Boats docked at Cais da Ribeira offer various cruises around the bridges and up the river to Peso da Régua and Pinhão.

FodorśChoice ★

❺ Casa-Museu de Guerra Junqueiro (Guerra Junqueiro House and Museum). This 18th-century white mansion, another of the city's buildings attributed by some to a pupil of Nicolau Nasoni and by others to Nicolau himself, was home to the poet Guerra Junqueiro (1850–1923). Although furnishings, sculptures, and paintings are labeled in Portuguese, English, and French (and there are brochures in English), the short tour of the elegant interior is less than enlightening if you don't speak Portuguese. ⊠ *Rua de Dom Hugo 32* ☎ *22/200-3689* ⊠ *Tues.–Fri. €1, free weekends* ☼ *Tues.–Sat. 10–12:30 and 2–5:30, Sun. 2–5:30.*

❸ Estação de São Bento. This train station was built in the early 20th century (King D. Carlos I laid the first brick himself in 1900) and inaugurated in 1915, precisely where the Convent of S. Bento de Avé-Maria was located. Therefore it inherited the convent's name—Saint Bento. The atrium is covered with 20,000 azulejos painted by Jorge Colaço (1916) depicting scenes of Portugal's history as well as ethnographic images. It is one of the most magnificent artistic undertakings of the early 20th century. The building was designed by architect Marques da Silva.

FodorśChoice ★

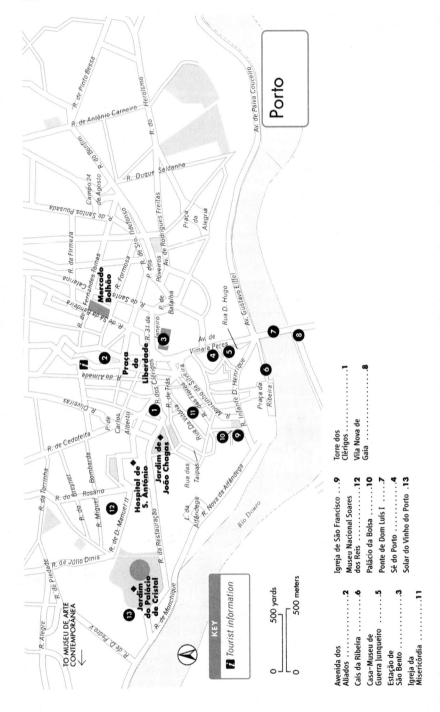

Porto

KEY

🛈 *Tourist information*

0 ———— 500 yards

0 ———— 500 meters

Avenida dos
Aliados **2**
Cais da Ribeira **6**
Casa–Museu de
Guerra Junqueiro **5**
Estação de
São Bento **3**
Igreja da
Misericórdia **11**

Igreja de São Francisco . .**9**
Museu Nacional Soares
dos Reis **12**
Palácio da Bolsa **10**
Ponte de Dom Luís I **7**
Sé do Porto **4**
Solar do Vinho do Porto .**13**

Torre dos
Clérigos **1**
Vila Nova de
Gaia **8**

TO MUSEU DE ARTE
CONTEMPORÂNEA

✉ *Praça Almeida Garret* 🚋 *22/205–1714* ☎ *808/208208 national call center* ⊕ *www.cp.pt.*

⑪ **Igreja da Misericórdia** (Mercy Church). Today's building represents a compromise between the church first built during the late 16th century and its reconstruction between 1749 and 1755 by painter and architect Nicolau Nasoni. At the church museum next door you can see *Fons Vitae* (Fountain of Life), a vibrant, anonymous, Renaissance painting, depicting the founder of the church, Dom Manuel I, his queen, and their eight children kneeling before a crucified Christ. ✉ *Rua das Flores 5* ☎ *22/207–4710* ⊕ *www.scmp.pt* ✉ *Church free, museum €1.50* ⊙ *Church Tues.–Fri. 8–12:30 and 2–5:30, museum weekdays 9:30–12:30 and 2–5:30.*

⑨ **Igreja de São Francisco** (Church of St. Francis). During the last days of Porto's siege by the absolutist army (the *miguelistas*) in July 1842, there was gunfire by the nearby São Francisco Convent. These shootings caused a fire that destroyed most parts of the convent, sparing only this church. The church is an undistinguished, late-14th-century Gothic building on the outside, but inside is an astounding interior: gilded carving—added in the mid-18th century—runs up the pillars, over the altar, and across the ceiling. An adjacent museum (Museu de Arte Sacra) houses furnishings from the Franciscan convent. A guided tour (call the day before) includes a visit to the church, museum, and catacombs. ✉ *Rua do Infante Dom Henrique 93* ☎ *22/206–2100* ✉ *€3* ⊙ *Nov.–Mar., daily 9–5; Apr.–Oct., daily 9–6; May–Sept., daily 9–7. Closed Dec. 25 for individual visits.*

★ ⑫ **Museu Nacional Soares dos Reis.** This art museum was the first in Portugal, founded in 1833 by King D. Pedro IV. In 1911 it was renamed after the 19th-century Portuguese sculptor whose works are contained within it. In 1940 it moved to this late-19th-century home, the Palácio dos Carrancas, which was once home to the royal family. The large art collection includes several Portuguese primitive works of the 16th century as well as superb collections of silver, ceramics, glassware, and costumes. Bus 78 runs here from Praça da Liberdade. ✉ *Palácio dos Carrancas, Rua de Dom Manuel II* ☎ *22/339–3770* ⊕ *www.ipmuseus. pt* ✉ *Tues.–Sat. €3, free Sun.* ⊙ *Tues. 2–6, Wed.–Sun. 10–12:30 and 2–6.*

⑩ **Palácio da Bolsa.** Porto's 19th-century, neoclassical stock exchange takes

Fodor'sChoice up much of the site of the former Franciscan convent at the Igreja de

★ São Francisco. Guided tours are the only way to see the interior of this masterpiece of 19th-century Portuguese architecture. The Arab-style ballroom, in particular, is one of the most admired chambers and was designed by civil engineer Gustavo Adolfo Gonçalves e Sousa. ✉ *Rua Ferreira Borges* ☎ *22/339–9013* ⊕ *www.palaciodabolsa.pt* ✉ *Tours €5* ⊙ *Apr.–Oct., daily 9–7; Nov.–Mar., daily 9–1 and 2–6.*

⑦ **Ponte de Dom Luís I** (Luís I Bridge). Though it was intended to replace the Pênsil bridge (also called D. Maria Pia), this two-tier bridge was completed in 1886 at another site. Designed by Teófilo Seyrig with two tiers for both vehicles and pedestrians, it leads directly to the city of Vila Nova de Gaia. Its real glory, however, is the magnificent vistas it affords of downtown Porto. A jumble of red-tile roofs on pastel-color buildings mixes with gray-and-white Gothic and baroque church towers, and all is reflected in the majestic Douro River; if the sun is shining just right, everything appears to be washed in gold.

4 **Sé do Porto** (Cathedral). Originally constructed in the 12th century by the parents of Afonso Henriques (Portugal's first king), Porto's granite cathedral has been rebuilt twice: first in the late 13th century and again in the 18th century, when the architect of the Torre dos Clérigos, Nicolau Nasoni, was among those commissioned to work on its expansion. Despite the renovations, it remains a fortresslike structure—an uncompromising testament to medieval wealth and power. Notice a low relief on the northern tower, depicting a 14th-century vessel and symbolizing the city's nautical vocation. Size is the only exceptional thing about the interior; when you enter the two-story, 14th-century cloisters, however, the building comes to life. Decorated with gleaming azulejos, a staircase added by Nasoni leads to the second level and into a richly furnished chapter house, from which there are fine views through narrow windows. Nasoni also designed the Paço dos Arcebispos (Archbishops' Palace), behind the cathedral. It has been converted to offices, so you can only admire its 197-foot-long facade. ⊠ *Terreiro da Sé* ☎ *22/205–9028* ✉ *Cathedral free; cloisters €2 per person if group is fewer than 10 people, €1.25 per person for groups of 10 or more* ☉ *Mon.–Sat. 9–12:30 and 2:30–6, Sun. 2:30–6.*

★ **13** **Solar do Vinho do Porto** (Port Wine Institute). Located in a 19th-century country house called the Quinta da Macierinha, the institute offers relaxed tastings of Porto's famous wine in much the same fashion as its counterpart in Lisbon, but it has a much friendlier reputation—and the wine has only had to travel across the river before being served. Tasting prices start at around €0.80 per glass. The Quinta da Macierinha is home to the **Museu Romântico da Quinta da Macierinha** (Romantic Museum), with displays of period furniture. ⊠ *Quinta da Macierinha, Rua de Entre Quintas 220* ☎ *22/609–4749 Port Wine Institute, 22/605–7033 museum, 22/606–6207 for guided tours* ⊕ *www.ivp.pt* ✉ *Port Wine Institute free; tasting prices vary. Museum €1.* ☉ *Port Wine Institute Mon.–Sat. 2–midnight; museum Tues.–Sat. 10–12:30 and 2–5:30, Sun. 2–6.*

☾ **1** **Torre dos Clérigos.** Designed by Italian architect Nicolau Nasoni and begun

Fodor'sChoice in 1754, the tower of the church Igreja dos Clérigos reaches an impressive height of 249 feet. There are 225 steep stone steps to the belfry, and the considerable effort required to climb them is rewarded by stunning views of the Old Town, the river, and beyond to the mouth of the Douro. The church itself, also built by Nasoni, predates the tower and is an elaborate example of Italianate baroque architecture. ⊠ *Rua S. Filipe Nery* ☎ *22/200–1729* ✉ *Tower €1.50* ☉ *Tower Sept.–May, daily 10–noon and 2–5; June and July, daily 9:30–1 and 2-7; Aug., daily 10–7. Church Mon.–Thurs. and Sat. 9–noon and 3:30–7:30, Sun. 10–1 and 8:30–10:30.*

Port Wine

Many of the more than 16 companies with caves in Vila Nova de Gaia are still foreign owned. They include such well-known names as Sandeman, Osborne, Cockburn, Kopke, Ferreira, Calém, Taylor's, Barros, Ramos-Pinto, Real Companhia Velha, Fonseca, Rozès, Burmester, Offley, Noval, and Graham's. All are signposted and within a few minutes' walk of the bridge and each other; their names are also displayed in huge white letters across their roofs. Each company offers free guided tours of its facility, which always end with a tasting of one or two wines and an opportunity to buy bottles from the company store. Children are usually welcome and are often fascinated by the huge warehouses and all sorts of interesting machinery. The major lodges are open weekdays 9–12:30 and 2–7, Saturday 9–12:30, from June through September; the rest of the year, tours end at 5 and are conducted only on weekdays. Tours begin regularly, usually when enough visitors are assembled. The tourist office at Vila Nova de Gaia offers a small map of the main lodges and can advise you on hours of the smaller operations.

★ ♻ ❽ **Vila Nova de Gaia.** A city across the Rio Douro from central Porto, Vila Nova de Gaia has been the headquarters of the port-wine trade since the late 17th century, when import bans on French wine led British merchants to look for alternative sources. By the 18th century, the British had established companies and a regulatory association in Porto. The wine was transported from vineyards on the upper Douro to port-wine caves at Vila Nova de Gaia, where it was allowed to mature before being exported. Very little has changed in the relationship between Porto and the Douro since those days, as wine is still transported to the city, matured in the warehouses, and bottled. Instead of traveling down the river on *barcos rabelos* (flat-bottom boats), however, the wine is now carried by truck. A couple of the traditional boats are moored at the quayside on the Vila Nova de Gaia side. For more on the port companies here, ⇨ *see* Shopping, *below.*

Vila Nova de Gaia isn't solely devoted to the port-wine trade. Combine a tour of the wine lodges with a visit to the **Casa-Museu de Teixeira Lopes,** the home of the sculptor António Teixeira Lopes (1866–1942). It contains some excellent sculpture as well as a varied collection of paintings by Teixeira Lopes's contemporaries. The collection of books, coins, and ceramics is also interesting. ⊠ *Rua Teixeira Lopes 32, Vila Nova de Gaia* ☎ *22/375–1224* ⊠ *Free* ☉ *Tues.–Sat. 9–12:30 and 2–5:30.*

OUTSIDE DOWNTOWN
Fodor'sChoice
★

Museu de Arte Contemporânea de Serralves. Designed by Siza Vieira, a former winner of the Pritzker Architecture Prize, this contemporary art museum is housed within the Serralves Mansion, which is surrounded by gardens. It displays the work of Portuguese painters, sculptors, and designers. Exhibitions change regularly, and the museum sometimes closes for two weeks at a time for rehanging. Check with the tourist office for the latest information. You can take either a taxi or Bus 78 from Praça da Liberdade. The journey takes about 30 minutes from the center of town. ⊠ *Rua D. João de Castro 210* ☎ *22/615–6500 or 808/200543* ⊕ *www.serralves.pt* ⊠ *Museum and garden €5, garden €2.50, car parking €0.75 per hr* ⊙ *Tues., Wed., and Fri.–Sun. 10–7, Thurs. 10–10.*

Where to Eat

$$$$ ✕ **Portucale.** Atop a modern building and hotel, the Portucale (whiting
Fodor'sChoice   loins) is known equally for the excellence of its food and the citywide
★   views from its windows. The tripe and game dishes are rich and imaginative; *lombos de pescada à moda do chefe* is a good bet. After dinner, sip some port from the impressive selection. ⊠ *Rua da Alegria 598* ☎ *22/ 537–0717* ⚑ *Reservations essential* ▤ *AE, DC, MC, V.*

$$$–$$$$ ✕ **Bull and Bear.** Chef-owner Miguel Castro Silva gives his northern Portugal dishes touches of French, Italian, and even Japanese flavors at his comfortable, modern restaurant in the Porto stock exchange building. The results are such unusual and successful combinations as *ameijoas com feijão manteiga* (clams with butter beans) and *linguado com molho de amêndoa* (sole with almond sauce). ⊠ *Av. da Boavista 3431* ☎ *22/ 610–7669* ▤ *AE, DC, MC, V* ⊙ *Closed Sun. No lunch Sat.*

★ $$$–$$$$ ✕ **Casa Nanda.** This restaurant is the epitome of a Portuguese tasca: a small, cozy tavern that offers home cooking. The cook and co-owner, Fernanda Maria, learned her skills from a legendary figure in the history of Porto restaurants, a tasca keeper of great fame. The experience shows. This is a great place to try cozido à portuguesa (boiled beef, pork, and chicken with vegetables, sausage, rice, and potatoes), but call first to see if it's available that day. ⊠ *Rua da Alegria 394* ☎ *22/537–0575* ▤ *No credit cards* ⊙ *Closed Sun.*

$$$–$$$$ ✕ **Tripeiro.** This spacious restaurant is just the place to try Porto-style tripe known as *tripas á moda do Porto* or the famous *cozido à portuguesa* (boiled meat with vegetables), which are nearly always on the menu in one form or another. In case you don't appreciate the city's favorite food, the menu has several meat and bacalhau specialties, too. Along with the typically Portuguese food comes typically Portuguese details: wooden ceiling beams, whitewashed walls, and potted plants throughout. There's an adjacent bar where you can eat cheaper. ⊠ *Rua de Passos Manuel 195* ☎ *22/200–5886* ▤ *AE, DC, MC, V* ⊙ *Closed Sun.*

★ $$–$$$$ ✕ **Bule.** In addition to some of the best cooking in town, Bule has a pretty little terrace with tables shaded by umbrellas, a spacious and comfortable interior dining room, and impeccable service throughout. The *pato assado* (roast duck) is a succulent specialty, as is the bacalhau *à lagareiro* (baked with onions and garlic in olive oil). ⊠ *Rua de Timor 128* ☎ *22/618–8777* ▤ *AE, DC, MC, V* ⊙ *Closed Sun. and 1st half of Aug.*

$$–$$$$ ✕ **O Escondidinho.** Near the main train station, this restaurant first opened in 1934 during the first great Portuguese Colonial Exhibition that took place in Palácio de Cristal. An entrance with hand-painted tiles from the 17th century announces a country-house decor. The menu has French-influenced dishes as well as high-quality Douro dishes. Steak is

prepared no less than six ways (try the woodsy-smoky version with truffles), and the sole is always deliciously fresh. The specialty is seafood, namely codfish, whiting, and lobster au gratin. The *pudim flan* (egg custard) is outstanding. ⊠ *Rua dos Passos Manuel 144* ☎ *22/200–1079* ⚖ *Reservations essential* ☐ *DC, MC, V* ⊘ *Closed Sun.*

$$–$$$$
Fodor'sChoice
★

✕ **Ó Macedo.** A 10-minute drive from the center of town, this agreeable little restaurant is in a restored old building overlooking the Douro estuary. The wine list is exceptionally good, and the menu has a tempting selection of meat and fish dishes. Try the *goraz assado no forno* (oven-baked sea bream) or the *bife de fillet mignon com natas à Macedo* (house-style filet mignon with cream sauce), not forgetting good old English roast beef. ⊠ *Rua do Passeio Alegre 552* ☎ *22/617–0166* ☐ *AE, MC, V* ⊘ *Closed Sun. and 2 wks in Aug. No lunch Sat.*

$$–$$$
Fodor'sChoice
★

✕ **Dom Tonho.** Seafood is the specialty of this riverfront restaurant, which occupies a building that goes back to the 16th century. Try one of the codfish dishes, the *robalo ao sal* (rock bass baked in salt), or *pescada da Póvoa grelhada* (grilled whiting from Póvoa). ⊠ *Cais da Ribeira 13–15* ☎ *22/200–4307* ☐ *AE, DC, MC, V.*

$–$$$

✕ **Cufra.** Dating to 1974, this restaurant named after the biggest oasis in the Sahara Desert is one of the best places in Porto to try the famous *francesinha* (rye bread, ham, sirloin steak, sausage, and Dutch cheese, all seasoned with seafood sauce). The seafood specialties are a good value. The more informal dining room has benches and tables, and the other area has individual tables, wood paneling, and a few reproduction paintings. ⊠ *Av. da Boavista 2504* ☎ *22/617–2715* ☐ *AE, DC, MC, V* ⊘ *Closed Mon. No lunch.*

$–$$$

✕ **Filha da Mãe Preta.** The pleasant first-floor dining room of this well-known Cais da Ribeira restaurant is decorated with azulejos and has arched windows that look across the river to the port-wine lodges of Vila Nova de Gaia. Stick with such simple fish specialties as *lulas grelhadas* (grilled squid) or *peixe espada* (grilled blade fish). Most of the grilled dishes come with an ample serving of rice; unless you're sharing with someone else, ask for a *meia dose* (half serving). Reservations are a good idea in summer. ⊠ *Cais da Ribeira 39–40* ☎ *22/205–5515* ☐ *AE, DC, MC, V* ⊘ *Closed Sun.*

★ **$–$$$**

✕ **Majestic Café.** Opened in 1921, this is one of Porto's grand old coffeehouses, and it serves double duty as a reasonably priced grill-restaurant. Sit amid the sculpted wood, carved nymphs, and mirrors and choose from a fair list of omelets, sandwiches, salads, burgers, and steaks. Or just have coffee and a pastry. The enclosed patio is the perfect place to dine on a summer's eve; if you come on Friday or Saturday night, your meal will be accompanied by piano music. There's an art gallery downstairs. ⊠ *Rua de Santa Catarina 112* ☎ *22/200–3887* ☐ *AE, DC, MC, V* ⊘ *Closed Sun.*

$–$$
Fodor'sChoice
★

✕ **Chez Lapin.** At this Cais da Ribeira restaurant overlooking the river, the service may be slow and the folksy decor may be overdone, but the food is excellent, and the outdoor terrace is attractive. The menu has such traditional but sometimes uncommon Porto dishes as bacalhau *e polvo assado no forno* (baked and with octopus) and *caldeirada de peixe* (fish stew), all served in generous portions. The restaurant also offers trips aboard its five traditional rabelo boats docked at the quay out front. ⊠ *Rua Canastreiros 40–42* ☎ *22/200–6418 or 22/208–0677* ⚎ *Reservations essential* ⊟ *AE, DC, MC, V.*

¢–$$ ✕**Traçadinho.** A long bar invites you to take an aperitif before descending to the vaulted dining room of this popular traditional restaurant. Many dishes are cooked over an open wood fire. The bacalhau *à Traçadinho* (baked with onions and tomatoes) is legendary, as is the cozido à portuguesa. ⊠ *Rua da Madeira 186* ☎ *22/200–5624* ⊟ *No credit cards* ⊘ *Closed Sun.*

Where to Stay

$$$–$$$$ ▦**Hotel Tivoli Porto.** This small hotel is west of the city center, off Avenida da Boavista, in a residential area near the Museum of Contemporary Art. The comfortable interior is unobtrusively modern. Rooms share a terrace and have every little amenity you could possibly want—right down to a shoe-shine kit. Bathrooms are marble clad and luxurious. ⊠ *Rua Afonso Lopes Vieira 66, 4100-020* ☎ *22/607–7900* ⊕ *www.tivolihotels.com* ⟿ *58 rooms* ⚐ *Restaurant, room service, in-room safes, minibars, cable TV, pool, bar, laundry service, business services, meeting rooms, car rental, Wi-Fi, free parking* ⊟ *AE, DC, MC, V* ⍾ *BP.*

$$$ ▦**Hotel Infante de Sagres.** Visiting royalty have been happy to stay at
Fodor'sChoice Porto's first luxury hotel, which was built after World War II. It does,
★ indeed, provide service fit for a king; it also has a great location close to Avenida dos Aliados. Intricately carved wood details, rare area rugs and tapestries, stained-glass windows, and 18th- and 19th-century antiques fill the public areas. In guest rooms, shades of beige, cream, and white complement dark-wood furnishings and lend a contemporary character; bathrooms are marble from floor to ceiling and have sophisticated lighting. ⊠ *Praça D. Filipa de Lencastre 62, 4050-259* ☎ *22/339–8500* ⊕ *www.hotelinfantesagres.pt* ⟿ *73 rooms* ⚐ *Restaurant, room service, minibars, cable TV, bar, Wi-Fi* ⊟ *AE, DC, MC, V* ⍾ *BP.*

$$ ▦**Grande Hotel do Porto.** The staff is efficient, and the rates are reason-
Fodor'sChoice able at the stately Grande, which is on the city's best shopping street.
★ The hotel has just the right mix of old and new. Public areas are full of turn-of-the-last-century details; streamlined guest rooms are loaded with modern amenities. ⊠ *Rua de Santa Catarina 197, 4000-450* ☎ *22/207–6690* ⊕ *www.grandehotelporto.com* ⟿ *100 rooms* ⚐ *Restaurant, room service, in-room safes, minibars, cable TV, bar, babysitting, laundry service, meeting rooms, free parking, no-smoking rooms, Wi-Fi* ⊟ *AE, DC, MC, V* ⍾ *BP.*

$$ ▦**Hotel Apartamento Fęnix Porto.** This modern apartment hotel is a good alternative if you feel like doing your own cooking. Each two-bed apartment has a fully equipped kitchenette plus amenities such as TV, direct-dial phone, and air-conditioning. If you tire of the kitchen stove, the Fęnix has another hotel (Hotel Tuela Porto) a block away with a good restaurant. The hotel is in the western part of the city, a 10-minute taxi ride from the center. Bus connections are frequent. ⊠ *Rua Gonçalo Sampaio 282, 1269-133* ☎ *22/607–1800* ⊕ *www.fenixporto.com*

🗪 *148 apartments* 🛇 *Kitchenettes, cable TV, ethernet, bar, laundry service, business services, meeting rooms, free parking, no-smoking rooms, Internet room* 🖃 *AE, DC, MC, V* ⅋ *EP.*

$$ 🏨 **Hotel Dom Henrique.** The Dom Henrique attracts business travelers who want a central base and an attentive staff. The ground-floor restaurant of this octagonal downtown tower has modern furnishings; the 17th-floor bar has classic bird's-eye views. The floors in between are full of spacious, well-appointed guest quarters. ⊠ *Rua Guedes de Azevedo 179, 4049-009* ☎ *22/340–1616* ⊕ *www.hoteldomhenrique. pt* 🗪 *112 rooms* 🛇 *Restaurant, minibars, cable TV, bar, babysitting, meeting rooms, ethernet, Wi-Fi, no-smoking rooms* 🖃 *AE, DC, MC, V* ⅋ *EP.*

$$ 🏨 **Hotel Mercure Batalha-Porto.** This attractive, modern hotel is a block or two from Avenida dos Aliados. Rooms are elegantly appointed and have the customary comforts. You can get sweeping views over the city from a wide terrace at the top of the building. ⊠ *Praça da Batalha 116, 4050-453* ☎ *22/204–3300* ⊕ *www.mercure.com* 🗪 *149 rooms* 🛇 *Restaurant, minibars, cable TV, bar, babysitting, laundry service, concierge, meeting rooms, airport shuttle, free parking* 🖃 *AE, DC, MC, V* ⅋ *BP.*

$$ 🏨 **Ipanema Park Hotel.** This elegant tower of a hotel may be a 15-minute taxi ride from the center of town, but it has loads of on-site facilities. Rooms are equipped with every modern convenience, and although the decor doesn't tell you you're in Portugal, the views—of the Douro estuary and the Atlantic—do. ⊠ *Rua de Serralves 124, 4150-702* ☎ *22/532–2100* ⊕ *www.ipanemaparkhotel.pt* 🗪 *281 rooms* 🛇 *Restaurant, in-room safes, minibars, cable TV, ethernet, 2 pools (1 indoor), health club, hair salon, massage, sauna, Turkish bath, squash, bar, shops, babysitting, business services, meeting rooms, free parking, no-smoking rooms, Wi-Fi* 🖃 *AE, DC, MC, V* ⅋ *BP.*

$$ 🏨 **Pestana Porto Carlton Hotel.** Right in Porto's historic heart, the Pestana is in a restored old building that's abutted by a medieval wall and surrounded by other old structures, some of which date from as far back as the 16th century. Rooms have city or sea views; all are contemporary, cozy, and almost cluttered with vibrant fabrics, plush carpets, throw pillows, and upholstered chairs. Bathrooms are sleek spaces, where the marble is polished to a high gloss. ⊠ *Praça da Ribeira 1, 4050-513* ☎ *22/340–2300* ⊕ *www.pestana.com* 🗪 *48 rooms* 🛇 *Restaurant, room service, in-room safes, minibars, cable TV, bar, laundry service, meeting rooms, no-smoking rooms, Wi-Fi, parking (fee)* 🖃 *AE, DC, MC, V* ⅋ *BP.*

Fodor'sChoice
★

$–$$ 🏨 **Hotel Ipanema Porto.** This modern building rises 10 floors and reserves some exclusively for nonsmokers and women. The rooms have an upbeat corporate look and include two suites for people with disabilities. There is also a good restaurant and popular bar with live music. ⊠ *Rua do Campo Alegre 156, 4150* ☎ *22/607–5059* ⊕ *www.ipanemaporto. com* 🗪 *140 rooms, 10 suites* 🛇 *Restaurant, in-room safes, minibars, cable TV with movies, bar, laundry service, business services, meeting rooms, free parking, Wi-Fi, some pets allowed, no-smoking rooms* 🖃 *AE, DC, MC, V* ⅋ *BP.*

7

$ ⊡ **Hotel BoaVista.** *Boa Vista* means "nice view." Overlooking the Douro
Fodor'sChoice estuary and the Atlantic Ocean, this hotel is a 10- to 15-minute taxi
★ ride or 20-minute bus ride west of the town center. The handsome mid-
19th-century building has small, tasteful guest rooms that are well
equipped. Ask for one with a view over the Atlantic Ocean and Douro
estuary, or settle for the view from the rooftop pool. ⊠ *Esplanada do
Castelo 58, 4150-196* ☎ *22/532–0020* ⊕ *www.hotelboavista.com*
☞ *71 rooms, 4 suites* ⌂ *Restaurant, snack bar, in-room safes, minibars, cable TV, pool, bar, meeting rooms, ethernet, free parking* ☐ *AE,
MC, V* ⎮◯⎮ *BP.*

$ ⊡ **Hotel Nave.** This moderately priced modern hotel is functional rather
than charming. It is, however, a mere 10-minute walk from the center,
and its rooms are comfortable and well equipped. ⊠ *Av. Fernão de Magalhães 247, 4300-190* ☎ *22/589–9030* ⊕ *www.hotelnave.com* ☞ *81
rooms* ⌂ *Restaurant, cable TV, bar, free parking, Wi-Fi* ☐ *AE, DC, MC,
V* ⎮◯⎮ *BP.*

$ ⊡ **Hotel Tuela Porto.** This hotel is a good option for those who want to
be close both to Porto's historic center and the airport (a 15-minute drive).
It's in a busy part of town that isn't of much interest to tourists, but the
small garden with shady trees and benches at the *Rotunda da Boavista*
(roundabout) is pleasant. Nearby is Arrábida bridge leading to Vila Nova
de Gaia and the port wine caves. The same bridge leads to the A1 mo-
torway, which links Porto to Lisbon and Spain, up north. The bathrooms'
amenities include hair dryers and phones. ⊠ *Rua Arq. Marques da
Silva 180–200, 4150* ☎ *22/600–4747* ⊕ *www.tuelaporto.com* ☞ *200
rooms* ⌂ *Restaurant, cable TV with movies, bar, laundry service, business services, meeting rooms, free parking, no-smoking rooms, Wi-Fi*
☐ *AE, DC, MC, V* ⎮◯⎮ *BP.*

$ ⊡ **Pensão Residencial dos Aliados.** The well-equipped, comfortable rooms
in this excellent *pensão* (pension) are usually in great demand, partly
because the location is right in the center of town. The delightfully ornate turn-of-the-last-century building is a listed city landmark. ⊠ *Rua
Elisio de Melo 27, 2nd fl., 4000-196* ☎ *22/200–4853* ⊕ *www.
residencialaliados.com* ☞ *43 rooms* ⌂ *Restaurant, room service, cable
TV, hair salon, bar, laundry service* ☐ *AE, MC, V* ⎮◯⎮ *EP.*

¢–$ ⊡ **Pensão Residencial Pão de Açúcar.** Just off the Avenida dos Aliados,
Fodor'sChoice this art nouveau pensão offers a lot for its relatively modest rates. You
★ can choose from among simple rooms, suites, or a top-floor room opening onto a terrace with tables and chairs. The owner also operates a car
rental agency. ⊠ *Rua do Almada 262, 4050-032* ☎ *22/200–2425*
⊕ *www.residencialpaodeacucar.com* ☞ *51 rooms* ⌂ *Room service,
minibars, cable TV, bar, laundry service, car rental, Wi-Fi* ☐ *AE, MC,
V* ⎮◯⎮ *CP.*

¢ ⊡ **Pensão Residencial Estoril.** The Estoril offers functional but comfortable rooms at very reasonable rates. It's in a quiet location near the city
center and has a terrace, a bar, and metered parking in a nearby square.
Ask for a room with a balcony overlooking the back garden area.
⊠ *Rua de Cedofeita 193, 4050-179* ☎ *22/200–2751* ⊕ *www.
pensaoestoril.com* ☞ *17 rooms* ⌂ *Cable TV, bar; no a/c* ☐ *DC, MC,
V* ⎮◯⎮ *EP.*

Nightlife & the Arts

Noted as a center for modern art, Porto enjoys regular and changing exhibitions at the Museu de Arte Contemporânea, as well as at a variety of galleries, many of which are on Rua Miguel Bombarda. Check local newspapers or with the tourist board for listings of current exhibitions as well as concerts.

Bars

Down on the Ribeira waterfront, **Aniki-bóbó** (⊠ Rua da Fonte Taurina 36–38 ☎ 22/332–4619) is where Porto's intellectual and artistic crowd hangs out until the early hours (it's open from 10 PM to about 4 AM daily). The odd name was the title of a film made by Portugal's famed director Manuel de Oliveira. The decor is old stone, set off by modern paintings; the little garden out back is great on warm nights.

FodorśChoice ★ Founded in 1933, the **Guarany Café** (⊠ Av. dos Aliados 89/85 ☎ 22/332–1272 ⊕ www.cafeguarany.com) is mostly known as a musicians' coffeehouse. It is a superb place combining the early-20th-century coffeehouse atmosphere with live concerts (jazz, classical) or literature presentations and discussions. The nicest places for an evening drink are the old-style cafés; try the **Majestic Café** (⊠ Rua de Santa Catarina 112 ☎ 22/208–7673), open Monday to Saturday until around PM. For

FodorśChoice ★ a glass of port, the best place is the **Solar do Vinho do Porto** (⊠ Rua de Entre Quintas 220 ☎ 22/609–4749), which is open until midnight every day but Sunday.

Dance & Music Clubs

Porto has a number of fashionable discos west of the city center in the commercial developments along the Douro estuary; these clubs usually open around 11 PM and close at 4 AM. A very funky, very hip crowd shows up late at **Indústria** (⊠ Av. do Brasil 843, Centro Comercial Foz, Loja A–F ☎ 22/617–6806), in the Centro Comercial da Foz. If you're into Latin-American music and want to dance salsa, look for **Mexcal Bar** (⊠ Rua da Restauração 39 ☎ 22/600–9188) which is free for women on weekdays. The **O Mal Cozinhado** (⊠ Rua do Outeirinho 13 ☎ 22/208–1319) is a lively restaurant with dancing and traditional folk music, including the plaintive sounds of fado, Monday–Saturday from 8:30 PM until 1 AM. Music from the 1960s and '70s is the draw at **Twins** (⊠ Rua do Passeio Alegre 994 ☎ 22/618–5740).

Theaters & Concert Halls

FodorśChoice ★ Porto's new cultural jewel, **Casa da Música** (⊠ Rua Eugénio de Castro 352, 1st fl. ☎ 22/605–9400 ⊕ www.casadamusica.com) is a work of art designed by Dutch architect Rem Koolhaas. Three esteemed Portuguese groups are in residency here: the Remix Ensemble, Remix Orchestra, and Opera Studio. **Coliseu do Porto** (⊠ Rua de Passos Manuel 137 ☎ 22/340–1910 or 800/108675 ⊕ www.tnsj.pt) is one of the biggest showrooms in Portugal, with 3,000 seats. Show biz greats who have appeared here and whose names you might recognize include Marcel Marceau, Pat Metheny, Diana Krall, Bob Dylan, BB King, Michael Nyman, Al Di Meola, Paco de Lucía, and Amália Rodrigues.

Designed in 1978, **Teatro Nacional de S. João** (⊠ Praça da Batalha ☎ 22/339–4940) hosts and produces a good range of classical and contemporary concerts and plays all year-round. Tickets can vary from €7 to €15.

Outdoor Activities

The main sporting obsession in Porto is *futebol* (soccer), and the city has one of the country's best teams, FC Porto, which rivals Lisbon's Benfica for domestic fame and fortune. Futebol matches are played September through May at the 52,000-seat **Estádio do Dragão** (Dragon Stadium; ⊠ Estádio do Dragão [near Av. Fernão de Magalhães] ☎ 22/557–0400) in the eastern part of the city, near the old Antas Stadium. Buses 6, 78, and 88 run past it, as does the tram system Metro do Porto.

Shopping

The best shopping streets are those off the Praça da Liberdade, particularly Rua 31 de Janeiro, Rua dos Clérigos, Rua de Santa Catarina, Rua Sá da Bandeira, Rua Cedofeita, and Rua das Flores. Traditionally, Rua das Flores has been the street for silversmiths. Gold-plated filigree is also a regional specialty, found along the same street and along Rua de Santa Catarina. Rua 31 de Janeiro and nearby streets are the center of the shoe trade, and many shops create made-to-measure shoes upon request.

You'll see port on sale throughout the city. But first taste the wine at either the Solar do Vinho do Porto or the caves at Vila Nova de Gaia. You may want to buy a bottle of the more unusual white port, drunk as an aperitif, as it's not commonly sold in North America or Britain. Try a Portonic, half tonic water and half white port served in a special glass that you'll see sold in most shops.

Books & Crafts

The **Artesanato Centro Regional de Artes Tradicionais** (Center for Traditional Arts; ⊠ Rua da Reboleira 37 ☎ 22/332–0201) has an excellent selection of regional arts and crafts. For a general handicrafts emporium, try **Artesanato dos Clérigos** (⊠ Rua da Assunção 33–34 ☎ 22/200–0257), next to Torre dos Clérigos. **Pedro A. Baptista** (⊠ Rua das Flores 237 ☎ 22/200–2880) deals in antique and modern silver.

Fodor'sChoice **Livraria Lello e Irmão** (⊠ Rua das Carmelitas 144 ☎ 22/200–2880) is
★ one of the most special and important bookshops in Portugal. It opened in 1906, and shelters more than 60,000 books. It is also famous for its neo-Gothic design and two-story interior with intricate wood-carved details.

Clothing

The designs of Luís Buchinho are sold at **Buchinho** (⊠ Rua Anibal Cunha 269 ☎ 22/201–0184). His winter wear features heavy wools, leather, and fur, but his evening dresses careen to slinky satin wear that occasionally tips its hat to lines reminiscent of the 1920s and 1940s. At **Maria Gambina** (⊠ Rua Fonte da Luz 197 ☎ 22/610–7083), the designer's street wear for men and women is sometimes subdued, sometimes splashed with bright red or yellow. Women's skirts might be bright and ringed with thick fringes or in neutral tones and given plenty of poof.

Markets & Malls

For a good general food market, visit the **Mercado Bolhão** (✉ Rua Fernandes Tomás, Edifício Mercado do Bolhão ☎ 22/332–6024 or 22/209–7200 ⊘ Weekdays 8–5, Sat. 8–1), within an enclosed building. After working up an appetite at the Mercado Bolhão, stop in at the **Confeitaria do Bolhão** (✉ Rua Formosa 339 ☎ 22/339–5220 ⊘ Mon.–Sat. 7–7:30), a delicious-smelling pastry shop.

One of the best shopping centers is **Via Catarina Shopping** (✉ Rua de Santa Catarina 312–350 ☎ 22/207–5600). Unlike most, this mall is centrally located in an old restored building. The top floor is occupied by little restaurants that re-create the Ribeira's architecture with small, medieval-style houses. The **Centro Comercial Brasília** (✉ Praça Mouzinho de Albuquerque ☎ 22/605–324), in the city's northwest section, is a popular mall. Take Bus 20, 52, or 3 from Praça da Liberdade; numbers 41, 56, or 76 from Cordoaria; or number 44 from Boavista. **Shopping Center Cidade do Porto** (✉ Rua do Bom Sucesso 161 ☎ 22/600–6584) is another one of Porto's contemporary malls. More than 13 bus lines, including numbers 3 and 56, reach the Bom Sucesso area and the center.

THE COAST & THE DOURO

Espinho, south of Porto, and the main resorts to the north—Vila do Conde, Póvoa de Varzim, Ofir, and Esposende—are the best places for watersports enthusiasts, with equipment-rental establishments often right on the beaches. Inland, the beautiful Douro Valley awaits, with its carefully terraced vineyards dotted with farmhouses stepping down to the river's edge. Drives along the river lead to romantic ancient towns. This is also the heart of prizewinning wine country, and every town has charming bars where you can pull up a chair, order a bottle and a plate of *petiscos* (mixed appetizers), and watch small-town life go by.

Vila do Conde

★ ⑭ *27 km (17 mi) north of Porto.*

Vila do Conde has a long sweep of fine sand, a fishing port, a lace-making school, and a struggling shipbuilding industry that has been making wooden boats since the 15th century. The yards are probably Europe's oldest, and the traditional boat-making skills used in them have changed surprisingly little over the centuries. It was here that the replica of Bartolomeu Dias's caravel was made in 1987 to commemorate his historic voyage around the Cape of Good Hope 500 years earlier. Urban and industrial sprawl mars the outer parts of town, but the center has winding streets and centuries-old buildings.

Vila do Conde has been known for its lace since the 17th century, and it remains the center of a flourishing lace industry. The tourist office can give you information about the Escola de Rendas (Lace-Making School), where you can see how the famed *rendas de bilros* (bone lace) is made. Local artisans also produce excellent sweaters.

The **Convento de Santa Clara** (Convent of St. Claire), now a center for children with disabilities, sprawls along the north bank of the Rio Ave (Ave River), on which Vila do Conde is situated. Dom Afonso Sanches and his wife, Dona Teresa Martins, established the convent in the 14th century, and it retains its original cloister and the beautiful tombs of its founders. The 16th-century **Igreja Paroquial** (Parish Church; ⊠ Av. Doutor Artur Cunha Araújo 46 ☎ 252/638730), in the center of town near the market, has a superb Gothic-style portal.

Created in 1919 by António Maria Pereira Júnior, the Escola de Rendas Lace-Making School is attached to the **Museu das Rendas de Bilros de Vila do Conde** (Museum of Lace Making). ⊠*Rua de S. Bento 70* ☎*252/ 248470* 🖼 *Free* ☉ *Weekdays 9–noon and 2–6.*

Colorful tents on the clean and coarse sand of the craggy beach **Praia de Mindelo** create a shield from inconvenient winds. From Vila do Conde, take the N13 7½ km (4 mi) to reach the beach's access at the small fishing village of Mindelo. The drive should take about 10 minutes.

The **Festival Internacional de Curtas Metragens** (International Short Film Festival; ☎ 252/646516 ⊕ www.curtasmetragens.pt), which started in 1993, takes place every July.

Where to Stay & Eat

$ ✕🏠 **Hotel Santana.** This hotel has a lovely landscaped setting on a hill above the River Ave. All rooms facing the river have their own balconies; if yours isn't facing the water, there are public areas to step out onto and enjoy. The decor is modern and streamlined, and rooms are well equipped with amenities. The restaurant ($$$–$$$$) offers a good selection of national dishes and views of the river and the Mosteiro de Santa Clara (Santa Clara Monastery). ⊠ *Monte Santana–Azurara, 4480-160* ☎ *252/640460* ⊕ *www.santanahotel. net* 🛏 *65 rooms, 10 suites* ⚒ *Restaurant, in-room safes, minibars, cable TV, indoor pool, health club, sauna, bar, public Internet, Wi-Fi* 🖃 *AE, DC, MC, V* 🍴 *BP.*

Póvoa de Varzim

⑮ *4 km (2½ mi) north of Vila do Conde, 31 km (19 mi) north of Porto.*

Póvoa de Varzim has a long beach, but the town has little of Vila do Conde's charm—except, perhaps, for the many shops and roadside stalls that sell similarly beautiful and reasonably priced hand-knit sweaters. It is, instead, a major resort, with high-rise hotels used mostly by vacationing Portuguese. The sandy beach is pleasant, but can become quite crowded in summer—possibly because not many people stay long in the water, where the summer temperature is usually about 16°C (60°F).

The 1930 waterfront **Casino da Póvoa** is a main attraction. It has an outstanding restaurant called Varandas do Mar, a disco, and nightly floor shows; you must be 18 to enter (take along your passport), and smart-casual dress is your best bet. The casino offers one gambling room where you can choose a range of activities from French or American roulette to blackjack or poker, and a room with 665 slot machines. There is also an entertainment area with special events and nightly shows that begin at 10:30 PM. International stars from crooners to jazz interpreters are regular guests. ⊠ *Edifício Casino da Póvoa do Varzim* ☎ *252/690870* ⊕ *www.casinos-estorilpovoa.com* ☾ *Daily 3 PM–3 AM.*

Where to Stay & Eat

$$$$
Fodor's Choice
★

✕ **Varandas do Mar.** This restaurant has a unique view over the coastline and a very refined style. It's a worthy choice, although it tends to be a bit pricey. Seafood is one of your best bets. Try *lombo de cherne grelhado com azeite perfumado de ervas aromáticas* (grilled fillet of turbot with an aromatic olive oil dressing). A jacket is not required, but you should dress smartly. ⊠ *Edifício Casino da Póvoa do Varzim* ☎ *252/690870* ⊟ *AE, DC, MC, V* ☾ *Closed Tues.*

$

🏨 **Hotel Mercure Povoa de Varzim.** This affordable beach hotel is part of a reliable Europe-wide chain and is within a few footsteps of the sea and casino. Rooms have modern decor and radio and Wi-Fi. ⊠ *Largo do Passeio Alegre 20, 4490-428* ☎ *252/290400* ⊕ *www.mercure.com* ⇨ *84 rooms, 2 suites* ⚐ *Restaurant, room service, in-room safes, minibars, cable TV, bar, public Internet, no-smoking rooms, Wi-Fi* ⊟ *AE, DC, MC, V* ⭤ *BP.*

Ofir & Esposende

⑯ *17 km (10 mi) north of Póvoa de Varzim, 46 km (29 mi) north of Porto.*

Ofir, on the south bank of the Rio Cávado, has a lovely beach with sweeping white sands, dunes, pinewoods, and water sports—a combination that has made it a popular resort. On the opposite bank of the river, Esposende, which also has a beach, retains elements of the small fishing village it once was. You'll have to drive here to appreciate these twin towns: the train line runs inland at this point, passing through Barcelos.

Espinho

⑰ *18 km (11 mi) south of Porto.*

Frequent trains and the N109 run past a string of quiet family beaches to Espinho, which has become an increasingly fashionable resort over the years. It has plenty of leisure facilities, including a casino, and a good selection of shops. The long, sandy beach is very popular in summer, but you can find some space by walking through the pinewoods to less developed areas to the south.

The **Casino Espinho** is by the beach. If the 500 slot machines, horse-racing machines, virtual roulette and blackjack, Portuguese dice, French and American roulette, or blackjack don't do it for you, come for the dining, dancing, and cabaret shows; foreign visitors must present their passports (18 is the minimum age), and although there's no formal dress code, smart and casual is most appropriate. ⊠ *Rua 19, 85* ☎ *22/733–5500* ☾ *Daily 3 PM–3 AM.*

Where to Stay & Eat

$$$$ ✕ **Restaurante Aquário Marisqueira de Espinho.** This oceanfront restau-
Fodor'sChoice rant by the casino is one of the most traditional in Espinho. Order roasted
★ fish on a spit or octopus fillet, two of the delicacies offered by this house.
There's an enormous variety of fresh seafood ready to be grilled, boiled,
or roasted in the oven. The wine list is well varied. ⊠ *Rua 4, 540* ☎ *22/
733–0370* ☰ *AE, DC, MC, V.*

$$ ⊡ **Hotel Solverde.** This five-star resort hotel is set on a hill, and most
rooms have an ocean view. A sandy beach lies some 110 yards away,
reached by foot by using a small tunnel under the train line that runs
parallel to the coast. For a calm float, you could also just dive into the
hotel's heated saltwater pools and enjoy a much warmer sea tempera-
ture. You can schedule a shuttle for the hotel's Casino Espinho, which
lies 2 km (1 mi) away on the beach. Convenient for late-night gamblers
is the 24-hour room service. ⊠ *Av. da Liberdade, Praia da Granja, S.
Felix da Marinha–Espinho 4405-362* ☎ *22/731–3162* ⊕ *www.solverde.
pt* ⇆ *166 rooms* ☖ *Restaurant, room service, in-room safes, minibars,
cable TV, miniature golf, 4 tennis courts, 2 saltwater pools, exercise equip-
ment, hot tub, massage, billiards, squash, bar, playground, laundry
service, no-smoking rooms, Wi-Fi* ☰ *AE, DC, MC, V* ❖❘ *BP.*

Outdoor Activities

For more on golf courses in the area, *see* Chapter 9.

The **Clube de Golfe de Miramar** (⊠ Av. Sacadura Cabral-Praia de Mira-
mar, Arcozelo–Vila Nova de Gaia ☎ 22/762–2067 ⊕ www.portugalgolf.
pt) has 9 holes and is 5 km (3 mi) north of Espinho. Nonmembers can
play here for €35 (9 holes–weekdays), €50 (18 holes–weekdays), or
€70 (18 holes–weekends/holidays). The golf club is closed Monday.
The 18-hole **Porto Golf Club** (⊠ Paramos ☎ 22/734–2008 ⊕ www.
portugalgolf.pt), founded in 1890 by members of the Port Wine Ship-
pers' Association, is just 2 km (1 mi) south of Espinho. Greens fees are
€60 on weekdays and €75weekends, when nonmembers can play
only until 10:30 AM.

Amarante

★ ⑱ *78 km (48 mi) northeast of Espinho, 60 km (37 mi) northeast of Porto.*

Small, agreeable Amarante is the one place in Porto's environs that re-
ally demands an overnight stop. Straddling the Rio Tâmega, its halves
are joined by a narrow 18th-century bridge that stretches above tree-
shaded banks. Although the river is polluted (which precludes swim-
ming), it's beautiful to look at. Rowboats and pedal boats are for hire
at several points along the riverside paths. The riverbank is also the site
of the local market, held every Wednesday and Saturday morning; at
these times, the usually peaceful town is disturbed by manic traffic rac-
ing along the main street and over the bridge.

★ The imposing **Convento de São Gonçalo** (St. Gonçalo Convent), built be-
tween the 16th and 20th century, is on the north side of the Rio Tâmega.
The effigy of the saint, in a room to the left of the altar, is reputed to
guarantee marriage to anyone who touches it. His features have almost

been worn away over the years, as desperate suitors try and, perhaps, try again. ✉ *Praça da República* ☎ *255/437425* 🖼 *Free* ☉ *Daily 8–6.*

NEED A BREAK?

Small cafés and restaurants with terraces overlooking the river line Rua 31 de Janeiro, the narrow main road leading to the bridge. Enjoy a drink, a snack, or a meal as you soak up the views. On the north side of the river, the big, modern **São Gonçalo Café** in the square beside the Igreja de São Gonçalo has outside tables in summer, ideal for a restful break. It also has lunch and dinner service.

Fodor'sChoice
★

The cloisters and associated buildings of a convent now house the tourist office and the **Museu Amadeo de Souza-Cardoso.** The museum has an excellent collection of modern Portuguese art, including important works by modernist painter Souza-Cardoso, who pursued variations of fauvism, cubism, futurism, and other avant-garde tendencies. He was born in the area and in 1906 shared an apartment with Amadeo Modigliani in Paris. He returned to Portugal in 1914, and died four years later at the age of 31. The museum also hosts temporary exhibitions and has some interesting archaeological pieces. The star attractions are the *diabos* (devils), a pair of 19th-century carved wooden figures connected with ancient fertility rites. They were venerated on St. Bartholomew's Day (August 24), when the devil was thought to run loose. The originals were destroyed by the French in the Peninsular War. In 1870, the Archbishop of Braga ordered the present two burned because of their pagan function. The São Gonçalo friars didn't go that far, but they did emasculate the male diabo. ✉ *Alameda Teixeira de Pascoaes* ☎ *255/420233* 🖼 *€1* ☉ *Tues.–Sun. 10–12:30 and 2–5:30. Closed holidays.*

Where to Stay & Eat

$–$$$$ ✕ **Restaurante Amaranto.** This spacious, well-appointed restaurant is atop the Amaranto Hotel on the river and near the center of town. The views are spectacular, and the menu has excellent regional fare with French touches. Try the *febras de porco à transmontana* (pork filled with smoked ham). ✉ *Edifício Amaranto, Rua Acácio Lino* ☎ *255/422006* 🖃 *AE, DC, MC, V.*

★ $ ✕ **A Quelha.** The restaurants along or near Rua 31 de Janeiro may have river views, but they don't necessarily serve the best food. This friendly, ham-and-garlic-bedecked place—behind a service station off a square at the end of the main street—has no views, but the regional fare served on its wooden tables is fantastic. The menu changes daily. Come early, around 7 PM, because it gets packed. ✉ *Rua da Olivença* ☎ *255/ 425786* 🖃 *No credit cards* ☉ *No dinner Mon.*

$$ ✕🏠 **Casa da Calçada.** Next to the old bridge and overlooking the Rio Tâmega are the carefully restored buildings of this hotel, which was once a nobleman's manor. Its ground-floor lounges are comfortable, and its guest rooms are elegant and individually furnished. The restaurant ($$$) serves regional, international, and vegetarian dishes. The gardens contain a swimming pool, a tennis court, and vineyards, and a stay here gets you a 25% discount at the Golfe de Amarante course, a 10-minute

Fodor'sChoice
★

drive away. ✉ *Largo do Paço 6, 4600-017* ☎ *255/410830* ⊕ *www.casadacalcada.com* ⌨ *30 rooms* ⚑ *Restaurant, minibars, cable TV, golf privileges, tennis court, pool, wading pool, bar, billiards, free parking, no-smoking rooms* 🖃 *AE, DC, MC, V* ⏏ *BP.*

\$\$ ✕⌂ **Pousada de São Gonçalo.** This modern pousada—20 km (12 mi) east of Amarante—is in the Serra do Marão at an altitude of nearly 3,000 feet. The rugged terrain and stone exterior are matched by a rustic interior, with lovely wood furniture, a large fireplace, and tile floors. The restaurant (\$\$\$\$) serves such satisfying regional fare as *cabrito da montanha* (mountain goat stew). A bottle of red wine from the carefully chosen list and a serving of the creamy, cinnamon-scented *arroz doce* (rice pudding) and you'll feel that all's right with the north of Portugal. ✉ *Curva do Lancete, Serra do Marão, 4604-909* ☎ *255/461113* ⊕ *www.pousadas.pt* ⌨ *15 rooms* ⚑ *Restaurant, minibars, cable TV, bar* 🖃 *AE, DC, MC, V* ⏏ *BP.*

¢–\$ ⌂ **Hotel Amaranto.** You'll have a good view over the old part of Amarante from the south bank of Rio Tâmega. This comfortable hotel is a good option if you are looking for a smart place for a fair value. The simple rooms have a standard, international look and include phone, TV, radio, and hair dryer. ✉ *Rua Acácio Lino Lote 53, 4600-045* ☎ *255/410840* ⊕ *www.hotelamaranto.com* ⌨ *35 rooms* ⚑ *Minibars, cable TV, bar, laundry service, public Internet* 🖃 *AE, DC, MC, V* ⏏ *CP.*

Outdoor Activities

For more on golf courses in the area, *see* Chapter 9.

Golfe de Amarante (✉ Fregim ☎ 255/446060), at the property of Quinta da Devesa, 5 km (3 mi) southwest of Amarante, is an 18-hole golf course with superb mountain views. The facilities include a bar, a restaurant, a golf shop, and a driving range. Greens fees are €39 on weekdays and €51 on weekends/holidays. A handicap certificate is required.

Pêso da Régua

⑲ *35 km (22 mi) southeast of Amarante, 108 km (67 mi) east of Porto.*

This small river port is in the heart of port-wine country, and all the wine from the vineyards of the Upper Douro Valley passes through it on its way to Porto. Local wine lodges offer tours of their cellars, which make a nice contrast to the large-scale operations in Vila Nova de Gaia. Combination train-boat tours begin and end in Régua (its shortened name).

Quintas

FodorśChoice **Quinta do Crasto** (Late Bottled Vintage). Dating to 1616, this large ★ wine estate was already marked on the first Douro Demarcated Region Map by Baron Forrester. Wines produced here include vintage Porto. This designates wine of ex-

> **WINE TASTING**
>
> To arrange a tasting with lunch or dinner (€50) and/or stays (€65–€176) at an inn, contact the **Gabinete da Rota do Vinho do Porto** (✉ Rua dos Camilos 90, Peso da Régua 5050-272 ☎ 254/320145 or 254/320146).

ceptional quality made in a single year. It must be bottled between the second and third year after the harvest; it is deep purple in color and full bodied. It also offers L.B.V. (Late Bottled Vintage), wines of a superior quality from a single year that are bottled between the fourth and sixth year after they were made, and others. Reservations must be made to visit this property. It lies on the north bank of Rio Douro in Sabrosa, between Peso da Régua and Pinhão. ⊠ *Gouvinhas–Ferrão, Sabrosa* ☏ *254/920020* ⊕ *www.quintadocrasto.pt.*

Fodor'sChoice
★ One of the oldest quintas in the region, **Quinta do Valado** is on the right bank of Rio Corgo near Rio Douro. This wine estate has been in the Ferreira family since 1818. It has 158 acres and vines more than 70 years old. Make reservations for a visit, which includes a wine tasting. This property holds a museum and a wine store. ⊠ *Vilarinho dos Freires, Peso da Régua 5050* ☏ *254/323147 or 254/324326.*

Bus & Train Tours

One way to reach Peso da Régua from Porto for a Sunday day trip is through tours of **Douro Azul** (⊠ Rua de S. Francisco 4-2°D, Porto ☏ 22/340–2500 ⊕ www.douroazul.pt). From March to October, a train departs Porto's S. Bento train station at 8:50 AM and arrives at Peso da Régua quay at 11:15 AM. The stay in Peso da Régua is brief: at 12:30 PM the boat departs for Porto, and lunch is served on board at 1 PM. Arrival at Vila Nova de Gaia quay is at 7 PM. The trip costs about €50.

Cenários d'Ouro (⊠ Praceta Aureliano Barrigas 6 1°E, Vila Real ☏ 259/338135 or 259/338136 ⊕ www.cenarios.com) offers a day trip that begins with transport from Porto by bus at 10 AM. At 12:30 PM you will arrive at one of Douro's quintas to lunch. At 3:35 PM you'll board a historic steam engine train in Peso da Régua for a trip to the small village Pinhão. Stretch your legs for 20 minutes and then it's on to the boat for the trip back to Peso da Régua, arriving at 6:30 PM. A bus then transports you back to Porto by 8 PM. The company also offers other boat and train combination trips from Peso da Régua. The trip costs about €82.

On Saturday, from May to October, there is a short, **historic train tour** along the Rio Douro (via steam or diesel, depending on availability). The train leaves Peso da Régua's station at 3:35 PM. In an hour the train reaches Tua, right on the Rio Tua's mouth. It returns to Régua at 5:55 PM, arriving there at 7:05 PM. For more information, call UVIR, the organization in charge of regional trains in Portugal, at the number below. ☏ *21/102–1129* ⊠ *€30 round-trip.*

Lamego

⓴ *13 km (8 mi) south of Peso da Régua, 121 km (75 mi) southeast of Porto.*

A prosperous wine-producing town, Lamego is rich in baroque churches and mansions. The town's most famous monument is the 18th-century Fodor'sChoice **Santuário de Nossa Senhora dos Remédios** (Our Lady of Cures Church and Shrine), which is on a hill west of the center of town and in a park of the same name. Leading to the shrine is a marvelous granite staircase of 686 steps decorated with azulejos. Landings along the way have statues and chapels. At the top, you can rest under chestnut trees and enjoy the views. During the Festas de Nossa Senhora dos Remédios, the annual pilgrimage to the shrine, many penitents climb the steps on their knees, just as they do at the shrine of Bom Jesus, near Braga. The main procession is September 8, but the festivities start at the end of August and include concerts, dancing, parades, a fair, and torchlight processions. Pilgrims use the stairs, but you can always drive up the road here to reach the shrine. ⊠ *Monte de Santo Estevão* ☎ *254/614392* ⊠ *Free* ☉ *Nov.–May, daily 7:30–6; June–Oct., daily 7:30–8.*

★ In the heart the Douro Valley, the wine estate **Quinta da Pacheca** has existed since 1551. A 17th-century stone marker bears a Feitoria inscription that indicates that the best-quality wine was made here, the only one that could be exported. The estate mansion has a chapel and a beautiful garden with trees that are hundreds of years old. Wine production is still done the old-fashioned way, with grapes crushed by men in a stone tank, and aging taking place in oak barrels. Reservations must be made if you want to visit this property. ⊠ *Cambes* ☎ *254/313228* ⊕ *www. quintadapacheca.com.*

THE MINHO & THE COSTA VERDE

The coastline of Minho Province, north of Porto, is a largely unspoiled stretch of small towns and sandy beaches that runs all the way to the border with Spain. The weather in this region is more inclement than elsewhere, a fact hinted at in its name: the Minho is green because it sees a disproportionate amount of rain. It's a land of emerald valleys, endless pine-scented forests, and secluded beaches that are beautiful but not for fainthearted swimmers. Summers can be cool, and swimming in the Atlantic is bracing at best. "These are real beaches for real people," is the reply when visitors complain about the water temperature.

You can break up your time on the coast with trips inland to medieval towns along the Rio Lima or through the border settlements along the Rio Minho. The remains of ancient civilizations are everywhere; you'll encounter dolmens, Iron Age dwellings, and Celtic and Roman towns. Old traditions are carefully incorporated into modern-day hustle and bustle. Up here, you'll see more than the occasional oxcart loaded with some sort of crop, being led by a long-skirted, wooden-shod woman on both highway and country lane.

Guimarães

★ *51 km (32 mi) northeast of Porto.*

Afonso Henriques was born in 1110 in Guimarães, and Portuguese schoolchildren are taught that *"aqui nasceu Portugal"* ("Portugal was born here") with him. Within 20 years he was referred to as king of *Portucale* (the united Portuguese lands between the Minho and Douro rivers) and had made Guimarães the seat of his power. From this first "Portuguese" capital, Afonso Henriques drove south, taking Lisbon back from the Moors in 1147. Today Guimarães is a town proud of its past, and this is evident in a series of delightful medieval buildings and streets. Today, the Old Town's narrow, cobbled thoroughfares pass delightful medieval buildings, small bars that open onto sidewalks, and pastel houses that overhang little squares and have flowers in their windowsills. In 2001 the historic center of Guimarães was classified as a World Heritage site by UNESCO.

The **castelo de Guimarães** (castle) was built (or at least reconstructed from earlier remains) by Henry of Burgundy; his son, Afonso Henriques, was born within its great battlements and flanking towers. Standing high on a solid rock base above the town, the castle has been superbly preserved. A path leads down from its walls to the tiny Romanesque Igreja de São Miguel de Castelo, the plain chapel where it's believed that Afonso Henriques was baptized. ⊠ *Rua D. Teresa de Noronha* ☎ *253/412273* 🖾 *€Castle 1.30, chapel free* ☉ *Castle Tues.–Sun. 9:30–12:30 and 2–5:30, chapel same hrs as castle.*

The **Paço dos Duques de Bragança** (Palace of the Dukes of Bragança), below the castle, is a much-maligned 15th-century palace belonging to the dukes of Bragança. Critics claim that the restoration during the Salazar regime (1936–59), which turned the building into a state residence, damaged it irrevocably. Certainly the palace's brick chimneys and turrets bear little relation to the original structure, which was an atmospheric ruin for many years. You can judge for yourself on a guided tour of the interior,

> ## CASTLES
>
> There are towers, castles, and forts galore to explore in this part of the country, some of them so complete they provide a virtual medieval playground. The best include those at Guimarães, Monção, Bragança, and Chaves. Don't miss the region's two vast ornamental staircases at the pilgrimage sights of Lamego and Bom Jesus do Monte.

where you'll find much of interest—from tapestries and furniture to porcelain and paintings. You can book guided tours at the main desk. ⊠ *Rua Conde D. Henrique* ☎ *253/412273* 🖾 *€3 (tour included), free Sun. until 12:30* ☉ *Daily 9:30–12:30 and 2–5:30.*

Fodor's Choice ★ The **Igreja de Nossa Senhora da Oliveira** (Church of Our Lady of the Olive Branch) is in the delightful square Largo da Oliveira. The church was founded in the 10th century to commemorate one of Guimarães's most enduring legends. Wamba, elected king of the Visigoths in the 7th century, refused the honor and thrust his olive-branch stick into the earth, declaring that only if his stick were to blossom would he accept the crown—whereupon the stick promptly sprouted foliage. In the square in front of the church, an odd 14th-century Gothic canopy sheltering a cross marks the supposed spot. ⊠ *Largo da Oliveira* 🖾 *Free* ☉ *Tues.–Sun. 7:15–noon and 3:30–5:30.*

The convent buildings surrounding the Colegiada de Nossa Senhora da Oliveira house the **Museu Alberto Sampaio,** with its beautiful displays of religious art, medieval statuary, sarcophagi, and coats of arms. The highlight is a 14th-century silver triptych of the Nativity that's full of animation and power. It's said to have been captured from the King of Castile at the crucial Battle of Aljubarrota and presented to the victorious Dom João I, whose tunic, worn at the battle, is preserved in a glass case nearby. ⊠ *Rua Alfredo Guimarães* 🕾 *253/423919* 🖃 *€2, free Sun. until 2* ☉ *Tues.–Sun. 10–12:30 and 2–5:30.*

Close to the Museu Alberto Sampaio, the **Museu de Arte Primitiva e Moderna** (Museum of Primitive and Modern Art) houses Portugal's most important collection of naïve art. The works are from several different countries and are attractively displayed. ⊠ *Antigos Paços do Concelho, Largo da Oliveira* 🕾 *253/414186* 🖃 *Free* ☉ *Weekdays 9–12:30 and 2–5:30.*

▮ NEED A BREAK? You can relax over coffee and a cake every day but Sunday at **A Medieval** (⊠ Largo da Oliveira 🕾 253/417583), an inexpensive café. If you're really thirsty, stop in at **Secos e Molhados** (⊠ Praça de Santiago 14 🕾 253/511303), a classy beer house that's open from 11 AM until 2 AM.

If you want to relax and enjoy a view of town, board the **Teleférico / Montanha da Penha,** a cable car that takes you 440 yards up to the top of Mount Penha in 10 minutes. The journey ends with a nice view over the city. ⊠ *Lugar das Hortas* 🕾 *253/515085* 🖃 *€3.30 round-trip* ☉ *Weekdays 11–7, weekends and holidays 10–8.*

The Old Town's streets peter out at the southern end of Guimarães in the Almeida da Liberdade, a swath of gardens whose benches and cafés are often full. Here the **Igreja de São Francisco** (Church of St. Francis) has a chancel decorated with 18th-century azulejos depicting the life of the saint. The church also has a fine Renaissance cloister. ⊠ *Largo de São Francisco* 🕾 *253/412228* ☉ *Daily 9–noon and 3–5.*

★ At the top of the Largo do Toural is the excellent **Museu Martins Sarmento,** contained within the cloister and buildings of a church, the Igreja de São Domingos. The museum has rich finds from the Celtic settlement of Citânia de Briteiros (northwest of Guimarães), as well as Lusitanian and Roman stone sarcophagi, a strange miniature bronze chariot, various weapons, and elaborate ornaments. Two finds stand out: the decorative, carved stone slabs known as the *pedras formosas* (beautiful stones)—one of which was found at a funerary monument at Briteiros—and the huge, prehistoric, granite *Colossus of Pedralva,* a figure of brutal power thought to have been used in ancient fertility rites. ⊠ *Rua Paio Galvão* 🕾 *253/414011* 🖃 *€1.50* ☉ *Tues.–Sun. 9:30–noon and 2–5. Closed holidays.*

Where to Stay & Eat

★ **$$–$$$**
Fodor$Choice
★

╳🖾 **Pousada de Santa Marinha.** This pousada is in a 12th-century monastery that was founded by the wife of Dom Afonso Henriques to honor the patron saint of pregnant women. Antiques and extraordinary azulejo wall panels fill the public rooms, and some guest rooms used to be monks' cells. The stone dining room ($$$$) serves regional and Continental dishes; the *rojões á Minhota* (pork simmered and served with pickled vegetables) is delicious; sop up the sauce with *broa* (chewy corn bread). A fitting dessert is *toucinho do céu,* which translates as "bacon from heaven" but is actually a rich egg-and-almond pudding cake. ⊠ *Largo Domingos Leite de Castro, 4810-011* ☎ *253/511249* ⊕ *www.pousadas.pt* ↩ *49 rooms, 2 suites* ⚭ *Restaurant, minibars, cable TV, bar, shops, pool, meeting rooms, Wi-Fi, free parking* ⊟ *AE, DC, MC, V* ⏏⏐ *BP.*

$$ ✕⊞ **Pousada da Nossa Senhora da Oliveira.** Town houses that date from the 16th and 17th centuries were remodeled and filled with antique reproductions to create this pousada. Service is courteous and efficient, and guest rooms are elegant, though not large; those facing the street can be noisy. The superb restaurant (reservations essential; $$$$) has a large fireplace and windows that overlook the Largo da Oliveira. The menu features Minho dishes; try the *coelho á fundador* (fricassee of rabbit with fennel and red wine). A dessert favorite is the *bolo de amêndoa* (almond cake made with flour and mashed potatoes). ⊠ *Rua de Santa Maria, 4801-910* ☎ *253/514157* ⊕ *www.pousadas.pt* ↩ *19 rooms, 6 suites* ⚭ *Restaurant, minibars, cable TV, bar, Wi-Fi, free parking* ⊟ *AE, DC, MC, V* ⏏⏐ *BP.*

Fodor'sChoice ★

Shopping

Guimarães is a center for the local linen industry. The fabric is handspun and handwoven, then embroidered, all to impressive effect; it is available in local shops or at the weekly Friday market. Shops owned by artisans themselves offer the best linen buys. Try **A Oficina** (⊠ Rua Paio Galvão, Loja 11 ☎ 253/515250).

EN ROUTE
The **Citânia de Briteiros,** 9 km (5½ mi) northwest of Guimarães, is the fascinating remains of a Celtic *citânia* (hill settlement). It dates from around 300 BC and was probably not abandoned until AD 300, making it one of the last Celtic strongholds against the Romans in Portugal. The walls and foundations of 150 huts and a meetinghouse have been excavated (two of the huts have been reconstructed to show their original size), and paths are clearly marked between them. Parts of a channeled water system also survive. The site was excavated in the late 19th century by Dr. Martins Sarmento, who gave his name to the museum in Guimarães, where most of the finds from Briteiros were transferred. If you intend to visit the site, don't miss the museum. ⊠ *Largo Martins Sarmento 51, 4810-241* ☎ *253/510322* ⊡ *Free* ☉ *Daily 9–noon and 1–5.*

Braga

㉒ *25 km (15 mi) northwest of Guimarães, 53 km (33 mi) northeast of Porto.*

Braga is one of northern Portugal's outstanding surprises. It first prospered in the 6th century—under the Visigoths—when it became an important bishopric. Braga's later archbishops often wielded greater power than the Portuguese kings themselves. In the 16th century, the city was beautified with churches, palaces, and fountains, many of which were altered in the 18th century.

Today Braga feels like the religious capital it is. Shops that sell religious items line the pedestrian streets around the cathedral. The Semana Santa (Holy Week) festivities here, including eerie torchlight processions of hooded participants, are impressive. There are also several interesting historical sights—most of them religious in nature—a short distance from the city. You can visit all of them by bus from the center of town; inquire at the tourist office for timetables.

The huge **Sé Catedral** was originally Romanesque but is now an impressive blend of styles. The delicate Renaissance stone tracery on the roof is particularly eye-catching. Enter from Rua do Souto through the 18th-century cloister; the cathedral interior is on your left, and there are various interesting chapels. Steps by the entrance to the cathedral lead to the **Museu de Arte Sacra** (Museum of Religious Art), which has a fascinating collection of religious art and artifacts, including a 14th-century crystal cross set in bronze. From the magnificent *coro alto* (upper choir), which you cross as part of the tour, there are views of the great baroque double organ. Across the cloister, you'll see the Capela dos Reis (Kings' Chapel), a 14th-century chapel containing the tombs of Afonso Henriques's parents, Henry of Burgundy and his wife, Teresa. ⊠ *Rua do Souto* ☎ *253/263317* 🖃 *Cathedral free, museum €2 (includes tour)* ☾ *Nov.–May, daily 8:30–5:30; June–Oct., daily 8:30–6:30.*

Across narrow Rua do Souto from the cathedral is the park Largo do Paço. It's flanked by the well-proportioned **Antigo Paço Arquiepiscopal Bracarense** (Archbishops' Palace), which overlooks a castellated fountain. Parts of the building date from the 14th century. Today it's occupied by faculties from the city's university and functions as the public library, one of the country's most impressive, with more than 300,000 volumes. ⊠ *Rua da Misericórdia.*

The pedestrian Rua Diogo de Sousa leads down from the cathedral and palace to one of the city's former gateways, the 18th-century Arco do Porta Nova. Beyond it and to the right is the Museu dos Biscainhos, within a baroque mansion known as **Palácio dos Biscaínhos.** The elegant rooms are furnished in 18th-century style and display silver and porcelain collections. The ground floor of the palace is flagstone, which allowed carriages to run through the interior to the stables beyond. At the back of the palace is a formal garden with decorative tiles. ⊠ *Rua dos Biscaínhos* ☎ *253/204650* ⊕ *www.ipmuseus.pt* 🖃 *€2* ☾ *Tues.–Sun. 10–12:15 and 2–5:30.*

Past the garden gateway of the Palácio dos Biscainhos is the **Zona Arqueológica** (Archaeological Zone), which usually isn't open to the public. It contains the excavations of an old Roman city known as Bracara Augusta, from which Braga derives its name. To the east, the Roman city stretched as far as the large Largo de São Tiago.

The city center is found at the **Praça da República,** the square at the head of Braga's elongated central gardens. The west side of the square is arcaded, and behind it stands the dominating 14th-century tower, the Torre de Menagem.

There are two inexpensive cafés in the arcade at the Praça da República. The **Café Astória** (☒ Av. Central ☎ 253/273944) has mahogany-paneled walls, mirrors, marble tables, and a molded ceiling. It's a good place to enjoy a coffee and to try some of the local pastries (best in morning). **Café Vianna** (☒ Av. Central-Arcada ☎ 253/262336) has been in business since 1871 and serves a wide variety of snacks. It's also a good place for breakfast and offers views of the fountain and gardens.

The **Capela de São Frutuoso de Montélios,** about 4 km (2½ mi) north of town on the EN201, is one of Portugal's oldest buildings. The original chapel is believed to have been constructed in the 7th century in the form of a Greek cross. It was partially destroyed by the Moors, and rebuilt in the 11th century. Some 6 km (4 mi) northwest of Braga on the EN201, turn on the EM564 to reach the impressive and romantic ruins ★ of the **Mosteiro de Tibães,** built as a Benedictine monastery in the 11th century and rebuilt at the end of the 19th century. You can tour four cloisters, which have some fine examples of azulejos. On a hilltop 5 km (3 mi) west of Braga on the N309 is the **Santuário Nossa Senhora do Sameiro,** after Fátima the most important Marian shrine (a shrine honoring the Virgin Mary, mother of Christ) in Portugal. Hundreds of thousands of pilgrims visit here annually. The church itself is of little architectural interest.

Fodor'sChoice Many people come to Braga specifically to see the **Bom Jesus do Monte,**
★ a pilgrimage shrine atop a 1,312-foot-high, densely wooded hill 5 km (3 mi) east of the city. The stone staircase, a marvel of baroque art that was started in 1723, leads to an 18th-century sanctuary-church, whose terrace commands wonderful views. Many pilgrims climb up on their knees. Fountains placed at various resting places represent the five senses and the virtues, and small chapels display tableaux with life-size figures illustrating the Stations of the Cross. If you don't want to climb up the staircase (which is worth the effort), you can drive up the winding road or pay €1 and take the funicular. There are restaurants, refreshment stands, and even a couple of hotels beside the sanctuary at the top. Buses run here every half hour from the center of Braga.

Where to Stay & Eat

$-$$$ ✕**Sameiro.** A meal in this restaurant is worth a climb (or drive) to the
Fodor'sChoice top of the hill that's home to the Santuário Nossa Senhora do Sameiro.
★ The dining room is spacious and pleasantly furnished, and the views are superb. The menu is unadulterated northern Portuguese cuisine. Try the *arroz de vitela com pastelinhos de marisco* (a veal and rice concoction with little seafood pastries) or one of the various bacalhau dishes. Lunch is served from noon to 3 PM and dinner from 7 PM to 10 PM. ☒*Sameiro–Espinho* ☎*253/675114* ☐*AE, DC, MC, V* ☺*Closed Mon.*

$$ ✕**Restaurante Inácio.** Just outside the 18th-century town gate, this well-known restaurant serves solid regional fare. Bacalhau is a good bet, as is the roast kid. The house wine is on the raw side, but the wine list is decent so you have plenty of other options. Service in the stone-clad interior is brisk and efficient. Reservations are essential on weekends. ✉ *Campo das Hortas 4* ☎ *253/613235* 🖃 *AE, DC, MC, V* ⊘ *Closed Tues.*

$–$$ ✕🖼 **Hotel do Elevador.** Many seasoned travelers to the north have made
Fodor'sChoice this charming hotel their top choice. In a 19th-century building on a
★ wooded hill 3 km (2 mi) outside Braga, it's named after the water-operated funicular that hoists the foot-weary up to the Bom Jesus do Monte sanctuary. The restaurant, Panorâmico do Elevador ($$–$$$$), scores highly for its food and for its gorgeous views. ✉ *Bom Jesus do Monte, 4710* ☎ *253/603400* ⊕ *www.hoteisbomjesus.web.pt* ⤵ *22 rooms* ♨ *Restaurant, minibars, cable TV, bar, meeting rooms, Wi-Fi* 🖃 *AE, DC, MC, V* ⊘ *BP.*

$ 🖼 **Albergaria Senhora-a-Branca.** This inn is in the center of town and offers very good value. Public areas have a contemporary, chic look. Guest rooms are on the small side, but they're attractively furnished. ✉ *Largo da Senhora a Branca 58, 4710-443* ☎ *253/269938* ⊕ *www.albergariasrabranca.pt* ⤵ *18 rooms, 2 suites* ♨ *Dining room, cable TV, bar, free parking* 🖃 *AE, DC, MC, V* ⊘ *BP.*

$ 🖼 **Hotel Residencial Dona Sofia.** Close to the cathedral, this pleasant, well-appointed hotel is one of Braga's best bargains. The only meal served is breakfast, but otherwise there's nothing lacking in terms of basic comforts, and the staff is friendly. ✉ *Largo São João do Souto 131, 4700-325* ☎ *253/263160* ✐ *hotel.d.sofia@oninet.pt* ⤵ *34 rooms* ♨ *Minibars, cable TV, bar, laundry service, free parking* 🖃 *AE, MC, V* ⊘ *BP.*

$ 🖼 **Hotel Turismo.** This smart, modern hotel is on a main road just a few minutes from the center of town. Rooms are well equipped and have balconies, although the views are mostly of traffic. The restaurant is good, and there's a rooftop pool. ✉ *Praceta João XXI, Av. da Liberdade, 4715-036* ☎ *253/206000* ⊕ *www.hotelturismobraga.com* ⤵ *132 rooms* ♨ *Restaurant, cable TV, pool, bar, no-smoking rooms, Wi-Fi* 🖃 *AE, DC, MC, V* ⊘ *BP.*

Nightlife

Braga has an active nightlife. The café-bars in the arcaded Praça da República are good places for a drink and are lively at any time of the day or night. **Populum Bar** (✉ Campo da Vinha 115 ☎ 253/610966) is a dance club with two rooms; anything from dance hits to ballroom to stand-up comedy can be taking place at the same time.

Barcelos

㉓ *12 km (7 mi) west of Braga, 27 km (17 mi) northeast of Guimarães.*

Barcelo, which is on the banks of the Rio Cávado, is the center of a flourishing handicrafts industry, particularly ceramics and wooden toys and models. It's worth coming here if you plan to carry home a host of souvenirs. The best time to visit is during the famous weekly market.

From the Campo da República, Rua Dom António Barroso leads down through the Old Town toward the river. On the left, the former medieval town tower now houses the tourist office and the **Centro de Artesanato** (Artisans' Center), which has some of the best local handicrafts. Ceramic dishes and bowls, often signed by the artist, are a good buy. Figurines, too, are popular, although none approach the individuality of those made by the late Rosa Ramalho and Mistério, local potters whose work first made famous the ceramics of Barcelos. ⊠ *Torre de Menagem, Largo de Porta Nova* ☎ *253/811882* 🖾 *Free* ☉ *Mon.–Sat. 9–noon and 1:30–5:30.*

The Rio Cávado, crossed by a medieval bridge, is shaded by overhanging trees and bordered by municipal gardens. High above the river stands the ruin of the medieval Paço dos Condes (Palace of the Counts), where you'll find the **Museu Arqueológico** (Archaeological Museum). Among the empty sarcophagi and stone crosses is the 14th-century crucifix known as the Cruzeiro do Senhor do Galo (Cross of the Rooster Man). According to local legend, after sentencing an innocent man to death, a judge prepared to dine on a roast fowl. When the condemned man said, "I'll be hanged if that cock doesn't crow," the rooster flew from the table and the man's life was spared. The Barcelos cock is on sale in pottery form throughout the town; indeed, it's become almost a national symbol. ⊠ *Largo do Município* ☎ *253/821252* 🖾 *Free* ☉ *Daily 10–5:30.*

NEED A BREAK? There are several attractive cafés in the center of town. From the market in the Campo da República, head for the **Avenida da Liberdade** and to the front of the tourist office building on the Largo Dr. José Novais for clean, well-lighted places to sit, have a cup of coffee and a pastry, and think about heading back to the market to get an extra suitcase for all the great stuff you just bought.

The **Museu de Olaria** (Pottery Museum), a five-minute walk from the medieval bridge, has more than 6,000 pieces. Look for selections from current and now-extinct Portuguese workshops, private donations, and excavation finds from both Portugal and all over the world. ⊠ *Rua Cónego Joaquim Gaiolas* ☎ *253/824741* 🖾 *€1.40* ☉ *Tues.–Fri. 10–5:30, weekends 10–12:30 and 2–5:30.*

Where to Stay & Eat

$–$$$ ✕ **Restaurante Bagoeira.** Vendors from the town's Thursday market favor this rustic restaurant, with its wooden ceiling, black-metal chandeliers, and vases of fresh flowers. *Grelhados* (grilled meats and fish) are prepared in full view of hungry customers on a huge old range that splutters and hisses. ⊠ *Av. Dr. Sidonio Pais 495* ☎ *253/811236* 🚭 *AE, DC, MC, V.*

FUN FESTIVALS

The **Feira de Barcelos** (Barcelos Market), held every Thursday in the central Campo da República, is one of the country's largest. Vendors cry out their wares, which include almost anything you can think of: traditional Barcelos ceramics (brown pottery with yellow-and-white decoration), workaday earthenware, baskets, rugs, glazed figurines (including the famous Barcelos cock), decorative copper lanterns, and wooden toys. There are also mounds of vegetables, fruits, cheese, fresh bread and cakes, clothes, shoes, leather, and kitchen equipment. The scent of roasting chestnuts wafts across the square, promising a snack to tide you over as you browse.

$ ⊞ **Quinta de Santa Combra.** Just 5 km (3 mi) from Barcelos on the road to Famalicão, this fine 18th-century manor house—full of wood beams and granite—offers bed and breakfast. It's a good deal for the money. ⊠ *Lugar de Crujães, Várzea de S. Bento 4750* ☎ *253/832101* ⊕ *www. stacomba.com* ⟿ *6 rooms* ♻ *Pool, horseback riding; no a/c* ▭ *AE* ⏍*I*⏐ *BP.*

Viana do Castelo

★ ㉔ *45 km (28 mi) northwest of Barcelos, 71 km (44 mi) north of Porto.*

At the mouth of the Rio Lima, Viana do Castelo has been a prosperous trading center since it received its town charter in 1258. Many of Viana's finest buildings date from the 16th and 17th centuries, the period of its greatest prosperity. Viana is regarded as the region's folk capital and specializes in producing traditional embroidered costumes. Although these make colorful souvenirs, you'll also find less elaborate crafts such as ceramics, lace, and jewelry. The large Friday market is a good place to shop. Before or after strolling through town, don't miss the excellent local beach, Praia do Cabedelo (reached by ferry from the riverside at the end of the main street).

The town's best face is presented in the old streets that radiate from the **Praça da República.** The most striking building here is the **Casa da Misericórdia**, an 18th-century almshouse, whose two upper stories are supported, unusually, by tall caryatids (carved, draped female figures). The square's stone fountain, also Renaissance in style, harmonizes perfectly with the surrounding buildings, which include the restored town hall and its lofty arcades.

▌**NEED A BREAK?** **Natário** (⊠ Rua Manuel Espregueira 37 ☎ 258/822376), a small café right off the main drag of Avenida dos Combatentes da Grande Guerra, is a perfect place to soak up the Minho atmosphere. The proprietor makes his own pastries, cakes, and croquettes. Brazilian writer Jorge Amado is rumored to have frequented this place when he was in town.

A 10-minute walk west from the Praça da República across the town's main avenue, the Avenida dos Combatentes da Grande Guerra, takes you to the impressive mansion that houses the **Museu Municipal de Viana do Castelo.** The early-18th-century interior has been carefully preserved, and the collection of 17th-century ceramics and ornate period furniture shows how wealthy many of Viana's merchants were. ⊠ *Largo de São Domingos* ☎ *258/820377* ▱ *€2* ⊙ *Tues.–Sun. 9:30–12:30 and 2–5. Closed holidays.*

A little ways beyond the Museu Municipal are the great ramparts of the **Castelo de Santiago da Barra,** the 16th-century fortification that added the words "do castelo" to the town's name and protected Viana against attack from pirates eager to share in its wealth. The castle has since been renovated and given a new function and name: Centro de Congressos Castelo de Santiago da Barra. The congress and meeting center has an auditorium, a translation center, and all the necessary equipment to hold conferences. Outside the castle walls, Viana holds a large market every Friday. ⊠ *Castelo Santiago da Barra* ☎ *258/820270.*

The **Basílica de Santa Luzia** is a white, domed basilica that overlooks the town from wooded heights. Unfortunately the funicular railway is closed for the foreseeable future, so you will have to walk up a narrow footpath, about 2 km (1 mi), or take a taxi. The views from the basilica steps are magnificent, and a staircase to the side allows access to the very top of the dome for some extraordinary coastal vistas. This steep climb, up a very narrow staircase to a little platform, is for the agile only. ⊠ *Av. 25 de Abril.*

Where to Stay & Eat

$$–$$$$ ✕ **Casa d'Armas.** This cozy, romantic restaurant is in a renovated mansion near the fishing docks. Although seafood is the reason to come here, the menu also has several grilled meat dishes. ⊠ *Largo 5 de Outubro 30, ground fl.* ☎☎ *258/824999* ▤ *DC, MC, V* ⊘ *Closed Mon. and 1 wk in Nov.*

$–$$$ ✕ **Os Três Potes.** The cellarlike dining room, converted from a 16th-century bakery, gets busy on summer weekends, when people crowd in for the folksinging and dancing sessions. Sitting at tables under stone arches or on the open-air terrace, you can choose from a fine range of regional dishes: start with the *aperitivos regionais* (a selection of cod pastries and cheeses); move on to the house bacalhau or the exceedingly tender *polvo grelhado* (grilled octopus). There's a good wine list and live music on weekends. ⊠ *Beco dos Fornos 7–9, off Praça da República* ☎ *258/829928* ⌂ *Reservations essential* ▤ *AE, DC, MC, V* ⊘ *Closed Mon. and holidays.*

★ **$$** ✕▣ **Pousada Santa Luzia do Monte.** A 1920s mansion, on a wooded outcrop behind the basilica, houses this pousada. The gardens and terrace are a delight, as are the grand public rooms—especially in winter, when the fireplaces add crackling, romantic warmth to the sometimes chilly lounges. Guest rooms are spacious and have glamorous marble baths. The restaurant ($$$$) serves regional and Continental cuisine and has sweeping views of both the countryside and the Atlantic. ⊠ *Monte de Santa Luzia, 4901-909* ☎ *258/800370* ⊕ *www.pousadas.pt* ⊲ *47 rooms* ⌂ *Restaurant, in-room safes, minibars, cable TV, tennis court, pool, billiards, bar, Wi-Fi* ▤ *AE, DC, MC, V* ▮◯▮ *BP.*

$ ▣ **Hotel Viana Sol.** Although the prices are low, this hotel has a few frills as well as comfortable, functional, modern rooms. It's in the center of town, not far from the river. ⊠ *Largo Vasco da Gama, 4900-322* ☎ *258/828995* ⌂ *hotelvianasol@mail.telepac.pt* ⊲ *65 rooms* ⌂ *In-room safes, cable TV, indoor pool, gym, sauna, squash, bar, dance club, ethernet* ▤ *AE, DC, MC, V* ▮◯▮ *BP.*

Nightlife

The motifs at the **Casting Bar** (⊠ Rua de S. Bento 120–121 ☎ 258/827396) come from the world of fashion. A young crowd flocks to **Foz Caffé** (⊠ Praia do Cabedelo–Darque ☎ 258/332485), a nightspot near the beach in the village of Darque. The popular bar **Glamour** (⊠ Rua da Bandeira 179 ☎ 258/822963) has an open-air esplanade, theme nights, and live music regularly.

EN
ROUTE Leaving Viana, both the train and the N13 continue north, following the coast and passing a succession of small villages with delightful beaches. There are good stretches of sand at the resorts of Vila Praia de Âncora and Moledo, and if you keep your eyes open, you'll find some side roads that lead to fairly isolated beaches.

Caminha

㉕ *25 km (15 mi) north of Viana do Castelo, 97 km (60 mi) north of Porto.*

At Caminha you reach the Rio Minho, which forms the border with Spain. The fortified town hall on the main square once was part of Caminha's defenses; its loggia, supported by graceful pillars, is very pleasing to the eye. There's a 16th-century clock tower in the square, too; the nearby parish church resembles a Gothic fortress and was built a century earlier, when Caminha was an important port. The rich interior of the church and the surviving mansions in the surrounding streets are reminders of the town's former wealth, but by the 17th century Caminha had lost much of its business to Viana do Castelo.

Vila Nova de Cerveira

㉖ *12 km (7 mi) northeast of Caminha.*

Granite hills border one side of Vila Nova de Cerveira, and the Rio Minho and Spain border the other. The town dates from the 13th century, when it was fortified to ward off any marauding Spaniards. Nowadays, the Spanish who come ashore on the ferry that connects Vila Nova to the Spanish town of Goian come for day trips and good shopping. A major monthlong event here is the biennial art show, **Bienal Internacional de Arte de Vila Nova de Cerveira** (☎ 251/794633 ⊕ www.bienaldecerveira.org).

Where to Stay & Eat

$$ ✕🖼 **Pousada de Dom Dinis.** Ancient, mottled buildings within the ram-
Fodor'sChoice parts of Vila Nova de Cerveira's 14th-century castle house this pousada.
★ Guest rooms have reproductions of traditional Minho furniture; some rooms also have private patios. The modern restaurant ($$$$) features local Minho dishes, including *robalo grelhado com molho manteiga* (grilled bass with butter sauce). For dessert, try the pears poached in red wine. ⊠ *Praça da Liberdade, 4920* ☎ *251/708120* ⊕ *www.pousadas. pt* 🛏 *29 rooms* 🝌 *Restaurant, cable TV, bar, recreation room, Wi-Fi* 🖃 *AE, DC, MC, V* 🍴 *BP.*

Valença do Minho

㉗ *15 km (9 mi) northeast of Caminha, 123 km (76 mi) northeast of Porto.*

Valença do Minho is the major border-crossing point in this area, with roads as well as rail service into Spain. Valença's Old Town is enclosed by perfectly preserved walls, which face the similarly defended Spanish town of Tuy. Strolling along the river and ramparts is very pleasant, especially in the evening, when the day-trippers from Spain have retreated to their own side of the river.

Where to Stay & Eat

$$ ✕🏠 **São Teotónio Pousada.** This pousada is on the highest point of
FodorsChoice Valença's old fortification. The view is superb, with the Rio Minho be-
★ neath you and Spain before you on the horizon. The restaurant's ($$$$)
core menu is based on Minho's dishes, and *rojões à moda do Minho*
(roasted pork) is one of the specialties. ✉ *Fortificações Praça Valença
do Minho, 4930-619* ☎ *251/800260* ⊕ *www.pousadas.pt* ☞ *18 rooms*
⌂ *Restaurant, bar, recreation room, Wi-Fi, travel services* ▤ *AE, DC,
MC, V* ⧈ *BP.*

Monção

㉘ *18 km (11 mi) northeast of Valença do Minho, 144 km (89 mi) north-
east of Porto.*

The riverside town of Monção is another fortified border settlement
with a long history of skirmishes with the Spanish. In town there are
the remains of a 14th-century castle that withstood a desperate siege
in 1368. When the Portuguese supplies ran low, a local woman baked
some cakes with the last of the flour and sent them to the Spaniards
with the message that there was plenty more where that came from.
The bluff worked, the Spanish retreated, and the little cakes are still
on sale in town. Try a glass of the local vinho verde, a noteworthy wine
available in several bars.

**EN
ROUTE** South of Monção the N101 traverses glorious rural countryside be-
fore descending to the valley of the Rio Vez, a tributary of the Lima.
Arcos de Valdevez, 35 km (22 mi) from Monção, makes a nice stop.
It's a typically serene little river town, where you can rent rowboats.
Five kilometers (3 mi) farther south you arrive at the Lima, one of the
country's most beautiful rivers. It was known to the Romans as the
River of Oblivion, because its blissful beauty was said to make trav-
elers forget their homes. Ask at the tourist office about walks along
the ancient Roman roads.

Ponte da Barca

㉙ *5 km (3 mi) south of Arcos de Valdevez on N101, 39 km (24 mi) south
of Monção.*

In Ponte da Barca, the *ponte* in question is a beautiful, 10-arched
bridge, built in the 15th century. At the junction of four main roads,
the small town has been an important commercial center for centuries,
and the Tuesday market held on the riverside here is well worth catch-
ing. On other days you can spend time quite happily walking along the
riverbank.

Ponte de Lima

★ **㉚** *18 km (11 mi) west of Ponte da Barca on N203, 57 km (35 mi) south-
west of Monção.*

Ponte de Lima's long, low, graceful bridge is of Roman origin. It's also
open only to foot traffic; drivers cross a concrete bridge at the edge of

town. The main square by the old bridge has a central fountain and benches and is ringed by little cafés—the perfect places to stop for a leisurely drink. The nearby square tower still stands guard over the town, and beyond, in the narrow streets, there are several fine 16th-century mansions and a busy market. Walking around town, you'll return again and again to the river, which is the real highlight of a visit. A wide beach usually displays lines of drying laundry, and a riverside avenue lined with plane trees leads down to the Renaissance Igreja de Santo António dos Capuchos. The twice-monthly Monday market, held on the riverbank, is the oldest in Portugal, dating from 1125. On market days and during the mid-September Feiras Novas (New Fairs) you'll see the town at its effervescent best.

> ## BEACHES
>
> The Atlantic is very cold, even at the height of summer, and beaches along the Minho are notoriously windswept. More pleasant is a dip in the Rio Lima or Rio Minho, although you should heed local advice about currents and pollution before plunging in. Ponte de Lima has a particularly nice wide, sandy beach. Espinho, south of Porto, and the main resorts to the north (Póvoa de Varzim and Ofir) are the best places for water-sports enthusiasts.

Where to Stay & Eat

The Ponte de Lima region is well known for its Turismo no Espaço Rural. There are 100 properties in the area, mostly along the Rio Lima's north bank, each no more than several miles from a town. Facilities are usually minimal; houses may have a communal lounge, tennis, a pool or access to local swimming facilities, fishing, and gardens. Rates include bed and breakfast, although some places will arrange other meals on request. The **Centro Nacional de Turismo no Espaço Rural** (Rural Tourism; ☎ 258/931750 ⊕ www.center.pt) is the central booking agency associated with the rural tourism program, and its Web site includes links to the Solares de Portugal and Aldeias de Portugal sites.

$–$$ ✕ **Restaurante Encanada.** The Encanada is adjacent to the tree-lined avenue along the riverfront. A terrace provides river views. The menu is limited, but you can count on good local cooking, with dishes that depend on what's available at the market. Try one of the Minho dishes such as rojões á Minhota accompanied by a vinho verde. ⊠ *Passeio 25 de Abril, Mercado Municipal* ☎ *258/941189* ▭ *AE, MC, V* ⊙ *Closed Thurs. and mid-May–early June.*

Parque Nacional da Peneda-Gerês

Lindoso, in the park's center section, is 30 km (18 mi) east of Ponte da Barca.

FodorsChoice The 172,900-acre **Peneda-Gerês National Park,** bordered to the north ★ by the frontier with Spain, was created in 1970 to preserve the region's diverse flora and fauna. Even a short trip to the main towns and villages contained within the park shows you wild stretches of land framed by mountains, woods, and lakes. Access is free, and general information is available at tourist offices in Braga and Viana do Castelo. There's also an information center at Caldas do Gerês, where you can get a walking map.

Accommodations are mostly in the attractive spa town of Caldas do Gerês, in the southern section around the Serra do Gerês (Gerês Mountains). It's a two-hour drive from Braga; turn off the N103 just after Cerdeirinhas, along the N304; there's bus service, too, from Braga to Cerdeirinhas and Caldas do Gerês. The park's central region is accessible from Ponte da Barca, from which the N203 leads to Lindoso, or from Arcos de Valdevez, from which the minor N202 leads to the village of Soajo. Both towns offer basic accommodations and superb hiking. To see the park's northern reaches, which encompass the Serra da Peneda (Peneda Mountains), it's best to approach from Melgaço, a small town on the Rio Minho, 25 km (15 mi) east of Monção. From Melgaço, it's 27 km (17 mi) on the N202 to the village of Castro Laboreiro, at the park's northernmost point. There are several information centers, including the Adere-Pg, an EU-assisted agency—which is probably the best for park resources. They can provide maps, leaflets, walks, and information on places to stay. ⊠ *Largo da Misericórdia 10, Ponte da Barca* ☎ *258/ 452250* ⊕ *www.adere-pg.pt.*

Where to Stay & Eat

$ ⊡ **Hotel Termas do Gerês/Hotel Universal.** One of the best values in the park are these adjacent sister properties, in the very heart of the park. Together they offer plenty of amenities, including a shared pool and restaurant. Service is friendly and the restaurant ($$) has a great variety of local dishes. ⊠ *Av. Manuel Francisco da Costa, Caldas do Gerês 4845-067* ☎ *253/391143 or 253/391144* ⊕ *www.ehgeres.com* ⤳ *Hotel Termas: 30 rooms, Hotel Universal: 80 rooms* ⅊ *Restaurant, cable TV, tennis court, pool, billiards, bar, recreation room* ▤ *AE, DC, MC, V* ⅋ *CP.*

TRÁS-OS-MONTES

The name means "Beyond the Mountains," and though roads built in the 1980s have made it easier to get here than in the past, exploring this beautiful region in the extreme northeast still requires a sense of adventure. Great distances separate towns, and twisting roads can test your patience. Medieval villages exist in a landscape that alternates between splendor and harshness, and the population, thinned by emigration, retains rural customs that have all but disappeared elsewhere. Many still believe in the evil eye,

GETTING AROUND

Having a car is the easiest way to tour the region, but making the trip by car would mean missing out on some of the finest train journeys in the country. The trip from Porto to Mirandela provides an excellent opportunity to see the changing landscape, and you can take a bus on to Bragança. But it is slow going. Both trains and buses stop at every village, and the journey could take more than nine hours.

witches, wolf men, golden-haired spirits living down wells, and even the cult of the dead.

Vila Real

③ *116 km (72 mi) northeast of Porto. By train from Porto, change at Peso da Régua to the Corgo line.*

The capital of Trás-os-Montes is superbly situated between two mountain ranges, and much of the city retains a small-town air. Although there's no great wealth of sights, it's worth stopping here to stroll down the central avenue, which ends at a rocky promontory over the gushing Rio Corgo. A path around the church at the head of the promontory provides views of stepped terraces and green slopes. At the avenue's southern end, a few narrow streets are filled with 17th- and 18th-century houses, their entrances decorated with coats of arms.

The finest baroque work in Vila Real is the **Capela dos Clérigos** (Chapel of the Clergy), also called the Capela Nova (New Chapel), a curious fan-shaped building set between two heavy columns. ⊠ *Rua 31 de Janeiro and Rua Direita* ☎ *No phone* 🖾 *Free* ☉ *Daily 10–noon and 2–6.*

An exceptional baroque mansion believed to have been designed by Nicolau Nasoni (architect of Porto's Clérigos Tower), the **Solar de Mateus** is 4 km (2½ mi) east of Vila Real. Its U-shaped facade—with high, decorated finials at each corner—is pictured on the Mateus Rosé wine label. Set back to one side is the chapel, with an even more extravagant facade. The elegant interior is open to the public, as are the formal gardens, which are enhanced by a "tunnel" of cypress trees that shade the path. The Casa de Mateus here is an international music school and hosts one of the most important music festivals of its kind in Portugal. It takes place around Trás-os-Montes every summer in July and August, presenting mostly classical musicians, but also one or two jazz or rock artists. ⊠ *N322 (road to Sabrosa), Mateus, 5000-291* ☎ *259/323121* ⊕ *www. casademateus.com* 🖾 *House, gardens, and tour €6; gardens only €3.50* ☉ *Dec.–Feb., daily 10–1 and 2–5; Mar.–May, Oct., and Nov., daily 9–1 and 2–6; June–Sept., daily 9–7.*

FodorsChoice ★

Where to Stay & Eat

$–$$$ ✕ **Terra de Montanha.** Not only is this an excellent restaurant, but it has a unique design as well. Tables and seating are within huge wine barrels. Most of the upper portions are cut away, giving you a view of the room, but some barrels are more enclosed for a sense of privacy. Try the specialty bacalhau *com presunto e broa no forno* (with smoked ham and corn bread from the oven), which is prepared to perfection. Service is friendly, and prices are quite reasonable. ⊠ *Rua 31 de Janeiro 16–18* ☎ *259/372075* 🖃 *AE, DC, MC, V* ☉ *Closed Sun.*

FodorsChoice ★

$$ ✕🏠 **Pousada do Barão de Forrester.** This pousada in Alijó, some 30 km (18 mi) southeast of Vila Real, is named for Baron Forrester, a 19th-century Scotsman whose family members were successful port vintners and whose remarkable map of the Rio Douro helped open the river to navigation. Time fades away as you sit reading by the fire in the lounge, glass of port at your side. The restaurant ($$$$) has two terraces for sunlit lunches and star-filled suppers. Try the river mackerel in marinade or the bacalhau *à Barão de Forrester* (fried with onion and baked potatoes). ⊠ *Rua José Rufino, Alijó 5070-031* ☎ *259/959467* ⊕ *www. pousadas.pt* ⇨ *21 rooms* ⚐ *Restaurant, cable TV, tennis court, pool, fishing, bar* ⊟ *AE, DC, MC, V* ⦾ *BP.*

$$–$$$ ⊞ **Vintage House Hotel.** With great views from the northern bank of the
Fodor'sChoice Rio Douro, this excellent hotel lies some 34 km (18½ mi) southeast of
★ Vila Real and around 16 km (10 mi) southwest of Alijó. Transformed from a warehouse of an 18th-century wine estate, the hotel and its decor are very much in tune with the setting. The hotel has a wine academy (Vintage House Wine Academy) whose activities include wine courses and wine tasting. The wine shop has a great selection of vintage ports. The hotel's restaurant ($$$$) has a refined atmosphere and menu. Try *salmão fumado com salada de ovo e caviar* (smoked salmon with egg salad and caviar). ⊠ *Lugar da Ponte, Pinhão–Alijó 5085-034* ☎ *254/ 730230* ⊕ *www.hotelvintagehouse.com* ⇨ *37 rooms, 7 suites* ⚐ *Restaurant, room service, in-room safes, minibars, cable TV, tennis court, pool, fishing, bar, library, recreation room, shop, no-smoking rooms, Wi-Fi* ⊟ *AE, DC, MC, V* ⦾ *BP.*

$ ⊞ **Hotel Miracorgo.** The reception area is handsome, the guest rooms are bright, and the service is good—all of which more than make up for the unattractive, modern exterior. Request a room facing the valley, with views of the dramatic stepped terraces. ⊠ *Av. 1 de Maio 76–78, 5000-651* ☎ *259/325001* ⊕ *www.hotelmiracorgo.com* ⇨ *166 rooms* ⚐ *Pool, bar, dance club, shop, Wi-Fi* ⊟ *AE, DC, MC, V* ⦾ *BP.*

**EN
ROUTE** The main road northeast of Vila Real (the N15) is straight for much of its length. You'll drive through exceptionally fine, high countryside; rolling, arable land continues as far as the small town of Murça, 40 km (25 mi) away. Unlike the Iron Age boar figures you'll see elsewhere in the region, Murça has it's own unique boar legend. According to a tale written down in 1875, a female wild boar of great ferocity and size menaced the region's inhabitants. The Lord of Murça succeeded in hunting her down, and in honor of his deed, a monolith in the shape of a wild boar was built in the center of town, known today as the *Porca de Murça*. This unlikely monument gives its name to Murça's fine wine and extraordinary olive oil.

Mirandela

③② *72 km (45 mi) from Vila Real.*

Mirandela, an attractive town midway between Vila Real and Bragança, has a medieval castle and a Roman bridge with 20 arches of uneven sizes. The grandest monument, however, is the 17th-century Paço dos Távoras (Távora Palace), right in the center of town. Its great facade has elaborate pediments and baroque ornaments. Once the residence of the prominent Távora family, it's now used as the town hall. Train service to Mirandela, via Tua from Peso da Régua, runs through pastures and barley fields, following the course of the Rio Tua, a tributary of the Douro.

Bragança

㉝ *60 km (37 mi) northeast of Mirandela, 255 km (158 mi) northeast of Porto.*

This ancient town in the very northeastern corner of Portugal has been inhabited since Celtic times (from about 600 BC). The town lent its name to the noble family of Bragança (or Branganza), whose most famous member, Catherine, married Charles II of England; the New York City borough of Queens is named for her. Descendants of the family ruled Portugal until 1910; their tombs are contained within the church of São Vicente de Fora in Lisbon. Unfortunately, since improved roads have encouraged development, the approaches to Bragança have been spoiled by many ugly new buildings.

Above the modern town rises the magnificent 15th-century Castelo (Castle), found within the ring of battlemented walls that surround the Cidadela (Citadel), the country's best-preserved medieval village and one of the most thrilling sights in Trás-os-Montes. Bragança has locally made ceramics, and there's also a good crafts shop within the walls of the Citadel. Baskets, copper objects, pottery, woven fabrics, and leather goods are all well made here.

The central cathedral is small and disappointing, but the modern town center is attractive in its way, with a wide central avenue and several cafés that open onto the sidewalk in summer. You'll easily exhaust all the sights in less than a day, but it's worth staying overnight for the views of the castle from the pousada on the outskirts of town.

Within the walls of the **Cidadela** (Citadel), you'll find the Castelo and the Domus Municipalis (City Hall), a rare Romanesque civic building dating from the 12th century. It's always open, but you may need to get a key from one of the local cottages for the Igreja de Santa Maria (Church of St. Mary), a building with Romanesque origins that has a superb 18th-century painted ceiling. A prehistoric granite boar stands below the castle keep, this one with a tall medieval stone pillory sprouting from its back. The keep, the Torre de Menagem, now contains the **Museu Militar,** which displays armament from the 12th century through to World War I. The most exciting aspect of the museum is the 108-foot-high Gothic tower, with its dungeons, drawbridge, turrets, battlements, and vertiginous outside staircase. ☎ *273/322378* 🖃 *Citadel free; museum €1.50, Sun. free* ☉ *Citadel daily sunrise–sunset, museum Mon.–Wed. and Fri.–Sun. 9–noon and 2–5.*

As you leave the castle walls on your way back down to town, you'll pass the Renaissance **Igreja de São Bento,** with a fine Mudèjar (Moorish-style) vaulted ceiling and a gilded retable. The church may or may not be open.

Housed in Bragança's former bishop's palace, the collections of the **Museu do Abade de Baçal** (Baçal Abbot Museum) include archaeological pieces such as the area's boarlike fertility symbols, tombstones, and coins, as well as furniture, local costumes, fine silver, ethnographic masks, and paintings. ⊠ *Rua Conselheiro Abílio Beça 27* ☎ *273/331595* ⊕ *www. ipmuseus.pt* 🎫 *€2* ☉ *Tues.–Fri. 10–5, weekends 10–6.*

Where to Stay & Eat

$$ **Fodor'sChoice**   ★

✗ **Restaurante Típico Dom Roberto.** The wooden balcony and signage outside may remind Americans of the old American West, but this rural house is very much a place rich in regional dishes, especially game specialties (hare, wild boar, pheasants) and smoked sausages. Inside are wood beams, fieldstone walls, and a red-tile floor. Service is helpful and gracious. ⊠ *Gimonde (IP4, Entrance Bragança-Nascente Estrada Nacional 218)* ☎ *273/302510* ⌀ *Reservations essential* ▭ *AE, DC, MC, V.*

$–$$ ✗ **Lá Em Casa.** This low-key but attractive restaurant is between the castle and the cathedral. It serves regional Portuguese food with a decent menu of fish and shellfish. As you might expect this far inland, however, such dishes are considerably more expensive than the excellent meat dishes which include veal and lamb. ⊠ *Rua Marquês de Pombal 7* ☎ *273/322111* ⌀ *Reservations essential* ▭ *AE, DC, MC, V.*

★ **$$**   ✗▥ **Pousada de São Bartolomeu.** On a hill just west of the town center, Bragança's modern, comfortable pousada offers terrific views of the Citadel. The bar-lounge has an open fireplace and wood furnishings, and the rustic guest rooms have balconies with dreamy citadel views. It doesn't really matter that the pousada is a few miles from all the in-town restaurants: the on-site dining room ($$$$), serves the area's best stews and game dishes. ⊠ *Estrada do Turismo, 5300-271* ☎ *273/331493* ⊕ *www.pousadas.pt* 🛏 *28 rooms* ⌂ *Restaurant, minibars, cable TV, tennis court, pool, bar, Wi-Fi* ▭ *AE, DC, MC, V* ▯◯▮ *BP.*

Vinhais

㉞ *31 km (19 mi) west of Bragança.*

Vinhais provides a welcome break from the beautiful although rather desolate scenery along the N103—bleak uplands with the mountains of Spain to the north and the distant mass of the Serra da Estrela (Estrela Mountains) to the south. Most probably a pre-Roman *castro* (settlement), the present town was founded in the 13th century by King Sancho II. The structure housing the former **Convento de São Francisco** (Convent of St. Francis) has a great baroque facade that incorporates two churches, one of which has a beautiful painted ceiling. ☎ *296/ 583532* ☉ *Daily 9–6.*

EN ROUTE   Shortly before reaching Chaves, you'll see the 13th-century **Castelo do Monforte** (Monforte Castle), built upon the site of an earlier Roman fort, a remote outpost of the great empire. You can walk around the ramparts.

Chaves

★ **㉟** *55 km (34 mi) west of Vinhais, 96 km (60 mi) west of Bragança.*

Chaves was known to the Romans as Aquae Flaviae (Flavian's Waters), in honor of the emperor Flavian. They established a military base here and popularized the town's thermal springs. The impressive 16-arch

Roman bridge across the Rio Tâmega, at the southern end of town, dates from the 1st century AD and displays two original Roman milestones. Today Chaves is characterized most by a series of fortifications built during the late Middle Ages, when the city was prone to attack from all quarters. The town lies only 12 km (7 mi) from the Spanish border. Its name means "keys"—whoever controlled Chaves held the keys to the north of the country.

The most obvious landmark is the great, blunt fortress overlooking the river, the 14th-century **Torre de Menagem** (castle keep). This houses the **Museu Militar**, and the grounds offer grand views of the town. The tower is surrounded by narrow, winding streets filled with elegant houses, most of which have carved wood balconies on their top floors. ⊠ *Praça de Camões* 🕾 *276/340500* 🖼 *Museum €0.50 (joint admission with Museu da Região Flaviense)* ⊗ *Tues.–Fri. 9:30–12:30 and 2–5, weekends 2–5:30.*

In Praça de Camões, the main square below the Torre de Menagem, the late-17th-century **Igreja da Misericórdia** (Church of Mercy) is lined with huge panels of blue-and-white azulejos that depict scenes from the New Testament. ⊠ *Praça de Camões* 🕾 *No phone* ⊗ *Daily 9–5:30.*

The **Museu da Região Flaviense** (Flaviense Regional Museum) adjacent to the Igreja da Misericórdia has a hodgepodge of local archaeological finds and relics that tell the town's history. ⊠ *Praça de Camões* 🕾 *276/ 340500* 🖼 *€0.50 (joint admission with military museum in Torre de Menagem)* ⊗ *Tues.–Fri. 9:30–12:30 and 2–5, weekends 2–5:30.*

Where to Stay & Eat

$–$$$ ✕ **Restaurante Cozinha do Convento.** The restaurant of the Hotel de São Francisco provides a refined and enjoyable meal within a remarkable structure that marries a 17th-century monastery fortress with modern additions. The menu is made up of regional delicacies including smoked sausages, *polvo à galega* (octopus), wild boar, and refined seafood dishes such as lobster with mayonnaise salad. ⊠ *Alto da Pedisqueira, Hotel Forte de S. Francisco* 🕾 *276/333700* ▤ *AE, DC, MC, V* ⊗ *Closed Mon.*

¢ ✕🖬 **Hotel Trajano.** The subdued basement restaurant ($$) of the Hotel Trajano is a good place to try the *presunto* (smoked ham) for which the town is famous. *Truta á transmontana* (river trout wrapped in paper-thin slices of smoked ham) is another good choice, served with boiled potatoes and salad. There's a reasonably priced selection of local wines to accompany your meal, which is served promptly on elegantly rustic monogrammed plates. The good service continues upstairs, where the hotel's pleasant guest rooms are cheerily decorated in Portuguese country style. There's a covered terrace to sit out on as well. ⊠ *Travessa Cândido dos Reis, 5400-164* 🕾 *276/301640* ⊕ *www. hoteltrajano.com* ⇱ *39 rooms* ⚭ *Restaurant, cable TV, bar, lounge* ▤ *AE, MC, V* ⦶ *BP.*

$$ 🖬 **Forte de São Francisco.** The ruins of a 17th-century Franciscan monastery have been transformed to create this remarkable hotel. Outside, massive walls surround extensive gardens and courtyards. The in-

Fodor'sChoice ★

terior is a sober blend of ancient stone and modern simplicity. The Franciscan monks would no doubt have frowned on the contemporary comforts of the elegant, well-equipped guest rooms and the sumptuous food served in the restaurant (Restaurante Cozinha do Convento). They might, however, have winked at the hotel's well-stocked wine cellar installed in their old water cistern. ⊠ *Alto da Pedisqueira, 5400-435* ☎ *276/333700* ⊕ *www.forte-s-francisco-hoteis.pt* 📭 *53 rooms, 5 suites* ⚫ *Restaurant, cafeteria, in-room safes, minibars, cable TV, tennis court, pool, bar* ⊟ *AE, DC, MC, V* ⦿ *BP.*

$ 🏨 **Hotel Aquae Flaviae.** Although it bears the ancient Roman name for Chaves, and it's a cannon shot away from the town's fortified tower, this is a gleaming, modern hotel. The facade has an art deco touch—it looks more like an enormous movie house than a hotel—and the interior impresses with its smooth lines and polished surfaces. The rooms are as spacious as they are attractive. ⊠ *Praça do Brasil, 5400-123* ☎ *276/ 309000* ⊕ *www.hoteis-arco.com* 📭 *167 rooms* ⚫ *Restaurant, in-room safes, minibars, cable TV, tennis court, pool, wading pool, gym, sauna, billiards, bar, shops, no-smoking rooms, Wi-Fi, meeting rooms* ⊟ *AE, DC, MC, V* ⦿ *BP.*

EN ROUTE If you continue west along the N103 for 35 km (22 mi), you'll come to an enormous system of lakes and hydroelectric dams along the Cávado. At this point you can make a short side trip to see the ruined castle at Montalegre, which is visible from miles around. Take a right turn onto the N308 and drive for 12 km (7 mi). The views are worth the detour. Back on the N103, you'll follow along the edge of the great lake system, skirting drowned valleys in an endless series of long loops. Allow plenty of time, because you're sure to want to stop often to take in the incredible views. To the north is the Parque Nacional da Peneda-Gerês; there are occasional access points along the road. Finally, after passing the village of Cerdeirinhas, the road runs for 30 km (18 mi) through rocky heights and down tree-clad slopes to reach Braga, where you are firmly in the center of the Minho province.

PORTO & THE NORTH ESSENTIALS

Transportation

BY AIR

Porto's Aeroporto F. Sá Carneiro, 13 km (8 mi) north of the city, is the gateway to all of northern Portugal. There's direct service from many European and South American cities, though not from the United States. TAP runs regular flights from Lisbon's Aeroporto Portela. Omni also has flights to regional airports in Bragança and Vila Real from Lisbon.

The Aerobus runs from the airport to downtown Porto. It takes up to an hour, depending on the traffic, to reach the stop Cordoaria, the area behind the Torre dos Clérigos (Clérigos Tower). A ticket will cost you €2.60. Taxis are available outside the terminal; the fare into town will run €18–€20, including the €1.50 baggage charge. If you are traveling outside the city's perimeter, tariffs are based on kilometers traveled.

The day rate until 10 PM is €0.50 per kilometer. Late night, weekends, and holidays, the tariff goes up 20%.

🖪 Airports **Aeroporto F. Sá Carneiro** 🕾 22/943-2400 ⊕ www.ana-aeroportos.pt. **Aeroporto Portela** 🕾 21/841-3500 for general information, 21/841-3700 for arrivals and departures information. **Bragança airport** 🕾 273/381175. **Vila Real airport** 🕾 259/336620.

🖪 Airlines **Aerocondor** 🕾 21/846-4964 in Lisbon, 259/328802 in Vila Real, 273/381298 in Bragança ⊕ www.aerocondor.com. **TAP** 🕾 707/205700 call center 8 AM-10 PM ⊕ www.tap-airportugal.com.

By Bus & Tram

IN PORTO Porto has a very good public transportation system of buses and trams. From 6 AM to 9 PM, 73 bus routes are served; after 9 PM, service is reduced to 14 routes. The tourist office provides a city map with the routes. Main stops are at Praça da Liberdade, Praça de Dom João I, and Cordoaria, behind the Torre dos Clérigos. Bus 78 runs from Praça da Liberdade, past the Museu Nacional Soares dos Reis and the Palácio de Cristal gardens, along the main Avenida da Boavista, to the Museu de Arte Contemporânea. Trams 1 and 18 make a pleasant run along the river.

Bus tickets are cheapest when purchased from STCP kiosks, newsagents, or tobacconists: €1.55 for round-trip within Porto and from €1.95 for outlying areas. Tickets bought on the bus are €1.30 for a single. There's also a €4 day pass available.

The latest means of transportation in Porto is the Metro do Porto, a tram network that runs mostly along the ground. Tickets start at €1.30 for a single ride but you can save money by investing in an Andante card covering metro, funicular, tram, and some bus routes. The initial card costs €0.50, and may then be recharged with more credit at vending machines at metro, train, and bus stations. For a detailed breakdown on the multitrip deals and season tickets pick up the *Transport Guide* pamphlet (in English) available at the city tourist offices.

🖪 **Blue Line** 🕾 808/200166. **Metro do Porto** ✉ Av. Fernão de Magalhães 1862, 7°, Porto 🕾 22/508-1000 or 808/205060 ⊕ www.metro-porto.pt. **Rodonorte** ✉ Rua Ateneu Comercial 19, Porto 🕾 22/200-5637. **STCP buses** ✉ Av. Fernão de Magalhães 1862 13°, Porto 🕾 22/507-1000 or 808/200166 ⊕ www.stcp.pt.

IN THE NORTH Several bus companies operate in the north. Major terminals are found at Porto, Braga, Guimarães, Vila Real, and Chaves. The best source of information about departures is the local tourist office, since bus station personnel invariably speak no English. Most bus stations do, however, have timetables that you should be able to decipher with the aid of a dictionary.

The main company operating in Trás-os-Montes is Rodonorte, whose terminal in Porto is at Rua da Ateneu Comercial. Bus trips in this region are slow and, on some of the minor routes, uncomfortable. One useful tip is to take the bus rather than the train between the neighboring towns of Guimarães and Braga. It's only 22 km (14 mi) on the road, but the circuitous train ride involves two changes.

🖪 **Rodonorte** ✉ Rua Ateneu Comercial 19, Porto 🕾 22/200-5637, 25/934-0710 in Vila Real.

BY CAR

The IP4 highway is a fast way to travel between Porto and Bragança, and there are quick routes from Porto to towns both north and south. The A4/E82 toll road connects Porto to Amarante. From here the three-lane IP4/E82 passes through Vila Real, Mirandela, and Bragança en route to the Spanish border at Quintanilha. The IP3 runs from Lamego to Peso da Régua, following N2 to Vila Real. The toll road A3/IP1 runs from Porto to Braga and on to Ponte de Lima and Valença on the Spanish border. The three-lane ICI travels from Porto to Viana de Castelo.

Given the nature of Portuguese terrain—particularly in the northeast—some journeys will never be anything but slow. Examples are the routes Bragança–Chaves–Braga (N103), Vila Real–Chaves (N2), and Bragança–Mirando do Douro (N218). It's best simply to accept the roads' limitations, slow down, and appreciate the scenery. Off the beaten track, always check with local tourist offices to make sure the routes you wish to follow are navigable. Roadwork and winter landslides can cause detours and delays. In isolated regions, take special care at night, because many roads are unlighted and unpaved.

BY TAXI

In Porto there's a taxi stand in Praça da Liberdade, or you can phone for a cab. Make sure the driver turns on the meter; if you have phoned for the cab, the cabbie will have already done so from wherever he picked up the call. Within the city's limits travelers are charged through a meter which starts at €1.80 or €2.10 if it is between 9 PM and 6 AM, the weekend, or a holiday. Outside the city's perimeter the rate is €0.34 per kilometer (plus 20% between 9 PM and 6 AM, the weekend, or a holiday). Taxis which run outside the city's perimeter have a letter "A" on the door. It's customary, but not obligatory, to tip up to 10% of the fare. Note that taxis add a surcharge for crossing the Ponte Dom Luís I to Vila Nova de Gaia, the suburb known for its port wine.
Rádio Táxis ☎ 22/507-3900.

BY TRAIN

Most trains into Porto (including those from Lisbon) arrive at Estação de Campanhã, just east of the city center. From here, you can take a five-minute connecting train ride to the central Estação de São Bento; connecting trains run regularly. When leaving Porto, be sure to budget plenty of time from the station to make your connection. For the express service to and from Lisbon, reserve your seat at least a day in advance.

Trains from Guimarães and from the coast immediately north of the city use the Estação da Trindade. The station is a few minutes' walk from downtown Porto, behind the town hall at the top of Avenida dos Aliados. From Spain, the Vigo–Porto train uses the Tuy/Valença do Minho border crossing and runs south down the Minho to Porto. These trains usually stop at the Campanhã and São Bento stations, but some stop only at Campanhã, and you'll have to change for São Bento.

All the region's train routes originate in Porto; from here some of the finest lines in the country stretch out into the river valleys and mountain ranges of the northeast. Even if you've rented a car, try to take a day trip on at least one of the beautiful lines that traverse the region.

The Douro Line runs from Estação de São Bento east to Pocinho via Livração, Peso da Régua, and Tua (a four-hour journey). Three narrow-gauge lines branch off from it: the Tâmega Line, linking Livração with beautiful Amarante (25 minutes); the Corgo Line from Peso da Régua to Vila Real (one hour); and the Tua Line from Tua to Mirandela (two hours). The trains on these lines generally have just one class of car, and usually stop at every station. Journeys are slow but rewarding. For reservations and current schedules contact Estação de São Bento or the tourist office in Porto.

Trains on the main route north along the Costa Verde depart approximately hourly from both São Bento and Campanhã stations and run through Barcelos and Viana do Castelo, as far as Valença do Minho. Branch lines connect with Braga and Guimarães.

🚉 **Estação de Campanhã** ⊠ Largo da Estação de Campanhã, Porto ☎ 22/519-1374, 808/208208 (between 7 ᴀᴍ and 11 ᴘᴍ). **Estação de Contumil** ⊠ Rua Dr. Deniz Jacinto 270, Porto ☎ 22/550-9405, 808/208208 (between 7 ᴀᴍ and 11 ᴘᴍ). **Estação de São Bento** ⊠ Praça Almeida Garrett, Porto ☎ 22/205-1714, 808/208208 (between 7 ᴀᴍ and 11 ᴘᴍ).

Contacts & Resources

EMERGENCIES

Pharmacies take turns staying open late. Schedules and addresses are posted on the door of each establishment, and listings of late-night services are carried in the local press.

🚑 **General** ☎ 112. **Hospital Escolar de São João** ⊠ Alameda Professor Hernâni Monteiro, Porto ☎ 22/551-2100. **Hospital Geral de Santo António** ⊠ Largo Professor Abel Salazar, Porto ☎ 22/207-7500. **Hospital Joaquim Urbano** ⊠ Rua Câmara Pestana 348, Porto ☎ 22/589-9550. **Hospital Magalhães Lemos** ⊠ Rua Prof. Álvaro Rodrigues, Porto ☎ 22/619-2400.

MAIL

The main post office in Porto is in Praça General Humberto Delgado. General-delivery mail (mark it ᴘᴏsᴛᴇ ʀᴇsᴛᴀɴᴛᴇ) is received here.

📮 **Post Office Porto** ⊠ Praça General Humberto Delgado ☎ 22/340-0472 ⊕ www.ctt.pt ⊙ Weekdays 8 ᴀᴍ–10 ᴘᴍ, Sat. 8–8.

TOURS

BOAT TOURS Several Porto-based companies offer cruises on the Rio Douro. These range from short trips taking in Porto's bridges and the local fishing villages to one- and two-day cruises that include meals and accommodations. Most of the short cruises (€7.50–€10) depart several times daily from the Cais da Ribeira, at the foot of Porto's Old Town. Porto Tours is a reservations center for the short tours.

The longer cruises, some in traditional rabelo riverboats, usually involve taking a train from the Estação de São Bento that connects with a boat farther up the Douro. These longer, upriver cruises usually leave once or twice a week from May to October.

One of the oldest companies is Endouro. Turisdouro specializes in rides on sailboats traditionally used to transport port wine downriver. Gabinete da Rota do Vinho do Porto can make reservations for boat and train tours, hotels, and wine tastings.

Douro Azul specializes in longer cruises from the upriver town of Peso da Régua. One of Douro Azul's most popular day tours is a steam train ride up the Rio Douro to Pinhão and Tua Railway Station, with a return trip by boat on Saturday; for trips on Sunday, Tuesday, and Thursday, you leave Porto by boat and return by train. Lunch is often included in the price, which is around €50 per person. Trains depart from the downtown Estação de São Bento; boats leave from the quay in Vila Nova de Gaia. Douro Azul also operates two air-conditioned hotel boats: the *Alto Douro* (37 double cabins, restaurant, and sundecks) and the *Invicta* (40 double cabins).

🚩 **Barcadouro** ✉ Rua Rei Ramiro, Edifício Vila Nova de Gaia 870, 1Lt, Vila Nova de Gaia ☎ 22/200-8882 ⊕ www.barcadouro.pt. **Cenários d'Ouro** ✉ Praceta Aureliano Barrigas 6, 1E, Vila Real ☎ 259/338135 or 259/338136 ⊕ www.cenarios.com. **Douro Azul** ✉ Rua de S. Francisco 4-2° D, Porto ☎ 22/340-2500 ⊕ www.douroazul.pt. **Douroacima** ✉ Praça da Ribeira 20dt°, Porto ☎ 22/200-6418 ⊕ www.douroacima.pt. **Gabinete da Rota do Vinho do Porto** ✉ Rua dos Camilos 90, Peso da Régua ☎ 254/320145 or 254/320146. **Porto Tours** ✉ Torre Medieval-Calçada D. Pedro Pitões 15, Porto ☎ 22/200-0073 ⊕ www.portotours.com. **Turisdouro** ✉ Rua Machado dos Santos 824, Porto ☎ 22/370-8429.

BUS TOURS Bus tours of Porto usually last a half day and take in all the principal sights, including the port-wine lodges in Vila Nova de Gaia. Contact the tourist office for more information. Cityrama and Diana Tours operate half- and full-day coach tours to destinations as diverse as the Douro Valley, the Minho, and Parque Nacional da Peneda-Gerês.

🚩 **Cityrama** ✉ Av. Praia da Vitória 12-B, Saldanha, Lisbon 1049-054 ☎ 21/319-1090 ⊕ www.cityrama.pt. **Diana Tours** ✉ Rua General Torres 344, Vila Nova de Gaia 4430-106 ☎ 22/377-1230 or 800/203983 ⊕ www.dianatours.pt.

HELICOPTER If you want to get above it all, Helitours offers 10-minute flights over
TOURS Porto and 20-minute flights that take you farther upriver. The three-hour tour includes a trip to Mesão Frio, with a stop for lunch. The heliport is in the Massarelos area overlooking the Douro River and next to the Helitours office.

🚩 **Helitours** ✉ Alameda Basílio Teles s/n, Porto ☎ 22/543-2464 ⊕ www.douroazul.com.

VISITOR INFORMATION

Alto Minho (✉ Castelo Santiago da Barra, Viana do Castelo ☎ 258/820270 ⊕ www.rtam.pt).

Alto Tâmega e Barroso (✉ Av. Tenente Valadim 39-1D, Chaves ☎ 276/340660 ⊕ www.rt-atb.pt).

Nordeste Transmontano (✉ Edifício Principal, Largo Principal, Bragança ☎ 273/331078 ⊕ www.rt-nordeste.pt).

Região de Turismo Serra do Marão (✉ Praça Luís de Camões 2, Vila Real ☎ 259/323560 ⊕ www.rtsmarao.pt).

Verde Minho (✉ Edifício Atlântico, Praça Dr. José Ferreira Salgado 90-6, Braga ☎ 253/202770 ⊕ www.rtvm.pt).

PORTO   There is an ICEP tourism office at the airport as well.

🚩 Tourist Offices Centro de Informação Turística do Porto, ICEP ✉ Praça Dom João I 43, east of Av. dos Aliados ☎ 22/205-7514, 808/781212 (Contact Center ICEP) ⊕ www.portoturismo.pt. **Posto de Turismo Municipal** ✉ Rua Clube dos Fenianos 25, at top of Av. dos Aliados ☎ 22/339-3470 ✎ turismo.central@cm-porto.pt ✉ Rua do Infante Dom Henrique 63, south of Praça da Liberdade ☎ 22/200-9770.

PORTO'S   **🚩 Tourist Offices Amarante** ✉ Alameda Teixeira de Pascoaes ☎ 255/420200. **Espinho**
ENVIRONS   ✉ Rua 23, 271 ☎ 22/733-5872. **Esposende** ✉ Av. Marginal ☎ 253/961354. **Lamego** ✉ Av. Visconde Guedes Teixeira ☎ 254/612005. **Póvoa de Varzim** ✉ Praça Marquês de Pombal ☎ 252/298120. **Vila do Conde** ✉ Rua 25 de Abril 103 ☎ 252/248473.

THE MINHO &   **🚩 Tourist Offices Arcos de Valdevez** ✉ Campo do Transladário ☎ 258/516001. **Barce-**
THE COSTA VERDE   **los** ✉ Torre de Menagem, Largo da Porta Nova ☎ 253/811882. **Braga** ✉ Av. da Liberdade 1 ☎ 253/262550. **Caminha** ✉ Rua Ricardo Joaquim de Sousa ☎ 258/921952 ✉ Av. Dr. Ramos Pereira ☎ 258/911384. **Guimarães** ✉ Alameda de S. Dâmaso 86 ☎ 253/412450. **Monção** ✉ Casa do Curro, Praça da República ☎ 251/652757. **Ponte da Barca** ✉ Largo da Misericórdia ☎ 258/452899. **Ponte de Lima** ✉ Praça da República ☎ 258/942335. **Terras do Bouro-Gerês** ✉ Vilar da Veiga ☎ 253/391133. **Valença do Minho** ✉ Av. de Espanha ☎ 251/823374. **Viana do Castelo** ✉ Rua do Hospital Velho ☎ 258/822620. **Vila Nova de Cerveira** ✉ Rua Dr. António Duro ☎ 251/708023.

TRÁS-OS-   **🚩 Tourist Offices Bragança** ✉ Av. Cidade de Zamora ☎ 273/381273. **Chaves** ✉ Ter-
MONTES   reiro de Cavalaria ☎ 276/340661. **Vila Real** ✉ Av. Carvalho Araújo 94 ☎ 259/322819.

Madeira

WORD OF MOUTH

"Madeira is a place of incredible natural beauty, and it was one of our favorite parts of our Portuguese experience. It is one of those places that you must experience, as the camera cannot do it justice (like the Grand Canyon). If you are at all into hiking (and I must admit I am not particularly athletic), you must do a Levada hike. It was the high point (literally and figuratively) of our trip there."

—newcomer

Updated by
Mary McLean

WINE CONNOISSEURS THROUGH THE AGES have savored Madeira's eponymous export, but a sip of this heady elixir provides only a taste of the island's many delights. Foremost among these is the balmy year-round temperature, ensured by warm Atlantic currents. Other draws include the promise of clear skies, the carpets of flowers, the waterfalls that cascade down green canyons, and the great hiking paths. Floral scents fill Madeira's sea-washed air. Bird-of-paradise flowers grow wild; pink and purple fuchsia weave lacy patterns up pastel walls; and jacaranda trees create purple canopies over roads and avenues. The natural beauty of this island is like no other, from the cliffs that plummet seaward to mountain summits cloaked in silent fog. The magic has captivated travelers for centuries.

Madeira is a subtropical island 900 km (558 mi) southwest of Lisbon—at roughly the same latitude as Casablanca. In the middle of the isle is a backbone of high, rocky peaks and the crater of a now-extinct volcano. Steep ravines fan out from the center like spokes of a wheel. Although Madeira is only 57 km (35 mi) long and 22 km (14 mi) wide, distances seem much greater, as the roads climb and descend precipitously from one ravine to the next. In the same island group are tiny Porto Santo, about 50 km (31 mi) northeast, which has a sandy beach popular with vacationers and its 5,000 inhabitants; the Ilhas Desertas, a chain of waterless, unpopulated islands 20 km (12 mi) southeast of Madeira; and the also-uninhabited Ilhas Selvagens, much farther south, near Spain's Canary Islands.

The British, who have roots on the island thanks to a 16th-century royal marriage, flock to Madeira—many via good-value hotel packages. It's also a popular destination for Germans and Scandinavians, who enjoy downtime in Funchal and hiking the island's famous network of *levadas,* inland irrigation canals converted into superb walking trails. An adventurous crowd puts Madeira's magnificent blend of sun and seascapes to good use, and when it needs to wind down, the food and lodging are good, tranquil gardens offer repose, and there's even afternoon teatime. Travelers whose priority is cosmopolitan action until dawn will be unimpressed by Madeira. Others—of almost any age, nationality, and fitness level—are likely to be caught in its spell.

The island's popularity has wrought change: its airport is now international, and its numerous new roads (construction projects continue) have halved many journey times. But such developments don't seem to overwhelm Madeira. Rather, it's the island's amazingly rugged interior that overwhelms all who experience it. Multiple microclimates, exotic topography and vegetation, and designated nature reserves create an amazing ecodestination. The Laurissilva forest that occupies a lofty coastal strip above the sea has been classified as part of the Madeira Nature and UNESCO World Natural Heritage. The island is the only region in the world where ancient forest dating back before the Ice Age can be found. Flora and fauna in the four nature reserves are still being discovered to this day. With this awesome heritage, Madeira has the power to keep its core a sanctuary for centuries to come.

A BIT OF HISTORY

The island was discovered entirely by accident in the early 15th century at the height of Portugal's "Golden Age of Discovery" as Henry the Navigator was putting together teams of explorers. In 1418 João Gonçalves Zarco and Tristão Vaz Teixeira were blown off course during a particularly savage storm on their way to Guinea. By the time the storm subsided, they had drifted hundreds of miles off course and were lucky enough to hit upon an uninhabited island that they christened Porto Santo (Holy Port). Based on the sea captains' reports, Henry the Navigator gave the order to colonize. When Zarco and Teixeira returned to the area in 1419, they disembarked on a larger island, then covered with a nearly impenetrable forest. Zarco named it Madeira, which means "wood" in Portuguese. The name of the first settlement, Funchal, was inspired by the word *funcho* (fennel). In the 15th and 16th centuries the colony grew rich from its sugar plantations. Later, Madeira's wine industry sustained the island's growth, and in recent decades, tourism has become big business, making the island one of Portugal's top travel destinations. A statue of João Gonçalves Zarco stands at the main intersection in Funchal, the island's capital.

Exploring Madeira

For ease of planning you can split Madeira into five regions: Funchal, the capital; its environs; the eastern side of Madeira; the peaks, gorges, and plateaus of the interior; and the powerful cliffs of the rocky northwest coast. Additionally, there are the neighboring islands of Porto Santo and Ilhas Desertas, although if time is limited, Madeira's pleasures are more than enough.

Restaurants & Cuisine

Restaurants are plentiful both in Funchal and on the rest of the island. The best and priciest meals on the island are served in the many five-star hotel restaurants, such as Quinta Palmeira (next to the Savoy) and Villa Cipriani (next to Reid's Palace), which serve international cuisine and offer buffets. Less-expensive regional specialties can be found in Estreito de Câmara de Lobos, São Roque, Estrada Conde Carvalhal, São Gonçalo, and Portela. Look for fish restaurants at the beaches of Praia Formosa or in Funchal's Old Town. There are plenty of places serving moderately priced local and international cuisine at Funchal Marina or the market area of the Old Town. Ajuda, Lido, and Vila Ramos are all worth exploring for restaurants. More modern, nouvelle cuisine tends to be expensive. Many restaurants serving such cuisine are clustered around Estrada Monumental–Lido and Funchal's city center. Chinese, Indian, and Italian options abound in Funcha's city center, the Lido area, and near hotels and larger shopping areas.

A soft, white, deep-sea fish known as *espada* (often called "scabbard fish" because of its long, swordlike shape) is served everywhere and pre-

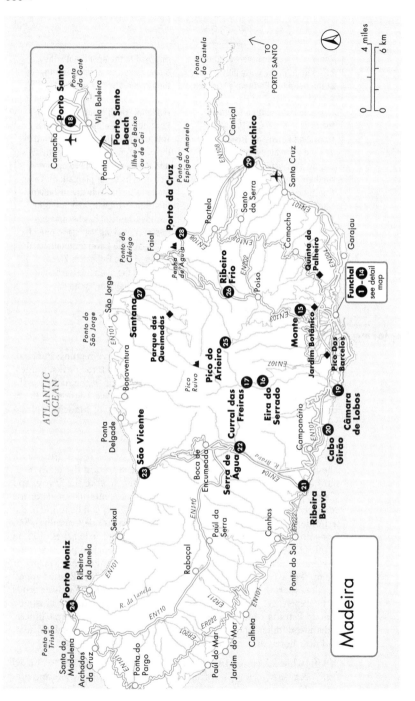

Madeira

ATLANTIC
OCEAN

Porto Santo
Camacha
18
Vila Baleira
Ponta
da Gaté
**Porto Santo
Beach**
Ponta
Ilhéu de Baixo
ou de Cai

TO
PORTO SANTO

4 miles
6 km

Ponta
do Castela

Ponta
do Espigão Amarelo

Caniçal

Machico
29
Santa Cruz
EN108

Porto da Cruz
28
Faial
Portela
Santo
da Serra
Camacha
EN101
EN102

Ponto do
Clérigo
Penha
de Águia
**Ribeiro
Frio**
26
EN202
Poiso
EN204
Garajau
Quinta da
Palheiro

São Jorge
Ponto do
São Jorge
Santana
27
Parque das
Queimadas
EN103
Funchal
1 – 14
see detail
map
15
Monte
Jardim Botânico

Bonaventura
Pico do Arieiro
25
Pico
Ruivo
EN101
**Pico Dos
Barcelos**
EN101

Ponta
Delgade
**Eira do
Serrado**
16
17
Curral das
Freiras
19
**Câmara
de Lobos**

São Vicente
23
Boca de
Encumeada
Serra de
Água
22
Campanário
EN101
**Cabo
Girão**
20

Seixal
EN110
Paúl da
Serra
Canhas
**Ribeira
Brava**
21

Porto Moniz
24
Ribeira
da Janela
EN101
Rabaçal
Ponta do Sol
EN101

R. da Janela
EN110
Paúl do Mar
Jardim do Mar
Calheta
EN101
ER211
ER222
ER209

Ponto do
Tristão
Santa da
Madalena
Archadas
da Cruz
Ponta do
Pargo

GREAT ITINERARIES

Three days are the minimum for exploring Funchal and its environs, along with some of the interior or the western coast; five days allows for a less hurried and more complete exploration of the island, including the northeast. You should use the old scenic roads as much as possible, and allow plenty of time for driving around. If, however, you're on a tight schedule or must travel at night, take advantage of the fast new roads.

IF YOU HAVE 3 DAYS

Devote your first day to the flower-bedecked capital city of 🔲 **Funchal** ❶– ⓮. Start Day 2 early, heading for the hills just outside the city. In the morning, visit the nearby Jardim Botânico, on the grounds of an aristocratic plantation, and the village of **Monte** ⓯, home of the unusual snowless sled ride. Next, go west from Funchal toward Pico dos Barcelos, whose view of the city can easily use up a roll of film. Then move on to the coast and a late lunch in or near the fishing village of **Câmara de Lobos** ⓲. Continue to **Cabo Girão** ⓴, with its spectacular views across the island. The terrain changes to forests as you continue along the coast to **Ribeira Brava** ㉑, another lovely seaside town. Turn inland through a rugged canyon and into a vivid green forest. You'll soon come to the mystical, cloud-shrouded peaks of the 🔲 **Serra de Água** ㉒. Plan well ahead to overnight at the charming pousada here. On your last day, wake up very early and walk in the mountains. Drive back to Funchal, where you can spend another night or catch a flight to Lisbon or home.

IF YOU HAVE 5 DAYS

Spend your first day getting into the island rhythm by touring 🔲 **Funchal** ❶– ⓮. In the morning of your second day, explore its environs, and visit the Jardim Botânico and the Quinta do Palheiro (Blandy Gardens). Next, head toward the village of **Monte** ⓯ for a quick look around. Afterward, using a good road map, follow the road to Poiso. Here, turn left and follow the signs to 🔲 **Pico do Arieiro** ㉓. Plan well ahead to overnight in the memorable pousada here, and the next day, head out for an exhilarating hike. If you're up to the challenge, try to reach Pico Ruivo. Later, backtrack to Poiso and head north to **Ribeiro Frio** ㉖. Walk along a levada and take a break at Victor's Bar, near the town's trout hatchery. Next head for **Santana** ㉗ to see the thatch-roof houses for which the village is famous, then west along the stunning coastal road toward 🔲 **São Vicente** ㉓. You can either overnight in São Vicente or push on to 🔲 **Porto Moniz** ㉔.

In Porto Moniz pick up picnic fare, then turn inland—past Santa Madalena—toward Rabaçal, full of waterfalls and quiet pools. Follow the road to Paúl da Serra, where you'll see sheep grazing across the moors. Next, follow the signs to the flower-filled town of Canhas and on to the coastal road back into Funchal. Spend your fourth night and the next day enjoying the capital; then bid the island a fond *até a prossima* (until next time).

8

pared dozens of ways—from poached à la Provençal to fried with bananas. In all the world, espada are fished commercially only in the
deep, offshore waters of Madeira and Japan. The fishermen set out in
the early evening in small boats, lower lines baited with specially prepared squid, and laboriously pull up the catch. Sunday is a day of rest,
however, so don't look for fresh espada on Monday.

Seafood fans should also try the Portuguese version of bouillabaisse,
caldeirada de peixes variados, a slowly simmered combination of fish,
shellfish, potatoes, tomatoes, onions, and olive oil. The other popular
fish plate is *bife de atum,* a hearty tuna steak. Those with more adventurous tastes should search out *polvo com vinagre*—a tangy octopus salad.

Another specialty is *carne de vinhos e alhos* (pork marinated in wine,
oil, garlic, and spices, then gently boiled and quickly browned over a
high flame). *Espetada,* a beef shish kebab seasoned with bay leaves and
butter, was traditionally a party dish prepared in the country over open
fires. The meat was once skewered on bay twigs, but nowadays it's served
on iron skewers hung vertically from special stands placed in the center of a table so that all diners can share. Espetada is usually accompanied by *milho frito* (fried cubes of savory corn pudding), a side dish native
to Madeira. Also on the table of many Madeiran restaurants is *bolo de
caco,* a round, flat bread smeared with garlic butter.

Typical desserts are bananas (small, sweet, silvery ones that aren't exported), mango, *paw paw* (papaya), *anonas* (custard apples), and
maracujá (passion fruit). Don't leave without trying the *bolo de mel,* a
spicy honey cake made with molasses and traditionally served with a
glass of Madeira, the unique wine
that has become synonymous with
the island. Most restaurants serve
Madeira (indeed, many offer diners a complimentary glass). Look
also for *vinho da casa,* a local table
wine. It's much cheaper than imported ones and generally of high
quality. Coral, a light lager, is the
local *cerveja* (beer). For a tasty non-
alcoholic drink, try *brisa* maracujá,
a sparkling passion-fruit soda.

About the Hotels

In Funchal your options range from
majestic old hotels to quiet *pensões* (pensions). Elsewhere on the island, consider staying in a *pousada.*
Here on Madeira, pousada is a commonly used term for an inn, or literally "resting place," and doesn't
mean the property is part of the licensed pousada network of mainland Portugal. Pousada do Pico do
Arieiro takes its name without being

MADEIRA WINE

MADEIRA'S WINE has been enjoyed for more than 500 years. It
has graced the tables of Napoléon,
the Russian czars, and even
George Washington. In fact, the
glasses raised to toast the signing
of America's Declaration of Independence were filled with it. The
fortified wine is served as an aperitif or with dessert, depending on
its sweetness. Unlike other wines,
Madeira is heated to produce its
distinctive mellow flavor—a process
that supposedly developed after
thirsty sailors sampled the
Madeira that had been shipped
through equatorial heat. The four
varieties, from driest to sweetest,
are Sercial, Verdelho, Boal, and
Malmsey.

part of the official pousada system, but you'll feel as if you're walking on air here because sometimes you actually are above the clouds. Several low-key inns and bed-and-breakfasts also dot the island.

Some of the larger Madeiran hotels cater to package-tour operators, who offer relatively low prices and reserve huge blocks of rooms during peak holiday-travel periods. This may be one place where do-it-yourself travelers are better off going through an agency.

WHAT IT COSTS In Euros					
	$$$$	**$$$**	**$$**	**$**	**¢**
RESTAURANTS	over €21	€16–€21	€11–€15	€7–€10	under €7
HOTELS	over €275	€176–€275	€101–€175	€60–€100	under €60

Restaurant prices are per person for a main course at dinner. Hotel prices are for a standard double room, including tax, in high season (off-season rates may be lower).

When to Go

The island's lower elevations are blessed by constant soft, warm breezes, and subtropical vegetation that perfumes the air year-round. Every day seems like spring. Historically Madeira has been a winter resort, but that—like much on the island—is changing. Christmas week, when every tree in Funchal is decorated with lights and the main boulevard becomes an open-air folk museum, is still the most popular time to visit, along with New Year's Eve, when cruise ships from everywhere pull into the harbor for an incomparable fireworks display from the hills surrounding Funchal. Book far in advance if you're coming at this time. Summer can also be crowded, especially during August, when the Portuguese take vacations. Festivals—celebrating flowers in April, the island's patron saint in August, and wine in September—are popular, too.

FUNCHAL

When colonists arrived in Madeira in July 1419, the valley they settled was a mass of bright yellow fennel, or *funchal* in Portuguese. Today the bucolic fields are gone, and the community that replaced them is the self-governing island's bustling business and political center.

Funchal's distinct British air stems from the mid-16th-century marriage of the Portuguese princess Catherine of Bragança to England's King Charles II, which marked the end of Spain's domination of Portugal. The marriage contract gave the English the right to live on Madeira, plus valuable trade concessions. Charles in turn gave Madeirans an exclusive franchise to sell wine to England and its colonies. The island's wine boom lured many British families to Funchal, and many blue-blooded Europeans and famous vacationers such as George Bernard Shaw and Winston Churchill followed the pack to enjoy the mild winters.

Exploring Funchal

To get to know Funchal best, spend time at the waterfront, market, and city squares—daily haunts of the islanders.

8

What to See

★ ➓ **Adegas de São Francisco.** The St. Francis Wine Lodge takes its original name from the convent that once stood on this site. Today the operation is owned by the island's famous wine-making Blandy family and is also known as the Old Blandy Wine Lodge. Here you can see how wine barrels are made, visit cellars where the wine is stored, and hear tales about Madeira wine. One legend has it that when the Duke of Clarence was sentenced to death in 1478 for plotting against his brother, King Edward IV, he was given his choice of execution methods. He decided to be drowned in a "vat of Malmsey," a barrel of the drink. There's plenty of time for tasting at the end of the visit. (Note that the production-line wineries are outside town and are closed to visitors.) ⊠ *Av. Arriaga 28* ☎ *291/ 740110* ⊕ *www.madeirawinecompany.com* ✉ *€3* ⊙ *Tours weekdays at 10:30 and 3:30, Sat. at 11. Wine shop weekdays 9:30–6:30.*

❹ **Antiga Alfândega.** The stately Old Customs House is home to Madeira's parliament (closed to the public). From here deputies govern the island, which is part of Portugal but enjoys greater autonomy than the mainland provinces. The building's original 16th-century Manueline style was given baroque touches during renovations that followed the devastating 18th-century earthquake that almost leveled faraway Lisbon. ⊠ *Av. do Mar and Av. das Comunidades Madeirenses* ☎ *No phone.*

⓭ **Convento de Santa Clara.** Inside the Santa Clara Convent, the painted wood walls and the ceiling are lined with ceramic tiles, giving the sanctuary an Arabic look. ⊠ *Calçada de Santa Clara* ☎ *291/742602* ⊙ *Daily 10–noon and 3–5.*

⓮ **Fortaleza do Pico.** The Fort of the Peak was built in the late 1500s to protect the settlement against pirate attacks. One of the worst raids on Funchal was in the 16th century by the pirating nobleman Bertrand de Montluc, who sacked the churches and stole barrels of Madeira. He resold the wine to his noble friends and unwittingly helped spread the reputation of the island's drink. The fortress has been in the possession of the navy since 1933, but you can view parts of it, including a balcony with a fine panorama of the city. ⊠ *Calçada do Pico* ☎ *No phone* ✉ *Free* ⊙ *Daily 9–6.*

❺ **Fortaleza de São Tiago.** This robust construction was started by 1614, if not earlier, when French corsairs began to threaten Funchal's coveted deepwater harbor. Thanks to continuous use—by British troops when their nation was allied with Portugal against Napoléon, and

---

TASTING

Madeira wine has a well-deserved reputation which dates back to Shakespeare's time. It is widely available throughout the island with the famous brands including Blandy's, Leacock's, and Cossart Gordon, to name a few. Although all are now produced by the Madeira Wine Company, each brand is blended to maintain its individual characteristics. To learn the history of these wines, see how they're made, and, better still, sample a few, you can visit the São Francisco Wine Lodge in Funchal or the Henriques & Henriques Vinhos (Winery) in Câmara de Lobos.

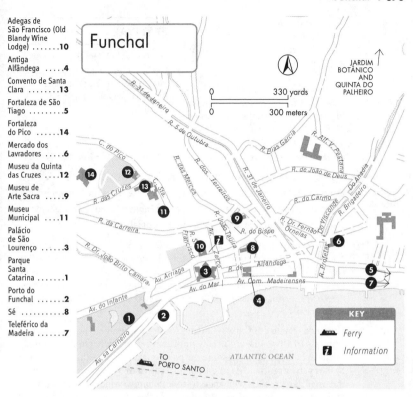

during the visit of the Portuguese king Dom Carlos in 1901—much of the military stronghold has been preserved. A former governor's house inside it is now the **Museu de Arte Contemporânea,** considered to be one of Portugal's top five modern art museums with changing exhibitions of works from the 1960s and later, most by local artists. ⊠ *Rua do Portão de São Tiago* ☎ *291/226456* ☑ *€2 for exhibitions, free at other times* ⊙ *Mon.–Sat. 10–12:30 and 2:30–5:45.*

FodorśChoice
★

❻ **Mercado dos Lavradores** (Farmers' Market). In the center patio of the Farmers' Market, women—sometimes in Madeira's native costume of a full, homespun skirt with yellow, red, and black vertical stripes and an embroidered white blouse—sell orchids, bird-of-paradise flowers (the emblem of Madeira), anthuriums, and other blooms. The lower-level seafood market displays the day's catch. Note the rows of fierce-looking espada. Their huge, bulging eyes are caused by the fatal change in pressure between their deepwater habitat and sea level. ⊠ *Rua Brigadeiro Oudinot* ⊙ *Weekdays 7 AM–8 PM, Sat. 7 AM–2 PM.*

❾ **Museu de Arte Sacra.** Funchal's Museum of Sacred Art has Flemish paintings, polychrome wood statues, and other treasures gathered from the island's churches. Most of the paintings were commissioned by the first merchants of Madeira, many of whom came from Brugge, Belgium. The

Adoration of the Magi was painted in 1518 for a wealthy trader from Machico and was paid for not in gold, but in sugar. You can tell how important this commodity was to the island by examining Funchal's coat of arms: it depicts five loaves of sugar in the shape of a cross. ⊠ *Rua do Bispo 21* ☎ *291/228900* 🎫 *€3* ⏱ *Tues.–Sat. 10–12:30 and 2:30–6. Also open for temporary exhibitions Sun. 10–1 and 2–6.*

> **FESTIVAL**
>
> The **Festival de Flores** in the last week of April, brightens downtown Funchal with a carpet of *flores* (flowers), a parade, and a lot of music.

NEED A BREAK?
A good place to stop for a light lunch or afternoon tea is **O Patio** (⊠ Av. Zarco 21 ☎ 291/227376), which entirely lives up to its name—it's a tiled open-air patio. At the same address, Livraria Inglesa is a rare English-language bookstore that sells magazines, novels, and books about Portugal.

⑪ Museu Municipal. Animals found on Madeira and in its seas—including a ferocious-looking collection of stuffed sharks—are on display in the city museum. Attached is a small aquarium, where you can watch the graceful movements of an octopus and view a family of sea turtles. ⊠ *Rua Mouraria 31* ☎ *291/229761* 🎫 *€2.10* ⏱ *Tues.–Fri. 10–6, weekends noon–6.*

⑫ Museu da Quinta das Cruzes (Crosses Manor Museum). The building and grounds of this museum are as impressive as its collection of antique furniture. Of special interest are the palanquins—lounge chairs once used to carry the grand ladies of colonial Madeira around town. Don't miss the small garden filled with ancient stone columns, window frames, arches, and tombstone fragments. ⊠ *Calçada do Pico 1* ☎ *291/740670* 🎫 *€3* ⏱ *Tues.–Sat. 10–12:30 and 2–5:30, Sun. 10–1.*

③ Palácio de São Lourenço. Built in the 17th century as Madeira's first fortress, the St. Lawrence Palace is still used as a military headquarters. On occasion its grand rooms are open to visitors (call the palace or ask at the tourist office for details); at other times its small Museu Militar (Military Museum) offers a glimpse inside the building. ⊠ *Entrance to Museu Militar on Av. Arriaga* ☎ *291/202530* 🎫 *Free* ⏱ *Weekdays 9:30–noon and 2–5:30, Sat. 9:30–noon.*

① Parque Santa Catarina. Abloom with flowers all year-round, St. Catarina Park covers an area of around 43,000 square yards with fantastic views over Funchal and its bay up to the Ponta do Garajau. At the top of the park is a pink mansion called **Quinta Vigia,** the residence of the president of Madeira (closed to the public). In the center of the park rests the tiny Capela de Santa Catarina (St. Catherine's Chapel), built by Madeira's discoverer João Gonçalves Zarco in 1425. It's one of the island's oldest buildings. ⊠ *Between Av. do Infante and Av. Sá Carneiro, overlooking the harbor.*

NEED A BREAK?
A classic spot to sit back and relax is the **Casa Minas Gerais** (⊠ Av. do Infante 2, at Rua João Brito Câmara ☎ 291/223381). Pick out your pastry from the central bar, and a waiter will bring it to your table with a pot of tea or coffee. The

The Azores: Portugal's Volcanic Isles

LOOKING FOR A VACATION from your vacation, or a unique destination that's far off the beaten path–by 1,410 km (875 mi)? The remote Portuguese archipelago collectively known as the Azores could be your place. With a total population of 237,000, these nine islands are a tranquil, pastoral escape from mainland Portugal and Europe.

Geologically, the Azores are relatively young volcanic isles. They were formed less than 6 million years ago, and eruptions are still possible. The most recent volcanic activity vented in 1958, creating a fascinating moonscape of lava rock and sand that is now the western tip of Faial island. The archipelago is quite spread out, requiring short flights between most islands. São Miguel is the largest and most populated of the group, and home to the political and economic capital, Ponta Delgada. Corvo is the smallest at 17 square km (6½ square mi) with around 400 inhabitants.

The mere existence of civilization on the Azores is impressive; volcanic rock terrain and a forbidding distance from the Portuguese mainland must have made the islands inhospitable to early inhabitants. Despite these natural obstacles, the first settlers arrived in the 1430s and became a successful Portuguese colony through perseverance and hard work. They imported livestock and cleared grazing fields to create a robust meat and dairy industry, grew grape vineyards in rock beds, and built a strong fishing industry. Then, for much of the 19th century, the Azores became the European hub of whaling–two museums on Pico island document its history, which concluded with the birth of petroleum production.

Today the islands are nurturing a budding tourism industry. Nature lovers come to witness the stunning beauty of the isles, with their dormant volcanoes, natural swimming holes, and–in spring–millions of wild, blooming hydrangeas. More adventurous travelers take advantage of the hiking, world-class fishing, and excellent whale watching available. Still others come for a brief glimpse into a simpler life that is rarely seen today in mainland Europe–small, pretty port towns of cobblestone streets, simple churches, and red-tile-roofed homes that thrive on cottage industries like fishing, cheese making, and ceramics.

Locals will explain that all nine islands are unique and each equally special, but if you're making a side trip from Lisbon and have limited time, you can get a good overview by sampling the four main islands: São Miguel with its two outstanding volcanic craters, Terceira with its many festivals and natural swimming coves, Faial and its legendary seafarers' port of Horta, and Pico which is dominated by a massive volcanic cone rising 7,715 feet into the clouds.

For more information and details, contact the Azores Tourist Board (Rua Ernesto Rebelo 14-P 9900-112, Horta, Faial ☎ 292/200-500 ⊕ www. drtacores.pt). Azores Express, part of SATA airlines (⊕ www.azores-express. com), is the main carrier to the islands and runs direct flights from Boston, and in high season, Oakland and Providence.

café retains many of its original 1920s fittings and has music to match: in the evening, from Wednesday through Sunday, a jazz band plays.

❷ Porto do Funchal. This is where growing numbers of cruise ships moor for one- or two-day visits to the island, and where big container ships— mostly from northern Europe—unload. Walk east on Avenida das Comunidades Madeirenses (known as Avenida do Mar), the seafront boulevard, and enjoy the view.

❽ Sé. Renowned for its ceiling with intricate geometric designs of inlaid ivory, Funchal's cathedral dates from 1514 and reveals an Arabic influence throughout. Don't miss the carved, gilded choir stalls in the side entrance and in the chancel (they depict the prophets and the apostles), or the intricate tile work at the side entrance and in the belfry. ⊠ *Av. Arriaga* ☎ *No phone* ⊗ *Mon.–Sat. 8–11:30 and 5–6:30.*

❼ Teleférico da Madeira. The sleek, Austrian-engineered cable-car service has more than 40 cars that travel from Funchal's waterfront up to Monte at 1,804 feet above sea level. The trip takes 15 minutes one way, and there are great views to enjoy as you float silently up and over the city.

From Monte you can buy a ticket back down to Funchal via the famous ★ **toboggan run** (⊠ Serra do Monte). No one in Madeira should miss this experience that will take 10 years off your life and stay with you forever. These basket cars have been whisking thrill seekers down the hill for more than a century and are driven by two men wearing white outfits and straw boaters, pushing and pulling you down the staggeringly steep 5-km (3-mi) descent back to Funchal. ⊠ *Campo Almirante Reis* ☎ *291/780280* ⊕ *www.madeiracablecar.com* ✉ *€9.50 1-way, €14.50 round-trip* ⊗ *Daily 10–6 (last round-trip 5:30, last uphill trip 5:45).*

OUTSIDE DOWNTOWN **Jardim Botânico.** The Botanical Garden is on the grounds of an old plantation 3 km (2 mi) northeast of Funchal. Its well-labeled plants—including anthuriums, bird-of-paradise flowers, and a large cactus collection—come from four continents. Savor wonderful views of Funchal, and check out the petrified trunk of a 10-million-year-old heather tree. There's also a natural-history museum, an orchid garden with more than 50,000 plants (unique in Europe), and a small exotic-birds garden. You can get here on Bus 30, which stops across the street from the market in front of Madeira's Electric Company. To hike up, turn uphill on Rua da Rochina, from Avenida Arriaga, to Caminho do Meio and follow it for at least 45 minutes. ⊠ *Caminho do Meio* ☎ *291/211200* ✉ *€3, orchid garden €3* ⊗ *Gardens daily 9–5:30, museum daily 9–1:30.*

Quinta do Palheiro. Also known as the Blandy Gardens, this 30-acre estate 5 km (3 mi) northeast of Funchal is owned by the Blandy wine family. The formal gardens have flowering perennials. You can stroll the gardens and the grounds, where camellia trees bloom between December and April, but you can't tour the family's house. To get here, head out of town on N101, the road to the airport. At the fork make a left onto N102 and follow the signs toward Camacha. Also, Bus 36 departs weekday mornings at 9:45 from in front of the Palácio de São Lourenço, on Avenida das Comunidades Madeirenses (next to the marina). It returns at 12:30. ☎ *291/793044* ✉ *€7* ☉ *Weekdays 9:30–12:30 PM.*

Where to Eat

Don't hesitate to join the locals in the small restaurants and snack bars spread all over the narrow backstreets (such as Rua da Carreira, Rua das Murças, Rua do Bispo, Rua Queimada de Cimão, Rua Queimada de Baixo), where you will often find freshly prepared daily specials at extremely reasonable prices.

$$–$$$$ ✕ **Casa Madeirense.** This restaurant—wedged into a restored house next to Reid's Palace hotel—has lavish tile work, hand-painted murals, and a bar that resembles one of Santana's thatch-roof dwellings. The menu is heavy on fresh seafood and regional dishes (including espada), which the chef likes to dress up with tropical fruits and flambé presentations. ✉ *Estrada Monumental 153* ☎ *291/766700* ▤ *AE, DC, MC, V* ☉ *Closed Sun. and Aug.*

★ **$$–$$$$** ✕ **Les Faunes.** Named for the series of Picasso lithographs that adorns its walls, Les Faunes is done in a sophisticated blue-gray, with tables on two tiers—guaranteeing stunning views of Funchal. A pianist plays romantic music during your meal. The nouvelle menu changes daily, but expect to find such dishes as artichoke custard with sweet red-pepper sauce, carpaccio of sea bass with caviar, duck breast baked with peaches, and hot passion-fruit soufflé. ✉ *Reid's Palace hotel, Estrada Monumental 139* ☎ *291/763001* ♙ *Reservations essential* 🏛 *Jacket and tie* ▤ *AE, DC, MC, V* ☉ *Closed June–Sept. No lunch.*

★ **$$–$$$$** ✕ **Quinta Palmeira.** Go down the steps beside this 1735 estate to reach the elegant, beautifully lighted restaurant (rather than the funky bar and diner at the front). You can sit in the airy, pastel dining room or out on the large terrace. Island specialties and international dishes are served with creative flair. Try espada *com bananas e molho de maracujá* (with a rich banana and passion-fruit sauce) or *filete de carneiro com molho de menta* (grilled lamb fillet with a fresh mint sauce). For dessert, give the unique *cassata de abacate* (homemade avocado ice cream) a try. ✉ *Av. do Infante 17–19* ☎ *291/221814* ▤ *AE, DC, MC, V.*

$–$$$$ ✕ **Casa Velha.** In the tiled dining room, exuberant floral arrangements, white-lace curtains, and green tablecloths rustle gently in the breeze of ceiling fans. The food is prepared with great care. Start with the cream of seafood soup or the salmon rillettes with shrimp, then move on to the seafood fricassee or lobster Thermidor. Dessert might be apple with kirsch flambé. ✉ *Rua Imperatriz D. Amelia 69* ☎ *291/225749* ⊕ *www.casavelharestaurant.com* ▤ *AE, MC, V.*

★ **$–$$$$** ✕ **O Celeiro.** The traditional Portuguese cooking seems right at home in the farmhouse decor. The dining room fills up with businesspeople at lunch and a mix of visitors and locals at dinner. Among the most popular items are the Algarve-style *cataplanas,* seafood stews served in special copper-lidded pots. *Pudim,* a flanlike pudding, makes a soothing dessert. ✉ *Rua das Aranhas 22* ☎ *291/230622* ▤ *AE, DC, MC, V.*

$–$$ ✕ **Golden Gate Grand Café.** Just across from the tourist office in the heart of Funchal, this restaurant-café has been open for business off and on

8

since 1814. Sit in the airy interior, capture one of the tables that flank the sidewalk, or—even better—bag a seat on the balcony. You can pop in for coffee, light local dishes, or British-style afternoon tea, or you can settle in for a feast of creative Portuguese and international dishes. Don't miss the delicious desserts such as *sorvete de banana e maracujá* (banana and passion-fruit sorbet). ⊠ *Av. Arriaga 29* ☎ *291/234383* ⊟ *AE, DC, MC, V.*

★ **$-$$** ✕ **A Seta.** It's not fancy, and the parking area is crammed with tour buses, but this restaurant on a hill above Funchal serves some of the island's best espetada. You'll share long narrow tables with other diners while waiters dodge in and out among folk dancers and fado singers. The meat is cooked over a charcoal fire; then the skewers are suspended from wrought-iron hooks at each table. ⊠ *Estrada do Livramento 80* ☎ *291/ 743643* ⊟ *AE, DC, MC, V* ☙ *Closed Wed.*

¢–$$ ✕ **Combatentes.** The inexpensive lunch specials at this large streamlined dining room behind the municipal gardens are popular with Funchal's businesspeople. Big portions of simple Madeiran cooking, such as es-pada, tuna, and grilled pork chops, are served with milho frito. If you want something lighter, try the *sopa de tomate e cebola com ovo* (tomato and onion soup, garnished with a poached egg). ⊠ *Rua Ivens 1* ☎ *291/ 221388* ⊟ *MC, V* ☙ *Closed Sun.*

¢–$$ ✕ **Pizzaria Xaramba.** When young Madeirans want a break from seafood, they head to this tiny restaurant behind a church in the old section of town. The ovens stay hot until 3 AM, and the place is often packed late at night. Individual-size pizzas are prepared behind a long bar while you watch. (Be careful not to confuse this restaurant with Pizzaria Xaram-binha—no relation—a few doors away, next to the church). ⊠ *Rua Portão São Tiago 11* ☎ *291/229785* ⌘ *Reservations not accepted* ⊟ *No credit cards* ☙ *No lunch.*

★ ¢–$ ✕ **Carochinha.** This deliberately old-fashioned restaurant beside the mu-nicipal gardens is an enduring, and to many, an endearing Funchal culi-nary oddity. Expect such English standards as steaks, and liver and onions, as well as such Continental classics as duck à l'orange, beef Stroganoff, and coq au vin. ⊠ *Rua São Francisco 2A* ☎ *291/223695* ⊟ *AE, DC, MC, V* ☙ *Closed Sun.*

Where to Stay

$$$$ ▦ **Reid's Palace.** In 1836 William Reid arrived in Madeira as a cabin
FodorśChoice boy with £5 in his pocket. He made his wealth on the island, but died
★ a few years before his dream hotel was finished in 1891. On its rocky point surrounded by 10 acres of gardens, Reid's is a destination as much as Madeira itself. Past residents include artists John dos Passos, Pablo Picasso, Rainer Maria Rilke, Gregory Peck (*Moby Dick* was filmed here), and an ailing Winston Churchill, who in 1950 occupied a suite on the ground floor. Reopened in April 2006 after refurbishment, the large rooms are dangerously comfortable, with wide balconies and sea views. Baths have power showerheads, towel warmers, and Molton Brown toiletries. There's hardly a whim that can't be catered to here. ⊠ *Estrada Monumental 139, 9000-098* ☎ *291/717030* 🖷 *291/717033* ⊕ *www.reidspalace.com* ⤶ *128 rooms, 35 suites* ☖ *5 restaurants,*

room service, in-room safes, minibars, cable TV, in-room VCRs, golf privileges, 2 tennis courts, 3 saltwater pools, gym, hair salon, massage, sauna, spa, dive shop, windsurfing, waterskiing, fishing, billiards, 3 bars, library, recreation room, shops, babysitting, children's programs (ages 4–12), Wi-Fi ⊟ AE, MC, V ⍾ BP, FAP, MAP.

$$$$ ⊞ **Savoy Hotel.** It may be hard to leave the grounds of the Savoy: everywhere you look there are fresh flowers, and every time you turn around there's yet another concert or cocktail party to attend. Do make the effort to get out and about, though, as this hotel is an easy 10-minute walk from downtown and is a hospitable base for explorations farther afield as well. Beyond lovely gardens is the Royal Savoy Resort, a sister establishment with time-share and hotel accommodations. The two properties share pool, spa, and other facilities. ⊠ *Rua Imperatriz D. Amelia 108/112, 9000-542* ☎ *291/213000* 🖷 *291/223103* ⊕ *www.madeiraroyalsavoy.com* ⇥ *325 rooms, 12 suites* ♨ *4 restaurants, 3 cafés, room service, in-room safes, minibars, cable TV, driving range, miniature golf, putting green, 2 tennis courts, 5 pools (2 indoor), hair salon, hot tub, 2 spas, 4 bars, library, shops, business services, convention center, meeting rooms, Wi-Fi ⊟ AE, MC, V ⍾ BP, FAP, MAP.*

$$$ ⊞ **Cliff Bay Resort.** This elegant hotel is on a spectacular promontory at the outskirts of town. Its cheerful guest quarters have marble baths with twin sinks. Rooms also take in sweeping views of the Atlantic, the Bay of Funchal, or the property's inviting gardens. ⊠ *Estrada Monumental 147, 9000-100* ☎ *291/707700* 🖷 *291/762524* ⊕ *www.portobay.com* ⇥ *211 rooms* ♨ *3 restaurants, room service, in-room safes, cable TV with movies, golf privileges, tennis court, indoor-outdoor pool, saltwater pool, fitness classes, gym, hot tub, massage, sauna, spa, Ping-Pong, squash, 4 bars, children's programs (ages 6–12), Wi-Fi ⊟ AE, DC, MC, V ⍾ BP, FAP, MAP.*

♻ **$$$** ⊞ **Crowne Plaza Resort Madeira.** On a spectacular oceanfront, the Crowne Plaza overlooks a stunning sea-level platform featuring bars, restaurants, and swimming pools, accessed by two panoramic elevators that take you down to the sea. Once there, you can sail, splash about in a pedal boat, or arrange to go diving at the PADI dive center. The hotel offers programs for children from 10 AM to 1 PM. Most rooms have ocean views and furniture designed by Philippe Starck. Suites have tubs with hydromassage jets. ⊠ *Estrada Monumental 176–177, 9000-100* ☎ *291/717700* 🖷 *291/717701* ⊕ *www.crowneplaza-madeira.com* ⇥ *276 rooms, 24 suites* ♨ *4 restaurants, room service, in-room safes, minibars, cable TV, ethernet, driving range, golf privileges, putting green, 2 tennis courts, 4 pools (2 indoor), fitness classes, gym, hair salon, massage, sauna, spa, steam room, beach, dive shop, snorkeling, windsurfing, boating, fishing, badminton, basketball, billiards, Ping-Pong, squash, volleyball, 3 bars, recreation room, children's programs (ages 4–12), playground, laundry service, public Internet, convention center, no-smoking rooms, Wi-Fi ⊟ AE, MC, V ⍾ BP, MAP.*

$$$ ⊞ **Eden Mar.** This six-story block sprouts from the island's busiest swimming complex known as the Lido. Although it won't win any exterior beauty contests, nor is it overloaded with sports and leisure facilities, it is one of several hotels in Funchal that offer good-value packages. It's

8

a favorite with families, who settle in for long stays and appreciate the kitchenettes in each unit. The lobby is full of stark, white marble, but rooms have homey floral-print fabrics, cheerful tiled bathrooms, and sea views. ⊠ *Rua do Gorgulho 2, 9004-537* ☎ *291/709700* 🖷 *291/761966* ⊕ *www.edenmar.com* 🛏 *70 suites, 37 studios* △ *Restaurant, coffee shop, in-room safes, kitchenettes, cable TV, ethernet, 4 pools (2 indoor), saltwater pool, gym, hot tub, massage, sauna, spa, squash, 2 bars, public Internet, meeting room, tennis court, squash, Wi-Fi* ⊟ *AE, DC, MC, V* ⦿ *BP, MAP.*

$$$ 🏨 **Tivoli Ocean Park Hotel.** At the end of Funchal's seafront promenade, this sleek hotel is about a 25-minute walk from town. All the well-equipped rooms have sea-view balconies; suites have hot tubs. The heated indoor pool is excellent. Sushi lovers might like to note that the resort has an excellent Japanese restaurant. ⊠ *Rua Simplicio dos Passos Gouveia 29, 9000-100* ☎ *291/702000* 🖷 *291/702020* ⊕ *www.tivolihotels.com* 🛏 *260 rooms, 57 suites* △ *3 restaurants, tea shop, room service, in-room safes, cable TV, 2 pools (1 indoor), health club, spa, squash, 3 bars, nightclub, recreation room, children's programs (ages 5–15), convention center, no-smoking floor, Wi-Fi* ⊟ *AE, MC, V* ⦿ *BP, FAP, MAP.*

$$–$$$ 🏨 **Pestana Casino Park.** Part of a complex designed by Oscar Niemeyer, the architect of Brasília (capital of Brazil), this drab concrete hotel sits next to what looks like a nuclear reactor but is actually the Casino da Madeira. Inside, though, the hotel is pleasant, having benefited from a recent total refurbishment, and is scheduled at press time to reopen in March 2007. The public rooms have lots of glass and mirrors and are flooded with light from floor-to-ceiling windows that overlook gardens and the sea. Guest rooms are bright and airy, and the restaurant is popular for its buffet dinner and folklore performances. ⊠ *Quinta da Vigia 67, 9000-513* ☎ *291/209100* 🖷 *291/232076* ⊕ *www.pestana.com* 🛏 *373 rooms* △ *2 restaurants, coffee shop, room service, cable TV, tennis court, saltwater pool, gym, health club, hot tub, sauna, billiards, 3 bars, casino, nightclub, convention center, meeting rooms, Wi-Fi* ⊟ *AE, DC, MC, V* ⦿ *BP, FAP, MAP.*

$$ 🏨 **Estalagem Jardins do Lago.** During the Napoleonic wars, General
Fodor'sChoice Beresford, commander of the British forces on the island, chose this beau-
★ tiful 18th-century quinta as his residence. A library, billiard room, numerous antiques, and a breakfast room with an exceptional 16th-century ceramic wall panel on its veranda give the hotel a timeless quality. The Beresford restaurant and the Visconde bar have garden seating for sunset cocktails and nightcaps. The Beresford's magnificent sideboard still adorns the dining room. The tranquil lake nestled in these mature and unique botanical gardens provided the hotel's name. Colombo, the quinta's giant tortoise, has lived here since 1949. Among the mango trees is a large heated swimming pool with bistro, sauna, Turkish bath, and Jacuzzi area. For the more energetic, the all-weather-surface tennis court and a well-equipped gym are available. ⊠ *Caminho Velho da Ajuda, 9000-113* ☎ *291/706600* 🖷 *291/764859* ⊕ *www.jardins-lago.com* 🛏 *36 rooms, 4 suites* △ *Restaurant, in-room safes, minibars, cable TV, tennis court, pool, gym, hot tub, sauna, Turkish bath, billiards, bar, library, public Internet* ⊟ *AE, MC, V* ⦿ *BP, FAP, MAP.*

★ **$$** ⊞ **Quinta da Bela Vista.** The hospitable staff at this hotel, in the hills above Funchal and formerly a doctor's estate, make you feel you're visiting a well-to-do friend. The original house contains a sophisticated restaurant and four guest rooms. Other rooms are in two buildings, constructed in the same gracious style as the main house. Guest quarters have French doors that open onto gardens and are filled with mahogany furniture—including four-poster beds—and beautifully framed pastoral prints. ⊠ *Caminho do Avista Navios 4, 9000-129* ☎ *291/706400* 🖷 *291/ 706411* ⊕ *www.belavistamadeira.com* ⟋ *72 rooms* ♵ *2 restaurants, room service, in-room safes, cable TV, ethernet, golf privileges, tennis court, pool, gym, hot tub, sauna, billiards, bar, library, ethernet* ⊟ *AE, DC, MC, V* ⦿ *BP, FAP, MAP.*

★ **$–$$** ⊞ **Pestana Carlton Madeira.** Ever since the 18-story, beachfront high-rise opened in 1971, it's seen many annual guests. They're no doubt attracted by the friendly service, the range of sports and health facilities, and the large guest rooms with pastel fabrics and tile baths as well as terraces overlooking the ocean or mountains. It's a 10-minute walk from central Funchal. Check the Web site for good deals. ⊠ *Largo António Nobre, 9004-531* ☎ *291/239500* 🖷 *291/223377* ⊕ *www.pestana.com* ⟋ *373 rooms* ♵ *3 restaurants, room service, in-room safes, cable TV, golf privileges, miniature golf, tennis court, indoor pool, 2 heated saltwater pools, health club, hair salon, hot tub, sauna, spa, steam room, dive shop, windsurfing, 3 bars, library, nightclub, shops, meeting rooms, Wi-Fi* ⊟ *AE, DC, MC, V* ⦿ *BP, FAP, MAP.*

$ ⊞ **Estrelicia.** Named for Madeira's bird-of-paradise flower, this Best Western accommodation is the topmost of three high-rise towers built uphill from the hotel strip. Perhaps because of its somewhat inconvenient location, the hotel is an especially good value. Large, carpeted guest rooms have gold bedspreads and brown leather chairs. ⊠ *Caminho Velho da Ajuda, 9000-113* ☎ *291/706600* 🖷 *291/764859* ⊕ *www.bestwestern. com* ⟋ *145 rooms* ♵ *Restaurant, in-room safes, minibars, cable TV, tennis court, saltwater pool, bar, piano bar, dance club, ethernet, free parking, no-smoking rooms* ⊟ *AE, MC, V* ⦿ *BP, FAP, MAP.*

$ ⊞ **Quinta da Fonte.** Halfway between Funchal and Monte, this Madeiran manor house dates back to 1850 and is set among gardens, tropical fruit trees, and breathtaking panoramic views of Funchal and its bay. Tastefully furnished, this live-in museum houses a vast collection of exquisite furniture, antiques, artwork, and Indo-Portuguese relics and artifacts. The breakfast buffet of fruit, scrambled eggs, cereals, bread, and homemade jams is served on a huge Pau Santo table that dates back to 1854. ⊠ *Estrada dos Marmeleiros 89, 9050-209* ☎ *291/235397* 🖷 *291/ 235397* ⊕ *www.madeira-island.com/hotels/quintas/quintadafonte* ⟋ *5 rooms* ♵ *Cable TV, lounge* ⊟ *No credit cards* ⦿ *BP.*

$ ⊞ **Quinta da Penha de França.** In an unbeatable location at unbeatable prices—just above Funchal Harbor—this place pleases those who prefer their resorts casual rather than glitzy. The white, four-story Portuguese manor house with green shutters is surrounded by gardens and a sun-drenched pool. Every room is slightly different, and the antique furnishings resemble that of an old English town house. There's a more modern seaside wing, about a five-minute walk from the main house, with large

8

terraces overlooking the sea, but its rooms aren't as charming. ✉ *Rua Imperatriz Dona Amélia 83, 9000-014* ☎ *291/204650* 🖷 *291/229261* ⊕ *www.hotelquintapenhafranca.com* ↩ *76 rooms* ♧ *Restaurant, in-room safes, minibars, cable TV, saltwater pool, billiards, bar* ▤ *AE, MC, V* ⦿ *BP, MAP.*

★ ¢–$ ▦ **Albergaria Dias.** Set in a quiet and historic part of the Old Town of Funchal, this friendly inn is a five-minute walk from the city center and handy for Barreirinha beach and some good bars and restaurants on the way. The restored classic Funchal town house has rambling gardens set around the pool. Each of the guest rooms has a marble bathroom, large balcony with sea view, high-quality modern furniture, and simple cream decor. The generous breakfast includes bacon and eggs. ✉ *Rua Bela de São Tiago 44 B, 9050-042* ☎ *291/206680* 🖷 *291/206681* ⊕ *www.albergariadias.com* ↩ *35 rooms* ♧ *Café, in-room safes, pool, gym, sauna* ▤ *AE, DC, MC, V* ⦿ *BP.*

★ ¢ ▦ **Albergaria Catedral.** This inexpensive option behind the cathedral is run by a local family whose hard work has made the hotel one of the best in its category. Most rooms look out onto the private Rua do Aljube and have their own spotless bathrooms with shower units. A light Continental breakfast is included with decent coffee and fresh seasonal fruit. ✉ *Rua do Aljube 13, 9000-067* ☎ *291/230091* 🖷 *291/230092* ↩ *25 rooms, 18 with bath* ♧ *Cable TV, laundry service* ▤ *No credit cards* ⦿ *CP.*

¢ ▦ **Hotel Madeira.** This hotel on a quiet street in central Funchal has a marble lobby and tiny rooftop pool. Rooms are basic, but each is carpeted and has a comfortable bed as well as a balcony with, in some instances, a view of the municipal gardens. ✉ *Rua Ivens 21, 9000-046* ☎ *291/230071* 🖷 *291/229071* ↩ *48 rooms, 5 suites* ♧ *Restaurant, coffee shop, cable TV, pool, billiards, bar, lounge, meeting rooms* ▤ *AE, MC, V* ⦿ *BP, MAP.*

¢ ▦ **Residencia Santa Clara.** This basic hostel has garnered a reputation for being the best bet for inexpensive accommodation on the island, and it is a particularly good value in terms of location and service. Nine of the rooms have twin beds, and five have a double bed. Although only one room has a private balcony, there is a large communal terrace that grants views over Funchal, the sea, and Ilhas Desertas. You can also relax at the small pool and a quiet garden area. ✉ *Calçada do Pico 16b, 9000* ☎ *291/742194* 🖷 *291/743280* ↩ *14 rooms* ♧ *Pool; no room TVs* ▤ *MC, V.CP*

Fodor's Choice
★

FOLKLORIC TRADITIONS

Madeira proudly makes the most of its folkloric traditions for visitors. No matter when you visit, there's a good chance you'll see folk dances performed at a restaurant or hotel. It may look as though the dancer has dropped a contact lens and is doing his or her level best to find it. One such dance, the Ponto do Sol, recalls the island's involvement with slavery, as the dancers move with bowed heads, their feet shuffling as though chained. Costumed dancers whirl to the music of a small guitarlike instrument called a *machête*.

Nightlife & the Arts

Nightlife

BARS If you prefer the company of trendsetters, try **Amarras Café** (⊠ Rua das Murças ☎ 291/241930), a funky, kitsch-filled space. Curl up on one of the cushy couches with a Coral (lager) or two. Another favorite bar is the quasi-English pub, the **Prince Albert Rua da Imperatriz Dona Amélia** (☎ 291/235793), which also shows big-screen sports and has imported beers and a buzzy atmosphere. On the same street, **Joe's Bar** is another popular place for downing a pint of English ale. At **Dó Fá Sol** (⊠ Galerias São Lourenço, next to Palácio de São Lourenço ☎ 291/241464), live bands (jazz, rock, blues) play regularly, and the crowds often spill out onto the terrace. Nothing much happens here until quite late—it's best to arrive around 11 PM. Wednesday through Saturday jazz bands play at **Jam** (⊠ Av. Sá Carneiro 9 ☎ 291/234800), a classy lounge. Shows start at 11 PM.

CABARET The somewhat informal **O Fugitivo** (⊠ Rua Imperatriz D. Amélia 68 ☎ 291/222003) has Brazilian-style cabaret. The glitziest of all the hotel floor shows takes place every weekend at the **Pestana Carlton Park Hotel** (⊠ Quinta da Vigia 67 ☎ 291/233111), where the theme is also usually Brazilian.

CASINO Gamblers can try their luck in the **Casino da Madeira** (⊠ Av. do Infante ☎ 291/209100 ⊕ www.casino-madeira.com), which is open Sunday–Thursday 3 PM–3 AM, and Friday and Saturday 4 PM–4 AM. Its unusual building was designed by architect Oscar Niemeyer. The entrance fee is €5, and you must be at least 18 years old; dress is smart casual (no sports shoes allowed).

DANCE CLUBS At **Copacabana** (⊠ Av. do Infante ☎ 291/233111), beneath the Casino da Madeira, there's often live Brazilian music. A lively, over-30 crowd dances to hits from the '70s and '80s—as well as some current tunes—at **O Farol** (⊠ Largo António Nobre ☎ 291/231031) in the Pestana Carlton Madeira hotel. Drum, bass, hip-hop, trance—or whichever type of music is currently in vogue—is on tap at **Vespas** (⊠ Av. Sá Carneiro 60 ☎ 291/231202), Madeira's largest disco situated next to the docks.

FADO You'll find good food as well as tear-jerking fado at **Arsénios** (⊠ Rua de Santa Maria 169 ☎ 291/224007). Reservations are a good idea. **Marcelino Pão y Vinho** (⊠ Travessa da Torre 22-A ☎ 291/230834) attracts fado aficionados as well as the just plain curious, who come to hear Portugal's soulful national music played each night from 9:30 until about 2 AM.

The Arts

The **Teatro Municipal Baltazar Diaz** (⊠ Av. Arriaga ☎ 291/220416) offers occasional concerts and plays. The local newspaper carries listings, but the easiest way to find out the schedule is to check at the tourist office or check out the posters outside the theater.

Outdoor Activities

Fishing

You can arrange fishing excursions at the Funchal Harbor through **Turipesca** (☎ 291/231063).

Golf

See Chapter 9, *Golf in Portugal: Where to Play,* for more information on Madeira's two courses.

The 18-hole course at **Palheiro Golf** (✉ São Gonçalo ☎ 291/790120 ⊕ www.palheirogolf.com) is in a pine forest at the edge of Blandy Gardens. Green fees are €90 for the day. The clubhouse restaurant has fine town views. Madeira's older course is the 27-hole, Robert Trent Jones Jr.–designed **Santo da Serra Golf** (✉ N102 ☎ 291/550100 ⊕ www.santodaserragolf.com), near the airport in Santo da Serra. Green fees start at €65 for 18 holes.

Scuba Diving

Madeira is too far north for colorful tropical fish, but divers enjoy the clear, still seas of summer and report lots of interesting marine life and coral formations. The diving center at the **Pestana Carlton Madeira** (✉ Largo António Nobre ☎ 291/239500) hotel rents scuba gear to nonguests and arranges guided dives with a qualified instructor. These range from €35 for a shore dive to €43 for a boat dive.

Shopping

For the best selection of Madeira wine, check out the **Madeira Wine Company** (✉ Av. Arriaga 28 ☎ 291/740100), which sells an exhaustive selection of the local tipple, covering virtually every vintage produced on the island for the past 35-odd years. The shop has an evocative setting, in a former 18th-century convent. Otherwise you can find Madeira wine sold in most of the island's delicatessens and better supermarkets. Despite its unpromising name, the **Casa do Turista** (✉ José S. Ribeiro 2, on corner with seafront ☎ 291/224907) sells museum-quality Madeiran crafts of all types. Prices are reasonable, if not the cheapest in town.

Baskets

In the village of Camacha, about 10 km (6 mi) northeast of Funchal, there's a large cooperative shop on the main square that sells every imaginable type of basket as well as some wicker furniture. Most of the work is done at home; on rural roads it's common to see men carrying large bundles of willow branches to be used for basketry. Although you'll find baskets and other wicker items all over Funchal, **Sousa & Gonçalves** (✉ Rua do Castanheiro ☎ 291/223626) is one of the largest manufacturers and exporters.

Clothing

Globe Line (✉ Av. Arriaga 43 ☎ 291/229551) has dressy women's clothes at moderate prices. **Rodier** (✉ Rua das Pretas 23 ☎ 291/228601), the upscale French chain, is a good place to go if you've forgotten your designer jeans or need a casual-chic outfit.

Flowers

Tropical flowers are available boxed from any florist for shipping home. (It's legal to bring flowers into the United States from Madeira as long as they're inspected at the U.S. airport upon arrival.) Flower stands in the market and behind the church in Funchal are good value and, like most island shops that deal with visitors, pack their bouquets in special boxes to withstand trips in luggage holds. The **Quinta da Boa Visita** (⊠ Rua Lombo da Boa Vista ☎ 291/220468), on the outskirts of town, sells orchid seedlings, orchids, and other exotic flowers.

EMBROIDERY
Thousands of local women spend their days stitching intricate floral patterns on organdy, Irish linen, cambric, and French silks. Their handiwork decorates tablecloths, place mats, and napkins, all of which are expensive (and almost all of which need ironing). When buying embroidery, make sure it has a lead seal attached, certifying it was made on the island and not imported.

Needlework

Needlepoint and tapestry making were introduced to Madeira in the early part of the 20th century by a German family, and you can visit their factory, **Kiekeben Tapestries** (⊠ Rua da Carreira 194 ☎ 291/222073). To buy pieces, stop by the shop, **Bazar Maria Kiekeben** (⊠ Av. do Infante 2 ☎ 291/227857), which also has a branch in Tampa, Florida.

One of the most popular embroidery shops is **Patricio & Gouveia** (⊠ Rua do Visconde de Anadia 33 ☎ 291/220801), where you can visit the upstairs workshop and see the white-uniformed employees stencil patterns and check production; the actual embroidery is done by an army of women in their homes.

8

SIDE TRIPS FROM FUNCHAL

Monte

★ ☉ ⓯ *6 km (4 mi) northeast of Funchal.*

The village of Monte is home to one of Madeira's oddest attractions: *tábuas de Madeira* or *carrinhos do Monte* (the snowless sled ride). The sleds were first created to carry supplies from Monte to Funchal; later, passenger sleighs hauled as many as 10 people at a time and required six drivers. Slippery cobblestones lined the hill, making the trip even faster than it is today. Nowadays the rides are just for fun, and no one in Madeira should miss this experience that will take 10 years off your life and stay with you forever.

Dressed in white and wearing goatskin boots with soles made of rubber tires, drivers line up on the street by the Nossa Senhora do Monte church. The sleds, which have cushioned seats, look like big wicker baskets; their wooden runners are greased with lard. Two drivers run alongside the sled, controlling it with ropes as it races downhill on a 20-minute trip nearly back to Funchal (you will have to walk about 1 km (½ mi) to reach Funchal). If the sled starts going too fast, the drivers jump on the back to slow it down. A ride costs €10 per person with a minimum of two riders. If you opted to have your photo taken at the top, you'll be free of another €10 when you retrieve the developed print at the bottom.

To drive up to Monte from Funchal, take Rua 31 de Janeiro. You can also hop a taxi or take Bus 20 or 21. But a ride up in a cable car on the Teleférico da Madeira seems the best complement to the singular trip back down by sled. Call 291/783919 for more information.

Only a five-minute walk from Funchal's town center, Quinta Palmeira was owned by the wealthy sugar industrialist Harry Hinton, and most of the **Palmeira Gardens** was designed in the early 20th century by his green-thumbed wife, Isabel Vasconcellos Welsh Hinton. Panoramic views look out onto Funchal Bay and the town. Look out for the pretty blue-and-white azulejo panels around the gardens and an impressive stone window salvaged from the house where Christopher Columbus lived. ⊠ *Rua da Levada da Santa Luzia 31A* ☎ *291/221091* 💳 *€6* 🕐 *Mon.–Sat. 9–noon and 2–5.*

The **Monte Palace Tropical Gardens** has indigenous flora as well as plants from all over the world. The Monte Palace was a grand hotel from 1897 until 1943, but with the death of the last owner, it went out of business and the building and grounds were neglected for more than 40 years. In 1987 millionaire entrepreneur José Manuel Rodrigues Berardo bought the property and transformed it into this garden. Antique statues, windows, niches, and other architectural artifacts dot the grounds, tiled panels recall the adventures of the Portuguese explorers, Asian pagodas and gateways lend touches of the exotic, and cannons pour their salvos of water from a stone galleon in a lake. All this and wonderful views down to Funchal, too. ⊠ *Caminho do Monte 174* ☎ *291/782339* ⊕ *www.montepalace.com* 💳 *€7.50* 🕐 *Daily 9–6.*

Standing tall at the highest point in Monte is the white-stucco church of **Nossa Senhora do Monte** (Our Lady of the Mountain). The tiny statue above the altar was found by a shepherdess in the nearby town of Terreira da Luta in the 15th century and has become the patron saint of Madeira. The church also contains the tomb of Emperor Charles I of Austria, the last Hapsburg monarch. He came to Madeira hoping that its more temperate climate would help him recover from tuberculosis, but he succumbed to the disease and died on the island in 1922. The church is open daily 8–6 and is reached by taking a cable car from the city center—an unforgettable 20-minute ride with stunning views of the harbor.

NEED A BREAK?   If you need refreshment before sledding back to Funchal, stop at the **Bar Alecrim**, just up the hill to the right of Nossa Senhora do Monte. The friendly owner makes a mean *poncha*, the island specialty drink of cane spirits, honey, and lemon juice. The food is also very good here. Notice the old photos of sleds and drivers. Not much has changed over the years.

Eira do Serrado

⑯ *16 km (10 mi) northwest of Funchal.*

The *miradouro* (viewpoint) at Eira do Serrado overlooks the Grande Curral—the crater of a long-extinct volcano in the center of the island, sometimes referred to as Madeira's belly button. From here, Pico Ruivo and the craggy central summits look like a granite city. Island legend says the peaks are the castle fortress of a virgin princess, who can be seen sleeping peacefully in the *rocha da cara* (rock face). It's said that she wanted to live in the sky like the clouds and the moon, and was so unhappy at being earthbound that her father—the volcano god—caused an earthquake that pushed the rocky cliffs high into the sky so she could live near the heavens. To get here from Funchal take Rua Dr. João Brito Câmara west, which turns into N101, and head for the miradouro at Pico dos Barcelos.

Curral das Freiras

⑰ *6 km (4 mi) north of Eira do Serrado.*

Along the N107 north from Eira do Serrado, you'll pass through a series of switchbacks and two tunnels that lead down to the village of Curral das Freiras (Nuns' Shelter). The sisters of the Convent of Santa Clara took refuge here from bands of lonely, marauding pirates. Nearly the geographic center of Madeira, the valley sits in the middle of a circle of extinct volcanoes that long ago pushed the island up from the bottom of the sea.

Porto Santo

⑱ *50 km (31 mi) northeast of Madeira.*

Beachcombers have long loved the tiny, dry island of Porto Santo, and you'll find it less crowded between March and June. A golden beach famous for its therapeutic properties runs over 10 km (6 mi) along the entire south coast. By packing themselves in the sand, locals cure their rheumatic pains and speed the healing of bone fractures or minor injuries. Look out for the island's famous traditional headwear for the men of Porto Santo—hats made of palm leaves. On Palm Sunday you will also see the *palmitos bordados* (palm leaves woven into the form of a crucifix).

The island's simple salâo houses are centuries old. Their unique roofs are made of salâo, a sandy clay noted for its strong adherent properties. This amazing roofing material fits extraordinarily well into the Porto Santo rural landscape. The houses are cool in summer because when the weather is very dry, cracks open up in the salâo, letting the air circulate. In winter, this material absorbs the rain. The price one pays for this natural convenience is labor: the roof needs to be replaced every year.

The Campo de Cima Airport is in the center of the island, and the 2½-hour ferry ride from Funchal ends in Vila Baleira, the island's main town.

A huddle of tidy, whitewashed cottages and town houses with terra-cotta tile roofs, Vila Baleira has a park containing an idealized statue of Christopher Columbus. Before gaining fame and his place in history, he married Isabela Moniz, daughter of Bartolomeu Perestrelo, the first governor of the island, in 1479. She died not long after, at the time of the birth of their son.

The **Casa de Cristóvão Colombo** (Columbus Museum and Home) is in the old governor's house. Inside, lithographs illustrate the life of Columbus. Copies of 15 portraits of the discoverer made between the 16th and 20th century prove there was little agreement on what he looked like. Ask to see the restored kitchen and bedroom in the upper part of the house. ✉ *Rua Cristóvão Colombo 12* ☎ *291/983405* 🎫 *Free* ⊙ *Tues.–Fri. 10–6, weekends 10–1.*

One of your first stops on Porto Santo should be at the **Portela** viewpoint, which overlooks the harbor, the town, and the long ribbon of beach. Move on to Serra de Foca, where a track passes old salt flats before winding down to a rocky beach popular with divers. As you continue around the island, you may have to dodge goats grazing along the edges of the road.

The island's series of 656- to 1,640-foot peaks make for great exploring. The summit **Pico do Castelo** has a small 16th-century fort that provided defense against the frequent attacks of French and Algerian pirates. Only four canons remain. On the 1½-km (1-mi) walk from Vila Baleira to the fort, you'll see an avenue of palm trees and a windmill. To the west is Porto Santo beach, and to the east is the conical shape of Pico de Baixo and the Ilhéu de Cima. You'll pass the chapel of Our Lady of Graça, built in 1851. From here it's an easy walk to **Pico do Facho** (1,552 feet), the island's highest point.

Because of frequent pirate attacks, locals once relied on hiding places. Opposite the Ilhéu das Cenouras there is a cave known as the **Furnas dos Amasiadas** (Furnaces of the Mistresses). You can still see basins dug in the rocks that were used for washing or keeping food. The Furna de Andresa, at S'tio de Dentro, was used for the same purposes. As you head to the southern tip of the island, you'll pass several windmills in disrepair and some still working that were once used for grinding wheat. The first one was built in 1794 and is the biggest surviving 18th-century construction on the island.

Pico das Flores—a lookout at the end of a bumpy ride—offers fine views of Madeira and the rocky, uninhabited islet called Ilhéu de Baixo. On the road that runs along the beach, development becomes apparent: you'll see a handful of high-rise apartment blocks, if not more by the time you arrive.

FISHING

Madeira and Porto Santo are meccas for those hoping to reel in huge blue marlin, yellowfin tuna, albacore, swordfish, and dorado. The list of gilled gentry inhabiting the surrounding waters also includes bigeye tuna, barracuda, dolphinfish, wahoo, and shark.

On an islet off the east side of Porto Santo, **Ilhéu de Cima** is the first lighthouse seen by ships coming from Europe. Between Porto Santo and Madeira you can see both the beams of this lighthouse and those of Ponta de São Lourenço, 50 km (31 mi) away.

Near the village of Camacha, the **Fonte da Areia** (Spring in the Sand) once had the purest water on the island and was used for medical treatments and considered sacred by locals. The water is hardly the same today, but the wind on the sandy rocks has created a fantastic erosion effect. To reach the spring, head west out of the village along the coastal road.

There is probably no better way to enjoy the whole island than to go **Calheta Point** at its far southwestern end and walk back along the beach during the sunset and admire the astonishing landscape.

Where to Stay & Eat

$–$$ ✕ **Arsénios.** Red-and-white-check tablecloths are your clue that this is the place for pizza, spaghetti, and lasagna. Portuguese specialties are also served in the rustic dining room. ✉ *Av. Dr. Manuel Pestana Jr., Vila Baleira* ☎ *291/984348* ▤ *AE, DC, MC, V.*

$–$$ ✕ **Baiana.** A covered patio serves as a combination sidewalk café and town meeting place, as just about everybody wanders by in the morning for coffee. Baiana also serves sandwiches, *feijoada* (bean stew), and carne de vinhos e alhos. ✉ *Rua Dr. Nuno S. Teixeira, Vila Baleira* ☎ *291/984649* ▤ *AE, MC, V.*

$–$$ ✕ **Gazela.** Not far from the Campo de Cima Airport, this large, modern restaurant is where islanders go for Sunday lunch or to celebrate special occasions. The menu is basic Madeiran—espada, espetada, and a seafood soup. ✉ *Campo de Cima* ☎ *291/984425* ▤ *AE, DC, MC, V.*

$–$$ ✕ **Pôr do Sol.** This fish restaurant is at the far end of the beach, near Ponta da Calheta. Just 24 tables fill the simple dining room slung with fishing nets. You can also dine on a sun terrace. There's a free shuttle to and from town. ✉ *Ponta da Calheta* ☎ *291/984380* ⌕ *Reservations not accepted* ▤ *AE, DC, MC, V.*

$–$$ ✕ **Teodorico.** In this farmhouse restaurant, authentic espetada is *the* dish (it is, in fact, the *only* dish), best accompanied by carafes of local dry red wine and *pão de caco*, the local bread. You can sit at outdoor tables made from tree stumps or in a tiny tiled dining room with a wood-burning oven. The town Serra de Fora is 3½ km (2¼ mi) northeast of Vila Baleira. ✉ *Serra de Fora* ☎ *291/982257* ▤ *No credit cards* ⊘ *No lunch.*

$$$ ▥ **Torre Praia Hotel.** Right on the beach, a five-minute walk from the center of town, this simple two-story chain hotel was built around an old watchtower that now holds the restaurant. The rooms are spacious and modern, and the hotel has all the amenities you need for a relaxing vacation in the sun. ✉ *Rua Goulart Medeiros, Vila Baleira 9400-164* ☎ *291/985292* ⎙ *291/982487* ⊕ *www.torrepraia.pt* ⬔ *62 rooms, 4 suites* ⌕ *2 restaurants, coffee shop, bar, in-room safes, kitchenettes, minibars, cable TV, pool, fitness classes, gym, hot tub, sauna, beach, squash, bar, public Internet, billiards, Wi-Fi* ⎰⎱ *BP, FAP, MAP.*

🐚 **$$** 🏨 **ApartHotel Luamar.** Part of the Torre Praia chain, the Luamar has apartments with a lounge and kitchenette overlooking the island's main beach. The hotel's swimming pool has a special area for children. The town Vila Beleira is 4 km (2½ mi) away. ⊠ *Cabeça da Ponta, 9400-030* ☎ *291/984121* 🖷 *291/983100* ⊕ *www.torrepraia.pt* 🖙 *114 apartments* 🖒 *Restaurant, coffee shop, in-room safes, kitchenettes, minibars, cable TV, pool, gym, hot tub, sauna, beach, bar, public Internet, meeting rooms, Wi-Fi* 🍴 *BP, FAP, MAP.*

$–$$ 🏨 **Praia Dourada.** This comfortable, modern hotel in the middle of the village is a five-minute walk from the beach and is popular with budget-minded German and Portuguese travelers. The corridors are dark, but the carpeted rooms are bright, and there's a small pool with a sundeck. ⊠ *Rua D. Estevão D'Alencastre, Vila Beleira 9400-161* ☎ *291/982315* 🖷 *291/982489* 🖙 *100 rooms* 🖒 *Cable TV, saltwater pool, bar, meeting room; no a/c* 🖃 *AE, DC, MC, V* 🍴 *BP.*

★ **$** 🏨 **Hotel Porto Santo.** On the beach about a 15-minute walk from town, this hotel is a beachcomber's dream—at least until more development comes. It's like a country club, with sports activities, a library-lounge, and rooms overlooking the interior instead of the shore. The hotel is often heavily booked throughout August, but in spring and fall you may have the place to yourself and the prices drop considerably. ⊠ *Campo de Baixo 9400-015* ☎ *291/980140* 🖷 *291/980149* ⊕ *www.hotelportosanto.com* 🖙 *96 rooms* 🖒 *Restaurant, in-room safes, cable TV, miniature golf, tennis court, saltwater pool, gym, Turkish bath, beach, bicycles, Ping-Pong, 2 bars, library* 🖃 *AE, DC, MC, V* 🍴 *BP, FAP, MAP.*

Outdoor Activities

Not just for walking tours on Porto Santo, the adventure travel company **Terras de Aventura** (⊠ Hotel Luamar ☎ 291/984121 ⊕ www.terrasdeaventura.com) organizes canoeing, paragliding, mountain biking, horseback riding, and water sports. The qualified guides have plenty of local knowledge and speak English well.

Camping
On Madeira there are really no organized campgrounds, but on Porto Santo **Parque Porto** (☎ 291/982361 for Porto Santo Tourist Office) is a stretch of beach just waiting for you to unroll your sleeping bag and pitch a tent.

Scuba Diving
For diving excursions off Porto Santo contact the **Dive Center** (⊠ Naval Clube de Porto Santo, Vila Beleira ☎ 291/983259).

WESTERN MADEIRA

The western region is the greenest and lushest part of Madeira: in some places you can see a dozen waterfalls spilling into a cool pine forest. On the dramatic north coast, a narrow highway clings to the cliff face.

Câmara de Lobos

⑲ *20 km (12 mi) west of Funchal.*

On coastal route N101, you'll pass many banana plantations on the way to Câmara de Lobos—a fishing village made famous by Winston Churchill, who came here (in a borrowed Rolls-Royce equipped with a bar) to paint pictures of the multicolored boats and the fishermen's tiny homes. A plaque marks the spot where he set up his easel. Although the coast here is changing as more and more people commute to jobs in Funchal, the boats are still pulled up onto the rocky beach during the day. Women still occasionally wash clothes in public fountains, while children run and play in the narrow streets and grizzled old fishermen stand around chatting. The promenade that protrudes from the main plaza offers magnificent views west to Cabo Girão.

> ### WINE TASTING
>
> If you're interested in sampling Madeira wine, visit the **Henriques & Henriques Vinhos,** a winery very close to Câmara de Lobos's promenade. You'll be made to feel right at home during a tour of a facility that combines state-of-the-art technology with down-home hospitality. And, yes, the bottles are for sale. ⊠ *Sítio de Belém* ☎ *291/941551* 🎟 *Free* ☉ *Weekdays 9–1 and 2:30–5:30.*

Where to Stay & Eat

$–$$$ ✕ **Coral Bar.** Just behind the cathedral and up the hill from the port, this welcoming restaurant has pleasant tables on the plaza and a simple rooftop terrace, with a great view of Cabo Girão and its dramatic cliffs. The day's catch is unloaded about a block away and served in big earthenware bowls. Try the delicious *peixe mista* (a combination of grilled fish, squid, and prawns) or the espada with fried bananas. ⊠ *Largo República 3* ☎ *291/942469* ▤ *AE, DC, MC, V.*

$$ ✕▥ **Estalagem Quinta do Estreito.** This onetime estate house is the perfect base from which to explore the Levada do Norte, one of Madeira's most popular walking trails. The views from here—across fields and down to the sea—are superb. Oak is lavishly used throughout the inn. Rooms have balconies and marble baths as well as such thoughtful touches as heated towel racks and a welcoming bottle of wine and a Madeira cake. Stairs lead up to a tower library that invites you to linger. The Bacchus Restaurant ($$–$$$), which serves nouvelle Madeira cuisine, may be reason enough for a visit. ⊠ *Rua José Joaquim da Costa, 9325-034* ☎ *291/ 910530* 🖷 *291/910549* ⊕ *www.charminghotelsmadeira.com* 🛏 *48 rooms* ♨ *2 restaurants, room service, in-room safes, cable TV with movies, indoor-outdoor pool, exercise equipment, hot tub, sauna, Turkish bath, 2 bars, library, dry cleaning, laundry service, public Internet, meeting room, no-smoking rooms, Wi-Fi* ▤ *MC, V* ⦿ *BP, MAP.*

Cabo Girão

⑳ *16 km (10 mi) west of Câmara de Lobos.*

At 1,900 feet, Cabo Girão is on one of the highest sea cliffs in the world. Totally uninhabited, from here you can see ribbons of terraces carved

8

out of even the steepest slopes and farmers daringly cultivating grapes or garden vegetables. Through centuries, thousands upon thousands of *poios* (terraces) have been built in Madeira. The poios rise from sea level up the mountainsides, and the mind boggles at the dangers involved and sheer labor that went into constructing the retaining walls that hold the terraces together. Neither machines nor animals are used on Madeiran farms because the plots are so small and difficult to reach. Not long ago, farmers blew into conch shells as a means of communication with neighbors across the deep ravines.

Ribeira Brava

㉑ *14 km (8½ mi) west of Cabo Girão.*

This pleasant village, with a pebbly beach and bustling seafront fruit market, was founded in 1440 at the mouth of the Ribeira Brava (meaning "wide river"); hence the name. It's one of the island's sunniest spots. Ribeira Brava is also the starting point for two popular levada walks. The first is one of the island's easiest and prettiest, taking around 40 minutes round-trip. At the lookout of Balcões (meaning "balconies") jagged peaks tower behind you, and there are views of a sleepy valley with minuscule houses here and there. A longer, 12-km (7-mi) hike leads along a levada to Portela. If you attempt this, it should take three to four hours. Arrange for a taxi back. Only a single tower remains of the 17th-century **Forte de São Bento,** built to protect the Ribeira Brava's citizens from pirates. It now houses the local tourist office.

Serra de Água

㉒ *7 km (4½ mi) north of Ribeira Brava.*

North from Ribeira Brava the N104 snakes through a sheer-sided canyon. In every direction you can see high waterfalls tumbling down canyon walls and into a pine forest. Eventually you'll come to Serra de Água, an ideal starting point for a trek into Madeira's interior. Even if you don't plan to hike, consider spending the night here at the stone pousada, surrounded by moss-green rocks, ferns, and more waterfalls.

Where to Stay & Eat

$ ✕⌧ **Pousada dos Vinháticos.** Guest rooms at this tiny stone lodge on the edge of a pine forest are inviting in shades of blue, green, and orange; some quarters are in log cabins. Do bring a good book in case fog weaves its otherworldly spell, forc-

HIKING IN MADEIRA

The island is covered with footpaths that run among peaks and alongside levadas, canals that crisscross the island and often flow through tunnels, bringing valuable water from the mountains to the tiny terraced farms. The footpaths were made so the *levadeiro,* the person tending the levadas, could clear anything that blocked the flow of water. Some date from as far back as the 15th century. One of the most breathtaking views is from Madeira's highest peak (6,102 feet) Pico Ruivo. On a clear day you can nearly see from one end of the island to the other.

ing you to forgo your hike. Madeira specialties are featured in the restaurant ($–$$), which has an outdoor terrace where you might feel truly part of the mountain scenery. Check the Web site for excellent deals on longer stays. ⊠ *Hwy. N104, 9350-306* ☎ *291/952344 or 291/765658* 🖷 *291/952140* ⊕ *www.pousadadosvinhaticos.com* ⇨ *21 rooms* ⚘ *Restaurant, cable TV, bar; no a/c* ▭ *AE, MC, V* ⦿ *BP.*

EN ROUTE From Serra de Água the road climbs north for 6 km (4 mi) to **Boca de Encumeada** (Mouth of the Heights). There are several trailheads here as well as good views of both the north and south coasts.

São Vicente

❷❸ *16 km (10 mi) northwest of Serra de Água.*

At the town of São Vicente, the road joins the one-lane north-coast highway that's chiseled out of the cliff face and is said to be one of the most expensive road projects, per mile, ever undertaken. In the early 19th century, workers in baskets were suspended by rope so they could carve out ledges and tunnels along the planned route. Proceed with caution and make sure to sound your horn when going around blind curves. Large tour buses constantly use this narrow road; if you happen to meet one, you may be forced to back up to a turnout.

Where to Stay

¢–$ ▦ **Estalagem do Mar.** All the rooms in this basic inn are done in sea green and white to complement the ocean views. The sparkling white-tile bathrooms are a comfortable place to freshen up after a day of exploring the area. Book from the Web site for serious savings. ⊠ *Fajã da Areia, 9240-2210* ☎ *291/840010* 🖷 *291/840019* ⊕ *www.hotelestalagemdomar. com* ⇨ *91 rooms, 8 suites* ⚘ *Restaurant, cable TV, tennis court, 2 pools (1 indoor), gym, hot tub, sauna, billiards, 2 bars* ▭ *AE, DC, MC, V* ⦿ *BP, MAP.*

EN ROUTE As you wind west along the coast, there are a number of waterfalls ahead: at one point the road passes behind a falls, and there's another delightful cascade right onto the road, so you have to drive through it. Stop at one of the viewpoints and notice the windbreaks—made of thick mats of purple heather—that protect the terraced vineyards such as the one in the pretty village of Seixal.

Porto Moniz

❷❹ *16 km (10 mi) west of São Vicente.*

Porto Moniz, with its natural pools formed by ancient lava, is the destination of nearly all visitors taking full-day trips in Madeira. There's not much to do here except splash around the pools (there are changing facilities), eat, and sunbathe: it's getting here that's the fun. The island's northernmost village was a whaling station in the 19th century. Thanks to modern development, however, little remains of its old houses and twisting cobblestone streets.

8

Where to Stay & Eat

¢ ✕⚏ **Residencial Orca.** Guest rooms here are tidy and pleasant though unremarkable unless you get one by the sea; if so, your large, tiled terrace will overlook the lava-walled pool and the blue-green ocean beyond. The Orca Restaurant (¢–$$), with equally good views, serves espada prepared in every way imaginable. Try it fried with orange, banana, kiwi, or passion fruit. ⊠ *Sitio das Poças, 9270-095* ☎ *291/850000* 📠 *291/ 850019* 💭 *12 rooms* ⌂ *Restaurant, cable TV, bar; no a/c* ⊟ *AE, MC, V* ⏍⏐ *BP, MAP.*

EN ROUTE As you drive along the winding uphill road out of Porto Moniz to the viewpoint near Santa Madalena, look back and see the patterns made by the scrub windbreaks. At the fork, turn left on N110, a road that crosses through Madeira's wildest area, providing a unique perspective of both sides of the island. If you have time, take the hair-raising lane to **Rabaçal,** a remote trailhead 22 km (14 mi) southeast of Porto Moniz. From here trails fan out in all directions. Madeirans love to come here to picnic alongside the cascades (bring food with you) or walk along a levada.

Past Rabaçal, the road heads into a moorland called **Paúl da Serra** (Desert Plain), where sheep and cattle graze and seagulls spiral overhead. This is the closest thing to flatland in Madeira, and its scrubby landscape looks out of place. From Paúl da Serra, you can turn right on N209 and follow signs south to the village of **Canhas.** The twisting road passes more terraced farms and, in 20 km (12 mi), joins the southern coastal road N101, which runs to Funchal. Or you can take the route to Boca de Encumeada and rejoin the main road (the N104).

CENTRAL PEAKS & SANTANA

The barren peaks of central Madeira offer spectacular views and great hikes. This part of the island includes the much-photographed village of Santana, with its thatch-roof A-frame houses.

Pico do Arieiro

★ ㉕ *7 km (4½ mi) northwest of Poiso, 30 km (18 mi) northeast of Funchal.*

Pico do Arieiro, at 5,963 feet, is Madeira's second-highest mountain. On your way here, you'll travel over a barren plain above the tree line: watch for errant sheep and goats wandering across the pavement on their way to graze on stubbly gorse and bilberry. Stop in the parking lot of the pousada and make the short climb to the lookout, where you can scan the rocky central peaks. There are often views of the clouds (below unless you're in them), and to the southeast is the Curral das Freiras valley—literally, Corral of the Sisters, so-named after the nuns of the Santa Clara convent who fled Funchal in 1565 to escape pirate raids. It's also known as the Grande Curral (Great Corral). Look in the other direction and try to spot the huge Penha de Aguia (Eagle Rock), a giant monolith on the north coast. The trail from the lookout that crosses the narrow ridge leads to Pico Ruivo (6,102 feet), the island's highest point.

Where to Stay & Eat

★ **$–$$** ✕🏨 **Pousada do Pico do Arieiro.** The air can be chilly high above the tree line, so there's often an inviting fire blazing in the bar of this pousada. The exterior may be unprepossessing, but inside you'll find cozy, chintz-adorned rooms with balconies. Hiking, playing chess, reading, and gazing out at the mountains are the main activities here. On clear days, the views from the large picture windows in the dining room ($$–$$$) are spectacular. The traditional island menu often includes delicious (and warming) soups. ⊠ *Pico do Arieiro* 🕆 *Funchal 9000* ☎ *291/230110 or 291/702030* 🖷 *291/228611* ↙ *21 rooms* ⚴ *Restaurant, coffee shop, cable TV, bar* ⊟ *AE, MC, V* ⟩⟨⟩⟨ *BP, FAP, MAP.*

Ribeiro Frio

★ ❷ *11 km (7 mi) north of Poiso, 17 km (10 mi) from Funchal.*

The landscape grows more lush on the northern side of the island, and the road is full of waterfalls. Ribeiro Frio is known for its beautiful gardens—native plants and nonindigenous flowers and plants can be found. This is an excellent place to start a walk with views from the Balcões looking down into the valley of Ribeiro do Faial and the rocky amphitheater of Machiço Central. Near here is the Pico Ruivo (Red Summit), the highest point on the island at 6,102 feet.

Where to Eat

$–$$ ✕ **Victor's Bar.** After your hike, stop at this family-owned mountain restaurant for afternoon tea and, some would say, the island's best bolo de mel. Full meals, including trout prepared many ways, are served here, too. Inside the rustic wood-and-glass building are a couple of welcoming fireplaces. The friendly owner, Victor Reinecke, is a font of island knowledge and can advise you on how to find Madeira's most remote and beautiful corners. ⊠ *N103* ☎ *291/575898* ⊟ *AE, DC, MC, V.*

EN ROUTE Continue north from Ribeiro Frio on N101 and follow signs to **Faial,** with the road descending in a series of steep curves into a deep ravine. The tiny A-frame huts that dot the terraces along the steep sides are barns for cows, which are prohibited from grazing. There's no horizontal pastureland, and they could easily fall off a ledge.

Santana

★ ❷ *18 km (11 mi) northwest of Ribeiro Frio, 39 km (24 mi) north of Funchal.*

Santana is a village famous for its A-frame, thatch-roof *palheiros* (cottages), which are painted in bright colors and look as if they've come straight from the pages of a fairy tale. Some are reproductions of more traditional versions; only a handful of islanders still live in earlier incarnations of these dwellings.

OFF THE BEATEN PATH **PARQUE DAS QUEIMADAS –** Five kilometers (3 mi) west of Santana there is a detour where the road quickly turns into a rough mountain track. Along a trail that passes by gorse bushes, hydrangeas, and wildflowers, this route leads right into a wonderful forest. There are picnic ta-

8

bles and toilet facilities at the Casa das Queimadas, which is used by forest rangers.

Where to Stay & Eat

$ ✕⌖ **Quinta do Furão.** In a peaceful setting, amid a vineyard high on the cliffs, this hotel with its nearby restaurant ($) have sweeping views of the sea. The place is such a north-coast draw that Funchal residents arrange to be flown here by helicopter for Sunday lunch. The food is a cut above the typical island fare, featuring such dishes as steak in pastry with Roquefort sauce, and prawns on a spit with avocado sauce. Regional wines are served. ⊠ *Achado do Gramacho, 9230-082* ☎ *291/570100* 🖷 *291/ 573560* ⊕ *www.quintadofurao.com* 🖙 *39 rooms, 4 suites* ♿ *Restaurant, room service, cable TV, indoor-outdoor pool, gym, sauna, bar, wine bar, recreation room* ▤ *AE, DC, MC, V* ⍾ *BP, FAP, MAP.*

Porto da Cruz

㉘ *20 km (12 mi) southeast of Santana.*

The road from Santana to Porto da Cruz skirts the back of the landmark **Penha de Aguia** (Eagle Rock), whose sheer cliffs tower over the village of São Roque do Faial. The fertile valley setting is filled with tiny farms and gardens. It's also where you can find the island's last working sugar mill, used during March and April to make *aguardente*. This firewater, a sugarcane brandy, can be tasted at the small no-name bar opposite the church. It's far more palatable when tasted as part of the island's famous cocktail, poncha, mixed with honey and lemon juice.

EN ROUTE Start your climb again on N101 and continue to **Portela,** where the view looks south over the gentler valley of Machico. From here it's an easy drive through pinewoods and sugarcane fields and into the town of Machico.

Machico

㉙ *15 km (9 mi) southeast of Porto da Cruz, 26 km (16 mi) northeast of Funchal.*

Local folklore says the bay of Machico was discovered in 1346 by two English lovers, Robert Machin and Anne d'Arfet, who set sail from Bristol to escape Anne's disapproving parents. The couple's ship was thrown off course by a storm and wrecked in this bay. Anne died a few days after becoming ill, and Robert then died of a broken heart. But their crew, according to legend, escaped on a raft, and news of the island made its way back to Portugal. (Legend also has it that Shakespeare heard the tale before he wrote *The Tempest.*) When the explorer Zarco arrived in 1420, he found a wooden cross with the lovers' story and the church—the island's first—where they were buried. He named the place in memory of Machin. You can visit the replacement church and wander through the old quarter. Among the handful of atmospheric restaurants is the Mercado de Velho, a café with a terrace in a former market.

**OFF THE
BEATEN
PATH**

CANIÇAL – Multicolored boats bob in water that has been witness to this village's long history as a whaling station, which it remained until the not-so-distant year of 1981. A whaling museum (closed Monday) tells the story. In 1985, 5 acres of the sea surrounding the town were designated a national marine park. On the way to Caniçal, 10 km (6 mi) northeast of Machico, stop for a coffee at Bar Crespo.

MADEIRA ESSENTIALS

Tranportation

BY AIR

Madeira is served by TAP Air Portugal, which has frequent flights daily from Lisbon (1¾ hours) and London (4 hours). British Airways has nonstops between London and Funchal several times a week. Numerous flights link Funchal with other European capitals.

The 15-minute interisland flight to Porto Santo from Madeira provides spectacular low-altitude views of Machico and São Lourenço Peninsula. TAP Air Portugal runs a shuttle between the islands several times a day. One-way fares start at €44. Reservations should be made in advance, especially for July and August.

The Aeroporto da Madeira is a 35-minute drive east of Funchal, near Santa Cruz. On Porto Santo, the tiny Aeroporto Campo de Cima is a 10-minute drive north of Vila Baleira. There are no buses on Porto Santo. A taxi transfer costs around €6.

🚩 Airports **Aeroporto Campo de Cima** ☎ 291/980120. **Aeroporto da Madeira** ☎ 291/520700.

8

BY BOAT

The *Lobo Marinho* ferry sails from Madeira to Porto Santo every day except Tuesday. Boats leave Funchal Harbor at 8 AM and return at 6 PM. The sometimes choppy one-way passage takes 2½ hours. Tickets cost €53 round-trip, and you can buy them on board or through the Porto Santo Line office, which is open weekdays 9–12:30 and 2:30–6. For sailings on summer weekends, buy tickets in advance.

🚩 **Porto Santo Line** ✉ Rua da Praia 6, Funchal ☎ 291/210300.

BY BUS

Madeira has two extensive bus systems. Yellow buses serve Funchal and its surrounding neighborhoods: lines 1 and 3 run west from the city and make stops along the Estrada Monumental, where most of the hotels are. Beige-and-red buses fan out to other points on the island. Both systems leave from an outdoor terminal at the end of Avenida do Mar. Generally, buses travel several times a day to each village on the island, but schedules change constantly, so inquire at your hotel or the tourist office for departure times.

🚩 **Bus Information** ☎ 291/705500.

BY CAR

Although the best way to explore Madeira is by car, the terrain is steep, and driving can be tortuous and slow. For example, the twisting, turning drive from Funchal to Porto Moniz in the west is only 156 km (97 mi) round-trip, but it takes all day if you go the scenic route. Road signs are generally adequate, but get an up-to-date map, particularly if you want to take advantage of Madeira's fast new highways.

Moinho ✉ Rua Levada Canha 2, Porto Santo, Vila Baleira ☎ 291/982780 ⊕ www. madeira-island.com/carhire/moinho.html.

BY TAXI

Taxis that are licensed to carry passengers within Funchal have a light on top, which is turned on if they are for hire. Taxis from outside Funchal won't pick up in the city limits. They're all metered, but if, for any reason, the meter is off or "not working," be sure to agree on a price before starting the journey. Rates are relatively inexpensive; a ride across town shouldn't cost much more than €5–€6, depending upon traffic. Porto Santo roads are easy to handle by car, but most visitors cover the 10-km-long (6-mi-long) island on foot or by taxi. It's fairly easy to hail cabs, and you can also phone for one.

Porto Santo Taxis ☎ 291/982334.

Contacts & Resources

EMERGENCIES

A 24-hour emergency service is provided by Clínica de Santa Luzia and Clínica de Santa Catarina. Pharmacies are open at night and on Sunday according to a rotating schedule. Dial 166 for information.

Funchal fire department ☎ 291/223056. **Funchal police** ☎ 291/208400. **General emergencies** ☎ 112. **Clínica de Santa Catarina** ✉ Rua 5 de Outubro 115, Funchal ☎ 291/741127. **Clínica de Santa Luzia** ✉ Rua da Torrinha 5, Funchal ☎ 291/233434.

MAIL

The post office branch in Funchal has hours weekdays 9–1 and 3–7 and on Saturday 9–1. Elsewhere on the island, post offices are generally open weekdays 9–12:30 and 2:30–5:30 and Saturday 9–12:30.

Post Office CTT Funchal ✉ Av. Zarco, Funchal.

TOUR OPTIONS

BOAT TOURS   Boat excursions around Funchal's coast take place year-round. Choose from a range of 2- to 2½-hour charters to Cabo Girão, Ponta do Sol, Machico, Ribeira Brava, or a shorter 1½-hour trip to Caniçal. Costs range from €15 to €20 per person.

Costa do Sol, Lda ✉ Marina do Funchal, Funchal ☎ 291/238538 or 291/224390.

HIKING TOURS   Viva Travel offers a different hiking tour through the mountains every day. Levels of difficulty vary, and each excursion includes something extra, such as a peek at local weavers or a wine tasting in a hidden cave. Other companies that organize walking tours are Turismo Verde e Ecologico da Madeira (TURIVEMA) and Terras de Aventura & Turismo.

Terras de Aventura & Turismo ✉ Caminho do Amparo 25, Funchal ☎ 291/66818. **TURIVEMA** ✉ Estrada Monumental 187, Funchal ☎ 291/763701 ⊕ www.madeira-levada-walks.com. **Viva Travel** ⊠ Largo António Nobre, Funchal ☎ 291/230724 ⊕ www. viva-travel.pt.

ISLAND TOURS Travel agencies specializing in island tours abound in Funchal. Visits in buses or minivans usually include lunch and multilingual guides. Trips generally take in Cabo Girão, the inland peaks, Porto Moniz, and the village of Santana. Among the best operators are Blandy's and Orion. Blandy's runs full-day (Thursday) excursions for wine lovers to vineyards on the east side of the island. Trips include a stop for lunch in the village of Santana.

🚩 **Blandy's** ⊠ Rua de São Francisco 20, Arcadas de São Francisco [behind winery], Funchal ☎ 291/200620 ⊕ www.blandys.com. **Orion** ⊠ Rua de João Gago 2-A, Funchal ☎ 291/228222 ⊕ www.orion-madeira.com.

VISITOR INFORMATION
In Funchal, Madeira's busy tourist office is open weekdays 9–8 and weekends 9–6. It dispenses maps, brochures, and up-to-date information on the constantly changing bus schedules. There are also tourist offices in other towns as well as on Porto Santo; their hours are generally weekdays 9–5:30, and Saturday 10 to 12:30.

🚩 **Madeira Tourist Offices** **Regional Tourism Office** ⊠ Av. Arriaga 18, Funchal 9004-519 ☎ 291/211902 🖶 291/232151 ⊕ www.madeiratourism.org. **Machico** ⊠ Forte do Amparo, Praça José António Almada, 9200 ☎ 291/962289. **Madeira Office in Lisbon** ⊠ Palácio da Foz, Praça dos Restauradores, 1250 ☎ 21/346–9113. **Porto Santo tourist office** ⊠ Av. Henrique Vieira de Castro, Vila Baleira 9400 ☎ 291/982361 ⊕ www. portosantoline.pt. **Ribeira Brava** ⊠ Forte de São Bento, Vila de Ribeira Brava 9350 ☎ 291/951675.

8

Golf in Portugal: Where to Play

WORD OF MOUTH

"Portugal is home to some of Europe's top class golf courses. Although the majority are located in the holiday playground of the Algarve, there are great, memorable courses located all over the country, particularly around Lisbon, and in Madeira. It is a sport that the Portuguese are really starting to take seriously, especially since the 2004 World Golf Championships, held at the prestigious Vilamoura course in the Algarve."

–Mary McLean

Updated by
Mary McLean

PORTUGAL, the country that gave the world Henry the Navigator, Madeira wine from its offshore dependency, and vintage port, has been attracting golfers from all over Europe since it was discovered that it had the perfect climate for winter golf, particularly on the Algarve's stunning coastline of sandy beaches. It was another Henry, Sir Henry Cotton, winner of three Open Championships and the father of golf on the Algarve, who turned a marshy field near the old fishing village of Portimão into the famous Penina golf course in the mid-1960s, thereby putting Portugal on the world golfing map.

Where to Play

Some of the finest layouts in continental Europe are to be found in the Algarve, which holds the majority of Portugal's courses and continues to boom as a tourism market. There is also golf on the west coast around Lisbon, and just two courses in the rather remote region of Beiras in the northern center of the country. Three fine 18-hole courses are on the island of Madeira, the best located at Palheiro and at Santo da Serra, which has an additional 9-hole layout in play.

Generally, winter weather is perfect for golf, particularly on the southern coast of the Algarve. January can be temperamental with rains, however. The northern courses suffer more in this regard in winter. In summer, high temperatures across the country are made more bearable by cool sea breezes. Motorized golf carts are available at most courses in Portugal, and major courses have caddies available on request. All courses are walkable.

Golf at the most popular courses is expensive, with fees varying with the seasons and ranging from around €60 to €150. Green fees are generally cheaper in the north, but if you shop around online, you can find some discounts for the Algarve.

The Algarve

The perfect golfing climate of the Algarve attracts golfers from all over northern Europe, who are eager to escape winter weather at home that often closes courses for days or weeks at a time. The Penina course led the early development of the region, and many others have followed since to take advantage of the coastal strip from the Spanish border to the east almost to Cape St. Vincent, the most westerly point of continental Europe. The rush to build courses quickly in the early part of the Algarve golf boom brought concerns over the condition of some of the courses, but these doubts have long since disappeared. You can be confident of playing on superbly presented fairways and greens.

Laguna Course Vilamoura. Water comes into play on many holes on this fine Vilamoura layout designed by Americans Joseph Lee and the late Rocky Roquemore. The layout close to the Atlantic is a fine complement to its more famous sister course, the Old Course. Tee times can be reserved online, and reservations are advised. ⊠ *Vilamoura, Quarteiro 8125-507* ☎ *289/310180* 🖷 *289/310183* ⊕ *www.vilamoura.net* 🏌 *18 holes. 6,111 m. Par 72. Slope 129* 🎫 *€60 per round* ☞ *Facilities: driving range, putting green, chipping area, golf carts, hand-pulled* carts, caddies on request, rental clubs, pro shop, golf academy/lessons, restaurant, bar.

Millennium Course Vilamoura. Martin Hawtree extended an existing 9-hole layout to create this visitor-friendly course on the vast Vilamoura estate. It shares the umbrella pine tree backdrop common to the other two Vilamoura courses but is a little shorter in length. Tee times can be reserved online, and reservations are advised. ⊠ *Vilamoura, Quarteiro 8125-507* ☎ *289/310188* 🖶 *289/310321* ⊕ *www.vilamoura.net* ⚑ *18 holes. 5,784 m. Par 72* 🏷 *€90 per round* ☞ *Facilities: driving range, putting green, chipping area, golf carts, hand-pulled carts, caddies on request, rental clubs, pro shop, golf academy/lessons, restaurant, bar.*

Fodor'sChoice **Morgado do Reguengo.** This inland layout north of Portimão opened in
★ 2003. Large greens are a feature on this European Golf–designed layout built on a vast 2,400 acre site through small undulating valleys. The course has good practice facilities and a clubhouse with spectacular views from its southern terrace. A sister course, Golfe dos Álamos, opened in March 2006 with a course that runs next to two large lakes and enjoys superb views of the Monchique mountain range. Both courses share the same clubhouse and require a handicap certificate. Both the Morgado do Requengo and Golfe dos Álamos courses may be booked via the following contact information. ⊠ *Apartado 293, Portimão 8501-912* ☎ *282/402150* 🖶 *282/402153* ⚑ *18 holes. 6,399 m. Par 73* 🏷 *€85 per round* ☞ *Facilities: driving range, putting green, chipping area, golf carts, hand-pulled carts, electric trolleys, rental clubs, pro shop, golf academy/lessons, restaurant, bar.*

★ **Ocean Course Vale do Lobo.** The Ocean Course emerged from an earlier design by Sir Henry Cotton and is a combination of the original "orange" and "green" courses of three 9-hole loops. The undulating fairways are fringed by pine, olive, orange, and eucalyptus trees. Accuracy is the key factor on what is otherwise a relatively short layout by today's standards. Practice facilities include play from mats and from grass. A handicap certificate is required. ⊠ *Vale do Lobo–Almancil 8135-864* ☎ *289/353535* 🖶 *289/353003* ⚑ *18 holes. 5,424 m. Par 71* 🏷 *€115 per round* ☞ *Facilities: driving range, putting green, chipping area, golf carts, hand-pulled carts, pro shop, restaurant, swimming pool, tennis academy, bar.*

Fodor'sChoice **Old Course Vilamoura.** One of the great golf courses of Europe, this Frank
★ Pennink layout needed considerable refurbishment a few years ago. Renamed the Old Course, it is the original and is widely regarded as the best of the Vilamoura layouts because of its subtle routing and challenging holes. Umbrella pines line the fairways, and the crack of ball on timber is almost a signature tune on this famous course. The maximum handicap for men is 24 and for women 28. ⊠ *Vilamoura, Quarteiro 8125-507* ☎ *289/310341* 🖶 *289/310321* ⊕ *www.vilamoura.net* ⚑ *Reservations essential* ⚑ *18 holes. 6,254 m. Par 73* 🏷 *€120 per round* ☞ *Facilities: driving range, putting green, chipping area, golf carts, hand-pulled carts, caddies on request, rental clubs, pro shop, golf academy/lessons, restaurant, bar.*

Fodor's Choice **Palmares.** Palmares is one of the lesser-known gems of European golf
★ and is partly a genuine seaside links. Five of the holes run alongside
the Atlantic Ocean, with the fifth hole a spectacular Par 5 that would
do justice to any links course in Scotland. The course is split by the
main coastal railway line with holes on the north side built high above
the sea amid beautiful pine forest. Almond trees abound, lending their
name to the famous Almond Blossom tournament played at Palmares
every spring. The handicap limit is 28 for men and 36 for women.
✉ *Apartado 74–Meia Praia, Lagos 8601-901* ☎ *282/790500* 🖷 *282/*
790509 ⊕ *www.palmaresgolf.com* ⅃. *18 holes. 5,961 m. Par 71*
🖼 *€85 per round* ☞ *Facilities: driving range, putting green, chip-*
ping area, golf carts, hand-pulled carts, rental clubs, pro shop, golf
lessons, restaurant, bar.

Fodor's Choice **Penina.** On what was once a flat and uninteresting field, Sir Henry Cot-
★ ton worked his design magic and created his most famous course 5 km
(3 mi) from the old fishing town of Portimão at the western end of the
Algarve. It is considered the masterpiece among his many layouts because of its difficult challenge and the beautiful setting he created by
planting more than 100,000 trees. Sir Henry held court here for years,
welcoming the great and good from world golf to the lavish Penina resort. The course that began the Portuguese golf boom in the 1960s has
had a face-lift and remains a stern test of golf. Le Meridien Penina hotel
guests are entitled to special green fee rates. On the championship
course, a handicap of 28 is required for men and 36 for women to play.
🕮 *Box 146, Penina, Portimão 8501-952* ☎ *282/420224* 🖷 *282/*
420300 ⊕ *www.penina.lemeridien.com* ⌕ *Reservations essential* ⅃. *18*
holes. 6,439 m. Par 73 🖼 *€100 per round* ☞ *Facilities: driving range,*
putting green, chipping area, golf carts, hand-pulled carts, electric trol-
leys, rental clubs, pro shop, golf academy/lessons, restaurant, bar.

Fodor's Choice **Pine Cliffs.** British motor racing ace and avid golfer Nigel Mansell was
★ president (1989–94) of this beautiful 9-hole golf course at the Sheraton
Algarve in Albufeira. Built in a pine forest and designed by Martin
Hawtree, it was opened to great acclaim in 1990. Only two of the holes
are more than 330 yards in length. The star attraction is the famous Par
3 ninth hole, with its championship tee built across a ravine requiring
a 187-yard carry across the cliffs to a narrow green. The course is always immaculately kept. A handicap certificate of 28 for men and 36
for women is required. ✉ *Praia da Falesia, Albufeira 8200-909* ☎ *289/*
500113 🖷 *289/501950* ⌕ *Reservations essential* ⅃. *9 holes. 2,051 m.*
Par 33 🖼 *€110 per round* ☞ *Facilities: driving range, 2 putting greens,*
chipping area, hand-pulled carts, electric trolleys, rental clubs, pro shop,
golf academy/lessons, restaurant, tennis courts, bar, hotel.

Pinheiros Altos. There are two very different nines on this layout close
to the Ria Formosa Nature Park. Peter McEvoy and Howard Swan were
brought in to make changes to the original Ronald Fream design. The
result is not always pleasing to the eye, but it remains a good test of
golf. Fairways carved through pine forest on the front nine and flat terrain with water on almost every hole on the back nine are the hallmarks.
The handicap limit is 28 for men and 36 for women. Reservations are

advised. ⊠ *Quinta do Lago, Almancil 8135-863* ☎ *289/359910* 🖷 *289/394392* ⊕ *www.algarvegolf.net* 🏌 *18 holes. 6,057 m. Par 71* 🏌 *€150 per round* ☞ *Facilities: driving range, putting green, chipping area, hand-pulled carts, rental clubs, pro shop, golf academy/lessons, restaurant, bar.*

Fodor'sChoice **Quinta de Cima.** This is the sister course to Quinta da Ria and is a stiffer
★ test. Also designed by Rocky Roquemore, water hazards abound, and length as well as accuracy are the premiums. The strength of the challenge is tempered by some wonderful views in a superb setting. Visitors are required to produce a handicap certificate. ⊠ *Apartado 161, Vila Nova de Cacela 8900-057* ☎ *281/950580* 🖷 *281/950580* ⊕ *www.quintadariagolf.com* 🏌 *18 holes. 6,256 m. Par 72. Slope 129* 🏌 *€90 per round* ☞ *Facilities: driving range, putting green, chipping area, golf carts, hand-pulled carts, electric trolleys, rental clubs, pro shop, golf lessons, restaurant, bar.*

Fodor'sChoice **Quinta do Lago South Course.** There are four loops of 9 holes at Quinta
★ do Lago at this beautiful complex only 12 km (7 mi) from Faro International Airport. The combination of the B and C courses is the most popular and is the layout used for major events. Always presented in fine condition, this William Mitchell–designed layout is very American in character, with wide fairways and large undulating greens. It is a substantial test from the back tees, but played a little farther forward, it provides excellent sport for all levels of ability. Handicap restrictions are 28 for men and 36 for women. ⊠ *Quinta do Lago, Almancil 8135-024* ☎ *289/390700* 🖷 *289/394013* ⊕ *www.quintadolago.com* 🖳 *Reservations essential* 🏌 *18 holes. 6,488 m. Par 72* 🏌 *€150 per round* ☞ *Facilities: driving range, putting green, chipping area, golf carts, hand-pulled carts, electric trolleys, rental clubs, pro shop, golf academy/lessons, restaurant, bar.*

★ **Quinta da Ria.** Set high on the cliff above the ocean, Quinta da Ria is a nice addition to the rich treasury of golf courses on the Algarve. The design has been cleverly incorporated into a tight location by Rocky Roquemore, and the result is a beautiful course perfect for holiday golf. The views alone are worth the visit. The handicap limit is 28 for men and 36 for women. Reservations are advised. ⊠ *Vila Nova de Cacela 8900-057* ☎ *281/950580* 🖷 *281/950589* ⊕ *www.quintadariagolf.com* 🏌 *18 holes. 6,016 m. Par 72. Slope 120* 🏌 *€90 per round* ☞ *Facilities: driving range, putting green, chipping area, hand-pulled carts, electric trolleys, rental clubs, pro shop, golf lessons, restaurant, bar.*

★ **Royal Course Vale do Lobo.** A much more difficult challenge than its sister course, Ocean Course Vale do Lobo, the Royal Course is much longer and is defended by more water and bunkers. Sir Henry Cotton laid out the original course, but significant changes have been introduced by Rocky Roquemore to bring it more up-to-date. The pick of the holes is the famous 16th, which requires a carry of 200 yards over three spectacular cliffs to reach the sanctuary green. A handicap limit of 27 for men and 35 for women is enforced here. ⊠ *Vale do Lobo–Almancil 8135-864* ☎ *289/353535* 🖷 *289/353003* 🖳 *Reservations essential* 🏌 *18* *holes. 6,175 m. Par 72 🖂 €135 per round ☞ Facilities: driving range, putting green, chipping area, golf carts, hand-pulled carts, pro shop, restaurant, swimming pool, tennis academy, bar.*

Fodor'sChoice ★ **San Lorenzo.** Regarded as the second-best course in continental Europe, San Lorenzo enjoys a beautiful and tranquil setting beside the Ria Formosa. This Joseph Lee–designed layout is best enjoyed by lower-handicap players, who will appreciate and be better able to contend with the demand for length and accuracy. This is golf not only in a beautiful setting but among some very imposing villas that do not in any way detract from the glorious golfing experience. Call 24 hours in advance for tee times. ⊠ *Quinta do Lago, Almancil 8135-901* 🕾 *289/396522* 🖷 *289/396908* ⌖ *Reservations essential* ⅃. *18 holes. 6,238 m. Par 72* 🖂 *€150 per round* ☞ *Facilities: driving range, putting green, chipping green, golf carts, hand-pulled carts, caddies on request, electric trolleys, rental clubs, pro shop, golf academy/lessons, restaurant, bar.*

★ **Vale da Pinta.** American course architect Ronald Fream carved the Vale da Pinta layout through an ancient olive grove where some of the trees are more than 700 years old. Fream was the perfect choice for the job, because he is highly regarded for his sensitivity to environmental issues. Five sets of tees on each hole make this an enjoyable course for all levels of ability. The greens are large, and there is a feeling of space here near the village of Carvoeiro. Handicap limits are 27 for men and 35 for women. ⊠ *Apartado 1011, Carvoeiro, Lagoa 8400* 🕾 *282/ 340900* 🖷 *282/340901* ⅃. *18 holes. 5,861 m. Par 71* 🖂 *€90 per round* ☞ *Facilities: driving range, putting green, chipping area, golf carts, hand-pulled carts, rental clubs, pro shop, golf academy/lessons, restaurant, bar.*

Fodor'sChoice ★ **Vila Sol.** The original 18-hole championship course at Vila Sol that hosted the Portuguese Open in 1992 and 1993 has been extended with a further 9-hole layout to create one of the finest golf facilities on the Algarve. Donald Steel from the United Kingdom was the designer, and some believe his original course represents some of his finest work. Many different species of trees have been incorporated to give a wonderfully natural feel to the place. The greens are large, undulating, and very fast. Handicap limits here are 28 for men and 36 for women. ⊠ *Alto do Semino, Vilamoura, Quarteiro 8125-307* 🕾 *289/300505 or 289/300522* 🖷 *289/316499* ⊕ *www.vilasol.pt* ⌖ *Reservations essential* ⅃. *18 holes. 6,335 m. Par 72* 🖂 *€100 per round* ☞ *Facilities: driving range, putting green, chipping area, golf carts, hand-pulled carts, pro shop, golf academy/lessons, restaurant, bar.*

Lisbon & Environs

Although less famous for its golf than for its culture and history, Portugal's capital, Lisbon, has much to offer the visiting golfer. There is a wide variety of fine courses in the area, although many are members' clubs that are particularly busy on the weekends.

Fodor'sChoice ★ **Aroeira 1.** The largest golf resort in the greater Lisbon area is set in a mature pine forest with two excellent 18-hole courses close to a popular stretch of sandy beach. Aroeira 1 is the shorter of the two courses but is a formidable challenge and has hosted several important championships, including the Portuguese Open in 1996 and 1997 and the Qualifying School for the Ladies European Tour. A handicap certificate is required here for Aroeira 1 and its sister course Aroeira 11: men 28 and women 36. ⊠ *Herdade da Aroeira, Fonte da Telha, Charneca da Caparica 2815-207* ☎ *21/297–9110* 🖷 *21/297–1238* ⊕ *www.aroeira. com* 🏌 *18 holes. 6,122 m. Par 72* 🎫 *€49 weekdays only, per round (weekends are reserved for members)* ☞ *Facilities: driving range, putting green, chipping area, golf carts, hand-pulled carts, caddies on request, rental clubs, pro shop, golf academy/lessons, restaurant, swimming pool, tennis courts, bar.*

★ **Belas.** Architect Rocky Roquemore built this tough but interesting layout in rolling countryside close to Lisbon and the Castle of Queluz with its famous gardens. Perhaps not the easiest golf course to walk—a golf cart is a must during the heat of summer—it is a serious test and will be better appreciated by lower-handicap players. The handicap limit here is 28 for men and 36 for women. ⊠ *Estrada Nacional, Belas 2605-199* ☎ *21/962–6640* 🖷 *21/962–6641* ⊕ *www.belasgolf.com* ⚑ *Reservations essential* 🏌 *18 holes. 6,380 m. Par 72* 🎫 *€75 weekdays, €86 weekends per round* ☞ *Facilities: driving range, putting green, chipping area, golf carts, hand-pulled carts, pro shop, golf academy/lessons, restaurant, bar.*

Fodor'sChoice **Oitavas Quinta da Marinha.** American architect Arthur Hills built this fine ★ golf course amongst pine woods and reforested dunes in an area of great natural beauty. The course lies within the Sintra-Cascais Natural Park, and Hills made the most of three distinct landscape forms: umbrella pine forest, dunes, and the open coastal transition area. Every hole has a view of the Atlantic Ocean and the Sintra Hills. This was the first course in Europe to be recognized as a Golf Certified Signature Sanctuary, which is awarded by American Audubon International. A handicap certificate is required to play here. ⊠ *25 Quinta da Marinha, Cascais 2750-15* ☎ *21/486–0000* 🖷 *21/486–9233* ⊕ *www.quinta-da-marinha.pt* 🏌 *18 holes. 6,303 m. Par 71* 🎫 *€90 weekdays, 150 weekends per round* ☞ *Facilities: driving range, putting green, chipping area, golf carts, hand-pulled carts, electric trolleys, rental clubs, pro shop, golf academy/lessons, restaurant, bar.*

Fodor'sChoice **Penha Longa.** With magnificent ocean views, the Sintra Hills, and Esto- ★ ril and Cascais in the foreground, architect Robert Trent Jones Jr. had a wonderful setting in which to create one of Portugal's most memorable courses. The Atlantic Course has great sweeping changes in elevation and often tight fairways that put a premium on driving accuracy. With the elevation often comes strong breezes that add another dimension to what is in any case a demanding layout. Lower-handicap players will savor the challenge, but there is plenty of enjoyment here for all abilities. A handicap certificate is required. ⊠ *Estrada do Lagoa Azul, Linhó, Sintra 2714-511* ☎ *21/924–9031* 🖷 *21/924–9024* ⊕ *www. penhalonga.com* ⚑ *Reservations essential* 🏌 *18 holes. 6,290 m. Par 72. Slope 124* 🎫 *€90 weekdays, €120 weekends per round* ☞ *Facilities: driving range, putting green, chipping area, golf carts, hand-pulled* carts, electric trolleys, rental clubs, pro shop, golf academy/lessons, restaurant, bar.

Fodor'sChoice **Praia d'El Rey.** Less than an hour's drive from Lisbon's international air-
★ port, Praia d'El Rey Golf & Country Club is an excellent beachfront resort with one of the most picturesque golf courses in Europe. Bold, deep bunkers, undulating greens, and natural sand-border areas are the hallmarks of this Cabell Robinson design, which has been rated 13th best in Europe by the United Kingdom's *Golf World* magazine. The architect was at great pains to make the course friendly to women players by creating sensible women's tees that are placed far enough forward. The handicap limit here is 28 for men and women. ⊠ *Obidos 2514-999* ☎ *262/905005* 📠 *262/905009* ⊕ *www.praia-del-rey.com* ⛳ *18 holes. 6,501 m. Par 72* 💲 *€90 weekdays, €110 weekends per round* ⚷ *Facilities: driving range, health club, 2 putting greens, chipping area, golf carts, hand-pulled carts, rental clubs, pro shop, restaurant, swimming pool, bar.*

★ **Quinta do Brínçal.** Quinta do Brínçal—it was originally known as Golden Eagle—is fast gaining a reputation as one of the finest golf courses in Portugal. This creation of American architect Rocky Roquemore is set in tranquil countryside and features rolling fairways, plenty of water, and stiff bunker protection around the greens. From the back tees it is a fine test for the better player, but it is much easier from the regular tees, which reduce the overall length by close to 545 yards. Women will also find much to like here. Handicap restrictions are 28 for men and 36 for women. ⊠ *Apartado 219, Rio Maior 2040-998* ☎ *243/908148* 📠 *243/908149* ⊕ *www.camin.pt* ⛳ *18 holes. 6,049 m. Par 72. Slope 126* 💲 *€50 weekdays, €60 weekends per round* ⚷ *Facilities: driving range, putting green, chipping area, golf carts, hand-pulled carts, pro shop, restaurant, bar.*

Fodor'sChoice **Quinta da Marinha.** Another creation of master architect Robert Trent
★ Jones, Quinta da Marinha has gained a well-deserved reputation as an excellent holiday golf destination. It's built on a relatively flat stretch of land in a private estate covered with pine trees and is only 25 km (15 mi) from the center of Lisbon. Relatively short by modern standards, this is nonetheless a fine test of golf good enough to have hosted a European Ladies' Tour event in 1988 and the Estoril Open on the PGA European Tour in 2002. Visitors always take back memories of the spectacular 13th hole, which slopes down toward the sea and presents wonderful views of the Atlantic from the green. There are no handicap restrictions here. ⊠ *Casa 36, Quinta da Marinha, Cascais 2750* ☎ *21/486–0180* 📠 *21/486–9032* ⊕ *www.quinta-da-marinha.pt* ⚷ *Reservations essential* ⛳ *18 holes. 6,014 m. Par 71* 💲 *€80 weekdays, €88 weekends per round* ⚷ *Facilities: driving range, putting green, golf carts, hand-pulled carts, rental clubs, pro shop, golf lessons, restaurant, bar.*

★ **Quinta do Peru.** Penncross bent grass on the greens and Tifton grass on the fairways adds up to a fine golfing experience at another of Rocky Roquemore's Portuguese creations. This one is slightly marred by the

9

property development going on around the course, but otherwise the layout is very playable for all levels and ideal for pleasant holiday golf. The club also boasts modern practice facilities and a good golf academy. The handicap limit here is 28 for men and 36 for women. ⊠ *Alameda da Serra 2, Quinta do Conde 2975-666* ☎ *212/134320 or 212/134322* 🖷 *212/134321* ⊕ *www.golfquintadoperu.com* ⌦ *Reservations essential* 🏌 *18 holes. 6,074 m. Par 72. Slope 137* 🏷 *€70 weekdays, €85 weekends per round* ☞ *Facilities: driving range, putting green, chipping area, golf carts, hand-pulled carts, rental clubs, pro shop, golf academy/lessons, restaurant, bar.*

Troia. What Robert Trent Jones had in mind when he laid out Troia back in 1981 is sometimes hard to figure out. Built on a peninsula close to the sea, there are hints of traditional links golf here, but some might say a little too much so. Without a doubt, it is a strategic layout requiring a great deal of thought and first-class shot making, but it might create too much of a test for the average player to find totally enjoyable. A lot of sand, maritime pines, and flora make for a very beautiful setting. The course is accessible by ferry from Setúbal, which is a much shorter journey than by road around the Sado Estuary. A handicap certificate is required. ⊠ *Complexo Turistico de Troia, Carvalhal 7570* ☎ *265/494112* 🖷 *265/494315* ⊕ *www.troiagolf.com* ⌦ *Reservations essential* 🏌 *18 holes. 6,320 m. Par 72* 🏷 *€60.50 weekdays, €72.50 weekends per round* ☞ *Facilities: driving range, putting green, chipping area, golf carts, hand-pulled carts, pro shop, restaurant, bar.*

Beiras

Golf in Portugal is centered around Lisbon and the Algarve, but there are other pockets where the game is played, including the region of Beiras. This area in the northern center of the country has just two courses that are worth visiting.

Curia. Opened in 2004 as part of the Grande Da Curia Golf & Spa complex, this 9-hole course will eventually expand to 18 holes. It is located just 20 minutes from Coimbra and the landscaping includes three artificial lakes. ⊠ *Curia* ☎ *231/516831* 🖷 *231/516831* ⊕ *www. curiagolfe.com* 🏌 *9 holes 2,457 m. Par 34* 🏷 *€17.50 weekdays, €25 weekends per round* ☞ *Facilities: driving range, putting green, chipping area, pro shop.*

Montebelo. Although hardly likely to be considered as a venue for the Ryder Cup, this interesting layout near Viseu lies in a picturesque region. It's the only course for many miles and has been built in hilly country, almost in the shadow of Portugal's highest mountain, the Serra da Estrela. This is much more informal golf than elsewhere in the country, and a handicap certificate is not required to play here. Walkers may find the hilly terrain a little hard going, but golf carts are available. ⊠ *Farminhão, Viseu 3510-643* ☎ *232/856464* 🖷 *232/856401* 🏌 *18 holes. 6,317 m. Par 72* 🏷 *€30 weekdays, €45 weekends per round* ☞ *Facilities: driving range, putting green, chipping area, golf carts, hand-pulled carts, pro shop, restaurant, bar.*

Porto & the North

Porto is the second-largest city in Portugal and is famous as a center of the port wine industry, which Portugal and Great Britain have to thank for their long-standing relationship. It was the British who took the game of golf to Portugal in the 19th century, and it is in this area that the only true links golf in the country can be found.

★ **Estela.** This is a genuine seaside links golf course only 24 km (15 mi) from the international airport. It was built in 1988 and quickly became renowned for its undulating and extremely fast greens. Architect Duarte Sotto-Mayor had a small piece of land with which to work, and although he did an excellent job, there are one or 2 holes that are very tightly squeezed into the site. Some 400,000 shrubs and trees—predominantly wild fig trees, willows, and oleanders—make this a walker's course. In summer, play before midday is often affected by morning mist that is slow to clear. ⊠ *Póvoa de Rio–Alto, Estela, Minho 4490* ☎ *252/ 601567* 🖷 *252/612701* ⊕ *www.estelagolf.pt* ⚑ *18 holes. 6,144 m. Par 72* 🏷 *€50 weekdays €75 weekends per round* ☞ *Facilities: driving range, putting green, chipping area, golf carts, hand-pulled carts, pro shop, restaurant, bar.*

Fodor'sChoice
★ **Oporto Golf Club.** Porto Golf Club is one of the most important clubs in the development of the game in Europe. British wine makers created the club in 1890, and it is, after Pau in France, the second-oldest golf course on the continent. By present-day standards it is not a long course, but it is a genuine, traditional links course beside the sea and subject to the vagaries of the north winds that often sweep down through that region. This is very much a private club (the restaurant is for members only), but visitors are made welcome and should take a handicap certificate. ⊠ *Sisto-Paramos, Espinho 4500* ☎ *22/734–2008* 🖷 *22/734–6895* ⚑ *Reservations essential* ⚑ *18 holes. 5,610 m. Par 71* 🏷 *€60 weekdays, €75 weekends per round* ☞ *Facilities: driving range, putting green, chipping area, golf carts, hand-pulled carts, pro shop, bar.*

Madeira

There are only a couple of golf courses on the delightful island of Madeira. Like everything else on this huge rock out in the Atlantic Ocean, they cling to a hillside. With the altitude come spectacular views, which, when added to the quality of the golf, make the trip here well worthwhile.

Fodor'sChoice
★ **Palheiro.** Memorable views over the capital, Funchal, and the southern coast of the island are the hallmarks of this delightful Cabell Robinson–designed course built high on the mountainside. Inevitably there are great changes in elevation, and although it is possible to walk this course, the sensible option is to take to buggy power, particularly in the hot summer months. It was a tight fit to contain 18 holes in this site, but there are a few great ones among them, and it's a pleasure to play all of them. A handicap certificate is required here. ⊠ *Sitio do Balançal, São Gonçado, Funchal 9050-296* ☎ *291/790125* 🖷 *291/792456* ⊕ *www. palheirogolf.com* ⚑ *Reservations essential* ⚑ *18 holes. 6,022 m. Par*

71 ✉ €80 per round ☞ Facilities: driving range (limited), putting green, chipping area, golf carts, hand-pulled carts, rental clubs, pro shop, restaurant, bar.

Santo da Serra. Golf at Santo de Serra often gives the impression of playing on top of the world. A setting high above the Atlantic Ocean means that the views at the end of the long climb are quite breathtaking. Occasionally the views are lost in the mist and low clouds that sometimes envelop the course, but when it is clear, there are few courses that command such a spectacular outlook. Use a golf cart to tackle the huge changes in elevation. Also, bring a handicap certificate. ✉ *N102, Casais Proximos, Antonio da Serra 9200-152* ☎ *291/550100* 🖷 *291/550105* ⊕ *www.santodaserragolf.com* ⚐ *18 holes. 6,039 m. Par 72* ✉ *€85 per round* ☞ *Facilities: driving range, putting green, chipping area, golf carts, hand-pulled carts, pro shop, restaurant, bar.*

UNDERSTANDING PORTUGAL

ART, ARCHITECTURE &
AZULEJOS

THE PLEASURES OF
PORTUGUESE WINE

PORTUGUESE
VOCABULARY

ART, ARCHITECTURE & AZULEJOS

PORTUGUESE SCULPTING and painting styles were inspired first by the excitement of the newly emerging nation and then by the baroque experimentation that the wealth from the colonies made possible. Sculpture found its first outlet in grand royal and noble funerary monuments, as witnessed by the realism of the Gothic tombs in the cathedrals of Lisbon, Guarda, and Braga. These were precursors of the masterpieces of their kind, including the 14th-century tombs of Pedro and Inês at Alcobaça and the eloquent hand-clasped figures of Dom João I and his queen, Philippa, in the chapel at Batalha.

Painting came into its own in the 15th century with the completion of Nuno Gonçalves's Flemish-inspired polyptych of São Vicente (St. Vincent), which portrayed the princes and knights, monks and fishermen, court figures and ordinary people of imperial Portugal in six panels. It's on display in Lisbon's Museu de Arte Antiga. The work of the next great Portuguese painter, the 16th-century Vasco Fernandes (known as Grão Vasco, or the Great Vasco), has an expressive, realistic vigor. His masterpieces are on display in Viseu.

The later baroque styles in art and sculpture said less about the country and more about its wealth. There were flamboyant creations, to be sure—including the unsurpassed granite-and-plaster staircases, pilgrimage shrines, and sculptures at Bom Jesus and Lamego, in the Minho—but these were built at a time when the monarchy had lost the vision and morals of earlier, greater periods. Nevertheless, there were always artists ready to work in styles that drew on the strengths of the Portuguese character and not the weaknesses.

The elaborate decoration that is the hallmark of Manueline architecture is inspiring in its sheer novelty. Buildings and monuments are supported by twisted stone columns and covered with sculpted emblems of Portugal's conquests on the high seas and in distant lands—particularly under Dom Manuel I (1495–1521). Representations of anchors, seaweed, and rigging mingle with exotic animals and strange, occasionally pagan, symbols—a fusion of diverse cultures and civilizations brought together under the umbrella of a Christian Portuguese empire.

Following the discovery of gold in Brazil at the end of the 17th century, buildings—churches, in particular—began to be embellished in an extraordinary rococo style, which employed *talha dourada* (polychrome and gilded carved wood) to stupendous pictorial effect. There are superb examples at the churches of São Francisco in Oporto and Santo António in Lagos, and at the Convento de Jesus at Aveiro. In contrast, to see rococo at its most restrained, you must visit the royal palace at Queluz, near Lisbon.

The 18th century saw the emergence of the sculptor Machado de Castro, who produced perhaps the greatest equestrian statue of his time, that of Dom José I in Lisbon's Praça do Comércio. Domingos António Sequeira (1768–1837) painted historic and religious subjects of international renown. Portrait and landscape painting became popular in the 19th century; the works of José Malhoã and Miguel Angelo Lupi can be seen in the Museu de José Malhoã in Caldas da Rainha. Museums throughout the country display the works of talented contemporaries. The Museu Soares dos Reis in Oporto—named after the 19th-century sculptor António Soares dos Reis (1847–89)—was the country's first national museum. His pupil was António Teixeira Lopes (1866–1942), who achieved great popular success, and who also has a museum named after him in the Oporto suburb of Vila Nova de Gaia.

Of all the country's artistic images, its *azulejos* (painted ceramic tiles) may well be the most enduring. The Moors introduced these tiles to Portugal, and although many of them are blue, the term they are known by doesn't come from *azul,* the Portuguese word for that color, but rather from the Arabic word *az-zulayj,* which means "little stones." By the 17th century the early styles were replaced by whole panels depicting religious or secular motifs. There are fine examples throughout the country, especially at the Fronteira palace on the outskirts of Lisbon.

The tiles, which feature geometric designs and come in a wide variety of colors, adorn many fountains, churches, and palaces. The Paço Real (Royal Palace) in Sintra is one of the most remarkable examples of their decorative effect. Look for delightful combinations on the nation's *quintas* or *solares* (country residences): for instance, an elegant pastel-color house whose outside walls and landscaped gardens are lavishly adorned with grandiose panels. The most interesting examples are found in the Minho region in the north. There are also well-preserved tile works on display in several museums, including Lisbon's Museu Nacional do Azulejo and Museu de Arte Antiga and Coimbra's Museu Machado de Castro.

THE PLEASURES OF PORTUGUESE WINE

WITH THE EXCEPTION OF those classic kings of wines, port and Madeira, the wines that Portugal produces are mainly honest and straightforward. This is a country where you can enjoy an endless procession of delicious experiments. You can also buy wines of a certain age at a very moderate cost.

Portuguese wine making stretches back beyond the Romans to the Phoenicians; it flourished under the teetotaling Muslims, and went through a checkered time after the Moors were expelled. A firm link with Britain enabled the wine trade to remain prosperous, especially where port was concerned. Trade between the two countries predates the 1386 Treaty of Windsor possibly by two centuries. After a long period of spasmodic development, with some regions flourishing and others, such as the Algarve, almost ceasing production, the situation was taken in hand by the Marquês de Pombal. In 1756 he demarcated the regions, geographically delineating growing areas and controlling their output and marketing; the port-making region was the first to be demarcated with stone borders.

Demarcation, and the attendant quality control, took off in the first years of the 20th century. Today there are at least 32 **Denominações de Origem** (origin denomination for wines whose originality and individuality is related to a certain region) resulting in 18 regions—*Vinho Verde, Trás-os-Montes, Douro, Távora-Varosa, Lafões, Bairrada, Dão, Beira Interior, Estremadura, Lourinhã, Bucelas, Carcavelos, and Colares, Ribatejo, Setúbal, Palmela, Alentejo, Algarve, Madeira,* and the *Azores.* Several areas that are still undemarcated also produce excellent wines. The official body that regulates wine production is the Instituto do Vinho e da Vinha, based in Lisbon. It controls all the facets of viniculture and of marketing, runs competitions, promotes cooperatives, and empowers growers to use a *selo de origem* (seal of origin). Rather like the French *appellation d'origine contrôlée,* the seal acts as a guarantee of a wine's pedigree.

The Algarve & the Alentejo

In the Algarve, wine is produced on a narrow strip of land between the mountains and the sea. Algarve wine is largely red. Among the better ones are Lagoa, Porche's, and Salira produced in Lagoa council. These reds are quite smooth, fruity, and full-bodied.

Alentejo vineyards are almost all in the top part of the province, around Évora and over toward the Spanish border. The wines they produce are now among the best in Portugal—Alabastro, Redondo, Borba (with its lovely dark color and slightly metallic astringent flavor), Monsaraz, and Vidigueira. The reds are rich in color, the whites pale and fruity.

Moscatel de Setúbal

Wines produced on the Setúbal Peninsula are well known abroad, mainly through the 150-year efforts of the House of Fonseca, based in Azeitão. The Moscatel that Fonseca—together with the small vine growers who make up the local cooperative a few miles east of Azeitão in Palmela—produces is best known as a fortified dessert wine, aged and with a mouthwatering taste of honey. If you find some that is, say, 25 years old, you'll see that it has developed a licorice color; enjoy its sweet scent and taste. Fonseca and the cooperative produce many other wines besides the Moscatel—fine reds (notably one called Periquita, or "little parrot"); rosés, of which Lancers and Faisca are often exported; and a few regular whites.

Bucelas, Carcavelos & Colares

The Bucelas region is about 30 km (19 mi) north of Lisbon, in the valley of the Rio Trancão (Trancão River). Although wine from here has a considerable history and was very popular with the British soldiers under Wellington in the Peninsular War, this is quite a small demarcated region, and all the wine it produces appears under the Caves Velhas label. Bucelas wine is usually straw color, with a distinctively full nose and a fruity taste that can sometimes verge on the citrusy. It goes extremely well with veal, poultry, and fish.

Carcavelos consists of just one small vineyard, the Quinta do Barão, between Lisbon and Estoril along a stretch of coast. This isn't an easy wine to find—the yearly output is small—but if you like wines with a history, it's worth looking for. Carcavelos is another fortified dessert wine, topaz color, with a nutty aroma and a slightly almond taste, mostly drunk as an aperitif.

The Colares region is at Portugal's westernmost tip, beyond Sintra. It's a fairly hostile place for vine growing, with sandy soil and exposure to the Atlantic winds. But it has a long and distinguished history of wine production, and it yields some very individual vintages. The red improves with age (it can be a little astringent when young) and has a full ruby color, an aromatic nose, and an aftertaste likened to black currants. One label to seek out is Colares Chita. The Colares whites are straw color, slightly nutty in taste, and—like the reds—improve with age. They should be served well chilled.

Bairrada, Lafões & Dão

Not far south of Porto is the coastal region of Bairrada. Although it wasn't that long ago—1979—that Bairrada was demarcated, the quality of its output suggests that it probably should have received that status long before. The region is made up mainly of small holdings, gathered into five cooperatives. Taken all together, they turn out a fairly large quantity of wine. The reds are of an intense color, with a delicious nose and a fruity, rich, and lasting taste. They mellow with age and go very well with stronger dishes such as game, roasts, and pungent cheeses. There aren't too many whites in this region, and most of them are slightly sparkling (*espumantes*). The whites have a slightly darkish straw color, with a heavy, rather spicy nose. They go well with fish, pasta, and pâtés. One of the biggest names in the region is Aliança, although several others such as São Domingos and Frei João are worth tracking down. The hotel at Buçaco has its own wines in an extensive cellar.

The Lafões region is just south of the Douro. Its name derives from the Moorish expression *Alafões* ("two brothers"), which refers to the two hills named *Castelo* and *Lafões*. Vines are cultivated along terraces. Red wines are acidic and age well. The fruity whites are very low in alcohol, rich in malic acid, and have a soft bubbly touch that recalls Minho's *vinho verde*. Look for Quinta da Comenda.

Also south of the Douro, and east of the Lafões, the mountainous Dão region is crossed by the valleys of the Dão, Mondego, and Alva rivers. The climate is capricious—cold, wet winters, scorchingly hot summers. Unlike the sandy or clay soils to the south, the terrain is made up of granite and schist, a rock that shatters easily. Much of the wine here is red and is matured in oak casks for at least 18 months before being bottled. When mature, Dão wines have a dark reddish-brown color—almost the hue of garnets—a "complex" nose, and a lasting velvety taste. They're best drunk at room temperature after being allowed to breathe well, and they go with roast lamb and pork. Look for São Domingos, Terras Altas, and Porta dos Cavaleiros, or any of the labels where "Dão" precedes the name of the supplier—Dão Aliança, Dão Caves Velhas, Dão Serra, or Dão Fundação. Dão whites are less common. They spend shorter times (10 months or so) maturing in casks and have the color of light straw, a full nose, and a dry, earthy flavor. The white Grão Vasco or the Meia Encosta is worth trying.

Douro & Port

The secret of port is found first of all in the nature of the arid, volcanic soil and the hothouse temperature of the Douro Valley. Some 800 years ago, when the father of Afonso Henriques took possession of his domain between Douro and Minho, he planted a stock brought from Burgundy. "Eating lava and drinking sunshine," the Burgundy vines stretched, little by little, to the river's edge. They fought a bitter fight, strangling in ravines, wandering in fits and starts, to force their roots through schistose soil. Nothing but the vine could survive in this torrid pass. With tireless obstinacy, the men of the Douro broke up slate, built terraces with stone retaining walls, struggled against drought and phylloxera (an insect plague that appeared for the first time in 1862 and inflicted great damage to the Douro vineyards), and made the lost valley the most prosperous in Portugal.

The region comes alive during the grape gathering, which lasts for several weeks. (In lower-level vineyards, the gathering is often finished long before the higher plantations are ripe.) From dawn until dusk women fill the baskets that the men carry on their backs, supporting as much as 150 pounds with the aid of a leather band looped over their foreheads. They descend in long files toward the *lagares* at the foot of the slopes and pile the fruit in these enormous vessels, ready for treading. More than 40 varieties of grape go into making port, creating a wide diversity of taste. The harvesters gather about the vats before the must has begun to ferment; the atmosphere is steamy, the feverish excitement of new wine induces singing and dancing. In spring the young wine goes down by road to the lodges in Vila Nova de Gaia. Since the building of a dam across the river the transporting of wine in traditional *rabelos,* boats that look somewhat like ancient Phoenician craft, has ceased.

Port, born as it is of a soil rich in schist, can be divided into two major categories: ruby and tawny. Ruby are wines where the evolution of their deep red color is restrained to maintain the fruit and strength of a young wine. This is the type of wine that you will find in the following categories, in ascending order of quality: Ruby, Reserve, Late Bottled Vintage (LBV), and Vintage. The finest category wines, especially Vintage, followed by LBV, are good for storing as they age well in bottle.

Tawny wines are made from a combination of different wines that have aged for different lengths of time in casks or in vats. With age, the color of the wine slowly develops into tawny, medium tawny, or light tawny, with a bouquet of dried fruits and wood; the older the wine, the stronger these aromas. The present categories for this type of port are: Tawny, Tawny Reserve, and Tawny with an indication of age (10, 20, 30, and 40 years old). A *colheita* is made from wines of a single year that are similar to an aged Tawny of the same age. These wines are ready to drink when they are bottled. Instituto do Vinho do Porto recommends a Tawny with an indication of age and colheita.

Vintage and Late Bottled Vintage (LBV) ports usually begin aging in casks. Vintages age for 2 to 3 years, and Late Bottled Vintages ages for 4 to 6. After these wines are bottled, characteristics improve considerably as their bouquet develops with little possibility of oxidation. The wine's longevity, due to their wealth of polyphenols, is extremely high, usually a maximum of about 20 years in the case of Vintage and of about 5 years in the case of LBV, although these frequently continue to improve for many more years.

For a long time, when England was the biggest market for port, the first choice was given to full-bodied tawnies; these were served at the end of dinner, with cheese or an apple and walnuts. However, there's a lot to be said for the white ports, either sweet, as an after-dinner drink, or dry, as an aperitif with ice and a twist of lemon.

In Porto you can visit a lodge to learn more about port, taste it, and maybe buy a bottle. Seeing these huge old cellars and finding out about the long, fascinating history of port is a memorable experience. Language won't be a problem, as there has been an alliance for more than 200 years between the English and Portuguese in the port trade, and many of the families are bilingual.

Not all the wine produced in the Douro region is port. The reds here are of a deep ruby color, extremely fruity, and with a rounded taste. They go well with richer foods, a variety of meats, casseroles, and stews—anything that tends to be well flavored with herbs. The whites are dry, by and large, and have a pleasant pale-yellow color with a full nose. They go well with salads, hors d'oeuvres, and chicken dishes. Contact **Instituto do Vinho do Porto** (⊕ www.ivp.pt).

Vinho Verde
Portugal's largest demarcated region amounts to 15% of Portugal's vineyards. It is divided into six subregions: Monção, Lima, Amarante, Basto, Braga, and Penafiel. Inland from the coast and threaded by a sequence of westward-flowing rivers, the region has a fairly mild climate and the country's highest rainfall. The vineyards here are often terraced, climbing hillsides away from the rivers like agricultural fortifications. In places they march alongside and arch over roads, the vines held up on colonnaded rows of pillars. The grapes hang so high they ripen in direct sunlight without any rising heat from the ground.

The name vinho verde, which translates as "green wine," refers not to the wine's color but to the fact that it's not aged. If you enjoy wine purely as a refreshing, mildly intoxicating beverage, vinho verde is *the* drink—gently sparkling (what the experts call *pétillant*), with a delicate fruity flavor, it embodies the coolness and fragrance of summer gardens. Vinho verde goes well with any kind of seafood. The reds are important to the region, but will mostly be found on their home ground; they don't travel much. They're also refreshingly thirst quenching, sharp rather than heavy, with a vermilion-to-purple color. They go ideally with any meat dish. Look for Alvarinho and Quinta de São Claudio.

Madeira
Like port, Madeira—the wine and its preparation—is a way of life, and a way of life in which Portuguese and British families are bound together. When Charles II married Catherine of Bragança in 1662 he, perhaps foolishly, declined to accept the island, which was offered as part of her dowry. Madeiran soil is volcanic, and its beaches, such as they are, are black. The temperate climate here, which can be humid in summer, provides exactly the conditions in which vines can thrive—although they seldom grow below 300 feet above sea level; that warmer zone is taken up by bananas and sugarcane.

Madeira is a fortified wine, and most often blended. Boal and Malmsey or Malvasia styles are sweet and heavy, and make excellent dessert wines; Verdelho, not so sweet, is a nice alternative to sherry; and Sercial, dry and light, makes an excellent aperitif. All are attractive—particularly when they're really aged—occasional wines. The labels to look for—and they date back in some cases for a couple of centuries—include Blandy, Cossart Gordon, Rutherford and Miles, Leacock, and Miles and Luís Gomes. A visit to a wine lodge in Funchal is an educational and delectable way to spend a couple of hours.

The Azores

Some say vines on the Azores were brought from Cyprus in 1470, others say the first vines came from Madeira. It will always be an unresolved matter. Just as on Madeira, the Azorean soil is volcanic, but wine produced in Pico, mainly white, is quite liquorous and full-bodied, with a spicy, complex aroma. Two other islands produce wine: Terceira, home to *Biscoitos* wine, and Graciosa. Try Terras de Lava from Pico.

PORTUGUESE WINE TERMS

Adamado	Medium sweet	*Generoso*	A sweet dessert wine, highly alcoholic
Adega	Wine vault	*Meio seco*	Medium dry
Adega cooperativa	Wine cooperative	*Região demarcada*	Demarcated region
Aguardente	Brandy	*Rosado*	Rosé
Branco	White	*Seco*	Dry
Bruto	Extra dry (for sparkling wines)	*Tinto*	Red
Caves	Wine cellars	*Velho*	Old
Colheita	Grape harvest (thus a vintage, e.g., Colh. 1980)	*Vinho da casa*	House wine
Doce	Sweet	*Vinho da mesa*	Table wine
Espumante	Sparkling wine	*Vinho do porto*	Port
Garrafeira or *Reserva*	Fine, mature wine, or a special vintage		

PORTUGUESE VOCABULARY

If you have reading knowledge of Spanish and/or French, you will find Portuguese easy to read. Portuguese pronunciation, however, can be somewhat tricky. Despite obvious similarities in Spanish and Portuguese spelling and syntax, the Portuguese sounds are a far cry—almost literally so—from their ostensible Spanish equivalents. Some of the main peculiarities of Portuguese phonetics are the following.

Nasalized vowels: If you have some idea of French pronunciation, these shouldn't give you too much trouble. The closest approach is that of the French *accent du Midi,* as spoken by people in Marseille and Provence, or perhaps an American Midwest twang will help. Try pronouncing *an, am, en, em, in, om, un,* etc., with a sustained *ng* sound (e.g., *bom = bong,* etc.).

Another aspect of Portuguese phonetics is the vowels and diphthongs written with the tilde: *ã, ão, ães.* The Portuguese word for wool, *lã,* sounds roughly like the French word *lin,* with the *-in* resembling the *an* in the English word "any," but nasalized. The suffix "-tion" on such English words as "information" becomes in Portuguese spelling *-ção,* pronounced *-sa-on,* with the *-on* nasalized: *Informação,* for example. These words form their plurals by changing the suffix to *-çoes,* which sounds like "*-son-ech*" (the *ch* here resembling a cross between the English *sh* and the German *ch:* hence *informações*).

The cedilla occurring under the "c" serves exactly the same purpose as in French: It transforms the "c" into a *ss* sound in front of the three so-called "hard" vowels ("a," "o," and "u"): e.g., *graça, Açores, açúcar.* The letter "c" occurring without a cedilla in front of these three vowels automatically has the sound of "k": *pico, mercado, curto.* The letter "c" followed by "e" or "i" is always *ss,* and hence needs no cedilla: *nacional, Graciosa, Terceira.*

The letter "j" sounds like the "s" in the English word "pleasure." So does "g" except when the latter is followed by one of the "hard" vowels: hence, *generoso, gigantesco, Jerónimo, azulejos, Jorge,* etc.

The spelling *nh* is rendered like the *ny* in "canyon": e.g., *senhora.*

The spelling *lh* is somewhere in between the *l* and the *y* sounds in "million": e.g., *Batalha.*

In the matter of syllabic stress, Portuguese obeys the two basic Spanish principles: (1) in words ending in a vowel, or in "n" or "s," the tonic accent falls on the next-to-the-last syllable: *fado, mercado, azulejos;* (2) in words ending in consonants other than "n" or "s," the stress falls on the last syllable: *favor, nacional.* Words in which the syllabic stress does not conform to the two above rules must be written with an acute accent to indicate the proper pronunciation: *sábado, república, politécnico.*

Numbers

1	um, uma
2	dois, duas
3	três
4	quatro
5	cinco
6	seis
7	sete
8	oito
9	nove
10	dez
11	onze
12	doze
13	treze
14	catorze
15	quinze
16	dezaseis
17	dezasete
18	dezoito
19	dezanove
20	vinte
21	vinte e um
22	vinte e dois
30	trinta
40	quarenta
50	cinquenta
60	sessenta
70	setenta
80	oitenta
90	noventa
100	cem
110	cento e dez
200	duzentos
1,000	mil
1,500	mil e quinhentos

Days of the Week

Monday	Segunda-feira
Tuesday	Terça-feira
Wednesday	Quarta-feira

Thursday	Quinta-feira
Friday	Sexta-feira
Saturday	Sábado
Sunday	Domingo

Months

January	Janeiro
February	Fevereiro
March	Março
April	Abril
May	Maio
June	Junho
July	Julho
August	Agosto
September	Setembro
October	Outubro
November	Novembro
December	Dezembro

Useful Phrases

Do you speak English?	Fala Inglês?
Yes	Sim
No	Não
Please	Por favor
Thank you	Obrigado/a
Thank you very much	Muito obrigado/a
Excuse me, sorry	Desculpe, Com licença
I'm sorry	Desculpe-me
Good morning or good day	Bom dia
Good afternoon	Boa tarde
Good evening or good night	Boa noite
Goodbye	Adeus
How are you?	Como está?
How do you say in Portuguese?	Como se diz em Português?
Tourist Office	Turismo
Fine	Optimo
Very good	Muito bem (muito bom)
It's all right	Está bem
Good luck	Felicidades (boa sorte)
Hello	Olá
Come back soon	Até breve

Where is the hotel?	Onde é o hotel?
How much does this cost?	Quanto custa?
How do you feel?	Como se sente?
How goes it?	Que tal?
Pleased to meet you	Muito prazer em o (a) conhecer
The pleasure is mine	O prazer é meu
I have the pleasure of introducing Mr., Miss, Mrs., or Ms. . . .	Tenho o prazer de lhe apresentar o senhor, a senhora . . .
I like it very much	Gosto muito
I don't like it	Não gosto
Don't mention it	De nada
Pardon me	Perdão
Are you ready?	Está pronto?
I am ready	Estou pronto
Welcome	Seja benvindo
What time is it?	Que horas são?
I am glad to see you	Muito prazer em o (a) ver
I don't understand	Não entendo
Please speak slowly	Fale lentamente por favor
I understand (or) It is clear	Compreendo (or) Está claro
Whenever you please	Quando quizer
Please wait	Faça favor de esperar
Toilet	Casa de banho
I will be a little late	Chegarei um pouco atrasado
I don't know	Não sei
Is this seat free?	Está vago este lugar?
Would you please direct me to . . . ?	Por favor indique-me . . . ?
Where is the station, museum . . . ?	Onde fica a estação, museu . . . ?
I am American, British	Eu sou Americano, Inglês
It's very kind of you	É muito amavel
Please sit down	Por favor sente-se

Sundries

cigar, cigarette	charuto, cigarro
matches	fosforos
dictionary	dicionário
key	chave
razor blades	laminas de barbear
shaving cream	creme de barbear

soap	sabonete
map	mapa
tampons	tampões
sanitary pads	pensos higiénicos
newspaper	jornal
magazine	revista
telephone	telefone
envelopes	envelopes
writing paper	papel de carta
airmail writing paper	papel de carta de avião
postcard	postal
stamps	selos

Merchants

bakery	padaria
bookshop	livraria
butcher's	talho
delicatessen	charutaria
dry cleaner's	limpeza a seco
grocery	mercearia
hairdresser, barber	cabeleireiro, barbeiro
laundry	lavandaria
shoemaker	sapateiro
supermarket	supermercado

Emergencies/Medical

ill, sick	doente
I am ill	Estou doente
I have a fever	Tenho febre
My wife/husband/child is ill	Minha mulher/marido/criança está doente
doctor	doutor/médico
nurse	enfermeira/o
prescription	receita
pharmacist/chemist	farmacia
Please fetch/call a doctor	Por favor, chame o doutor/medico
accident	acidente
road accident	acidente na estrada
Where is the nearest hospital?	Onde é o hospital mais proximo?
Where is the American/British Hospital?	Onde é o hospital Americano/Britanico?

dentist	dentista
X-ray	Raios-X
aspirin	aspirina
painkiller	analgésico
bandage	ligadura
ointment for bites/stings	pomada para picadas
cough mixture	xarope para a tosse
laxative	laxativo
thermometer	termómetro

On the Move

plane	avião
train	comboio
boat	barco
taxi	taxi
car	carro/automovel
bus	autocarro
seat	assento/lugar
reservation	reserva
smoking/no-smoking compartment	compartimento para fumadores/ não fumadores
rail station	estação caminho de ferro
subway station	estação do Metropolitano
airport	aeroporto
harbor	estação mártima
town terminal	estação/terminal
shuttle bus/train	autocarro/comboio com ligação constante
sleeper	cama
couchette	beliche
porter	bagageiro
baggage/luggage	bagagem
baggage trolley	carrinho de bagagem
single ticket	bilhete de ida
return ticket	bilhete de ida e volta
first class	primeira classe
second class	segunda classe
When does the train leave?	A que horas sai o comboio?
What time does the train arrive at . . . ?	A que horas chega o comboio a . . . ?

Portugal
Essentials

PLANNING TOOLS, EXPERT INSIGHT, GREAT CONTACTS

There are planners, and there are those who fly by the seat of their pants. We happily place ourselves among the planners. Our writers and editors try to anticipate all the issues you may face before and during any journey, and then they do their research. This section is the product of their efforts. Use it to get excited about your trip to Portugal, to inform your travel planning, or to guide you on the road should the seat of your pants start to feel threadbare.

GETTING STARTED

We're really proud of our Web site: Fodors.com is a great place to begin any journey. Scan Travel Wire for suggested itineraries, travel deals, restaurant and hotel openings, and other up-to-the-minute info. Check out Booking to research prices and book plane tickets, hotel rooms, rental cars, and vacation packages. Head to Talk for on-the-ground pointers from travelers who frequent our message boards. You can also link to loads of other travel-related resources.

▌ RESOURCES

ONLINE TRAVEL TOOLS

You'll find general and business information at ⊕ www.portugal.org, which has a link to the slow-to-load but rich-in-wisdom ⊕ www.portugalinsite.com—the official tourism site. You can order tourist-board brochures with information on a variety of travel-related topics and activities through ⊕ www.orderportugal.com (for U.S. and Canadian citizens only).

The Institute of Portuguese Museums (⊕ www.ipmuseus.pt) encompasses 29 museums and has an English-language option on its Web site. The Portuguese National Trust has a site (⊕ www.ippar.pt) with information (in Portuguese) on the many historic buildings and monuments that it oversees. The sites www.portugal-info.net, www.portugaltravelguide.com, and www.portugalvirtual.com provide quick access to a variety of information, including many links.

ALL ABOUT PORTUGAL

An interesting Web site that may save you money with its publicized deals on accommodation, flights, and so on, is www.portugal-secrets.com. For a cultural look at the country from an immigrant's point of view, check out www.portcult.com. If you are interested in Portuguese literature (and speak Portuguese), click on www.

instituto-camoes.pt/cvc, or, if architecture and monuments are more your thing, check out www.360portugal.com.

Currency Conversion Google ⊕ www.google.com does currency conversion. Just type in the amount you want to convert and an explanation of how you want it converted (e.g., "14 Swiss francs in dollars"), and then voilà. **Oanda.com** ⊕ www.oanda.com also allows you to print out a handy table with the current day's conversion rates. **XE.com** ⊕ www.xe.com is a good currency conversion Web site.

Safety Transportation Security Administration (TSA) ⊕ www.tsa.gov.

Time Zones Timeanddate.com ⊕ www.timeanddate.com/worldclock can help you figure out the correct time anywhere in the world.

Weather Accuweather.com ⊕ www.accuweather.com has especially good coverage of hurricanes. **Weather.com** ⊕ www.weather.com is the Web site for the Weather Channel.

Other Resources CIA World Factbook ⊕ www.odci.gov/cia/publications/factbook/index.html has profiles of every country in the world. It's a good source if you need some quick facts and figures.

VISITOR INFORMATION

Portuguese National Tourist Offices Canada ✉ 60 Bloor St. W, Suite 1005, Toronto, Ontario M4W 3BS ☎ 416/921-1353. **Portuguese National Tourist Office Web site** ⊕ www.portugal.org. **United Kingdom** ✉ 22-25A Sackville St., London W1X 1DE ☎ 020/7494-1441. **United States** ✉ 590 5th Ave., 4th fl., New York, NY 10036 ☎ 212/354-4403.

▌ THINGS TO CONSIDER

GOVERNMENT ADVISORIES

As different countries have different world views, look at travel advisories from a range of governments to get more of a sense of what's going on out there. And be sure to parse the language carefully. For example, a warning to "avoid all travel" carries more weight than one urging you to "avoid nonessential travel," and both are much stronger than a plea to "exercise caution." A U.S. government travel warning is more permanent (though not necessarily more serious) than a so-called public announcement, which carries an expiration date.

■ TIP→ **If you're a U.S. citizen traveling abroad, consider registering online with the State Department (https://travelregistration. state.gov/ibrs/), so the government will know to look for you should a crisis occur in the country you're visiting. If you travel frequently, look into the TSA's Registered Traveler program. The program, which is still being tested in several U.S. airports, is designed to cut down on gridlock at security checkpoints by allowing prescreened travelers to pass quickly through kiosks that scan an iris and/or a fingerprint. How sci-fi is that?**

The U.S. Department of State's Web site has more than just travel warnings and advisories. The consular information sheets issued for every country have general safety tips, entry requirements (though be sure to verify these with the country's embassy), and other useful details.

General Information & Warnings Australian Department of Foreign Affairs & Trade ⊕ www.smartraveller.gov.au. **Consular Affairs Bureau of Canada** ⊕ www.voyage.gc. ca. **U.K. Foreign & Commonwealth Office** ⊕ www.fco.gov.uk/travel. **U.S. Department of State** ⊕ www.travel.state.gov.

GEAR

Older generations of Portuguese citizens tend to dress up more than their counterparts in the United States or the United Kingdom. That said, attitudes toward clothes have become more relaxed in recent years among the younger generations. Jeans, however, are generally still paired with a collared shirt and, if necessary, a sweater or jacket. Dressier outfits are needed for more expensive restau-

rants, nightclubs, and fado houses, though, and people still frown on shorts in churches. Away from the beaches, wearing bathing suits on the street or in restaurants and shops is not considered good taste. Sightseeing calls for casual, comfortable clothing (well-broken-in low-heel shoes, for example). Summer can be brutally hot; spring and fall, mild to chilly; and winter, cold and rainy. Sunscreen and sunglasses are a good idea any time of the year, since the sun in Portugal is very bright.

SHIPPING LUGGAGE AHEAD

Imagine globe-trotting with only a carry-on in tow. Shipping your luggage in advance via an air-freight service is a great way to cut down on backaches, hassles, and stress—especially if your packing list includes strollers, carseats, and so on. There are some things to be aware of, though. First, research carry-on restrictions; if you absolutely need something that's isn't practical to ship and isn't allowed in carry-ons, this strategy isn't for you. Second, plan to send your bags several days in advance to U.S. destinations and as much as two weeks in advance to some international destinations. Third, plan to spend some money: it will cost least $100 to send a small piece of luggage, a golf bag, or a pair of skis to a domestic destination, much more to places overseas. Some people use Federal Express to ship their bags, but this can cost even more than air-freight services. All these services insure your bag (for most, the limit is $1,000, but you should verify that amount); you can, however, purchase additional insurance for about $1 per $100 of value.

PACKING 101

Why do some people travel with a convoy of huge suitcases yet never have a thing to wear? How do others pack a duffle with a week's worth of outfits *and* supplies for every contingency? We realize that packing is a matter of style, but there's a lot to be said for traveling light. These tips help fight the battle of the bulging bag.

MAKE A LIST. In a recent Fodor's survey, 29% of respondents said they make lists (and often pack) a week before a trip. You can use your list to pack and to repack at the end of your trip. It can also serve as record of the contents of your suitcase—in case it disappears in transit.

THINK IT THROUGH. What's the weather like? Is this a business trip? A cruise? Going abroad? In some places dress may be more or less conservative than you're used to. As you create your itinerary, note outfits next to each activity (don't forget accessories).

EDIT YOUR WARDROBE. Plan to wear everything twice (better yet, thrice) and to do laundry along the way. Stick to one basic look—urban chic, sporty casual, and so on. Build around one or two neutrals and an accent (e.g., black, white, and olive green). Women can freshen looks by changing scarves or jewelry. For a week's trip, you can look smashing with three bottoms, four or five tops, a sweater, and a jacket.

BE PRACTICAL. Put comfortable shoes atop your list. (Did we need to say this?) Pack lightweight, wrinkle-resistent, compact, washable items. (Or this?) Stack and roll clothes, so they'll wrinkle less. Unless you're on a guided tour or a cruise, select luggage you can readily carry. Porters, like good butlers, are hard to find these days.

CHECK WEIGHT AND SIZE LIMITATIONS. In the United States you may be charged extra for checked bags weighing more than 50 pounds. Abroad some airlines don't allow you to check bags over 60 to 70 pounds, or they charge outrageous fees for every excess pound—or bag. Carry-on size limitations can be stringent, too.

CHECK CARRY-ON RESTRICTIONS. Research restrictions with the TSA. Rules vary abroad, so check them with your airline if you're traveling overseas on a foreign carrier. Consider packing all but essentials (travel documents, prescription meds, wallet) in checked luggage. This leads to a "pack only what you can afford to lose" approach that might help you streamline.

RETHINK VALUABLES. On U.S. flights, airlines are liable for only about $2,800 per person for bags. On international flights, the liability limit is around $635 per bag. But items like computers, cameras, and jewelry aren't covered, and as gadgetry can go on and off the list of carry-on no-no's, you can't count on keeping things safe by keeping them close. Although comprehensive travel policies may cover luggage, the liability limit is often a pittance. Your home-owner's policy may cover you sufficiently when you travel—or not.

LOCK IT UP. If you must pack valuables, use TSA-approved locks (about $10) that can be unlocked by all U.S. security personnel.

TAG IT. Always tag your luggage; use your business address if you don't want people to know your home address. Put the same information (and a copy of your itinerary) inside your luggage, too.

REPORT PROBLEMS IMMEDIATELY. If your bags—or things inside them—are damaged or go astray, file a written claim with your airline *before leaving the airport*. If the airline is at fault, it may give you money for essentials until your luggage arrives. Most lost bags are found within 48 hours, so alert the airline to your whereabouts for two or three days. If your bag was opened for security reasons in the United States and something is missing, file a claim with the TSA.

Luggage Concierge ☎ 800/288-9818 ⊕ www.luggageconcierge.com. **Luggage Express** ☎ 866/744-7224 ⊕ www. usxpluggageexpress.com. **Luggage Free** ☎ 800/361-6871 ⊕ www.luggagefree.com. **Sports Express** ☎ 800/357-4174 ⊕ www. sportsexpress.com specializes in shipping golf clubs and other sports equipment. **Virtual Bellhop** ☎ 877/235-5467 ⊕ www. virtualbellhop.com.

PASSPORTS & VISAS

Citizens of Australia, Canada, New Zealand, and the United States need a valid passport to enter Portugal for stays of up to 60 days. Visas are required for longer stays and, in some instances, for visits to other countries in addition to Portugal. Citizens of the European Union need a valid passport but can stay indefinitely.

U.S. citizens can stay in Portugal for up to 90 days in any half year without a visa. If you are planning to stay longer you must apply for a visa in advance; you can do it in person or by mail. When you apply by mail, you send your passport to a designated consulate, where your passport will be examined and the visa issued. Expediters—usually the same ones who handle expedited passport applications—can do all the work to obtain your visa for you; however, there's always an additional cost (often more than $50 per visa).

Most visas limit you to a single trip—basically during the actual dates of your planned vacation. Other visas allow you to visit as many times as you wish for a specific period of time. Remember that requirements change, sometimes at the drop of a hat, and the burden is on you to make sure that you have the appropriate visas. Otherwise, you'll be turned away at the airport or, worse, deported after you arrive in the country. No company or travel insurer gives refunds if your travel plans are disrupted because you didn't have the correct visa.

PASSPORTS

We're always surprised at how few Americans have passports—only 25% at this writing. This number is expected to grow in coming years, when it becomes impossible to reenter the United States from trips to neighboring Canada or Mexico without one. Remember this: A passport verifies both your identity and nationality—a great reason to have one.

U.S. passports are valid for 10 years. You must apply in person if you're getting a passport for the first time; if your previous passport was lost, stolen, or damaged; or if your previous passport has expired and was issued more than 15 years ago or when you were under 16. All children under 18 must appear in person to apply for or renew a passport. Both parents must accompany any child under 14 (or send a notarized statement with their permission) and provide proof of their relationship to the child.

■ TIP→ Before your trip, make two copies of your passport's data page (one for someone at home and another for you to carry separately). Or scan the page and e-mail it to someone at home and/or yourself.

There are 13 regional passport offices, as well as 7,000 passport acceptance facilities in post offices, public libraries, and other governmental offices. If you're renewing a passport, you can do so by mail. Forms are available at passport acceptance facilities and online.

The cost to apply for a new passport is $97 for adults, $82 for children under 16; renewals are $67. Allow six weeks for processing, both for first-time passports and renewals. For an expediting fee of $60 you can reduce this time to about two weeks. If your trip is less than two weeks away, you can get a passport even more rapidly by going to a passport office with the necessary documentation. Private expediters can get things done in as little as 48 hours, but charge hefty fees for their services.

VISAS

A visa is essentially formal permission to enter a country. Visas allow countries to keep track of you and other visitors—and generate revenue (from application fees). You *always* need a visa to enter a foreign country; however, many countries routinely issue tourist visas on arrival, particularly to U.S. citizens. When your passport is stamped or scanned in the immigration line, you're actually being issued a visa. Sometimes you have to stand in a separate line and pay a small fee to get your stamp before going through immigration, but you can still do this at the airport on arrival. Getting a visa isn't always that easy. Some countries require that you arrange for one in advance of your trip. There's usually—but not always—a fee involved, and said fee may be nominal ($10 or less) or substantial ($100 or more).

If you must apply for a visa in advance, you can usually do it in person or by mail. When you apply by mail, you send your passport to a designated consulate, where your passport will be examined and the visa issued. Expediters—usually the same ones who handle expedited passport applications—can do all the work of obtaining your visa for you; however, there's always an additional cost (often more than $50 per visa).

U.S. Passport Information U.S. Department of State ☎ 877/487-2778 ⊕ http://travel. state.gov/passport.

U.S. Passport & Visa Expediters A. Briggs Passport & Visa Expeditors ☎ 800/806-0581 or 202/464-3000 ⊕ www.abriggs.com. **American Passport Express** ☎ 800/455-5166 or 603/559-9888 ⊕ www. americanpassport.com. **Passport Express** ☎ 800/362-8196 or 401/272-4612 ⊕ www. passportexpress.com. **Travel Document Systems** ☎ 800/874-5100 or 202/638-3800 ⊕ www.traveldocs.com. **Travel the World Visas** ☎ 866/886-8472 or 301/495-7700 ⊕ www.world-visa.com.

GENERAL REQUIREMENTS FOR PORTUGAL	
Passport	Must be valid for six months after date of arrival.
Visa	Required for Americans ($100)
Vaccinations	Yellow fever (recommended for Madeira, Azores) and diphtheria as needed
Driving	International Driving Permit; CDW is compulsory on car rentals and will be included in the quoted price
Departure Tax	US$20, payable in cash only

SHOTS & MEDICATIONS

No special shots are required before visiting Portugal (except for yellow-fever shots if you want to visit Madeira and have come from an infected area). You might consider a tetanus-diphtheria booster if you haven't had one recently.

■ TIP→ **If you travel a lot internationally—particularly to developing nations—refer to the CDC's** *Health Information for International Travel* **(aka Traveler's Health Yellow Book). Info from it is posted on the CDC Web site (www. cdc.gov/travel/yb), or you can buy a copy from your local bookstore for $24.95.**

For more information *see* Health *under* On the Ground in Portugal, *below.*

Health Warnings National Centers for Disease Control & Prevention (CDC) ☎ 877/394-8747 international travelers' health line ⊕ www.cdc.gov/travel. **World Health Organization** (WHO) ⊕ www.who.int.

TRIP INSURANCE

What kind of coverage do you honestly need? Do you even need trip insurance at all? Take a deep breath and read on.

We believe that comprehensive trip insurance is especially valuable if you're booking a very expensive or complicated trip (particularly to an isolated region) or if you're booking far in advance. Who knows what could happen six months down the road? But whether or not you get insurance has more to do with how comfortable you are assuming all that risk yourself.

Comprehensive travel policies typically cover trip-cancellation and interruption, letting you cancel or cut your trip short because of a personal emergency, illness, or, in some cases, acts of terrorism in your destination. Such policies also cover evacuation and medical care. Some also cover you for trip delays because of bad weather or mechanical problems as well as for lost or delayed baggage. Another type of coverage to look for is financial default—that is, when your trip is disrupted because a tour operator, airline, or cruise line goes out of business. Generally you must buy this when you book your trip or shortly thereafter, and it's only available to you if your operator isn't on a list of excluded companies.

If you're going abroad, consider buying medical-only coverage at the very least. Neither Medicare nor some private insurers cover medical expenses anywhere outside the United States besides Mexico and Canada (including time aboard a cruise ship, even if it leaves from a U.S. port). Medical-only policies typically reimburse you for medical care (excluding that related to preexisting conditions) and hospitalization abroad, and provide for evacuation. You still have to pay the bills and await reimbursement from the insurer, though.

Expect comprehensive travel insurance policies to cost about 4% to 7% of the total price of your trip (it's more like 12% if you're over age 70). A medical-only policy may or may not be cheaper than a comprehensive policy. Always read the fine print of your policy to make sure that you are covered for the risks that are of most concern to you. Compare several policies to make sure you're getting the best price and range of coverage available.

■ TIP➔ OK. You know you can save a bundle on trips to warm-weather destinations by traveling in rainy season. But there's also a chance that a severe storm will disrupt your plans. The solution? Look for hotels and resorts that offer storm/hurricane guarantees. Although they rarely allow refunds, most guarantees do let you rebook later if a storm strikes.

Trip Insurance Resources

INSURANCE COMPARISON SITES		
Insure My Trip.com	800/487-4722	www.insuremytrip.com
Square Mouth.com	800/240-0369	www.quotetravelinsurance.com
COMPREHENSIVE TRAVEL INSURERS		
Access America	866/807-3982	www.accessamerica.com
CSA Travel Protection	800/873-9855	www.csatravelprotection.com
HTH Worldwide	610/254-8700 or 888/243-2358	www.hthworldwide.com
Travelex Insurance	888/457-4602	www.travelex-insurance.com
Travel Guard International	715/345-0505 or 800/826-4919	www.travelguard.com
Travel Insured International	800/243-3174	www.travelinsured.com
MEDICAL-ONLY INSURERS		
International Medical Group	800/628-4664	www.imgglobal.com
International SOS	215/942-8000 or 713/521-7611	www.internationalsos.com
Wallach & Company	800/237-6615 or 504/687-3166	www.wallach.com

BOOKING YOUR TRIP

Unless your cousin is a travel agent, you're probably among the millions of people who make most of their travel arrangements online. But have you ever wondered just what the differences are between an online travel agent (a Web site through which you make reservations instead of going directly to the airline, hotel, or car-rental company), a discounter (a firm that does a high volume of business with a hotel chain or airline and accordingly gets good prices), a wholesaler (one that makes cheap reservations in bulk and then resells them to people like you), and an aggregator (one that compares all the offerings so you don't have to)? Is it truly better to book directly on an airline or hotel Web site? And when does a real live travel agent come in handy?

ONLINE

You really have to shop around. A travel wholesaler such as Hotels.com or Hotel-Club.net can be a source of good rates, as can discounters such as Hotwire or Price-line, particularly if you can bid for your hotel room or airfare. Indeed, such sites sometimes have deals that are unavailable elsewhere. They do, however, tend to work only with hotel chains (which makes them just plain useless for getting hotel reservations outside major cities) or big airlines (so that often leaves out upstarts like jetBlue and some foreign carriers like Air India). Also, with discounters and wholesalers you must generally prepay, and everything is nonrefundable. And before you fork over the dough, be sure to check the terms and conditions, so you know what a given company will do for you if there's a problem and what you'll have to deal with on your own.

■ TIP→ To be absolutely sure everything was processed correctly, confirm reservations made through online travel agents, discounters, and wholesalers directly with your hotel before leaving home.

Booking engines like Expedia, Traveloc-ity, and Orbitz are actually travel agents, albeit high-volume, online ones. And airline travel packagers like American Airlines Vacations and Virgin Vacations—well, they're travel agents, too. But they may still not work with all the world's hotels.

An aggregator site will search many sites and pull the best prices for airfares, hotels, and rental cars from them. Most aggregators compare the major travel-booking sites such as Expedia, Travelocity, and Orbitz; some also look at airline Web sites, though rarely the sites of smaller budget airlines. Some aggregators also compare other travel products, including complex packages—a good thing, as you can sometimes get the best overall deal by booking an air-and-hotel package.

WITH A TRAVEL AGENT

If you use an agent—brick-and-mortar or virtual—you'll pay a fee for the service. And know that the service you get from some online agents isn't comprehensive. For example Expedia and Travelocity don't search for prices on budget airlines like jetBlue, Southwest, or small foreign carriers. That said, some agents (online or not) *do* have access to fares that are difficult to find otherwise, and the savings can more than make up for any surcharge.

A knowledgeable brick-and-mortar travel agent can be a godsend if you're booking a cruise, a package trip that's not available to you directly, an air pass, or a complicated itinerary including several overseas flights. What's more, travel agents that specialize in a destination may have exclusive access to certain deals and insider information on things such as charter flights. Agents who specialize in types of travelers (senior citizens, gays and lesbians, naturists) or types of trips (cruises, luxury travel, safaris) can also be invaluable.

A top-notch agent planning your trip to Russia will make sure you get the correct

Online Booking Resources

AGGREGATORS		
Kayak	www.kayak.com	looks at cruises and vacation packages.
Mobissimo	www.mobissimo.com	comprehensive airfare search
Qixo	www.qixo.com	compares cruises, vacation packages, and even travel insurance.
Sidestep	www.sidestep.com	compares vacation packages and lists travel deals.
Travelgrove	www.travelgrove.com	compares cruises and packages.
BOOKING ENGINES		
Cheap Tickets	www.cheaptickets.com	a discounter.
Expedia	www.expedia.com	a large online agency that charges a booking fee for airline tickets.
Hotwire	www.hotwire.com	a discounter.
lastminute.com	www.lastminute.com	specializes in last-minute travel; the main site is for the U.K., but it has a link to a U.S. site.
Luxury Link	www.luxurylink.com	has auctions (surprisingly good deals) as well as offers on the high-end side of travel.
Onetravel.com	www.onetravel.com	a discounter for hotels, car rentals, airfares, and packages.
Orbitz	www.orbitz.com	charges a booking fee for airline tickets, but gives a clear breakdown of fees and taxes before you book.
Priceline.com	www.priceline.com	a discounter that also allows bidding.
Travel.com	www.travel.com	allows you to compare its rates with those of other booking engines.
Travelocity	www.travelocity.com	charges a booking fee for airline tickets, but promises good problem resolution.
ONLINE ACCOMMODATIONS		
Hotelbook.com	www.hotelbook.com	focuses on independent hotels worldwide.
Hotel Club	www.hotelclub.net	good for major cities worldwide.
Hotels.com	www.hotels.com	a big Expedia-owned wholesaler that offers rooms in hotels all over the world.
Quikbook	www.quikbook.com	offers "pay when you stay" reservations that let you settle your bill at check out, not when you book.
OTHER RESOURCES		
Bidding For Travel	www.biddingfortravel.com	a good place to figure out what you can get and for how much before you start bidding on, say, Priceline.

10 WAYS TO SAVE

1. Join "frequent guest" programs. You may get preferential treatment in room choice and/or upgrades in your favorite chains.

2. Call direct. You can sometimes get a better price if you call a hotel's local toll-free number (if available) rather than a central reservations number.

3. Check online. Check hotel Web sites, as not all chains are represented on all travel sites.

4. Look for specials. Always inquire about packages and corporate rates.

5. Look for price guarantees. For overseas trips, look for guaranteed rates. With your rate locked in you won't pay more, even if the price goes up in the local currency.

6. Look for weekend deals at business hotels. High-end chains catering to business travelers are often busy only on weekdays; to fill rooms they often drop rates dramatically on weekends.

7. Ask about taxes. Verify whether local hotel taxes are included in quoted rates. In some places taxes can add 20% or more to your bill.

8. Read the fine print. Watch for add-ons, including resort fees, energy surcharges, and "convenience" fees for such things as unlimited local phone service you won't use or a free newspaper in a language you can't read.

9. Know when to go. If your destination's high season is December through April and you're trying to book, say, in late April, you might save money by changing your dates by a week or two. Ask when rates go down, though: if your dates straddle peak and non-peak seasons, a property may still charge peak-season rates for the entire stay.

10. Weigh your options (we can't say this enough). Weigh transportation times and costs against the savings of staying in a hotel that's cheaper because it's out of the way.

visa application and complete it on time; the one booking your cruise may get you a cabin upgrade or arrange to have bottle of champagne chilling in your cabin when you embark. And complain about the surcharges all you like, but when things don't work out the way you'd hoped, it's nice to have an agent to put things right.

■ TIP→ Remember that Expedia, Travelocity, and Orbitz are travel agents, not just booking engines. To resolve any problems with a reservation made through these companies, contact them first.

If it is your first trip to Portugal or you are combining this trip with a visit to other European countries, you may want to let a travel agent book your flights, although in these days of Internet travel you'll undoubtedly pay more for the convenience. If you do opt to go it alone, try to use the same airline for your transfers in case of delay on one leg of the journey.

Agent Resources American Society of Travel Agents ☎ 703/739-2782 ⊕ www.travelsense. org.

Portugal Travel Agents Intervisa ⊠ Praça ona Filipa de Lencastre 1, Porto ☎ 222/079200. **Tagus** ⊠ Rua Campo Alegre 261, Lisbon ☎ 226/094146. **Top Atlântico** ⊠ Rua Alferes Malheiro 96, Lisbon ☎ 222/074020. **Wasteels** ⊠ Rua Pinto Bessa 29, Lisbon ☎ 225/194230.

▌ ACCOMMODATIONS

There are many different types of lodging options in Portugal. Many who travel to the Algarve region book themselves into luxurious resorts and never step outside them thanks to amenities such as a golf course, tennis courts, and entertainment. Though there are international chain hotels in Portugal, *residências* and *pensãos* (simple accommodations with private bathroom and breakfast as the only meal served) in former private homes are just as popular and very affordable. They can be found in cities and rural towns as well. *Pousadas* (inns) are within historic structures, often former castles, and are usually decorated with local crafts or antique reproductions. They still offer modern amenities, such as television.

Most hotels and other lodgings require you to give your credit-card details before they will confirm your reservation. If you don't feel comfortable e-mailing this information, ask if you can fax it (some places even prefer faxes). However you book, get confirmation in writing and have a copy of it handy when you check in.

Be sure you understand the hotel's cancellation policy. Some places allow you to cancel without any kind of penalty—even if you prepaid to secure a discounted rate—if you cancel at least 24 hours in advance. Others require you to cancel a week in advance or penalize you the cost of one night. Small inns and B&Bs are most likely to require you to cancel far in advance. Most hotels allow children under a certain age to stay in their parents' room at no extra charge, but others charge for them as extra adults; find out the cutoff age for discounts.

■ TIP➜ Assume that hotels operate on the European Plan (**EP**, no meals) unless we specify that they use the Breakfast Plan (**BP**, with full breakfast), Continental Plan (**CP**, Continental breakfast), Full American Plan (**FAP**, all meals), Modified American Plan (**MAP**, breakfast and dinner) or are all-inclusive (**AI**, all meals and most activities).

APARTMENT & HOUSE RENTALS

The rental properties in the Algarve are in high demand. Most apartments and villas are privately owned, with a local management company overseeing the advertising, maintenance, and rent collection. Two reliable Algarve-based agencies are Villas & Vacations and Jordan & Nunn. For lists of rental properties and reputable agents elsewhere in Portugal, contact tourist offices. Avoid time-share touts on the street; they'll try to lure you in to view a property with the promise of free vacations and cash. These are often sophisticated (and costly) scams.

Online Booking Resources

At Home Abroad	212/421-9165	www.athomeabroadinc.com
Barclay International Group	516/364-0064 or 800/845-6636	www.barclayweb.com
Drawbridge to Europe	541/482-7778 or 888/268-1148	www.drawbridgetoeurope.com
Homes Away	800/374-6637 or 416/920-1873	www.homesaway.com
Hometours International	865/690-8484	thor.he.net/~hometour
Interhome	954/791-8282 or 800/882-6864	www.interhome.us
Jordan & Nunn	Av. Duarte Pacheco 226, Almancil 8135; 289/399943	www.jordannunn.com
Suzanne B. Cohen & Associates	207/622-0743	www.villaeurope.com
Vacation Home Rentals Worldwide	800/633-3284 or 201/767-9393	www.vhrww.com
Villanet	800/964-1891 or 206/417-3444	www.rentavilla.com
Villas & Apartments Abroad	212/213-6435 or 800/433-3020	www.vaanyc.com
Villas & Vacations	Apartado 3498, Almancil 8135-906; 8135-906; 289/390501	www.villas-vacations.com
Villas International	415/499-9490 or 800/221-2260	www.villasintl.com
Villas of Distinction	800/289-0900 or 707/778-1800	www.villasofdistinction.com
Wimco	800/449-1553	www.wimco.com

BED & BREAKFASTS

Reservation Services **Bed & Breakfast.com** ☎ 800/462-2632 or 512/322-2710 ⊕ www. bedandbreakfast.com also sends out an on-line newsletter. **Bed & Breakfast Inns Online** ☎ 800/215-7365 or 615/868-1946 ⊕ www. bbonline.com. **BnB Finder.com** ☎ 888/547-8226 or 212/432-7693 ⊕ www.bnbfinder.com.

COUNTRY HOUSES

Throughout the country, though particularly in the north, many *solares* (manors) and *casas de campo* (farm- or country houses) have been remodeled to receive small numbers of guests in a venture called Turismo de Habitação (TURIHAB; Country House Tourism). These guesthouses are in bucolic settings, near parks or monuments or in historic *aldeias* (villages). If they are larger properties, such as farmhouses, guests stay in self-contained cottages on the grounds. Breakfast is always included in the price. The Central Nacional de Turismo no Espaço Rural (National Center for Rural Tourism) serves as a clearinghouse for information from several organizations involved in this endeavor.

Central Nacional de Turismo no Espaço Rural ✉ Praça da República, Ponte de Lima 4990 ☎ 258/741672, 258/742827, or 258/742829 ⊕ www.center.pt. **TURIHAB** ⊕ www. turihab.pt.

HOME EXCHANGES

With a direct home exchange you stay in someone else's home while they stay in yours. Some outfits also deal with vacation homes, so you're not actually staying in someone's full-time residence, just their vacant weekend place.

Exchange Clubs **Home Exchange.com** ☎ 800/877-8723 ⊕ www.homeexchange. com; $59.95 for a 1-year online listing. **Home-Link International** ☎ 800/638-3841 ⊕ www. homelink.org; $80 yearly for Web-only membership; $125 includes Web access and two catalogs. **Intervac U.S.** ☎ 800/756-4663 ⊕ www.intervacus.com; $78.88 for Web-only membership; $126 includes Web access and a catalog.

HOSTELS

Hostels offer bare-bones lodging at low, low prices—often in shared dorm rooms with shared baths—to people of all ages, though the primary market is young travelers, especially students. Most hostels serve breakfast; dinner and/or shared cooking facilities may also be available. In some hostels you aren't allowed to be in your room during the day, and there may be a curfew at night. Nevertheless, hostels provide a sense of community, with public rooms where travelers often gather to share stories. Many hostels are affiliated with Hostelling International (HI), an umbrella group of hostel associations with some 4,500 member properties in more than 70 countries. Other hostels are completely independent and may be nothing more than a really cheap hotel.

Membership in any HI association, open to travelers of all ages, allows you to stay in HI-affiliated hostels at member rates. One-year membership is about $28 for adults; hostels charge about $10–$30 per night. Members have priority if the hostel is full; they're also eligible for discounts around the world, even on rail and bus travel in some countries.

There are over 40 hostels in Portugal, and all are affiliated with Hostelling International (HI). Most hostels are open year-round and offer simple clean accommodation; the majority have kitchens and many have cafés and Internet terminals. Some hostels have a curfew of 11 PM or midnight. Overall the hostels are used by students with accommodation in dormitories, although a few have double rooms available for couples for a higher cost. Check Movijovem for information on these.

Hostelling International–USA ☎ 301/495-1240 ⊕ www.hiusa.org. **Movijovem** ☎ 217/232100 in Lisbon ⊕ www.pousadasjuventude. pt.

HOTELS

Portugal has many excellent and reasonably priced hotels, though good properties can be hard to come by in remote inland areas. The government officially grades accommodations with one to five stars or with a category rating. Ratings, which are assigned based on the level of comfort and the number of facilities offered, can be misleading, because quality is difficult to grade. In general, though, the system works.

Most hotel rooms have such basic amenities as a private bathroom and a telephone; those with two or more stars may also have air-conditioning, cable or satellite TV, a minibar, and room service. (Note that all hotels listed in this guide have private bath unless otherwise indicated, although most hotels up to three stars will have a shower, rather than bathtub.) Note that you will also generally have a choice of twin or double (queen-size) bed. There are no king-size beds in Portugal. The Web sites of the Portuguese National Tourist Office and Mais Turismo have search engines for accommodations throughout the country.

High season means not only the summer months, but also the Christmas and New Year's holiday period on Madeira, Easter week throughout the country, and any time a town is holding a festival. In the off-season (generally November through March), however, many hotels reduce their rates by as much as 20%.

SOME USEFUL VOCABULARY

Twin beds	duas camas
Double (queen-size)	duplo
With a bathroom	com banho
With a shower	com duche
With a view	com vista
Is there?	Há
Air-conditioning	ar condicionado
Heating	aquecimento
Television	televisão
Room service	service de quartos

Mais Turismo ⊕ www.hotelguide.pt. **Portuguese National Tourist Office** ✉ 590 5th Ave., New York, NY 10036 ☎ 212/354-4403 or 212/354-4404 ⊕ www.portugalinsite.pt.

POUSADAS

The term *pousada* is derived from the Portuguese verb *pousar* (to rest). Portugal has a network of more than 45 of these state-run hotels, which are in restored castles, palaces, monasteries, convents, and other charming buildings. Each pousada is in a particularly scenic and tranquil part of the country and is tastefully furnished with regional crafts, antiques, and artwork. All have restaurants that serve local specialties; you can stop for a meal or a drink without spending the night. Rates are reasonable, considering that most pousadas are four- or five-star hotels and a stay in one can be the highlight of a visit. They're extremely popular with foreigners and Portuguese alike, and some have 10 or fewer rooms; make reservations well in advance, especially for stays in summer. Also check for seasonal and senior-citizen discounts, which can be as high as 40%. **Keytel International** ✉ 402 Edgeware Rd., London W2 1ED ☎ 020/7616-0330 ⏰ 020/7616-0317 ⊕ www.keytel.co.uk. **Marketing Ahead** ✉ 433 5th Ave., New York, NY 10016 ☎ 800/223-1356 or 212/686-9213 ⊕ www.marketingahead.com. **Pousadas de Portugal** ✉ Av. Santa Joana Princesa 10, Alvalade, Lisbon 1749-090 ☎ 21/844-2001 ⏰ 21/844-2085 ⊕ www.pousadas.pt.

SPAS

Concentrated mostly in the northern half of the country is a profusion of *termas* (thermal springs), whose waters reputedly can cure whatever ails you. In the smaller spas, hotels are rather simple; in the more famous ones, they're first-class. Most are open from May through October. **Associação das Termas de Portugal** ✉ Av. Miguel Bombarda 110-2, Saldanha, Lisbon 1050 ☎ 21/794-0574 ⊕ www.termasdeportugal.pt.

▌ AIRLINE TICKETS

Most domestic airline tickets are electronic; international tickets may be either electronic or paper. With an e-ticket the only thing you receive is an e-mailed receipt citing your itinerary and reservation and ticket numbers. The greatest advantage of an e-ticket is that if you lose your receipt, you can simply print out another copy or ask the airline to do it for you at check-in. You usually pay a surcharge (up to $50) to get a paper ticket, if you can get one at all. The sole advantage of a paper ticket is that it may be easier to endorse over to another airline if your flight is canceled and the airline with which you booked can't accommodate you on another flight.

▌ TIP➡ Discount air passes that let you travel economically in a country or region must often be purchased before you leave home. In some cases you can only get them through a travel agent.

Consider flying to London first and picking up an onward no-frills budget airline or charter flight: you might save money *and* have a wider choice of destinations in Portugal. There are often good deals to Faro, in particular, because the Algarve is popular with British vacationers. In summer, last-minute, round-trip flights have cost as little as $150. From Australia or New Zealand, look for a cheap charter to London or Amsterdam and then a second direct charter to Portugal.

Air Pass Info Budget & Charter Flights
easyJet ⊕ www.easyjet.com. **Monarch** ⊕ www.flymonarch.com. **Ryanair** ⊕ www. ryanair.com.

CHARTER FLIGHTS

Charter companies rent aircraft and offer regularly scheduled flights (usually nonstops). Charter flights are generally cheaper than flights on regular airlines, and they often leave from and travel to a wider variety of airports. For example, you could have a nonstop flight from Columbus, Ohio, to Punta Cana, Dominican Republic, or from Chicago to Dubrovnik, Croatia. You don't, however, have the same protections as with regular airlines. If a charter can't take off for mechanical or other reasons, there usually isn't another plane to take its place. If not enough seats are sold, the flight may be canceled. And if a company goes out of business, you're out of luck (unless, of course, you have insurance with financial default coverage; ⇨ Trip Insurance *under* Things to Consider *in* Getting Started, *above*).

▌ RENTAL CARS

When you reserve a car, ask about cancellation penalties, taxes, drop-off charges (if you're planning to pick up the car in one city and leave it in another), and surcharges (for being under or over a certain age, for additional drivers, or for driving across state or country borders or beyond a specific distance from your point of rental). All these things can add substantially to your costs. Request car seats and extras such as GPS when you book.

Rates are sometimes—but not always—better if you book in advance or reserve through a rental agency's Web site. There are other reasons to book ahead, though: for popular destinations, during busy times of the year, or to ensure that you get certain types of cars (vans, SUVs, exotic sports cars).

The airports are relatively small and easy to navigate in Portugal so you only need allow an extra 30 minutes or so for drop-off time. In general, it's a good idea to reserve your car two weeks in advance, and a month in advance if possible, for car rentals in the Algarve between May and September. ▌ TIP➡ Make sure that a confirmed reservation guarantees you a car. Agencies sometimes overbook, particularly for busy weekends and holiday periods.

Rates in Lisbon begin at around $75 a day, with three-day rates starting at around $135 and weeklong rates starting at about $230 for a standard economy car with unlimited mileage. The Value-Added Tax

(V.A.T.) on car rentals is 17% and is included in the rate.

Car-rental prices in the Algarve can be considerably higher than those quoted above due to the increase in demand from holidaying tourists. Automatic cars are more expensive and harder to find than standard ones. The good news is that most rental cars have air-conditioning and, increasingly, use diesel gas which equals a lot more mileage. Among the most common car makes are Citroën, Opel, Nissan, Fiat, and Ford. Four-wheel drive vehicles are only available from the larger international car-rental agencies, such as Avis and Hertz.

To rent a car in Portugal you must be a minimum of 25 years old and a maximum of 75 years old and have held your driving license for over a year. According to Portuguese law, children under 12 years old must ride in the back seat in age-appropriate restraining devices, and children under 18 months must be in backward-facing child car seats.

There's generally a surcharge of around $75 for each additional driver, and most agencies charge a small surcharge of around $6 per day for children's car seats which must be reserved at the time of booking.

You may not be able to rent a car without an International Driving Permit (IDP), which can be used only in conjunction with a valid driver's license and which translates your license into 10 languages. Check the AAA Web site for more info as well as for IDPs ($10) themselves.

CAR-RENTAL INSURANCE

Everyone who rents a car wonders whether the insurance that the rental companies offer is worth the expense. No one—including us—has a simple answer. It all depends on how much regular insurance you have, how comfortable you are with risk, and whether or not money is an issue.

If you own a car, your personal auto insurance may cover a rental to some degree,

11 WAYS TO SAVE

1. Nonrefundable is best. If saving money is more important than flexibility, then nonrefundable tickets work. Just remember that you'll pay dearly (as much as $100) if you change your plans.

2. Comparison shop. Web sites and travel agents can have different arrangements with the airlines and offer different prices for exactly the same flights.

3. Beware those prices. Many airline Web sites—and most ads—show prices *without* taxes and surcharges. Don't buy until you know the full price.

4. Stay loyal. Stick with one or two frequent-flier programs. You'll rack up free trips faster and you'll accumulate more quickly the perks that make trips easier.

5. Watch those ticketing fees. Surcharges are usually added when you buy your ticket anywhere but on an airline Web site. (That includes by phone—even if you call the airline directly—and paper tickets regardless of how you book).

6. Check early and often. Start looking for cheap fares up to a year in advance.

7. Don't work alone. Some Web sites have tracking features that will e-mail you immediately when good deals are posted.

8. Jump on the good deals. Waiting even a few minutes might mean paying more.

9. Fly mid-week. Look for departures on Tuesday, Wednesday, and Thursday, typically the cheapest days to travel.

10. Be flexible. Check on prices for departures at different times and to and from alternative airports.

11. Weigh your options. What you get can be as important as what you save. A cheaper flight might have a long layover rather than being nonstop, or it might land at a secondary airport, where your ground transportation costs might be higher.

Car Rental Resources

AUTOMOBILE ASSOCIATIONS		
Automóvel Clube de Portugal	21/318-0202	www.acp.pt
American Automobile Association	315/797-5000	www.aaa.com
National Automobile Club	650/294-7000	www.thenac.com
LOCAL AGENCIES & INTERNET-BASED AGENCIES		
Advantage		www.arac.com
Auto Jardim	21/846-3187 Lisbon Airport	www.autojardim.pt
Car Rentals		www.carrentals.co.uk
Holiday Autos		www.holidayautos.com
MAJOR AGENCIES		
Alamo	800/462-5266	www.alamo.com
Avis	800/230-4898	www.avis.com
Budget	800/527-0700	www.budget.com
Hertz	800/654-3131	www.hertz.com
National Car Rental	800/227-7368	www.nationalcar.com
WHOLESALERS		
Auto Europe	888/223-5555	www.autoeurope.com
Europe by Car	212/581-3040 in New York, 800/223-1516	www.europebycar.com
Eurovacations	877/471-3876	www.eurovacations.com
Kemwel	877/820-0668	www.kemwel.com

though not all policies protect you abroad; always read your policy's fine print. If you don't have auto insurance, then seriously consider buying the collision- or loss-damage waiver (CDW or LDW) from the car-rental company, which eliminates your liability for damage to the car. Some credit cards offer CDW coverage, but it's usually supplemental to your own insurance and rarely covers SUVs, minivans, luxury models, and the like. If your coverage is secondary, you may still be liable for loss-of-use costs from the car-rental company. But no credit-card insurance is valid unless you use that card for *all* transactions, from reserving to paying the final bill. All companies exclude car rental in some countries, so be sure to find out about the destination to which you are traveling.

■ TIP→ Diners Club offers primary CDW coverage on all rentals reserved and paid for with the card. This means that Diners Club's company—not your own car insurance—pays in case of an accident. It *doesn't* mean your car insurance company won't raise your rates once it discovers you had an accident.

In Portugal CDW will cost around $25 a day depending on the type of car and will reduce your liability to a few hundred euros. For an additional fee, you can take out a Super CDW where you will be completely covered.

■ TIP→ You can decline the insurance from the rental company and purchase it through a third-party provider such as Travel Guard (www.travelguard.com)—$9 per day for $35,000 of coverage. That's sometimes just under half the price of the CDW offered by some car-rental companies.

■ VACATION PACKAGES

Packages *are not* guided excursions. Packages combine airfare, accommodations, and perhaps a rental car or other extras (theater tickets, guided excursions, boat trips, reserved entry to popular museums, transit passes), but they let you do your own thing. During busy periods packages may be your only option, as flights and rooms may be sold out otherwise. Packages will definitely save you time. They can also save you money, particularly in peak seasons, but—and this is a really big "but"—you should price each part of the package separately to be sure. And be aware that prices advertised on Web sites and in newspapers rarely include service charges or taxes, which can up your costs by hundreds of dollars.

■ **TIP→** Some packages and cruises are sold only through travel agents. Don't always assume that you can get the best deal by booking everything yourself.

Each year consumers are stranded or lose their money when packagers—even large ones with excellent reputations—go out of business. How can you protect yourself? First, always pay with a credit card; if you have a problem, your credit-card company may help you resolve it. Second, buy trip insurance that covers default. Third, choose a company that belongs to the United States Tour Operators Association, whose members must set aside funds to cover defaults. Finally, choose a company that also participates in the Tour Operator Program of the American Society of Travel Agents (ASTA), which will act as mediator in any disputes. You can also check on the tour operator's reputation among travelers by posting an inquiry on one of the Fodors.com forums.

Portugal is a relatively small country with sights within easy reach of each other so you may want to consider renting a car, rather than a package to allow more flexibility.

Organizations American Society of Travel Agents (ASTA) ☎ 800/965–2782 or 703/739–

---

10 WAYS TO SAVE

1. Beware of cheap rates. Those great rates aren't so great when you add in taxes, surcharges, and insurance. Such extras can double or triple the initial quote.

2. Rent weekly. Weekly rates are usually better than daily ones. Even if you only want to rent for five or six days, ask for the weekly rate; it may very well be cheaper than the daily rate for that period of time.

3. Don't forget the locals. Price local companies as well as the majors.

4. Airport rentals can cost more. Airports often add surcharges, which you can sometimes avoid by renting from an agency whose office is just off airport property.

5. Wholesalers can help. Investigate wholesalers, which don't own fleets but rent in bulk from firms that do, and which frequently offer better rates (note that you must usually pay for such rentals before leaving home).

6. Look for rate guarantees. With your rate locked in, you won't pay more, even if the price goes up in the local currency.

7. Fill up farther away. Avoid hefty refueling fees by filling the tank at a station well away from where you plan to turn in the car.

8. Pump it yourself. Don't buy the tank of gas that's in the car when you rent it unless you plan to do a lot of driving.

9. Get all your discounts. Find out whether a credit card you carry or organization or frequent-renter program to which you belong has a discount program. And confirm that such discounts really are a deal. You can often do better with special weekend or weekly rates offered by a rental agency.

10. Check out package rates. Adding a car rental onto your air/hotel vacation package may be cheaper than renting a car separately on your own.

2782 ⊕ www.astanet.com. **United States Tour Operators Association** (USTOA) ☎ 212/599-6599 ⊕ www.ustoa.com.

■ TIP➡ Local tourism boards can provide information about lesser-known and small-niche operators that sell packages to only a few destinations.

▌ GUIDED TOURS

Guided tours are a good option when you don't want to do it all yourself. You travel along with a group (sometimes large, sometimes small), stay in prebooked hotels, eat with your fellow travelers (the cost of meals sometimes included in the price of your tour, sometimes not), and follow a schedule. But not all guided tours are an if-it's-Tuesday-this-must-be-Belgium experience. A knowledgeable guide can take you places that you might never discover on your own, and you may be pushed to see more than you would have otherwise. Tours aren't for everyone, but they can be just the thing for trips to places where making travel arrangements is difficult or time-consuming (particularly when you don't speak the language). Whenever you book a guided tour, find out what's included and what isn't. A "land-only" tour includes all your travel (by bus, in most cases) in the destination, but not necessarily your flights to and from or even within it. Also, in most cases prices in tour brochures don't include fees and taxes. And remember that you'll be expected to tip your guide (in cash) at the end of the tour.

Package Tours **Euro Adventures** ⊕ www.euroadventures.net/vacations. **My Visual Travel** ⊕ www.myvisualtravel.com/tours. **Tour Vacations to Go** ⊕ www.tourvacationstogo.com/portugal_tours.cfm.

▌ CRUISES

Portugal is a port of call for many cruise liners, including those listed below. Most stop at Lisbon, while a few include Madeira in their itinerary. There are also companies which offer more localized cruising opportunities, including River Cruise Tours which offer luxury boat trips along the Douro River from Porto to the Spanish border.

Cruise Lines **Celebrity Cruises** ☎ 800/437-3111 or 305/539-6000 ⊕ www.celebrity.com. **Costa Cruises** ☎ 800/462-6782 or 954/266-5600 ⊕ www.costacruise.com. **Crystal Cruises** ☎ 800/446-6620 or 310/785-9300 ⊕ www.crystalcruises.com. **Cunard Line** ☎ 800/728-6273 or 661/753-1000 ⊕ www.cunard.com. **Holland America Line** ☎ 877/932-4259 or 206/281-3535 ⊕ www.hollandamerica.com. **Mediterranean Shipping Cruises (Madeira only)** ☎ 800/666-9333 or 212/764-4800 ⊕ www.msccruises.com. **Norwegian Cruise Line** ☎ 800/327-7030 or 305/436-4000 ⊕ www.ncl.com. **Oceania Cruises** ☎ 800/531-5658 or 305/514-2300 ⊕ www.oceaniacruises.com. **Princess Cruises** ☎ 800/774-6237 or 661/753-0000 ⊕ www.princess.com. **Regent Seven Seas Cruises** ☎ 800/477-7500 or 954/776-6123 ⊕ www.rssc.com. **River Cruise Tours** ☎ 888/942-3301 ⊕ www.rivercruisetours.com in the U.S. **Royal Caribbean International** ☎ 800/327-6700 or 305/539-6000 ⊕ www.royalcaribbean.com. **Seabourn Cruise Line** ☎ 800/929-9391 or 305/463-3000 ⊕ www.seabourn.com. **SeaDream Yacht Club** ☎ 800/707-4911 or 305/631-6110 ⊕ www.seadreamyachtclub.com. **Silversea Cruises** ☎ 800/722-9955 or 954/522-4477 ⊕ www.silversea.com. **Star Clippers** ☎ 800/442-0551 or 305/442-0550 ⊕ www.starclippers.com. **Windstar Cruises** ☎ 800/258-7245 or 206/281-3535 ⊕ www.windstarcruises.com.

TRANSPORTATION

▮ BY AIR

The flying time to Lisbon is 6½ hours from New York, 9 hours from Chicago, and 15 hours from Los Angeles. The flight from London to Lisbon is about 2½ hours.

Note that several budget airlines, such as U.K.-based easyJet and Ryanair, don't allocate seats. Also, that they generally don't serve meals but do sell (overpriced) sandwiches and other items. If you're on a special diet, pack appropriate snacks in your carry-on bag. Regardless of your dietary concerns, it's always good to bring a small (plastic) bottle of water.

Airlines & Airports Airline and Airport Links.com ⊕ www.airlineandairportlinks.com has links to many of the world's airlines and airports.

Airline Security Issues Transportation Security Administration ⊕ www.tsa.gov has answers for almost every question that might come up.

▮ **TIP→ Ask the local tourist board about hotel and local transportation packages that include tickets to major museum exhibits or other special events.**

AIRPORTS

The major gateway to Portugal is Lisbon's Aeroporto Portela (LIS), approximately 8 km (5 mi) northeast of the center of the city. A convenient AeroBus departs from outside Arrivals and goes to the center of the city (45 minutes) roughly every 20 minutes from 7:45 AM to 9 PM.

A new international airport is due to open at Ota, 48 km (77 mi) north of the city, in 2010. Porto's Aeroporto Francisco Sá Carneiro (OPO) also handles international flights and, like Lisbon, operates an AeroBus to the city center (25 minutes) from 6:45 AM to 6:15 PM. The Aeroporto de Faro (FAO) handles the largest number of charter flights because of its location in the popular tourist destination of the Algarve. There are several buses that run into town

(15 minutes), while a taxi will cost approximately €12. The organization that oversees Portugal's airports, Aeroportos de Portugal (ANA), has a handy Web site with information in English (⊕ www.ana-aeroportos.pt).

International airport taxes, normally levied by countries of both origin and destination, are generally included in the price of your flight.

Airport Information Aeroporto de Faro ✉ Faro ☎ 289/800617, 289/800801 for flight information. **Aeroporto Francisco Sá Carneiro** ✉ Porto ☎ 229/412141. **Aeroporto Portela** ✉ Lisbon ☎ 21/841-3500 or 21/841-3700. **ANA** ⊕ www.ana-aeroportos.pt.

FLIGHTS

Domestic air travel options are limited and expensive. You're better off renting a car or taking the train or bus, unless time is an issue. TAP Air Portugal and PGA (Portugália Airlines) fly between Lisbon, Porto, and Faro; Aerocondor and Omni have some intercity flights. TAP also has daily flights from Lisbon to Funchal, Madeira.

TAP Air Portugal has daily nonstop flights from New York (Newark Liberty International Airport) to Lisbon with connections to Faro and Porto. During the summer months there are also direct flights from New York to Faro in the Algarve.

Continental's daily nonstop flights between Newark Liberty International Airport and Lisbon are scheduled to provide convenient connections from destinations elsewhere in the eastern and southern United States. The carrier also has a second daily flight from New York (Newark) to Lisbon via Amsterdam, with the connecting flight on KLM, Continental's codeshare partner.

British Airways, PGA, and TAP have regular nonstop flights from the United Kingdom to several destinations in Portugal.

FLYING 101

Flying may not be as carefree as it once was, but there are some things you can do to make your trip smoother.

MINIMIZE THE TIME SPENT STANDING LINE. Buy an e-ticket, check in at an electronic kiosk, or—even better—check in on your airline's Web site before leaving home. Pack light and limit carry-on items to only the essentials.

ARRIVE WHEN YOU NEED TO. Research your airline's policy. It's usually at least an hour before domestic flights and two to three hours before international flights. But airlines at some busy airports have more stringent requirements. Check the TSA Web site for estimated security waiting times at major airports.

GET TO THE GATE. If you aren't at the gate at least 10 minutes before your flight is scheduled to take off (sometimes earlier), you won't be allowed to board.

DOUBLE-CHECK YOUR FLIGHT TIMES. Do this especially if you reserved far in advance. Schedules change, and alerts may not reach you.

DON'T GO HUNGRY. Ask whether your airline offers anything to eat; even when it does, be prepared to pay.

GET THE SEAT YOU WANT. Often, you can pick a seat when you buy your ticket on an airline Web site. But it's not guaranteed; the airline could change the plane after you book, so double-check. You can also select a seat if you check in electronically. Avoid seats on the aisle directly across from the lavatories. Frequent fliers say those are even worse than back-row seats that don't recline.

GOT KIDS? GET INFO. Ask the airline about its children's menus, activities, and fares. Sometimes infants and toddlers fly free if they sit on a parent's lap, and older children fly for half price in their own seats. Also inquire about policies involving car seats; having one may limit seating options. Also ask about seat-belt extenders for car

seats. And note that you can't count on a flight attendant to produce an extender; you may have to ask for one when you board.

CHECK YOUR SCHEDULING. Don't buy a ticket if there's less than an hour between connecting flights. Although schedules are padded, if anything goes wrong you might miss your connection. If you're traveling to an important function, depart a day early.

BRING PAPER. Even when using an e-ticket, always carry a hard copy of your receipt; you may need it to get your boarding pass, which most airports require to get past security.

COMPLAIN AT THE AIRPORT. If your baggage goes astray or your flight goes awry, complain before leaving the airport. Most carriers require this.

BEWARE OF OVERBOOKED FLIGHTS. If a flight is oversold, the gate agent will usually ask for volunteers and offer some sort of compensation for taking a different flight. If you're bumped from a flight *involuntarily*, the airline must give you some kind of compensation if an alternate flight can't be found within one hour.

KNOW YOUR RIGHTS. If your flight is delayed because of something within the airline's control (bad weather doesn't count), the airline must get you to your destination on the same day, even if they have to book you on another airline and in an upgraded class. Read the Contract of Carriage, which is usually buried on the airline's Web site.

BE PREPARED. The Boy Scout motto is especially important if you're traveling during a stormy season. To quickly adjust your plans, program a few numbers into your cell: your airline, an airport hotel or two, your destination hotel, your car service, and/or your travel agent.

Aer Lingus has a regular service from Dublin to Lisbon. There are no direct flights from Australia or New Zealand, but the national Australian airline, Qantas, has a code-sharing agreement with British Airways for flights via the United Kingdom. There are no direct flights from Canada to Portugal. Most airlines route through New York or Europe.

From Spain, TAP, Iberia, and Spanair have daily Madrid-Lisbon flights. Elsewhere in Europe TAP flies to Lisbon and Porto daily from Amsterdam, while PGA has regular direct flights to Lisbon from Berlin, Stuttgart, Cologne, and Hamburg.

Airline Contacts Aer Lingus ☎ 0818/365000 in Ireland, 351/21892-5831 in Portugal ⊕ www.aerlingus.com. **American Airlines** ☎ 800/433-7300 ⊕ www.aa.com. **British Airways** ☎ 800/247-9297 in U.S., 0845/773-3377 in U.K., 351/2141-4151 in Portugal ⊕ www.ba.com. **Continental Airlines** ☎ 800/523-3273 for U.S. and Mexico reservations, 800/231-0856 for international reservations, 351/2141-59102 (Portugal office) ⊕ www.continental.com. **Delta Airlines** ☎ 800/221-1212 for U.S. reservations, 800/241-4141 for international reservations ⊕ www.delta.com. **Hi Fly** ☎ 21/006-2480 ⊕ www.hifly.aero, formerly Air Luxor, flies to Lisbon and Porto from major European capitals and to/from former Portuguese colonies in Africa, Guinea-Bissau, and São Tomé. **Iberia** ☎ 800/772-4642 ⊕ www.iberia.com. **Northwest Airlines** ☎ 800/225-2525 ⊕ www.nwa.com. **TAP Air Portugal** ☎ 800/221-7370 in U.S., 0845/601-0932 in U.K., 28/980-0218 in Portugal ⊕ www.tap.pt. **United Airlines** ☎ 800/864-8331 for U.S. reservations, 800/538-2929 for international reservations ⊕ www.united.com. **USAirways** ☎ 800/428-4322 for U.S. and Canada reservations, 800/622-1015 for international reservations ⊕ www.usairways.com.

Smaller Carriers Aerocondor ☎ 21/846-4964 in Portugal ⊕ www.aerocondor.com. **Omni** ☎ 21/445-8600 in Portugal ⊕ www.omni.pt. **PGA** ☎ 21/842-5559 in Portugal ⊕ www.pga.pt. **Spanair** ☎ 808/261-261 in Portugal ⊕ www.spanair.com.

▌BY BUS

Bus service within Portugal is fairly comprehensive, and in some places, such as the Algarve, buses are the main form of public transportation. Overall, bus services throughout the country are punctual. Some luxury coaches even have TVs and food service—a comfortable way to travel. Note that all buses have a strict no-smoking policy. Three of the largest bus companies are Rede Expressos, which serves much of the country; Rodo Norte, which serves the north; and Eva Transportes, which covers the Algarve and also has service to and from major cities, like Évora.

Note that bus travel can be slow; it can also be difficult to arrange on your own, especially given the baffling number of privatized bus companies operating across the country. In Porto alone there are at least 18 bus companies, most based at different terminals.

▌ TIP➔ **For schedules within Portugal it's best to inquire at tourist information offices or, alternatively, the bus station should be able to provide you with a printout of the routes you are interested in. Be prepared for routes and companies to change frequently, however, and note that bus company personnel rarely speak English.**

If you plan to buy a ticket directly from a specific bus company's office, give yourself plenty of time to purchase before you depart. Most travel agents can sell you a bus ticket in advance; it's always wise to reserve a ticket at least a day ahead, particularly in summer for destinations in the Algarve.

There are three classes of bus service: *expressos* are comfortable, fast, direct buses between major cities; *rápidas* are fast regional buses; and *carreiras* stop at every crossroad. Expressos are generally the best cheap way to get around (particularly for long trips, where per-kilometer costs are lowest). An under-26 card should get you a discount of around 20%, at least on the long-distance services.

The Eurolines/National Express consortium runs regular bus service from the United Kingdom (out of London's Victoria Coach Station) to Lisbon, Porto, Coimbra, Fátima, Faro, Lagos, and other destinations. The company also has service from Paris, its other major hub. The Eurolines agent at the Gare do Oriente train and bus station in Lisbon handles inquiries about Eurolines transportation.

Buses Eva Transportes ⊕ www.eva-bus.com. **Rede Expressos** ⊕ www.rede-expressos.pt. **Rodo Norte** ⊕ www.rodonorte.pt.

Eurolines ⊠ Loca 203, Gare do Oriente, Parque das Nações, Lisbon ☎ 21/895-7398 ⊠ Centro Comercial Central Shopping, Campo 24 de Agosto 125, Porto ☎ 225/189299.

▌BY CAR

In general, Portugal's roads are in good condition and, obviously, driving allows you a lot more freedom. On the downside, the tolls here can add up and the drivers are among the worst in Europe, although a crack down on drunk driving has resulted in a 10% decrease in road death rates in recent years.

Red tape wise, your driver's license from home is recognized in Portugal. However, you should learn the international road-sign system (charts are available to members of most automobile associations).

GASOLINE

Gas stations are plentiful although, increasingly, they are self-service. Prices are controlled by the government and are the same everywhere. At press time gasoline cost €1.39 a liter (approximately ¼ gallon) for 98 and 95 octane *sem chumbo* (unleaded) and €1.10 for diesel. Credit cards are frequently accepted at gas stations. If you require a receipt, request *un recibo*.

ROAD CONDITIONS

Commercially operated *autoestradas* (toll roads with four or more lanes identified with an "A" and a number) link the prin-

cipal cities, including Porto, with Lisbon, circumventing congested urban centers. The autoestrada from Lisbon to Faro and a toll road (E90) links Lisbon with Portugal's eastern border with Spain at Badajoz (from which the highway leads to Madrid). Many main national highways (labeled with "N" and a number) have been upgraded to toll-free, two-lane roads identified with "IP" (Itinerario Principal) and a number. Highways of mainly regional importance have been upgraded to IC (Itinerario Complementar). Roads labeled with "E" and a number are routes that connect with the Spanish network. Because road construction is still under way, you may find that one road has several designations—A, N, IP, E, and so on—on maps and signs.

Autoestrada tolls are steep, costing, for example, €17.60 between Lisbon and Porto, but time saved by traveling these roads usually makes them worthwhile. Minor roads are often poor and winding with unpredictable surfaces.

⚠ The local driving may be faster and less forgiving than you're used to, and other visitors in rental cars on unfamiliar roads can cause problems: drive carefully.

In the north the IP5 shortens the drive from Aveiro to the border with Spain, near Guarda. Take extra care on this route, however. It's popular with trucks (you may get stuck behind a convoy), *and* it has curves and hills. The IP4 connects Porto through Vila Real to once-remote Bragança. You can pick up the IP2 just southwest of Bragança and continue to Ourique in the Alentejo, where it connects to the IP1 straight down to Albufeira on the southern coast. This same IP1 is an autoestrada from Albufeira and runs east across the Algarve to the Spanish border near Ayamonte, 1½ hours east of Seville.

Heading out of Lisbon, there's good, fast access to Setúbal and to Évora and other Alentejo towns, although rush-hour traffic on the bridge Ponte 25 de Abril across the Rio Tejo (Tagus River) can be frustrating. An alternative is taking the 17-km-long (11-mi-long) Ponte Vasco da Gama (Europe's second-longest water crossing after the Channel Tunnel) across the Tejo estuary to Montijo; you can then link up with southbound and eastbound roads. Signposting on these fast roads isn't always adequate, so keep your eyes peeled for exits and turnoffs.

ROADSIDE EMERGENCIES

If you are unfortunate enough to be involved in a mild accident, you will be required to fill out Constat Aimable (European Accident Statement) which will be used by the respective insurance companies (including those relating to rental cars) to exchange information. All large garages in and around towns have breakdown services, and you'll see orange emergency (SOS) phones along turnpikes and highways. The national automobile organization, Automóvel Clube de Portugal, provides reciprocal membership with AAA and other European automobile associations. Car theft is common with rental cars. Never leave anything visible in an unattended car and contact the rental agency immediately, as well as the local police, if your car is stolen.

Emergency Services The 24-hour emergency help number is ☎ 707/509510. **Automóvel Clube de Portugal** ☎ 21/942-9103 for breakdowns south of Pombal, ☎ 22/834-0001 for breakdowns north of Pombal ⊕ www.acp.pt.

RULES OF THE ROAD

Driving is on the right. At the junction of two roads of equal size, traffic coming from the right has priority. Vehicles already in a traffic circle have priority over those entering it from any point. The use of seat belts is obligatory. Horns shouldn't be used in built-up areas, and you should always carry your driver's license, proof of car insurance, and a reflective red warning triangle, for use in a breakdown. The speed limit on the autoestrada is 120 kph (74 mph); on other roads it's 90 kph (56 mph), and in built-up areas, 50 kph–60 kph (30 mph–36 mph).

According to Portuguese law, children under 12 years old must ride in the back seat in age-appropriate restraining devices and facing backwards for children under 18 months. Motorcyclists and their passengers must wear helmets and motorcycles must have their headlights on day and night.

Billboards warning you not to drink and drive dot the countryside, and punishable alcohol levels are just 0.2g/L—equivalent to a single glass of wine. Portuguese drivers are notoriously rash, and the country has one of the highest traffic fatality rates in Europe—drive defensively.

■ BY TRAIN

Portugal's train network, Caminhos de Ferro Portugueses (CP), covers most of the country, though it's thin in the Alentejo region. The cities of Lisbon, Coimbra, Aveiro, and Porto are linked by the fast, extremely comfortable Alfa and Alfa Pendular services. Most other major towns and cities are connected by InterCidade trains, which are reliable, though slower and less luxurious than the Alfa trains. The regional services that connect smaller towns and villages tend to be infrequent and slow, with stops at every station along the line.

The standards of comfort vary from *alfa pendular* train luxury—with air-conditioning, food service, and airline-type seats at which you can use a telefax and plug in your laptop—to the often spartan conditions on regional lines. Most InterCidade trains have bar and restaurant facilities, but the food is famously unappealing. A first-class ticket will cost you 40% more than a second-class one and will buy you extra leg- and elbow room but not a great deal more on the Alfa and InterCidade trains. The extra cost is definitely worth it on most regional services, however. Smoking is restricted to special carriages on all Portuguese trains.

A direct, nightly train connects Spain and Portugal. The train departs from Madrid's

Chamartin station at 10:45 PM and arrives at Lisbon's Santa Apolónia station at 8:15 the following morning; for the reverse trip, the train leaves Lisbon at 10 PM, arriving in Madrid at 8:25 AM the next day. There's also a daily train service between Lisbon's Santa Apolónia station and Paris (Montparnasse and Austerlitz stations). On some trips, you change onto a French TGV (high-speed train) at the Spain–France border to go on to Paris; note that you may need special reservations for this leg of the journey.

There are three main classes of long distance train travel in Portugal: *regional* trains which stop at every town and village; reasonably fast *interregional* trains and express trains appropriately known as *rápido*. Currently only operating between Lisbon and Porto (via Coimbra) is the *alfa pendular* a deluxe, marginally faster train. In addition there is a network of suburban *(suburbano)* train lines throughout the country.

■ TIP→ **To save money, look into rail passes. But be aware that if you don't plan to cover many miles, you may come out ahead by buying individual tickets.**

Portugal is one of the countries in which you can use a Eurail pass, which provides unlimited first-class rail travel, in all of the participating countries, for the duration of the pass. If you plan to rack up the miles, get a standard pass. These are available in units from 15 days to three months. In addition to a standard Eurail pass, ask about special rail-pass plans. Among these are the Eurail Youthpass (in second class for those under age 26), the Eurail Saverpass (which gives a discount for two or more people traveling together), a Eurail Flexipass (which allows 10 or 15 travel days within a two-month period), the Euraildrive Pass and the Europass Drive (which combine travel by train and rental car). It's best to purchase your pass before you leave for Europe.

There are also special tourist tickets (bilhetes turísticos) valid for unlimited travel during 7/14/21 consecutive days, cost €112/€189/€277 (half price for those aged under 12 and over 65). Toddlers who need a seat of their own cost half price.

Many travelers assume that rail passes guarantee them seats on the trains they wish to ride. Not so. You need to book seats ahead even if you are using a rail pass; seat reservations are required on some European trains, particularly high-speed trains, and are a good idea on trains that may be crowded—particularly in summer on popular routes. You will also need a reservation if you purchase sleeping accommodations.

If you speak Portuguese, you can call the general information number of the Caminhos de Ferro Portugueses (CP) for schedule and other information. Otherwise check the Web site, or head to a train station information desk for a printed timetable.

Major credit cards (Visa, MasterCard, American Express) or cash are the best forms of payment. Traveler's checks may or may not be accepted, depending on the size of the station.

Advance booking is mandatory on long distance trains and is recommended in the case of popular services such as the Alfa trains. Reservations are also advisable for other trains if you want to avoid long lines in front of the ticket window on the day the train leaves. You can avoid a trip to the station to make the reservation by asking a travel agent to take care of it for you.

CP ☎ 800/200904, 808/208208, or 21/888-4025 ⊕ www.cp.pt. **Rail Europe** ☎ 800/942-4866, 800/274-8724, 0870/584-8848 U.K. credit-card bookings ⊕ www.raileurope.com.

ON THE GROUND

■ COMMUNICATIONS

INTERNET

Better hotels increasingly have a Wi-Fi zone available for laptop users and many hotels will have Internet connection available in the rooms. If you are traveling with a laptop take extra precautions against theft, including extra insurance, if feasible. **Cybercafes** ⊕ www.cybercafes.com lists over 4,000 Internet cafés worldwide.

PHONES

The good news is that you can now make a direct-dial telephone call from virtually any point on Earth. The bad news? You can't always do so cheaply. Calling from a hotel is almost always the most expensive option; hotels usually add huge surcharges to all calls, particularly international ones. In some countries you can phone from call centers or even the post office. Calling cards usually keep costs to a minimum, but only if you purchase them locally. And then there are mobile phones (⇨ *below*), which are sometimes more prevalent—particularly in the developing world—than land lines; as expensive as mobile phone calls can be, they are still usually a much cheaper option than calling from your hotel.

The country code for Portugal is 351. When dialing a Portuguese number from abroad, dial the nine-digit number after the country code.

CALLING WITHIN PORTUGAL

All phone numbers have nine digits. Numbers in the area in and around Lisbon and Porto begin with a two-digit area code; phone numbers anywhere else in the country begin with a three-digit area code. All fixed-phone area codes begin with 2; mobile numbers, which also have nine digits, begin with 9.

For general information, dial 118 (operators often speak English). The international information and assistance numbers are 171 for operator-assisted calls, 172 for collect calls, and 177 for information (the operators speak English).

To make calls to other areas within Portugal, precede the provincial area code with 0 (most phone booths have a chart inside listing the various province codes). The 0 is unnecessary when dialing from outside Portugal.

You can ask to use the phone in cafés or bars, where they're often metered. The waiter or bartender will charge you after you've finished, though you should expect to pay a higher rate than the one you would pay in a public phone booth.

The easiest way to call from a public booth is to use a Portugal Telecom *cartão telefônico* (calling card), which you can buy at post offices, newspaper shops, and tobacconists for either €5 or €10. The phones that accept them have digital readouts, so you can see your time ticking away. Instructions in several languages, including English, are posted in the booths. A second option is a HelloCardPT or PT CARD Europe which cost €5 each. You call an access number then key in the pass code at the back of the card. This is the cheapest way of making international calls. There are plenty of competing cards offering much the same service. Avoid using coins which disappear rapidly. The minimum cost for a local call is €0.20; it's €0.50 to call another area, for which you must dial the area code.

Portugal Telecom ⊕ www.telecom.pt. **Yellow Pages** ⊕ ww.paginasamarelas.pt

CALLING OUTSIDE PORTUGAL

Calling abroad is expensive from hotels, which often add a considerable surcharge. The best way to make an international call is to go to the local telephone office and have someone place it for you. Every town has such an establishment, and big cities

LOCAL DO'S & TABOOS

SIGHTSEEING

Portugal has a strong Catholic influence. If you're visiting a church or place of worship, wear conservative clothing.

OUT ON THE TOWN

If you're invited to dinner by a Portuguese family, a bottle of good wine is a thoughtful gift. Shake hands with everyone, including youngsters, on arriving and leaving. If you're more closely acquainted, a kiss on both cheeks is normal (right cheek always first), except between men. Address men as *senhor*, women as *senhora*, and highly respected or older women as *dona* followed by the first name.

Dining in the rural countryside is rarely formal; in fact, don't be surprised to see people eating with their fingers or talking with their mouths full.

DOING BUSINESS

It's prudent to use a title, such as senhor and senhora, during introductions. Shake hands with every man and his dog, and have business cards at the ready. Dress is generally casual (slacks and nice shirts, with jackets optional), but more formal (suits and ties) in Lisbon and Porto.

Don't expect things to start on time: everybody in Portugal runs late—period. During meetings, avoid direct criticism or confrontation; strive instead for win-win situations. For a lunch or dinner meeting, it's generally understood that the person who issued the invitation will be the one to pay. Giving gifts when conducting business is never really considered appropriate.

LANGUAGE

One of the best ways to avoid being an Ugly American is to learn a little of the local language. You need not strive for fluency; even just mastering a few basic words and terms is bound to make chatting with the locals more rewarding.

Portuguese is the seventh-most-spoken language in the world. It can be difficult to pronounce and understand (most people speak quickly and elliptically). If, however, you have a fair knowledge of a Latin language, you may be able to read a little Portuguese. Just be aware that, with some cognates, appearances can be deceptive—it's best to double-check terms in a pocket Portuguese-English dictionary. Any attempt you make to speak Portuguese will be well received. In large cities and major resorts many people speak English and, occasionally, Spanish or French.

---

have several. When the call is connected, you'll be directed to a quiet cubicle and charged according to the meter. If the price is €10 or more, you can pay with Visa or MasterCard. Lisbon's main phone office is in the Praça dos Restauradores, right off the Rossío.

The country code for the United States is 1.

To make an international call yourself, dial 00 followed directly by the country code (1 for the United States, 44 for the United Kingdom, 61 for Australia, and 64 for New Zealand) and the area code and number. The Portuguese telephone directory contains a list of all the principal world country codes and the codes for principal cities.

If all else fails, call from a local telephone office or pay phone.

Access Codes AT&T Direct ☎ 800/800128 in Portugal, 800/222-0300 for other areas. **MCI WorldPhone** ☎ 800/800123 in Portugal, 800/444-4141 for other areas. **Sprint International Access** ☎ 800/800187 in Portugal, 800/877-4646 for other areas.

CALLING CARDS

Purchasing a phone card from a post office, newsagent, or tobacconist can save you money and the aggravation of finding enough change for a pay phone. Cards come in denominations of €5 and €10 and can be used from both private and public phones for national and international calls.

MOBILE PHONES

If you have a multiband phone (some countries use different frequencies from what's used in the United States) and your service provider uses the world-standard GSM network (as do T-Mobile, Cingular, and Verizon), you can probably use your phone abroad. Roaming fees can be steep, however: 99¢ a minute is considered reasonable. And overseas you normally pay the toll charges for incoming calls. It's almost always cheaper to send a text message than to make a call, since text messages have a very low set fee (often less than 5¢).

▣ TIP→ **If you travel internationally frequently, save one of your old mobile phones or buy a cheap one on the Internet; ask your cell phone company to unlock it for you, and take it with you as a travel phone, buying a new SIM card with pay-as-you-go service in each destination.**

If you just want to make local calls, consider buying a new SIM card (note that your provider may have to unlock your phone for you to use a different SIM card) and a prepaid service plan in the destination. You'll then have a local number and can make local calls at local rates. If your trip is extensive, you could also simply buy a new cell phone in your destination, as the initial cost will be offset over time.

Cellular Abroad ☎ 800/287-5072 ⊕ www.cellularabroad.com rents and sells GMS phones and sells SIM cards that work in many countries. **Mobal** ☎ 888/888-9162 ⊕ www.mobalrental.com rents mobiles and sells GSM phones (starting at $49) that will operate in 140 countries. Per-call rates vary throughout the world. **Planet Fone** ☎ 888/988-4777 ⊕ www.planetfone.com rents cell phones, but the per-minute rates are expensive.

▮ CUSTOMS & DUTIES

You're always allowed to bring goods of a certain value back home without hav-

CON OR CONCIERGE?

Good hotel concierges are invaluable—for arranging transportation, getting reservations at the hottest restaurant, and scoring tickets for a sold-out show or entree to an exclusive nightclub. They're in the know and well connected. That said, sometimes you have to take their advice with a grain of salt.

It's not uncommon for restaurants to ply concierges with free food and drink in exchange for steering diners their way. Indeed, European concierges often receive referral *fees*. Hotel chains usually have guidelines about what their concierges can accept. The best concierges, however, are above reproach. This is particularly true of those who belong to the prestigious international society of Les Clefs d'Or.

What can you expect of a concierge? At a typical tourist-class hotel you can expect him or her to give you the basics: to show you something on a map, make a standard restaurant reservation (particularly if you don't speak the language), or help you book a tour or airport transportation. In Asia concierges perform the vital service of writing out the name or address of your destination for you to give to a cab driver.

Savvy concierges at the finest hotels and resorts can arrange for just about any good or service imaginable—and do so quickly. You should compensate them appropriately. A $10 tip is enough to show appreciation for a table at a hot restaurant. But the reward should really be much greater for tickets to that U2 concert that's been sold out for months.

ing to pay any duty or import tax. But there's a limit on the amount of tobacco and liquor you can bring back duty-free, and some countries have separate limits for perfumes; for exact figures, check with your customs department. The values of so-called "duty-free" goods are included in these amounts. When you shop abroad, save all your receipts, as customs inspectors may ask to see them as well as the items you purchased. If the total value of your goods is more than the duty-free limit, you'll have to pay a tax (most often a flat percentage) on the value of everything beyond that limit.

Visitors age 15 and over are permitted to bring in 200 cigarettes, or 100 cigarillos, or 50 cigars, or 250 grams of loose tobacco. Those 17 years of age and older may bring in 1 liter of liquor over 22 proof and 2 liters of wine. Perfume is limited to 50 grams, eau de cologne to ¼ liter. Food items can be the trickiest items to bring home unless they include baked goods, sweets or chocolates, which are simple to import. Avoid bringing home meats, fruits, or vegetables, and, while dairy items such as milk, yogurt, and hard cheese are allowed, soft cheeses such as Brie and ricotta are not. It's a good idea to carry sales receipts for expensive personal items to avoid paying export duties when you leave. There's no more duty-free shopping in Portugal's airports. Travelers to Portugal may bring a maximum of two pets with them and a rabies vaccination is usually compulsory. Check at your local Portugal Consulate or Embassy for more information about when the vaccine must be administered and customs regulations in general.

Information in Portugal Direção Geral das Alfândegas ✉ Rua da Alfândega 5, Alfama, Lisbon ☎ 21/881-3700.

Telephone numbers can also be found through www.118.pt.

U.S. Information U.S. Customs and Border Protection ⊕ www.cbp.gov.

▌ EATING OUT

The explosion of fast-food restaurants in recent years hasn't dented the Portuguese affection for old-fashioned, white-tablecloth dining—even though the tablecloth and napkins may now be made of paper. Hamburger places do a roaring lunchtime trade in towns all over the country, but so do the traditional little restaurants that offer office workers home cooking at a modest price. Don't expect much in the way of decor, and if you have trouble squeezing in, remember the rule of thumb: if it's packed, it's probably good.

Although Portugal's plush, luxury restaurants can be good, they seldom measure up to their counterparts in other European countries. The best food by far tends to be found in the moderately priced and less-expensive spots. Restaurants featuring charcoal-grilled meats and fish, called *churasqueiras*, are also popular (and often economical) options, and the Brazilian *rodízio*-type restaurant, where you are regaled with an endless offering of spit-roasted meats, is entrenched in Lisbon, Porto, and the Algarve. Shellfish restaurants, called *marisqueiras*, are numerous along the coast; note that lobsters, mollusks, and the like are fresh and good but pricey. Restaurant prices fall appreciably when you leave the Lisbon, Porto, and Algarve areas, and portion sizes increase the farther north you go.

▌ TIP→ While you ponder the menu, you may be served an impressive array of appetizers. If you eat any of these, you'll probably be charged a small amount called a *couberto* or *couvert*. If you don't want these appetizers, you're perfectly within your rights to send them back. However, you should do this right away.

Portuguese restaurants serve an *ementa* (or *prato*) *do dia*, or set menu of three courses. This can be a real bargain—usually 80% of the cost of three courses ordered separately.

Vegetarians can have a tough time in Portugal, although *sopa de legumes* (vegetable soup) is often included as a starter, together with the inevitable *salada* (salad). In general, the only other option (for vegetarians) are omelets. The larger cities and the Algarve have a few vegetarian restaurants and Chinese and Italian restaurants are increasingly common and always have plenty of vegetarian (and vegan) options. The restaurants we list in this book, each indicated by a knife-and-fork icon, ✕, are the cream of the crop in each price category. Establishments marked with ✕⊡ are hotels that stand out equally for their restaurants.

For information on food-related health issues, *see* Health *below.*

MEALS & MEALTIMES

Breakfast (*pequeno almoço*) is the lightest meal, usually consisting of nothing more than a croissant or pastry washed down with coffee; lunch (*almoço*), the main meal of the day, is served between noon and 2:30, although nowadays, office workers in cities often grab a quick sandwich in a bar instead of stopping for a big meal. Some cafés and snack bars serve light meals throughout the afternoon. About 5 PM there's a break for coffee or tea and a pastry; dinner (*jantar*) is eaten around 8 PM, and restaurants generally serve from 7 PM to 10 PM. Monday is a common day for restaurants to close, although this does vary and is noted in the restaurant listings in this guide. Unless otherwise noted, the restaurants listed in this guide are open daily for lunch and dinner.

PAYING

Major credit cards are accepted in better restaurants and those geared towards tourists, particularly on the Algarve. Humbler establishments generally only accept cash. Always check first, or you may end the evening washing dishes. For guidelines on tipping *see* Tipping *below.*

RESERVATIONS & DRESS

Regardless of where you are, it's a good idea to make a reservation if you can. In some places (Lisbon, for example), it's expected. We only mention them specifically when reservations are essential (there's no other way you'll ever get a table) or when they are not accepted. For popular restaurants, book as far ahead as you can (often 30 days), and reconfirm as soon as you arrive. (Large parties should always call ahead to check the reservations policy.) We mention dress only when men are required to wear a jacket or a jacket and tie.

WINES, BEER & SPIRITS

Portuguese wines are inexpensive and, in general, good. Even the *vinho da casa* (house wine) is perfectly drinkable in most restaurants. Among the most popular are Bairrada from the Coimbra/Aveiro region, Ribatejo and Liziria from the Ribatejo region, and the reds from the Dão region. The light, sparkling *vinhos verdes* (green wines, named not for their color but for the fact that they're drunk early and don't improve with age) are also popular. Both the Instituto de Vinho de Porto (Port Wine Institute) and the Comissão de Viticultura da Região dos Vinhos Verdes (Vinho Verde Region Viticulture Commission) have fascinating Web sites—with information in several languages, including English—that will help you learn more about Portuguese wines.

The leading brands of Portuguese beer—including Super Bock, Crystal, Sagres, and Imperial—are available on tap and in bottles or cans. They're made with fewer chemicals than the average American beers, and are on the strong side with a good, clean flavor. Local brandy—namely Macieira and Constantino—is cheap, as is domestic gin, although it's marginally weaker than its international counterparts.

Portugal has the world's highest alcohol consumption after Russia, so licensing laws are lax. Amazingly there is no minimum age for drinking alcohol here although you still have to be over 16 to buy alcohol at shops, supermarkets, bars, and restaurants. Note that having brandy with your morning coffee will mark you as a local.

Wine Information **Comissão de Viticultura da Região dos Vinhos Verdes** ⊕ www. vinhoverde.pt. **Instituto de Vinho de Porto** ⊕ www.ivp.pt.

▮ ELECTRICITY

The electrical current in Portugal is 220 volts, 50 cycles alternating current (AC); wall outlets take plugs with two round prongs. Consider making a small investment in a universal adapter, which has several types of plugs in one lightweight, compact unit. Most laptops and mobile phone chargers are dual voltage (i.e., they operate equally well on 110 and 220 volts), so require only an adapter. These days the same is true of small appliances such as hair dryers. Always check labels and manufacturer instructions to be sure. Don't use 110-volt outlets marked FOR SHAVERS ONLY for high-wattage appliances such as hair-dryers.

Steve Kropla's Help for World Traveler's ⊕ www.kropla.com has information on electrical and telephone plugs around the world. **Walkabout Travel Gear** ⊕ www. walkabouttravelgear.com has a good coverage of electricity under "adapters."

▌ EMERGENCIES

The national number for emergencies is 112, which is the universal emergency number within the European Union. The ambulance service in Portugal is run by volunteers and free. Contact details of English-speaking doctors can by obtained from American consular offices. Pharmacies *(farmácias)* will have a notice posted on the door with directions to the nearest 24-hour pharmacy.

Foreign Embassies **U.S. Embassy** ✉ Av. das Forças Armadas, Sete Rios, Lisbon ☎ 21/727–3300 ⊕ www.american-embassy.pt.
Australia **Australian Consular Section** ✉ Av. da Liberdade 200, 2nd fl., Centro, Lisbon ☎ 21/310–1500 ⊕ www.portugal.embassy.gov.au.
Canada **Canadian Embassy** ✉ Av. da Liberdade 196, Centro, Lisbon ☎ 21/316–4600 ⊕ www.dfait-maeci.gc.ca.
United Kingdom **U.K Embassy** ✉ Rua de São Bernardo 33, Rato, Lisbon ☎ 21/396–1191.
General Emergency Contacts

▌ HEALTH

The most common types of illnesses are caused by contaminated food and water. Especially in developing countries, drink only bottled, boiled, or purified water and drinks; don't drink from public fountains or use ice. You should even consider using bottled water to brush your teeth. Make sure food has been thoroughly cooked and is served to you fresh and hot; avoid vegetables and fruits that you haven't washed (in bottled or purified water) or peeled yourself. If you have problems, mild cases of traveler's diarrhea may respond to Imodium (known generically as loperamide) or Pepto-Bismol. Be sure to drink plenty of fluids; if you can't keep fluids down, seek medical help immediately.

Infectious diseases can be airborne or passed via mosquitoes and ticks and through direct or indirect physical contact with animals or people. Some, including Norwalk-like viruses that affect your digestive tract, can be passed along through contaminated food. If you are traveling in an area where malaria is prevalent, use a repellant containing DEET and take malaria-prevention medication before, during, and after your trip as directed by your physician. Condoms can help prevent most sexually transmitted diseases, but they aren't absolutely reliable and their quality varies from country to country. Speak with your physician and/or check the CDC or World Health Organization Web sites for health alerts, particularly if you're pregnant, traveling with children, or have a chronic illness.

For information on travel insurance, shots and medications, and medical-assistance

---

WORD OF MOUTH

Was the service stellar or not up to snuff? Did the food give you shivers of delight or leave you cold? Did the prices and portions make you happy or sad? Rate restaurants and write your own reviews in Travel Ratings or start a discussion about your favorite places in Travel Talk on www.fodors.com. Your comments might even appear in our books. Yes, you, too, can be a correspondent!

companies *see* Shots & Medications *under* Things to Consider *in* Getting Started, *above.*

SPECIFIC ISSUES IN PORTUGAL

Sunburn and sunstroke are common problems in summer in mainland Portugal and virtually year-round on Madeira. On a hot, sunny day, even people not normally bothered by strong rays should cover up. Sunscreen can be found in pharmacies and supermarkets, and some U.S. brands are available. The sun protection factor (SPF) is always noted. Carry sunscreen for nose, ears, and other sensitive areas; be sure to drink enough liquids; and above all, limit your sun exposure for the first few days until you become accustomed to the heat. Mosquitoes are found throughout Portugal and, while they don't carry malaria, they can cause irritation so pack or buy a local insect repellent.

OVER-THE-COUNTER REMEDIES

If your system is sensitive to new and different foods, note that mild cases of diarrhea may respond to Imodium, Lomotil (known generically as loperamide), or kompensam pills, a Portuguese medicine stocked by most pharmacies. Pepto-Bismol (not as strong) can also be purchased over the counter. Drink plenty of purified water or *chá* (tea). *Camomila* (chamomile tea) is a good folk remedy. In severe cases, rehydrate yourself with a salt-sugar solution: ½ teaspoon *sal* (salt) and 4 tablespoons *açúcar* (sugar) per quart of *agua* (water). The word for aspirin is *aspirinha*; Tylenol is pronounced *tee*-luh-nawl. For insect bites, try *fenistil.* Sunburn sufferers may gain some relief from *diprosoal,* which comes in the form of a soothing gel.

▌HOURS OF OPERATION

Lunchtime is taken very seriously throughout Portugal. Many businesses, particularly outside urban areas, close between 1 and 3 and then reopen for business until 6 or 7. Government offices are typically open from 9 to noon and 2 to 5. It's worth noting religious and public holidays, as most businesses grind to a halt, and even the local transport service may be reduced. Also, if the holiday falls at a weekend, then typically a Friday or Monday will also be a holiday.

Banks are open weekdays 8:30–3. Money exchange booths at airports and train stations are usually open all day (24 hours at Portela Airport in Lisbon).

Most gas stations on main highways are open 24 hours. In more rural areas, stations are open 7 AM to 10 PM. Note that gas stations can seem few and far between away from the towns and cities, so if you are planning to explore in the hinterland, always start out with a full tank of gas.

Museums and palaces generally open at 10, close for lunch from 12:30 to 2, and then reopen until 5; a few, however, remain open at midday. The 29 sites of the nationwide Portuguese Institute of Museums (IPM) are closed Monday, as well as Easter Sunday, May 1, Christmas, and January 1. Some IPM museums don't open until 2 PM on Tuesday.

Pharmacies are usually open weekdays 9 to 1 and 3 to 7, and Saturday 9 to 1.

Most shops are open weekdays 9 to 1 and 3 to 7, and Saturday 9 to 1. In December, Saturday hours are the same as weekdays. Shops often close Sunday. *Hipermercados* (giant supermarkets), *supermercados* (regular supermarkets), and shopping centers are typically open seven days a week from 10 AM to midnight. In the seaside resorts of the Algarve, many shops, including souvenir shops and supermarkets, open all day between May and September.

HOLIDAYS

New Year's Day (January 1); Mardi Gras (better known as Carnaval, held during the last few days before Lent); Good Friday; Easter Sunday; Liberty Day (April 25); Labor Day (May 1); Corpo de Deus (May 30); Camões Day (June 10); Assumption (August 15); Republic Day (October 5); All Saints' Day (November 1); Independence Day (December 1); Immaculate Conception (December 8); Christmas Day (December 25).

If a national holiday falls on a Tuesday or Thursday, many businesses also close on the Monday or Friday in between, for a long weekend called a *ponte* (bridge). There are also local holidays when entire towns, cities, and regions grind to a standstill. Check the nearest tourist office for dates.

▌ MAIL

You can expect a letter to take 7–10 days to reach the United States, Australia, or New Zealand and 4–5 days to the United Kingdom or elsewhere in the European Union. All post is sent airmail unless otherwise specified.

The Portuguese postal service—the CTT—has a Web site in English and Portuguese with information such as how to trace mail and the location and hours of countrywide post offices.

Airmail letters to the United States and Canada cost €0.75 for up to 20 grams. Letters to the United Kingdom and other EU countries cost €0.60 for up to 20 grams. Letters within Portugal are €0.30. Postcards cost the same as letters. You can buy *selos* (stamps) at *correios* (post offices) or at kiosks and shops displaying a red CORREIOS–SELOS sign. Stamp-vending machines are scattered about Lisbon.

If you're on the move, it's best to have your mail sent to American Express; call for lists of offices in Portugal. An alternative is to have mail held at a Portuguese post office; have it addressed to *poste restante* in a town you'll be visiting. Postal addresses should include the name of the province and district—for example, Figueira da Foz (Coimbra). You will need photo ID to collect your mail, for which there's a charge of around €1 per item.

CTT ⊕ www.ctt.pt.

SHIPPING PACKAGES
Although you can send packages by registered air mail, it's best to ship them through the more reliable courier services. In short, don't send anything from a Portuguese post office that you can't afford to lose. The largest national courier company is Correia Azul, which has branches in cities, large towns, and major resorts. Expect to pay slightly over three times as much as normal postage, with delivery time generally two to three days. Other companies include DHL, TNT, and Federal Express. Overnight courier service is available only within Europe.

Express Services Correia Azul ☎ 800/206868. **DHL** ☎ 21/810-0099 ⊕ www.dhl.com. **Federal Express** ☎ 800/244144 ⊕ www.federalexpress.com. **TNT** ☎ 21/854-5050 ⊕ www.tnt.com.

American Express ☎ 800/543-4080 ⊕ www.americanexpress.com.

▌ MONEY

Lisbon isn't as expensive as most other international capitals, but it's not the extraordinary bargain it used to be. The coastal resort areas from Cascais and Estoril down to the Algarve can be expensive, though there are lower-price hotels and restaurants catering mainly to the package-tour trade. If you head off the beaten track, you'll find substantially cheaper food and lodging.

Transportation is still cheap in Portugal when compared with the rest of Europe. Gas prices are controlled by the government, and train and bus travel are inexpensive. Highway tolls are steep but may be worth the cost if you want to bypass the small towns and villages. Flights within the country are costly.

Here are some sample prices. Coffee in a bar: €0.60 (standing), €0.80 (seated). Draft beer in a bar: €0.60 (standing), €0.80 (seated). Bottle of beer: €0.80. Port: €1.50–€10, depending on brand and vintage. Table wine: €5.50 (bottle), €3.50 (half bottle), €0.70 (small glass). Coca-Cola: €1. Ham-and-cheese sandwich: €1.50. One-kilometer (½-mi) taxi ride: €3. Local bus ride: €1. Subway ride:

€0.65. Ferry ride in Lisbon: €1–€2 one-way. Opera or theater seat: €25–€50. Nightclub cover charge: €10–€25. Fado performance: €16 for the show plus a drink or €25–€40 for dinner and a show. Movie ticket: €4.50–€5 (most cinemas offer cheaper tickets on Monday). Foreign newspaper: €2.50–€5.

Museums that are part of the Portuguese Institute of Museums (IPM) are free on Sunday until 2 PM. The IPM also sells "season tickets" for two, five, and seven days that grant you entrance to all permanent and temporary exhibits during that time period. Lisbon and Porto sell cost-saving passes that cover city transport and entry to museums and other sights. The respective tourist office can fill you in. You can often also save as much as 50% on accommodations if you visit Portugal out of season.

If you're undeterred by potentially wet weather, consider traveling November to March, when many hotels discount their rates by up to 20%. In Lisbon and Porto, check with the tourist office about discount cards offering travel deals on public transport, reduced or free entrance to certain museums, and discounts in some shops and restaurants.

Prices throughout this guide are given for adults. Substantially reduced fees are almost always available for children, students, and senior citizens.

■ TIP→ Banks never have every foreign currency on hand, and it may take as long as a week to order. If you're planning to exchange funds before leaving home, don't wait until the last minute.

ATMS & BANKS

Your own bank will probably charge a fee for using ATMs abroad; the foreign bank you use may also charge a fee. Nevertheless, you'll usually get a better rate of exchange at an ATM than you will at a currency-exchange office or even when changing money in a bank. And extracting funds as you need them is a safer option than carrying around a large amount of cash.

■ TIP→ PIN numbers with more than four digits are not recognized at ATMs in many countries. If yours has five or more, remember to change it before you leave.

ATMs are ubiquitous, and the Portuguese use them for banking as well as for paying bills and taxes. The Multibanco, or MB, system is state-of-the-art and reliable. The cards most frequently accepted are Visa, MasterCard, American Express, Eurocheque, Eurocard, Cirrus, and Electron. You need a four-digit PIN to use ATMs in Portugal. Always have a couple of different cards with you in case there is a temporary hiccup with accepting a particular type of card (it does happen!).

Always be wary when using an ATM machine that nobody is looking over your shoulder. Similarly, if the machine appears tampered with, stay away. There is a scam throughout Europe whereupon a dummy cover is placed over the machine and/or a tiny camera notes your PIN number. There is usually a limit of €300 a day withdrawal.

ATM Locations Cirrus ☎ 800/424-7787 ⊕ www.mastercard.com. **Plus** ☎ 800/843-7587 ⊕ www.visa.com.

CREDIT CARDS

Throughout this guide, the following abbreviations are used: **AE**, American Express; **DC**, Diners Club; **MC**, MasterCard; and **V**, Visa.

It's a good idea to inform your credit-card company before you travel, especially if you're going abroad and don't travel internationally very often. Otherwise, the credit-card company might put a hold on your card owing to unusual activity—not a good thing halfway through your trip. Record all your credit-card numbers—as well as the phone numbers to call if your cards are lost or stolen—in a safe place, so you're prepared should something go wrong. Both MasterCard and Visa have general numbers you can call (collect if you're abroad) if your card is lost, but you're better off calling the number of your issuing bank, since MasterCard and

Visa usually just transfer you to your bank; your bank's number is usually printed on your card.

If you plan to use your credit card for cash advances, you'll need to apply for a PIN at least two weeks before your trip. Although it's usually cheaper (and safer) to use a credit card abroad for large purchases (so you can cancel payments or be reimbursed if there's a problem), note that some credit-card companies *and* the banks that issue them add substantial percentages to all foreign transactions, whether they're in a foreign currency or not. Check on these fees before leaving home, so there won't be any surprises when you get the bill.

■ TIP➡ **Before you charge something, ask the merchant whether or not he or she plans to do a dynamic currency conversion (DCC). In such a transaction the credit-card *processor* (shop, restaurant, or hotel, not Visa or MasterCard) converts the currency and charges you in dollars. In most cases you'll pay the merchant a 3% fee for this service in addition to any credit-card company and issuing-bank foreign-transaction surcharges.**

Dynamic currency conversion programs are becoming increasingly widespread. Merchants who participate in them are supposed to ask whether you want to be charged in dollars or the local currency, but they don't always do so. And even if they do offer you a choice, they may well avoid mentioning the additional surcharges. The good news is that you *do* have a choice. And if this practice really gets your goat, you can avoid it entirely thanks to American Express; with its cards, DCC simply isn't an option.

Reporting Lost Cards American Express ☎ 800/992-3404 in U.S., 336/393-1111 collect from abroad ⊕ www.americanexpress.com. **Diners Club** ☎ 800/234-6377 in U.S., 303/799-1504 collect from abroad ⊕ www.dinersclub.com. **MasterCard** ☎ 800/622-7747 in U.S., 636/722-7111 collect from abroad ⊕ www.mastercard.com. **Visa** ☎ 800/847-2911 in U.S., 410/581-9994 collect from abroad ⊕ www.visa.com.

American Express ☎ 21/392-5727 call collect to report loss or theft. **MasterCard** ☎ 800/811272.

CURRENCY & EXCHANGE

Portugal is one of the 25 European Union countries to use a single currency—the euro (€). Coins are issued in denominations of 1, 2, 5, 10, 20, and 50 euro cents, as well in denominations of €1 and €2. Notes are issued in denominations of €5, 10, 20, 50, 100, 200, and 500. At press time, the exchange rate was US$1 to €0.78.

■ TIP➡ **Even if a currency-exchange booth has a sign promising no commission, rest assured that there's some kind of huge, hidden fee. (Oh . . . that's right. The sign didn't say no *fee*.) And as for rates, you're almost always better off getting foreign currency at an ATM or exchanging money at a bank.**

TRAVELER'S CHECKS & CARDS

Some consider this the currency of the caveman, and it's true that fewer establishments accept traveler's checks these days. Nevertheless, they're a cheap and secure way to carry extra money, particularly on trips to urban areas. Both Citibank (under the Visa brand) and American Express issue traveler's checks in the United States, but Amex is better known and more widely accepted; you can also avoid hefty surcharges by cashing Amex checks at Amex offices. Whatever you do, keep track of all the serial numbers in case the checks are lost or stolen.

American Express now offers a stored-value card called a Travelers Cheque Card, which you can use wherever American Express credit cards are accepted, including ATMs. The card can carry a minimum of $300 and a maximum of $2,700, and it's a very safe way to carry your funds. Although you can get replacement funds in 24 hours if your card is lost or stolen, it doesn't really strike us as a very good deal. In addition to a high initial cost ($14.95 to set up the card, plus $5 each time you "reload"), you still have to pay a 2% fee for each purchase in a foreign currency (similar to that of any credit card). Further, each time you use the card in an ATM you pay a transaction fee of $2.50 on top of the 2% transaction fee for the conversion—add it all up and it can be considerably more than you would pay when simply using your own ATM card. Regular traveler's checks are just as secure and cost less.

American Express ☎ 888/412-6945 in U.S., 801/945-9450 collect outside the U.S. to add value or speak to customer service ⊕ www.americanexpress.com.

▌RESTROOMS

Restaurants, cinemas, theaters, libraries, and service stations are required to have public toilets. Restrooms can range from marble-clad opulence to little better than primitive, but in most cases they're reasonably clean and have toilet paper, although it's always useful to carry a small packet of tissues just in case! Few are adapted for travelers with disabilities. Restrooms are occasionally looked after by an attendant who customarily receives a tip of €0.30. Train stations are likely to have pay toilets.

Find a Loo The Bathroom Diaries ⊕ www.thebathroomdiaries.com is flush with unsanitized info on restrooms the world over—each one located, reviewed, and rated.

▌SAFETY

Be particularly cautious in crowded areas and in the poorer areas of large cities. Be wary of anyone stopping you on the street to ask for directions, the time, or where you're from—particularly if there's more than one person and if you have recently visited the bank or an ATM.

There's enough of a police presence in Portugal that women traveling solo are relatively safe. Take normal precautions, though, and avoid dark, empty streets at night. Ask your hotel staff to recommend a reliable cab company, and whenever possible, call for a taxi instead of hailing one on the street at night. Avoid eye con-

WORST-CASE SCENARIO

All your money and credit cards have just been stolen. In these days of real-time transactions, this isn't a predicament that should destroy your vacation. First, report the theft of the credit cards. Then get any traveler's checks you were carrying replaced. This can usually be done almost immediately, provided that you kept a record of the serial numbers separate from the checks themselves. If you bank at a large international bank like Citibank or HSBC, go to the closest branch; if you know your account number, chances are you can get a new ATM card and withdraw money right away. **Western Union** (☎ 800/325-6000 ⊕ www.westernunion.com) sends money almost anywhere. Have someone back home order a transfer online, over the phone, or at one of the company's offices, which is the cheapest option. The U.S. State Department's **Overseas Citizens Services** (☎ 202/647-5225) can wire money to any U.S. consulate or embassy abroad for a fee of $30. Just have someone back home wire money or send a money order or cashier's check to the state department, which will then disburse the funds as soon as the next working day after it receives them.

tact with unsavory individuals. If such a person approaches you, discourage him politely but firmly by saying, "*Por favor, me dê licença*" ("Excuse me, please") and then walk away with resolve.

Shopkeepers, restaurateurs, and other business owners are generally honest, and credit card receipts are rarely subject to copying. There have been occasional incidents of highway robbery, where the thief slashes the victim's tires during a stop at a gas station and then follows the victim, offering to "help" when the tire goes completely flat. In other cases, the thief takes advantage of an unwary traveler who has left car keys in the ignition or money or a handbag on the seat while stopped at a gas station by telling the driver(s) that they have a puncture in a back tire and urging them to get out of the car to inspect.

■ TIP➡ **Distribute your cash, credit cards, IDs, and other valuables between a deep front pocket, an inside jacket or vest pocket, and a hidden money pouch. Don't reach for the money pouch once you're in public.**

■ TAXES

Value-added tax (IVA, pronounced *ee-vah*) is 12% for hotels. By law prices must be posted at the reception desk and should indicate whether tax is included. Restaurants are also required to charge 12% IVA. Menus generally state at the bottom whether tax is included (*IVA incluido*) or not (*mas 12% IVA*). When in doubt about whether tax is included in a price, ask: *Está incluido o IVA?*

The sales tax is 19% on shop goods. A number of Portuguese stores, particularly large ones and those in resorts, will refund this amount on single items worth more than €60. Sometimes the store will subtract the tax when you make your purchase, particularly if they are arranging the shipment of goods to your home.

When making a purchase, ask for a V.A.T. refund form and find out whether the merchant gives refunds—not all stores do, nor are they required to. Have the form stamped like any customs form by customs officials when you leave the country or, if you're visiting several European Union countries, when you leave the EU. After you're through passport control, take the form to a refund-service counter for an on-the-spot refund (which is usually the quickest and easiest option), or mail it to the address on the form (or the envelope with it) after you arrive home. You receive the total refund stated on the form, but the processing time can be long, especially if you request a credit-card adjustment.

Global Refund is a Europe-wide service with 225,000 affiliated stores and more than 700 refund counters at major airports and border crossings. Its refund form, called a Tax Free Check, is the most common across the European continent. The service issues refunds in the form of cash, check, or credit-card adjustment.

V.A.T. Refunds Global Refund ☎ 800/566-9828 ⊕ www.globalrefund.com.

■ TIME

Portugal sets its clocks according to Greenwich Mean Time, five hours ahead of the U.S. East Coast. Portuguese summer time (GMT plus one hour) requires an additional adjustment from late March to late October.

■ TIPPING

Service is included in café, restaurant, and hotel bills, but waiters and other service people are poorly paid, and you can be sure your contribution will be appreciated. If, however, you received bad service, never feel obligated (or intimidated) to leave a tip. An acceptable tip is 5%–10% of the total bill, and if you have a sandwich or *petiscos* (appetizers) at a bar, leave less, just enough to round out the bill to the nearest €0.50. Cocktail waiters get €0.30–€0.50 a drink, depending on the bar.

Taxi drivers get about 10% of the meter, more for long rides or extra help with luggage (note that there's also an official surcharge for airport runs and baggage). Hotel porters should receive €1 a bag; a doorman who calls you a taxi, €0.50. Tip €1 for room service and €1–€2 per night for maid service. Tip a concierge for any additional help he or she gives you.

Tip tour guides €2–€5, depending on how knowledgeable they are and on the length of the tour. Ushers in theaters or bullfights get €0.50; barbers and hairdressers (for a wash and a set) at least €1. Washroom attendants are tipped €0.30.

EFFECTIVE COMPLAINING

Things don't always go right when you're traveling, and when you encounter a problem or service that isn't up to snuff, you should complain. But there are good and bad ways to do so.

TAKE A DEEP BREATH. This is always a good strategy, especially when you are aggravated about something. Just inhale, and exhale, and remember that you're on vacation. We know it's hard for Type A people to leave it all behind, but for your own peace of mind, it's worth a try.

COMPLAIN IN PERSON WHEN IT'S SERIOUS. In a hotel, serious problems are usually better dealt with in person, at the front desk; if it's something quick, you can phone.

COMPLAIN EARLY RATHER THAN LATE. Whenever you don't get what you paid for (the type of hotel room you booked or the airline seat you pre-reserved) or when it's something timely (the people next door are making too much noise), try to resolve the problem sooner rather than later. It's always going to be harder to deal with a problem or get something taken off your bill after the fact.

BE WILLING TO ESCALATE, BUT DON'T BE HASTY. Try to deal with the person at the front desk of your hotel or with your waiter in a restaurant before asking to speak to a supervisor or manager. Not only is this polite, but when the person directly serving you can fix the problem, you'll more likely get what you want quicker.

SAY WHAT YOU WANT, AND BE REASONABLE. When things fall apart, be clear about what kind of compensation you expect. Don't leave it to the hotel or restaurant or airline to suggest what they're willing to do for you. That said, the compensation you request must be in line with the problem. You're unlikely to get a free meal because your steak was undercooked or a free hotel stay if your bathroom was dirty.

CHOOSE YOUR BATTLES. You're more likely to get what you want if you limit your complaints to one or two specific things that really matter rather than a litany of wrongs.

DON'T BE OBNOXIOUS. There's nothing that will stop your progress dead in its tracks as readily as an insistent "Don't you know who I am?" or "So what are you going to do about it?" Raising your voice will rarely get a better result.

NICE COUNTS. This doesn't mean you shouldn't be clear that you are displeased. Passive isn't good, either. When it comes right down to it, though, you'll attract more flies with sugar than with vinegar.

DO IT IN WRITING. If you discover a billing error or some other problem after the fact, write a concise letter to the appropriate customer-service representative. Keep it to one page, and as with any complaint, state clearly and reasonably what you want them to do about the problem. Don't give a detailed trip report or list a litany of problems.

INDEX

PHOTO CREDITS

NOTES

NOTES

NOTES

NOTES

NOTES

NOTES

NOTES

NOTES

NOTES

ABOUT OUR WRITERS

Journalist Mary McLean is from England and has worked in California, the Middle East, and, since 1990, in Spain and Portugal. Mary writes for many magazines and travel publications, including in-flight magazines and guidebooks. She has covered Portugal, Italy, and various regions of Spain, and contributes to travel-related Web sites. In her spare time she likes nothing better than exploring the wilder regions of the Iberian peninsula, taking along a sketch pad as well as her portable computer.

Norman Renouf was born in London and educated at Charlton Secondary School, Greenwich. Always interested in travel, he started writing travel guides, articles, and newspaper contributions in the early 1990s and has covered destinations throughout Europe. Now living in Spain, he has also written several guides about Washington, D.C., and the mid-Atlantic region.